THE MACLEAN'S
MONEY COMPANION

Ted M. Ohashi, CFA

RAINCOAST BOOKS

Vancouver

Thank you to my son Adam for the enthusiastic support and assistance.
Thank you to my mother for everything. — TO

First published in 2000 by

Raincoast Books
8680 Cambie Street
Vancouver, B.C.
V6P 6M9
(604) 323-7100

www.raincoast.com

1 2 3 4 5 6 7 8 9 10

CANADIAN CATALOGUING IN PUBLICATION DATA

Ohashi, Ted, 1944-
The Maclean's Money Companion

ISBN 1-55192-197-9

1. Finance – Dictionaries. 2. Investments – Dictionaries. I. Title.

HG151.O32 1999   332'.03 C98-910642-X

THE CANADA COUNCIL | LE CONSEIL DES ARTS
FOR THE ARTS | DU CANADA
SINCE 1957 | DEPUIS 1957

*Raincoast Books gratefully acknowledges the support of the
Government of Canada, through the Book Publishing Industry
Development Program, the Canada Council for the Arts and
the Department of Canadian Heritage. We also acknowledge
the assistance of the Province of British Columbia, through the
British Columbia Arts Council.*

Interior Design by Bruce Collins

Printed and bound in Canada

Foreword

At *Maclean's* we pride ourselves on being a thorough, reliable, accessible source of information of relevance for Canadians. Thus it seemed a natural fit when Raincoast Books approached us for permission to apply our name to participate in Ted Ohashi's Money Companion. Within the covers of this most Canadian of financial compendia, Ted Ohashi has factored three decades of experience in the financial world, rendered with an acute sense of observation and leavened with a warmth all too rare in financial writing. Money, or an informed understanding thereof, is fundamental to survival in our fast-changing times. This book is an essential reference to a complex and, on occasion, overwhelming field. But, more than just an exemplary reference, this book truly is a companion – a reliable desktop tutor in the basics of making sense of our finances, and those of our nation. We are delighted to see publication of this first edition of *The Maclean's Money Companion*, and we look forward to taking part in its evolution through future editions.

Michael Benedict
Editorial Director, New Ventures
Maclean's

Introduction

No one just sits down and writes a book like *The Maclean's Money Companion*. At least I didn't. A book such as this evolves over time. It grows entry by entry, sometimes more quickly and other times a little more slowly. And, as parents and gardeners will appreciate, it is the hard work behind the scenes that is so crucial to the final result.

I first recognized the need for a Money Companion more than 15 years ago. At the time, I was actively involved in communicating financial information to the public through the media and seminars. I realized that the average Canadian was having difficulty keeping pace with the changes in business, economics and personal finance. I wrote the Money Companion to fill that knowledge and information gap, and by the time I submitted a draft manuscript to the publisher in 1997, I calculated it to be the equivalent of adding two new entries every day for more than 12 years.

In a way, *The Maclean's Money Companion* chronicles my business career, because I have been involved in so many different aspects of the financial services industry. Many of the investment terms in the book are grounded in my years in the brokerage industry as a chartered financial analyst. The financial planning, insurance and estate planning entries come from my professional experience helping Canadian families plan their financial strategies. The institutional and investment management entries come from my career as a portfolio manager. So, although you may be surprised to find a financial reference book that feels warm and fuzzy, I hope this one does. For me, it's a journal of my three decades in the financial services industry.

Once I had amassed a manuscript containing some 10,000 entries, more work went into refining this book's focus. As we went through an extensive editing process, I received pages and pages back from the editor marked with the question, "Why does this belong?" In the end, our criterion for including a term was simply that it had to explain money or concepts related to money.

The result is that you will find this book useful, not only if you are a savvy investor, but also if you are simply someone with a credit card, a debit card, a chequing or savings account, a mortgage, life insurance, an employee benefit plan, guaranteed investment certificates, Canada Savings Bonds, term deposits, stocks, bonds, mutual funds or a will. If you don't have most of the above, you may need this book even more.

The Maclean's Money Companion will be useful to you whether you have a job or run your own business; if your finances are doing well or if you're having difficulties. While it is well suited to the needs of the financial novice, it is just as useful for the working professional. As I like to tell people, this book contains everything about money from AAA (the first entry) to ZZZZ Best (the last), and everything in between.

But remember, this book is not just a dictionary: it is also a *companion*. It's like a mentor you can always approach with a tough question and expect a sensible answer. Over the years, I hope the cover of your copy becomes wrinkled from constant use, some of the pages smudged with fingerprints, a drop of coffee, a blob of ketchup. All these will be signs that it has been there for you in times of need.

Like any good friend, *The Maclean's Money Companion* will not break up existing relationships. It will, instead, make them better. It is not intended to replace your accountant, financial planner, stockbroker, mutual fund agent, life insurance specialist, estate planner or money advisor. However, in the end this book can help facilitate your active involvement in important personal financial decisions.

While most books have a beginning, middle and end, this book has a beginning and a middle, but there can be no end. In business, new terms are being coined constantly, and existing terms are given a new spin every day. With this in mind, it will be revised and updated regularly. If you look for a term and can't find it, let me know. I plan to give written credit to the first person who contributes each new term that is included in the next edition.

A few years ago, I spotted a sign in a restaurant window that read, "Come in or we'll both starve." I feel that way now. If you've read this far, read on. You'll be better off, and so will I.

Ted M. Ohashi, CFA
December 1999
www.tedohashi.com

Acknowledgements

I thought my job was finished when I submitted my first draft, but it turned out that writing a manuscript is only a small part of the publishing process. Here is what happened to me: First, many of my friends and associates were very supportive of my project. One of them introduced me to Beverley Slopen, a highly regarded Toronto-based literary agent. In the roller-coaster world that is book publishing, I discovered that a five-minute telephone conversation with Beverley is like a walk in a sun-shower. It's exhilarating and uplifting. I was fortunate to make this association.

Beverley put me in touch with Raincoast Books and arranged for me to meet with Mark Stanton, then president, and Brian Scrivener, editorial director. With their actions speaking louder than words, it became evident that they cared as much about this book as I did. Everyone at Raincoast has been very helpful, and I am grateful for their confidence and contributions.

Beverley then proposed the *Maclean's* magazine connection, Raincoast agreed, and I had the good fortune to meet Michael Benedict, *Maclean's* editorial director, new ventures. I am flattered that *Maclean's* has lent its name to this project. Having someone as diligent as Michael with his hand on the quality control lever, one must live up to very demanding standards.

Raincoast's project editor, Rachelle Kanefsky, ably guided me through an exacting editorial process. I am truly indebted to Rachelle, to copy editor Joanne Richardson and to everyone else who participated in the editing. I hope they share my pride in the final product.

Help *The Maclean's Money Companion* Help You

It's easy to get the most out of your book. Terms are listed alphabetically. Multiple-word terms such as Initial Public Offering are treated as if they were one word (e.g., initialpublicoffering). Acronyms are listed as a word (e.g., ARM) and you will find a reference to the full term, Adjustable Rate Mortgage (ARM), with the appropriate definition. Numbers are treated as words (e.g., 30 is "Thirty").

Each term is defined with specific reference to how it is used in business. If a term has more than one meaning, or applications in different aspects of finance, multiple definitions are provided, often with a reference to the area involved.

I have included many "see" and "see also" cross-references to direct you to related terms. Examining the cross-references will not only help you understand the term but also provide more insight into the context in which it applies. On occasion, you may want to find a term without being certain what you are looking for. In such cases, look up a general category or related term such as Annuity or Bond and review the many cross-references listed there.

Where a constellation of terms clusters around a specific subject (e.g., Life Insurance, Registered Retirement Savings Plan, Mutual Fund), you will find a more extensive sidebar, a sort of mini-primer on the topic. Finally, many tables and charts have been provided to help you further.

A

AAA: the highest credit rating granted to a government or company by a bond rating agency. Also known as Triple A. *See also* Canadian Bond Rating Service, Dominion Bond Rating Service.

AAMOF: Internet acronym for "as a matter of fact."

ABA: *see* American Banker's Association.

Abacus: a manual calculator, probably developed in Asia, that has moveable counters that are strung on rods. *See also* Computer.

Abandonment: the loss of title to an asset, resulting from the failure to claim ownership for an extended period of time (e.g., a dormant bank account).

Abatement: a reduction or rebate (e.g., a tax abatement is a tax reduction). *See also* Taxes.

ABC Agreement: an agreement that explains the terms and conditions in place when a brokerage firm purchases a New York Stock Exchange seat.

ABE: *see* Euro Banking Association.

Abeyance: the condition of an unresolved issue (e.g., an unsettled estate may be in abeyance).

ABIL: *see* Allowable Business Investment Loss.

Ability to Pay: a principle of taxation theory that asserts that people should be taxed according to their ability to pay, i.e., the higher one's income, the higher the tax rate. Ability to pay is the basis for progressive taxation. *See also* Progressive Income Tax, Taxes.

Ab Initio: reference to the date on which a contract or statute becomes legally valid.

ABM: *see* Automated Banking Machine.

Abnormal Return: in an asset class, the rate of return that is in excess of the expected rate of return, which is based on risk, term to maturity and liquidity. *See also* Rate of Return.

Above Par: a market price that is higher than the face value or par value of a security. *See also* Par Value, Premium.

Above the Market: an order to sell shares at a price that is higher than the current market price.

Abrogate: to annul, revoke or repeal an old law and replace it with a new law.

ABS: 1. *see* Asset Backed Security. **2.** *see* Automated Bond System.

Absentee Landlord: a landlord not in residence (usually carries the implication that he/she lives in another country). *See also* Landlord.

Absolute Priority: in U.S. bankruptcy, the rule that gives creditors a financial claim ahead of an owner.

Absorbed: a term used to describe the condition of a new issue that has been completely sold. Also known as Assimilated.

Absorption Point: the point at which a market cannot accept added buying or selling without a price change.

Abstinence Theory: an economic theory stating that the buyer of goods or services should only pay for actual usage if that is less than the amount contracted (e.g., if a car lease allows for 25,000 km per year but actual mileage is only 15,000 km).

Abstract: a summary of a report.

Abstract of Title: a condensed history of the title of a property, it is available in the land registry office. *See also* Land Registry Office, Title.

Abuttal: the bounding of a property by another property, street or other boundary.

A/C: abbreviation for "account."

Accelerate: an increase in the rate of change, as in "economic growth is expected to accelerate."

Accelerated Amortization: to write off a cost faster than normal in order to reduce taxable income and, therefore, income tax. Also known as Accelerated Depreciation.

Accelerated Benefit: *see* Living Benefit.

Accelerated Depreciation: *see* Accelerated Amortization.

Accelerated Funds Transfer: an electronic funds transfer system used to move funds between accounts, pay bills and collect receivables. Also known as Automatic Transfer. *See also* Electronic Funds Transfer.

Acceleration Clause: a clause in an indenture that makes a debt immediately repayable in full if payments go into default, sinking fund payments fall behind or the borrower becomes insolvent. *See also* Indenture.

Acceleration Theory: an economic theory that states that investment spending varies directly with overall economic output.

Accelerator Principle: an economic theory that states that, in an economic upturn, the demand for capital goods recovers before the demand for consumer goods.

Acceptance: a voluntary act by which a party agrees to be bound by the terms of a contract.

Acceptance Supra Protest: an arrangement in which a party other than the debtor agrees to pay off a debt.

Access: in family law the right to visit with a child.

Access Card: a magnetically coded card that enables a person to enter a building or, for example, use an automated banking machine. *See also* Automated Banking Machine.

Access Control: a function that limits access to part of a computer network. *See also* Authentication, Biometric Authentication, Challenge-Response Token, Computer, Firewall, Password, Public Key, Secret Key.

Accession Rate: the initial exchange rate at which 11 members of the European Common Market agreed to convert their currencies into the Euro.

Accessory: in law, one who performs acts that facilitate others committing a crime. *See also* Accessory after the Fact, Accessory before the Fact.

Accessory after the Fact: one who gets involved with an action knowing that a crime has already been committed. *See also* Accessory, Accessory before the Fact.

Accessory before the Fact: one who counsels another to commit a crime but does not take part in it. *See also* Accessory, Accessory after the Fact.

Accidental Death Benefit: in life insurance, an option that pays an extra amount, usually equal to the face value, if the insured dies by accident. *See also* Double Indemnity, Life Insurance.

Accident, Death and Dismemberment Insurance: insurance that covers death or loss of a limb(s) as a result of an accident. *See also* Accidental Death Benefit.

Accident Year: an insurance claim based on the date of an accident rather than the year the accident is reported or the year the claim is settled.

Accommodation Endorsement: authorization, granted by someone with adequate financial standing, that serves as a guarantee for someone of lesser financial strength.

Accord: in law, the acceptance of less than total payment to fully satisfy an obligation.

Account: 1. a facility for doing business. *See also* Account Agreement, Account Analysis, Account Balance, Chequing Account, Savings Account. **2.** in law, a detailed statement of receipts and disbursements of money between parties. *See also* Account Balance.

Account Agreement: a document between an account holder and a financial institution that lists the rights and responsibilities of both parties. *See also* Account.

Account Analysis: a detailed summary of transactions in an account provided by a financial institution to its corporate customers. *See also* Account.

Accountant: a person with specialized training, mainly with regard to financial record keeping and auditing for businesses and individuals. *See also* Certified General Accountant, Chartered Accountant.

Accountant's Opinion: *see* Auditor's Report.

Accountant's Review: a report that states that a chartered accounting firm has reviewed but not audited a company's financial statements. Reviews are less rigorous than audits, and lenders and investors have less confidence in them. *See also* Chartered Accountant.

Account Balance: in an account, the difference between debits and credits. *See also* Account, Credit Balance, Debit Balance.

Account Executive: a term, more commonly used in the U.S. than in Canada, that refers to a licensed stockbroker. *See also* Broker.

Accounting Cycle: a summary of financial activities for a fixed period, starting with an opening balance and including all debits, credits and other transactions leading to an ending balance.

Accounting Period: the time covered by a financial statement, normally one year (often a calendar year).

Accounting Policies: the rules and procedures used in preparing financial statements. *See also* Generally Accepted Accounting Principles.

Accounting Principles Board (APB): a board of the American Institute of Certified Public Accountants, it issues the accounting opinions that are the basis for Generally Accepted Accounting Principles. *See also* Generally Accepted Accounting Principles.

Account Reconciliation: the process of reviewing chequing and savings account records to make sure that they agree with personal records. Also known as Reconciliation. If the account reconciliation involves a bank account, it is known as a Bank Reconciliation.

Accounts Payable: money not yet paid for goods and services received. *See also* Accounts Receivable.

Accounts Receivable: money not yet received in payment for goods and services provided. *See also* Accounts Payable.

Accounts Receivable Financing: short-term loans made with accounts receivable as security.

Account Statement: any summary of transactions and balances for a specific period. Account statements are issued for chequing and savings accounts (bank statements), brokerage accounts (brokerage statements), credit accounts, etc.

Accretion: 1. to grow or increase in size gradually. **2.** to add value to a property.

Accretion Bond: a bond that does not pay interest but matures at a higher value, representing return of principal plus interest. *See also* Bond, Residual, Stripped Bond, Stripped Coupon, Zero Coupon Bond.

Accretive: adding to, as in "the merger is accretive."

Accrual Accounting: 1. an accounting and income tax system that records income earned even if it is not received and that records expenses incurred even if they are not paid. Also known as Accrual Basis Accounting. *See also* Cash Accounting. **2.** in income tax, the reporting of taxable income earned even if it has not been received. *See also* Cash Accounting.

Accrual Basis Accounting: *see* Accrual Accounting.

Accrued Benefits: *see* Vesting.

Accrued Income: income earned but for which payment has not yet been received. *See also* Accrual Accounting.

Accrued Interest: interest that accumulates between interest payment dates. The price of a bond between interest payment dates is adjusted for accrued interest. *See also* Bond, Price Plus Accrued.

Accrued Liabilities: amounts owed for expenses incurred but not yet paid. *See also* Accrual Accounting.

Accumulate: to gather up or build over time by making regular contributions to, as in "accumulate mutual fund shares." The term implies that buying is done in a manner that avoids pushing the price of the asset up.

Accumulated Dividend: a dividend owed to holders of a cumulative preferred share, usually because a payment has been missed. *See also* Cumulative Preferred Share.

Accumulated Interest: interest payable but not yet paid.

Accumulation Area: a technical stock-trading term that refers to a fairly narrow price range within which investors buy stock. *See also* Technical Analysis.

Accumulation Plan: in mutual funds, a program in which investors make regular purchases by reinvesting dividends. *See also* Contractual Plan, Mutual Fund, Periodic Payment Plan, Systematic Savings Plan, Voluntary Accumulation Plan.

Accused: the defendant(s) in a criminal trial.

ACES: *see* Advanced Computerized Execution System.

ACI: *see* Financial Markets Association.

Acid Gas Removal: an antipollution measure that consists of removing hydrogen sulphide from refinery discharges. Hydrogen sulphide is the main cause of acid rain. *See also* Acid Rain.

Acid Rain: rain that, having picked up pollutants in the atmosphere, has an abnormally high level of acidity. *See also* Acid Gas Removal.

Acid Ratio: a ratio calculated by dividing cash, liquid assets and current accounts receivable by current debts. An acid ratio of 1.0 is considered reasonable. This is a key ratio that is often used by banks in assessing a borrower's credit worthiness. Also known as Acid Test Ratio.

Acid Test Ratio: *see* Acid Ratio.

Acknowledgement: verification that a signature on a document is valid and has been verified by an authorized person. An acknowledgement is required to transfer a brokerage account.

Acquis Communautaire: the body of principles, policies, law, judgements and practices of the European Court of Justice that have been adopted by the European Community. *See also* European Court of Justice.

Acquisition: the purchase of an entire company (or control of a company) by another company.

Acquisition Cost: the commissions incurred to purchase securities or mutual funds. *See also* Mutual Fund.

Acquisition Fee: a fee, usually related to value, that is charged on the purchase of assets. The term frequently applies to the charges applied when investing in mutual funds. Also known as Commission. *See also* Deferred Sales Charge, Front End Load.

Acquisition Stage Financing: financing provided to a business to acquire a new product line, division or company. *See also* Stage of Development Financing.

Acquit: in law, to discharge from an accusation of guilt. *See also* Acquittal.

Acquittal: in law, a judicial discharge from an accusation of guilt. *See also* Acquit.

Acre: a measure of area, usually applied to land, equal to 4,840 square yards. *See also* Acreage.

Acreage: a reference to a large piece of property. *See also* Acre.

Across-the-Board: in compensation, a percent or dollar amount of change applicable to all employees (e.g., an across-the-board pay increase of 3 percent).

Acting in Concert: a reference to two or more investors buying or selling a security on a cooperative basis. This is illegal if done to manipulate the price of the security. *See also* Wash Trading.

Action: in law, a proceeding in which one party prosecutes another.

Actionable: having a legal basis to prosecute.

Active Account: an account with a financial institution in which a transaction has taken place within the past year. Also known as Live Account. *See also* Dormant Account.

Active Assets: assets used by a company in its day-to-day operations.

Active Bond Crowd: the bond traders of the New York Stock Exchange. *See also* Cabinet Bond Crowd.

Active Business: in Canadian tax law, any corporate business except a specified investment business or a personal service business. *See also* Active Business Income, Investment Business, Personal Service Business.

Active Business Income: income from an active business that is entitled to a lower federal tax rate. *See also* Active Business.

Active Investor: an investor who plays a day-to-day role in the operations or management of the business he/she has invested in. Also known as Hands-On Investor. *See also* Passive Investor.

Active Management: *see* Active Portfolio Management.

Active Market: a stock or stock exchange with a high volume of trading.

Active Portfolio Management: a portfolio management technique in which managers use buy-and-sell strategies to try to add value to average returns. Also known as Active Management. *See also* Indexing, Passive Portfolio Management.

Active Reward: the additional portfolio return that results from active management. Active reward is gained through good market timing, security selection and industry weightings, as well as from trading efficiency. *See also* Active Management, Active Risk.

Active Risk: the additional portfolio return that results from active management. Active risk arises from management's decisions to move market timing, security selection and industry weightings away from a benchmark. *See also* Active Management, Active Reward.

Active Window: in computers, the screen currently in use (i.e., the screen on which the keyboard is functioning). *See also* Computer.

Activity: 1. usually, a reference to the volume of trading on a stock exchange, a group of stocks or an individual stock. **2.** the amount of buying and selling of securities in an individual's stock brokerage account.

Act of God: something that cannot be foreseen and, therefore, cannot be insured.

Actual: any commodity (e.g., gold, wheat, pork bellies) that can be used to deliver (or complete) a futures trade. An actual is in contrast to a financial future, in which settlement is made in cash or securities.

Actuarial Reserves: an actuary's calculation of the amount of reserves required by a fund (e.g., a pension fund) for it to be able to honour liabilities. *See also* Actuary, Pension Fund.

Actuarial Risk: the risk that an insurance company covers in return for a premium. So termed because the risk of premature death, for example, is calculated by an actuary. *See also* Actuary, Risk.

Actuary: a mathematician who calculates life insurance, annuity and pension liabilities using estimated future costs, investment returns and life expectancy. *See also* Actuarial Reserves, Actuarial Risk.

ACUIC: *see* Associate of the Credit Union Institute of Canada.

ADB: *see* Asian Development Bank.

Add-On: something added as a supplement (e.g., a warrant added to a common share to make an underwriting more attractive to investors).

Address: 1. in computers, a number assigned to a specific memory location. *See also* Computer. **2.** on the Internet, a code leading to a specific Web site. The standard form for Internet addresses is the user name followed by the "@" sign, the location and the organization type or country of origin. *See also* .com, .edu, E-Mail Address, .gov, Internet, .mil, .net, .org, Organization Type, Universal Resource Locator.

Addressable: in computers, any block of information or data that can be assigned an address and stored in memory. *See also* Computer, Word.

Ademption: the situation that exists when a specific asset given in a will is no longer a part of the estate or is not clearly identified. In such cases, the gift is adeemed and the beneficiary of that gift receives nothing. *See also* Will.

Ad Hominem: in an argument, an attack on a person's character rather than on what he/she is saying.

Ad Infinitum: forever. For eternity.

Adjustable Rate Mortgage (ARM): a mortgage that allows interest rate changes at specific points before maturity. *See also* Mortgage.

Adjustable Rate Preferred Share: *see* Floating Rate Preferred Share.

Adjusted Balance Method: the calculation of financing costs or interest payable based on the amount owing at the end of a period, after payments and credits are posted. This method of calculating balance results in low interest payable and is used in many interest-paying savings or chequing accounts. *See also* Average Daily Balance Method, Minimum Monthly Balance, Past Due Balance Method, Previous Balance Method.

Adjusted Cost Base: an income tax term referring to a tax cost that may differ from the amount actually paid for the asset. *See also* Taxes.

Administered Registered Retirement Savings Plan: *see* Registered Retirement Savings Plan – Administered or Directed.

Administration Fee: generally, any fee paid for the performance of administrative services. *See also* Trustee Fee.

Administrative Relief: relief provided by Canada Customs and Revenue Agency when the strict application of the Income Tax Act leads to unintended or unfair results. *See also* Canada Customs and Revenue Agency.

Administrator: 1. a court-appointed person who takes charge of an estate if the deceased did not leave a will or appoint an executor, or if the executor will not serve. *See also* Administratrix, Executor, Executrix, Will. **2.** in law, any person empowered to act for another person whom a court has deemed incapable of acting for himself/herself. **3.** *see* Pension Plan Administrator.

Administratrix: a female administrator. *See also* Administrator.

ADN: Internet acronym for "any day now."

Ad Nauseam: to a sickening degree, as in "he/she went on ad nauseam."

Adopt: in law, to take a person into a family.

ADR: *see* American Depository Receipt.

Ad Referendum: a signed contract that has certain unresolved issues.

Adultery: in family law, voluntary sexual intercourse between a married person and someone other than his/her lawful spouse. In Canada, evidence of adultery is grounds for divorce. *See also* Marriage Breakdown, Mental Cruelty.

Ad Valorem: in proportion to value. *See also* Ad Valorem Tax.

Ad Valorem Tax: a tax (e.g., a property tax) calculated as a percentage of value. *See also* Ad Valorem.

Advance: 1. a rise in price or value, as in a "stock market advance." *See also* Rally. **2.** a payment ahead of time, as in a "cash advance."

Advanced Computerized Execution System (ACES): an automated order-entry execution and reporting system for the NASDAQ stock market.

Advance/Decline Line: an indicator that, over time, compares the number of stocks advancing in price with the number of stocks declining in price.

Advance Directive: *see* Living Will.

Advances: in a trading session, the number of listed stocks rising in price. *See also* Breadth Ratio, Declines.

Advancing Volume: in a trading session, the volume of trades made at a higher price. *See also* Declining Volume.

Adventure Capital: capital used to invest in high-risk ventures. Such ventures are entered upon as much for excitement as for expected profit. *See also* Venture Capital.

Adversarial System: in a court of law, an approach to a dispute whereby each party presents evidence for its side and against the other side(s).

Adverse Opinion: *see* Qualified Opinion.

Adverse Selection: *see* Antiselection.

Advertorial: advertising, including direct-response marketing, that provides information through what appears to be editorial or objective commentary. *See also* Advocacy Advertising, Direct-Response Marketing, Infomercial, Infotainment, Institutional Advertising, Situmercial.

Advising Bank: in a transaction involving a letter of credit, the bank that acts on behalf of the seller of goods and, ultimately, receives a letter of credit for payment. *See also* Issuing Bank, Negotiating Bank.

Advisor: someone with experience and expertise who recommends or counsels action.

Advisory Letter: *see* Investment Letter.

Advocacy Advertising: advertising that appears to provide objective information but that actually promotes a group's, often a government's, special interests. *See also* Advertorial, Direct-Response Marketing, Infomercial, Infotainment, Institutional Advertising, Situmercial.

Advocacy Group: a group that lobbies on behalf of a cause or person.

Aeroplane Rule: a maxim stating that "complexity increases the chance of failure."

AFAIK: Internet acronym for "as far as I know."

Affidavit: a sworn, notarized written statement. *See also* Motion.

Affiliate: 1. a relationship between two or more parties wherein one of the parties is in a position of influence over the other(s). **2.** *see* Affiliated Companies.

Affiliated Companies: a situation in which one company owns less than 50 percent of the voting shares of another company, or two companies are subsidiaries of another company. *See also* Affiliate, Parent Company, Subsidiary Company.

Affiliated Person: 1. an income tax term that defines those people or parties who are considered to be related and not to be at arm's-length. **2.** in investment, a person who is in a position to influence the actions of a company, including individuals who own more than 10 percent of the voting shares of the company as well as the directors, senior officers and the members of their immediate families. Also known as Control Person.

Affinity Group: a group of people with a common interest or profession (e.g., the Institute of Chartered Financial Analysts).

Affirmative Action: a policy to compensate those who often suffer from discrimination, it entails employing or promoting people partially on the basis of race, colour, creed or gender.

Affordability Index: a real estate index based on the average income, borrowing costs and housing prices in a region. Lower average incomes and higher interest rates and real estate prices make housing less affordable. Higher average incomes and lower interest rates and real estate prices make housing more affordable. Also known as Housing Affordability Index.

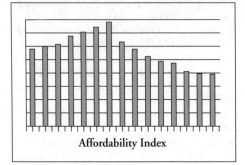

Affordability Index

Afgani: the prime currency of Afghanistan.

A Fortiori: a more logical conclusion.

After Acquired Clause: a mortgage provision that allows for the addition of another property in order to secure a loan. *See also* Mortgage.

After Market: 1. the trading of a company's securities shortly after an initial public offering or new issue. *See also* Primary Market, Secondary Market. **2.** the market into which materials and components are sold to service products that have already been manufactured and sold (e.g., an after market supplier of automobile tires). *See also* Original Equipment Manufacturer, Retrofit.

Aftershock: a response to a significant event (e.g., the aftershock of the Bre-X Minerals Ltd. fraud was a loss of investor confidence which, in turn, drove down prices of other mining exploration company shares). *See also* Bre-X Minerals Ltd.

After Tax Income: income after payment of income taxes. *See also* Pretax Income.

After Tax Return: the rate of return on investment after taking into account payment of income taxes. Also known as After Tax Yield. *See also* Pretax Return.

After Tax Yield: *see* After Tax Return.

After the Bell: after the stock market close. Derived from the New York Stock Exchange, where the end of a trading day is announced by the ringing of a bell. *See also* At the Bell.

AG: *see* Attorney General.

Ag: *see* Silver.

Against the Box: 1. short selling a security that is owned, usually to avoid disclosure or for tax benefits.

2. buying or selling a security when the specialist or market maker is on the opposite side of the transaction. *See also* Market Maker, Specialist.

Against the Crowd: *see* Contrary Opinion.

Age Credit: a deduction from federal income taxes payable, it applies to Canadians aged 65 and over.

Age Discrimination: the illegal act of discriminating against an employee on the basis of his/her age. This often involves a company attempting to lay off older employees because they earn more than younger employees. *See also* Wrongful Dismissal.

Agent: 1. an individual or company authorized to act on behalf of someone else (who is known as the principal). *See also* Principal **2.** *see* Life Insurance Agent.

Agent for Executor: usually a trust company engaged to provide advice to the executor of an estate. *See also* Executor.

Age of Majority: the age at which a person becomes responsible for such legal actions as signing contracts. It is 18 in all provinces except British Columbia, New Brunswick, Newfoundland, Nova Scotia, the Yukon and Northwest Territories, where it is 19. *See also* Minor.

Aggressive Growth: a strategy for higher income growth, it accepts the involvement of higher risk.

Aggressive Growth Fund: a mutual fund that focuses on aggressive growth investments. *See also* Mutual Fund – Other.

Aging: this refers to measuring the length of time that accounts receivable or payable have been outstanding.

AGM: *see* Annual General Meeting.

Agreement for Sale: a written agreement that, according to the terms specified, binds the buyer and seller of goods or services to a transaction.

Agricultural Cooperative: *see* Marketing Board.

AI: *see* Artificial Intelligence.

AIM: *see* Alternative Investment Market.

AIMR: *see* Association for Investment Management and Research.

AIP: *see* Automatic Investment Program.

Air Mile: *see* Nautical Mile.

Air Pocket: a term used to describe a sudden fall in the price of a stock.

Aladdin: the new security that is created when an old security is converted according to preestablished terms and conditions.

Alberta: *see* Canada's Provinces and Territories.

Alberta Stock Exchange (ASE): a stock exchange located in Calgary, Alberta. From incorporation in 1913 until 1974, it was known as the Calgary Stock Exchange. The ASE is best known for Junior Capital Pools, also called JCPs or "blind pool" underwritings. Under an agreement in principle announced in March 1999, the ASE will merge with the Vancouver Stock Exchange to form a national junior equities market known as the Canadian Venture Exchange. The Toronto Stock Exchange will become the senior securities market, and the Montreal Exchange will focus exclusively on futures and derivatives trading. Web site: www.alberta.net/ *See also* Canadian Venture Exchange, Montreal Exchange, Toronto Stock Exchange, Vancouver Stock Exchange.

Alberta Stock Exchange Combined Value Index: a stock market index for the Alberta Stock Exchange.

Aleatory Contract: an agreement, the outcome of which is uncertain because it depends on an unpredictable future event (e.g., a variable annuity).

ALGOL: short for **Algo**rithmic Language. The first structured procedural computer language, it was developed in the late 1950s and was geared for scientific applications. *See also* Computer, FORTRAN, Machine Language.

Algorithm: 1. a set of step-by-step instructions that perform a function or solve a problem. **2.** In computers, a set of instructions that perform a common programming task. *See also* Computer.

Alien Company: any company that operates in a jurisdiction other than the one in which it was incorporated. *See also* Company.

Alimony: *see* Spousal Support.

Alligator Spread: an options strategy that involves so many puts and calls that the commission cost virtually eliminates any opportunity for profit. *See also* Option.

All-In: *see* All-in-Cost.

All-In Cost: cost inclusive of everything, including cash costs, implied costs and opportunity costs. Also known as All-In. *See also* Implied Cost, Opportunity Cost.

Allodial: a term used to describe free and clear ownership of land.

All Ordinaries Index: *see* Australian Stock Exchange All Ordinaries Index.

All or None Order: 1. an order to buy or sell a stock as long as the entire amount is bought or sold. *See also* Order. **2.** in underwriting, the right of the issuer to cancel the offering if it is not fully sold.

Allotment: 1. the number of shares of a new issue allocated to a brokerage firm to sell to its clients. **2.** the number of shares of a new issue allocated to a broker to sell to his/her clients.

Allowable Business Investment Loss (ABIL): for Canadian income tax purposes, a loss incurred on the sale of securities of a small business corporation.

All Risks Insurance: property insurance that covers all perils (e.g., fire or theft). Each contract is different, however, and should be read carefully.

All Weather Fund: a mutual fund that performs well during both favourable and unfavourable economic conditions. *See also* Mutual Fund – Other.

Alpha (α): the proportion of an investment's return that arises from specific or non-market risk. A positive or high alpha stock is one that provides or is expected to provide a higher return than the average return for stocks of similar risk. In terms of measuring portfolio returns, a positive alpha indicates an above-average return and above-average investment management. *See also* Historical Alpha, Industry Specific Risk, Judgmental Alpha, Market Specific Risk, Positive Alpha, Required Alpha, Specific Risk.

Alphabet Stock: shares that are given a letter designation when used to acquire another company. The designation is required because the shares frequently have different terms and conditions (e.g., General Motors issued "E" stock to acquire Electronic Data Systems and "H" stock to acquire Hughes Aircraft).

Alphanumeric: made up of both letters and numbers, as in a code, name or reference (e.g., AB123X).

Alphanumeric Memory: the ability to store both words and numbers, as in a cellular telephone.

Alpha Stock: in the London Stock Exchange's former system of ranking stocks, alpha stocks were those that rated highest in terms of size and trading volume. Beta, Delta and Gamma were other rankings, each of which represented a smaller underlying company and less actively traded stock. *See also* Beta Stock, Delta Stock, Gamma Stock.

Alternate Appointment: an executor who is appointed if the executor named in a will cannot or will not act. *See also* Executor.

Alternative Investment Market (AIM): a market made up of the shares of emerging or smaller companies, such as the AIM market associated with the London Stock Exchange.

Alternative Minimum Tax (AMT): a tax calculation made by Canada Customs and Revenue Agency to ensure that a person pays a minimum amount of income tax. If a person uses certain tax preference items to reduce or eliminate taxes payable, such as his/her contributions to Registered Retirement Savings Plans or resource expenditures, then Canada Customs and Revenue Agency requires that he/she add back such tax preference items so that a minimum amount of tax is paid. *See also* Taxes.

Alternative Order: an order to a broker to buy or sell a security that is made up of two separate orders, the execution of one cancelling the other. For example, in a buy minus/buy stop order, the former triggers a market order if the price falls to a certain level and the latter triggers a buy order if the stock rises to a certain level. Also known as One Cancels the Other Order. *See also* Buy Minus, Buy Stop, Order.

A.M. Best Company, Inc.: *see* Best (A.M.) Company, Inc.

Ambulance Chaser: a lawyer who actively seeks clients with personal injury claims.

American Banker's Association (ABA): an industry association for the American banking industry.

American Bond Fund: *see* Foreign Bond Fund.

American Common Stock Fund: *see* American Equity Fund.

American Depository Receipt (ADR): a system for trading foreign securities. A U.S. bank or trust company holds a foreign security registered in its own name in safekeeping and issues a receipt against the certificate. The receipts are traded as American Depository Receipts. This system is used because re-registering foreign securities can be a time-consuming process. *See also* American Depository Share, Global Depository Receipt, International Depository Receipt.

American Depository Share (ADS): a share that is issued under a deposit arrangement and that represents the actual share trading on an exchange. An American Depository Receipt is a certificate that represents an American Depository Share. *See also* American Depository Receipt.

American Equity Fund: 1. *see* U.S. Equity Fund. **2.** *see* U.S. Small to Mid Cap Equity Fund. Also known as American Common Stock Fund.

American Money Market Fund: *see* Foreign Money Market Fund.

American National Standards Institute (ANSI): established in 1918, a voluntary, nonprofit organization of U.S. business and industry groups that develop trade and communication standards.

American Standard Code for Information Interchange (ASCII): created in 1968 to standardize transmission among different hardware and software systems, a coding scheme that assigns numeric values to up to 256 keyboard characters, including letters, numerals, control characters, etc. *See also* Text File.

American Stock Exchange (AMEX): a secondary U.S. stock exchange headquartered in New York City, it lists common shares of smaller companies than the New York Stock Exchange. In early 1998 an agreement was reached for a merger with the National Association of Securities Dealers. Also known as the Curb, Little Board, New York Curb Exchange. Web site: www.amex.com/

American-Style Option: the North American style of

option that can be exercised at any time, including the last trading day. *See also* European-Style Option, Option.

AMEX: *see* American Stock Exchange.

Amman Financial Market: the major stock market of Jordan, located in its capital, Amman. Also known as Jordan Stock Market. Web site: www.accessme.com/afm/index.html

Amortization: 1. an accounting adjustment that spreads the cost of an asset, such as a patent, over its estimated useful life. **2.** the amount of reduction in mortgage (or other loan) principal over time. *See also* Amortization Period, Mortgage.

Amortization Period: the number of years over which a loan is to be repaid. *See also* Mortgage.

Amsterdam Exchanges Index: a market capitalization weighted index of 25 stocks listed on the Amsterdam Stock Exchange.

Amsterdam Stock Exchange: the major stock exchange of the Netherlands, located in its capital, Amsterdam. Founded in 1602, it is the oldest stock exchange in the world. Web site: www.aex.nl

AMT: *see* Alternative Minimum Tax.

Analog Computer: a computer that measures continuously variable physical changes. *See also* Computer, Digital Computer.

Analyst: *see* Financial Analyst.

And Interest: *see* Price Plus Accrued.

Anecdotal Evidence: nonscientific or statistically unfounded evidence based on personal observations.

Angel: 1. an investment-grade bond. *See also* Fallen Angel. **2.** a financial backer. Also known as Backer.

Anglophone: an English-speaking person. More generally, in Canada, a person of English descent. *See also* Francophone.

Ankle Biter: a small cap company that is being underwritten. *See also* Small Cap

Anniversary: the yearly return of a significant date (e.g., the anniversary date of a mortgage falls one year from when it was first taken out). It is usually on this date that one can make changes to a mortgage. *See also* Mortgage.

Annual: occurring once a year. *See also* Biennial, Triennial.

Annual Audit: the yearly review of a business' or organization's financial statements by independent auditors. Also known as Year-End Audit. *See also* Audited Financial Statement, Auditor's Report.

Annual Cleanup: a lending term that indicates that a borrower must have a line of credit balance of zero at a specific time each year.

Annual General Meeting (AGM): a yearly meeting of the stockholders of a company. During this meeting, the board of directors is elected and other formal business (e.g., approval of financial statements) is conducted. Also known as Annual Meeting. *See also* Annual Report.

Annualized Rate: the rate of return or growth over less than one year but extrapolated over one year (e.g., a 1 percent return over one month is a 12 percent annualized rate of return). Also known as Annualized Return. If the most recent period is annualized, it is known as Run Rate. *See also* Rate of Return.

Annualized Return: *see* Annualized Rate.

Annual Meeting: *see* Annual General Meeting (AGM).

Annual Percentage Rate (APR): a U.S. legislated calculation intended to show the true rate of interest charged on credit cards and loans.

Annual Renewable Term Insurance: term insurance that can be renewed each year, usually at a higher premium that is established when the insurance is acquired. *See also* Term Insurance.

Annual Report: a comprehensive document that, at the year end, provides a company's financial statements. Public company annual reports must be audited. *See also* Annual General Meeting.

Annual Return: the total financial benefit from owning an investment for one year, expressed as a percentage of the amount invested.

Annuitant: 1. the party that receives or will receive an annuity benefit. *See also* Annuity. **2.** the income tax term used to describe RRSP holders. *See also* Registered Retirement Savings Plan.

Annuity: 1. a contract that requires periodic payments to the annuitant for a specified time period (often related to a lifetime). **2.** An RRSP maturity option. *See also* Annuitant, Annuity Certain, Annuity Due, Apportionable Annuity, Commutation Payment, Complete Annuity, Curtate Annuity, Decreasing Annuity, Deferred Annuity, Equal Annuity, Fixed Annuity, Hybrid Annuity, Immediate Annuity, Increasing Annuity, Indexed Annuity, Joint and Last Survivor Annuity, Joint Life Annuity, Life Annuity, Life Annuity with Guarantee, Non-Apportionable Annuity, Ordinary Annuity, Periodic Purchase Deferred Annuity, Reversionary Annuity, Single Life Annuity, Straight Life Annuity, Substandard Health Annuity, Terminable Annuity, Term to Age 90 Annuity, Variable Annuity, Variable Deferred Annuity.

Annuity Bond: a bond that, over its term, repays principal and interest in a series of equal payments. *See also* Bond.

Annuity Certain: an annuity that provides payments at specified times for a specified period without reference to the life or death of an annuitant. Also known as Certain Term Annuity, Period Certain Annuity, Term Certain Annuity. *See also* Annuity.

Annuity Due: an annuity that pays for the period ahead. In other words, the payment at the beginning of the month is for the month ahead. *See also* Annuity, Ordinary Annuity.

Annulment: the action of declaring a law or marriage void.

Anomaly: in resource exploration, an area of interest based on abnormal amounts of mineralization, chemistry or magnetics.

ANSI: *see* American National Standards Institute.

Answer Mode: in computers, the setting on a modem that allows it to receive incoming calls from another modem. *See also* Automatic Answering, Computer.

Antedate: to date earlier than the actual date. Also known as Backdate, Predate. *See also* Postdate.

Anti-Avoidance Rules: regulations that enable Canada Customs and Revenue Agency to prevent taxpayers from taking steps to avoid or reduce tax payment. *See also* Taxes.

Annuity

In some ways, an annuity is life insurance in reverse. It is a financial contract that is purchased to provide a series of payments in the future.

The most common terms for annuities include the life of one person; the longer of two lives; a person's life with a minimum guarantee of a fixed number of years; or a fixed number of years with no reference to lifespan.

The start-up of payments from an annuity also varies. It can be immediate, after a fixed period of time or after an event, such as the death of another person (e.g., a spouse or parent).

Annuity means annual payment, but with modern contracts, payments are often monthly, quarterly or semiannually. In addition, they can be fixed over the term of the contract or they can increase or decrease over time according to a prearranged formula.

The annuity is one maturity option for a Registered Retirement Savings Plan (RRSP). It is well suited to those individuals who are interested in a simple means of obtaining a guaranteed life income. For example, at age 65 a person may choose to take the capital in his/her RRSP and purchase an annuity to provide a monthly income for as long as he/she (or his/her spouse) is living.

Anticipation: the right to prepay a financial obligation, with or without penalty, before it is due. *See also* Anticipation Rate, Mortgage, Mortgage Prepayment, Penalty, Prepayment Clause, Prepayment Penalty, Prepayment Privilege, Right of Anticipation.

Anticipation Rate: a specific discount rate or other penalty attached to the right to prepay a financial obligation before it is due. *See also* Anticipation, Mortgage, Mortgage Prepayment, Penalty, Prepayment Clause, Prepayment Penalty, Prepayment Privilege, Right of Anticipation.

Antidilution Clause: 1. a clause in a warrant agreement that allows for changes in the event of a stock split or the issue of a stock dividend or additional shares (e.g., a warrant to buy one share of stock at $50 per share would be changed to $25 per share if the shares were split two-for-one). **2.** a clause in a private company shareholders' agreement that allows the company to issue additional shares only if existing shareholders are given an opportunity to buy a sufficient quantity to maintain their proportionate ownership.

Antiselection: in life insurance, the tendency of individuals in high-risk situations (e.g., people in dangerous jobs) to want more insurance. Antiselection can result in poor claims experience and financial loss for an insurance company. Also known as Adverse Selection.

Antitrust: a term derived from the U.S. Sherman Anti-Trust Act of 1890, it refers to laws created to prevent monopolies, price fixing and/or restraint of trade.

Any Occupation: a stipulation in some disability income insurance contracts that states that benefits will continue until the insured is able to perform any type of occupation, and not necessarily the occupation he/she was performing when he/she was disabled. *See also* Disability Income Insurance, Same Occupation.

Any or All Order: an order to buy or sell a stock, especially in a takeover or issuer bid, in which the buyer will accept any shares tendered. *See also* All or None Order, Order.

APB: *see* Accounting Principles Board.

API Gravity: a scale to measure the density of liquid petroleum products. The higher the API, the lighter the crude oil.

A Posteriori: reasoning that moves from specific facts to general principles.

Appellant: someone who appeals a court decision.

Appellate Court: a court with the jurisdiction to hear an appeal of a previous court decision.

Apple Computer, Inc.: one of the leading companies in the development of the personal computer. Also known as Mac, Macintosh; that is, for its best-known product line. Apple designs, manufactures and markets personal computers and related products. Web site: www.apple.com *See also* Computer.

Applicant: the party that issues a letter of credit in payment of goods to be received. *See also* Beneficiary.

Application: 1. in computers, a program designed to assist in the performance of a specific task (e.g., word processing). *See also* Computer. **2.** the form used to apply for life insurance. *See also* Policy. **3.** a form to be filled out with personal information when applying for a job or loan.

Apportionable Annuity: an annuity that pays a pro rata amount of the final payment to the annuitant's estate. *See also* Annuity.

Appraisal: the process of estimating the fair market value of an asset, often real estate. Appraisals may vary, depending on their purpose (e.g., appraisals for insurance purposes are often higher than appraisals for tax purposes). *See also* Mortgage, Property Assessment.

Appraisal Fee: the fee charged by a professional appraiser to perform an appraisal.

Appraisal Surplus: the amount by which the appraised value of an asset exceeds its book value or cost.

Appraised Value: an estimated market value for a property. The appraised value is normally calculated by a professional appraiser and is used by a lender to determine the maximum amount of a loan that will be advanced.

Appraiser: a person who estimates the value of property, often real estate.

Appreciation: *see* Capital Appreciation.

Approved List: in investment, a list of assets that a financial institution or investor is allowed to acquire. The approved list may be established by legislation. *See also* Legal for Life, Unauthorized Investment.

Appurtenance: added rights appended to real property (e.g., an easement).

APR: *see* Annual Percentage Rate.

A Priori: a conclusion based on theory rather than experience.

Aquaculture: the commercial cultivation of fish and/or shellfish for food. *See also* Fish Farm.

Arabian Light Crude: a sour, light crude oil produced in Saudi Arabia.

Arabic Numeral: one of the symbols 1, 2, 3, 4, 5, 6, 7, 8, 9 and 0.

Arab Oil Embargo: the action by the Organization of Petroleum Exporting Countries (OPEC) in the fall of

1973 to withhold sales of oil to the rest of the world. The embargo was a political tactic to enable the members of OPEC to take back control of their petroleum resources and establish a stronger position in world affairs. The subsequent rise in oil prices added to inflation and triggered a worldwide economic slowdown, including a recession in the U.S. that lasted until 1975. Also known as Oil Embargo. *See also* Organization of Petroleum Exporting Countries.

Arbiter: in a commercial dispute, someone with the power to make a decision.

Arbitrage: the simultaneous purchase and sale of an asset that takes advantage of price discrepancies in the same or similar asset. In theory, arbitrage is a low risk activity. *See also* Risk Arbitrage.

Arbitrageur: a person who practises arbitrage.

Arbitrage Trading Program (ATP): computerized trading in which simultaneous orders are placed for index options and the underlying stocks. The objective is to take advantage of small price variations. Sometimes referred to as Program Trading. *See also* Option, Program Buying, Program Selling, Program Trading.

Arbitration: the process of a mutually acceptable third party facilitating the settlement of a dispute.

Architecture: in computers, the organization and structure of a system from a design perspective. *See also* Computer.

Area Play: 1. in mining or oil and gas exploration, interest in a region near a major discovery. **2.** a company owning property in the vicinity of a major discovery.

Argental Gold: gold ore that contains silver.

Argentina Merval Index: a stock index based on a portfolio of shares listed on the Buenos Aires Stock Exchange.

Argentinian Stock Exchange: *see* Buenos Aires Stock Exchange.

Arithmetic Average: the number derived by dividing the sum of the quantities in a set by the number of quantities in the set. Also known as Arithmetic Mean, Average. *See also* Mean, Median, Mode.

Arithmetic Mean: *see* Arithmetic Average.

ARM: *see* Adjustable Rate Mortgage.

Arm's-Length Transaction: a contract or agreement made by independent parties. *See also* Non-Arm's-Length Transaction.

Arraign: to call an accused to court to answer a charge.

Array: the arrangement of mathematical quantities in rows and columns. *See also* Spreadsheet

Arrears: 1. an amount past due. **2.** an amount to be paid at the end of a period.

Articles of Clerkship: *see* Articling.

Articles of Incorporation: a legal document that provides many details of a company, including shareholder voting rights and how to call a special meeting. Also known as Corporate Charter. *See also* Special Meeting of Shareholders.

Articling: the act of serving of an apprenticeship before being admitted to the practice of law. Also known as Articles of Clerkship.

Artificial: not real (e.g., for Canada Customs and Revenue Agency, a non-arm's-length sale of an asset for the purpose of triggering a capital loss is considered artificial, and such losses are, therefore, not permitted).

Artificial Currency: a substitute for currency (e.g., special drawing rights). *See also* Special Drawing Rights.

Artificial Intelligence (AI): the study of and methods by which machines and computers simulate rational human behaviour and learning skills. *See also* Computer.

Artificial Person: in law, a nonhuman legal entity that is recognized as a person (e.g., a company).

Ascending Tops: a technical stock market term used to describe a price pattern wherein subsequent highs are higher. *See also* Descending Tops, Technical Analysis.

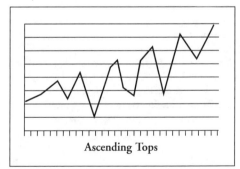

Ascending Tops

Ascending Trend: a pattern in prices or in an economic series wherein subsequent highs are higher and subsequent lows are higher. *See also* Descending Trend.

ASCII: *see* American Standard Code for Information Interchange.

ASCII-Art: *see* Emoticon.

ASCIIbetical Order: computer data in ASCII-collated order rather than alphabetical order. *See also* Computer.

ASCII-Glyph: *see* Emoticon.

ASE: *see* Alberta Stock Exchange.

Asia Ex-Japan Equity Fund: one of the 31 Canadian fund categories developed by the Investment Funds Standards Committee. Mutual funds in this category must have a minimum of 50 percent of the total assets, and 75 percent of the non-cash assets, of the portfolio in equities or equity equivalents of companies that are located in Asia (excluding Japan), Australia or New Zealand, or they must have derivative-based exposure to such markets. The calculations to determine whether a mutual fund fits this definition are based on median values from fund data over three years, unless otherwise noted. The derivatives are weighted on an extended value basis. Each of the categories may be refined by a fund manager (e.g., a Canadian Large Cap Equity Fund might be described as "growth" or "value" to reflect the manager's style). *See also* Extended Value, Mutual Fund – Category.

Asian Contagion: the severe downturn in economic growth, stock markets and currency values that hit Asia in the latter part of the 1990s. Japan led the way, but countries such as Indonesia, Hong Kong and South Korea were also severely impacted. Also known as Asian Flu.

Asian Development Bank (ADB): an international bank that is owned by 50 countries and that promotes social and economic growth by making loans to underdeveloped Asian countries.

Asian Flu: *see* Asian Contagion.

Asian Tigers: a group of Asian nations made up of the Four Tigers (Hong Kong, the Republic of Korea [South Korea], Singapore and Taiwan) and the four Mini Tigers (Indonesia, Malaysia, the Philippines and Thailand). Also known as Eight Tigers, Tigers of Asia. *See also* Four Tigers, Mini Tigers of Asia.

Asia/Pacific Rim Equity Fund: one of the 31 Canadian fund categories developed by the Investment Funds Standards Committee. Mutual funds in this category must have a minimum of 50 percent of the total assets, and 75 percent of the non-cash assets, of the portfolio in equities or equity equivalents of companies that are located in Asia, Australia or New Zealand, or they must have derivative-based exposure to such markets. The calculations to determine whether a mutual fund fits this definition are based on median values from fund data over three years, unless otherwise noted. The derivatives are weighted on an extended value basis. Each of the categories may be refined by a fund manager (e.g., a Canadian Large Cap Equity Fund might be described as "growth" or "value" to reflect the manager's style). *See also* Extended Value, Mutual Fund – Category.

As Is: a condition of sale, often used for sale items on display or at auction, that alerts the buyer that the product is in the condition as viewed. *See also* Auction, Caveat Emptor.

As Is, Where Is: a condition of sale, often used for larger items on display or at auction, that alerts the buyer that the product is in the condition as viewed and that it is the buyer's responsibility to remove the item purchased. *See also* Auction, Caveat Emptor.

Ask: *see* Offer Price.

Ask Price: *see* Offer Price.

ASP General Index: the Russian/State Press Stock Market General Index. A market capitalization weighted index of the 100 largest companies on the exchange.

ASPIRIN: *see* Australian Stock Price Riskless Indexed Notes.

Aspirin Count Theory: a tongue-in-cheek market indicator that states that stock prices will move in the opposite direction of aspirin production. *See also* Boston Snow Indicator, Frivolity Theory, Hemline Indicator, Super Bowl Indicator, Tie Theory, Yellow Market Indicator.

Assay: 1. a test of a metal's purity to ensure that it meets the standards for settlement of a commodities trade. **2.** scientific analysis of a resource sample for specific minerals in a measurable quantity.

Assembler: a computer language that can be understood by humans and that translates instructions into a code that can be read by computers. *See also* Computer.

Assessed Value: the value of a property set by a municipality as the basis for calculating property taxes. *See also* Mill Rate.

Assessment: notification from Canada Customs and Revenue Agency that an income tax return has been accepted. An assessment may or may not include changes. Canada Customs and Revenue Agency can still make further changes to a return at a later date.

Assessment Roll: a list of all properties in a municipality and their assessed values. *See also* Assessed Value.

Assessor: a person who determines the value of a property for tax purposes.

Asset: a thing of value owned by an individual or legal entity.

Asset Allocation: the distribution of investments into different asset classes (e.g., cash, bonds and stocks) to minimize risk and to maximize income and/or capital appreciation potential. Some studies indicate that 90 percent of portfolio performance can be attributed to asset allocation. *See also* Strategic Asset Allocation, Tactical Asset Allocation.

Asset Allocation Fund: a portfolio in which the manager shifts investments to the asset classes expected to provide the most attractive rate of return. Such funds are popular because the asset allocation decision is turned over to a professional manager and does not have to be made by the individual investor. Also known as Flexible Mutual Fund. *See also* Mutual Fund – Other.

Asset Backed Financing: a loan to purchase an asset in which the asset being purchased is the only collateral for the loan.

Asset Backed Security (ABS): a financial security supported by an asset, such as a mortgage. *See also* Mortgage Backed Security.

Asset Classes: an almost endless number of categories of assets, such as real assets, financial assets, real estate, fixed income and equities. Distinctions can also be made within such groups; for example, fixed income can be divided into bonds, preferred shares and mortgages. *See also* Asset Allocation.

Asset Coverage: a calculation of the extent to which the net assets of a company cover a debt or class of shares. Asset coverage indicates to an investor the extent of protection available in the event of liquidation.

Asset Financing: the use of assets, such as accounts receivable or inventory, to secure loans for working capital purposes. Also known as Commercial Financing.

Asset/Liability Management: *see* Matching.

Asset Mix: the proportion of cash, bonds, equities and other asset classes held in a portfolio at any given time.

Asset Play: in investment, a security that is attractive for the value of the underlying corporate assets (e.g., shares of a company that has real estate assets valued at a cost far below current market value).

Asset Stripper: a person engaged in acquiring companies with the intention of selling their assets. After the assets of a particular company are sold, the stripper estimates the net cost of investment.

Asset Structure: the type of assets owned by a business.

Asset Swap: a trade in which a holder of "Asset A" wants to hedge by switching part of the holding into "Asset B." This is facilitated by a broker, who finds a holder of "Asset B" who wants to hedge into "Asset A." Also known as Swap. *See also* Interest Rate Swap.

Asset Value (Per Share): the estimated market value (net of debt) of a company's assets divided by common shares outstanding. A key measure for a value investor who is looking for opportunities to invest in companies at a price well below asset value per share. *See also* Book Value.

Assign: to transfer ownership from one party to another, often temporarily.

Assignee: the one to whom title is transferred under an assignment.

Assignment: 1. the process of transferring ownership. **2.** the process by which an interest in a life insurance policy is transferred from one person to another. **3.** the document and process by which a party voluntarily goes into bankruptcy. The assets are assigned to creditors who liquidate them to satisfy debts. **4.** notification from an option buyer to an option seller that the option has been exercised. *See also* Option.

Assignor: the party that endorses and surrenders title under an assignment.

Assimilated: *see* Absorbed.

Associate of the Credit Union Institute of Canada (ACUIC): a standing attained by credit union employees who have completed course work offered by the Credit Union Institute of Canada to prepare them for middle and senior management positions.

Association Bancaire pour l'Euro (ABE): *see* Euro Banking Association.

Association Cambiste Internationale (ACI): *see* Financial Markets Association.

Association for Investment Management and Research (AIMR): the primary U.S.-based professional organization for financial analysts, portfolio managers and others engaged in investment decision-making. AIMR is, among other things, responsible for enforcing the code of ethics and standards of professional conduct for its members. *See also* Financial Analysts Federation, Institute of Financial Analysts. Web site: www.aimr.com

Assumable Mortgage: a mortgage that, with the credit approval of the lender, can be transferred from the seller of a property to the buyer. *See also* Mortgage, Non-Assumable Mortgage, Wrap-Around Mortgage.

Assumed Interest Rate: the rate of interest used by an insurance company to establish the payments under an annuity contract. To allow the insurance company a margin of safety, the assumed interest rate is normally well below current interest rates. The higher the assumed interest rate, the higher the annuity payments.

Assumption: the act of taking responsibility for the obligations of another. *See also* Assumption Agreement.

Assumption Agreement: an agreement under which someone other than the mortgager agrees to undertake the mortgage obligations. Under such agreements, the original mortgager may have ongoing responsibilities for the mortgage until it is paid off or until the mortgagee provides a release. Also known as Mortgage Assumption. *See also* Mortgage.

Assurance: a term that is interchangeable with insurance, especially in Britain.

ASX All Ordinaries Index: *see* Australian Stock Exchange All Ordinaries Index.

Asynchronous: 1. in computers, a data transmission mode (used by most modems) in which each character is sent individually and begins with a start bit and ends with one or two stop bits. *See also* Computer. **2.** not occurring at the same time or at the same rate. *See also* Autosynch, Synchronous.

At Close Order: an order to buy or sell within 30 seconds of the market close or the order is cancelled. *See also* At Opening Order.

ATDP: *see* Automatic Dial Pulse.

ATDT: *see* Automatic Dial Tone.

ATES: *see* Automated Trade Execution System.

Athens Stock Exchange: the major stock exchange of Greece, located in its capital, Athens. Web site: www.ase.com

ATM: *see* Automated Teller Machine.

At Opening Order: a securities order to be filled at the opening trade or the order is cancelled. *See also* At Close Order.

ATP: *see* Arbitrage Trading Program.

At Par: at a price equal to par value (or face value) of a security. If the price is above par, it is at a premium. If the price is below par, it is at a discount. *See also* Discount, Par Value, Premium.

At Risk: exposed to the danger of economic loss. *See also* At Risk Rules.

At Risk Rules: in the Canadian Income Tax Act, rules limiting losses that partners can apply to the cost of investment (plus profits and minus losses and adjustments). In order to claim tax deductions, investors in limited partnerships must establish that they are at risk of economic loss. *See also* At Risk.

Attained Age: the age at which a person is eligible to receive benefits (e.g., from a pension plan).

Attachment: 1. a writ ordering the seizure of property. **2.** the legal seizure of a property or person.

At the Bell: just prior to the end of a trading session on the stock exchange. Also known as At the Close. *See also* After the Bell.

At the Close: *see* At the Bell.

At the Market Order: *see* Market Order.

At the Money: a circumstance in which the strike price of a financial option (e.g., a put or call) is equal to or near the price of the underlying security. Also known as On the Money. *See also* Deep in the Money, Deep out of the Money, In the Money, Option, Out of the Money.

Attorney General (AG): in Canada, the chief law officer of the Crown.

Attribute: in computers, a code that determines a file status as read-only, hidden, archive or system. *See also* Computer.

Attribution Rules: Canadian income tax rules that state that if the ownership of a property or asset is transferred to a spouse or certain children, the income from that property may be deemed to remain with the transferor. This prevents income splitting among family members for the sole purpose of reducing income taxes.

Au: *see* Gold.

Auction: 1. a public sale in which goods are sold to the highest bidder in an open process. *See also* As Is; As Is, Where Is; Presale Estimate; Reserve Bid. **2.** the system of bidding that forms the basis for virtually all financial markets. *See also* Open Outcry.

Auction Market: a market in which prices are set by open and competitive bids and offerings. Most financial markets are auction markets. Also known as Double Auction System.

Audit: the act of evaluating financial records for their accuracy, using the standards established by the Canadian Institute of Chartered Accountants. *See also* Annual Audit, Auditor.

Audited Financial Statement: a financial statement that has met the standards of an audit. *See also* Unaudited Financial Statement.

Auditor: one qualified to perform an audit. *See also* Audit.

Auditor's Report: a report signed by the auditor of a set of financial statements. The standard auditor's report has three paragraphs. The first paragraph states that the auditor has examined each of the financial statements presented. The second paragraph states that the audits were done according to generally accepted standards. The third paragraph expresses the auditor's opinion that the financial statements are a fair representation of the facts. If there are more than three paragraphs, the report may be qualified and should be read carefully. Also known as Accountant's Opinion. *See also* Annual Audit, Going Concern Opinion, Qualified Opinion.

Audit Trail: a record that traces financial data back to the original transaction.

Aunt Millie: a term used (mainly in the U.S.) to describe an unsophisticated investor. *See also* Jane Q. Public, John Q. Public.

Australian Stock Exchange: the major stock exchange of Australia, located in Sydney. Web site: www.asx.com.au

Australian Stock Exchange All Ordinaries Index: a market capitalization weighted index of the Australian Stock Exchange. Also known as All

Ordinaries Index, ASX All Ordinaries Index.

Australian Stock Price Riskless Indexed Notes (ASPIRIN): a four-year bond that has its interest rate determined by the increase in the Australian Stock Exchange All Ordinaries Index.

Austrian Stock Exchange: *see* Vienna Stock Exchange.

Austrian Traded Index: a market capitalization weighted index of the Vienna Stock Exchange.

Autex System: a computer network that alerts brokers of other brokers seeking to buy or sell large blocks of stocks.

Authenticated Copy: a copy of a document that an accepted authority (e.g., a notary public) has certified as real. *See also* Notary Public.

Authentication: in computers, the act of verifying a user's identity with passwords, challenge-response tokens or through biometric authentication. *See also* Biometric Authentication, Challenge-Response Token, Password.

Autocracy: a government in which one person has total power. *See also* Big Brother.

Authorized Capital: the total number of shares that a company is authorized to sell. In order to provide management with enough flexibility to issue a large number of shares without obtaining shareholder approval (e.g., to make an acquisition), authorized capital is often far in excess of current needs. Also known as Shares Authorized. *See also* Issued and Outstanding Capital.

AUTOEXEC.BAT: a DOS file that contains some start-up commands that help to configure a computer. It runs automatically when the computer is turned on. *See also* Computer.

Automated Banking Machine (ABM): a machine that accepts deposits, dispenses cash and provides other services to people who have valid access cards. On average, it costs $.27 to process a cheque by ABM compared with $.91 to process it by a teller. In 1998 there were 15,481 ABMs, or 1.9 for every bank branch in Canada. Also known as Automated Teller Machine, Bank Machine.

Automated Bond System (ABS): a computer system on the New York Stock Exchange that records bids and offerings of infrequently traded bonds. *See also* Cabinet Bond.

Automated Exchange Trade System (XTS): the automated trading system on the Athens Stock Exchange. *See also* Athens Stock Exchange.

Automated Teller Machine (ATM): *see* Automated Banking Machine.

Automated Trade Execution System (ATES): a fully automated trading system used by the Alberta Stock Exchange.

Automatic Answering: in computers, a feature that enables a modem to answer a telephone call after a specified number of rings. *See also* Automatic Dialling, Computer.

Automatic Dialling: in computers, a process by which a modem dials a telephone call. *See also* Automatic Answering, Computer.

Automatic Dial Pulse (ATDP): in computers, a modem command that initiates automatic pulse dialling. *See also* Automatic Dial Tone, Computer, Pulse Dialling.

Automatic Dial Tone (ATDT): in computers, a modem command that initiates automatic touch-tone dialling. *See also* Automatic Dial Pulse, Computer, Tone Dialling.

Automatic Investment Program (AIP): any investment program that features automatic purchases or withdrawals. The more common AIPs include monthly investments with a mutual fund, automatic dividend reinvestment with a mutual fund or company and payroll deduction plans. *See also* Mutual Fund.

Automatic Premium Loan: in a cash value life insurance policy, a clause that provides for a loan to be taken on the cash surrender value and used to pay premiums. *See also* Cash Surrender Value, Life Insurance, Whole Life Insurance.

Automatic Transfer: *see* Accelerated Funds Transfer.

Automatic Withdrawal Program: the act of taking a fixed amount of money from a bank account regularly for the purpose of making insurance payments, mutual fund investments and loan or other payments. *See also* Life Insurance, Mutual Fund.

Automobile Insurance: insurance that covers liabilities stemming from automobile accidents, it is subject to deductible amounts and coverage limits.

Autosync: in computers, a protocol that allows a modem to adjust to synchronous or asynchronous data transmissions. *See also* Asynchronous, Computer, Synchronous.

Average: 1. *see* Arithmetic Average. 2. *see* Stock Market Index.

Average Cost: the average of the cost per share of all shares purchased when the same security is purchased more than once (e.g., a dollar cost averaging program). *See also* Dollar Cost Averaging.

Average Daily Balance Method: the calculation of financing costs or interest payable based on the amount owing at the end of each day, divided by the number of days in a period. This method of calculating balance is used by many department store credit cards and results in less interest payable than with the Previous Balance Method, which is used by most

general purpose credit cards. *See also* Adjusted
Balance Method, Minimum Monthly Balance, Past
Due Balance Method, Previous Balance Method.

Average Down: the act of buying additional shares at
lower prices to lower the average price of all the
shares owned. *See also* Average Up.

Average Income: an annual household income of
$57,146 (1997). Also known as Middle Income.

Average Investor: the typical individual investor.

Average Life: an estimate of the term to maturity of a
bond, it takes into account possible early repayments.

Average Number of Shares Outstanding: a time-
weighted calculation of the number of shares outstanding during the year (e.g., if a company issues
shares at the end of the third quarter, then only one
quarter of the total number of shares would be
included in the calculation). This is an important calculation because it affects earnings per share. *See also*
Earnings per Share.

Average Tax Rate: total income taxes payable divided
by total taxable income. *See also* Effective Tax Rate,
Marginal Tax Rate, Taxable Income, Tax Bracket,
Taxes.

Average Up: the act of buying additional shares at
higher prices to raise the average price of all the
shares owned. *See also* Average Down.

Averaging: the act of investing over time, and at dif-
ferent prices, rather than all at once. Also known as
Price Averaging. *See also* Average Down, Average Up,
Dollar Cost Averaging.

Avocation: an activity in addition to a person's occupation (e.g., a hobby). *See also* Occupation

Avoirdupois Weight: the system of weights based on
one pound equalling 16 ounces, or 7,000 grains.

Away from the Market: a bid for securities that is
below, or an offering that is above, the current market.

Away from Me: a comment, often used by market
makers on the New York Stock Exchange, that indicates that a more attractive bid or offer is available
elsewhere.

BA: *see* Banker's Acceptance.

Baby Bells: the separate companies into which the Bell System was broken up in 1984, including Ameritech, Bell Atlantic, BellSouth, Cincinnati Bell, NYNEX, SBC Communications and U.S. West.

Baby Bond: a bond with a par value of under $1,000. *See also* Bond.

Baby Boom: the large increase in births after the Second World War.

Baby Boomer: a person born shortly after the Second World War, generally between the years of 1947 and 1959. Also known as Boomer. *See also* Echo Generation, Generation X, Generation Y, Sandwich Generation.

Back and Fill: a term used to describe a financial market's tendency to consolidate after a rise. The consolidation is often marked by prices falling part of the way back for a period of time before moving ahead to new highs.

Backbencher: a member of a legislative body who is not a cabinet minister, an opposition critic or a party leader.

Backdate: *see* Antedate.

Back Door Listing: this occurs when a company that does not qualify for a stock exchange listing acquires a listed company in order to become listed.

Back End Load: *see* Deferred Sales Charge.

Backer: 1. *see* Angel. **2.** someone who lends financial support.

Background: in computers, an application that takes place behind the active window. *See also* Active Window, Computer.

Back In: a right (usually in a resource property agreement) that allows the original property owner to increase his/her interest in a property if exploration is successful.

Backlog: orders received but not fulfilled. A high backlog usually indicates a positive business environment.

Back Month: *see* Furthest Out.

Back Office: the accounting or operations departments of a financial institution. *See also* Front Office.

Back Office Crunch: this occurs when the volume of trading on the stock exchange is so high that brokerage firm back offices cannot keep up with the number of buy and sell orders. In the past, stock exchanges have been forced to shorten trading hours to allow record keeping to catch up.

Backstop: to provide last-resort support or security.

Back Taxes: tax payments that are overdue.

Back-to-Back Letter of Credit: a letter of credit issued on the security of an existing letter of credit. A back-to-back letter of credit is often used by an agent who purchases goods from one country and sells them in another country. *See also* Letter of Credit.

Backup: 1. in computers, to save data in a secondary storage area. *See also* Computer. **2.** in bond trading, the swap of one security for another with a shorter maturity. *See also* Bond. **3.** in financial markets, a sudden change in the overall trend.

Backwardation: in commodities and foreign exchange, this occurs when near-term deliveries trade at a higher price than later deliveries. Opposite of Contango. *See also* Contango.

Bad Debt: 1. in business, accounts receivable that cannot be collected. **2.** slang for loans that have non-tax-deductible interest. *See also* Good Debt, Non-Deductible Interest Expense.

Bad Delivery: a term used to describe a stock certificate that is not in transferable form when submitted to settle a trade (e.g., a certificate without a proper signature or signature guarantee). *See also* Bounce, Good Delivery.

Bad Faith: to mislead another party or to purposefully neglect the fulfillment of an obligation. *See also* Good Faith.

Bad Title: title to property (often real estate) that does not clearly confer ownership. A bad title can arise from unpaid property taxes, an incorrect survey or a building violation. *See also* Clear Title, Cloud on Title, Defective Title, On Title, Title, Title Deed, Title Defect, Title Search.

Bag Man: someone who organizes the collection of financial donations, especially for political parties.

Bahrain Stock Exchange (BSE): the major stock exchange of Bahrain, located in its capital, Manama. Web site: www.bahrainstock.com/

Bahrain Stock Exchange Index: a market capitalization weighted index for the Bahrain Stock Exchange.

Baht: the prime currency of Thailand.

Bail: a security deposit used to guarantee that an arrested person will appear for trial.

Bail Bond: a document that secures the pretrial release of a person in custody.

Bailiff: a court official who executes writs and arrests.

Bailout: this occurs when a government provides financial assistance not available from conventional sources in order to prevent a company from going bankrupt. *See also* Bankrupt.

Bail Out: to sell a security, often at a loss, in order to avoid future expected losses.

Bailsman: one who provides bail for another.

Bait and Switch: an unethical sales tactic by which bargain-priced items are used to attract customers who are then sold more expensive items.

Baker's Dozen: 13 items. Derived from the Middle Ages, when severe penalties were levied against bakers who delivered bread that was short in weight. Because it was not easy to measure weight back then, bakers routinely delivered an extra loaf for every 12 ordered.

Baksheesh: from the Middle East, a term that means an extravagant gratuity or bribe.

Balance: 1. the difference between debits and credits in an account. **2.** in banking, the amount of money in an account.

Balanced Budget: a budget in which revenue or income matches expenses or outflow. *See also* Budget Deficit, Budget Surplus.

Balanced Fund: *see* Balanced Mutual Fund.

Balanced Mutual Fund: a mutual fund that holds both lower risk, lower return fixed income securities and higher risk, higher return equities. Also known as Balanced Fund. *See also* Mutual Fund – Other.

Balance of Payments: a system used by countries to measure financial inflows and outflows. The balance of payments is usually divided into a country's current account, capital account and gold account. *See also* Capital Account, Current Account, Gold Account.

Balance of Sale: *see* Vendor Financing.

Balance of Trade: the difference between a country's exports (the goods and services flowing out and the payment flowing in) and imports (the goods and services flowing in and the payment flowing out). *See also* Favourable Balance of Trade, Unfavourable Balance of Trade.

Balance Sheet: a financial statement that lists assets, liabilities and equity. So termed because in the balance sheet equation, assets equal liabilities plus shareholder's equity; in other words, they balance. The balance sheet provides a picture of financial position at a point in time. Also known as Statement of Financial Position. *See also* Financial Position.

Balboa: the prime currency of Panama.

Baleboss: the person in charge of a business.

Balloon Loan: a loan with one large final payment. Balloon loans are used to keep regular payments at a low level when a refinancing at maturity is expected.

Also known as Partially Amortized Loan. *See also* Balloon Payment.

Balloon Payment: the one large final payment due under a balloon loan. *See also* Balloon Loan.

Bamboozle: to swindle or cheat.

Bandwidth: the rate at which data can be transmitted by a communications system in bits per second. *See also* Computer.

Bangkok SET Index: a market capitalization weighted index of the Stock Exchange of Bangkok.

Bangladesh Stock Exchange: *see* Dhaka Stock Exchange.

Bank: 1. a financial institution that accepts deposits to safeguard money or facilitate the transfer of funds, makes loans, guarantees creditworthiness and exchanges currency. A bank generates profits by borrowing money at a lower rate of interest (e.g., through savings accounts, term deposits, etc.) and lending money at a higher rate of interest (e.g., through credit cards, mortgages, etc.) as well as through service charges. In Canada, banks are often referred to as Chartered Banks. *See also* Commercial Banking, Consumer Banking. **2.** to do business with a bank. **3.** to operate a bank.

Bankable: a term used to describe a business transaction that is sufficiently secure to warrant financing from a bank.

Bank Accommodation: a bank loan made on the basis of a note signed by the customer. An accommodation is a quick and less expensive form of borrowing that is available to the bank's better clients.

Bank Account: 1. *see* Chequing Account. **2.** *see* Savings Account.

Bank Act: the federal statute that regulates the banking industry in Canada.

Bankbook: a booklet in which all transactions in an bank account are recorded. Also known as Passbook.

Bank Card: a card issued by a bank to enable customers to access an automated banking machine or to make payments directly from a bank account. Also known as Cash Card. *See also* Debit Card.

Bank Cheque: a cheque that is payable from the bank's own account.

Banker's Acceptance (BA): a short-term draft guaranteed by a bank.

Banker's Hours: a work day that starts late and ends early. Derived from the time when banks would open later and close earlier than other commercial establishments.

Banker's Pool: a group, led by Richard F. Whitney (1888-1974), that purchased hundreds of millions of dollars worth of stocks during the stock market crash of 1929 in an effort to restore public confidence.

Bank for International Settlements (BIS): established in 1930 and based in Basel, Switzerland, the BIS is a central bank of central banks. There are 41 National Central Banks that are voting shareholders in the BIS. Since 1986, the BIS has been the clearing and settlement agent for the Euro Banking Association. *See also* Euro Banking Association.

Banking Group: *see* Underwriting Syndicate.

Bank Insurance Fund (BIF): the unit of the U.S. Federal Deposit Insurance Corporation that provides deposit insurance for banking institutions. *See also* Federal Deposit Insurance Corporation.

Bank Line: *see* Line of Credit.

Bank Machine: *see* Automated Banking Machine.

Bankmail: an agreement between a bank and a party to a takeover offer in which the bank will not finance a competing offer. *See also* Blackmail, Greenmail, Whitemail.

Bank Note: often, paper currency.

Bank of Canada: the central bank of Canada, which is regulated under the Bank of Canada Act. The Bank of Canada is responsible for managing Canada's monetary policy and providing central bank services, such as supporting the cheque clearing system, managing the federal government debt and issuing Canadian currency.

Bank of Canada Act: the federal statute that regulates the Bank of Canada.

Bank of Canada Notes: Canadian currency. Money.

Bank of Canada Rate: *see* Bank Rate.

Bank of England: the central bank of the United Kingdom, established on July 27, 1694.

Bank of Japan: the central bank of Japan.

Bank Quality: *see* Investment Grade.

Bank Rate: an interest rate charged by the Bank of Canada on loans made to chartered banks. The bank rate is the average of 91-day treasury bill rates plus one-quarter of one percent. Also known as Bank of Canada Rate.

Bank Reconciliation: *see* Account Reconciliation.

Bankroll: 1. to underwrite or finance a project. **2.** a large amount of paper currency.

Bankrupt: 1. legally declared unable to meet one's financial obligations. Also known, informally, as Belly Up, Broke, Busted. *See also* Insolvent, Solvent. **2.** a person who is in a state of bankruptcy. *See also* Bankruptcy, Creditor's Committee, Discharge of Bankruptcy, Proposal, Trustee in Bankruptcy.

Bankruptcy: a legal process. If a creditor cannot satisfy all debts in full, then bankruptcy ensures that debts are satisfied in an equitable manner and that the bankrupt party is also treated fairly. *See also* Bankrupt, Creditor's Committee, Discharge of Bankruptcy, Trustee in Bankruptcy, Voluntary Bankruptcy.

Bank Statement: *see* Account Statement.

Bank Wire: a subscription-based private wire service for North American financial institutions.

Barbell: a bond portfolio investment strategy in which holdings are concentrated in very short and very long maturities. Also known as Dog Bone, Dumbbell.

Bar Code: a series of vertical bars of varying widths printed on consumer product packaging to record prices and control inventory.

Barefoot Pilgrim: an unsophisticated investor who has lost everything in the stock market.

Bargain: 1. an investment or product that can be purchased at an attractive price. **2.** to negotiate.

Bar Graph: a graph that consists of rectangular bars representing quantities. *See also* Pie Chart, Point and Figure Chart.

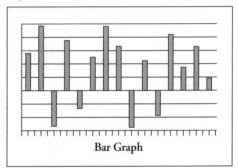

Bar Graph

Barings Bank (Barings PLC): the 233-year-old bank that collapsed in early 1995 under $1.4 billion of losses stemming from unauthorized derivatives trading by Nick Leeson. Barings' best-known customer was the Queen of England. *See also* Leeson, Nick.

Barings PLC: *see* Barings Bank.

Barometer: an instrument that measures atmospheric pressure in order to forecast the weather. The stock market is often referred to as a barometer because it can be used to forecast the economy. *See also* Bellwether.

Barometer Stock: a stock that has a price trend indicative of the market as a whole. *See also* Bellwether Stock.

Barra: a recognized standard for measuring the inherent risks and returns of various asset classes.

Barrel of Oil (Bbl): 42 American gallons of oil at 60 degrees Fahrenheit.

Barrel of Oil Equivalent (BOE): conversion of gas reserves into the equivalent of a barrel of oil. As a rule, 10 mcf of gas is equivalent to one barrel of oil.

Barriers to Entry: factors that make it difficult for new competitors to enter an industry, these include large upfront capital requirements, regulatory approval or licensing and significant research and development time.

Barrister: a member of the legal profession who is qualified to plead cases in the superior courts. In Canada (excluding Quebec), all barristers are also solicitors. *See also* Lawyer, Solicitor.

Barron's Confidence Index: an index published in *Barron's* magazine, a leading U.S. financial publication of Dow Jones & Company, it compares the yield on 10 high-grade bonds with the yield on 40 average-grade bonds. A declining spread indicates increasing confidence because it means that money is flowing into the lower grade bonds. Also known as Confidence Index. *See also* Dow Jones.

Barter: to trade goods and services without money. On an international level, bartering can facilitate trade between countries when one country does not have sufficient hard currency to make payment. *See also* Hard Currency, Sale.

Base Building: a period of flat or trendless prices after a prolonged decline in the financial markets.

Baseline: a line that forms the basis for measurement or comparison.

Basement: the low point for prices.

Base Period: the starting point for a comparison of change (e.g., the Toronto Stock Exchange 300 Index started with a value of 1,000 in 1975. The base period is 1975). *See also* Base Value, Base Year.

Base Value: the starting value for a comparison of change (e.g., the Toronto Stock Exchange 300 Index started with a value of 1,000 in 1975. The base value is 1,000). *See also* Base Period, Base Year.

Base Year: a base period that is one year. Often used to compare the rate of growth in a company's sales or earnings (e.g., the earnings per share for the Toronto Dominion Bank increased from $2.14 for the year ending October 1994 to $3.62 for the year ending October 1998. The base year is the 12 months ending October 1994). *See also* Base Period, Base Value.

Basis: 1. the difference between the cash price and the futures price of a commodity. **2.** the difference between the price of a financial futures contract and the price of the underlying security. *See also* Underlying Security.

Basis Point: one one-hundredth of one percent. A 50 basis point change in interest rates is a move of one-half of one percent. Also known as Beep, as in "interest rates rose 10 beeps today." *See also* Point.

Basis Trading: a trading strategy in which either the stock index futures or the underlying stocks are

owned. The portfolio switches between the stock index futures and the underlying stocks, depending on which asset is determined to be relatively cheap.

Basket: a group of selected securities or items. *See also* Market Basket.

Basket Clause: a section of the Pension Benefits Standards Act that specifies what proportion of a pension portfolio can be invested in securities that do not qualify for pension fund investment under the usual requirements of the act. *See also* Pension Benefits Standards Act.

Basket Delivery: the system that allows different futures contracts on cash instruments to be delivered at the same time.

Basket Trade: buying or selling a specific set of securities (generally 15 or more) in one order. Used by program traders or institutions to invest a large sum of money in the same securities and in the same proportion as a particular index or portfolio. *See also* Institutional Investor, Market Basket, Program Trading.

Baud: a unit of speed in computer data transmission. One baud equals one event or signal change per second. *See also* Baud Rate, Computer.

Baud Rate: the speed at which a computer communicates with a modem. Not to be confused with the speed at which a modem transfers data in bits per second (BPS) (e.g., a 9,600-baud modem actually operates at 9,600 BPS but has a 2,400 baud rate if it encodes four bits per event). *See also* Baud, Bits per Second, Computer.

Bay Street: the main financial district of Toronto and the financial centre of Canada. *See also* Howe Street, Main Street, Threadneedle Street, Wall Street.

BBA: *see* British Banker's Association.

Bbl: *see* Barrel of Oil.

BBS: *see* Bulletin Board System.

BCT-Costa Rica Index: a market capitalization weighted index of the Costa Rica Stock Exchange.

Bean Counter: slang for an accountant. *See also* Accountant.

Bear: 1. in general, one who is pessimistic about the economy or financial markets. **2.** a person who expects stock or bond prices to decline. *See also* Bull.

Bear Campaign: selling securities short in the expectation that prices will fall and provide the seller with an opportunity to cover his/her position at a profit. *See also* Short Sale.

Bear Clique: a group that sells a security short in order to drive down the price. Such groups are illegal. *See also* Bear Raid.

Bear Covering: *see* Short Covering.

Bearer Bond: *see* Bearer Security.

Bearer Form: a form of security registration that is not in an owner's name but makes the security negotiable by the person having physical possession of the certificate. *See also* Bearer Security.

Bearer Security: a security registered in bearer form. A bond registered in bearer form is known as a Bearer Bond. A stock registered in bearer form is known as a Bearer Stock. *See also* Bearer Form.

Bearer Stock: *see* Bearer Security.

Bear Hug: a term used to describe a takeover offer so attractive that it is highly unlikely to be refused.

Bearish: a sense of pessimism about financial markets or the economy. *See also* Bullish.

Bear Market: a market in which prices have declined sharply, or have declined over an extended period of time or have declined sharply over an extended period of time. *See also* Bull Market, Elliott Wave Theory, Kondratieff Wave, Peak, Presidential Election Cycle, Stock Market Cycle, Trough.

Bear Panic: this occurs when prices rebound unexpectedly, and bearish investors, who have sold short, panic and begin to cover their positions. *See also* Bearish, Buying Panic, Panic, Short Sale.

Bear Pool: a group of people who, illegally, act together to try to manipulate a stock price so it will fall. *See also* Bull Pool.

Bear Raid: a move to manipulate stock prices so that they will decline. *See also* Bear Clique, Bull Raid.

Bear Spread: a reference to buying one option and selling another in order to profit if the price of the underlying security falls as well as to minimize losses if the price of the underlying security rises sharply. *See also* Option.

Bear Straddle: a strategy that involves writing an uncovered call option and a covered put option on the same underlying stock with the same strike price and expiration date. The writer profits if the stock price remains stable. *See also* Bull Straddle, Covered Put Option, Expiration Date, Option, Strike Price, Uncovered Call Option, Underlying Stock.

Bear Squeeze: *see* Short Squeeze.

Bear Trap: a sharp, brief drop in the market that recovers quickly. Those induced to sell or sell short during the decline are said to have "fallen into a bear trap." *See also* Bull Trap.

Beat the Market: to manage a portfolio so as to produce a rate of return that is higher than the return from a benchmark (e.g., the Toronto Stock Exchange 300 Index). Also known as Beat the Tape.

Beat the Tape: *see* Beat the Market.

Beep: *see* Basis Point.

Beige Book: an economic summary produced for the U.S. Federal Open Market Committee meetings.

Authorship of the document rotates among the Federal Reserve banks represented on the committee. *See also* Federal Open Market Committee, Federal Reserve Banks, Federal Reserve Board.

Beirut Stock Exchange: the major stock exchange of Lebanon, located in its capital, Beirut. Web site: www.lebanon.com/financial/stocks/index.htm

Belgium Stock Exchange: *see* Brussels Stock Exchange.

Bell: 1. *see* Closing Bell. **2.** *see* Opening Bell.

Bell Curve: a graphic depiction of a normal distribution of data. *See also* Normal Distribution.

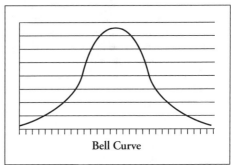

Bell Curve

Bells and Whistles: features added to a product to induce prospective purchasers. *See also* Sweetener.

Bellwether: a leader or leading indicator of trends. *See also* Barometer.

Bellwether Bond: a single bond used to gauge the performance of the bond market in general. *See also* Bond.

Bellwether Stock: a stock looked upon as a leading indicator of the market. General Motors was a bellwether stock, hence the old adage: "What is good for General Motors is good for America." *See also* Barometer Stock, General Motors Indicator.

Belly Up: *see* Bankrupt.

Belly Up to the Bar: 1. to make a commitment. **2.** to get involved in a market or market play.

Belt Tightening: a reduction in spending or expenses.

BEL20: *see* Brussels Stock Exchange BEL20 Index.

Benchmark: a standard against which other things can be measured or compared. *See also* Bogie, Stock Bet.

Bench Warrant: a court order authorizing the legal arrest of a person.

Beneficial Interest: an interest that is represented by the ownership of some other asset of value (e.g., an interest in a company through owning shares). *See also* Beneficial Owner, Beneficial Use.

Beneficial Owner: the person (or institution) that benefits from ownership of an asset even though he/she is not registered as the owner (e.g., shares held by a brokerage company in a nominee name even though the real owner is a client). *See also* Nominee, Nominee Name.

Beneficial Use: with respect to property, the right to its use as distinct from its legal title (e.g., a person may retain legal title to a residence in order to control ownership but may grant the use of the property to another person). *See also* Beneficial Interest.

Beneficiary: 1. the person who receives an inheritance by being named in a will. *See also* Will. **2.** the person who receives payments from an annuity. *See also* Annuity. **3.** the person who receives the death benefit from a life insurance policy. *See also* Life Insurance. **4.** the party in whose favour a letter of credit is issued. *See also* Letter of Credit. **5.** the person who inherits the assets of a Registered Retirement Savings Plan. *See also* Registered Retirement Savings Plan. **6.** the party for whom a trust is established. *See also* Trust.

Benefit: an entitlement under an employment agreement, insurance policy or welfare program.

Benefit/Cost Analysis: *see* Cost/Benefit Analysis.

Benefit Plan: *see* Employee Benefit Plan.

Bequeath: to leave something to another through a will. *See also* Will.

Bequest: something left to another through a will. Also known as Legacy. *See also* Will.

Bermuda Stock Exchange (BSX): the stock exchange of Bermuda, located in its capital, Hamilton. Web site: www.bsx.com

Bessemer Process: the act of making steel by blasting air through molten iron to burn away impurities.

Best Efforts: a type of underwriting in which the underwriter agrees to sell a fixed number of securities to investors at an agreed-upon price without a guarantee of how many securities will be sold. This form of underwriting entails risk for the issuer because there is no guarantee that the security offering will be successful. *See also* Bought Deal, Standby Commitment, Underwriting Risk.

Best Interests Test: in law, the intent to resolve disputes regarding custody of and access to children on the basis of what will best serve the children's interests.

Best (A.M.) Company, Inc.: established in 1899, Best's provides a widely recognized rating of the financial strength of life, health, property and casualty insurance companies in 65 countries. Best's ratings can be used to judge an insurer's ability to satisfy potential insurance claims and the payment of obligations under annuity contracts. Also known as A.M. Best Company, Inc. Web site: www.ambest.com *See also* Best's Financial Performance Ratings, Best's Ratings.

Best's Financial Performance Ratings: ratings of small, less well-established insurance companies by Best (A.M.) Company, Inc. Ratings range from 9 ("very strong") to 1 ("poor"). A rating of 4 or less indicates that the insurer is "vulnerable." *See also* Best (A.M.) Company, Inc.; Best's Ratings.

Best's Ratings: ratings of large, well-established insurance companies by Best (A.M.) Company, Inc. A rating of A++ or A+ is "superior," A or A- is "excellent," and B++ or B+ is "very good." A rating of B or lower indicates that the insurer is "vulnerable." *See also* Best (A.M.) Company, Inc.; Best's Financial Performance Ratings.

Bet: *see* Stock Bet.

Beta (ß): a statistical measure of the volatility of a security or portfolio compared with a benchmark. The higher the beta, the more volatile the stock or portfolio and the higher the risk. Average risk is a beta of 1.0. A beta of 0.8 has 20 percent less risk than the market. A beta of 1.2 has 20 percent more risk than the market. Conservative investors should focus on lower beta stocks, while aggressive investors should favour higher beta stocks. *See also* Historical Beta, Long-Term Beta, Normal Beta, Portfolio Beta, Short-Term Beta, Standard Deviation, Volatility.

Beta Fundamental: a systematic risk coefficient estimated on the basis of the fundamental operating characteristics of a company. *See also* Beta, Systematic Risk.

Beta Risk: the level of risk of a specific security in the context of a portfolio of securities. *See also* Non-Systematic Risk.

Beta Stock: in the London Stock Exchange's former system of ranking stocks, beta stocks were those that rated just below alpha stocks (the highest ranking) in terms of size and trading volume. Delta and Gamma were other rankings, each of which represented a smaller underlying company and less actively traded stock. *See also* Alpha Stock, Delta Stock, Gamma Stock.

Beta Test: a round of testing in the field prior to commercial production (e.g., new computer software is often given to a group of users for testing and debugging before it is offered for sale). Also known as Field Test. *See also* Bug, Debug.

Beta Test Site: a location chosen for a beta test.

B4N: Internet acronym for "bye for now."

Biannual: *see* Semiannual.

Bid: the price quote for a security is comprised of a bid and offer. The bid is the price at which a buyer will purchase a security. When the bid equals the offer, then a trade occurs. Also known as the Bid Price. *See also* Offer.

Bid Price: see Bid.

Bid Up: a term used to describe the process that occurs when a buyer is willing to raise his bid price to successively higher levels in order to accumulate a security.

Bid Wanted: when there are no bids, a notice given by a broker who is interested in selling a security. *See also* Offered Without, Offer Wanted.

Bid Without: a market in which there is a bid but no offer. *See also* Offered Without, Offer Wanted.

Biennial: occurring every two years. Also known as Biyearly. *See also* Annual, Triennial.

BIF: *see* Bank Insurance Fraud.

Big Bang: 1. the reform of the London Stock Exchange, which occurred on October 27, 1986. *See also* May Day. **2.** a reference to the reform of the stock exchanges of Japan proposed in mid-1998.

Big Blue: *see* International Business Machines Corporation.

Big Board: a nickname for the New York Stock Exchange. *See also* New York Stock Exchange.

Big Brother: a symbol of oppressive state control, taken from George Orwell's *Nineteen Eighty-four*. *See also* Autocracy.

Big Dragon of Asia: *see* Big Tiger of Asia.

Big Eight: *see* Big Five.

Big Five: the five largest U.S. accounting firms, as of 1999: Anderson Worldwide, Deloitte & Touche, Ernst & Young, KPMG and Price Waterhouse Cooper. Formerly known as Big Eight and Big Six (prior to mergers).

Big Five Chartered Banks: in Canada, the Bank of Montreal, Bank of Nova Scotia, Canadian Imperial Bank of Commerce, Royal Bank of Canada and Toronto Dominion Bank.

Big Four: the four major brokerage companies that dominate trading in equities and bonds in Japan (1998): Daiwa Securities Ltd., Nikko Securities Ltd., Nomura Securities Ltd. and Yamaichi Securities Ltd. (Yamaichi went out of business in early 1998, so the term may soon change to Big Three.)

Big Mac Index: an index based on the theory that if currencies are valued properly, a relatively homogeneous product, such as a McDonald's Big Mac, will cost the same in every country and in any currency. *See also* Purchasing Power Parity.

Big Producer: in the investment industry, a stockbroker who generates a large amount of commissions (e.g., over $1 million a year).

Big Six: *see* Big Five.

Big Three: 1. originally, General Motors, Ford and Chrysler. As of November 14, 1998, following Chrysler's merger with Daimler-Benz (into DaimlerChrysler AG), the Big Three is now the Big Two. **2.** in Switzerland, a reference to the country's three largest banks: Credit Suisse, Swiss Bank Corporation and Union Bank of Switzerland.

Big Ticket: a consumer product with a high price.

Big Tiger of Asia: Japan. Also known as Big Dragon of Asia. *See also* Mini-Tigers of Asia, Tigers of Asia.

Big Two: *see* Big Three.

Big Uglies: large, unglamorous companies that are out of favour with investors.

BIL: *see* Business Improvement Loan.

Bilateral: an agreement made between two parties or countries with the consent of both sides.

Bilk: to cheat or defraud.

Bill: 1. a statement of charges or a request for payment. **2.** a reference to paper money (e.g., a ten-dollar bill). **3.** in government, proposed legislation. **4.** short form for treasury bill. *See also* Treasury Bill. **5.** short form for bill of exchange. *See also* Bill of Exchange. **6.** short form for bill of lading. *See also* Bill of Lading. **7.** short form for bill of sale. *See also* Bill of Sale. **8.** short form for due bill. *See also* Due Bill.

Billing Cycle: the time, usually after one month, when bills are sent to customers.

Billionaire: 1. an individual whose personal wealth exceeds one billion or more units of currency. **2.** a general reference to a person of great wealth.

Bill of Exchange: 1. a short-term debt secured by a commodity or product in transit. *See also* Eurobill of Exchange. **2.** a requirement to pay a sum of money to a specified person. Also known as Draft.

Bill of Goods: 1. a consignment of merchandise. **2.** a misleading or dishonest statement.

Bill of Lading: a document that lists and acknowledges the receipt of goods.

Bill of Sale: a document that attests to the transfer of goods or property through sale.

Bimonthly: every two months.

Binary Digit: either of the two digits in the binary number system, 0 and 1. *See also* Binary Number System, Binary Scale, Binary System.

Binary Number System: a system using only two symbols, 0 and 1, to express information. *See also* Binary Digit, Binary Scale, Binary System.

Sample Binary Scale
0 is expressed as 00
1 is expressed as 01
2 is expressed as 10
3 is expressed as 11
4 is expressed as 100
5 is expressed as 101
6 is expressed as 110
7 is expressed as 111
8 is expressed as 1000
9 is expressed as 1001
10 is expressed as 1010
and so on …

Binary Scale: a scale in which all of the numbers are made up of combinations of 0 and 1. *See also* Binary Digit, Binary Number System, Binary System.

Binary System: a system based on two elements (e.g., an on/off electrical switch is a binary system). Modern digital computers use a binary number system operated by positive and negative electrical charges. *See also* Binary Digit, Binary Number System, Binary Scale, Computer.

Binding Agreement: an agreement that legally requires participants to fulfill their obligations.

Binding Arbitration: a process of dispute resolution by which two parties agree to abide by the decision of a third party. *See also* Negotiation.

Binder: 1. a temporary document that puts an agreement into effect until the final contract is prepared. **2.** in insurance, a temporary agreement that puts coverage into effect until the final contract is issued. **3.** in real estate, a refundable deposit that stays in place until the sale is closed.

Biochip: a computer chip that uses organic molecules to form a semiconductor. *See also* Computer.

Biogas: a methane and carbon dioxide mixture produced by bacteria and used as fuel.

Biomass: plant material, vegetation or agricultural waste used as fuel.

Biometric Authentication: in computers, a method for identifying users through tests such as fingerprint readers, retinal scans or voice verification. *See also* Access Control, Authentication, Challenge-Response Token, Computer, Firewall, Password, Public Key, Secret Key.

BIOS: a set of low-level instructions needed by a computer to perform basic operations. The computer's BIOS (Basic Input/Output System) is usually stored on a special kind of memory chip and loaded at start-up. *See also* Computer.

Biotechnology: the use of biological substances to perform industrial or manufacturing processes.

Bipartisan: supported by members of two parties (e.g., in the House of Commons, a bill upheld by two major political parties constitutes a bipartisan agreement).

Bipartite: an agreement that has two participants.

Bird in the Hand . . . : in investment, the idea that a smaller profit today is better than the promise of a larger profit in the future.

Birr: the prime currency of Ethiopia.

Birthrate: in a given region, the number of live births divided by the total population for a specific period of time.

Birthright: a right, privilege or possession belonging to one from birth.

BIS: *see* Bank for International Settlements.

Bit: short for **bi**nary digi**t**, a bit is the smallest unit of information stored by a computer. One bit expresses either the numerals 0 or 1 of a binary number. Eight bits make up a byte. *See also* Binary Digit, Binary Number System, Byte, Computer, Gigabyte, Kilobyte, Megabyte.

Bite the Dust: in investment and business, to fail, go bankrupt or experience a serious decline in value.

Bitmap: on a computer, a picture or image composed of tiny dots or pixels. A common bitmapped image file is identified with the extension .BMP. *See also* Computer.

Bits per Second (BPS): in computer data transmission, a unit of speed. *See also* Baud Rate.

Biweekly: occurring every two weeks.

Biyearly: *see* Biennial.

Blackball: a negative vote, often used to prevent admitting someone to membership in an organization.

Black Box: any device in which the inputs and outputs are known but the internal processes are unknown.

Black Friday: any Friday during which stock prices decline sharply. The original Black Friday was September 24, 1869, when an attempt to corner the gold market created a panic. Another Black Friday was October 16, 1987, when the Dow-Jones Average fell 108 points prior to the Crash of '87. *See also* Black Monday, Black Thursday, Black Tuesday, Black Wednesday, Golden Wednesday, Grey Monday, Silver Thursday.

Black Gold: slang for oil.

Black Knight: a party that makes a hostile takeover offer on a target company. *See also* Grey Knight, White Knight, Yellow Knight.

Black List: 1. to put on a list of people or businesses to be avoided. *See also* Blackball. **2.** a list of people or businesses to be avoided. *See also* White List.

Blackmail: extortion. *See also* Bankmail, Greenmail, Whitemail.

Black Market: illicit traffic in officially controlled or scarce goods or services.

Black Monday: any Monday during which stock prices decline sharply. Notable Black Mondays include October 19, 1987, when the Dow-Jones Average fell 504 points, and August 31, 1998, when the Dow fell 512 points. *See also* Black Friday, Black Thursday, Black Tuesday, Black Wednesday, Golden Wednesday, Grey Monday, Silver Thursday.

Black Out: a complete loss of electric power, often caused by an unexpected increase in demand for power. *See also* Brown Out.

Black-Scholes Option Pricing Model: a mathematical model used to estimate option prices based on exercise price, underlying security price, term to expiry, interest rates and underlying security price volatility. Created in 1973 by the late Fischer Black and Nobel Prize winner Myron S. Scholes, professor of Finance at Stanford University, the model has gained broad application in option valuation and trading. *See also* Option.

Black Thursday: any Thursday during which stock prices decline sharply. Notable Black Thursdays include October 24, 1929, when security prices plunged in one of the most memorable down days in the history of the New York Stock Exchange, and October 23, 1997, when the Hong Kong market fell 10.4 percent. *See also* Black Friday, Black Monday, Black Tuesday, Black Wednesday, Golden Wednesday, Grey Monday, Silver Thursday.

Black Tuesday: any Tuesday during which stock prices decline sharply. Notable Black Tuesdays include October 29, 1929, the date of the greatest frenzy on the New York Stock Exchange during the Crash of '29, and October 28, 1997, when the Hong Kong market fell 13.7 percent. *See also* Black Friday, Black Monday, Black Thursday, Black Wednesday, Crash of '29, Golden Wednesday, Grey Monday, Silver Thursday.

Black Wednesday: 1. any Wednesday during which stock prices decline sharply. A notable Black Wednesday was October 23, 1929, the date of the major stock market decline that marked the end of the Roaring Twenties. *See also* Black Friday, Black Monday, Black Thursday, Black Tuesday, Golden Wednesday, Grey Monday, Roaring Twenties, Silver Thursday. **2.** a reference to September 16, 1992, the day that the Bank of England was forced to withdraw the pound from the European Exchange Rate Mechanism.

Blank Cheque: 1. a signed cheque with the amount unspecified. **2.** total freedom to act. Also known as Carte Blanche.

Blank Cheque Offering: *see* Junior Capital Pool.

Blank Cheque Preferred Share: a preferred share issued to provide voting rights to friendly investors in an attempt to fend off or avoid a hostile takeover.

Blank Endorsement: the endorsement of a financial instrument by a person or company of great financial strength. Such an endorsement makes the instrument negotiable without qualification.

Blanket Bond: insurance used by brokerage companies to cover fraud or losses caused by employees.

Blanket Mortgage: *see* Inter Alia Mortgage.

Blanket Recommendation: a widely disseminated recommendation by a brokerage firm to buy or sell a

stock. So termed because it is made without consideration of individual investment objectives.

Blank Stock: shares in a junior capital pool. *See* Junior Capital Pool.

Bleed: the process of losing large amounts of money.

Blended Payment: any payment, often a mortgage payment, that consists of a principal and interest component. The amount of the blended payment remains the same over time, but the principal portion increases and the interest portion decreases. *See also* Mortgage.

Blind Pool: *see* Junior Capital Pool.

Blind Trust: a trust fund established to protect certain people, such as politicians, from conflict of interest. The trust investments are managed by a fiduciary, but the beneficiary is not told how the funds are invested.

Bloc: a group of countries united by a common cause.

Block: a relatively large amount of a security or securities that is either owned or traded.

Blocking Minority: on the European Council, 62 of 87 votes is required to pass most legislation. A blocking minority is 26 votes. *See also* Voting Rights of the European Council.

Block Order: an order to buy or sell a block of shares, usually defined as having a value of $1 million or more or constituting an amount of 10,000 shares or more. *See also* Block Trade, Order.

Block Trade: the purchase or sale of a large number of shares, usually defined as having a value of $1 million or more or constituting an amount of 10,000 shares or more. *See also* Block Order.

Bloodbath: generally, a reference to a sizable investment loss within a short period of time.

Bloodletting: a period of major investment losses.

Bloomberg L.P.: a major financial news and data distributor. Bloomberg also provides software to analyze the financial information that they distribute. Services are offered to subscribers through proprietary hardware that can be operated by a personal computer as well through television, radio and magazine circulation. *See also* Dow Jones & Company, Inc.; Reuters Holdings Plc.

Blotter: a written record of daily security trades.

Blow Off: an indiscriminate sale of a large number of shares without consideration of the market impact.

Blow Out: a new issue of securities that, due to high demand, sells almost immediately.

Blue Book: *see* Kelly Blue Book Official Guide.

Blue Chip: a well-established, large company.

Blue Chip Stock: the shares of a large, well-managed company. Also known as Quality Stock. *See also* Secondary Stock.

Blue-Collar: skilled or semiskilled manual labour. *See also* White-Collar.

Blue Law: the regulation of Sunday business activities.

Blue Pacific: billed as the world's fastest computer in late 1998. Built by International Business Machines, it is 15,000 times faster than the average personal computer and can perform 3.9 trillion calculations per second. *See also* Computer, Deep Blue, Deeper Blue, International Business Machines Corporation.

Blue Room: a small trading room on the floor of the New York Stock Exchange, located adjacent to the main trading room.

Blue Sheets: a daily U.S. publication that lists quotes for over-the-counter municipal bonds. *See also* Yellow Sheets.

Blue Sky Law: a U.S. term that refers to legislation requiring the issuers of securities to provide a standard set of financial reports for each offering and to register each offering with regulatory authorities before a sale. Similar rules exist in Canada.

.BMP: *see* Bitmap.

BNA Act: *see* British North America Act.

Board: 1. in computers, a panel on which electronic circuitry is printed. *See also* Computer. **2.** formerly, the blackboard wall of a stock exchange on which prices were written using chalk.

Board Foot: a measure of lumber, it is one foot long by one foot wide by one inch thick.

Board Lot: a minimum quantity of shares (or a multiple thereof) for trading, usually 100. Also known as Regular Lot, Round Lot.

Board Lotter: an investor who buys and sells in board lots. Also known as Round Lotter. *See also* Odd Lotter.

Board Meeting: a meeting, usually quarterly, of a company's board of directors. Its purpose is to review financial results, progress relative to budgets, business plans and any other business items that may come before the meeting.

Board of Directors: a group that is elected by a company's shareholders and is responsible for making top-level policy decisions and reviewing senior management performance and compensation. *See also* Director, Inside Director, Interlocking Director, Outside Director.

Board of Trade: a group of individuals who share the goal of expanding or improving business in a certain region. *See also* Chamber of Commerce.

Bo Derek: a term used to describe an investment, usually a particular stock, that is perfect. Also known as Ten.

Body Shopping: the process of recruiting an employee for a specific, specialized function. *See also* Head Hunter.

BOE: *see* Barrel of Oil Equivalent.

Bogeyman: a widely accepted reason for not making an investment (e.g., a bogeyman for real estate stocks is the threat of higher interest rates).

Bogie: a target rate of return set for a professional portfolio manager. Also known as Crossbar. *See also* Benchmark.

Bogota Stock Exchange: the stock exchange of Colombia, located in its capital, Bogota. Also known as Bolsa de Bogota SA. Web site: www.bolsabogota.com.co/

Bogus: fake.

Boilerplate: legal wording, often found in a contract, that is considered standard and is used repeatedly in different applications.

Boiler Room: a room full of telephones and salespeople using high-pressure tactics to sell speculative stocks that are often fraudulent. *See also* Bucketing, Bucket Shop, Confidence Man, Dialling for Dollars, Front Running, Salting, Scam, Tailgating.

Bolivar: the prime currency of Venezuela.

Boliviano: the prime currency of Bolivia.

Bolsa de Bogota SA: *see* Bogota Stock Exchange.

Bolsa de Comercio de Buenos Aires: *see* Buenos Aires Stock Exchange.

Bolsa de Comercio de Santiago: *see* Santiago Stock Exchange.

Bolsa de Madrid: *see* Madrid Stock Exchange.

Bolsa de Valores de Caracas: *see* Caracas Stock Exchange.

Bolsa de Valores de Lisboa: *see* Lisbon Stock Exchange.

Bolsa de Valores de Lisboa General Index: a stock price index of all shares listed on the official market of the Lisbon Stock Exchange.

Bolsa de Valores de Montevideo: *see* Stock Exchange of Montevideo.

Bolsa de Valores de Panama: *see* Panama Stock Exchange.

Bolsa de Valores de Quito: *see* Quito Stock Exchange.

Bolsa de Valores de Rio de Janeiro: *see* Rio de Janeiro Stock Exchange.

Bolsa Mexicana de Valores: *see* Mexican Stock Exchange.

Bombay Stock Exchange: *see* National Stock Exchange of India.

Bombed Out: a term used to describe a stock that has fallen sharply in price within a short period of time.

Bona Fide: real. Genuine.

Bonanza: 1. a major business or investment profit. **2.** a rich ore vein or mine.

Bond: a security that represents a loan from an investor to an issuer. The bond stipulates all terms and conditions of the loan. *See also* Accretion Bond, Accrued Interest, Annuity Bond, Baby Bond, Backup, Bellwether Bond, Bond Fund, Bondholder, Bond Rating, Bond Rating Agency, Bulldog Bond, Call Feature, Call Price, Canada Savings Bond, Canadian Bond Rating Service, Collateral Trust Bond, Compound Interest Bond, Convertible Bond, Corporate Bond, Coupon, Coupon Bond, Credit Risk, Cushion Bond, Debenture, Deep Discount, Denomination, Discount Bond, Dollar Bond, Dominion Bond Rating Service, Dragon Bond, Duration, Eurobond, Eurodollar Bond, Extendable Bond, Extending Term, First Mortgage Bond, Fixed Income, Foreign Bond Fund, Funded Debt, Gilt, Global Bonds, Gold Bond, Government Bond, Government Guaranteed Bond, High-Grade Bond, Income Bond, Indenture, Interest Rate Risk, Joint Bond, Junk Bond, Long-Term Bond, Low Coupon Bond, Municipal Bond, Par Value, Perpetual Bond, Premium, Rating, Real Return Bond, Registered Bond, Reset Bond, Residual, Retractable Bond, Samurai Bond, Secured Bond, Separately Traded Residual and Interest Payment Bond, Serial Bond, Shogun Bond, Short-Term Bond, Sinking Fund Bond, Sour Bond, Split Coupon Bond, Strip, Stripped Bond, Stripped Coupon, Term to Maturity, Yankee Bond, Yield to Maturity, Zero Coupon Bond. **2.** an amount of money or securities pledged as a sign of good faith. **3.** *see* Performance Bond.

Bond Certificate: evidence of ownership of bonds. A bond certificate will usually include the name of the issuer, the name of the registered owner, the par value and some (if not all) of the terms and conditions relating to the bond. Also known as Certificate.

Bond Fund: *see* Bond Mutual Fund.

Bondholder: the owner of a bond. *See also* Bond.

Bond Market: a market in which bonds are traded. *See also* Commodity Exchange, Financial Market, Futures Exchange, Money Market, Stock Market.

Bond Mutual Fund: a mutual fund that invests its portfolio in bonds. Also known as Bond Fund. *See also* Bond, Mutual Fund – Other.

Bonds

A bond is a security that represents a loan. The borrower or issuer is usually a government or corporation, and the bond purchaser is considered a lender as well as an investor.

The conditions of a bond are detailed in the indenture and specify, among other things, how much and when interest is to be paid, when the loan is to be repaid and what assets secure the loan.

The amount of interest to be paid is called the coupon. Payments are often made annually but can be made more frequently. As the interest payment is normally at a set rate, a bond is called a fixed income security. The loan is repaid by the issuer on the maturity date. The time remaining at any date on or after the issue date until the bond matures is the term to maturity.

Once a bond is issued it can be traded among investors. If interest rates decline, then already issued bonds become more attractive because new bonds pay less interest. As a result, the price of existing bonds rises.

If interest rates rise, then already issued bonds become less attractive because new bonds pay more interest. Under these conditions the price of existing bonds will normally fall.

The bond yield is a calculation of the rate of return on investment, taking into account the current price, future interest payments and any capital gain or loss at maturity. If the bond price is higher, then the yield is lower, and vice versa.

There are two major risks for bond investors, one of which is the interest rate risk described above. If interest rates rise while the bond is owned, then the value of the bond will decline. The second risk concerns credit – specifically, the possibility that the issuer's credit rating will decline while the bond is owned. In extreme cases, the issuer may not be able to make interest payments or to repay the bond at maturity.

Canada Savings Bonds (CSB) are a unique form of bond because they are cashable at face value on demand. CSB prices do not change if interest rates change. Other forms of bonds include compound interest bonds, which pay not only regular interest but also interest on the interest; real return bonds, which pay either more or less interest to offset the effect of inflation; and stripped bonds, which are bonds in which interest payments and repayment at maturity have been separated into different securities.

Treasury bills, or T-bills, are a form of short-term government bond known as an accretion bond. T-bills do not pay interest but trade at one price and mature (in less than a year) at a higher price. The increase in price at maturity provides the return. T-bills are very safe because payment is guaranteed by the government and term to maturity is short, so prices do not decline significantly if interest rates rise.

As a rule, regular bonds are safer than common stocks and riskier than treasury bills, guaranteed investment certificates and term deposits.

Bond Rating: a professional assessment of a bond's investment quality. AAA (or "Triple A") is normally the highest rating, and D is often the lowest. *See also* Bond, Bond Rating Agency, Canadian Bond Rating Service, Dominion Bond Rating Service, Moody's Investors Service, Rating, Standard & Poor's Corporation.

Bond Rating Agency: an independent agency that assesses a bond's investment quality. The Canadian Bond Rating Service and Dominion Bond Rating Service are well known Canadian agencies. In the U.S., Standard & Poor's Corporation and Moody's Investors Service are widely followed. Also known as Rating Agency. *See also* Bond, Bond Rating, Canadian Bond Rating Service, Dominion Bond Rating Service, Moody's Investors Service, Rating, Standard & Poor's Corporation.

Bond Ratio: *see* Debt/Equity Ratio.

Bondsman: one who obtains surety bonds for others for a fee.

Bond Trader: 1. an employee of a brokerage firm engaged in buying and selling bonds based on client orders. **2.** an employee of a financial institution engaged in buying and selling bonds based on instructions from a portfolio manager. **3.** an investor who actively buys and sells bonds for his/her own account. *See also* Stock Trader, Trader.

Bond Yield: *see* Yield to Maturity

Bond Yield Average: an index that measures the performance of a selection of bonds over time. The most widely used bond indexes in Canada are published by ScotiaMcLeod. Averages are available for different types of bonds (e.g., provincial and corporate) as well as for bonds with different terms to maturity (e.g., short-term, mid-term and long-term). *See also* Bond.

Bonus: an amount of money given in addition to regular pay, often in recognition of outstanding performance or as a supplement at certain times of the year (e.g., Christmas bonus). *See also* Bonus Plan, Compensation, Perquisite, Phantom Stock Plan, Profit Sharing Plan.

Bonus Plan: any method of compensation that provides for additional payment if certain conditions are met (e.g., profit sharing, productivity quotas). Also known as Variable Pay Program. *See also* Bonus, Compensation, Perquisite, Phantom Stock Plan, Profit Sharing Plan.

Book Debts: a banking term that refers to trade debts or receivables.

Book Entry: completion of a trade through making a note in the accounts of the buyer and seller rather than through physically exchanging documents.

Book Entry Stock: shares held by a brokerage firm in street form or in nominee name on behalf of clients. Mutual fund shares/units are often held as book entry stock. *See also* Nominee Name, Street Form.

Bookkeeper: a dated term for the accountant of a business or organization.

Book Loss: *see* Paper Loss.

Book Profit: *see* Paper Profit.

Book Value: 1. generally, the value of an asset at cost less accumulated depreciation. **2.** corporately, the value of an asset or liability as reported on a company's financial statements. *See also* Book Value per Share, Price to Book Value.

Book Value per Share: the book value of corporate assets less liabilities and divided by the number of shares outstanding. Book value per share is a rough estimate of the liquidation value of a company, except when the current value of assets varies greatly from the book value. *See also* Asset Value, Book Value, Price to Book Value.

Boom: an extended period of growth and prosperity in the economy and/or the stock market. *See also* Boom or Bust, Bust.

Boomer: *see* Baby Boomer.

Boomerang: an investment that backfires.

Boom or Bust: conditions that are always either outstanding or terrible but never in between. *See also* Boom, Bust.

Boondoggle: a trivial or wasteful expenditure.

Bootleg: to make, transport or sell illegally.

Bootleg Copy: *see* Knock-off.

Bootstrap: to develop a company or business from its very beginnings, often with very little capital.

Bootstrap Acquisition: a takeover in which the target company exchanges some its assets for the shares of dissident shareholders. The acquiring company is then able to take over the target company at a lower price because some of the latter's assets are used to finance part of the takeover.

Boot Up: the process of starting or resetting a computer. *See also* Computer.

Borrower: a person who obtains money and agrees to pay it back by a specific date and at a specific interest rate.

Borrowing Factoring: this occurs when accounts receivable are sold for a percentage of face value. *See also* Factoring.

Borsa Valori di Milano: *see* Italian Stock Exchange.

Boston Snow Indicator: a theory stating that snow on the ground in Boston on Christmas Day means stock prices will rise. For obvious reasons, also known as the BS Indicator.

Boston Stock Exchange: a regional U.S. stock exchange located in Boston, Massachusetts. Web site: www.bostonstock.com

Botswana Share Market Index: a price index for the Botswana Stock Exchange.

Botswana Stock Exchange: the major stock market of Botswana, located in its capital, Gaborone. Web site: www.mbendi.co.za/exbo.htm

Bottleneck: an obstruction that slows down a manufacturing or production process.

Bottom: 1. in investment, the low point in a financial market or in the price of an individual security before an advance begins. *See also* Top. **2.** the low point in an economic cycle. *See also* Trough.

Bottom Fishing: a strategy that involves buying securities or buying into financial markets that have declined drastically in price.

Bottom Line: net income or net profit. So termed because it is the lowest or last line of an income statement. *See also* Top Line.

Bottom Quartile: *see* Fourth Quartile.

Bottom-Up: a portfolio management style that involves buying and selling securities based on individual investment merits and with minimal regard to overall trends in the economy or in financial markets. *See also* Growth Investor, Portfolio Management Style, Sector Rotation, Top-Down, Value Investor.

Bought Deal: a new share issue that an underwriter purchases to resell to investors. This occurs when the underwriter is confident that the securities can be sold. Also known as Firm Commitment. *See also* Best Efforts, Standby Commitment, Underwriting Risk.

Bounce: 1. in financial markets, a brief upward movement in price after an extended decline. *See also* Dead Cat Bounce, Rally. **2.** in banking, to refuse to honour a cheque, usually due to insufficient funds. Also known as Dishonour. *See also* Not Sufficient Funds Cheque. **3.** in securities, to refuse to accept a security for delivery. *See also* Bad Delivery.

Bourse: *see* Paris Stock Exchange.

Bourse de Bruxelles, Beurs van Brussel: *see* Brussels Stock Exchange.

Bourse de Montreal: *see* Montreal Exchange.

Bourse des Valeurs Mobilieres de Tunis: *see* Tunisian Stock Exchange.

Bourse des Valeurs Mobilieres de Tunisie Index: a stock price index for the Tunisian Stock Exchange.

Boutique: a financial firm, often a broker, that specializes in certain clients, products or services (e.g., an institutional boutique deals primarily [or entirely] with institutional clients).

Bovespa Index: a market capitalization weighted index of the Sao Paulo Stock Exchange in Brazil.

Box: 1. an account that buys and sells a particular stock to maintain an orderly and active market. **2.** in a brokerage firm, the physical location where securities are held in safekeeping.

Box Spread: option arbitrage in which an investor is able to buy a combination of options that produces a locked-in profit. *See also* Bear Spread, Bull Spread, Option.

Box Store: a new style of retail store that is very large and sells one general line of merchandise. Home Depot is an example of a box store.

Boycott: a form of protest that entails refusing to buy a certain product, use a certain service or deal with a certain person or firm.

BPS: *see* Bits per Second.

Bracket: *see* Tax Bracket.

Bracket Creep: this occurs when inflation pushes income into successively higher tax brackets, resulting in no increase in real purchasing power but more income tax payable. In Canada, bracket creep is a special problem because many income tax credits and personal exemptions are only increased following years in which inflation exceeds 3 percent. Also known as Tax Bracket Creep.

Brady Bonds: named after Nicholas F. Brady (1930-), U.S. secretary of the treasury from 1988 to 1993. Brady bonds are issued by developing countries and are backed by U.S. treasury bonds.

Brain Drain: the loss of a large number of skilled professionals, often due to high taxes. Between 1955 and 1965, Canada suffered a brain drain to the U.S. *See also* Brain Gain.

Brain Gain: the gain of a large number of skilled professionals, often due to lower taxes. Between 1965 and 1972, Canada enjoyed a brain gain from the U.S. *See also* Brain Drain.

Branch: 1. in banking, a facility that offers many, if not all, financial services and is often located in a community for the convenience of customers. **2.** in securities, a brokerage office that is located apart from the head office and is under the supervision of a branch manager. *See also* Branch Manager.

Branch Manager: 1. in banking, a senior person who is generally responsible for the administration and management of a branch. **2.** in securities, usually a senior broker who supervises other brokers. If a branch manager supervises more than three other brokers, he/she must pass tests administered by the regulatory authority. *See also* Branch.

Brand: a name or symbol strongly associated with a product or service. *See also* Brand Name, Logo, Symbol, Trademark.

Brand Name: a name strongly associated with a product or service. *See also* Brand.

Bratislava Stock Exchange: the major stock exchange of Slovakia, located in its capital, Bratislava. Web site not available.

Brazilian Stock Exchange: *see* Rio de Janeiro Stock Exchange.

BRB: Internet acronym for "be right back."

Breach of Contract: a failure to fulfill a contractual duty that results in the innocent party having an action for damages.

Breach of Duty: failure to perform a duty owed to another (e.g., a trustee failing to act in the interest of a beneficiary). *See also* Fiduciary Responsibility.

Breadth: the number of stocks participating in a market trend. If a large number of stocks are involved, then the market is said to "move broadly."

Breadth Ratio: the number of advances divided by the number of declines. *See also* Advances, Declines.

Breadwinner: the main income earner for a group of dependents.

Break: 1. in investment, a sharp, sudden, unexpected drop in security prices. **2.** in marketing, the point at which a price changes due to a volume discount. *See also* Break Point. **3.** a signal that interrupts a computer process. *See also* Computer. **4.** *see* Bust.

Breakaway Gap: a technical reference to a change in the price of a stock on abnormally high trading volume, which creates a price gap between the last trade and the next trade. It is "bullish" if the gap is on the upside and "bearish" if the gap is on the downside. *See also* Gap, Technical Analysis.

Breakdown: this occurs when the price of a security begins to falter and decline.

Break-Even: a position of zero profit or loss.

Break-Even Analysis: an analysis of revenue, fixed costs, variable costs and profits. *See also* Break-Even Point.

Break-Even Point: the level of sales, in dollars or units, at which there is no profit or loss. *See also* Break-Even Analysis.

Breakfast Club: often, a group of business people who meet regularly (at breakfast, lunch or dinner) to share information and promote their respective businesses. Also known as Luncheon Club, Supper Club.

Breaking the Spread: a term used to describe the activity of trading a security outside of the difference (or "the spread") between the bid price and the ask price (e.g., buying at the ask price and then selling to a higher bidder). Such activity has the effect of changing the prevailing bid and ask prices, thus "breaking the spread."

Breaking the Syndicate: to terminate the group underwriting a security, thus allowing members to sell holdings without restriction.

Breakout: a technical stock-trading term used to describe a stock or market that rises above its previous high or above a long-term trend. *See also* Technical Analysis.

Break Point: 1. the point at which the price per $1,000 of insurance drops (e.g., the cost for $50,000 of life insurance may be more per $1,000 than the cost for $50,001 to $100,000 of life insurance). **2.** any level at which a price or commission charge changes.

Break Up: in resource exploration, this occurs when the frozen ground melts and it becomes difficult to move ground-based equipment.

Break-Up Value: *see* Private Market Value.

Breather: a pause in a security price advance.

Brent Crude Oil: a light, intermediate-grade oil produced in the United Kingdom/North Sea. *See also* West Texas Intermediate Crude Oil.

Bretton Woods System: a foreign exchange rate system that was based on the U.S. dollar pegged to gold at $35 per ounce. Other currencies in this system were pegged to the U.S. dollar at fixed but floating rates. Each country was to attempt to keep their currency within the designated value, plus or minus one percent.

Bre-X Minerals Ltd.: this company was involved in what is probably the largest stock swindle in history. Its Busang gold property in Indonesia, which reportedly contained as much as 200 million ounces of gold, was proven fraudulent in May 1997. At its high, Bre-X had a market value of $4.4 billion U.S. *See also* Equity Funding Corporation, Ponzi Scheme, Salad Oil Scandal, ZZZZ Best.

Bribe: any form of payment or favour used to induce a person to act dishonestly. *See also* Baksheesh, Payola.

Bricks and Mortar: physical facilities such as office buildings, retail outlets or manufacturing plants.

Bridge Building: *see* Networking.

Bridge Financing: the making of a bridge loan. *See also* Bridge Loan.

Bridge Loan: a temporary loan that covers the period until permanent financing is approved. Also known as Swing Loan.

Brief: a short, concise statement, especially in law.

Brinkmanship: the act of pushing a negotiation to a dangerous position in order to force an opponent to concede.

British Banker's Association (BBA): founded in 1919, an industry association for the UK banking industry. The BBA participates in the European Banking Federation and also sponsors the Euro

LIBOR and the Euro Overnight Index Average (EURONIA). Web site: www.bba.org.uk

British Columbia: *see* Canada's Provinces and Territories.

British Commonwealth: an association of the United Kingdom, its dependencies and many former colonies including Canada.

British North America Act (BNA Act): a statute of the British Parliament, passed on March 29, 1867. The principal document of the Canadian Constitution. *See also* Canadian Charter of Rights and Freedoms, Constitution.

British Thermal Unit (BTU): the amount of heat required to raise the temperature of one pound of water one degree Fahrenheit.

Broadcast: 1. to make known over a wide area. *See also* Narrowcast. **2.** to transmit, especially over radio or television.

Broad Market: the overall market, taking into account the majority of securities traded (e.g., the Dow-Jones Average can rise based on the 30 stocks in the index, but the broad market is based on all listed stocks). *See also* Broad Market Index.

Broad Market Index: a stock market index, such as the Toronto Stock Exchange 300 Index, that measures market changes with a large or broad sample of stocks. *See also* Broad Market.

Broadtape: a term used to describe the wide paper on which Dow Jones & Company used to publish business news. It stands in contrast to the narrow paper (i.e., ticker tape) they used for stock quotes.

Brochure: a brief pamphlet used to advertise a product or service.

Broke: *see* Bankrupt.

Broken Story: a term used to describe a widely held investor expectation regarding a company that failed to materialize. Also known as Busted Story. *See also* Fallen Angel.

Broker: 1. a person who acts as an intermediary between a buyer and a seller. **2.** a brokerage firm employee who advises clients and trades client accounts for a commission, salary or a combination of the two. To be a broker, an individual must pass the required tests, be registered with the province in which he/she works and be properly supervised. Also known as Customer's Man, Independent Broker, Investment Advisor, Investment Dealer, Registered Representative, Stockbroker. *See also* Broker-Dealer. **3.** in insurance, a person licensed to place insurance with more than one insurance company. *See also* Agent, Chartered Financial Consultant, Chartered Life Underwriter, Life Insurance Agent. **4.** in real estate, an agent who acts for the seller of real estate and receives a commission from the proceeds of the sale.

Brokerage Account: a facility with a brokerage firm through which the purchase and sale of securities is conducted, recorded and settled.

Brokerage Statement: *see* Account Statement.

Brokerage Firm: a company engaged in buying and selling securities for clients.

Broker-Dealer: a firm that acts as an intermediary between security buyers and security sellers (i.e., a broker) and that also acts as a principal in buying or selling a security (i.e., a dealer). *See also* Broker, Dealer.

Broker Loan: *see* Call Loan.

Broker Loan Rate: *see* Call Loan Rate.

Broker Overnight Loan: *see* Call Loan.

Brown Out: a reduction in electric power, it causes lights to dim and appliances to work less efficiently. *See also* Black Out.

Browser: *see* Web Browser.

Brussels Stock Exchange: the major stock exchange of Belgium, located in its capital, Brussels. Also known as Bourse de Bruxelles, Beurs van Brussel. Web site: www.bourse.be/

Brussels Stock Exchange BEL20 Index (BEL20): a modified market capitalization weighted index of the 20 largest and most liquid stocks on the Brussels Stock Exchange.

Brussels Treaty: *see* Treaty of Brussels.

BSE: 1. *see* Bahrain Stock Exchange. **2.** *see* Bulgarian Stock Exchange.

BSE Index: a stock price index for the Bulgarian Stock Exchange.

BS Indicator: *see* Boston Snow Indicator.

BSX: *see* Bermuda Stock Exchange.

BTU: *see* British Thermal Unit.

BTW: Internet acronym for "by the way."

Bubble: a speculative market or venture in which values rise rapidly before they fall rapidly, or before "the bubble bursts."

Bucharest Stock Exchange: the major stock exchange of Romania, located in its capital, Bucharest. Web site: www.bse.ccir.ro

Bucharest Stock Exchange BET Index: a market capitalization weighted stock price index for the Bucharest Stock Exchange. The BET is denominated in both U.S. dollars and the Romanian leu.

Buck: an informal reference to one dollar.

Bucketing: an illegal activity whereby, in an attempt to make a short-term profit, a broker confirms an order to a client without actually executing it. *See also* Boiler Room, Bucket Shop, Confidence Man, Dialling for Dollars, Front Running, Salting, Scam, Tailgating.

Bucket Shop: a brokerage firm that uses high-pressure sales tactics to sell securities of questionable merit. *See also* Boiler Room, Bucketing, Confidence

Man, Dialling for Dollars, Front Running, Salting, Scam, Tailgating.

Buck the Trend: to act in a way that is contrary to overall market trends (e.g., a stock that rises while the overall stock market declines is said to "buck the trend").

Budapest Stock Exchange: the stock exchange of Hungary, located in its capital, Budapest. Web site: www.fornax.hu/fmon/indexe.html

Budapest Stock Exchange Index: a market capitalization weighted stock price index for the Budapest Stock Exchange. Also known as Bux Index.

Budget: a series of financial statements used to make up a financial plan for a fiscal year or a project.

Budget Deficit: the balance of a budget when expenditures exceed income. *See also* Balanced Budget, Budget Surplus, Tax and Spend.

Budget Deficit – Federal: the yearly amount by which federal government spending exceeds income. *See also* Tax and Spend.

Budget Deficit – Provincial: the yearly amount by which provincial government spending exceeds income. *See also* Tax and Spend.

Budget – Federal Government: a series of financial statements that detail federal government income and spending plans for the ensuing year.

Budget – Provincial Government: a series of financial statements that detail provincial government income and spending plans for the ensuing year.

Budget Surplus: the balance of a budget when income exceeds expenditures. *See also* Balanced Budget, Budget Deficit.

Budget Surplus – Federal: the yearly amount by which federal government income exceeds spending.

Budget Surplus – Provincial: the yearly amount by which provincial government income exceeds spending.

Buenos Aires Stock Exchange: the major stock exchange of Argentina, located in its capital, Buenos Aires. Also known as Bolsa de Comercio de Buenos Aires. Web site: www.bcba.sba.com.ar/

Buffer: in computer memory, a storage area in which data are accumulated until they can be processed. *See also* Computer.

Buffett, E. Warren (1930-): generally considered one of the best U.S. money managers of all time because of the investment results produced by Berkshire Hathaway, where Buffett is chairman and chief executive officer. Buffett stresses the investment principle of buying excellent companies and holding them for a long time while ignoring short-term changes in the market. As of mid-1998, Buffett's personal wealth was estimated at $36 billion. Also known as Oracle of Omaha.

Bug: 1. a defect in a system or design. **2.** a hardware defect or an error in computer software. *See also* Computer, Debug, Leap Year Bug, Year 2000 Conversion, Year 2000 Problem.

Build or Buy: the corporate decision to either create a product or service or to buy it from an existing supplier. Also known as Buy or Build.

Bulgarian Stock Exchange (BSE): the major stock exchange of Bulgaria, located in its capital, Sofia. Successor to the First Bulgarian Stock Exchange (FBSE). Web site: www.kenpubs.co.uk/investguide/bulgaria/bul_st_ex.htm

Bulge Bracket: in a tombstone, the bulge bracket contains the list of underwriters who sold the largest amount of the issue. *See also* Mezzanine Bracket, Tombstone.

Bulge Line of Credit: *see* Temporary Line of Credit.

Bull: 1. in general, one who is optimistic about the economy or financial markets. **2.** a person who expects stock or bond prices to rise. *See also* Bear.

Bulldog Bond: a sterling-denominated bond issued in the UK by a non-British firm or institution. *See also* Bond.

Bullet Immunization: the use of a bond portfolio with a highly secure yield to fund a specific liability.

Bulletin Board: 1. an electronic service offered by the National Association of Securities Dealers, it lists quotes on over-the-counter stocks. Quotations on the bulletin board are firm. Also known as Over-the-Counter Bulletin Board. *See also* National Association of Securities Dealers, Over-the-Counter. **2.** on the Internet, a system for exchanging messages and files. *See also* Internet.

Bulletin Board System (BBS): a host system into which callers may dial to read and send electronic mail, upload and download files and chat with other callers. *See also* Sysop.

Bulletproof: a term used to describe a contract that has no loopholes.

Bullion: a refined amount of a precious metal that has been poured into bars, ingots or plates. *See also* Precious Metal, Unparted Bullion.

Bullion Coin: a coin that derives its value from its precious metal content. *See also* Gold Coin, Numismatic Coin.

Bullish: a sense of optimism about financial markets or the economy. *See also* Bearish.

Bull Market: an extended period of rising stock prices. *See also* Bear Market, Elliott Wave Theory, Kondratieff Wave, Peak, Presidential Election Cycle, Stock Market Cycle, Trough.

Bull Pool: a group of people who, illegally, act together to try to manipulate a stock price so that it will rise. *See also* Bear Pool.

Bull Raid: a move to manipulate stock prices so that they will rise. *See also* Bear Raid, Raid.

Bull's Eye: a term used to describe an estimate or forecast that proves to be very accurate.

Bull Spread: a reference to buying one option and selling another in order to profit if the price of the underlying security rises as well as to minimize losses if the price of the underlying security falls sharply. *See also* Option.

Bull Straddle: a strategy of writing an uncovered put option and a covered call option on the same underlying stock with the same strike price and expiration date. The writer profits if the stock price remains stable. *See also* Bear Straddle, Covered Call Option, Expiration Date, Option, Strike Price, Uncovered Put Option, Underlying Stock.

Bull Trap: a sharp, brief rise in the market. Those induced to buy during the rise are said to have "fallen into a bull trap." *See also* Bear Trap.

Bumph: a moderately derogatory term used to describe information geared to encourage or generate sales.

Bum Steer: misleading advice.

Bunched Trade: several trades, occurring simultaneously and at the same price, that are reported as one trade.

Bundesbank: *see* Deutsche Bundesbank.

Bundle: to package products and/or services together so that the buyer must buy them all in order to receive one. *See also* Unbundle.

Buoyant: a term used to describe a favourable financial market.

Burden of Proof: the onus on the Crown prosecutor to prove a case. In criminal law, the Crown must prove its case by a preponderance of evidence or beyond a reasonable doubt. In civil law, the plaintiff must prove his/her case on a balance of probabilities. *See also* Plaintiff, Prosecutor.

Burn Rate: the rate at which a company spends cash each month. The term is often used with reference to research and development companies. *See also* Death Valley Curve.

Bursary: financial assistance that is provided to a student and that does not need to be repaid.

Business: 1. any ongoing commercial, industrial, financial or professional dealings. **2.** a company or corporation. **3.** a person's occupation or profession.

Business Cycle: *see* Economic Cycle.

Business Day: 1. by convention, Monday to Friday, excluding statutory holidays. **2.** in the stock market, any day that the major stock exchanges are open for trading.

Business Development Bank of Canada: prior to 1995, known as the Federal Business Development Bank. Currently, a bank that complements con-

ventional financial institutions with business lending that ranges from term financing to venture capital. A second function of the bank is management-support consulting.

Business Expansion Loan: a loan made to purchase fixed assets or any other asset used to produce income. A business expansion loan is not used to finance day-to-day operations. *See also* Working Capital Loan.

Business Improvement Loan (BIL): a loan that is issued by an approved lender and guaranteed by the federal government to a maximum of $100,000 at one percent over the prime rate.

Business Interruption Insurance: insurance that, under specific conditions, protects loss of income when a business shutdown occurs. Also known as Loss of Income Insurance.

Businessman's Risk: an aggressive but not speculative investment.

Business Risk: the variability of a company's earnings, stemming from economic and industry factors. *See also* Interest Rate Risk, Inventory Risk, Risk.

Busman's Holiday: a vacation during which one engages in activities that are similar to those one usually engages in when at work.

Bust: 1. a severe downturn, usually in an economy. *See also* Boom or Bust. **2.** to reverse or break a trade.

Busted: *see* Bankrupt.

Busted Story: *see* Broken Story.

Busted Takeover: an acquisition, often a leveraged buyout, in which assets of the acquired company must be sold to help pay for the acquisition. *See also* Leveraged Buyout.

Butter and Guns Curve: *see* Guns and Butter Curve.

Butterfly Spread: an option strategy, combining two long call options and two short call options, that will produce a profit if the underlying security price remains within a narrow range. Also known as Dumbbell Strategy. *See also* Option.

Buttonwood Tree Agreement: the first formal agreement (1792) to regulate stockbroker activity in New York. This led to the formation of the New York Stock Exchange in 1817. *See also* New York Stock Exchange.

Bux Index: *see* Budapest Stock Exchange Index.

Buy: 1. a recommendation to purchase a security. Also known as Buy Recommendation. **2.** to acquire an asset in exchange for money. In the financial market, also known as Buy Long. **3.** a security that is being recommended for purchase, as in "it's a buy." **4.** an order to purchase. Also known as Buy Order.

Bux Index: a stock market index for the Budapest Stock Exchange.

Buy and Hold: an investment strategy that involves purchasing securities with the intention of long-term ownership. *See also* One Decision Stock.

Buy and Write: an investment strategy that involves purchasing securities with the intention of writing and selling options against them. *See also* Option.

Buyback: 1. *see* Normal Course Issuer Bid. **2.** *see* Short Covering.

Buy Down: a cash payment on a mortgage in return for a lower interest rate. *See also* Mortgage.

Buyer: in a transaction, the party that acquires goods or services in return for payment.

Buyer's Market: a market in which supply exceeds demand, thus giving buyers an advantage over sellers. *See also* Seller's Market.

Buyer's Monopoly: *see* Monopsony.

Buy In: the forcible repurchase of securities that occurs when a selling broker or selling client does not provide timely delivery of securities. *See also* Sell Out.

Buy-In Notice: notification from a broker to a client informing him/her of an amount of a security that must be delivered immediately or the broker will begin buying the securities that the client has failed to deliver. The client is liable for any remaining balance. *See also* Buy In, Sell-Out Notice.

Buying: in financial markets, trading that is initiated by orders to purchase. *See also* Selling.

Buying Back: *see* Short Covering.

Buying Climax: a short period of explosive buying, near the end of a long-term price advance, that pushes prices up rapidly. The buying frenzy usually ends quickly, and prices then collapse. *See also* Selling Climax.

Buying Panic: this occurs when investors, speculators, traders and institutions believe that, due to a period of rapidly rising stock prices, they must buy securities immediately. *See also* Bear Panic, Selling Panic.

Buying Power: 1. generally, an investor's financial ability to buy securities. **2.** the dollar value of additional securities that an investor can buy with his/her margin account. *See also* Margin Account.

Buying Pressure: this occurs when orders to buy a security outweigh orders to sell it and, consequently, the price rises. *See also* Selling Pressure.

Buying Program: a policy, often set up by a large institutional investor, to buy a stock or stocks over a certain period of time. *See also* Selling Program.

Buying Range: the price range within which a security is considered to be attractively priced. *See also* Selling Range.

Buy Long: *see* Buy.

Buy Low, Sell High: a widely followed investment rule. *See also* Chase the Market.

Buy Minus: an order to a broker to buy at a price below the current market. *See also* Order, Sell Plus.

Buy on Margin: to purchase securities with money borrowed from a lender (often a broker).

Buy on Mystery, Sell on History: an investment adage that reflects the market's tendency to discount events in advance. Therefore, stock prices rise in anticipation of news and fall once it has become actual. Also known as Buy on Rumour, Sell on News; Sell on News.

Buy on Rumour, Sell on News: *see* Buy on Mystery, Sell on History.

Buy on the Come: *see* On the Come.

Buy or Build: *see* Build or Buy.

Buy Order: *see* Buy.

Buyout: normally, the purchase by one party of all that is owned by another party.

Buy Recommendation: *see* Buy.

Buy-Sell Agreement: an agreement between two or more major partners or shareholders that outlines the conditions under which each may sell his/her interest should he/she become disabled, retire, die or simply choose to sell. *See also* Shotgun Clause.

Buy Side (of the Street): the investing institutions, such as mutual funds, pension funds or insurance companies, that are considered to be buyers of securities. *See also* Sell Side (of the Street).

Buy Signal: an indication that the price of a security or the overall market will rise. *See also* Sell Signal.

Buy Stop Order: *see* Stop Buy Order.

Buy the Book: to purchase all shares offered at a certain price.

Buy Ticket: the paper form used by a broker to enter a client's order to buy shares. Most order-entry systems are now electronic. *See also* Sell Ticket.

Buzzword: a specialized term or acronym, often used with the intent to impress or confuse.

Bylaw: normally, a law or rule regarding the internal matters of an organization.

By-Product: something of use that is produced as a result of processing or manufacturing something else.

Byte: in computers, the basic unit of data storage, which is made up of eight bits. *See also* Bit, Computer, Gigabyte, Kilobyte, Megabyte.

By These Presents: a phrase, often used in legal documents, that refers to the document itself or to the words and statements used in it.

C: in Roman numerals, the number 100.

C: 1. *see* Celsius. **2.** *see* Centigrade.

Cabinet Bond: a bond that is listed on a major exchange but trades infrequently. So termed because, at one time, bids and offerings for such bonds were kept in a cabinet. *See also* Automated Bond System.

Cabinet Bond Crowd: the traders who trade cabinet bonds. *See also* Active Bond Crowd.

Cabinet Minister: in the federal or provincial governments, an elected member appointed to a senior position in a department (e.g., finance minister).

CA: *see* Chartered Accountant.

CAC-40 Index: a market capitalization weighted index of the Paris Stock Exchange.

Cache: in computers, a high-speed memory area where contents of a hard drive or secondary storage unit are duplicated for faster access. *See also* Computer.

CAD: *see* Computer Assisted Design.

Cadillac Plan: *see* Top Hat Plan.

Cafeteria Employee Benefit Plan: an employee benefit plan that provides some flexibility in the type and amount of benefits selected. Also known as Cafeteria Plan. *See also* Employee Benefit Plan.

Cafeteria Plan: *see* Cafeteria Employee Benefit Plan.

CAFP: *see* Canadian Association of Financial Planners.

Cage: *see* Securities Cage.

CAGR: *see* Compound Annual Growth Rate.

CAIFA: *see* Canadian Association of Insurance and Financial Advisors.

Cairo Stock Exchange: the major stock exchange of Egypt, located in its capital, Cairo. Web site: www.egyptse.com/borsanet_new/Default.htm

Caisses Populaires: the Quebec counterpart of credit unions.

Calcinator: equipment that uses heat to drive off moisture and gaseous impurities in petroleum.

Calculate: to compute through mathematical processes.

Calculated Risk: an investment or business decision made after careful consideration of the facts.

Calculator: a small electronic device for performing (at least) the four basic mathematical functions.

Calculus: a mathematical specialty including, among other things, the calculation of areas and volumes.

Caldera: craters, formed by ancient volcanic processes, that are often associated with ore bodies.

Calendar: 1. a schedule of securities to be underwritten in the near future. **2.** a schedule of upcoming events or economic announcements.

Calendarization: the effect of dates on reported financial results (e.g., Easter sometimes falls in the first three months and sometimes in the second three months of the calendar year). This can cause shifts in the sales of retailers from one year to the next.

Calendar Quarters: the four three-month periods of the calendar year, ending in March, June, September and December.

Calendar Spread: the simultaneous purchase and sale of more than one option of the same type (e.g., calls, puts) on the same underlying security and with different expiration dates. Also known as Horizontal Spread. *See also* Option, Vertical Spread.

Calendar Year: the 12-month period starting January 1 and ending December 31. *See also* Fiscal Year.

Calendar Year End: December 31.

Calgary Stock Exchange: *see* Alberta Stock Exchange.

Call: 1. to buy a stock according to the terms of an option, which enable one to acquire a fixed number of shares at a fixed price by a fixed date. **2.** *see* Call Option. **3.** a demand made by a bank to a borrower to repay the full amount of a loan immediately. A call is generally triggered by the borrower's failure to meet an obligation (e.g., an interest payment). **4.** to redeem a bond prior to maturity. *See also* Redeemable Bond.

Callable: *see* Redeemable.

Callable Bond: *see* Redeemable Bond.

Callable Preferred Share: *see* Redeemable Preferred Share.

Call Date: the date that a redeemable security can be called. *See also* Redeemable Bond, Redeemable Preferred Share.

Called Away: a term used to describe what happens to an investor when a redeemable bond is called, an option is exercised or a security sold short must be delivered.

Call Feature: a condition of a bond that makes it callable. *See also* Bond.

Call Loan: a loan made to a brokerage firm with securities as collateral. Brokers often use the money to finance margin accounts. A call loan can be terminated by either the lender or borrower on demand. Also known as Broker Loan, Broker Overnight Loan. *See also* Call Loan Rate, Margin Account.

Call Loan Rate: the interest rate that banks charge on call loans. This rate is important because it is the basis for interest charges on margin accounts. Also known as Broker Loan Rate.

Call Money: demand loans made by banks to brokerage firms. Also known as Day-to-Day Money, Demand Money.

Call Option: a stock option that gives the holder the right to buy a fixed number of shares at a fixed price by a fixed date. Also known as Call. *See also* Option, Put Option.

Call Price: the price at which a bond or other callable security may be redeemed. *See also* Bond.

Call Protection: the period of time during which a redeemable security cannot be redeemed by the issuer. *See also* Redeemable Bond, Redeemable Preferred Share.

Call Provision: the clause in a bond or preferred share prospectus that outlines the terms and conditions under which the security may be redeemed.

Call Risk: the risk that a security may be called away. If the cost of the investment was higher than the call price, a capital loss may be triggered. If interest rates have declined, it may not be possible to replace the yield in the portfolio. Also known as Redemption Risk, Risk of Redemption. *See also* Called Away, Call Price.

Calorie: the amount of heat needed to raise the temperature of one gram of water by one degree Celsius at one atmosphere of pressure.

Camp Out: to stay on the Internet for an extended period of time. *See also* Internet.

Can: slang for to fire from a job.

Canada Business Service Centres: located in each province, a distributor of business-related government programs and services.

Canada Customs and Revenue Agency (CCRA): the federal government agency that promotes compliance with Canada's tax, trade and border legislations and regulations. Prior to November 1, 1999, Revenue Canada processed and enforced Canada's income tax legislation. *See also* Internal Revenue Service.

Canada Deposit Insurance Corporation: a federal Crown corporation that insures the deposits of Canadians at banking, trust and loan companies. Individual accounts are insured for losses of up to $60,000 resulting from the financial failure of a member company. In Quebec, the service is provided by the Quebec Deposit Insurance Board. Web site: www.cdic.ca *See also* Federal Deposit Insurance Corporation.

Canada Education Savings Grant: a federal government grant of 20 percent of an annual registered education savings plan contribution, to a maximum grant of $400.

Canada Mortgage and Housing Corporation (CMHC): a Crown agency originally formed in 1946, CMHC began by building housing for veterans of the Second World War. In 1954, CMHC began insuring mortgage loans made by private investors, an activity that increased dramatically when Canadian chartered banks were permitted to offer loans for mortgages. CMHC administers Canada's National Housing Act. *See also* Mortgage.

Canada's Provinces and Territories

Province	Capital	Population	Economic Base
Alberta	Edmonton	2,696,826	agriculture, forestry, oil & gas, services
British Columbia	Victoria	3,724,500	forestry, mining, fishing, manufacturing, tourism
Manitoba	Winnipeg	1,113,898	resources, manufacturing, services
New Brunswick	Fredericton	738,133	agriculture, fishing, forestry, hydroelectric power
Newfoundland	St. John's	551,792	fishing, hydroelectric power, mining, oil & gas
Northwest Territories	Yellowknife	64,402	mining, oil & gas, services
Nova Scotia	Halifax	909,282	fishing, manufacturing, mining, petroleum refining
Ontario	Toronto	10,753,573	manufacturing, mining, services
Prince Edward Island	Charlottetown	134,557	agriculture, services, tourism
Quebec	Quebec City	7,138,795	forestry, mining, manufacturing, services
Saskatchewan	Regina	990,237	agriculture, manufacturing, mining
Yukon	Whitehorse	30,766	fishing, mining, services, tourism

(*Source:* Statistics Canada, based on the 1996 Census. *See also* Nunavut.)

Canada Mortgage and Housing Corporation Chattel Loan Insurance Program: a mortgage insurance program available for mortgages on manufactured homes. *See also* Mortgage.

Canada Mortgage and Housing Corporation Insurance: insurance provided to protect a mortgagor from financial loss in the event a mortgagee defaults. A borrower is required to purchase CMHC Insurance for any high ratio mortgage.

Canada Pension Plan (CPP): a mandatory, defined benefit pension plan started by the government of Canada in 1966. Benefits are payable to individuals who have been income earners and contributed to the plan for at least 10 years. Recipients include retirees, widowed spouses, orphans, disabled persons and children of disabled contributors. The CPP also pays death benefits to the spouse and dependent children of beneficiaries. *See also* Registered Pension Plan, Survivor's Benefit.

Canada Pension Plan Survivor's Benefit: an amount paid by the Canada Pension Plan to eligible spouses after a beneficiary's death, including a lump-sum payment and an ongoing pension. *See also* Canada Pension Plan, Survivor's Benefit.

Canada Pension Plan

The Canada Pension Plan (CPP), which began in 1966, provides a pension to employees and self-employed individuals with employment income. Quebec residents are covered by the Quebec Pension Plan (QPP). In 1998, 4.5 million people received CPP and QPP benefits.

Unlike private pension plans, which are funded by a pool of investment capital made up of contributions from plan members, the CPP is a "pay as you go" plan. In other words, benefits are paid to retired people from the contributions of working people. The investment pool only represents two years of pension payments.

The CPP pays retirement, disability and survivor pensions, the latter being made up of a lump-sum payment to a pensioner's spouse and an ongoing portion of the regular pension payment.

Today, the CPP faces the challenge of an aging population. Currently (1998), there are five workers for every retired person. By 2030, it is estimated that there will be only three workers to support every retiree, and 23 percent of Canadians will be over 65 years old.

To fund this change, the annual CPP premium must rise from 5.6 percent of incomes (1998) to 14.2 percent. Two questions must be considered. First, is it fair to ask young Canadians to pay so much? Second, will they agree to do so?

Canadas: government of Canada bonds. *See also* Bond.

Canada Savings Bond (CSB): a bond issued by the Bank of Canada, normally in the fall. Canada Savings Bonds are redeemable at any time at par and offer regular and compound interest features. Also known as Savings Bond. *See also* Bond.

Canada-U.S. Free Trade Agreement of 1989 (FTA): a bilateral treaty between Canada and the U.S. to reduce (and ultimately eliminate) all trade barriers. The FTA was expanded to the North American Free Trade Agreement with the inclusion of Mexico. Also known as U.S.-Canada Free Trade Agreement. *See also* North American Free Trade Agreement.

Canada-U.S. Social Security Agreement: an agreement between Canada and the U.S. that coordinates the social security programs of the two countries.

Canada-U.S. Tax Convention of 1980: *see* Convention Between the United States of America and Canada with Respect to Taxes on Income and Capital.

Canadian Asset Allocation Fund: one of the 31 Canadian fund categories developed by the Investment Funds Standards Committee. Mutual funds in this category must have over 75 percent of the market value of the portfolio in one, or a combination of, the following groups: Canadian fixed income, Canadian equities or Canadian cash and equivalents. The calculations to determine whether a mutual fund fits this definition are based on median values from fund data over three years, unless otherwise noted. The derivatives are weighted on an extended value basis. Each of the categories may be refined by a fund manager (e.g., a Canadian Large Cap Equity Fund might be described as "growth" or "value" to reflect the manager's style). *See also* Extended Value, Mutual Fund – Category.

Canadian Association of Financial Planners (CAFP): an association for financial planners who were issued the Registered Financial Planner (RFP) designation. The RFP designation has now been replaced by the Certified Financial Planner (CFP) designation.

Canadian Association of Insurance and Financial Advisors (CAIFA): successor to the Life Underwriters Association of Canada (LUAC), CAIFA offers professional development programs, sets standards of conduct and acts as an advocacy group for its members. It also offers courses leading to the designations of Chartered Life Underwriter, Certified Financial Planner and Chartered Financial Consultant. CAIFA is a founding member of the Financial Planners Standards Council (FPSC).

Canadian Association of Petroleum Producers (CAPP): an industry association for Canadian oil and gas producers whose membership develops, produces and explores for more than 95 percent of Canada's natural gas and crude oil. Each year CAPP holds a conference in Calgary at which its members make presentations to a select audience of senior oil and gas financial analysts and portfolio managers.

Canadian Balanced Fund: one of the 31 Canadian fund categories developed by the Investment Funds Standards Committee. Mutual funds in this category must have a minimum of 75 percent of the market value of the portfolio in a combination of Canadian equity and Canadian fixed income. The equity component of the portfolio must be between 25 and 75 percent. Fixed income and cash must constitute between 25 and 75 percent of the portfolio. The calculations to determine whether a mutual fund fits this definition are based on median values from fund data over three years, unless otherwise noted. The derivatives are weighted on an extended value basis. Each of the categories may be refined by a fund manager (e.g., a Canadian Large Cap Equity Fund might be described as "growth" or "value" to reflect the manager's style). *See also* Extended Value, Mutual Fund – Category.

Canadian Banker's Association (CBA): an industry association for the Canadian banking industry. The CBA provides banks with information and research and contributes to the development of public policy on financial services. It also provides industry information to the public. Web site: www.cba.ca

Canadian Bill of Rights: an act that recognizes and protects human rights and fundamental freedoms, passed by the federal Parliament in 1960 as an amendment to the British North America Act.

Canadian Bond Fund: one of the 31 Canadian fund categories developed by the Investment Funds Standards Committee. Mutual funds in this category must have over 75 percent of the market value of the portfolio in Canadian-dollar-denominated government and/or corporate bonds, debentures and short-term notes. The average term to maturity of the portfolio, including short-term investments, must be greater than three years. The calculations to determine whether a mutual fund fits this definition are based on median values from fund data over three years, unless otherwise noted. The derivatives are weighted on an extended value basis. Each of the categories may be refined by a fund manager (e.g., a Canadian Large Cap Equity Fund might be described as "growth" or "value" to reflect the manager's style). *See also* Extended Value, Mutual Fund – Category.

Canadian Bond Rating Service (CBRS): an independent company that rates commercial paper from A-1+ (highest) to A-3 (lowest), bonds from A++ to D and preferred shares from P-1 to P-5. *See also* Bond Rating Agency.

Canadian Charter of Rights and Freedoms: Part I of the Constitution Act of 1982, which can only be altered by constitutional amendment. Some of the rights and freedoms contained in the charter and entrenched in the Canadian Constitution include freedom of expression, the right to a democratic government, the right to live and seek employment anywhere in Canada, the right to equality, including the equality of men and women, the right to use either official language and to receive an education in the language of one's choice and the protection of Canada's multicultural heritage. *See also* British North America Act.

Canadian Commercial Corporation (CCC): a federal Crown corporation that acts as prime contractor for Canadian exporters selling to foreign governments, agencies and international organizations.

Canadian Common Stock Fund: *see* Canadian Equity Fund.

Canadian-Controlled Private Corporation: a company controlled directly or indirectly by a resident person or persons who are not public companies.

Canadian Dealing Network, Inc. (CDN): the organized over-the-counter market in Canada. The CDN is now a wholly owned subsidiary of the Toronto Stock Exchange. Previously known as the Canadian Over-the-Counter Automated Trading System (COATS). *See also* Over-the-Counter.

Canadian Dividend Fund: one of the 31 Canadian fund categories developed by the Investment Funds Standards Committee. Mutual funds in this category must have a minimum of 50 percent of the total assets, and 75 percent of the non-cash assets, of the portfolio in dividend-paying securities of Canadian corporations, equity securities convertible into the securities of Canadian corporations or royalty and income trusts (to a maximum of 25 percent of the portfolio) listed on a recognized exchange. The calculations to determine whether a mutual fund fits this definition are based on median values from fund data over three years, unless otherwise noted. The derivatives are weighted on an extended value basis. Each of the categories may be refined by a fund manager (e.g., a Canadian Large Cap Equity Fund might be described as "growth" or "value" to reflect the manager's style). *See also* Extended Value, Mutual Fund – Category.

Canadian Education Savings Grant (CESG): a federal government grant of up to $400 a year, to be placed into a Registered Education Savings Plan (RESP) if at least $2,000 is contributed to the RESP in that year.

Canadian Equity Fund: one of the 31 Canadian fund categories developed by the Investment Funds Standards Committee. Mutual funds in this category must have a minimum of 50 percent of the total assets, and 75 percent of the non-cash assets, of the portfolio in Canadian equities listed on a recognized exchange. In addition, a minimum of six of the Toronto Stock Exchange 300 sub-indexes should be represented with a weighting equal to 50 percent (at least) of each sub-index weighting, or the mean Industry Sector Concentration (ISC) value must not exceed 40. The calculations to determine whether a mutual fund fits this definition are based on median values from fund data over three years, unless otherwise noted. The derivatives are weighted on an extended value basis. Each of the categories may be refined by a fund manager (e.g., a Canadian Large Cap Equity Fund might be described as "growth" or "value" to reflect the manager's style). Also known as Canadian Common Stock Fund. *See also* Extended Value, Industry Sector Concentration (ISC), Mutual Fund - Category, Toronto Stock Exchange 300 Sub-Index (Communications and Media Index - Utilities Index).

Canadian High Income Balanced Fund: one of the 31 Canadian fund categories developed by the Investment Funds Standards Committee. Mutual funds in this category must have a minimum of 25 percent of the total assets, including cash and equivalents, in interest income-bearing securities and 50 percent of the total assets in non-interest, but income-producing, investments. The calculations to determine whether a mutual fund fits this definition are based on median values from fund data over three years, unless otherwise noted. The derivatives are weighted on an extended value basis. Each of the categories may be refined by a fund manager (e.g., a Canadian Large Cap Equity Fund may be described as "growth" or "value" to reflect the manager's style). *See also* Extended Value, Mutual Fund – Category.

Canadian Institute of Chartered Accountants (CICA): an industry association that awards the chartered accountant designation. The CICA governs members, sets accounting and auditing standards, establishes ethical standards and generally promotes the profession of the chartered accountant.

Canadian Institute of Financial Planners (CIFP): now inactive, this group offered the Chartered Financial Planner (CFP) designation and was a founder of the Financial Planners Standards Council (FPSC). Former Chartered Financial Planners were grandfathered as Certified Financial Planners (CFP) under the FPSC.

Canadian Intellectual Property Office: administers and processes patents, trademarks, copyrights, industrial design and integrated circuit board topographies. It also maintains a Canadian trademark database.

Canadian Investment Manager (CIM): a designation issued by the Canadian Securities Institute that indicates qualifications in the areas of portfolio and wealth management.

Canadian Investor Protection Fund (CIPF): established in 1969 as the National Contingency Fund, the CIPF protects the customers of brokerage firms that are members of a Sponsoring Self-Regulatory Organization (SSRO) from losses resulting from the insolvency of a member firm. In January 1999 the insurance was $500,000 per account. The five SSROs are the Toronto, Alberta and Vancouver stock exchanges, the Montreal Exchange and the Investment Dealers Association of Canada.

Canadian Large Cap Equity Fund: one of the 31 Canadian fund categories developed by the Investment Funds Standards Committee. Mutual funds in this category must have a minimum of 50 percent of the total assets, and 75 percent of the non-cash assets, of the portfolio in companies of the Toronto Stock Exchange 100 Index (TSE100). A minimum of 50 percent of the equity weighting must represent at least two of the four major sub-indexes of the TSE100. The calculations to determine whether a mutual fund fits this definition are based on median values from fund data over three years, unless otherwise noted. The derivatives are weighted on an extended value basis. Each of the categories may be refined by a fund manager (e.g., a Canadian Large Cap Equity Fund might be described as "growth" or "value" to reflect the manager's style). *See also* Extended Value, Mutual Fund – Category, Toronto Stock Exchange 100 Sub-Index (Consumer Index)-(Resource Index).

Canadian Life and Health Insurance Association (CLHIA): an industry association for life insurance companies.

Canadian Life and Health Insurance Compensation Corporation (COMPCORP): a life insurance and deposit-guarantee company funded by the Canadian life insurance industry. If a member company experiences financial failure, their contracted death benefits are guaranteed to $200,000 and cash values are guaranteed to $60,000.

Canadian Money Market Fund: one of the 31 Canadian fund categories developed by the Investment Funds Standards Committee. This definition makes reference to the statutory definition of money market funds. In summary, mutual funds in this category must invest in government obligations maturing in 25 months or less or in high-quality corporate securities maturing in 13 months or less. The portfolio must have a weighted average term to maturity of not more than 180 days, and 95 percent of the portfolio must be invested in assets denominated in the same currency as the units of the mutual fund. The calculations to determine whether a mutual fund fits this definition are based on median values from fund data over three years, unless otherwise noted. The derivatives are weighted on an extended value basis. Each of the categories may be refined by a fund manager (e.g., a Canadian Large Cap Equity Fund might be described as "growth" or "value" to reflect the manager's style). Also known as Money Market Fund. *See also* Extended Value, Mutual Fund – Category.

Canadian Mortgage Fund: one of the 31 Canadian fund categories developed by the Investment Funds Standards Committee. Mutual funds in this category must have over 75 percent of the market value of the portfolio in Canadian industrial, commercial and/or residential mortgages, including mortgage backed securities. The calculations to determine whether a mutual fund fits this definition are based on median values from fund data over three years, unless otherwise noted. The derivatives are weighted on an extended value basis. Each of the categories may be refined by a fund manager (e.g., a Canadian Large Cap Equity Fund might be described as "growth" or "value" to reflect the manager's style). *See also* Extended Value, Mortgage, Mortgage Backed Security, Mutual Fund – Category.

Canadian Over-the-Counter Automated Trading System (COATS): *see* Canadian Dealing Network, Inc.

Canadian Payments Association: the organization that handles the national clearing and settling of interbank payments Established in 1980, members include chartered banks, trust and loan companies, some credit unions and the caisses populaires.

Canadian Radio-Television and Telecommunications Commission (CRTC): the body that regulates broadcasting and telecommunications in Canada by setting guidelines, applying policy and granting operating licences.

Canadian Securities Course (CSC): a general investment course offered by the Canadian Securities Institute (CSI) and often a requirement for employment in the financial services industry.

Canadian Securities Institute (CSI): the national educational association for the Canadian investment industry and members of the public.

Canadian Shareowner's Association (CSA): an educational and investment institute that offers services to individuals who want to learn more about investing without using a stockbroker. *See also* National Association of Investment Clubs.

Canadian Short-Term Bond Fund: one of the 31 Canadian fund categories developed by the Investment Funds Standards Committee. Mutual funds in this category must have over 75 percent of the market value of the portfolio in Canadian short-term bonds and in mortgage-backed securities with a term to maturity of less than five years and more than one year. The calculations to determine whether a mutual fund fits this definition are based on median values from fund data over three years, unless otherwise noted. The derivatives are weighted on an extended value basis. Each of the categories may be refined by a fund manager (e.g., a Canadian Large Cap Equity Fund might be described as "growth" or "value" to reflect the manager's style). *See also* Extended Value, Mutual Fund – Category.

Canadian Small to Mid Cap Equity Fund: one of the 31 Canadian fund categories developed by the Investment Funds Standards Committee. Mutual funds in this category must have a minimum of 50 percent of the total assets, and 75 percent of the equity holdings, of the portfolio in Canadian equities with a market capitalization of not more than $3 billion (Canadian). The calculations to determine whether a mutual fund fits this definition are based on median values from fund data over three years, unless otherwise noted. The derivatives are weighted on an extended value basis. Each of the categories may be refined by a fund manager (e.g., a Canadian Large Cap Equity Fund might be described as "growth" or "value" to reflect the manager's style). Also known as Mid Cap Equity Fund, Small Cap Equity Fund. *See also* Extended Value, Market Capitalization, Mutual Fund – Category.

Canadian Standards Association (CSA): *see* CSA International.

Canadian Stock Exchange: *see* Montreal Curb Market.

Canadian Trademark Database: *see* Canadian Intellectual Property Office.

Canadian Venture Exchange (CDNX): the new exchange created in late 1999 as a result of the merger of Vancouver and Alberta stock exchanges. *See also*

Alberta Stock Exchange, Monteal Stock Exchange, Toronto Stock Exchange, Vancouver Stock Exchange.

Cancel Former Order (CFO): a client order to a broker to cancel a previous unfilled order.

Cancelled Charter: the status of a former company, indicating that it is no longer in business. *See also* Articles of Incorporation.

Candle Chart: a chart that displays a stock's open, high, low and close value over time.

Cap: 1. generally, an upper limit placed on prices, interest rates and so on. *See also* Capped Rate Mortgage, Collar, Floor. **2.** the highest interest rate that can be paid on a floating rate security. *See also* Floating Rate, Floating Rate Debt, Floating Rate Mortgage, Floating Rate Preferred Share. **3.** *see* Stock Market Capitalization.

Capacity Utilization Rate: a statistic that measures the percentage of the production capacity of the economy that is in use. A figure of over 85 percent is considered to be inflationary. *See also* Inflation, Operating Rate.

CAPEX: *see* Capital Expenditure.

Capital: 1. relating to financial assets or the financial value of assets. **2.** the plant, machinery and equipment in the economy. *See also* Social Capital. **3.** an investor's financial resources. **4.** *see* Shareholder's Equity.

Capital Account: in measuring the balance of payments, the capital account measures the value of investment flows in and out of a country. *See also* Balance of Payments, Current Account, Gold Account.

Capital Appreciation: 1. the rise in the value of an asset. Also known as Appreciation, Growth. **2.** one of the principal investment objectives. *See also* Income, Safety.

Capital Asset: a long-term asset that is not bought or sold in the day-to-day course of business (e.g., land, buildings). *See also* Operating Asset.

Capital Asset Pricing Model (CAPM): a theoretical calculation of value based on discounting expected income at a risk-free return plus a risk premium. A key to the model is the direct relationship between expected return and expected risk (i.e., an investor will demand additional return to accept a higher risk, and vice versa).

Capital Budget: a budget that itemizes long-term outlays (e.g., a new plant, research and development). *See also* Operating Budget.

Capital Consumption Allowance: an estimated amount of depreciation that reduces gross national product to net national product. Gross national product is more useful because the capital consumption allowance estimate is not reliable.

Capital Cost Allowance (CCA): a depreciation rate for an asset allowed by the Canadian Income Tax Act. The CCA is often greater than the actual depreciation rate, which reduces income tax payable.

Capital Cost Allowance Recapture: when there is a disposition of real estate for income tax purposes, the proceeds of the actual sale may exceed the original cost less capital cost allowance claimed. In such cases, the amount by which the proceeds of the sale exceeds the original cost less capital cost allowance must be added back to income and is recaptured capital cost allowance. Also known as Tax Recapture.

Capital Dividend Account (CDA): an account in a private corporation where the untaxed portion of capital gains is credited. This amount can be distributed to shareholders without additional tax.

Capital Expenditure (CAPEX): : the outlay to acquire capital assets or to upgrade existing capital assets. *See also* Capital Asset.

Capital Flight: *see* Flight of Capital.

Capital Formation: the economic process by which goods produce other goods in order to stimulate economic growth.

Capital Gain: 1. the increase in the value of an asset. **2.** the profit realized from selling an asset.

Capital-Gains Tax: a tax charged on profits realized from the disposition of assets for tax purposes. In Canada, 75 percent of the net capital gain is added to taxable income in the year of disposition. This results in a lower rate of tax on capital gains than on wages, salaries and interest income.

Capital Intensive: a business that requires a relatively large investment in capital assets (e.g., a steel producer).

Capital Investment: investment in land, buildings, machinery and other fixed assets.

Capitalism: an economic system in which the means of production and distribution are privately owned and operated for profit. *See also* Centrally Planned Economy, Communism, Free Market Economy, Market Economy, Socialism.

Capitalist: a person who believes in or works successfully under capitalism.

Capitalization: 1. the long-term capital of a company, including bonds, preferred shares and common stocks. Also known as Cap. **2.** *see* Stock Market Capitalization.

Capitalization Rate: 1. *see* Discount Rate.

Capitalization Ratio: the proportion of a company's total capital that is represented by long-term debt, preferred and common shares, retained earnings and capital surplus. *See also* Debt/Equity Ratio.

Capitalize: 1. to categorize items such as research and development costs as long-term assets and charge the amount against earnings over many years.

2. to convert a lease into an asset (reflecting the value of asset that is leased) with an offsetting liability (reflecting the financial obligation under the lease). *See also* Capital Lease. **3.** to convert a stream of income into a principal value. **4.** to record capital expenditures as additions to assets and not as current expenses. *See also* Capital Expenditure. **5.** to take advantage of an opportunity.

Capital Lease: a lease in which substantially all of the benefits and risks of ownership are transferred to the lessee. Capital leases are recorded as assets on the balance sheet with an offsetting liability. *See also* Financial Lease, Graduated Lease, Ground Lease, Lease, Open-End Lease, Operating Lease.

Capital Loss: 1. the decrease in the value of an asset. **2.** the loss realized from selling an asset.

Capital Loss Deduction: for Canadian income tax purposes, capital losses in a taxation year are first used to reduce or eliminate taxable capital gains in that year. Any capital losses still remaining are next used to reduce or eliminate taxable capital gains reported in the previous three years. Any capital losses that still remain unused can be carried forward indefinitely to be written off against future capital gains.

Capital Market: a market in which capital assets, such as bonds or stocks, are traded.

Capital Outflow: *see* Flight of Capital.

Capital Property: assets, including bonds, stocks and real estate, that may appreciate or decline in value and are held to generate income.

Capital Requirement: 1. the amount of cash and liquid securities certain regulated companies such as stock brokerage firms are required to maintain. **2.** the total working capital and long-term capital needed by a business to finance ongoing operations.

Capital Risk: the risk related to the preservation of money invested.

Capital Share: the share of a dual purpose mutual fund that is entitled to the capital appreciation generated by the portfolio. *See also* Dual Purpose Mutual Fund, Income Share.

Capital Stock: a company's common shares outstanding.

Capital Structure: the value of a company's long-term debt plus preferred shares plus shareholder's equity.

Capital Surplus: the amount by which the balance sheet value of capital exceeds the par value. The main source of capital surplus is the issuance of common shares at a price above par value.

Capital Tax: a tax levied annually on corporate capital; often considered unfair and anti-business because it is a wealth tax; that is, a tax on the same assets and/or earnings year after year.

Capitation: *see* Poll Tax.

CAPM: *see* Capital Asset Pricing Model.

CAPP: *see* Canadian Association of Petroleum Producers.

CAPP Conference: *see* Canadian Association of Petroleum Producers.

Capped Rate Mortgage (CRM): a mortgage stipulating the maximum rate of interest that can be charged. *See also* Cap, Mortgage.

Captive Agent: an insurance agent who sells the products of one insurance company. A captive agent will often have more in-depth product knowledge of a shorter list of products available. *See also* Independent Agent.

Captive Finance Company: a company, often a subsidiary, that is in business to finance products sold by its parent company (e.g., Ford Motor Credit Company).

Caracas Stock Exchange: the major stock exchange of Venezuela, located in its capital, Caracas. Also known as Bolsa de Valores de Caracas. Web site: www.caracasstock.com/

Carat: a measure of weight used for gems. One carat equals 200 milligrams or 315 grains. In North America, Karat is used as a measure of the proportion of fine gold in an alloy. In other regions, Carat and Karat are more or less synonymous. *See also* Karat.

Cardinal Number: a number that is used in counting and that indicates how many elements there are in an assemblage.

Cardinal Rule: a most important rule. In investing, "buy low, sell high" is a cardinal rule.

Car Insurance: *see* Automobile Insurance.

Carpetbagger: an outsider who arrives to take financial advantage of a situation. Derived from the post-American Civil War period, when northerners went south seeking financial opportunities.

Carpet Bomb: on the Internet, an advertisement or solicitation sent randomly to many different newsgroups. This is considered poor "netiquette." *See also* Internet.

Carriage Trade: to cater to very wealthy customers.

Carried Interest: an interest in a resource property under which the owner is not required to make a proportionate contribution to expenditures.

Carrier: in computers, a steady tone that is altered by a modem in order to communicate data across telephone lines. *See also* Computer.

Carrot: a reward used as a motivation, as in a bonus paid an employee for attaining a certain level of sales.

Carrot and Stick: to motivate by offering a reward for good performance and a penalty for poor results.

Carry: the net cost of financing an investment position. The income from the investment less the cost of funds borrowed to purchase the position.

Carry Back: an income tax term referring to the use of an unused deduction against taxes already paid. A capital loss, for example, can be "carried back" and applied against capital gains reported in the three preceding years.

Carry Forward: an income tax term referring to the use of an unused deduction against future taxes. A capital loss, for example, can be "carried forward" and applied against any future capital gains.

Carrying Charge: 1. in investment, the amount of money a broker charges a client on borrowed funds. *See also* Margin Account. **2.** the cost of holding, storing and insuring a physical inventory of commodities. Also known as Cost of Carry. **3.** *see* Carrying Cost.

Carrying Cost: generally, the interest on borrowed money. Also known as Carrying Charge.

Cartage: the cost of transporting goods by land.

Carte Blanche: total freedom to act. Also known as Blank Cheque.

Cartel: a small group of producers of a good or service that agrees to regulate supply in an effort to control or manipulate prices (e.g., the Organization of Petroleum Exporting Countries [OPEC] is an oil cartel).

Casablanca All Share Index: a stock price index of all stock s listed on the Casablanca Stock Exchange.

Casablanca Stock Exchange: the major stock exchange of Morocco, located in Casablanca.

Caseload: the number of clients or patients being handled, especially in law, medicine, psychiatry and the social services.

Cash: 1. a negotiable currency in spendable form. **2.** a balance sheet account that records the amount of cash (and equivalents) of a business. *See also* Balance Sheet. **3.** to convert into cash, as in "cash a cheque."

Cashable Guaranteed Investment Certificate: a GIC that, through the payment of an interest penalty, can be converted to cash before maturity.

Cashable Term Deposit: a term deposit that, through the payment of an interest penalty, can be converted to cash before maturity.

Cash Account: an account, often with a brokerage firm, in which the customer must settle purchase transactions in cash. *See also* Margin Account.

Cash Accounting: 1. an accounting system that records revenue when payment is received and records expenses when payment is made. Also known as Cash Basis Accounting. *See also* Accrual

Accounting. **2.** in income tax, the reporting of taxable income only when it is received. *See also* Accrual Accounting.

Cash Advance: a cash loan made on a credit card. A cash advance may be charged a higher interest rate or interest charges may start immediately.

Cash and Carry: 1. a transaction in which an investor buys an asset today and simultaneously sells it in the futures market. In an efficient market, the return will be equivalent to short-term interest rate returns for the holding period. **2.** a somewhat dated condition of sale; that is, payment in cash, with the buyer responsible for removing the goods.

Cash Basis Accounting: *see* Cash Accounting.

Cash Board: the place where cash commodity sales are listed on a commodities exchange. *See also* Cash Commodity, Cash Delivery, Cash Market, Cash Price, Cash Security, Cash Settlement, Cash Trade.

Cash Budget: an analysis of the timing of the receipt and disbursement of cash in a business. A cash budget is useful in determining when purchases can be made and how much credit can be extended to customers.

Cash Buying: the purchase of commodities or securities for immediate delivery and settlement in cash or equivalent. *See also* Cash Board, Cash Commodity, Cash Delivery, Cash Market, Cash Price, Cash Security, Cash Settlement, Cash Trade.

Cash Card: *see* Bank Card.

Cash Commodity: a commodity that is owned immediately upon the purchase transaction being completed (in contrast to a futures commodity that is not owned until a future date). *See also* Cash Board, Cash Delivery, Cash Market, Cash Price, Cash Security, Cash Settlement, Cash Trade.

Cash Conversion: *see* Currency Conversion.

Cash Conversion Cycle: the time between a manufacturing company paying for raw materials and being paid for a final product. A short cash conversion cycle means less cash is needed to fund a business. *See also* Cash Turnover.

Cash Cow: any business or investment that generates a high level of cash flow.

Cash Crop: an agricultural crop cultivated for its commercial value.

Cash Cycle: *see* Cash Conversion Cycle.

Cash Delivery: this occurs when securities are traded and delivered the same day. Also known as Same Day Delivery. *See also* Cash Board, Cash Buying, Cash Commodity, Cash Market, Cash Price, Cash Security, Cash Settlement, Cash Trade.

Cash Discount: 1. a typical trade practice of offering a price discount for early payment (e.g., "2 percent,

10 days, net 30" means a 2 percent discount is available if payment is made within 10 days, the full amount being due in 30 days. **2.** a retail practice of offering a discount for payment in cash at the time of purchase.

Cash Dividend: a cash distribution of profits to common or preferred shareholders. *See also* Dividend, Optional Dividend, Stock Dividend.

Cash Earnings: *see* Cash Flow.

Cash Equivalents: high-quality, liquid investments that are considered to be the same as cash.

Cash Flow: the net income of a company adding back non-cash expenses. Non-cash expenses are expenses such as depreciation and depletion that are charged in calculating net income but do not represent cash paid out. In investment, the future flow of cash back to the investor.

Cashier: an employee of a financial institution who handles the disbursement and receipt of money as well as other transactions.

Cashier's Cheque: the U.S. equivalent of a certified or guaranteed cheque.

Cashless Society: a society in which cash has been totally replaced by debit and credit cards.

Cash Management: the process of managing corporate short-term assets. Also, managing a portfolio invested in the money market.

Cash Management Account: an account with a brokerage firm that allows for credit card payments to be made from investment account balances.

Cash Market: a market in which securities trade for immediate payment. *See also* Cash Board, Cash Buying, Cash Commodity, Cash Delivery, Cash Price, Cash Security, Cash Settlement, Cash Trade.

Cash on Cash Return: a rate of return calculation that measures the annual cash income as a percentage of the total cash invested. Cash on cash is often used in real estate investment because a small cash down-payment and a mortgage are frequently used to finance purchases.

Cash on Delivery (COD): 1. a settlement method for a brokerage account that requires payment for the purchase of a security upon simultaneous receipt of the shares purchased. **2.** a notation indicating payment is due when merchandise is delivered.

Cash or Deferred Arrangement (CODA): a U.S.-defined benefit pension plan in which payments can be directed to the person or to a qualified plan in which income taxes can be deferred.

Cash Position: *see* Cash Reserves.

Cash Price: 1. the price of a commodity for immediate delivery. *See also* Cash Board, Cash Buying, Cash Commodity, Cash Delivery, Cash Market, Cash

Security, Cash Settlement, Cash Trade. **2.** the selling price of an article for immediate payment in cash.

Cash Ratio: cash and marketable securities divided by current liabilities. The cash ratio is a measure of the liquidity of a business. *See also* Quick Ratio.

Cash Reserves: the amount of a portfolio that is uninvested (i.e., held as cash). The higher the cash position, the more defensive the portfolio strategy. Also known as Cash Position.

Cash Security: a security traded for immediate settlement. *See also* Cash Board, Cash Buying, Cash Commodity, Cash Delivery, Cash Market, Cash Price, Cash Settlement, Cash Trade.

Cash Settlement: a settlement method for a brokerage account that makes payment on the same day a security is purchased or receives payment on the same day a security is sold. Also known as Same Day Settlement. *See also* Cash Board, Cash Buying, Cash Commodity, Cash Delivery, Cash Market, Cash Price, Cash Security, Settlement, Three-Day Settlement.

Cash Surrender Value (CSV): in some life insurance products, the amount of cash that will be paid out if the contract or policy is cancelled. The cash surrender value does not have to be paid out (e.g., it can be used to continue premium payments). Also known as Cash Value, Surrender Value. *See also* Life Insurance.

Cash Trade: a security transaction in which the transaction, payment and delivery occurs on the same day. *See also* Cash Board, Cash Buying, Cash Commodity, Cash Delivery, Cash Market, Cash Price, Cash Security, Cash Settlement.

Cash Turnover: the number of cash conversion cycles in a year. Cash turnover is a measure of the efficient use of cash. *See also* Cash Conversion Cycle.

Cash Value: *see* Cash Surrender Value.

Cash Value Life Insurance: *see* Whole Life Insurance.

Cash Yield: a bond yield calculation that is the annual cash interest received divided by the market price. Unlike yield to maturity, cash yield does not take into account the fact that a bond will mature at par. *See also* Yield to Maturity.

Casino Finance: an investment program of exceptionally high risk, often involving bank loans and the use of options on stocks or stock market indexes. *See also* Option.

Casualty Insurance: the U.S. term for liability insurance.

Catalytic Cracker: equipment that upgrades petroleum distillates to higher value, lighter products.

Catastrophe: in general insurance, any short-term event, such as a storm, that produces many claims.

Cathode-Ray Tube (CRT): a television screen often used as an output device for a personal computer. *See also* Computer, Computer Screen, Interactive Terminal, Laser Printer, Line Printer, Monitor, Optical Character Recognition, Peripheral, Printer, Printout, Readout, Remote Access, Terminal.

CATS: 1. *see* Certificate of Accrual on Treasury Certificates. **2.** *see* Computer Assisted Trading System.

Cats and Dogs: speculative securities.

CATV: *see* Community Antenna Television.

Caveat: 1. a cautionary statement or warning. Caveats are often used in the investment industry to point out that forecasts are not totally reliable. *See also* Caveat Emptor, Caveat Venditor. **2.** in law, a process to suspend proceedings until something is done.

Caveat Emptor: a principle in commerce meaning, "let the buyer beware."

Caveat Subscriptor: *see* Caveat Venditor.

Caveat Venditor: a principle in commerce meaning, "let the seller beware."

Cayman Islands Stock Exchange: a stock exchange for the Cayman Islands.

Cayman Islands Stock Exchange Index: a stock price index for the Cayman Islands Stock Exchange.

CBA: *see* Canadian Banker's Association.

CBOE: *see* Chicago Board Options Exchange.

CBRS: *see* Canadian Bond Rating Service.

cc: at the end of a letter, abbreviation for "carbon copy." It shows that a copy has been sent to the person indicated, as in "cc: Mr. Jones."

CCA: *see* Capital Cost Allowance.

CCC: *see* Canadian Commercial Corporation.

CCITT: *see* Comité Consultatif International Télégraphique et Téléphonique.

CCRA: Canada Customs and Revenue Agency.

CD: 1. *see* Certificate of Deposit. **2.** *see* Compact Disc.

CDA: *see* Capital Dividend Account.

CDIC: *see* Canada Deposit Insurance Corporation.

CDN: *see* Canadian Dealing Network, Inc.

CDNX: *see* Canadian Venture Exchange

CD-ROM: *see* Compact Disc – Read Only Memory.

Cease Trading Order: a directive from a regulatory body, such as a securities commission or stock exchange, indicating that the shares of a specific company should not be traded until further notice.

Cedi: the prime currency of Ghana.

Ceiling: *see* Cap.

Cell: 1. the geographic area one cellular telephone tower covers. **2.** a unique location on a spreadsheet identified by the intersection of a column by a row. *See also* Spreadsheet.

Cell Phone: *see* Cellular Telephone.

Cellular Telephone: a portable telephone, named after the system of cells used to gather and connect telephone signals. Also known as Cell Phone. *See also* Personal Communications Service, Roam.

Celsius (C): a temperature scale in which water boils at 100 degrees and freezes at zero degrees.

Censure: an expression of criticism or disapproval sometimes used formally by organizations with respect to the actions of their members.

Cent: a penny. One one-hundredth of a dollar.

Centi: in the decimal system, the prefix denoting one part in 100, as in a centilitre, which is one one-hundredth of a litre. *See also* Metric System.

Centigrade (C): the descriptive form of Celsius.

Central Africa Republic Franc: the currency of countries making up the Central Africa Republic including Cameroon, Central Africa Republic, Chad, Congo, Equatorial Guinea and Gabon.

Central America: the isthmus between North and South America including Belize, Guatemala, El Salvador, Honduras, Nicaragua, Costa Rica and Panama. Mineral resources of the region include gold, silver, lead, zinc, copper, nickel, oil and gas.

Central Bank: a government banking agency that issues currency and government bonds, manages monetary policy and facilitates banking services by managing cheque clearing systems. Canada's central bank is the Bank of Canada.

Central Depository for Securities: a central location that holds investment certificates in member accounts.

Central Limit Theorem: a statistical principle that the average of a large number of observations approximates the true value and deviations follow a normal distribution. This forms the basis of many life insurance industry calculations.

Centrally Planned Economy: an economy such as that under Communism in which government bureaucrats and ministries make all resource allocation decisions. *See also* Capitalism, Communism, Free Market Economy, Market Economy, Socialism.

Centrally Planned Economy: an economy, such as that under Communism, in which a person or persons make all resource allocation decisions. *See also* Capitalism, Communism, Free Market Economy, Market Economy, Socialism.

Central Processing Unit (CPU): the main control device in a computer, where instructions are interpreted and calculations are carried out. Also known as Processor. *See also* Computer.

Central Selling Organization (CSO): the marketing system through which De Beers Centenary controls most of the world's diamond marketing.

CEO: *see* Chief Executive Officer.

Certain Term Annuity: *see* Annuity Certain.

Certificate: 1. *see* Bond Certificate. **2.** *see* Certificate of Deposit. **3.** *see* Share Certificate.

Certificate of Accrual on Treasury Certificates (CATS): a noninterest-paying U.S. Treasury Bond sold at a deep discount. Created by Salomon Brothers Inc.

Certificate of Charge: provincial government acknowledgement of the registration of a mortgage in a land titles office. *See also* Mortgage.

Certificate of Deposit (CD): a term deposit, usually with a fixed interest rate and maturity date of up to six years. CDs issued by members of the Canada Deposit Insurance Corporation are guaranteed in value up to $60,000 per issuer. Also known as Certificate. *See also* Canada Deposit Insurance Corporation, Term Deposit.

Certificate of Title: a provincial government receipt for the registration of a title deed in a land titles office.

Certified Cheque: a personal cheque, with payment guaranteed by the issuing institution.

Certified Financial Planner (CFP): a financial planner's designation, issued by the Institute of Certified Financial Planners in the U.S. and licensed for use in Canada by the Financial Planners Standards Council.

Certified General Accountants Association of Canada: an association representing CGAs.

Certified Public Accountant (CPA): a person who, upon passing a series of exams, meets U.S. state requirements for becoming a certified public accountant. In most cases, only CPAs are permitted to render opinions on the fairness of financial statements.

Certify: 1. to formally acknowledge the creation of a labour union as the bargaining unit for a group of workers. *See also* Decertify. **2.** in general, to formally recognize an accomplishment by issuing a certificate.

CESG: *see* Canadian Education Savings Grant.

CFA: *see* Chartered Financial Analyst.

CFA Franc BEAC: *see* Central Africa Republic Franc.

CFO: 1. *see* Cancel Former Order. **2.** *see* Chief Financial Officer.

CFP: 1. *see* Certified Financial Planner. **2.** *see* Chartered Financial Planner.

CFR (Cost and Freight): a transaction in which the seller assumes all costs and risks of delivering the goods to a specific port of destination and the buyer is responsible for all insurance. *See also* CIF, EXW, FAS, FOB, FOR, FOT.

CFTC: *see* Commodity Futures Trading Commission.

CGA: *see* Certified General Accountant.

Chaebol: a term that refers to the largest industrial conglomerates in South Korea, including Daewoo, Hyundai and Samsung.

Chain Letter: a letter that instructs the recipient to send money or an item of value to the person at the top of the list of names included, to remove the name at the top of the list, add the recipient's name to the bottom of the list and send out a number of copies to people who will keep the letter going. A chain letter with 10 names already on it and requiring the recipient to send it to 10 additional people will have to reach 10 billion people (roughly two letters to every person on earth) if the chain is unbroken when the recipient's name reaches the top of the list.

Chain Reaction: a series of events in which each step is induced by the one preceding it. Chain reactions can sometimes trigger the buying or selling of stocks.

Chain Store: one of many stores under the same name dealing in substantially the same merchandise.

Chair: the officer in charge of running meetings. Also known as Chairman, Chairwoman or Chairperson.

Chairman: *see* Chair.

Chairman of the Board: a member of the board of directors elected to preside as chair at meetings. The chairman of the board is the highest ranking officer of a company but is usually not involved in the day-to-day operations of the business. *See also* Chief Executive Officer.

Chairman of the Federal Reserve Board: the senior member of the seven-member Federal Reserve Board. This person is important because he/she can influence Federal Reserve Board policies and is a spokesperson for the Federal Reserve.

Chairperson: *see* Chair.

Challenge-Response Token: in computers, an authentication system that makes use of multiple codes. A user must provide these codes in order to gain access to a computer or network. *See also* Access Control, Authentication, Biometric Authentication, Computer, Firewall, Password, Public Key, Secret Key.

Chamber of Commerce: a group of business people that promotes the activities and interests of its members, especially by promoting a city or region to attract new businesses or tourism. *See also* Board of Trade.

Chameleon: an investor who continuously changes his/her objectives.

Chancellor of the Exchequer: the United Kingdom's equivalent of Canada's Finance Minister or the U.S.'s Secretary of the Treasury.

Change of Use: in Canadian taxation, this refers to what occurs when an owner of real estate converts

the use of a property, thus triggering tax consequences (e.g., changing a rental property to a principal residence).

Characters per Second (CPS): in computers, a data
transmission rate and/or printer speed expressed in
characters per second. *See also* Baud, Baud Rate,
Computer.

Charitable Donation: a gift to a registered charity,
providing an income tax deduction to the donor.

Charity: aid given to a worthwhile cause. The donor
may or may not receive an income tax deduction,
depending on whether the recipient has been
approved as a registered charity for income tax purposes.

Charge Account: a credit facility usually offered by a
merchant to enable a customer to purchase a good or
service today and pay for it in the future.

Charitable Lead Trust: a trust that pays income to a
charity while the donor is living and the balance of
the trust to beneficiaries upon the donor's death. *See
also* Charitable Remainder Trust, Trust.

Charitable Remainder Trust: a trust established by a
living person in which the remaining value of the
trust is irrevocable transferred to a charity. The contributor receives a current tax deduction for the
donation and is entitled to receive the income from
the trust, net of expenses, during his/her life or
his/her life and the life of his/her spouse.

Charitable Trust: a trust established to benefit charity
without naming a specific beneficiary (e.g., to benefit
health care rather than the Heart Fund). *See also*
Beneficiary, Charity.

Chart: a graphic illustration of data over time.

Charter Cancelled: the status indicating that a company has gone out of business.

Chartered Accountant (CA): a person meeting the
qualifications, and agreeing to abide by the standards,
set by the Canadian Institute of Chartered
Accountants.

Chartered Bank: *see* Bank.

Chartered Financial Analyst (CFA): a professional
designation awarded by the Institute of Chartered
Financial Analysts to persons qualified in accounting,
financial analysis and management of portfolios. *See
also* Securities Analyst.

Chartered Financial Consultant (CH.F.C.): a designation offered by the Canadian Association of
Insurance and Financial Advisors. The CH.F.C. has
been replaced by the Certified Financial Planner designation. *See also* Agent, Broker, Chartered Life
Underwriter.

Chartered Financial Consultant (ChFC): a professional financial planner completing a series of courses

and examinations in economics, insurance, real estate
and tax shelters. The designation is awarded by the
American College of Bryn Mawr, Pennsylvania.

Chartered Financial Planner (C.F.P.): a financial
planning designation issued by the Canadian
Institute of Financial Planners. The C.F.P. designation has been phased out in favour of the Certified
Financial Planner (CFP) designation.

Chartered Life Underwriter (CLU): a person who
has completed certain courses of study in life and
health insurance and employee benefits offered by
the Canadian Association of Insurance and Financial
Planners. *See also* Agent, Broker, Chartered Financial
Consultant.

Chartered Property Casualty Underwriter (CPCU):
a professional designation in the field of property and
casualty insurance.

Chartist: a person who examines the past price trends
of assets in order to find patterns on which to base
forecasts of future price trends. *See also* Technical
Analyst, Fundamental Analyst.

Chase the Market: a term used to describe the investment practice of buying at higher prices after the
market has been rising or selling at lower prices after
the market has been falling. Generally, the opposite
of the investment rule "Buy low, sell high." *See also*
Buy Low, Sell High.

Chastity Bonds: bonds that are redeemable at par
value if the issuer is taken over. *See also* Bond,
Macaroni Defence, Par Value, Redeemable.

Chat Room: a site on the Internet where people dis-
cuss certain topics. *See also* Internet.

Chattel: all moveable possessions (e.g., land is not a
chattel but a house built on that land is a chattel).
See also Goods and Chattels, Personal Property.

Chattel Interest: an interest in leasehold property. *See
also* Chattel, Goods and Chattels, Personal Property.

Chattel Loan: *see* Chattel Mortgage.

Chattel Mortgage: a loan on personal property of a
moveable nature, as opposed to land. *See also* Chattel,
Mortgage.

Cheap: a security that is low in price relative to income
or assets. A value investor buys cheap securities.

Check: U.S. spelling for cheque. *See also* Cheque.

Check Assays: in the mining industry, assays conducted by an independent firm in order to confirm
initial results.

Check the Market: to review the current bids and
offerings for a stock or the change in the indexes.

Cheque: a written order to a financial institution to
pay a sum from funds on deposit.

Cheque Book: a pad of blank cheques relating to an
account.

Cheque Register: a place, usually in a cheque book, where records of cheques written are kept.

Chequing Account: a deposit account intended to be used actively. The cost of processing a cheque is lower with a chequing account than with a savings account, and the interest paid on cash balances is lower. Also known as Bank Account. *See also* Combination Account, Demand Deposit, Deposit, Savings Account.

Cherry Picking: looking through a list of assets or investments and choosing only the very best.

CH.F.C: *see* Chartered Financial Consultant.

Chicago Board Options Exchange (CBOE): the largest U.S. exchange for the trading of financial options. Web site: www.chicagostockex.com *See also* Option.

Chicago Mercantile Exchange (CME): an organized exchange established in 1919 for the trading of futures contracts in various American agricultural commodities. Web site: www.cme.com/

Chicago Stock Exchange: a regional U.S. stock exchange located in Chicago, Illinois. Formerly, the Midwest Stock Exchange. Web site: www.chicagostockex.com *See also* Cincinnati Stock Exchange.

Chicken: a nervous, risk-averse investor.

Chicken Feed: an insignificant amount of money.

Chief Executive Officer (CEO): a senior corporate officer responsible for the overall administration and management of a company. *See also* Chairman of the Board, Chief Financial Officer, Chief Operating Officer, Corporate Secretary.

Chief Financial Officer (CFO): a senior corporate officer responsible for the management of a company's finances and record keeping. *See also* Chairman of the Board, Chief Executive Officer, Chief Operating Officer, Corporate Secretary.

Chief Information Officer (CIO): a senior corporate officer responsible for the management of a company's information technology. *See also* Information Technology.

Chief Investment Officer (CIO): a senior corporate officer responsible for the management of the investment activities of an investment firm.

Chief Operating Officer (COO): a senior corporate officer responsible for the management of a company's day-to-day operations. *See also* Chairman of the Board, Chief Executive Officer, Chief Financial Officer, Corporate Secretary.

Child Support: a payment by agreement or court order, usually by the non-custodial parent to the custodial parent, to assist in the raising of children. Child support payments by agreement before May 1, 1997, and not changed are tax deductible for the paying spouse and taxable for the receiving spouse. Payments by agreement or court order or that have changed since May 1, 1997, are not tax deductible for the paying spouse and are not taxable for the receiving spouse.

Child Tax Benefit: a single federal benefit that replaced the former family allowance, the refundable child tax credit and non-refundable tax credit for dependent children in 1993. It is a non-taxable monthly benefit paid to families for each child, generally increasing with the number of children and decreasing for higher income families. Also known as Non-Refundable Tax Credit for Dependent Children.

Chilean Stock Exchange: *see* Santiago Stock Exchange.

Chill Factor: the climate in which a news report or article is moderated or cancelled in response to external pressure, real or perceived, from an advertiser, for example.

Chinese Lunar Cycle: in Asian countries, a 12-year cycle in which each year is represented by an animal.

Chinese Lunar Cycle	
1998, 2010	The Tiger
1999, 2011	The Rabbit
2000, 2012	The Dragon
2001, 2013	The Snake
2002, 2014	The Horse
2003, 2015	The Goat
2004, 2016	The Monkey
2005, 2017	The Rooster
2006, 2018	The Dog
2007, 2019	The Pig
2008, 2020	The Rat
2009, 2021	The Ox

Chinese Market: a situation in which buyers will pay above, and sellers will sell below, the offering price if there is a sufficient volume of trading to be done.

Chinese Stock Exchange: *see* Shanghai Securities Exchange.

Chinese Wall: *see* Firewall.

Chip: a tiny piece of semiconducting material that may contain millions of integrated circuits.

Chiphead: slang for someone very actively involved in computers and related areas. *See also* Computer, Computer Geek, Cracker, Hacker.

Christmas Tree: *see* Wellhead.

Chronological Order: in order according to date.

Churning: unnecessary trading of securities in a client's account in order to increase commissions for the broker.

CICA: *see* Canadian Institute of Chartered Accountants.

CIF (Cost, Insurance and Freight): a transaction in which the seller assumes all costs and risks to a specific port of destination. *See also* CFR, EXW, FAS, FOB, FOR, FOT.

CIFP: *see* Canadian Institute of Financial Planners.

C+I+G+FT: a basic economic formula stating that economic output for a period equals the total of consumption plus investment plus government spending plus the effect of foreign trade.

CIM: *see* Canadian Investment Manager.

Cincinnati Stock Exchange: a regional U.S. stock exchange located in Chicago, Illinois, it was the first fully automated stock exchange in the U.S. *See also* Chicago Stock Exchange.

CINS: *see* CUSIP International Numbering Service.

CIO: 1. *see* Chief Information Officer. 2. *see* Chief Investment Officer.

CIPF: *see* Canadian Investor Protection Fund.

Circle: the process an underwriter goes through to estimate commitments for a new issue of securities dependent on price. If a client indicates interest, the underwriter circles the name and amount reserved. *See also* Fully Circled, Indication of Interest.

Circle of Influence: a concept used extensively by brokers and financial planners in seeking clients who have a large circle of influence; that is, individuals who influence the thoughts and actions of others.

Circuit Breaker: a reference to New York Stock Exchange rules which halt all trading for one hour if the Dow-Jones Average falls 10 percent before 2:00 p.m. and 30 minutes if it takes place between 2:00 and 2:30 p.m.; two hours if it falls 20 percent before 1:00 p.m., one hour if it takes place between 1:00 and 2:00 p.m. and for the balance of the day if it takes place after 2:00 p.m.; and for the balance of the day if it falls 30 percent at any time.

Circuit Court: a province's superior court, which travels throughout various communities for sittings.

City Council: the group of officials elected to manage a city, usually led by a mayor.

City Desk: the news department responsible for local news and events.

City Gate: the point on a distribution system at which a gas utility receives gas from the transmission system.

City Hall: 1. the building housing the city council and administrative employees. 2. term used to describe a municipal government.

City Manager: the administrative employee in municipal government.

Civil Disobedience: the disobeying of civil laws, usually in a nonviolent fashion, in order to force change in government policy or legislation.

Civil Law: the body of laws that deal with the rights of private citizens. In Canada, Quebec has a legal system based on the French civil code. The other provinces use a system based on English common law. *See also* Common Law.

Civil Liberties: basic individual rights (e.g., freedom of speech and religion).

Civil Rights: rights that belong to an individual as a result of citizenship (e.g., the right to equal protection under the law and the right to freedom from discrimination).

Civil Service: permanent professional branches of government services, excluding elected politicians, the judiciary and the military. Also known as Service.

Claim: 1. notification to an insurance company that a benefit is payable to the insured under the provisions of an insurance contract. *See also* Coverage, Death Benefit, Policy, Settlement Options. 2. a title or right to something. 3. in mining, an area of land (approximately 16.2 hectares) to which a company holds rights of exploration or production granted by the federal or a provincial government.

Claimant: one who makes a claim.

Class: a category of security that has similar qualities (e.g., bonds, preferred shares, common shares).

Class A Share: *see* Classified Stock.

Class B Share: *see* Classified Stock.

Classified Stock: common shares that are different by virtue of the issuing company's bylaws (e.g., Class A shares and Class B shares where one is voting, or entitled to multiple votes, and one is non-voting).

Claw Back: a term used to describe how the government reduces (or eliminates) a benefit as the recipient's income rises.

Clean Opinion: an auditor's unqualified opinion attesting to the accuracy of a financial statement. Also known as Unqualified Opinion.

Clear: 1. in underwriting, to satisfy regulatory requirements, as in "clear a prospectus." *See also* Prospectus. 2. in banking, to collect and make payment of funds drawn by a cheque, as in "the cheque has been cleared." 3. in securities, to successfully settle a trade, as in "the trade has cleared." 4. *see* Clear Title.

Clear Day: under certain provincial legislation, a day following a Sunday or statutory holiday that is added to a stated period for a takeover.

Clear-Cut Logging: a controversial logging method that entails all the growth in an area being logged at once.

Clearing and Settlement: the process comparing the details of a transaction between brokers and making the final exchange of payment and delivery of securities.

Clearing Corporation: a company that clears option trades by becoming the buyer for every seller and the seller to every buyer of options. *See also* Options Clearing Corporation.

Clearing System: an organization established in order to facilitate the settlement of security trades or, in banking, a system to clear cheques and other financial instruments.

Clear Title: a title of ownership that is clear of any claims or dispute. Also known as Good Title, Just Title. *See also* Bad Title, Cloud on Title, Defective Title, On Title, Title Deed, Title Defect, Title Search.

CLEC: *see* Competitive Local Exchange Carrier.

CLHIA: *see* Canadian Life and Health Insurance Association.

Client Computer: *see* Network Computer.

Client/Server: this describes a relationship between two pieces of computer software, where a data storage and retrieval device (the server) handles directions from personal computers or workstations (the client). *See also* Computer.

Climax: a period of sharp price changes and heavy volume at the end of a long-term trend.

Climb a Wall of Worry: an expression indicating that stock prices can only rise if actual results are better than expected results. The more things investors worry about, the more likely it is that results will exceed expectations, and so "stock prices climb a wall of worry."

Clinton Bond: *see* Quayle Bond.

Cliometrics: the use of data processing and analysis to study history.

Clone: a new mutual fund established to emulate a successful mutual fund within the same family of funds. *See* Mutual Fund.

Close: 1. a reference to the price of a security or a stock market index at the end of a trading session. *See also* Closing Bell, Opening. **2.** in real estate, to consummate a sale, as in "close the sale." **3.** in accounting, to conclude entering data at the end of an accounting period, as in "close the books." Also known as Closing the Books.

Closed End Fund: *see* Closed End Mutual Fund.

Closed End Mutual Fund: a mutual fund in which investors buy shares or units from current owners and sell shares or units to new investors. *See also* Mutual Fund – Other.

Closed Fund: *see* Closed Up Mutual Fund.

Closed Mortgage: a mortgage in which the interest rate cannot be changed until maturity. *See also* Mortgage.

Closed Out: selling securities owned by a client who is unable to meet a margin call or cover a short sale.

Closed Shop: a facility that employs only union members. Also known as Union Shop. *See also* Open Shop.

Closed Up Mutual Fund: an open-ended mutual fund that has discontinued the sale of new shares to the public. *See also* Mutual Fund.

Closely Held: a term used to describe shares (often held by a controlling group) that will be held for the long term. The holders of such shares consider themselves owners of the underlying business and their decision to continue as shareholders is not influenced by the ups and downs of the financial markets in the same way as an investor/shareholder.

Close Out: 1. *see* Closed Out. **2.** a sale, usually held just before closing an outlet, at which merchandise is sold at a deep discount.

Closet Indexer: an active portfolio manager whose style is to have portfolios closely replicate a widely followed index or benchmark.

Closing: 1. generally, the end of a trading day on a securities market. *See also* Closing Bell. **2.** the price of a security at the end of a trading day on a securities market. *See also* Closing Price, Closing Trade. **3.** the completion of a financial transaction (e.g., the underwriting of securities or the sale of an asset, such as real estate).

Closing Bell: the end of a trading session on a securities exchange, so termed because of the ringing of a bell to announce the end of each day's trading on the New York Stock Exchange. Also known as the Bell. *See also* Opening Bell.

Closing Costs: the costs associated with finalizing a real estate sale, including appraisal fees, lawyer's fees, title searches and fees relating to financing. *See also* Fees and Disbursements, Title Search.

Closing Date: the date the underwriter of a new issue turns over proceeds to the issuing company.

Closing Out: 1. the process of completing a short sale by voluntarily buying back the same number of shares. *See also* Short Sale. **2.** this occurs when an option seller buys back an option identical to the one previously sold (or an option buyer sells an option identical to the one previously purchased). The option purchased (or sold) cancels out the option sold (or purchased) and the position is effectively liquidated. Also known as Closing Purchase, Closing Sale. *See also* Option.

Closing Period: on some commodity and futures exchanges, a time set aside at the end of the day's trading to complete At Close Orders. *See also* At Close Order, Market on Close Order.

Closing Price: the price of the last trade of a security at the end of a trading session.

Closing Purchase: *see* Closing Out.

Closing Quote: the final posted bid and offer of a security when a trading session ends. *See also* Opening Quote.

Closing Sale: *see* Closing Out.

Closing the Books: *see* Close.

Closing Tick: the net of the plus ticks and minus ticks on the last trade of all stocks traded on an exchange. If the total is positive, the market is considered to have closed on a positive note and vice versa. *See also* Minus Tick, Plus Tick, Tick, Zero-Minus Tick, Zero-Plus Tick.

Closing Trade: 1. on any given day, the last transaction in a security. *See also* Opening Trade. **2.** the last trade in a series of trades. *See also* Closing Transaction.

Closing Transaction: the trade that closes out a position (e.g., buying back shares that were sold short). *See also* Closing Out, Closing Trade, Opening Transaction.

Closure: a parliamentary procedure used to end debate and move to an immediate vote.

Cloud on Title: a legally registered charge against the title of a property. *See also* Bad Title, Clear Title, Defective Title, On Title, Title, Title Deed, Title Defect, Title Search.

CLU: *see* Chartered Life Underwriter.

CMBS: *see* Commercial Mortgage Backed Security.

CME: *see* Chicago Mercantile Exchange.

CMHC: *see* Canada Mortgage and Housing Corporation.

CMHC Chattel Loan Insurance Program: *see* Canada Mortgage and Housing Corporation Chattel Loan Insurance Program.

CMHC Insurance: *see* Canada Mortgage and Housing Corporation Insurance.

CNIL: *see* Cumulative Net Investment Losses.

COATS: *see* Canadian Over-the-Counter Automated Trading System.

Coattail Agreement: an agreement that specifies how one group of shareholders will be treated if an offer is made to another group of shareholders.

Coattail Investing: copying the investments of an individual or institution when these portfolios are made public. Many individuals invest on the coattails of Warren Buffett because of his excellent long-term track record. *See also* Buffett, E. Warren.

Co-Branding: a special offering made by a merchant in association with a credit card.

Cockroach Theory: in the stock market, a theory that states that bad news, like cockroaches, comes in bunches.

Cocooning: the theory that people tend to spend their leisure time in the security and comfort of their own homes.

COD: *see* Cash on Delivery.

CODA: *see* Cash or Deferred Arrangement.

Code of Conduct: a formalized set of rules that defines acceptable behaviour.

Codicil: a document amending a will but not having all of the latter's components. A codicil should be registered with the Department of Vital Statistics. *See also* Will.

COD Transaction: a trade in which the buyer provides payment on receipt of, or on an undertaking to deliver, a security.

Coefficient of Determination: the fraction of change in the dependent variable that is explained by the independent variable. The range is from zero to one, where one means that the change in the independent variable explains all of the change in the dependent variable. *See also* Correlation Coefficient, Regression Analysis.

Coextensive: having the same limits or boundaries (e.g., the U.S. capital of Washington and the District of Columbia are coextensive).

Cogeneration: a system producing electricity or heat from waste energy.

Cohabitation: living together as spouses, often with the implication of being unmarried.

Cohabitation Agreement: a domestic contract between a couple who intend to live together but not marry. Such agreements may cover ownership and division of property and any other matter except the custody and access to children.

Co-Heir: a person who inherits property jointly with one or more other persons.

Co-Insurance: 1. an insurance plan in which the insurer provides indemnity for only a certain part of the insured's loss. **2.** a situation in which the total insurance risk is shared between more than one underwriter.

Coincident Economic Indicator: an economic series that changes at the same time and in the same direction as does the overall economy.

Coincident Indicator: an economic series that changes at the same time and in the same direction as does the series being forecast.

Co-Insurance: an insurance plan in which the insurer provides indemnity for only a certain part of the insured's loss.

COLA: *see* Cost of Living Adjustment.

Cold Call: 1. a call made to a prospective client without the benefit of a personal introduction. *See also* Prospect, Suspect. **2.** an unsolicited call. This type of prospecting is often restricted or, in some cases, prohibited. *See also* Dialling for Dollars.

Cold Comfort Letter: *see* Comfort Letter.

Collapse: 1. a sudden drop in a market or security price. **2.** a term used to describe the withdrawal of all money from a Registered Retirement Savings Plan, especially during the year in which the plan holder attains the age of 69. Collapsing an RRSP does not apply when the individual selects a maturity option (e.g., a Registered Retirement Income Fund).

Collar: 1. the maximum rate of interest payable on a variable interest rate security. A collar is made up of a cap and a floor. *See also* Cap, Floor. **2.** in general, any restriction on market activities. *See also* Cap, Floor.

Collateral: an asset pledged in order to secure a loan. *See also* Security Value.

Collateral Bond: a bond used to secure a loan.

Collateral Mortgage: a loan made up of a promissory note and the security of a mortgage on a property. *See also* Mortgage.

Collateral Term Life Insurance: life insurance used to repay a bank loan or other obligation if the borrower dies. *See also* Creditor's Group Insurance.

Collateral Trust Bond: a bond secured by stocks, bonds or other securities held in trust. *See also* Bond.

Collateral Value: *see* Security Value.

Collectible: an item whose value is derived from its rarity, beauty or historical significance (e.g., baseball cards, stamps).

Collection Department: the department in a business specializing in the collection of past due accounts.

Collection Period: the average number of days required to collect accounts receivables. The faster accounts receivable are collected, the faster a dollar of sales becomes a dollar of cash.

Collection Risk: the risk that a borrower will not be able to repay a loan. Also known as Risk of Collection.

Collective: 1. a business or activity owned and operated by the workers. **2.** sometimes used to describe farms or factories under a Communist regime.

Collective Bargaining: a process wherein union representatives negotiate on behalf of a large number of union members.

Collectivism: an economic system where the means of production is owned by "the people"; that is, the government. It is the opposite of free enterprise, which is based on individual ownership and profit.

Collect on Delivery: *see* Cash on Delivery.

Collusion: the act of making an agreement with one or more other people with the intention of perpetrating a fraud.

Colombian Stock Exchange: *see* Bogota Aires Stock Exchange.

Colombo All Share Index: a stock price index for the Colombo Stock Exchange.

Colombo Stock Exchange: a major stock exchange of Sri Lanka, located in its capital, Colombo. Web site: www.lanka.net

Colon: the prime currency of Costa Rica and El Salvador.

Column: in a computer matrix, the vertical lines. *See also* Row, Spreadsheet.

.com: an appendage to an e-mail or Internet address that identifies a commercial location. *See also* .edu, .gov, Internet, .mil, .net, .org.

Combination Account: a deposit account with some features of a savings account (e.g., payment of interest on a minimum balance) as well as of a chequing account (e.g., the ability to write cheques on the account). *See also* Chequing Account, Savings Account.

Combination Annuity: *see* Hybrid Annuity.

Combination in Restraint of Trade: a merger or other joining of two competing companies that significantly changes the competitive balance in their favour. *See also* Restraint of Trade.

Combines Investigation Act: a Canadian act intended to prevent monopolies and other illegal trade practices.

Come to Market: to offer securities for sale in order to raise capital.

Come to Terms: to reach or make an agreement.

COMEX: *see* Commodity Exchange of New York.

Comfort Letter: 1. a letter provided by a broker's former employer that is required before the broker's licence can be transferred to a new employer. A comfort letter may be delayed if there are outstanding credit or legal problems. *See also* Broker. **2.** in underwriting, an auditor's letter that confirms the financial statements in a prospectus have been prepared properly and that no material changes have taken place in the interim period. Also known as Cold Comfort Letter. *See also* Prospectus, Underwriting. **3.** a letter between parties to a contract that certain actions will or will not be taken.

Comité Consultatif International Télégraphique et Téléphonique (CCITT): the international committee representing the United Nation's International Telecommunications Union. It establishes telecommunication standards and protocols.

Comité des Représentants Permanents dela CEE: *see* Committee of Permanent Representatives.

Commercial: a term used to describe a product or activity that will generate enough income to sustain a business.

Commercial Bank: a financial institution that provides commercial banking services. *See* Commercial Banking.

Commercial Banking: providing the services of gathering deposits, making loans and providing other services to businesses. *See also* Bank, Consumer Banking.

Commercial Financing: *see* Asset Financing.

Commercial Hedge: using futures contracts to establish future selling prices or operating costs. Commercial Hedging is done by those who actually produce or use the commodities hedged. *See also* Direct Hedge, Hedge.

Commercial Letter of Credit: *see* Letter of Credit.

Commercial Loan: a short-term loan to finance operations rather than long-term, fixed assets.

Commercial Mortgage: a loan secured by real estate where the borrowed funds are used to finance a business. *See also* Mortgage, Residential Mortgage.

Commercial Mortgage Backed Security (CMBS): a financial asset secured by commercial mortgages. *See also* Asset Backed Security, Mortgage, Mortgage Backed Security.

Commercial Orebody: a property with sufficient reserves to justify the cost of going into production.

Commercial Paper: generally, an unsecured corporate note that matures in less than one year.

Commercial Property: real estate that is used for business purposes. Commercial property usually includes hotels, industrial parks, office buildings, shopping centres and warehouses. *See also* Residential Property.

Commercial Reorganization: an effort by an insolvent company to reorganize finances in order to avoid bankruptcy and/or receivership.

Commercial Wells: a well producing enough oil and/or gas to justify the cost of production.

Commingle: 1. in general, to mix cash or securities belonging to different owners. **2.** in the securities industry, the mixing of client-owned securities with firm-owned securities. This is allowed with client approval.

Commingled Fund: an investment fund consisting of assets of several individual accounts that have been "comingled" in order to reduce the cost of managing them separately.

Commission: 1. a charge for executing purchases and/or sales of securities and other financial products. **2.** a payment to an agent by the seller of real estate for finding a buyer and concluding a sale. **3.** *see* Acquisition Fee.

Commissioner for Taking Oaths: an official appointed by law to take affidavits.

Commission Only: a financial planner or investment advisor compensated only by the commissions charged on transactions in recommended securities. *See also* Fee and Commission, Fee Only, Financial Planner, Investment Advisor.

Commitment Fee: a fee payable to a lender that holds credit available to a borrower.

Committee of Permanent Representatives: a committee that ensures only the most sensitive issues of policy for the European Union are presented for discussion at the ministerial level of the European Council. Also known as Comité des Représentants Permanents dela CEE, Coreper. *See also* European Union.

Committee on Uniform Security Identification Procedures (CUSIP): a nine-character alpha-numeric security identification code. The fist six characters identify the issuer, the next two identify the issue and the final character is a check digit. CUSIP was established by the American Bankers Association and is maintained by the CUSIP Service Bureau, which is owned and operated by Standard & Poor's Corporation. *See also* CINS.

Commodities: agricultural products, minerals or other materials used in manufacturing that are often traded on a commodities exchange.

Commodity Exchange: 1. an organization whose function is to facilitate buying and selling of commodities as well as financial securities representing commodities. *See also* Bond Market, Commodities, Financial Market, Futures Exchange, Money Market, Stock Market. **2.** *see* Commodity Exchange of New York.

Commodity Exchange of New York (COMEX): a division of the New York Mercantile Exchange, the COMEX operates in New York City and offers facilities for the trading of futures and futures options in metals. Also known as the Commodity Exchange. Web site: www.nymex.com/ *See also* New York Mercantile Exchange, Option.

Commodity Future: a contract to buy or sell a fixed amount of a commodity at a fixed price at an agreed-upon future date.

Commodity Futures Trading Commission (CFTC): a U.S. federal agency that regulates and supervises the trading of commodity futures and commodity options.

Commodity Hedging: 1. the act of selling commodity futures in order to fix future revenue from the sale of a product. **2.** the act of buying commodity futures in order to fix future costs stemming from the purchase of a product (e.g., a gold mine sells half of its annual production for future delivery. The seller is guaranteed the current price of gold and the buyer fixes costs at that price).

Commodity Trading: the buying and selling of commodities.

Common Area Costs: in certain types of real estate, such as condominiums or shopping malls, the cost of areas shared with other owners or tenants. Also known as Common Costs.

Common Costs: *see* Common Area Costs.

Common Disaster Clause: a clause in a will that addresses the possibility of a beneficiary dying at about the same time as the devisor; that is, the person whose estate is covered by the will. If a husband and wife are killed in a traffic accident, for example, there can be significant differences if it is determined one person died first. The common disaster clause addresses these issues and avoids the possibility of taxes and expenses for two estates in a short period. Also known as Simultaneous Death Clause.

Common Law: a legal system based on precedents set by custom and prior court decisions rather than by statute. In Canada, all provinces except Quebec operate under common law. *See also* Civil Law.

Common Law Marriage: a relationship established by people with a history of conjugal living. In Canada, a common law marriage is recognized if two people have cohabited for the preceding year or are the parents of the same child.

Common Law Spouses: 1. for income tax reporting purposes, two people of the opposite sex in a conjugal relationship who have cohabited for the preceding year or are the parents of the same child. The concept of "two people of the opposite sex" was ruled unconstitutional in 1999 and changes in this and many other areas will result. **2.** two people who have attained the status of spouses for some legal purpose.

Common Market: an economic alliance between Austria, Belgium, Denmark, Finland, France, Germany, Greece, Italy, Ireland, Luxembourg, Netherlands, Portugal, Spain, Sweden and the United Kingdom. Formally, the European Economic Community.

Common Share: a unit of ownership in a company. A common shareholder is a residual owner because all other claims on the company must be satisfied before any distributions are made on the common shares. Also known as Common Stock, Ordinary Share, Ordinary Stock, Share. *See also* Preferred Share.

Common Shareholder: the owner of common shares.

Common Stock: *see* Common Share.

Common Stock Equivalent: a security that is similar to common stock, including convertible bonds, convertible preferred stock, options, and warrants.

Common Stock Fund: *see* Equity Mutual Fund.

Commonwealth of Independent States: a federation of self-governing states in Europe and Asia that were formerly republics of the Soviet Union.

Commonwealth of Nations: *see* British Commonwealth.

Communications Port (COM Port): a serial port on a personal computer. *See also* Computer.

Communism: a system in which a government controls the means of production and distribution of goods and services and in which economic decisions are centralized. *See also* Capitalism, Centrally Planned Economy, Free Market Economy, Market Economy, Socialism.

Communist: a person who believes in or supports communism.

Community Antenna Television (CATV): a now infrequently used term referring to cablevision.

Community Property: property owned by both spouses. The legal concept of community property holds that, excepting gifts and inheritance, all property acquired by husband and wife during a marriage is equally owned by each spouse.

Commutable Annuity: an annuity in which the beneficiary has the option of cancelling the future payments for a specified lump sum payment.

Commutation: in law, a substitution, change or reduction of penalty.

Commutation Payment: a single or lump sum payment in the place of all future payments (e.g., from an annuity). *See also* Annuity.

Commuted Value: the present value of a series of payments due under an insurance contract. If the beneficiary has the option to receive a lump sum payment, the amount of that payment is the commuted value.

Compact Disc (CD): a plastic disc that contains optically readable information such as audio, video or data, primarily for entertainment. Also known as Optical Disc.

Compact Disc-Read Only Memory (CD-ROM): a compact disc that data can be read from but not recorded on.

Companies' Creditors Arrangement Act: in Canada, this is an act that protects a company while it develops a plan to deal with severe creditor problems.

Company: an entity created by law and owned by its shareholders. A company may own assets, incur debt, be party to a contract and do virtually anything a person can do. The main features of a company are limited liability for its shareholders, easy transfer of ownership through the buying and selling of its shares and the ongoing existence of the organization. Also known as Corporation, Limited Company. *See also* Going Concern, Legal Entity, Limited Liability, Stock Company.

Company Doctor: an executive who specializes in turning around a company that is in financial trouble. *See also* Turnaround Candidate.

Company Maker: an event or transaction that can ensure the long-term success of a business (e.g., a major exploration discovery for an oil and gas company).

Company Owned Insurance: *see* Corporate Owned Insurance.

Company Specific Risk: an influence on the price of a security that stems entirely from the company (e.g., stock prices rising after an exceptionally favourable earnings report). Also known as Specific Risk. *See also* Event Risk, Industry Specific Risk, Market Specific Risk, Non-Systematic Risk, Risk, Systematic Risk.

Comparables: in valuing a specific stock, parallels are drawn between shares of similar companies. These companies are referred to as comparables.

Compatible: in computers, a device that can be used with another device or system (e.g., IBM compatible means a device will work with an IBM computer). *See also* Computer.

COMPCORP: *see* Canadian Life and Health Insurance Compensation Corporation.

Compensating Balance: most common in the U.S., an amount which must be kept on deposit with a bank while money is owed to the bank. Also known as Compensatory Balance.

Compensation: 1. payment for services rendered (e.g., salary, wages). Also known as Remuneration. *See also* Bonus, Bonus Plan, Perquisite, Phantom Stock Plan, Salary, Wage. **2.** a payment to offset loss or damage (e.g., injury while at work). *See also* Workers' Compensation Board.

Compensatory Balance: *see* Compensating Balance.

Competent: in law, the capacity to understand and act reasonably. *See also* Incompetent, Non Compos Mentis.

Competitive Bid: 1. a system that awards a contract to the most attractive bid from a number of competing bidders. **2.** a system sometimes used by a company to choose an investment firm to lead an underwriting. *See also* Underwriter.

Competitive Local Exchange Carrier (CLEC): a provider of local telephone services in competition with the traditional monopolistic service.

Competitor: anyone offering similar goods and services.

Complainant: in law, the party that initiates the complaint in an action or proceeding.

Complete Annuity: an annuity that pays a pro rata amount of the final payment to the annuitant's estate. *See also* Annuity, Apportionable Annuity, Curtate Annuity, Non-Apportionable Annuity.

Completion of Contract Accounting: a method of recognizing revenues and costs from a long-term project. Profit is recorded only when the project is complete.

Compliance: in a regulated company, the act of ensuring that all rules are followed and that all requirements are met. *See also* Compliance Department, Compliance Officer.

Compliance Department: 1. in a regulated company (e.g., a brokerage firm), the department that is responsible for compliance. *See also* Compliance, Compliance Officer. **2.** *see* Surveillance Department.

Compliance Officer: the employee of a regulated company, this person is responsible for ensuring that regulations are followed. *See also* Compliance, Compliance Department.

COM Port: *see* Communications Port.

Composite: a term that indicates a stock market average is made up of price changes from several other averages (e.g., the Vancouver Stock Exchange Composite Index combines the Vancouver Stock Exchange Resource, Commercial/Industrial and Venture indexes).

Composite Tape: a security price service that includes all transactions on each of the exchanges and in the over-the-counter market.

Compos Mentis: in law, to be mentally competent.

Compound Annual Growth Rate (CAGR): the percentage change applied to a base year number and each subsequent number to produce the ending number. For example, if a company's sales double from $10 million to $20 million in five years, the CAGR is 14.87 percent, as in:

Base Year	$10,000,000
Year One	$11,487,000
Year Two	$13,195,117
Year Three	$15,157,231
Year Four	$17,411,111
Year Five	$20,000,143

Compound growth is widely used in assessing investment attractiveness (the higher the growth rate, the better the investment). It is important to note that CAGR measures only the rate of growth between the Base Year and the ending number (e.g., $10 million and $20 million). The actual results for Years One through Four may have varied considerably.

Compound Interest: interest calculated on the original principal and accumulated interest. Also known as Interest on Interest. *See also* Simple Interest.

Compound Interest Bond: a bond that gives the holder the option to have annual interest reinvested at an interest rate equal to the yield. *See also* Bond.

Compound Interest Depreciation: a method of accounting for depreciation in which the amount of depreciation for each period is reduced by the interest that would be earned on the amount of depreciation.

Compound Number: a quantity expressed in different units (e.g., five pounds, six ounces).

Compression: in computers, coding data so it uses less memory to be transmitted or stored. *See also* Computer, Conventional Memory, Data, Data Bank, Database, Datawarehouse, Memory, Memory Unit, Primary Memory, Random Access Memory (RAM), Read-Only Memory (ROM), Save, Secondary Memory.

Compressor: a unit attached to a pipeline in order to raise the volume of gas transmitted.

Comptroller: *see* Controller.

Computer: an electronic device having four basic functions: it performs arithmetic calculations (i.e., it has a logic unit); it retains information (i.e., it has memory); it receives data and sends out results (i.e., it has input-output units); and maintain a set of instructions to govern its actions (i.e., it has control). *See also* Abacus, Active Window, Address, Addressable, ALGOL, Algorithm, Architecture, Artificial Intelligence, ASCIbetical Order, Assembler, Asynchronous, Attribute, AUTOEXEC.BAT, Autosync, Background, Backup, Bandwidth, Biochip, BIOS, Bitmap, Board, Boot Up, Break, Buffer, Cache, Carrier, Central Processing Unit (CPU), Client/Server, Compression, Communications Port, Compatible, Computer Assisted Design (CAT), Computer Literate, Control Unit, Conventional Memory, Copy Protection, Cursor, Cyberia, Cyberspace, Data Carrier, Data Processing, Delimiter, Demodulation, Desktop Publishing, Dialog Box, Digital Transmission, Directory, Document, Download, Driver, Dump, Emulate, Encode, Ethernet, Export, Failsafe, File, File Server, File Transfer, Firmware, First Generation, Format, FORTRAN, Freeware, Function Key, Garbage In-Garbage Out (GIGO), Global, Hang, Hardware, Hardwired, Hash Function, Icon, Import, Incompatible, Initialize, Input-Output Unit (I/O Unit), Installation, Installed Base, Interface, Iteration, Label, Lag, Legacy System, Local Area Network (LAN), Lag, Logic Unit, Loopback, Machine Language, Macro, Mailbox, Memory Unit, Microprocessor, Migration, Mission Critical, Modem, Monitor, Morphing, Mouse, MS-DOS, Multitasking, Negotiation, Network, Networking, Noise, Null Character, Object Linking and Embedding, Off-Load, Open System, Operating Platform, Operating System, Override, Overwrite, Packet, Parallel, Parallel Port, Parallel Processing, Patch, PC-DOS, Personal Computer, Personal Computer Memory Card International Association (PCMCIA), Pixel, Plug and Play, Plug-In, Point-to-Point Protocol, Port, Primary Memory, Printer Driver, Processor, Program, Programmer, Prompt, Protocol, Pull-Down Menu, Pulse Dialling, Queue, Random Access Memory, Read-Only Memory, Routine, RS-232C, Save, Scan, Seamless, Search, Secondary Memory, Serial, Serial Port, Server, Shareware, Sleep Mode, Software, Spoofing, Subdirectory, Subprogram, Subroutine, Suite, Synchronous, System, Task Switching, Terminal, Text File, Timeshare, Toggle, UNIX, Upgrading, Upload, User Friendly, Video Display Terminal, Virtual Reality, What-If, What You See Is What You Get, Word, Word Processing, Word Processor, Workstation, Write.

Computer Assisted Design (CAD): the use of computer software to design new products or processes. *See also* Computer.

Computer Assisted Trading System (CATS): an automated system for trading securities on an exchange.

Computer Disk (CD): a disc on which computer texts, data or programs are written and stored. *See also* Computer, Disk, Floppy Disk, Hard Disk, Magnetic Disk.

Computer Geek: an affectionate term for a person whose life is largely devoted to computers and computer-related matters. *See also* Chiphead, Computer, Cracker, Hacker.

Computerized Trading: portfolio management techniques that use buy-and-sell decisions based on computerized mathematical relationships.

Computer Literate: a person who is comfortable with and able to handle basic consumer-oriented computer applications. He/she is not necessarily a computer expert. *See also* Computer.

Computer Network: *see* Network.

Computer Screen: 1. *see* Screen. **2.** a cathode-ray tube used as a computer output device. *See also* Cathode-Ray Tube, Computer, Disk Drive, Input/Output Device (IO Device), Interactive Terminal, Joystick, Keyboard, Keypad, Laser Printer, Line Printer, Monitor, Optical Character Recognition, Peripheral, Printer, Printout, Readout, Remote Access, Terminal.

Concentrate: ore with some waste material removed so that the metal content is increased.

Concentration: a relatively large holding in a margin account. The brokerage firm providing the margin for such an account may require additional security. *See also* Margin Account.

Concept Stock: a common stock whose value reflects its potential rather than its current tangible assets and earnings.

Concession: 1. the amount members of the selling group pay for securities in a new corporate underwriting. **2.** a discount on either price or commission, usually to facilitate a trade. Also known as Selling Concession. **3.** the right to explore a defined area for resources.

Condensate: a high-value, light petroleum liquid often found with natural gas.

Condensed Prospectus: *see* Simplified Prospectus.

Conditional Offer: an offer to buy an asset if certain conditions are met (e.g., an offer to buy a house on the condition that a mortgage can be arranged). Also known as Subject Offer. *See also* Firm Offer.

Conditional Sales Agreement: an agreement that details the terms under which the sale will be completed. Conditional sales agreements are commonly used when purchasing real estate. *See also* Conditional Offer.

Conditional Sales Contract: a contract in which the property remains with the seller until all the installments on the purchase price have been fully paid.

Conditional Will: a will that is in effect only for a brief time (e.g., for the duration of short-term military service). *See also* Will.

Condominium: a real estate interest in which part of the asset, usually part of the physical building, is owned individually, while common areas, land and improvements are owned by tenants in common.

Condonation: 1. the forgiveness of a matrimonial offense (e.g., infidelity) with full knowledge of the circumstances and the acceptance of the offending spouse back into the family. A forgiven offence cannot be revived at a later date as a basis for divorce. *See also* No-Fault. **2.** a general term regarding the pardoning of any offense.

Conduit Theory: the theory that because certain forms of investment companies (e.g., mutual funds) pass through all interest, dividends and capital gains to shareholders or unitholders, income taxes should not be levied at the company level. This theory ensures investors are taxed only once on the same income. In regular companies, investors are taxed twice: once when the company reports net income

and again when investors receive the income as dividends. *See also* Double Taxation, Mutual Fund.

Conference Call: a telephone call in which three or more people are connected at one time.

Confidence Index: *see* Barron's Confidence Index.

Confidence Man (Con Man): a person who perpetrates a swindle by inducing a victim to hand over valuables based on confidence in his/her supposed honesty. *See also* Boiler Room, Bre-X Minerals Ltd., Bucketing, Bucket Shop, Dialling for Dollars, Front Running, Salting, Scam, Tailgating.

Confidentiality: legal protection ensuring that people in certain officially recognized relationships do not have to give evidence or reveal information that has been exchanged under the auspices of those relationships (e.g., lawyer/client, accountant/client).

Confidentiality Agreement: a legal document under which "Party A" (often a prospective investor) agrees to keep all information learned about "Party B" strictly confidential and to return all relevant materials upon request. Also known as Non-Disclosure Agreement.

Confirmation: 1. a written verification of a transaction from a brokerage firm to a client. **2.** when one stock market indicator corroborates a trend or turning point indicated by another.

Confirming: the financing of accounts payable, often on an international basis.

Conflict of Interest: a situation wherein there is the potential for a party to a decision to allow personal benefit to influence that decision. *See also* Non-Arm's-Length Transaction, Self-Dealing.

Conformed Copy: in law, a document that contains all the essential legal features required (e.g., original signature, corporate seal).

Conforming Use: in law, the use of land or buildings in compliance with current zoning. *See also* Zoning.

Congestion Area: an area in which supply and demand for a stock is equal. Technicians will wait until a stock breaks out of a congestion area before buying. *See also* Technical Analysis.

Conglomerate: a company made up of many separate companies from diverse industries. *See also* Pure Play.

Conjugal Rights: the rights of married couples, including cohabitation, the profits of their joint efforts and the intimacies of domestic relations.

Con Man: *see* Confidence Man.

Connivance: marital misconduct of one spouse caused by, or knowingly permitted by, the other. A divorce application based on connivance may be rejected.

Consensus: the view held by most investors. *See also* Conventional Wisdom.

Consensus Ad Idem: agreement to the same thing; of the same mind; similar in all essential matters.

Consensus Estimate: 1. the earnings estimate held by most analysts. *See also* Conventional Wisdom. **2.** the generally accepted estimate. *See also* Conventional Wisdom.

Conservative: generally, a condition of being averse to taking risks.

Conservative Investor: a person who is averse to taking risks. *See also* Gambler, Investor, Nervous Nellie, Speculator.

Conservative Portfolio: a holding of securities focused on safety.

Conservator: a temporary court-appointed guardian of property (often the assets of individuals deemed incompetent). *See also* Incompetent.

Consideration: something of value, such as an asset or an act, that may be offered for compensation.

Consignment: goods sent or delivered to an agent on the understanding that payment is due only upon sale.

Consolidate: to combine two or more assets or operations into one.

Consolidated Financial Statement: a financial statement such as a balance sheet or income statement for a company and its subsidiaries that reports the results as one rather than separately for each company.

Consolidated Tape: a network that reports all securities transactions on U.S. exchanges. Network A reports the New York Stock Exchange and Network B reports the American Stock Exchange. Regional data are also reported.

Consolidation Loan: *see* Debt Consolidation.

Consortium: a group of companies that combines resources in order to attain a common goal.

Constant Dollar Plan: a formula for investing in which a constant amount of money is kept in stocks, and the remainder is kept in bonds or short-term securities. The term is sometimes incorrectly used to describe Dollar Cost Averaging.

Constant Dollars: currency adjusted over time to reflect declining purchasing power due to inflation. The Financial Accounting Standards Board in the U.S. has adopted the symbol "C$" to denote constant dollars. *See also* Financial Accounting Standards Board.

Constant Ratio Plan: a formula plan for investing in which the market value of all stocks in a portfolio is kept at a fixed percentage (e.g., 50 percent) of the total. The portfolio is rebalanced from time to time. *See also* Portfolio Rebalancing.

Constituency: 1. supporters. **2.** in politics, the voters represented by an elected official.

Constitution: a written document describing the laws and principles authorizing and limiting government powers and defining the rights of citizens. *See also* British North America Act, Canadian Charter of Rights and Freedoms.

Constrained Share Companies: companies that have restrictions on the number of shares that can be owned by non-Canadian citizens and/or residents (e.g., banks, insurance companies, broadcasting companies).

Construction Lien: a right to protect the payment to suppliers of goods and services for improving a piece of real property.

Construction Loan: a short-term mortgage to finance the construction of a real estate project before permanent long-term financing is obtained. *See also* Mortgage.

Constructive Dismissal: this term describes an attempt to remove a person from an employment arrangement by changing his/her job description or forcing him/her to resign (e.g., by giving him/her a much smaller office). In law, constructive dismissal amounts to wrongful dismissal. *See also* Dismissal for Cause, Severance, Severance Pay, Wrongful Dismissal.

Constructive Total Loss: an insurance term implying the insured asset was abandoned because total loss was unavoidable or recovery would have cost more than the value of the asset. Often arises in maritime cases when a ship sinks.

Consul: a government-appointed official who represents his/her government's interests while residing in another country.

Consulate: the official residence of a consul.

Consumer: in economics, the sector of the economy that purchases goods and services for personal use.

Consumer Advocate: a person who fights for the rights of the consumer.

Consumer Bank: a financial institution that provides consumer banking services. *See also* Consumer Banking.

Consumer Banking: providing the services of gathering deposits, making loans and providing other services to individuals. *See also* Bank, Commercial Banking.

Consumer Confidence: the mood of the population with regard to spending on consumer goods and services.

Consumer Confidence Index: a leading indicator of consumer spending. It measures consumer confidence through the use of surveys.

Consumer Credit: debt taken out by a consumer for any purchase except a home mortgage.

Consumer Durable: an item, such as a washing machine or automobile, that is purchased by a consumer and will last three years or longer.

Consumer Goods: products and services purchased for personal or household use.

Consumer Price Index (CPI): an index that measures the change in the cost of living for consumers over a period. The rate at which the CPI increases is a measure of consumer inflation. Canada's CPI is produced by Statistics Canada. Also known as Price Index. *See also* Gross National Product Deflator, Price Index.

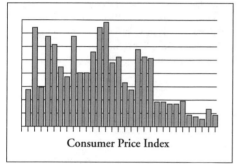

Consumer Price Index

Consumer Proposal: a proposal under the Canadian Bankruptcy Act in which a debtor makes an offer, totalling up to $75,000, to creditors. If half the creditors accept this offer, then all must accept it. *See also* Bankruptcy.

Consumer Sovereignty: the fundamental principle in a free market economy that a consumer is free to spend money. In so doing, consumers collectively determine which products and services are in demand.

Consumer Spending: the purchase of goods and services by the personal sector of the economy, in contrast to by the corporate or government sectors.

Consumer Tax Index: an index, calculated by the Fraser Institute, that measures the percent change from a base year in the average Canadian family's tax bill.

Consumption: one of the fundamental measures of an economy, it uses up goods and services (especially at the consumer level).

Consumption Tax: *see* Value-Added Tax.

Contact: a business association with an influential person.

Contango: 1. in commodities and foreign exchange, when longer-term deliveries trade at a higher price than near-term deliveries. The opposite of backwardation. *See also* Backwardation. **2.** a fee paid by a buyer of a security to delay delivery until a future date.

Contempt of Court: wilful disobedience of a court order. Contempt of court is punishable by fine, imprisonment or both.

Contested Divorce: this occurs when either spouse disputes the grounds for divorce, child care or support payments. *See also* Joint Petition, Uncontested Divorce.

Contiguous: adjacent and touching, as in "contiguous mining properties."

Contingency: something that may happen, or will happen, if certain conditions are met.

Contingency Fee: a payment arrangement with a lawyer, popular in large, personal liability cases, to determine the legal fee as a percentage of the award or settlement if successful. *See also* Performance Fee, Success Fee.

Contingent Beneficiary: a person named in a life insurance contract to receive the death benefit if the beneficiary dies before the benefit is payable. *See also* Life Insurance.

Contingent Deferred Sales Charge: 1. *see* Deferred Declining Redemption Fee – At Cost. **2.** *see* Deferred Declining Redemption Fee – At Market Value.

Contingent Liabilities: potential liabilities (e.g., loss of an outstanding lawsuit).

Contingent Order: an order to sell one security and buy another in which each order is dependent on the other; that is, one cannot happen without the other. Also known as Net Order, Swap Order.

Continuance: the postponement of a court action to a specified future date.

Continuous Disclosure: the requirement of a public company to inform the public as soon as a material change occurs and, in any case, within 10 days.

Continuous Inventory: an inventory accounting method in which book inventory is kept in continuous agreement with physical inventory. Also known as Perpetual Inventory.

Continuous Settlement: settling transactions between brokerage firms using a central clearing house where the settlement is made by adding the shares to the buying broker's account and deducting the shares from the selling broker's account.

Continuous Trading: this occurs when brokers execute orders as soon as they are received. It is through continuous trading that securities are bought and sold on most stock exchanges.

Contraband: prohibited goods.

Contra Broker: the broker on the opposite side of a transaction. To a buying broker the contra broker represents the seller, and vice versa.

Contract: 1. a legally binding agreement stipulating the essential elements of a transaction. To be legal and binding, a contract must be between competent parties, involve a legal transaction, require each party to perform certain duties and represent a meeting of the minds. **2.** notice from a broker to a client regarding a purchase or sale of securities.

Contracting Out: the practice of assigning work to independent service providers. Contracting out is often less costly than using internal unionized employees.

Contraction: the stage in an economic cycle during which the economy shrinks. *See also* Cyclical, Economic Cycle, Expansion, Peak, Trough.

Contract Month: the month that a futures or options contract expires. *See also* Option.

Contract Size: in options and futures, the agreed-upon number of units each contract represents (e.g., a call option is for 100 shares, a gold contract is for 100 ounces). *See also* Futures Contract, Option, Options Market.

Contractual Plan: a plan that requires an investor to make mutual fund contributions of a fixed amount on a regular basis for an agreed-upon period. Such contracts are rarely used today. *See also* Accumulation Plan, Mutual Fund, Periodic Payment Plan, Systematic Savings Plan, Voluntary Accumulation Plan.

Contra Cyclical: a cycle that is opposite to the prevailing economic or market cycle.

Contrarian: a person whose mode of investment is to do the opposite of the majority. *See also* Contrary Market Indicator, Contrary Opinion, Investment Services Bearish, Investment Services Bullish, Theory of Contrary Opinion, Wall of Worry.

Contrary Opinion: a view that runs opposite to the prevailing view (i.e., a nonconventional outlook). Also known as Against the Crowd. *See also* Contrarian, Contrary Market Indicator, Investment Services Bearish, Investment Services Bullish, Theory of Contrary Opinion.

Contrary Market Indicator: a stock market indicator that points in a direction opposite to that of the majority. *See also* Contrarian, Contrary Opinion, Investment Services Bearish, Investment Services Bullish, Theory of Contrary Opinion, Wall of Worry.

Contributed Capital: *see* Paid-In Capital.

Contributed Surplus: *see* Paid-In Surplus.

Contribution: *see* Contribution to Overhead.

Contribution Holiday: a period in a pension plan or life insurance in which the participant is not required to make payments. *See also* Payment Holiday.

Contribution to a Registered Retirement Savings Plan: *see* Registered Retirement Savings Plan – Contribution.

Contribution to Overhead: an accounting term for the amount of variable costs paid after payment of all direct costs. Also known as Contribution.

Contributory Negligence: conduct on the part of a plaintiff that, in law, contributes to his/her own harm or injury.

Contributory Pension Plan: a pension plan in which members make a financial contribution. Also known as a Contributory Plan. *See also* Noncontributory Pension Plan.

Contributory Plan: 1. an employee benefit plan in which both the employee and employer contribute to the cost. *See also* Employee Benefit Plan, Noncontributory Plan. **2.** *see* Contributory Pension Plan.

Control and Compliance: *see* Compliance.

Control and Compliance Officer: *see* Compliance Officer.

Control Block: a share holding that gives the owner control over a company. *See also* Two Tier Pricing.

Controlled Commodities: in the U.S., primarily domestically produced agricultural products.

Controller: a senior person in the accounting department of a company. Also known as Comptroller.

Controlling Interest: a group that has control, or a control block, when its members' interests are pooled. Often members of the family of the founder. *See also* Control Stock.

Control Person: *see* Affiliated Person.

Control Premium: a value in excess of the market value that is accorded a block of shares representing control of a company.

Control Stock: shares owned by a person or persons having a controlling interest. *See also* Controlling Interest.

Control Unit: one of the four basic units of a computer, the control unit manages and guides all computer activities. *See also* Computer, Input/Output Unit, Logic Unit, Memory Unit.

Covenant: an agreement in a trust indenture or loan agreement that the borrower will or will not do certain things. *See also* Restrictive Covenant.

Convenantee: the lender in a mortgage deed. *See also* Mortgage.

Convenantor: the borrower in a mortgage deed. *See also* Mortgage.

Conventional Memory: in computers, the standard memory base used by DOS-based systems. *See also* Compression, Computer, Data, Data Bank, Database, Datawarehouse, Memory, Memory Unit, Primary Memory, Random Access Memory, Read-Only Memory, Save, Secondary Memory.

Conventional Mortgage: a residential mortgage loan of not more than 75 percent of the appraised value and with no unusual terms and conditions. *See also* Mortgage.

Conventional Wisdom: the prevailing or accepted view of the majority of investors. *See also* Consensus Estimate.

Convention Between the United States of America and Canada with Respect to Taxes on Income and Capital: a bilateral tax treaty ensuring that Canadians earning income in the U.S. and Americans earning income in Canada are not taxed twice. Under the convention, the higher rate of tax imposed by either country is usually charged. Also known as Canada-U.S. Tax Convention of 1980, Tax Treaty. *See also* Protocol Amending the Canada-U.S. Tax Treaty.

Convergence: 1. the trend of the businesses of the telephone companies and cable television companies in Canada to become more alike. **2.** describes the price of an option contract moving toward its intrinsic value as it nears expiry. *See also* Option. **3.** the movement of two variables toward each other. *See also* Divergence.

Convergence Criteria: the guidelines set forth in the Maastricht Treaty for countries to participate in the Economic and Monetary Union in Europe. The criteria includes budget deficits not to exceed 3 percent of Gross Domestic Product (GDP), debt to GDP not to exceed 60 percent, observance of normal European Monetary System fluctuation margins for two years and long-term interest rates within 2 percent of the three best-performing members.

Conversion: 1. the act of exchanging one type of security for another (e.g., a convertible bond into shares). *See also* Convertible. **2.** the illegal practice of a broker issuing a cheque to him/herself from a client account. **3.** the no-cost or low-cost transfer of one mutual fund into another within the same family of funds. *See also* Family of Funds, Mutual Fund. **4.** in insurance, the switch from term to a cash-value policy (often when leaving an employee benefit plan). *See also* Conversion Clause, Life Insurance. **5.** the exchange of one currency for another.

Conversion Clause: a provision in most group and term insurance contracts that allows the insured to convert them to any cash-value policy at standard rates without having to provide evidence of insurability.

Conversion Premium: a convertible security (e.g., a convertible bond or preferred) will often trade at a price above its conversion value. The amount by which the price exceeds the conversion value is the conversion premium. Also known as Premium Over Conversion Value. *See also* Conversion Value, Convertible.

Conversion Value: relating to a convertible security, the value calculated by multiplying the number of shares the holder is entitled to by the market price of the shares. This will often be less than the market price of the convertible because convertible securities generally trade at a premium over conversion value. *See also* Conversion Premium.

Convertible: a security, normally a bond, debenture or preferred share, that can be converted into another security (usually common shares). *See also* Forced Conversion, Residual Security.

Convertible Bond: a bond that is convertible into another security (usually common shares). *See also* Bond, Residual Security.

Convertible Currency: a currency that is not restricted from being exchanged for another currency.

Convertible Debenture: a debenture that is convertible into another security (usually common shares). *See also* Debenture, Residual Security.

Convertible Preferred Share: a preferred share that is convertible into another security (often common shares). *See also* Preferred Share, Residual Security.

Convertible Term Insurance: a term insurance contract that allows the insured to convert it to any cash-value policy at standard rates without having to provide evidence of insurability.

Convexity: a measure of the sensitivity of a bond price to interest rates. Higher convexity describes a bond that will change more in price for a given change in interest rates than a lower convexity bond.

Conveyance: the process of transferring ownership of real estate from one person to another. *See also* Transfer.

COO: *see* Chief Operating Officer.

Cook the Books: an act (often fraudulent) that entails falsifying corporate financial records.

Co-op: *see* Cooperative.

Cooperative: a non-profit organization owned by its members. A cooperative is operated for the benefit of its members, who use the goods and/or services. Also known as Co-op. *See also* Cooperative Housing, Credit Union, Marketing Board.

Cooperative Housing: a multiunit residential property owned by a cooperative. The title is not held by individuals but by a separate entity (e.g., a company). *See also* Cooperative.

Coparceners: persons who become equal and concurrent owners in the estate of a common ancestor. *See also* Will.

Copartner: a joint partner.

Copenhagen Stock Exchange: the major stock exchange of Denmark, located in its capital, Copenhagen. Also known as Kobenhavns Fondsbors. Web site: www.xcse.dk/

Copenhagen Stock Exchange Total Share Index: a stock price index of the Copenhagen Stock Exchange.

Copy Protection: a method of preventing the unauthorized reproduction of computer software, especially through the use of instructions incorporated within the software itself. *See also* Computer.

Copyright: protection of the works of authors and artists through statute or common law. Copyrights in Canada last for the life of the person plus 50 years. *See also* Logo, Symbol, Trademark.

Cordoba: the prime currency of Nicaragua.

Core Assets: the most important company assets.

Core Holding: a long-term or semipermanent part of a portfolio.

Coreper: *see* Committee of Permanent Representatives.

Co-respondent: a person charged with adultery with the defendant in a divorce action. *See also* Adultery, Respondent.

Corner: *see* Corner the Market.

Corner the Market: in securities markets, an illegal activity that involves acquiring sufficient control of a market for a stock so as to be able to manipulate the price. Also known as Corner. *See also* Natural Corner, Trap the Shorts.

Corp.: abbreviation for "corporation." Often used in conjunction with a company name, as in "ABC Corp."

Corporate Bond: a bond issued by a corporation. *See also* Bond.

Corporate Charter: *see* Articles of Incorporation.

Corporate Culture: the ethical and social values that pervade a company's workplace.

Corporate Finance: activities that deal with raising money through the underwriting of securities. Also mergers, acquisitions and other related activities. *See also* Deal Flow.

Corporate Gadfly: a person who persistently criticizes the management of companies, often at annual general meetings.

Corporate Governance: the activity of shareholders in influencing the actions and ethical conduct of corporate management.

Corporate Income Tax: the income taxes levied on corporate profits.

Corporate Owned Insurance: insurance owned by a company on the lives of its shareholders. If a shareholder dies, the insurance is used to repurchase the deceased's shares. Also known as Company Owned Insurance. *See also* Life Insurance.

Corporate Reorganization: a method of saving a company from bankruptcy and liquidation by enabling it to change its financial structure (perhaps its management) and to deal with other issues (e.g., unions).

Corporate Resolution: a document that defines the authority of company officers. A corporate resolution is often required by a bank before it will open an account for a company. Also known as Resolution.

Corporate Secretary: a corporate officer responsible for records, minutes of meetings, official company correspondence and administration. Also known as Secretary. *See also* Chairman of the Board, Chief Executive Officer, Chief Financial Officer, Chief Operating Officer.

Corporate Share Repurchase Agreement: in jurisdictions that allow corporations to buy their own shares, this is an agreement arrived at by corporate partners in order to require a company to buy back shares from a shareholder who becomes disabled, retires or dies.

Corporate Shell: a company with minimal assets and liabilities (other than a stock exchange listing).

Corporate Web Site: a commercial Web site used to advertise products and services and to keep the public up to date on recent developments. *See also* Address, .com, Internet.

Corporation: *see* Company.

Corporeal: in law, having material form (e.g., a house is corporeal but the annual rent to live in the house is incorporeal). *See also* Incorporeal.

Corpus: 1. in Latin, the body. **2.** the assets in a trust. *See also* Trust. **3.** the principal amount or capital value of an investment (i.e., as distinct from the income). **4.** the assets of an estate. *See also* Estate.

Corpus Delicti: in law, the major ingredients of an offence.

Correction: *see* Reaction.

Correlation: the amount of variance in one variable that can be explained by another variable.

Correlation Coefficient: a mathematical measure of the relationship between a dependent variable and an independent variable. A correlation coefficient of 1.0 means the relationship is direct (e.g., housing starts and lumber prices move up and down together). A correlation coefficient of -1.0 means the relationship is indirect (e.g., housing starts and interest rates move in opposite directions). A correlation coefficient of zero means there is no relationship. The correlation coefficient is the square root of the Coefficient of Determination. Also known as Regression Coefficient. *See also* Coefficient of Determination, Covariance, Dependent Variable, Independent Variable, Regression Analysis.

Correspondent: 1. a financial institution (e.g., a brokerage firm) that performs services for another organization in a jurisdiction in which the latter does not have direct access. **2.** *see* Correspondent Bank.

Correspondent Bank: a bank that performs services for another bank (e.g., accepting deposits, transferring funds) in a jurisdiction in which the latter does not have direct access. *See also* Correspondent.

Cost: usually the price paid for an item adjusted for directly related charges (e.g., commissions).

Cost and Freight: *see* CFR.

Costa Rican Stock Exchange: *see* Bolsa Nacional de Valores, SA

Cost/Benefit Analysis: decision-making based on assigning dollar values to costs and benefits. Also known as Benefit/Cost Analysis.

Cost Centre: a business division where costs are segregated and profit and loss is calculated.

Cost for Tax Purposes: usually the price paid for an item adjusted up or down by various elections in the Income Tax Act.

Cost, Insurance and Freight: *see* CIF.

Cost of Capital: the weighted average cost of all capital (e.g., bonds, preferred shares, common shares) employed by a business.

Cost of Carry: *see* Carrying Charge.

Cost of Living Adjustment (COLA): adjustments made to income in order to offset changes in the cost of living. *See also* Consumer Price Index, Inflation.

Cost of Living Index: *see* Consumer Price Index.

Cost Plus: a contractual agreement in which the charge for goods or services is the cost plus a fixed percentage.

Cost-Push Inflation: inflation caused by rising wages and materials costs passed through as higher prices for the final products. *See also* Demand-Pull Inflation.

Costs: the sum payable for legal services. A judge may have discretion to order the losing party to pay a portion of the successful party's legal costs.

Co-Tenancy: property ownership by two or more owners. *See also* Tenants in Common.

Cougar: a certificate evidencing ownership of a U.S. Treasury bond principal or amount of interest payable in the future.

Council: a group of people assembled to administer, advise or legislate.

Council of Economic Advisors: a group of economists selected by the U.S. president to advise on economic policies and the budget.

Council of Europe: *see* European Council.

Council of Ministers: *see* Council of the European Union.

Council of the European Union: the supreme legislative body of the European Union, made up of

representatives of the 15 member countries. Also known as Council of Ministers.

Councilor: 1. a council member. **2.** a member of a municipal government.

Countercharge: a charge made in opposition or response to another charge.

Counter Cheque: a cheque that is not coded for a particular account so it can be adapted for use for any account.

Counterclaim: a claim made in opposition or response to another claim.

Countercyclical: a regular cyclical pattern that is opposite to that of the economy and/or financial markets. *See also* Countercyclical Stock.

Countercylical Stock: the shares of a company that has a cyclical pattern opposite to that of the economy (e.g., an employment agency is busier during a recession and high unemployment). *See also* Countercyclical.

Counterfeit: an unlawful imitation of something (usually paper money and securities) with a view to defraud.

Counterparties: the two parties involved in a swap. *See also* Swap.

Countersign: to add a second or confirming signature to a document.

Country Fund: *see* Country Specific Fund.

Country Risk: the risk that a country will or will not be able to honour its commitments. *See also* Risk, Sovereign Risk.

Country Specific Fund: one of the 31 Canadian categories developed by the Investment Funds Standards Committee. Mutual funds in this category must have a minimum of 50 percent of the total assets, and 75 percent of the non-cash assets, of the portfolio invested in a specific country. The calculations to determine whether a mutual fund fits this definition are based on median values from fund data over three years, unless otherwise noted. The derivatives are weighted on an extended value basis. Each of the categories may be refined by the fund manager (e.g., a Canadian Large Cap Equity Fund might be described as "growth" or "value" to reflect the manager's style). Also known as Single Country Mutual Fund. *See also* Extended Value, Mutual Fund – Category.

County Court: a federal court that hears intermediate civil cases and serious criminal cases.

Coup D'état: the overthrow of a government by force.

Coupon: 1. the part of a bond representing the interest payment. **2.** in bond parlance, the yearly interest rate paid by a bond. **3.** on a stripped bond, the interest payment separated from the bond. *See also* Bond.

Coupon Bond: a bond with attachable coupons that may be removed and cashed in to collect interest payments. *See also* Bond.

Coupon Yield: *see* Nominal Yield.

Court of First Instance: the court that comprises the judiciary of the European Community along with the European Court of Justice. It was established to deal with certain actions brought by individuals and corporations as well as competition cases. Appeals on matters of law may be taken to the European Court of Justice.

Court Order: a court-issued order to do something or to refrain from doing something.

Covariance: a statistical measure of the extent to which two variables move together. A high covariance between two stocks indicates that adding one to a portfolio that already owns the other does not result in further diversification. *See also* Correlation Coefficient.

Covenant: a legally binding term of an agreement.

Coverage: 1. an individual or company's income or cash flow divided by interest expense. **2.** protection provided by insurance. *See also* Life Insurance.

Covered Call Option: a call option on a stock written and sold against a position in the stock sufficient to satisfy an exercise of the call option by the buyer. *See also* Covered Option, Option, Uncovered Call Option.

Covered Option: an option on a stock written and sold against a position in the stock sufficient to satisfy an exercise of the option by the buyer. *See also* Option, Uncovered Option.

Covered Position: a term used to describe the circumstance of having written a covered option. *See also* Option, Uncovered Position.

Covered Put Option: a put option on a stock written and sold against sufficient collateral to take delivery of the security in case the option is exercised. *See also* Covered Option, Option, Uncovered Put Option.

Covered Transaction: the act of buying or selling a security while holding an offsetting position. A neutralizing transaction. *See also* Uncovered Transaction.

Covered Writer: a person who sells options against a security he/she owns. A covered writer profits if the price of the underlying security remains stable or moves in an opposite direction to the option sold. *See also* Option, Uncovered Writer.

Covered Writing: the process of writing options against an existing stock position. *See also* Option, Uncovered Writing.

Cover Your Ass (CYA): to take steps to protect oneself from future problems or prosecution.

CPA: *see* Certified Public Accountant.

CPCU: *see* Chartered Property Casualty Underwriter.

CPI: *see* Consumer Price Index.

CPP: *see* Canada Pension Plan.

CPS: *see* Characters per Second.

CPU: *see* Central Processing Unit.

Crack: a sudden drop in the market.

Cracker: a programmer who overcomes a computer's security system in order to gain unauthorized access to information. *See also* Computer, Hacker.

Cracking: the breaking down of crude oil and/or natural gas into various component chemicals.

Cram-Down Transaction: an offer that shareholders are forced to accept for lack of a more attractive alternative.

Crapshoot: a very risky venture.

Crash: *see* Stock Market Crash.

Crash of '29: a general reference to the stock market decline that began in 1929 and lasted for many years. The key dates relating to this crash are Black Thursday (October 24, 1929) and Black Tuesday (October 29, 1929). *See also* Black Thursday, Black Tuesday, Crash of '87.

Crash of '87: a reference to October 19, 1987, when the Dow-Jones Average fell 508 points, or 22.6 percent. *See also* Black Monday, Crash of '29.

Craton: a large, immoveable structure made up of rock belonging to the oldest division of geologic time. When a craton is near the surface of the earth it is associated with large mineral deposits. *See also* Pluton, Volcanic.

Crayon Test: a comment by investment expert Peter Lynch that you should never invest unless you can take a crayon and one piece of paper and illustrate the company's business. *See also* Peter Lynch.

Credential: an accomplishment or written warrant that entitles a person to a position of confidence or authority.

Credit: 1. *see* Credit Balance. **2.** a term used to describe a deposit to a savings or chequing account, so termed because it results in a credit entry in the institution's accounting system. **3.** money lent or agreed to be lent. **4.** an accounting entry that increases liabilities.

Credit Analyst: 1. a financial analyst who assesses the creditworthiness of individuals or corporations. **2.** a financial analyst who determines a creditor's bond rating. *See also* Bond Rating Agency.

Credit Approval: the process of analyzing a person or company's financial position and history to see if the individual or company is worthy of credit. *See also* Credit.

Credit Balance: 1. the amount of cash remaining in a brokerage account after all outstanding trades have been settled. *See also* Brokerage Account, Debit Balance. **2.** a positive balance in an account (e.g., a savings account). *See also* Debit Balance.

Credit Bureau: in Canada, an agency that maintains credit information on people.

Credit Card: a card that allows its owner to make purchases with borrowed money. *See also* Credit Limit, Debit Card, Secure Electronic Transaction.

Credit Department: any business department that analyzes customer financial histories for the purpose of extending loans.

Credit Limit: with respect to a credit card, the maximum amount the cardholder is allowed to borrow. *See also* Credit Card.

Credit Loss: a loan that is uncollectible and that has been written off.

Creditor: of the two parties to a loan, the one to whom money is owed. *See also* Debtor.

Creditorproof: to be protected from the claims of creditors.

Creditor's Committee: a group representing the creditors of a company facing bankruptcy. *See also* Bankrupt, Bankruptcy, Discharge of Bankruptcy.

Creditor's Group Insurance: insurance offered through a lender in order to offset any debt that may remain at the time of a borrower's death. Also known as Creditor's Insurance. *See also* Collateral Term Life Insurance, Life Insurance.

Creditor's Insurance: *see* Creditor's Group Insurance.

Credit Rating: for a government or corporation, a formal assessment of the ability to repay debts. *See also* Bond Rating Agency.

Credit Risk: 1. the risk that a borrower will be unable to repay a loan. *See also* Risk. **2.** the risk that the quality of a bond will decline should the issuer's financial situation worsen. *See also* Bond, Risk.

Credit Sale: a sale that allows the buyer time to pay.

Credit Scoring: the method used by lenders to establish the amount of credit to offer a borrower. *See also* Z-Score.

Credit Spread: an option strategy that involves owning a higher-value call option and a lower-value put option on the same underlying security. *See also* Call Option, Option, Put Option.

Credit Union: a cooperative organization that provides financial services for its members. Each year, most excess revenue over expenses is returned to members. In the U.S., also known as a Thrift. *See also* Cooperative.

Credit Union Deposit Insurance Corporation (CUDIC): insurance to protect deposits at credit unions up to $100,000 per account. *See also* Credit Union.

Credit Union Institute of Canada: an organization formed to provide educational and training programs for credit union employees. *See also* Credit Union.

Creeping Tender: the purchase of a takeover target's stock through the open market rather than through a formal tender offer.

Criss-Cross Insurance: an arrangement in which shareholders own a life insurance policy on each other. If a shareholder dies, the insurance proceeds are used to buy the deceased's shares from his/her estate.

Critical Growth Period: a time when a business must grow or face severe financial problems.

Critical Illness Insurance: insurance that pays in the event the insured is diagnosed with having suffered a heart attack, coronary artery disease needing a bypass operation, a stroke, cancer, kidney failure, total blindness, any condition requiring an organ transplant, multiple sclerosis, deafness or paralysis. *See also* Dread Disease Rider.

CRM: *see* Capped Rate Mortgage.

Croatia CROBEX Index: a market capitalization weighted index of the Zagreb Stock Exchange.

Croatian Stock Exchange: *see* Zabreb Stock Exchange.

Crop Year: the time between one harvest and the next. This usually differs for each agricultural commodity.

Cross: this occurs when a broker has an order to buy and sell the same security at the same price and so makes a simultaneous trade between one client and another. Also known as Cross Order. *See also* Two-Sided Market.

Crossbar: *see* Bogie.

Crosscurrents: conflicting ideas concerning financial markets and/or the economy.

Crossed Market: a market in which a bid is inadvertently above an offer or in which an offer is below a bid.

Crossed Trade: a practice, outlawed on most major stock exchanges, in which buy and sell orders for the same stock in the same amount are offset without recording the trade through the stock exchange.

Cross Order: *see* Cross.

Cross Shareholding: this occurs when Company A owns shares of Company B and vice versa.

Cross-Trading: this occurs when a portfolio manager sells a security out of one account over which he/she has discretionary trading authority and buys it in another account in which he/she has discretionary authority.

Crowding Out: this occurs when a government borrows so much that there are insufficient savings left over to satisfy the borrowing needs of corporations.

Crown Corporation: a corporation established, owned and often regulated by a government. *See also* Government.

Crown Jewel: a prized asset. In a takeover, the acquirer is often after a corporate crown jewel. *See also* Crown Jewel Defence.

Crown Jewel Defence: this entails thwarting a hostile takeover by agreeing to sell the target company's most valuable asset before the takeover can be completed. *See also* Crown Jewel.

CRT: *see* Cathode-Ray Tube.

CRTC: *see* Canadian Radio-Television and Telecommunications Commission.

Crude Oil: hydrocarbons found in a liquid state in underground reservoirs.

Crunch: a crisis that is the result of financial pressures.

Crystallization: the point at which a floating charge becomes immediately enforceable by the creditor.

Crystallize: in taxation, to intentionally cause the realization of a capital gain or loss. Also known as to Trigger.

CSA: 1. *see* Canadian Shareowner's Association. **2.** *see* CSA International.

CSA International: the new name for the Canadian Standards Association effective January, 1999. Established in 1919, it develops and applies standards through product certification, management systems registration and information products. Web site: www.csa-international.org *See also* International Organization for Standardization.

CSB: *see* Canada Savings Bond.

CSC: *see* Canadian Securities Course.

CSE – All Share Index: *see* Cyprus Stock Exchange General.

CSI: *see* Canadian Securities Institute.

CSO: *see* Central Selling Organization.

CSV: *see* Cash Surrender Value.

CU: Internet acronym for "see you."

Cuban Missile Crisis: the events in 1962 that led to President John Kennedy forcing Premier Nikita Kruschev to remove Russian missiles from Cuba. Although the world was close to a nuclear war, the stock market fell only around 6.5 percent.

CUDIC: *see* Credit Union Deposit Insurance Corporation.

Cuff Quote: a security price quote that is given without checking the actual market. Cuff quotes are commonly given on rarely traded bonds.

CUL: Internet acronym for "see you later."

Culpable: in law, deserving of blame.

Cum Dividend: the condition in which the buyer of a security is entitled to a dividend that has been declared but not paid. *See also* Dividend, Ex Dividend.

Cum Right: the condition in which the buyer of a security is entitled to a right that has been declared but not paid. Also known as Rights On. *See also* Ex Rights, Right.

Cumulative Net Investment Losses (CNIL): the amount by which accumulated investment expenses exceeded accumulated investment income in 1987 and later years. Investment expenses include items such as interest expense and other carrying charges, various limited partnership expenses and losses, other tax shelter claims, 50 percent of deductions attributed to resource flow-through shares and the loss from any property.

Cumulative Preferred Share: a preferred share for which all past and current dividends must be paid before dividends on common shares can be paid. *See also* Noncumulative Preferred Share, Preferred Share.

Cumulative Voting: the form of voting for corporate directors in which each share is entitled to one vote multiplied by the number of directors to be elected (e.g., a shareholder with 1,000 shares and eight directors to be elected is entitled to 8,000 votes). Cumulative voting is to the advantage of smaller shareholders because all of the votes can be given in favour of one nominee. Also known as Proportional Representation. *See also* Statutory Voting.

Cum Warrants: the condition in which the buyer of a security is entitled to receive a warrant that has been declared but not distributed. *See also* Ex Warrants.

Curb: 1. a reference to the over-the-counter market. **2.** *see* American Stock Exchange.

Curb Exchange: until 1921, the name of the American Stock Exchange. *See also* American Stock Exchange.

Curb Market: 1. the original name of the American Stock Exchange, founded in 1849, which was so termed because trading was conducted on the street. Trading moved indoors in 1921. **2.** a reference to the over-the-counter market. *See also* American Stock Exchange.

Currency: money in circulation. *See also* Cash.

Currency and Demand Deposits: the narrowest definition of money supply. *See also* M1.

Currency Conversion: the change in the price quote for a security based on the previous currency it was convertible into prior to the Euro. Also known as Cash Conversion.

Currency Crisis: a condition that occurs when the weakness of a country's currency threatens to produce severe economic hardship.

Currency Devaluation: a significant decline in a country's currency value relative to the U.S. dollar.

Currency Future: contracts in the futures market for delivery in a major world currency. Companies engaged in international trade use currency futures to hedge exchange rate risk. *See also* Currency Hedge, Futures Exchange.

Currency Hedge: a way of protecting oneself against a change in currency value. It entails buying and selling currency futures. *See also* Currency Future.

Current Account: in measuring a country's balance of payments, the current account measures the value of imports and exports. *See also* Balance of Payments, Capital Account, Gold Account.

Current Assets: those assets that a company can convert to cash in less than one year.

Current Disbursement Funding: a term used to describe a pension plan that pays current obligations from current revenues. *See also* Unfunded Pension Plan.

Current Liabilities: those liabilities that a company must pay within one year.

Current Market Price: the most recent quoted price of a security.

Current Ratio: current assets divided by current liabilities. Normally, a ratio of 1.0 is considered reasonable.

Current Yield: 1. for a bond, the annual interest divided by the current market price expressed as a percentage. **2.** for a money market mutual fund, the portfolio's average earnings in the most recent seven-day period converted to an annualized rate of return. *See also* Annualized Rate, Canadian Money Market Fund.

Cursor: in a computer, the small line that blinks on the screen to show where the next entry will occur. *See also* Computer.

Curtate Annuity: an annuity that makes no final payment to the annuitant's estate. *See also* Annuity.

Curtilage: in common law, the land around a dwelling place.

Curtsy: the portion of his wife's assets that a widower acquired during their marriage.

Cushion: the time between the issue of a bond and the date it can be called.

Cushion Bond: a callable bond that has a price that is artificially low because of its call feature. Cushion bonds have more interest rate stability and will decline much less than average during a period of rising interest rates. *See also* Bond.

Cushion Theory: the theory that a short position in a stock will eventually exert upward pressure on the price as investors cover their positions. The original

justification for allowing short selling. *See also* Short Sale.

CUSIP: *see* Committee of Uniform Security Identification Procedures.

CUSIP International Numbering Service (CINS): a uniform code for identifying international securities. *See also* Committee on Uniform Security Identification Procedures.

Custodian: 1. a financial institution (e.g., bank, trust company) that holds a mutual fund's cash and securities in safekeeping. Also known as Mutual Fund Custodian. *See also* Mutual Fund. **2.** an agent that stores investments for safekeeping.

Custody: the court-ordered guardianship of a child.

Customer's Man: *see* Broker.

Customs: duties charged on commodities imported into or exported out of a country.

Cut and Run: to terminate losses on an investment by selling.

Cut Back: to reduce expenditures by retrenching or curtailing operations or employment.

Cut Both Ways: to have both positive and negative consequences.

Cut Down: to reduce expenditures by retrenching or curtailing operations or employment.

Cut Losses, Let Profits Run: an investment adage meaning it is better to sell losing investments quickly while holding on to stronger performers. Also known as First Loss, Best Loss; Take Losses, Let Profits Run.

Cutoff Grade: in mining, the grade below which it is not profitable to mine. Material below this grade is not included in reserves.

Cut Rate: reduced in price. Also, of low quality.

Cutting Losses: selling a losing position and accepting the loss rather than risking more losses.

CYA: *see* Cover Your Ass.

Cyberia: in computers, where one is located when trapped by an inability to make technology function properly. *See also* Computer.

Cybernaut: one who spends a lot of time using the Internet or e-mail. *See also* Internet.

Cyberserf: a slave to the Internet. *See also* Internet.

Cybersleuth: a person, often non-professional, who uncovers investment fraud on the Internet.

Cyberspace: 1. a computer-created virtual reality environment inside which people may interact. Cyberspace is a three-dimensional computer environment made up of audio, text and video signals. **2.** a nickname for the Internet. *See also* Computer.

Cybrarian: 1. a program that allows electronic access to a database via the Internet. **2.** a person who does full-time research or retrieval from the Internet. *See also* Internet.

Cycle: a regular pattern of ups and downs. *See also* Bear Market, Bull Market, Business Cycle, Contraction, Contra Cyclical, Cycle Down, Cycle Up, Cyclical, Cyclical Stock, Cyclical Trend, Depression, Economic Cycle, Elliott Wave Theory, Expansion, Industry Life Cycle, Kondratieff Wave, Life Cycle, Market Cycle, Mature, Peak, Presidential Election Cycle, Recession, Seasonal Trend, Secular Trend, Startup, Stock Market Cycle, Trough.

Cycles

In a market economy, conditions tend to change in a cyclical fashion. A cyclical change generally relates to a short-term cycle lasting less than five years or so, while a secular change relates to a long-term cycle lasting one or more decades.

The overall economy moves in cycles. There is an expansion phase followed by a peak. Then there is a contraction (often called a recession), which is followed by a trough. A severe recession is called a depression.

Since the Second World War, economic cycles in Canada and the U.S. have averaged around eight years. Stock markets move in cycles. The rising stage is called a "bull market" and is followed by a peak; the falling stage is called a "bear market" and is followed by a trough. Stock market cycles average about five years in length in both Canada and the US.

Many, but not all, stock market declines are associated with recessions. This has led to the observation that the stock market has forecast nine out of the last five recessions.

Other economic variables, such as interest rates and inflation, have tended to follow secular patterns. Generally, the decades of the 1960s and 1970s saw a secular rise in interest rates and inflation. Since the early 1980s, both have been in a secular decline.

Cycles in the economy and financial markets are likely the result of people's expectations swinging from being overly optimistic to being overly pessimistic. As long as economic variables reflect the collective actions of a large number of people, cycles will continue to be a fact of life.

Cycle Down: regular pattern of ups and downs wherein successive peaks are lower than preceding peaks and successive troughs are lower than preceding troughs. *See also* Cycle.

Cycle Up: a regular pattern of ups and downs wherein successive peaks are higher than preceding peaks and successive troughs are higher than preceding troughs. *See also* Cycle.

Cyclical: subject to cycles. *See also* Cycle.

Cyclical Stock: shares of a company sensitive to the economic cycle. Generally, a cyclical stock moves up and down over a cycle but makes little headway over successive cycles. *See also* Cycle.

Cyclical Trend: the short-term trend within which seasonal trends take place which, in turn, form a part of the secular trend. *See also* Cycle.

Cyprus Stock Exchange: the major stock exchange of Cyprus, located in its capital, Nicosia (Lefkosia).

Cyprus Stock Exchange General: a stock market index for the Cyprus Stock Exchange. Also known as CSE – All Share Index.

Czech Stock Exchange: *see* Prague Stock Exchange.

D: in Roman numerals, the number 500.

Dabble: to make small or frivolous investments.

Daily Limit: the maximum amount some commodity or option prices can rise or fall in a day before trading is halted until the next day. Also known as Daily Trading Limit. *See also* Commodities, Option.

Daily Trading Limit: *see* Daily Limit.

Daisy Chain: an illegal activity in which a number of investors trade a stock among themselves, thus creating the illusion of activity. When other investors are drawn in, the members of the daisy chain sell stock to them. *See also* Surveillance Department, Wash Trading.

Dalasi: the prime currency of Gambia.

Damages: money ordered by the court to be paid as compensation for loss or injury. *See also* Punitive Damages.

Damper: an event that depresses the financial market.

D&B: *see* Dun & Bradstreet Corporation.

Danish Stock Exchange: *see* Copenhagen Stock Exchange.

DAP: *see* Delivery Against Payment.

Data: 1. factual information. **2.** a common reference to alphanumeric information used in computer processing. *See also* Computer.

Data Bank: a facility for housing information, frequently on a computer. *See also* Computer.

Database: any collection of data, especially on a computer. *See also* Computer.

Data Carrier: a medium for communicating, recording, transporting or storing computer-based data. *See also* Computer.

Data Communications Equipment (DCE): a hardware device that uses a certain kind of serial connection. Most modems are configured as DCE.

Data Compression: in data communications, facsimile transmission and CD-ROM publishing, a way of reducing the amount of space or bandwidth required to store or transmit a block of data.

Data Fitting: a flawed statistical technique that consists of drawing a theory from a set of data and using the latter to prove the former.

Data Processing: working with data in a computer. *See also* Computer.

Datawarehouse: in computers, a large database that allows user access. *See also* Computer.

Dated Date: the date from which interest accrues on debt securities.

Date of Maturity: *see* Maturity Date.

Date of Record: *see* Record Date.

Dating: in commercial transactions, an allowance to make payment beyond the standard terms. Because dating is used to cover off periods of high seasonal activity, it is also known as Seasonal Dating. *See also* Full Trade Credit, Trade Credit.

Datum: 1. the singular form of "data." **2.** a fact used to make a decision.

DAX Index: a total return index of the Frankfurt Stock Exchange.

Day Labour: workers hired by the day.

Daylight Loan: a loan that lasts less than one working day.

Daylight Overdraft: when a deposit account is overdrawn during part of a business day.

Daylight Trade: *see* Day Trading.

Day Order: an order (to buy or sell a security) that expires if not filled on the day it is entered. *See also* Order.

Day-to-Day Money: *see* Call Money.

Day Trading: buying and selling a security during the same day. Day trading has mushroomed into a significant stock market factor facilitated by stock brokerage services offered over the Internet. Also known as Daylight Trading. *See also* Short-Term Trading.

Day Tripper: an investor with a pattern of buying and selling the same security on the same day.

DBRS: *see* Dominion Bond Rating Service.

DCE: *see* Data Communications Equipment.

Dead: any business transaction that is no longer in effect.

Dead Account: *see* Dormant Account.

Deadbeat: slang for one who does not pay his/her debts.

Dead Cat Bounce: in stocks, describes an initial recovery after a prolonged decline, as in "even a dead cat will bounce if it is dropped from high enough."

Dead in the Water: at a standstill, as in "the economy is dead in the water."

Deadlock: a standstill between two forces, as in "a deadlock in negotiations."

Deal: a business agreement or transaction.

Deal Breaker: *see* Showstopper.

Dealer: a securities firm that acts as a principal in a securities transaction (e.g., buys a new issue of securities and sells it to its clients). *See also* Broker-Dealer.

Dealership: a franchise to sell certain items in a certain area (e.g., a General Motors dealership).

Dealer's Turn: a profit made by a dealer who buys a security at the bid and immediately sells at the offering.

Deal Flow: the rate at which new corporate finance projects are being brought in for consideration. *See also* Corporate Finance.

Deal Maker: 1. a person with an acknowledged ability to conclude transactions. **2.** an event that results in a transaction being concluded (e.g., a favourable tax ruling). *See also* Showstopper.

Deal Stock: shares that are being traded based on rumours of a takeover, merger or acquisition.

Dear John Letter: notification that a specific relationship (e.g., employment) is being terminated.

Deathbed Gift: *see* Donatio Mortis Causa.

Death Benefit: the amount payable on death, usually from life insurance. *See also* Life Insurance.

Death Play: a stock that is purchased in the belief it will rise in value based on the imminent death of a key executive or shareholder.

Death Rate: the number of deaths as a percentage of the population for a given area in a given time period.

Death Star: a term applied by the analog-based cable television industry to the satellite used to transmit digital satellite television.

Death Stock: the shares of a company facing bankruptcy.

Death Valley Curve: a venture capital term that describes the period in the development of a new company during which capital must be spent but potential income is many months or years away. *See also* Burn Rate.

Debenture: an unsecured bond. In banking, debenture often refers to a formal loan agreement. *See also* Bond.

Debit: 1. *see* Debit Balance **2.** a term used to describe a withdrawal from a savings or chequing account, so termed because it results in a debit entry in the institution's accounting system.

Debit Balance: 1. the amount owing in a brokerage account after all outstanding trades have been settled. *See also* Brokerage Account, Credit Balance. **2.** a negative balance in an account (e.g., a savings account). *See also* Credit Balance.

Debit Card: a card that enables its user to pay for a purchase by deducting the requisite funds from a bank account. The opposite of a credit card. *See also* Bank Card, Credit Card.

Debt: an amount owing. A financial obligation.

Debt Bomb: the failure of a major financial institution that has a negative impact on financial markets locally and, on occasion, worldwide (e.g., the failure of the savings and loans companies in the U.S. in the late 1980s).

Debt Capacity: an estimate of the total amount of debt that can be serviced and repaid.

Debt Consolidation: a strategy of taking a number of debts and refinancing them into one loan, also known as a Consolidation Loan. Debt consolidation is done before serious credit problems have arisen. *See also* Debt Restructuring.

Debt Conversion: a process that occurs when a party in financial difficulty arranges with creditors to transform his/her debt into, for example, common shares.

Debt/Equity Ratio: a financial ratio of the amount of long-term debt divided by shareholders' equity. The debt/equity ratio is a measure of leverage. Generally, a ratio of over 33 percent indicates high leverage, except for certain businesses (e.g., public utilities), where the stable nature of revenues allows for higher leverage. Also known as Bond Ratio. *See also* Capitalization Ratio, Leverage.

Debt Financing: the use of borrowed money.

Debt Instrument: any document that gives evidence of a loan.

Debtor: of the two parties to a loan, the one that owes money. *See also* Creditor.

Debt Ratio: a financial ratio derived by dividing total debt by total assets. A person's debt ratio is often important to financial institutions considering a personal loan application.

Debt Restructuring: this occurs when a party in financial difficulty arranges with creditors to change the terms and conditions of a loan(s) so that operations can continue. *See also* Debt Consolidation.

Debt Retirement: repayment of a loan.

Debt Security: *see* Bond.

Debt Service: this refers to the funds required to pay interest and principal due on debt. Also known as Service.

Debt to Equity Ratio: *see* Debt/Equity Ratio.

Debt to Gross Domestic Product: a ratio that indicates the level of a country's government debt. For industrialized nations, a ratio of over one dollar in debt for every one dollar in gross domestic product is very high. Canada and Italy are in this range.

Debug: to find and to correct computer programming errors. *See also* Bug, Computer.

Deca: in the decimal system, the prefix denoting 10 (e.g., a decalitre is equal to ten litres). *See also* Metric System.

Decade: a period of 10 years.

Decedent: a deceased person.

Decennial: occurring every 10 years.

Decennial Cycle: first observed by Edgar Lawrence Smith in *Common Stocks and Business Cycles,* since 1880, the fifth year of each decade has been an up year for the stock market. *See also* Pentaphilia Theory.

Decentralize: to spread authority and responsibility throughout an organization rather than to keep it all in the head office.

Decertify: 1. to formally terminate a labour union as the bargaining unit for a group of workers. *See also* Certify. **2.** in general, to formally terminate recognition by withdrawing a certificate.

Decessit Sine Prole: died without issue (i.e., children).

Deci: in the decimal system, the prefix denoting one part in ten (e.g., a decilitre is equal to one-tenth of a litre). *See also* Metric System.

Decile: a ranking into 10 equal groups, with the first decile being the top 10 percent and tenth decile being the bottom 10 percent. *See also* Quartile, Quintile.

Decimal: based on, or ordered by, groups of 10.

Decimalization of Sterling: when the British pound was changed to 100 new pence from the previous system in which the pound was 20 shillings and one shilling was 12 pennies.

Decimal System: a number system based on groups of 10.

Decimal System
Milli:	one one-thousandth
Centi:	one one-hundredth
Deci:	one-tenth
Gram:	a unit of weight
Litre:	a unit of volume
Metre:	a unit of length
Deca:	a multiple of 10
Hecto:	a multiple of 100
Kilo:	a multiple of 1,000

Declaration Date: the date on which a company announces a dividend payment.

Declaration of Trust: in law, an acknowledgement by a person that he/she holds property in trust for another.

Declination: the decision by an insurer not to accept an application for life insurance.

Decline: 1. move lower, as in "the stock price is expected to decline following a report of lower earnings." **2.** a phase in an industry life cycle in which activity falls. *See also* Industry Life Cycle.

Declines: the number of listed stocks that decline in price during a trading session. *See also* Advances, Breadth Ratio.

Declining Volume: in a trading session, the volume of trades made at a lower price. *See also* Advancing Volume.

Decontrol: to take away control, mainly from a government.

Decreasing Annuity: an annuity in which the amount of the payment declines over time. *See also* Annuity.

Decreasing Term Insurance: life insurance for a fixed term, during which premiums remain the same but the death benefit declines in stages. This type of insurance is often popular with young couples who need a higher insurance when their families are young. *See also* Life Insurance.

Decree: a law, judgement or order of the court.

Decree Absolute: under the Divorce Act, a decree that finalizes a divorce (usually occurring three months after a decree nisi).

Decree Nisi: a provisional decree of divorce.

Decrement: the amount lost by gradual reduction, often used to describe the reduction of the number of members in a pension plan because of factors such as retirement, death or termination from employment.

Decriminalize: to abolish criminal penalties for a particular act.

Decryption: the process of converting an encrypted message to its original form. *See also* Encryptian.

DECS: *see* Dividend Enhanced Convertible Stock.

Dedicated Line: a communication line used only to connect one entity to another.

Dedicated Portfolio: *see* Portfolio Dedication.

Deductible: 1. in certain forms of liability insurance, the initial amount of a claim that is not covered (e.g., with a $500 deductible on automobile collision insurance, the owner is responsible for the first $500 of damages and his/her insurance is responsible for the rest). **2.** *see* Tax Deductible.

Deductible Expense: a sum that may be subtracted from one's income before the calculation of one's income tax. *See also* Tax Deductible, Taxes.

Deductible Interest: interest on money borrowed that is a deductible expense for tax purposes because the loan is used to make investments in the expectation of earning income.

Deduction: in income tax, a sum that can be subtracted from one's income in order to reduce taxable income.

Deed: a document that gives evidence of ownership of real property. It is used to transfer and record title. Also known as Title Deed. *See also* Title Deed.

Deemed Disposition: a transaction under the Income Tax Act in which, for income tax purposes, a disposition is said to have occurred even though it has not. *See also* Disposition.

Deemed Realization: *see* Deemed Disposition.

Deemed Trust: trusts that are imposed by statute. Such trusts are "deemed" to exist.

Deep: substantial (e.g., if a bid is deep, it is good for a sizeable number of shares). *See also* Deep Bid.

Deep Bid: a bid for a large number of shares, often away from the market.

Deep Blue: the IBM computer that chess champion Gary Kasparov defeated in 1996. *See also* Blue Pacific, Computer, Deeper Blue, International Business Machines Corporation.

Deep Cyclical Stock: the common stock of a company engaged in a business that is effected greatly by the economy (e.g., mining). Deep cyclical stocks usually perform best in the late stages of an economic recovery. *See also* Cyclical.

Deep Discount: a price substantially below a stated value (e.g., a bond price far below par value). *See also* Bond.

Deeper Blue: the IBM computer that defeated chess champion Gary Kasparov in 1997. Deeper Blue can analyze 200 million moves per second compared to Kasparov's three, and, within the space of three minutes, it can look 100 moves ahead. *See also* Blue Pacific, Computer, Deep Blue, International Business Machines Corporation.

Deep in the Money: a condition in which the strike price of a put option is far above or the strike price of a call option is far below the price of the underlying security. *See also* At the Money, Deep out of the Money, In the Money, Option, Out of the Money.

Deep Money: profits made from investment in trends of your own making, such as Michael Milken's profits from the junk bond market he created. *See also* Shallow Money.

Deep out of the Money: a condition in which the strike price of a put option is far below or the strike price of a call option is far above the price of the underlying security. *See also* At the Money, Deep in the Money, In the Money, Option, Out of the Money.

Deep Pockets: 1. to have deep pockets is to have sizeable financial resources. **2.** in a lawsuit, the party or parties with the greatest ability to pay a judgement.

Deep Pocket Syndrome: in insurance, the tendency to make claims against those who can pay rather than those who are at fault.

De Facto: in fact.

Defalcation: without the implication of criminal fraud, a condition when a person entrusted with money fails to pay when it is due.

Defame: to damage someone's reputation. *See also* Libel, Slander.

Default: this occurs when a debtor fails to meet an interest or principal payment.

Default Judgement: a judgement granted after the defendant fails to appear or file a statement of defence.

Default Settings: in computers, automatic changeable settings on hardware or software. *See also* Computer, Factory Default Settings.

Defeasance: the process or provision that renders an instrument, such as a will or loan, null and void. *See also* Will.

Defective Title: a legally invalid property title (e.g., a title is defective if the original vendor did not have title to the property sold or if the property was illegally acquired). *See also* Bad Title, Clear Title, Cloud on Title, On Title, Title, Title Deed, Title Defect, Title Search.

Defendant: in a court action, the party that is charged by a plaintiff.

Defensive Industry: an industry, such as utilities, that does not suffer as much as do others during economic slowdowns.

Defensive Investment: an investment that is more attractive for its lack of risk than for its potential return.

Defensive Investment Strategy: a strategy used more to protect capital from loss than to increase its value.

Defensive Portfolio: a portfolio structured to protect value, sometimes in the expectation of poor markets.

Deferred Annuity: an annuity in which payments do not begin until a future date. *See also* Annuity, Immediate Annuity.

Deferred Charge: an expense or cost that has been pushed to a future date.

Deferred Commission: a commission charged when money is withdrawn. In most cases, the amount of the charge declines each year until it reaches zero. Often used by mutual funds. Also known as Deferred Sales Charge. *See also* Back End Load, Front End Load, Load, No Load Fund.

Deferred Declining Redemption Fee – At Cost: a commission charged when money is withdrawn, with the amount of the charge declining each year until it reaches zero. The applicable percentage commission charge is based on the cost of the original investment. Also known as Contingent Deferred Sales Charge. *See also* Back End Load, Deferred Commission, Deferred Declining Redemption Fee – At Market Value, Deferred Sales Charge, Exit Fee, Front End Load, Life Insurance, Load, Loading Charge, Mutual Fund, No Load Fund, Rear End Load.

Deferred Declining Redemption Fee – At Market Value: a commission charged when money is withdrawn, with the amount of the charge declining each year until it reaches zero. The applicable percentage commission charge is based on the market value of investment at the time of redemption. Also known as Contingent Deferred Sales Charge. *See also* Back End Load, Deferred Commission, Deferred Declining Redemption Fee – At Cost, Deferred Sales Charge, Exit Fee, Front End Load, Life Insurance, Load, Loading Charge, Mutual Fund, No Load Fund, Rear End Load.

Deferred Interest Bond: a bond that does not pay current interest but has payment deferred to a future date (e.g., a zero coupon bond).

Deferred Load: *see* Deferred Sales Charge.

Deferred Profit Sharing Plan (DPSP): a plan in which a company contributes to an investment account for employees. Within limits, the employer's contributions are tax deductible, and the employee is not taxed on the money until he/she withdraws it. Often the funds are invested in the employer's company shares. *See also* Profit Sharing Plan.

Deferred Sales Charge: a commission charged when money is withdrawn from a mutual fund. In most cases, the amount of the charge declines each year until it reaches zero. Also known as Back End Load, Deferred Commission, Deferred Load, Exit Fee and Rear End Load. *See also* Deferred Declining Redemption Fee – At Cost, Deferred Declining Redemption Fee – At Market Value, Front End Load, Load, Loading Charge, Mutual Fund, No Load Fund.

Deferred Taxes: taxes whose payment has been postponed to a future date.

Deficiency Letter: a letter, written by a regulator, that seeks more information in a prospectus that an underwriter has submitted for regulatory approval. Also known as Letter of Deficiency.

Deficit: a financial condition in which expenses exceed revenue or liabilities exceed assets.

Deficit Financing: the process of using borrowed funds to finance the amount by which spending exceeds revenue.

Deficit Spending: in governments, the process of spending money in excess of taxation revenue that results in a budget deficit. Deficit spending must be covered by additional debt. *See also* Budget Deficit, Budget Surplus.

Deficit to Gross Domestic Product: a ratio measuring the level of a country's government deficits. For industrialized nations, a ratio of 5 percent to 7 percent is high.

Defined Benefit Pension Plan: a pension determined by formula, usually combining years of plan membership and a percentage of salary based on career earnings (or the average of last or best earnings) for a

specified period (e.g., the formula might be years of service times 2 percent times the average income for the last five years of employment). Also known as Unit Benefit Pension Plan. *See also* Money Purchase Plan.

Defined Contribution Pension Plan: *see* Money Purchase Pension Plan.

Deflation: a period during which the Consumer Price Index and similar price indexes are declining. *See also* Disinflation, Inflation, Reflation.

Deflator: a statistical factor that adjusts prices for inflation over time.

Defraud: to swindle.

Defray: to pay out or disburse money.

Defunct: no longer in business.

Dehire: a modern euphemism for to fire or to lay off.

Deindustrialization: this occurs when a mature economy changes from being primarily dependent upon producing goods to being primarily dependent upon producing services.

Deinstitutionalize: to remove the status of institution.

De Jure: legal; lawful; legitimate.

Delayed Delivery: a securities trade in which delivery of securities occurs after the normal delivery date.

Delayed Opening: normally, after the announcement of a major event, the postponement of trading in a security due to an imbalance of either buy orders or sell orders.

Delayed Settlement: a securities transaction in which settlement occurs after the normal settlement date.

Delegate: 1. to assign responsibility for a task to another person. **2.** someone who attends a meeting as a representative, as in "a delegate to a political convention."

Delimiter: in computers, a character that marks the beginning or ending of any given part of a program or data collection. *See also* Computer.

Delinquent: 1. to be behind in payments or obligations. **2.** in law, a juvenile who is guilty of antisocial or criminal behaviour.

Delisted: shares removed from trading on a recognized stock exchange. In many but not all cases, the companies have gone out of business. In some cases, companies delist their shares from one exchange because the shares have been accepted for listing on a more senior exchange.

Delisting: removing shares from trading on a recognized stock exchange. In many but not all cases, the companies have gone out of business.

Delivery: the completion of a securities transaction through the physical handing over of a stock certificate.

Delivery Against Payment (DAP): a form of trade settlement in which security delivery and payment are simultaneous.

Delivery Date: the date on which delivery is due in order to settle a transaction (normally three business days after the trade).

Delivery Notice: notification from the seller of a commodity futures contract to the buyer of a commodity futures contract to confirm when physical delivery of the commodity will take place.

Delphi Forecast: a market forecast in which a group of experts present their predictions and justifications. The group then analyzes what each person said and, after discussion, puts together a composite forecast. Also known as Jury of Executive Opinion.

Delta: expected change in the value of an option upon a one-dollar change in the price of an underlying security. *See also* Option.

Delta Hedge: the practice of a financial option writer to reduce risk by purchasing or selling the underlying securities. *See also* Option.

Delta Stock: the London Stock Exchange formerly used a system for ranking stocks Alpha, Beta, Delta and Gamma, each representing a smaller underlying company and less actively traded stock. Delta stocks ranked below Alpha and Beta stocks in terms of size and trading volume. *See also* Alpha Stock, Beta Stock and Gamma Stock.

Demand: the amount of a product, service or financial instrument that will be purchased at a given price. *See also* Equilibrium Price, Supply.

Demand Curve: a chart with selling price on the vertical axis and units for sale on the horizontal axis. A demand curve usually falls from left to right, indicating that demand for units increases as the price decreases. *See also* Supply Curve.

Demand Deposit: any account from which funds can be withdrawn immediately. *See also* Chequing Account, Combination Account, Deposit, Savings Account.

Demand Draft: a draft payable on demand. *See also* Sight Draft, Term Draft.

Demand Loan: a loan that does not mature and on which one makes (usually) only interest payments. The loan is repayable in full upon demand.

Demand Money: *see* Call Money.

Demand Note: a note that is repayable upon demand.

Demand-Pull Inflation: a situation in which overwhelming demand for goods and services causes prices to rise, thus creating inflation. *See also* Cost-Push Inflation

Demise: 1. to transfer or convey an estate for a fixed term or life. **2.** death.

Democracy: a social, political and economic system based on the election of government representatives by secret ballot.

Demodulation: in computers, the retrieval of modulated information and its conversion from the analog signal received over the telephone line into the digital information used by the computer. *See also* Computer.

Demographics: the study of population characteristics for the purpose of making economic and related assessments.

Demography: the study of human populations.

Demogrowthics: trends of population change that influence economic growth.

Demonetize: to divest of money or currency (e.g., withdrawing gold as a currency for settlement of international trade in 1978).

Demutualization: the process of changing a corporate entity from a mutual company to some other form of company (e.g., limited liability company). Several Canadian insurance companies made this change following the passing of federal legislation on March 12, 1999. *See also* Mutual Company, Mutual Life Insurance Company.

Denary: to have a base of 10, as in the decimal system.

Denigrate: to attack a person's reputation.

Denizen: an inhabitant or resident.

DENKS: *see* Dual Income, No Kids.

Denomination: usually, the units of a financial security (e.g., the face value or the par value of bonds). *See also* Bond.

Denominator: 1. in a fraction, the number below the line. **2.** in division, the number divided into the other.

Dental Plan: an employee benefit that covers part of the cost of dental work for the employee and usually members of his/her family as well. *See also* Employee Benefit Plan.

Dependence Adjustment Factor: when more than one money manager is used to manage a large portfolio, a measure of the relative independence of one manager's judgement relative to all others. If the manager is totally independent, the factor is one. If the manager adds no new judgement to the group, the factor is zero.

Dependent: one who relies on another, especially for financial support (e.g., a child).

Dependent Variable: in correlating two variables, the one that is contingent on the independent variable. *See also* Independent Variable, Multiple Regression Analysis.

Depletion: an accounting method for writing off the cost of a consumable natural asset (e.g., oil or gas) as a non-cash charge over its expected reserve life.

Depletion Allowance: under the Income Tax Act, the amount of depletion deductible from pretax earnings.

Deponent: 1. a witness. **2.** one who gives information under oath.

Depose: 1. to remove from office, often forcibly. **2.** in law, to give a deposition.

Deposit: 1. to put money into an account with a financial institution. *See also* Chequing Account, Combination Account, Demand Deposit, Savings Account, Withdrawal. **2.** money or other consideration given as a pledge for fulfillment of an agreement or to protect the other party in the event the agreement is not fulfilled. **3.** sums lodged with landlords for security (e.g., a damage deposit). **4.** securities or money placed with a bank or other institution for a particular purpose (e.g., to secure a loan). **5.** a property containing minerals.

Deposit Cutoff: the time during a business day by which a deposit must be made to be credited to an account that day. This is important for companies when large sums of money are involved, either to earn one extra day of interest or to ensure the funds are available to cover outstanding cheques.

Deposition: a witness statement, under oath and in question-and-answer form, given at a pretrial examination for discovery.

Deposit Taking Institution: a bank, trust depreciation. company, credit union or financial institution that accepts deposits.

Depreciate: 1. to reduce in value. **2.** in accounting, the writing down of an asset over its useful life by allocating a non-cash charge against earnings.

Depreciated Cost: an accounting value calculated as original cost less accumulated

Depreciation: an accounting method for writing off the cost of a fixed asset (e.g., machinery or equipment) over its useful life. *See also* Straight Line Depreciation, Sum-of-the-Year's Digits Method.

Depress: to cause financial and economic trends to turn down or decline.

Depressed: generally, financial and economic trends that are down substantially, as in "the economy is depressed."

Depression: an extended period of above average economic contraction. *See also* Dirty Thirties, Great Depression

Deputy: a person appointed to act for another.

Deregistering a Registered Retirement Savings Plan: *see* Registered Retirement Savings Plan – Deregistration.

Deregulation: the reduction or elimination of government control over industries in order to promote competition.

Derivative: a security whose value is derived from the value of another security. *See also* Option.

Derogate: 1. to prejudice. **2.** to evade a right or obligation.

Descendant: a person related to another by birth.

Descending Tops: a technical stock market term used to describe a price pattern wherein subsequent highs are lower. *See also* Ascending Tops, Technical Analysis.

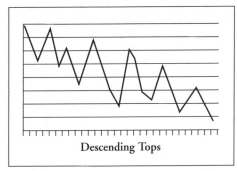

Descending Tops

Descending Trend: a pattern in prices or in an economic series wherein subsequent highs are lower and subsequent lows are lower. *See also* Ascending Trend.

Desertion: a unilateral decision by one spouse not to live with the other spouse.

Desktop Publishing: the production of professional-quality printed documents through the use of a personal computer, word processing and a high-quality printer. *See also* Computer.

Destabilize: to unbalance the equilibrium. When economic or market forces are out of balance, they are said to be destabilized.

Destination Shopping: an outlet to which customers are willing to travel in order to make purchases.

Determinable Fee: an interest in a real property that may last forever but that will be terminated if certain conditions are not met (e.g., a property given as long as it is used as a church). *See also* Fee.

Deterministic Model: a mathematical model that assumes the values of variables are known. *See also* Stochastic Model.

Deutsche Bundesbank: the central bank of Germany, often referred to as the Bundesbank.

Deutschemark: the prime currency of Germany. Also known as the Mark or D-mark.

Devaluation: a lowering of value, with particular reference to currency.

Developer: in real estate, one engaged in development.

Development: 1. changing real estate to a more valuable use, such as raw land to housing. **2.** in resources, the stage of preparing a property for production. *See also* Exploration Company, Integrated Oil Company, Oil Company, Production Company, Refining and Marketing.

Development Company: 1. in real estate, a company engaged in development. **2.** in resources, a company involved in bringing resource properties into production.

Development Drilling: drilling for oil and gas in proximity to existing production. Also, drilling to expand reserves in a proven field or to raise production. Development drilling is lower in risk than is wildcat drilling. *See also* Wildcat Drilling.

Devil's Advocate: a person who challenges a position by asking difficult or unpopular questions in order to provoke argument or discussion.

Devise: a gift of real property through a will. *See also* Beneficiary, Devisee, Devisor, Heir, Heir Apparent, Heiress, Ultimate Beneficiary, Will.

Devisee: one who receives a gift of real property through a will. *See also* Beneficiary, Devise, Devisor, Heir, Heir Apparent, Heiress, Ultimate Beneficiary, Will.

Devisor: one who gives a gift of real property through a will. *See also* Beneficiary, Devise, Devisee, Heir, Heir Apparent, Heiress, Ultimate Beneficiary, Will.

Devolution: the act of passing something (e.g., an inheritance) on to a successor.

Devolution of Power: the granting of power, generally political, from a senior to a lower level or from a central authority to a regional authority.

Devolve: to pass by succession (e.g., through a will or estate).

DEWKS: *see* Dual Employed, With Kids.

Dhaka Stock Exchange: the major stock exchange of Bangladesh, located in its capital, Dhaka.

Diagonal Spread: the simultaneous purchase and sale of more than one option of the same type (e.g., calls, puts) on the same underlying security with different strike prices and expiration dates. *See also* Option.

Dialling and Smiling: *see* Dialling for Dollars.

Dialling for Dollars: a term used to describe making unsolicited calls in the hope of identifying new clients or customers. In investment, the term has a negative connotation and is often used to refer to the activities of workers in a boiler room. Also known as Dialling and Smiling. *See also* Boiler Room, Bucketing, Bucket Shop, Cold Calling.

Dialog Box: in computers, a window in which there appears a question or a request for more information. *See also* Computer.

Dial-Up Network: a network accessed by a telephone connection (e.g., the Internet). *See also* Internet.

Diamond: a valuable gemstone. Historically, South Africa, Russia and Australia have been major producers. In recent years, discoveries in the Northwest Territories and promising exploration in the provinces will result in Canada becoming a major producer. *See also* Four Cs, Uncut.

Diamond Drilling: a form of mining exploration that, for the purposes of analysis, extracts a core from the Earth.

Diamonds: index participation units, offered by the American Stock Exchange, which replicate movements in the Dow-Jones Average. It is a basket of securities that provides index-like returns and that investors can buy as a single common share. *See also* Index Participation Unit, Spider, TIPs, TIPs35, TIPs100.

Dictum: an authoritative, often official, pronouncement.

Diesel: a fuel that is a heavier distillate of petroleum.

Diet: a legislative assembly.

Die Without Issue: *see* Failure of Issue.

Differential: usually, the difference between two financial or economic variables.

Differential Voting Shares: *see* Restricted Voting Shares.

Diffusion Index: an index that comprises several other economic series and that measures an overall trend (e.g., the Index of Leading Economic Indicators).

Digit: any one of the Arabic numerals between zero and nine. *See also* Arabic Numeral.

Digital Cash: *see* Electronic Cash.

Digital Computer: a computer that performs calculations on discrete elements, usually using the binary number system. *See also* Analog Computer, Computer.

Digital Signature: a coded electronic password that has been made secure by data encryption.

Digital Transmission: in computers, the act of sending data as a stream of discrete electrical pulses. *See also* Computer.

Digital Versatile Disc (DVD): *see* Digital Versatile Disc – Read Only Memory.

Digital Versatile Disc – Read Only Memory (DVD–ROM): a high-speed, read-only compact disc capable of storing 4.7 gigabytes of text, sound, graphics and video.

Digital Video Disc (DVD): a DVD–ROM next-generation replacement for the VCR and VHS tape.

Digits Deleted: in reporting stock trading, the practice of sometimes reporting the price change without reporting the stock price.

Dike: in mining, a geological formation created as a result of magma forcing its way into cracks in the Earth. These cracks are hundreds of metres wide and several kilometres long. Also known as Dyke. *See also* Sill.

Dilution: a lessening of a shareholder's claim or interest in a company's earnings or assets through the issuance of additional shares without an offsetting increase in earnings or assets. *See also* Watered Stock.

Dime: an informal reference to the 10-cent coin.

Dinar: the prime currency of Bahrain, Iraq, Jordan, Kuwait, Libya, Tunis, Yemen and Yugoslavia.

Dioxin: any of the carcinogenic chemicals in petroleum-based herbicides.

Dip: a mild and temporary drop in prices.

Diplomat: one appointed to manage a country's international relations.

Direct Cost: *see* Direct Expense.

Direct Deposit: for regular payments such as salary or pension payments, an option in which the money is deposited into the recipient's account by the payer.

Direct Distribution: a distribution channel in which there is only one level between the manufacturer of a product and the customer (e.g., telemarketing, corporate sales force).

Directed Registered Retirement Savings Plan: *see* Registered Retirement Savings Plan – Administered.

Directed Trust: a trust in which the beneficiary can instruct the trustee how to invest his/her capital.

Directed Verdict: a verdict brought in by a jury at the direction of a judge. In civil cases, a directed verdict can be for either party; in criminal cases, a directed verdict can be only for acquittal.

Direct Expense: a business expense that is attributable to a specific department (e.g., salaries). *See also* Indirect Expense.

Direct Funding: when a company raises money from an investor(s) without using an agent or underwriter.

Direct Hedge: the purchase or sale of options for the purpose of reducing risk in an investment portfolio. *See also* Commercial Hedge, Hedge.

Direct Heir: an unbroken line of ancestry from father to son.

Direct Holding: an individual or corporate interest in an asset that is owned directly rather than indirectly through another company. (e.g., if Company A owns a 50 percent interest in Company B, which owns a 50 percent interest in Company C, Company A has a 50 percent direct holding in Company B and a 25 percent indirect holding in Company C). *See also* Indirect Holding.

Directional Drilling: in the mining and petroleum industries, a recent innovation that enables the operator to drill in different directions off the vertical. *See also* Horizontal Drilling.

Direct Investment: 1. an investment made directly from an issuer without the services of an agent. **2.** the purchase of an investment of size sufficient to enable the investor to control management.

Direct Labour Cost: wages paid to employees who are involved in the actual production of a product (e.g., automobile assembly workers). *See also* Indirect Labour Cost.

Direct Lease: a lease arranged by a leasing company at the time of the original transaction (e.g., a leased car). *See also* Indirect Lease, Leveraged Lease.

Direct Mail: advertising mailed to customers, often with an invitation to reply.

Director: a member of a board of directors. *See also* Board of Directors, Inside Director, Interlocking Director, Outside Director.

Directorate: the office of a director.

Director Liability: a reference to a director's personal liability for the obligations incurred by his/her company.

Directors' and Officers' Liability Insurance: insurance that protects a firm's directors and officers against lawsuits.

Director's Resolution: a formal directive approved by the board of directors (e.g., declaring the payment of a dividend). Also known as Resolution.

Directory: in computers, a list of the files contained in a storage device. *See also* Computer.

Direct Payment: a settlement system using a debit card in which payment is made electronically from the purchaser's account to the merchant's account.

Direct Placement: a transaction wherein an issuer sells a new security to an investor without the use of a broker.

Direct Reduction Mortgage: a mortgage that is retired by making equal payments for the life of the loan. *See also* Mortgage.

Direct-Response Marketing: any of the marketing approaches geared to soliciting a purchase order for goods or services directly from the consumer *See also* Advertorial, Advocacy Advertising, Infomercial, Infotainment, Institutional Advertising, Situmercial.

Direct Sales: sales made to the ultimate user of specific goods or services.

Direct Sales Force: a sales and marketing team that targets the ultimate user of specific goods or services.

Direct Tax: a tax visible to the party paying it, such as a sales tax added at the time of a purchase. A tax levied directly on the ones who bear the burden. *See also* Taxes.

Direct to Home Television (DTH): the delivery of television signals, via satellite, directly to the viewer's home.

Dirham: the prime currency of Morocco, United Arab Emirates.

Dirt Cheap: very low in price.

Dirty Float: a term used to describe the practice of a central bank intervening in the foreign exchange market of its currency while publicly denying it is doing so.

Dirty Price: the price of a bond including the accrued interest that must be paid to the seller. *See also* Price Plus Accrued.

Dirty Stock: a slang term for shares that do not meet the requirements for good delivery. *See also* Good Delivery.

Dirty Thirties: the decade of the 1930s. So termed because of the Great Depression, which began in 1929 and lasted throughout most of the 1930s. *See also* Depression, Great Depression.

Disability: a physical or mental impairment preventing normal activities, often in the context of the ability to work.

Disability Benefit: 1. an option attached to life insurance calling for a moratorium on premium payments if the insured becomes totally and permanently disabled. **2.** the benefit from a disability insurance contract which may be either a lump sum or series of regular payments.

Disability Income Insurance: income replacement insurance that protects an individual from the loss of employment income resulting from the inability to work because of accident or illness. One key variable in disability insurance is whether payments continue until the insured can perform his/her own occupation or any occupation. Another is the time between the disabling event and when benefit payments begin. Also known as Loss of Income Insurance. *See also* Any Occupation, Elimination Period, Same Occupation.

Disability Table

Age	Percent Disabled
20	78.9 percent
30	72.3 percent
40	63.5 percent
50	48.9 percent
60	22.1 percent

The number of people per 1,000 in a given age group that will be disabled for a period of at least 90 days before reaching age 65.

Disability Table: a table that shows the number of people out of 1,000 in a given age group that will be disabled for a period of at least 90 days before reaching age 65.

Disaster Out Clause: *see* Force Majeure.

Disbar: to revoke a lawyer's right to practise law by rescinding the necessary certificate.

Disburse: to pay out or expend.

Disbursement: the paying out of funds; funds paid out; out-of-pocket expenses incurred by a lawyer on behalf of a client.

Discharge: a release from a lender upon complete repayment of an obligation.

Discharge of Bankruptcy: the final stage in a bankruptcy proceeding, after which the bankrupt person is usually absolved of responsibility for the specified debts. *See also* Bankrupt, Bankruptcy, Creditor's Pool.

Discharge of Lien: a legal removal of a lien after the originating obligation has been satisfied. *See also* Lien.

Disclaimer: a statement that repudiates the responsibility to limit legal liability (e.g., "The information herein was gathered from usually reliable sources but its accuracy is not guaranteed"). Also known as Hedge Clause. *See also* Errors and Omissions Excepted.

Disclaimer Clause: a clause required by various jurisdictions to indicate that regulators have not approved of the merits of an offering (in the case of a prospectus) or the significance of the news (in the case of a news release). A typical disclaimer clause is: "The Vancouver Stock Exchange has neither approved nor disapproved the information contained herein."

Disclaimer of Opinion: *see* Qualified Opinion.

Disclosure: the actions of a company whereby it releases all information that might impact a decision to invest in the securities of the company. *See also* Full Disclosure, Public Disclosure, Selective Disclosure, Soft Disclosure, Structured Disclosure, Timely Disclosure.

Disclosure Statement: a document providing information about an estate prepared by the executor or administrator for the probate fees department. *See also* Probate Fee, Will.

Discomfort Index: an economic index created by U.S. economist Arthur M. Okun (1928-) in the 1970s which adds the inflation and unemployment rates. The higher the number, the greater the discomfort. *See also* Okun's Law.

Discontinuance: an end to a court proceeding through the voluntary action of the plaintiff.

Discount: 1. the process of reducing future income to a present value that recognizes the time value of money (e.g., if interest rates are 10 percent, $1.00 due in one year is worth $.909 today because $.909 can be invested at 10 percent, to be worth $1.00 in one year. For the same reason, $1.00 in two years has a present value of $.8264). *See also* Discounted Value, Discount Rate, Discount the News, Present Value, Time Value of Money. **2.** the amount a price is reduced for sale. **3.** *see* At Par. **4.** the way treasury bills are priced at less than face value. *See also* Treasury Bill. **5.** the method used by some lenders of taking the interest payment for a loan in advance.

Discount Bond: a bond that trades below (often substantially below) face value. *See also* At Par, Bond.

Discount Broker: a stockbroker who executes purchases and sales of securities for a low commission rate. This is offset by the provision of fewer services.

Discounted Dividend Model: a mathematical model that estimates the current value of a stock as the present value of future dividends to be paid.

Discounted Value: *see* Present Value.

Discounting: 1. the process by which investors adjust security prices based on expectations. As the likelihood of a positive development increases, the stock price rises to reflect the change and, as a result, when the news is announced, the stock price almost always fully reflects the news. Also known as Discounting the News. **2.** reducing the price to promote a sale. **3.** pricing a security below par so that the price increase to par at maturity provides the return.

Discounting Accounts Receivable: using accounts receivable as security for a short-term loan. Also known as Pledging Accounts Receivable. *See also* Factoring.

Discounting the News: *see* Discounting.

Discount Rate: 1. the interest rate Canadian and U.S. banks pay to the central bank on secured loans. **2.** the rate of interest used in calculating present value. Also known as Capitalization Rate. *See also* Present Value.

Discovery: *see* Examination for Discovery.

Discretionary Account: an investment account that allows an advisor to make changes to the holdings without prior consent.

Discretionary Income: income available for non-essential consumption (e.g., for things other than food, clothing and shelter).

Discretionary Order: an order to buy or sell securities that allows the broker to exercise his/her judgement over timing and price. *See also* Order.

Discretionary Trust: a trust that empowers the trustee(s) to distribute any amount of income or principal. *See also* Trust.

Discretionary Trading: trading, conducted on behalf of a person's account or portfolio, that does not require his/her prior approval.

Disenfranchise: to deprive of a privilege, especially the right to vote.

Dishonour: *see* Bounce.

Disinflation: a period during which inflation continues at lower and lower rates (i.e., a period of declining inflation). *See also* Deflation, Inflation.

Disinherit: to exclude from the right to inherit.

Disinheritance: the act by which a donor dissolves a person's right to inherit a property to which he/she previously had a right.

Disintermediation: 1. the removal of layers or levels of activities between the product or service provider and consumer. **2.** in finance, withdrawal of funds from financial intermediaries such as banks and life insurance companies for investment in higher-yielding investments such as treasury bills or money market mutual funds. *See also* Money Market Mutual Fund, Treasury Bill.

Disinvestment: the divestiture, liquidation or sale of a segment of a firm.

Disk: in computers, a small, circular, magnetic device for the external storage of data. *See also* Computer, Computer Disk, Floppy Disk, Hard Disk, Magnetic Disk.

Disk Drive: a computer device that stores and reads information from a disk. *See also* Cathode-Ray Tube, Computer, Computer Screen, Input/Output Device, Interactive Terminal, Joystick, Keyboard, Keypad, Laser Printer, Line Printer, Monitor, Optical Character Recognition, Peripheral, Printer, Printout, Readout, Remote Access, Terminal.

Disk Operating System (DOS): an early, general term for the software on a personal computer that supports all the other programs and enables them to run. PC-DOS and MS-DOS were specific operating systems common to most personal computers. *See also* Computer, MS-DOS, PC-DOS.

Dismal Science: a reference to economics.

Dismiss: to discharge from employment.

Dismissal for Cause: firing a person from a job for legitimate reason. *See also* Constructive Dismissal, Severance, Severance Pay, Wrongful Dismissal.

Disposable Income: *see* Personal Disposable Income.

Disposition: 1. the sale of an asset for purposes of calculating income tax. *See also* Deemed Disposition. **2.** getting rid of an asset by sale or any other method.

Disseminate Information: the process of spreading news to interested parties. *See also* Inside Information, Timely Disclosure.

Dissenting Opinion: in law, a written judgement by a member of the court that does not agree with the majority view.

Dissident Shareholders: unhappy or dissatisfied shareholders. In practice, a reference to a large number of unhappy shareholders who are organizing to force changes to management.

Dissolve: to disband a company.

Distaff Side: the maternal side of a family (e.g., a female heir is sometimes referred to as a distaff).

Distant Thunder: early warnings of bad news.

Distillate: a liquid, sometimes petroleum-based, condensed through the process of distillation. *See also* Distillation.

Distillation: the process of evaporating a liquid, sometimes petroleum-based, and condensing its vapours in order to separate its components.

Distress: the power of a commercial landlord to seize a tenant's property should the latter's rent be in arrears.

Distress Sale: the sale of a security out of necessity (e.g., to meet a margin call). *See also* Margin Call.

Distribution: 1. a payment to shareholders (e.g., a dividend) **2.** in mutual funds, the payment to unitholders of interest, dividends and net realized capital gains earned during the year. *See also* Mutual Fund. **3.** the payment or allocation of assets from an estate under the guidance of a will and with the approval of the court. *See also* Will.

Distribution Area: the price range in which a security trades for an extended time. In theory, because a large number of shares have traded in the distribution area, investors should be able to liquidate his/her holdings in this price range at a later date.

Distribution Channel: generally, the method used by a manufacturer to get a product to market. Also known as Marketing Channel. *See also* Agent, Direct Distribution, Distributor, Retailer, Strategic Alliance.

Distribution Date: the date upon which a company pays interest or dividends.

Distributor: a seller of goods (normally on a wholesale basis), often under licence (or franchise).

Diurnal: 1. an event that occurs during a 24-hour period or every 24-hours. **2.** an event that occurs during the day (as opposed to during the night).

Dive: a rapid, pronounced decline in price.

Divergence: 1. the movement of a trend away from that which is expected. **2.** the movement of two variables away from each other. *See also* Convergence.

Diversification: 1. in a portfolio, spreading risk by holding many different securities. *See also* Don't Put All Your Eggs in One Basket, Modern Portfolio Theory, Put All Your Eggs in One Basket and Watch

the Basket. **2.** in a company, reducing risk through different products or businesses.

Diversify: to spread activities or investments over several areas in order to reduce risk.

Divest: to sell an investment.

Divestiture: the sale or spinoff or a corporate subsidiary or other asset.

Dividend: 1. the amount of money distributed by a company to preferred or common shareholders. *See also* Cash Dividend, Income, Optional Dividend, Stock Dividend. **2.** the return of an overcharged premium on a participating life insurance policy. *See also* Insurance Dividend. **3.** the amount to be divided by another number.

Dividend Discount Model: a method used to estimate the current value of a stock by forecasting future dividends and discounting the value to the present. If the value is higher than the stock price, the shares are considered undervalued, and vice versa. *See also* Dividend, Present Value.

Dividend Enhanced Convertible Stock (DECS): redeemable preferred shares that automatically convert into a common share at maturity.

Dividend Omission: *see* Passed Dividend.

Dividend Options: choices a life insurance policy holder has regarding dividends, including buying more life insurance, leaving the money on deposit, taking a cash payment or applying it against future premiums.*See also* Life Insurance.

Dividend Payout Ratio: the dividend per share divided by the earnings per share. High growth companies usually reinvest earnings into the business and have low dividend payout ratios.

Dividend Record: the history of dividend payments.

Dividend Reinvestment Plan (DRIP): a plan that allows an investor to use cash dividends in order to acquire additional common shares, often without commissions. *See also* Reinvestment.

Dividend Tax Credit: an income tax calculation that bestows a lower personal tax rate on dividend income. Canadians add 25 percent of qualifying dividend income to the amount of dividends received. The income tax payable on this "grossed up" amount is calculated and 16.67 percent of the actual dividend received is then deducted from the federal portion of the income tax payable.

Divining Rod: a forked instrument, often a tree branch, used to indicate the presence of water or minerals below ground.

Divisor: in arithmetic, the number by which another number is to be divided.

Divorce: 1. the legal dissolution of a marriage. **2.** in some cases, the male person divorced.

Divorce Act: in Canada, a federal act that outlines the law pertaining to separation and divorce.

Divorcee: in some cases, a female person divorced. In current usage, any divorced person.

DJBA: *see* Dow-Jones Bond Average.

DJCA: *see* Dow-Jones Composite Average.

DJIA: *see* Dow-Jones Industrial Average.

DJTA: *see* Dow-Jones Transportation Average.

DJUA: *see* Dow-Jones Utilities Average.

DLL: *see* Dynamic-Link Library.

D-mark: *see* Deutschemark.

DOA: *see* Documents on Acceptance.

Dobra: the prime currency of Sao Tome and Principe.

Docket: the calendar of cases awaiting court action.

Dockworker: a person engaged in the loading and unloading of ships (or related activities).

Doctorate: a degree conferring the status of an academic doctor. A Ph.D. (Doctor of Philosophy).

Doctrine: a body of principles that guides policies, including those of government.

Doctrine of Equivalents: in patent law, the doctrine under which protection is provided to products or pro-cesses that are similar but not identical to the invention.

Document: 1. a paper that formalizes information or an agreement. **2.** a computer file that holds information. *See also* Computer.

Documentary Credit: *see* Letter of Credit.

Documentary Letter of Credit: *see* Letter of Credit.

Documents on Acceptance (DOA): the forms necessary to release goods to the buyer. The DOA is issued only after the buyer has accepted the draft in payment from the seller. *See also* Documents on Payment.

Documents on Payment (DOP): the forms necessary to release goods to the buyer. The DOP is issued only after payment has been made. *See also* Documents on Acceptance.

Dog: a poor or unsuccessful investment.

Dog and Pony Show: a seminar that introduces new issues of securities, financial products and so on.

Dog Bone: *see* Barbell.

Dog-Eat-Dog: ruthlessly competitive, as in "it's a dog-eat-dog market."

Dogfight: a heated battle (e.g., a competitive takeover).

Dog House: where one is when out of favour, as in "management is in the dog house."

Dogma: a principle or belief considered to be absolutely true.

Do-It-Yourself Investor: an investor who makes personal financial decisions without the help of an advisor (e.g., financial planner, broker, agent).

Doldrums: a period of stagnation (e.g., the summer doldrums is a quiet time in the financial markets during the summer).

Dollar: the prime currency of Antigua, Australia, Bahamas, Barbados, Belize, Bermuda, Brunei, Canada, Christmas Island, Cocos (Keeling) Island, Dominica, East Caribbean, Fiji, Grenada, Guam, Guyana, Heard and McDonald Islands, Hong Kong, Jamaica, Johnston Islands, Kiribati, Liberia, Midway Island, Montserrat, Namibia, Nauru Islands, New Zealand, Nieue, Norfolk Islands, Pitcairn Island, Puerto Rico, Samoa (American), Singapore, Solomon Islands, St. Christopher, St. Kitts, St. Lucia, St. Vincent, Taiwan, Tokelau, Trinidad/Tobago, Turks & Caicos, Tuvalu, U.S., Virgin Islands, Zimbabwe.

Dollar Bear: an investor who believes the U.S. dollar is overvalued. *See also* Bear.

Dollar Bond: foreign-issued bonds denominated in U.S. dollars. *See* Bonds.

Dollar Bull: an investor who believes the U.S. dollar is undervalued. *See also* Bull.

Dollar Cost Averaging: the act of accumulating an asset by investing a fixed amount of money at regular intervals. *See also* Averaging, Monthly Investment Plan, Scale In.

Dollar Denominated: U.S. currency-based investments, such as bonds and stocks, that are attractive to foreign investors whenever the U.S. dollar is strong.

Dollarization: a term used to describe the idea that Canada and the U.S. should have the same currency.

Dollar Stock: U.S. stocks traded and settled in dollars.

Dollar Weighted: in a portfolio, calculating the respective proportion of each asset after converting all values into dollars.

Dollar Weighted Rate of Return: the rate of return on a portfolio measuring the effect of cash flow for a specific period.

Domestic Violence: the act of one spouse intimidating the other through threat or physical violence.

Domicile: where one resides. Domicile is determined by, among other things, having a permanent residence, being in residence for at least 183 days (may vary according to the jurisdiction), having a driver's licence and being registered to vote. In Canada, for purposes of marriage, divorce, payment of taxes and both testate and intestate succession, domicile is the province of residence at the time. *See also* Intestate, Taxes, Testate, Will.

Dominant Estate: in an easement, the party that benefits from the use granted by the servient estate. *See also* Easement, Servient Estate.

Dominion Bond Rating Service (DBRS): an independent company that rates commercial paper from R-1 to R-3, bonds from AAA (highest) to C (lowest) and preferred shares from Pfd-1 to D. *See also* Bond, Bond Rating, Bond Rating Agency, Canadian Bond Rating Service, Moody's Investors Services, Rating, Standard & Poor's Corporation.

Domino Effect: this occurs when one event sets off a chain of other events.

Donatio Mortis Causa: a gift made in anticipation of death from a particular cause and within a particular time. Also known as Deathbed Gift.

Donation: an income tax deductible gift to a registered charity.

Donee: the recipient of a gift or donation.

Dong: the prime currency of Vietnam.

Donor: the giver of a gift or donation.

Do Not Reduce: on a buy minus or stop sell order, an instruction to the broker to not reduce the price when the stock goes ex dividend. *See also* Buy Minus, Ex Dividend, Stop Sell Order.

Don't Fight the Tape: an expression meaning, "Don't invest against the primary trend in the market." *See also* Fight the Tape.

Don't Put All Your Eggs in One Basket: an investment adage advising diversification. *See also* Diversification, Put All Your Eggs in One Basket and Watch the Basket.

DOP: *see* Documents on Payment.

Dormant Account: an account with a financial institution in which a transaction has not taken place in the past year. Also known as Dead Account. *See also* Active Account.

DOS: *see* Disk Operating System.

Dossier: papers that provide information about a person or topic.

Dot.Com Stock: *see* Internet Stock.

Double: to increase by a factor of two. A 100 percent return.

Double Auction System: *see* Auction Market.

Double Blind: a testing procedure in which neither the administrators nor the subjects know who is receiving the experimental treatment until the study is finished.

Double Bottom: a price that falls to approximately the same low point twice in a relatively short period of time. A graphic depiction of a double bottom looks like the letter "W." *See also* Triple Bottom.

Double-Dealing: deceitfulness, especially in business practices.

Double Digit: numbers between 10 and 99 (e.g., Double Digit Inflation is inflation between 10 percent and 99 percent; Double Digit Growth is growth between 10 percent and 99 percent).

Double Digit Inflation: inflation rates exceeding 10 percent.

Double Dipping: a situation in which a person is drawing two or more benefits or incomes from the government (e.g., a person who is a paid consultant to a government from which a pension is also received).

Double Eagle: a U.S. gold coin with a $20 face value.

Double Entry Bookkeeping: a form of accounting wherein a change in one entry is offset by an equal change in one or more other entries.

Double Indemnity: a type of insurance that pays double if loss results from certain specific causes (e.g., accidental death). *See also* Accidental Death Benefit.

Double Jeopardy: a principle of common law that a person cannot be tried twice for the same crime.

Doublespeak: deliberately ambiguous language.

Double Standard: a situation in which it is more difficult for one group of people (e.g., minorities or women) to attain a promotion or higher level of income than another group (e.g., white males).

Double Taxation: a situation in which the same earnings are taxed twice (e.g., corporate earnings are taxed and dividends are taxed when the tax-paid earnings are paid to shareholders). *See also* Conduit Theory.

Double Top: a price that reaches its high point twice in a relatively short period of time. A graphic depiction of a double top looks like the letter "M." *See also* Triple Top.

Double Witching Hour: this occurs when stock index options and futures expire on the same day (e.g., the last hour of trading on the third Friday of January, February, April, May, July, August, October and November). *See also* Option, Option Cycle, Triple Witching Hour, Witching Hour.

Dow, Charles H. (1851-1902): along with Edward D. Jones, the founder of Dow Jones & Company in 1882. Began publishing the *Wall Street Journal* in 1889. Also initiated the calculation and publication of the Dow-Jones Averages. *See also* Dow-Jones Composite Average, Dow-Jones Industrial Average, Dow-Jones Transportation Average, Dow-Jones Utilities Average, Dow Theory.

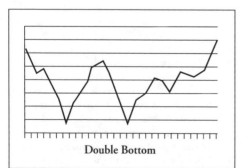

Double Bottom

Dow Dogs: *see* Dow Ten.

Dower: the rights of a wife or widow with regard to freehold property owned by her husband. *See also* Endowment.

Dow Five: any one of a number of formula plans based on an investment in 5 of the 30 stocks making up the Dow-Jones Industrial Average and on rebalancing the portfolio at the start of every calendar year. A Dow Five based on the 5 lowest priced stocks is also known as the Flying Five. Any of these formula plans is also known as the Rule of Five. *See also* Dow-Jones Industrial Average, Dow Ten, Formula Plan, Rebalancing.

Dow-Jones Average

The Dow-Jones Average was created by Charles H. Dow as the first regularly published stock market index in the U.S. It was first calculated as a 12-stock average on May 26, 1896, was increased to 16 stocks in 1916 and then was increased again to its current 30 stocks on October 1, 1928.

Because it was created during a period of manual calculation, the formula had to be simple. The prices of the stocks were totalled and divided by 30. Because of this the Dow-Jones Average is a price-weighted index. To adjust for stock splits and stock dividends (which lowered stock prices artificially), the divisor was reduced.

As an average of only 30 stocks, the Dow is also a "blue-chip" index that reflects the larger, higher quality stocks on the New York Stock Exchange. As of September 1999, the components of the Dow-Jones Average were: Allied Signal Inc., Aluminum Company of America, American Express Company, AT&T Corp, Boeing Co., Caterpillar Inc., Chevron Corp., Citigroup, Inc., Coca-Cola Company, The Walt Disney Co., Du Pont (E.I.) De Nemours, Eastman Kodak Co., Exxon Corp., General Electric Co., General Motors Corp., Goodyear Tire & Rubber Co., Hewlett-Packard Co., International Business Machines Corp., International Paper Co., Johnson & Johnson, McDonald's Corporation, Merck & Co., Inc., Minnesota Mining & Manufacturing Co., J.P. Morgan & Company, Philip Morris Companies Inc., Procter & Gamble Co., Sears, Roebuck and Co., Union Carbide Corp., United Technologies Corp, Wal-Mart Stores Inc.

Because of its long, continuous record on the New York Stock Exchange, the Dow-Jones Average remains a popular market index despite some of its statistical shortcomings. To this day, when investors ask "How's the market?" they mean "What's the Dow-Jones Average doing?"

Dow Jones: almost always a reference to the Dow-Jones Industrial Average but possibly a reference to Dow Jones & Company, Inc. or any of the financial products or services bearing its name. Also known as The Dow. *See also* Dow, Charles, H., Dow Jones & Company, Inc., Dow-Jones Bond Average, Dow-Jones Commodity Futures Index, Dow-Jones Composite Average, Dow-Jones Industrial Average, Dow-Jones Transportation Average, Dow-Jones Utilities Average.

Dow Jones & Company, Inc.: a business and financial news publisher. Its best-known publications are the *Dow-Jones Average* and the *Wall Street Journal.* Dow Jones co-owns CNBC television operations in Asia and Europe. Web site: www.dowjones.com *See also* Bloomberg L.P., Reuters Holdings Plc.

Dow-Jones Bond Average (DJBA): an index of six bond groups that indicates trends in the bond market.

Dow-Jones Commodity Futures Index: an index of 12 commodities that indicates trends in the commodity markets.

Dow-Jones Composite Average (DJCA): an average of the 30 Dow-Jones Industrial stocks, the 20 Dow-Jones Transportation stocks and the 15 Dow-Jones Utilities stocks. *See also* Dow, Charles, H., Dow-Jones Industrial Average, Dow-Jones Transportation Average, Dow-Jones Utilities Average, Dow Theory.

Dow-Jones Industrial Average (DJIA): a price-weighted average of 30 blue-chip stocks listed on the New York Stock Exchange. First published on May 26, 1896, and published continuously in its current form since October 1, 1928. *See also* Dow, Charles, H., Dow-Jones Composite Average, Dow-Jones Transportation Average, Dow-Jones Utilities Average, Dow Theory.

Dow-Jones Transportation Average (DJTA): a price-weighted average of 20 transportation company shares listed on the New York Stock Exchange. Began as the Dow-Jones Railroad Average. *See also* Dow, Charles, H., Dow-Jones Composite Average, Dow-Jones Industrial Average, Dow-Jones Utilities Average, Dow Theory.

Dow-Jones Utilities Average (DJUA): a price-weighted average of 15 utility companies listed on the New York Stock Exchange. First published on January 2, 1929. *See also* Dow, Charles, H., Dow-Jones Composite Average, Dow-Jones Industrial Average, Dow-Jones Transportation Average, Dow Theory.

Down and Out: lacking financial resources.

Downdraft: a sudden decline in prices. *See also* Updraft.

Downgrading: 1. the process of selling a higher quality security to buy a lower quality security. *See also*

Upgrading. **2.** when an investment professional reduces an earnings estimate or lowers a recommendation for a company. *See also* Upgrading.

Download: the process of moving data files to one's own computer from a remote computer. *See also* Computer, Upload.

Downpayment: a partial payment made at the time of purchase. A downpayment is usually refundable if the purchase does not proceed. *See also* Earnest Money.

Downside: the possible amount by which a market or stock could fall in value. *See also* Upside.

Downside Risk: an estimate of how far a market or security might decline in price under adverse conditions. *See also* Upside Potential.

Downsize: when a company reduces its size, particularly its number of employees.

Downsloping Yield Curve: *see* Negative Yield Curve.

Downstream: 1. in the oil and gas industry, the functions of refining and marketing. *See also* Refining and Marketing, Upstream. **2.** in general, a point in the manufacture or distribution of a product or service that is close to the ultimate consumer of the product or service.

Downstream Merger: the merger of a parent company with a subsidiary.

Downtick: *see* Minus Tick.

Downtick Volume: the number of shares traded on downticks. *See also* Downtick, Tick Index, Uptick, Uptick Volume.

Downtime: a period during which a facility (e.g., a factory) is not operating.

Down Trend: a price trend in which successive peaks are lower than preceding peaks and successive troughs are lower than preceding troughs. *See also* Up Trend.

Downturn: this occurs when a trend ceases to rise and begins to fall.

Down Under Bond: an Australian or New Zealand Eurobond not registered in the U.S.

Dowry: money or property brought by, or given on behalf of, a bride to the groom.

Dow Ten: any one of a number of formula plans based on an investment in 10 of the 30 stocks making up the Dow-Jones Industrial Average and on rebalancing the portfolio at the start of every calendar year. A Dow Ten based on the 10 highest yielding stocks is also known as the Dow Dogs. Any of these formula plans is also known as the Rule of Ten. *See also* Dow Five, Dow-Jones Industrial Average, Formula Plan, Rebalancing.

Dow Theory: 1. a belief that a sustained stock market trend is indicated only if both the Dow-Jones Industrial and Transportation Averages are in the same trend. **2.** a variation states the Dow-Jones Utilities Average must join the Industrial and Transportation Averages to support a long-term trend. **3.** a third form of the Dow Theory states that a change in trend is indicated when the Dow-Jones Industrial and Transportation averages both break through previous highs or lows. *See also* Dow, Charles, H., Dow-Jones Composite, Dow-Jones Industrial, Dow-Jones Transportation, Dow-Jones Utilities.

DPSP: *see* Deferred Profit Sharing Plan.

Drachma: the prime currency of Greece.

Draft: a document to transfer money, as in a bank draft. *See also* Bill of Exchange.

Dragon Bond: an Asian bond whose denomination is in U.S. dollars. Also known as Dragons. *See also* Bond.

Dragons: *see* Dragon Bond.

Drain: to deplete gradually, as in "the underperforming security drained the portfolio."

Dram: 1. the prime currency of Armenia. **2.** a unit of weight equal to 1.772 grams.

Drawback: the reimbursement of import duties paid if the item is subsequently exported. *See also* Duty.

Dread Disease Rider: an addition to a life insurance contract that pays a fixed amount or a fixed percentage of the death benefit if the insured suffers a "dread disease" (e.g., a major organ transplant, cancer, a stroke). *See also* Critical Illness Insurance, Rider.

Dress Up: 1. to make an investment more attractive or seem more attractive in preparation for sale. **2.** *see* Window Dressing.

Drift: to move aimlessly, as in "stock prices are drifting."

Drill Core: the sample recovered from subsurface rock through the process of drilling. Analysis of the core provides important information for resource exploration.

DRIP: *see* Dividend Reinvestment Plan.

Driver: in computers, a program to run other devices (e.g., printers, mice or joysticks). *See also* Computer.

Drop: to fall, descend, become less, as in "stock prices are dropping."

Drop-Dead Day: the day of a significant deadline (e.g., when government debt reaches its legal limit).

Drop Dead Money: money set aside for extreme emergencies. *See also* Fun Money, Nest Egg.

Drop Lock: 1. the right to fix the yield on a floating rate security if the interest rate falls to a prescribed level. **2.** a floating rate security that offers the right to fix the yield if the interest rate falls to a prescribed level. *See also* Floating Rate.

Dry Goods: in retailing, textiles and clothing.

Dry Hole: an oil or gas well that is not economic.

DSE All-Share Price Index: a market capitalization weighted stock index for the Dhaka Stock Exchange.

DTH: *see* Direct to Home Television.

Dual Employed, No Kids (DENKS): *see* Dual Income, No Kids.

Dual Employed, With Kids (DEWKS): a family in which both spouses work and there are children. Marketing of long-term investment and insurance products are directed toward DEWKS.

Dual Income, No Kids (DINKS): a family in which both spouses work and do not need to support children. DINKS are important in the economy because they have high disposable incomes. Also known as Dual Employed, No Kids (DENKS).

Dual Listed Stock: a stock that is listed on more than one stock exchange.

Dual Listing: listing a stock on more than one stock exchange.

Dual-Mode Handset: a telephone handset that supports both analog and digital technology. *See also* Analog, Digital.

Dual Purpose Fund: *see* Dual Purpose Mutual Fund.

Dual Purpose Mutual Fund: a mutual fund, trust or other investment structure with two classes of shareholders. One class of shares (income shares) receive all the interest, dividends and other income from the portfolio of investments. The other class of shares (capital shares) receive all the capital gains. *See also* Capital Share, Income Share, Mutual Fund – Other.

Ducat: any of various gold or silver coins, formerly used in most European countries.

Due: payable immediately.

Due Bill: in the securities industry, a bill to indicate a further payment is due (e.g., a buyer of a security that is ex dividend but before the dividend is paid will provide a due bill stating the dividend payment belongs to the seller).

Due Date: the date on which interest and/or principal is payable.

Due Diligence: 1. to analyze an investment in detail prior to an underwriting. **2.** a formal process required in certain instances (e.g., insolvency).

Due-on-Sale Clause: a clause in a mortgage that specifies the loan is repayable on the day the property securing the mortgage is sold, transferred or otherwise encumbered. A due-on-sale clause is found in a non-assumable mortgage. *See also* Mortgage, Non-Assumable Mortgage.

Due Process: an established course for judicial proceedings.

Duff & Phelps Credit Rating Co.: a credit rating service headquartered in Chicago, Illinois, that rates

the ability of insurance companies to pay future claims.

Dumbbell: *see* Barbell.

Dumbbell Strategy: *see* Butterfly Spread.

Dummy Director: a corporate director who acts and votes according to the wishes of a nonboard member. *See also* Board of Directors.

Dummy Shareholder: a person holding shares in his/her name when the stock is really owned by someone else. *See also* Shareholder.

Dump: 1. in financial markets, to sell a large number of shares at almost any price. **2.** in computers, to print out or remove data from memory. *See also* Computer.

Dumping: 1. indiscriminate selling of shares without regard for price. **2.** in international trade, the action of one country selling products into another country at a very low price.

Dun: to aggressively seek repayment from a debtor.

Dun & Bradstreet Corporation (D&B): a financial service that provides credit information on companies based on information from the company and its creditors. D&B is the parent company of Moody's Investors Service. *See also* Moody's Investors Service.

Dunning Letter: a letter from a creditor requesting payment of an overdue amount.

Duopoly: a circumstance in which there are only two suppliers of a product or service or in which two suppliers dominate the market of a product or service. *See also* Monopoly, Monopsony, Natural Monopoly, Oligopoly, Oligopsony.

Duplex: a residential housing unit divided into or built as two separate living units. *See also* Multi-Family Residential Housing, Single Family Residence, Triplex.

Durable Power of Attorney: a power of attorney that stays in effect even if the person who issues it becomes incompetent. In most jurisdictions, a power of attorney ceases to be in effect if the principal becomes incompetent. *See also* Incompetent, Power of Attorney.

Duration: a measure of term to maturity taking into account reinvestment of interest payments. Duration is shorter than term to maturity for all bonds except zero coupon bonds when duration equals term to maturity. The greater the duration, the more a bond price will fluctuate for a given change in yield. *See also* Bond.

Dust Bowl: a reference to the drought conditions affecting the central U.S. during the early 1930s. *See also* Dirty Thirties.

Dutch Auction: 1. in securities, a sale in which a number of independent bidders enter secret bids. All bidders above the minimum price set by the seller buy at that price. **2.** a sale where the seller reduces the price regularly until the item(s) is sold. *See also* Auction, English Auction.

Duty: *see* Tariff.

DVD: 1. *see* Digital Versatile Disc. **2.** *see* Digital Video Disc.

DVD–ROM: *see* Digital Versatile Disc – Read Only Memory.

Dwelling House: in law, one's residence.

Dyke: *see* Dike.

Dynamic-Link Library (DLL): a file that contains a routine that is only loaded when needed by a program. The same dynamic-link library can be used with other programs.

E

e-: a symbol that, when used as a prefix, describes a computerized or electronic service provided through the Internet. For example, e-mail is electronic mail through the Internet; e-forms are forms (such as expense accounts) handled electronically. *See also* Electronic Commerce, Internet.

EAFE Index: a widely followed stock price index for Europe, Australasia and the Far East calculated by Morgan Stanley.

E&OE: *see* Errors and Omissions Excepted.

Early Retirement: taking a pension before standard retirement age. Often an option offered by employers to encourage employees to voluntarily terminate employment.

Early Settlement: the settling of a security trade before it is due.

Early Stage Financing: financing provided to a business prior to commercial operations or production. *See also* Stage of Development Financing.

Early Withdrawal Penalty: a penalty that is assessed if a fixed term investment is cashed in before maturity (e.g., a two-year term deposit cashed after one year).

Earmark: to set aside for a certain purpose, as in "money earmarked for a new car."

Earned Income: *see* Registered Retirement Savings Plan – Earned Income.

Earned Surplus: *see* Retained Earnings.

Earnest Money: money put up in a business transaction to signify a commitment. Earnest money is usually forfeited if the purchase does not proceed. *See also* Downpayment.

Earning Power: an estimate of the earnings of a company under normal conditions.

Earnings: revenue less all expenses, including income taxes.

Earnings Before Income Taxes (EBIT): revenues less all expenses except income taxes.

Earnings Before Interest, Taxes, Depreciation and Amortization (EBITDA): a financial calculation of net earnings plus interest expense, income taxes, depreciation and amortization.

Earnings Estimate: a forecast of a company's future net income.

Earnings Momentum: a pattern of accelerating growth in earnings. Earnings momentum is one of the attributes favoured by momentum investors. *See also* Momentum, Momentum Investor.

Earnings per Share: net income after taxes and preferred dividends divided by the number of outstanding common shares.

Earnings Quality: the extent to which a company's earnings accurately reflect the facts. High-quality earnings result from conservative accounting practices.

Earnings Report: *see* Profit and Loss Statement.

Earnings Statement: *see* Profit and Loss Statement.

Earnings Surprise: reported earnings that are higher or lower than the concensus estimate. *See also* Concensus Estimate.

Earnings Yield: a company's earnings per share divided by share price. The inverse of the price/earnings ratio.

EASDAQ: *see* European Association of Securities Dealers Automated Quotation.

EASDAQ Index: a market capitalization weighted index of all companies traded on the EASDAQ.

Easement: a right to use something that is not one's own (e.g., a path across a neighbour's property). *See also* Dominant Estate, Public Easement, Servient Estate, Trespass.

Easier: a mild drop in price, as in "stocks were easier."

Easy Monetary Conditions: this occurs when money supply is increasing, short-term interest rates are falling and credit is readily available.

Easy Money: 1. the initial profits realized in an investment. **2.** the conditions constituted by a rising money supply and falling short-term interest rates.

Eating Stock: being forced to purchase shares (e.g., an underwriter that is unable to sell an issue may have to "eat stock for his/her own account").

Eat Well, Sleep Well: an investment adage to explain the relationship between risk and reward in the stock market says, "How you invest in the stock market depends on whether you want to eat well or sleep well." In other words, if you invest very safely (so you can sleep well), you will realize a lower rate of return (so you cannot eat well), and vice versa. Also known as Sleep Well, Eat Well.

EBA: *see* Euro Banking Association.

EBF: *see* European Banking Federation.

EBIT: *see* Earnings Before Income Taxes.

EBITDA: *see* Earnings Before Interest, Taxes, Depreciation and Amortization.

EBS: *see* Electronic Bourse System.

e-business: *see* Electronic Commerce.

EC: *see* European Community.

e-cash: *see* Electronic Cash.

ECB: *see* European Central Bank.

Echo Generation: the generation consisting of the children of the baby boomers. *See also* Baby Boomer, Generation X, Generation Y, Sandwich Generation.

ECN: *see* Electronic Communication Network.

E-Commerce: *see* Electronic Commerce.

Econometric Model: a mathematical formula that, for predictive purposes, replicates an economy.

Econometrics: the application of mathematics, especially statistics, to economic data.

Economic: relating to the production, development and management of resources.

Economic and Monetary Union (EMU): a three-stage integration of Europe. Stage One began July 1, 1990, and involved closer coordination of economic and monetary policies. Stage Two began on January 1, 1994, and started the process of economic conversion. Stage Three began on January 1, 1999, and involved establishing a European Central Bank and single currency for its 11 founding members: Austria, Belgium, Finland, France, Germany, Ireland, Italy, Luxembourg, the Netherlands, Portugal and Spain.

Economic Calendar: a schedule that indicates the dates upon which important economic data will be released.

Economic Cycle: the ups and downs in the economy. A complete economic cycle includes four stages: expansion (a period of growth), peak (a topping out), contraction (a decline in activity) and trough (a bottoming out). Also known as Business Cycle. *See also* Contraction, Cyclical, Expansion, Peak, Trough.

Economic Growth: generally, the percentage growth in gross national product or gross domestic product.

Economic Indicators: various economic series that, relative to the economy, change in a consistent manner.

Economic Life: the useful life of an asset.

Economic Model: a conceptual or mathematical rendition of a business or industry. Often, a computer model that emulates a real-life situation.

Economic Refugee: a person who seeks refugee status in a new country when in reality, he/she is actually attempting to improve his/her economic potential.

Economics: the study of the production, distribution and consumption of goods and services. Economics is often described as the system that efficiently allocates scarce resources. *See also* Economic Cycle, Economic Growth, Economic Indicators, Economic Model, Economic Theory.

Economic Theory: a conceptual explanation of the functioning of the economy (e.g., Keynesian Economic Theory maintains that government plays a key role in economic growth).

Economies of Scale: an economic theory that as the volume of production rises, the cost per unit will fall. Economies of scale arise because large production plants are often more efficient than small production plants, and the ability to order large volumes of materials usually lowers the cost per unit.

Economic Theory and Practice

Economics is the science (some call it art) of allocating scarce resources. In a circumstance where there is not enough of everything to satisfy everyone, there must be a system that decides who gets what and at what price.

Most of the "free world" practices a form of free market economics in which the allocation of resources is determined by consumers spending money for goods and services. If people choose not to buy Kaiser automobiles, not enough are sold to enable the manufacturer to continue in business. But if consumers decide they like Ford Mustangs, the manufacturer will be profitable. The company will then have the capital to build more cars that the people will buy, and so on. This system is sometimes compared with Darwin's theory of the survival of the fittest.

For this reason, competition is a key ingredient for an economic system. The consumer must be able to choose between a Kaiser and a Mustang. Entrepreneurs must have the ability to introduce new ideas and products to the public. The pricing of goods and services must be competitive. This ensures profits will be kept at a reasonable level.

In a centrally planned economy such as the former Soviet Union, government officials or bureaucrats make resource allocation decisions. Since people make decisions for selfish or political reasons, this form of economics does not reward efficiency and will fail in time.

Under socialism, the government believes some income should be taxed from people who work hard, are productive and successful and given to those who are less productive or are in need. This can function to a point but if taxation becomes too high and the advantage for hard work and success becomes too small, the system breaks down. Economists have theorized this occurs when taxes take more than half a person's income.

A literal translation of economics is "management of the household." In a futuristic world where robots cater to our every whim, there will be no scarcity of resources and, as a result, no need for economics. Until then, economics will remain vital to our lives.

Economize: to reduce spending or to increase efficiency.

Economy: 1. the system of economic activity, as in "the Canadian economy." **2.** the efficient use of resources.

ECSC: *see* European Coal and Steel Community.

EC Treaty: *see* Treaty of Brussels.

ECU: *see* European Currency Unit.

ECU Banking Association: *see* Euro Banking Association.

ECU-Index: *see* Indice Nacional de Precios y Cotizaciones del Mercado Ecuatoriano.

ECU LIBOR: *see* European Currency Unit LIBOR.

EDCC: *see* Export Development Credit Corporation.

Edict: an order issued by an authority.

EDP: *see* Enterprise Development Program.

.edu: an appendage to an e-mail or Internet address that identifies an educational location. *See also* .com, .gov, Internet, .mil, .net, .org.

Educational Assistance Payments: payments taken from a registered education savings plan and put toward a beneficiary's post-secondary education.

Educational Leave Option: *see* Registered Retirement Savings Plan – Educational Leave Option.

Education Savings Plan: *see* Registered Education Savings Plan.

Edutainment: the combining of education and entertainment (as in some computer programs).

EEA: *see* European Economic Area.

EEC: *see* European Economic Community.

EFFAS: *see* European Federation of Financial Analysts' Societies.

Effective Control: a controlling interest that is made up of less than 50 percent of a company's shares.

Effective Interest Rate: the annual rate of interest that reflects the effect of compounding. More frequent compounding results in a higher effective interest rate.

Effective Life: the time during which a piece of machinery or equipment is functional (e.g., a personal computer might continue to be operational for many years but its effective life is probably two years). Also known as Useful Life. *See also* Expected Life.

Effective Tax Rate: total income taxes payable divided by total taxable income. *See also* Average Tax Rate, Income Tax, Negative Income Tax, Progressive Income Tax, T4, Tax, Taxable Income, Tax Bracket, Tax Return.

Effective Yield: 1. the yield on a bond assuming interest received is invested and earns interest. Also known as Realized Compound Yield. **2.** the yield on a bond or debenture based on the purchase price. *See also* Yield to Maturity.

Efficient Frontier: in portfolio management, an arc described by various combinations of assets held. An efficient portfolio will lie on the efficient frontier at the point of highest return with the lowest risk. *See also* Efficient Portfolio, Modern Portfolio, Modern Portfolio Theory, Portfolio Optimization.

Efficient Market Hypothesis: a theory that all information that is known or knowable is reflected in financial market prices. To earn an above-average level of profit in an efficient market, it is necessary to forecast something that is not known or knowable. The weak form of the hypothesis is that the past cannot be used to predict the future. The semi-strong form is that all public information is reflected in prices. The strong form is that all information (public or not) is reflected in prices. This latter form suggests prices cannot be predicted at all.

Efficient Portfolio: a portfolio that either provides the maximum expected return for the level of risk or the minimum level of risk for an expected return. Also known as Optimum Portfolio. *See also* Efficient Frontier, Modern Portfolio, Modern Portfolio Theory, Portfolio Optimization.

e-file: to file income taxes electronically.

EFT: *see* Electronic Funds Transfer.

EFTA: *see* European Free Trade Association.

e.g.: for example. From the Latin *exempli gratia*.

Egalitarian: to be in favour of universal political, economic and social equality.

Egress: 1. the right of a lessee to leave the premises of a leasehold. Usually, "ingress and egress," which is the right of a lessee to enter and leave a leasehold property. **2.** generally, a way out.

Egyptian Stock Exchange: *see* Cairo Stock Exchange.

EI: *see* Employment Insurance.

Eight Dragons of Asia: *see* Eight Tigers of Asia.

Eight Tigers of Asia: a group of Asian nations made up of the Four Tigers (Hong Kong, Republic of Korea [South Korea], Singapore and Taiwan) and the four Mini Tigers of Asia (Indonesia, Malaysia, Philippines and Thailand). Also known as Eight Dragons of Asia, Tigers of Asia. *See also* Big Tiger of Asia, Four Tigers of Asia, Mini Tigers of Asia.

Eighty/Twenty Rule: *see* Pareto's Law.

Either-Or Order: *see* Alternative Order.

Either Way: *see* Two-Sided Market.

Elasticity of Demand: a measure of how much demand changes in relation to price. Demand is very elastic if small price changes result in large demand changes. *See also* Inelasticity of Demand, Price Conscious.

Elasticity of Supply: a measure of how much supply changes in relation to price. Supply is very elastic if small price changes produce large supply changes. *See also* Inelasticity of Supply.

Electorate: a group of voters, often in one region or area.

Electronic Bourse System (EBS): the system used for trading Swiss shares in Switzerland.

Electronic Business (e-business): *see* Electronic Commerce.

Electronic Cash: 1. a token-based currency that translates into real currency units guaranteed by a bank. **2.** a bank card with a computer chip embedded into it, allowing the user to store cash electronically and use the card to make everyday payments.

Electronic Commerce (e-commerce): business activity based on computers and electronic records instead of paper. E-commerce includes telephone, fax, ABM, credit card, debit card, television shopping and the Internet.

Electronic Communication Network (ECN): a trading agreement that allows direct trading among several institutional investors on a less costly basis than trading on an organized stock exchange.

Electronic Funds Transfer (EFT): the electronic movement of money. An instantaneous money transfer means that no interest is lost while waiting for paperwork to be done, for mail or for courier delivery. *See also* Accelerated Funds Transfer.

Electronic Mail (E-Mail): a message sent via the Internet or other electronic network. *See also* Free Mail, Internet, Snail Mail.

Electronic Mall (E-Mall): an Internet site that features a number of merchants offering goods and services for sale. *See also* Internet.

Electronic Market: a stock market in which orders are entered into a computer that concludes transactions by matching orders to buy securities at a certain price with orders to sell securities at the same price. *See also* Auction Market, Quote Driven Market.

Electrophotograhy: *see* Xerography.

Elephant: a large, institutional investor. The term implies that elephants tend to make the same investment decisions at the same time and drive security prices up and down.

Eligible Investments: *see* Registered Retirement Savings Plan – Eligible Investments.

Elimination Period: for disability income insurance, the period after disability and before benefit payments begin. Also known as Qualification Period, Waiting Period. *See also* Disability Income Insurance.

ELKS: *see* Equity Linked Debt Securities.

Elliott Wave Theory: Ralph N. Elliott's 1938 theory that long-term cycles in the Dow-Jones Industrial Average consist of either a five-wave bull market

(three up and two down) or a three-wave bear market (two down and one up). *See also* Bear Market, Bull Market, Dow-Jones Industrial Average, Kondratieff Wave, Peak, Presidential Election Cycle, Stock Market Cycle, Trough.

E-Mail: *see* Electronic Mail.

E-Mail Address: an identifier used to send electronic mail to a specific destination. *See also* Electronic Mail, Internet.

E-Mall: *see* Electronic Mall.

Embargo: the prohibition of exports to and/or imports from another country.

Embassy: the official residence of an ambassador or consul in a foreign country.

Embezzlement: the act of stealing money, often through misrepresentation or violation of trust. In Canada, embezzlement is not defined as a specific crime.

Emergency Repair Program (ERP): a federal government program that provides non-repayable contributions to pay for emergency repairs by homeowners in rural and remote areas of Canada.

Emerging Growth Stock: the shares of a young firm that has very good growth prospects.

Emerging Markets: immature markets in developing countries, often following the World Bank definition of a country with less than $8,956 per capita income, including Argentina, Armenia, Bangladesh, Barbados, Bolivia, Botswana, Brazil, Bulgaria, Chile, China, Colombia, Costa Rica, Côte d'Ivoire, Croatia, Cyprus, the Czech Republic, Ecuador, Egypt, Ghana, Greece, Honduras, Hungary, India, Indonesia, Iran, Jamaica, Jordan, Kenya, Korea, Lithuania, Malaysia, Malta, Mauritius, Mexico, Morocco, Namibia, Nepal, Nigeria, Oman, Pakistan, Panama, Peru, the Philippines, Poland, Portugal, Russia, Saudi Arabia, the Slovak Republic, Slovenia, South Africa, Sri Lanka, Swaziland, Taiwan, Thailand, Trinidad & Tobago, Tunisia, Turkey, Uruguay, Venezuela and Zimbabwe. Also known as Less Developed Countries.

Emerging Markets Common Stock Fund: *see* Emerging Markets Equity Fund.

Emerging Markets Equity Fund: one of the 31 Canadian categories developed by the Investment Funds Standards Committee. Mutual funds in this category must have a minimum of 50 percent of the total assets, and 75 percent of the non-cash assets, of the portfolio in equities or equity equivalents of emerging markets countries or derivative-based exposure to such markets. The calculations to determine whether a mutual fund fits this definition are based on median values from fund data over three years, unless otherwise noted. The derivatives are weighted on an extended value basis. Each of the categories may be refined by the fund manager (e.g., a Canadian Large Cap Equity Fund might be described as "growth" or "value" to reflect the manager's style). Also known as Emerging Markets Common Stock Fund. *See also* Emerging Markets, Extended Value, Mutual Fund – Category.

EMI: *see* European Monetary Institute.

Emigrant: one who moves out of his/her own country to settle in another. *See also* Emigrate, Emigration, Immigrant.

Emigrate: to move out of one's own country to settle in another. *See also* Emigrant, Emigration, Immigrate.

Emigration: the act of moving out of one's own country to settle in another. *See also* Emigrant, Emigrate, Immigration.

Eminent Domain: the right of a government to usurp personal property for the common good. *See also* Expropriate.

Emir: a political leader in the Middle East.

Emirate: a region ruled by an emir.

Emissary: an agent sent to represent another person.

Emolument: 1. anything by which a person benefits. **2.** payment for holding an office or job.

Emoticon: in computers, a combination of symbols designed to communicate a message without words (e.g., the happy face sideways: :-)). An emoticon is often used in e-mail messages or on newsgroups as a comment on the writing that precedes it. Also known as ASCII-Art, ASCII-Glyph, Smiley.

Emperor: the male ruler of an empire.

Empirical Evidence: evidence based on observation or experience rather than on theory.

Employee: a person who works for compensation.

Employee Benefit Plan: a program of insurance and other financial benefits usually offered by employers for employees and by associations and other groups. Also known as Benefit Plan, Group Insurance Plan, Group Plan. *See also* Cafeteria Employee Benefit Plan, Contributory Plan, Dental Plan.

Employee Retirement Income Security Act (ERISA): the U.S. laws governing the operation of most private pension and employee benefit plans.

Employee Stock Option: *see* Stock Option – Executive and/or Employee.

Employee Share Ownership Plan (ESOP): a U.S. plan allowing employees to buy their employer company's stock.

Employee Turnover: total number of employees divided by the number of employees who are replaced, usually on an annual basis. Employee turnover is one measure of management/employee relations. Also known as Turnover.

Employment: 1. a person's occupation **2.** the condition of having a job. *See also* Unemployment.

Employment Equity: the concept that there should be no discrimination in the employment process because of colour, race, creed or sex.

Employment Insurance (EI): a government program that provides certain benefits to unemployed persons. Previously, and also known as Unemployment Insurance (UI). *See also* Social Safety Net.

Employment Insurance

Originally established in 1940 as the Unemployment Insurance Act and revised as the Employment Insurance Act effective July 1, 1996, employment insurance (EI) is now an important feature of Canada's social safety net. In the last 20 years or so, EI has almost doubled in size relative to the economy and federal budget. This has come about due to increased benefits and higher overall unemployment rates. Approximately three million Canadians receive a benefit annually.

EI is not a true insurance plan. Like the Canada Pension Plan, EI has been run on a "pay-as-you-go" basis. In other words, employed people make contributions to EI on the understanding that, should they become unemployed, they will receive financial benefits.

However, some important changes have been introduced in recent years. The number of weeks of work needed to qualify for EI depends on the region in which a person resides and the unemployment rate in that area. The higher the rate, the shorter the qualifying period. In addition, an "Intensity Rule" means that those who make extensive use of EI will see benefits reduced in subsequent periods. In addition, the new regulations contain harsher penalties for fraud.

At present, the new EI Act seems to focus less on cash benefits and more on retraining programs.

Emporium: a large variety retail store.

Empress: the female ruler of an empire.

EMS: *see* European Monetary System.

EMU: 1. *see* Economic and Monetary Union. **2.** *see* European Monetary Union.

Emulate: in computers, for a hardware or software system to imitate another hardware or software system (e.g., a printer that can be driven by the same software that drives a popular, branded model). *See also* Computer.

Encipher: to put a message into code. *See also* Encryption.

Encl.: an abbreviation for "enclosure," encl. is placed at the end of a letter or other formal message. It indicates that additional information has been included.

Encode: 1. in computers, to convert into machine language. *See also* Computer. **2.** to translate a non-text file to an ASCII text format for e-mail. *See also* E-mail.

Encroach: to reduce the capital value of a trust by paying out or spending assets. *See also* Trust.

Encroachment: unlawful trespass.

Encryption: to use sophisticated mathematical formulae to encode information so that people cannot read it. Often used to maintain business security on the Internet. *See also* Decryption, Internet.

Encumbered: a property owned by one person but subject to another person's or institution's claim (e.g., a home subject to a mortgage). *See also* Mortgage, Unencumbered.

Encumbrance: a legal claim, lien or liability registered against property.

End Date Bias: the impact that the selected base date has on a rate of return calculation (e.g., stock market returns calculated from January 1, 1991, are higher than those calculated from January 1, 1990, because the stock market was higher on January 1, 1990, than it was on January 1, 1991).

End Game: taken from chess, the final stages of a long-term corporate plan, during which its objective becomes clear to all.

Endorse: to provide a signature authorizing payment or transfer of title (e.g., signing the back of a cheque in order to cash it). *See also* Joint Endorsement, Qualified Endorsement, Restricted Endorsement.

Endorsed Security: a security issued by one party and guaranteed by another.

Endow: to provide with property, income or both.

Endowment: 1. in law, a dower that goes to a woman. *See also* Dower. **2.** the property or assets that provide the initial funding for a society. *See also* Society.

Endowment Insurance: an insurance contract that pays a lump sum benefit on a certain date or on the death of the insured, whichever is sooner.

End Product: the final useable form of a product.

End User: the party that is the intended ultimate user of a product or service.

Energy Fund: *see* Energy Mutual Fund.

Energy Mutual Fund: *see* Specialty/Miscellaneous Fund.

Enfranchise: 1. to bestow a franchise. **2.** to grant an individual the rights of a citizen, especially the right to vote.

English Auction: in securities, a sale in which independent bidders enter secret bids. If the bid is above the minimum price the seller will accept, the independent bidder will buy at the bid price. *See also*

Auction, Dutch Auction.

English Form Will: the most common form of will in the common-law provinces of Canada. *See also* Holographic Will, International Will, Living Will, Notarial Will, Oral Will, Other Wills, Will.

Enjoin: in law, to prohibit or restrict through the use of an injunction.

Entail: 1. a line of heirs of one's body. **2.** to limit inheritance to a specified succession of heirs.

Entente: an agreement among a number of governments to engage in a cooperative action.

Enterprise: a business organization.

Enterprise Development Program (EDP): a federal program that provides loans and loan guarantees to businesses.

Enterprise Value (EV): a widely used mandate for the value of a company as a takeover candidate. EV is market capitalization plus preferred equity plus short- and long-term debt minus cash and equivalents.

Enterprise Value to EBITDA: a valuation method sometimes used as an alternative or in conjunction with the price to earnings ratio, it is Enterprise Value (EV) divided by EBITDA. *See also* Earnings Before Interest, Taxes, Depreciation and Amortization; Enterprise Value; Price/Earnings Ratio.

Enter the Market: to begin to participate in the buying or selling of a security.

Entitlement: a legal right to ownership.

Entitlement Program: a government program that provides benefits to all members of a defined group.

Entrapment: an act that involves the police (or government) drawing a person into committing an offence.

Entrepreneur: generally, a person willing to risk his/her own capital in a start-up or high-risk business venture.

Entrust: to give something into another person's care.

Enumerate: to count and list by name.

Environmentalism: a movement whose concern is the care and protection of the natural environment.

Environmentalist: an advocate for the care and protection of the natural environment.

Envoy: a government representative engaged in a special mission.

EOC: *see* Euroclear Operations Centre.

EONIA: *see* Euro Overnight Index Average.

Equal: having the same value, qualities, effect, status or rights.

Equal Annuity: an annuity in which the amount of the payment is unchanged over time. *See also* Annuity, Decreasing Annuity, Increasing Annuity.

Equal Dollar Weighted: a stock market index calcu-

lated to give all components an equal weighting at
the base period so that a 5 percent change in a high-
priced share has the same effect as a 5 percent change
in a low-priced share.

Equalized Billing: a method of payment in which the
monthly payments are equal even though the actual
monthly charges may vary (e.g., equal monthly electrical utility bills, even though summer use may be
less than winter use).

Equilibrium Price: the price at which supply equals
demand. *See also* Demand, Supply.

Equity: 1. a synonym for common shares. **2.** the
excess of assets over liabilities. **3.** the value of an asset
over debt against the asset. **4.** in a brokerage account,
the market value of securities held long less the market value of securities sold short less any debit balance plus any credit balance. *See also* Account, Buy,
Credit Balance, Debit Balance, Short Sale.

Equity Capital: the money a company raises by selling common and preferred shares. *See also* Common
Share, Preferred Share.

Equity Earnings: the amount, not reported by the
parent company, by which a subsidiary's earnings
exceed dividends paid.

Equity Financing: the raising of money by or for a
company through the sale of preferred or common
shares.

Equity Fund: *see* Equity Mutual Fund.

Equity Funding: a U.S. investment that combines life
insurance and mutual funds.

Equity Funding Corporation: an insurance company which reported the sale of more insurance policies than it had actually sold. For a nine-year period
starting in 1964, the company escaped detection
even though some 40 senior executives were
involved. The hero was Ray Dirks, a securities analyst, who uncovered the scam. Total losses are estimated to have exceeded $2 billion. *See also* Bre-X
Minerals Ltd., Ponzi Scheme, Salad Oil Scandal,
ZZZZ Best.

Equity Investment: an investment in common shares
or in securities whose characteristics are similar to
those of common shares.

Equity Kicker: in the issue of securities, an amount
of common shares or other equities added to make
the transaction more attractive.

Equity Linked: related to common shares, often in
performance or rate of return. *See also* Equity Linked
Guaranteed Investment Certificate, Kicker.

Equity Linked Debt Securities (ELKS): a debt security created by Salomon Brothers Inc., with a value
that is linked to an unrelated common stock value.

Equity Linked Guaranteed Investment Certificate:

a guaranteed investment certificate whose interest
return varies with the returns from a selected stock
market index. *See also* Equity Linked.

Equity Mutual Fund: a mutual fund that invests in a
broadly based portfolio of common stocks. Also
known as Equity Fund. *See also* Mutual Fund –
Other.

Equity of Redemption: *see* Right of Redemption.

Equity Risk Premium: the amount of extra return
from common stocks over a more conservative
investment asset, to compensate for the former's
higher risk.

Equity Security: any security that represents ownership in a company, including preferred shares, common shares and share purchase warrants.

Erg: a unit of work.

Ergo: therefore.

Ergonomics: the science of designing equipment,
including office furniture, in such a way that operator fatigue and discomfort will be reduced.

ERISA: *see* Employee Retirement Income Security
Act.

ERM: *see* Exchange Rate Mechanism.

ERM-2: *see* Exchange Rate Mechanism-2.

ERP: *see* Emergency Repair Program.

Erratum: an error in printed text.

Errors and Omissions Excepted (E&OE): a disclaimer that limits liability in case of error.

Errors and Omissions Insurance: insurance that protects advisors from losses if the advice they give is
incomplete. *See also* Disclaimer.

Escalator Clause: in a contract, a clause that allows
certain costs to be passed along or (under specific
conditions) prices to be raised.

ESCB: *see* European System of Central Banks.

Escheat: conveyance of property to the Crown upon a
person dying without a will and without heirs. In
some cases such property can be reclaimed. *See also*
Will.

Escrow: money and/or property held by a third party
pending fulfillment of obligations.

Escrowed Share: a share of a company that is issued
and outstanding but that may not be sold until certain conditions are met and approval (often from a
regulatory authority) is received.

Escudo: the prime currency of Portugal.

ESOP: *see* Employee Share Ownership Plan.

ESP: *see* Exchange Stock Portfolio.

Establishment: 1. a place of business. **2.** an exclusive
or influential group of society.

Estate: a person's possessions at time of death. *See
also* Estate Creation, Estate Freeze, Estate Liquidity,
Estate Planning, Estate Preservation, Estate Tax,

Will.

Estate Creation: a benefit of life insurance to the family of a person who dies at a young age. *See also* Estate, Estate Freeze, Estate Liquidity, Estate Planning, Estate Preservation, Estate Tax, Will.

Estate Freeze: a sophisticated estate planning device in which an older person with a large estate transfers the growth potential of its assets to younger beneficiaries. *See also* Estate, Estate Creation, Estate Liquidity, Estate Planning, Estate Preservation, Estate Tax, Will.

Estate Liquidity: cash, often from life insurance, that enables an estate to cover necessary expenditures. *See also* Estate, Estate Creation, Estate Freeze, Estate Planning, Estate Preservation, Estate Tax, Will.

Estate Planning: a term applied to activities that involve maximizing wealth, minimizing taxes at death and preparation of wills. *See also* Estate, Estate Creation, Estate Freeze, Estate Liquidity, Estate Preservation, Estate Tax, Will.

Estate Preservation: a basic reason for life insurance, which is to pay taxes triggered by death. *See also* Estate, Estate Creation, Estate Freeze, Estate Liquidity, Estate Planning, Estate Tax, Will.

Estate Tax: a tax applied to estate assets before they are transferred to heirs. Also known as Succession Duty or Succession Tax. *See also* Estate, Estate Creation, Estate Freeze, Estate Liquidity, Estate Planning, Estate Preservation, Will.

Estimate: 1. to calculate or forecast an approximate amount. An estimate may form a part of a forecast or projection. **2.** an approximation of the cost of a service (e.g., an estimate on the cost of fixing a dented fender on a car).

Estonian Stock Exchange: *see* Tallinn Stock Exchange.

Et Al.: and others.

Etc.: et cetera (Latin for "and the rest," usually translated as "and so on").

Ethernet: in computers, a common type of local area network standard that defines the medium through which computers are connected to each other. *See also* Computer.

Ethical Investing: investing in companies meeting certain ethical criteria (e.g., only in companies that are equal opportunity employers). Compared with socially responsible investing, ethical investing is less likely to sacrifice rate of return for social benefit. *See also* Socially Responsible Investing.

Ethical Mutual Fund: a mutual fund investing in companies meeting certain ethical criteria (e.g., investing only in equal opportunity employers). Compared with a socially responsible mutual fund, an ethical mutual fund is less likely to sacrifice rate of return for social benefit. *See also* Mutual Fund –

Other, Socially Responsible Mutual Fund.

Et Non: and not.

EU: *see* European Union.

EUR: the ISO 4217 currency code for the Euro.

Euratom: *see* European Atomic Energy Community.

EURIBOR: the inter-bank offered rate for the Euro in the Euro area. *See also* LIBOR.

Euro: the single currency for members of the European Common Market. Initially, 11 countries adopted the Euro: Austria, Belgium, Finland, France, Germany, Ireland, Italy, Luxembourg, Netherlands, Portugal and Spain. The Euro will be not be used for retail transactions. Euro notes and coins will be introduced on January 1, 2002, and the national currencies to be withdrawn by July 1, 2002. The basic unit will be the Euro and it will be made up of 100 cents. *See also* EUR.

Euro Area: *see* Euroland.

Euro Banking Association (EBA): formerly known as the ECU Banking Association, the EBA operates the Euro Clearing System to settle transactions in the Euro on a daily basis. The EBA is overseen by the European Monetary Institute. The EBA is headquartered in Paris, where it is known as Association Bancaire pour l'Euro (ABE).

Eurobill of Exchange: a bill of exchange in a foreign currency but payable outside the country of origin. *See also* Bill of Exchange.

Eurobond: a bond issued internationally in which interest and principal are due in the currency specified by the issuer. The general form is Euro (e.g., a Eurodollar bond pays interest and principal in Eurodollars. A Euro Canadian bond pays in Canadian dollars held in European banks). *See also* Bond.

Euroclear System: the clearing and settlement system for Eurobonds. It is owned by around 2,000 users and operated by Morgan Guaranty Trust Company of New York through the Euroclear Operations Centre (EOC). Also known as Euroclear Operations Centre.

Euroclear Operations Centre: *see* Euroclear System.

Eurocurrency: funds deposited in a bank (usually European) in a currency different from the domestic currency of the bank.

Eurodollar: U.S. currency that is held in European banks and is used to settle international transactions.

Eurodollar Bond: a bond issued internationally in which interest and principal are due in Eurodollars. *See also* Bond, Euro Non-Dollar Bond.

Eurodollar Certificate of Deposit: a certificate of deposit issued by a bank outside the U.S., payable in U.S. dollars. *See also* Certificate of Deposit.

Eurodollar Security: any foreign security denominated in U.S. dollars, with the dollars deposited in

European banks.

Euro Economy: the economy represented by the 11 European nations using the EURO as its currency. This group represents 19.4 percent of world economic output (the U.S. represents 19.6 percent and Japan represents 7.7 percent). It will be the world's leading trader, with 18.6 percent of all trade (the U.S. has 16.6 percent and Japan has 8.2 percent); however, 90 percent of the Euro economy's trade takes place within Euroland.

Euro – 11: *see* European Monetary Union.

Eurofed: *see* European System of Central Banks.

Euroland: an informal name to describe the emerging Europe made up of a single currency and other financial and business arrangements. Also known as the Euro Area, Euro Zone.

Euro LIBOR: the London interbank offer rate for the Euro. The Euro LIBOR is based on the rates of 16 banks active in the Euro market. *See also* ECU LIBOR.

Euroline: a line of credit to a Canadian or U.S. citizen by a foreign bank in the currency of the foreign bank. *See also* Line of Credit.

EURONIA: *see* Euro Overnight Index Average (EURONIA).

Euro Non-Dollar Bond: a bond issued by a U.S. company in a foreign country in non-U.S. dollar currency. *See also* Eurodollar Bond.

Euro Overnight Index Average (EONIA): the domestic overnight rate for the Euro.

Euro Overnight Index Average (EURONIA): the offshore overnight rate for the Euro.

European Association of Securities Dealers Automated Quotation (EASDAQ): a market set up in Europe to be similar to the National Association of Securities Dealers Automated Quotations in the U.S. It is an over-the-counter market listing new, high-growth companies. Prices across Europe are quoted and shares are traded in U.S. dollars.

European Atomic Energy Community: one of the three original European communities (along with the European Economic Community and the European Coal and Steel Community). It was formed by the Treaty of Rome to develop the safe and peaceful use of nuclear energy by Belgium, France, Italy, Luxembourg, the Netherlands and West Germany. *See also* Treaty of Rome.

European Banking Federation (EBF): the body that represents the European Union's banking industry. Also known as Fédération Bancaire de l'Union Européenne.

European Central Bank (ECB): the central bank for Europe established on June 1, 1998, and based in Frankfurt, Germany. The ECB is governed by the Executive Board, the Governing Council, and the General Council. The ECB replaced the European Monetary Institute. *See also* European Central Bank Executive Board, European Central Bank General Council, European Central Bank Governing Council, European System of Central Banks.

European Central Bank Executive Board: a six-member board responsible for day-to-day operations of the European Central Bank. *See* European Central Bank, European System of Central Banks.

European Central Bank General Council: a 21-member board responsible for issues between the Euro nations and rest of the European Community. *See also* European Central Bank, European System of Central Banks.

European Central Bank Governing Council: a 17-member board responsible for formulating the monetary policy of the European Central Bank. *See also* European Central Bank, European System of Central Banks.

European Coal and Steel Community: one of the three original European communities (along with the European Economic Community and the European Atomic Energy Community). It was formed by the Treaty of Paris to pool the coal and steel resources of Belgium, France, Italy, Luxembourg, the Netherlands and West Germany. *See also* Treaty of Paris.

European Commission: effectively, the civil service of the European Union (EU). The commission proposes legislative changes, implements decisions and manages the EU annual budget.

European Common Market: *see* European Economic Community.

European Common Stock Fund: *see* European Equity Fund.

European Community (EC): an economic alliance of Austria, Belgium, Denmark, Finland, France, Germany, Greece, Italy, Ireland, Luxembourg, the Netherlands, Portugal, Spain, Sweden and the United Kingdom. The term "European Community" replaced "European Economic Community" on February 7, 1992.

European Council: a policy-making body made up of the European Community (EC) members' heads of state or government. Also known as the Summit, it sets priorities and political direction for the EC. *See also* Troika.

European Court of Justice: with the Court of First Instance, forms the supreme judiciary of the European Community. *See also* Court of First Instance.

European Currency Unit (ECU): a currency unit

made up of a package of European Economic Community members' currency adjusted regularly to reflect exchange rate changes. The ECU was converted into the Euro on a one-for-one basis on January 1, 1999.

European Currency Unit LIBOR (ECU LIBOR): the London Interbank Offer Rate for the European Currency Unit. The ECU LIBOR was replaced by the Euro LIBOR on January 1, 1999.

European Economic Area (EEA): the countries of the European Community and the European Free Trade Association. The latter group comprises Iceland, Liechtenstein, Norway and Switzerland.

European Economic Community (EEC): one of the three original European communities (along with the European Coal and Steel Community and the European Atomic Energy Community). It was formed by the Treaty of Rome to phase out trade barriers, create a common external tariff and abolish obstacles to the free movement of labour, capital and enterprise among Belgium, France, Italy, Luxembourg, the Netherlands and West Germany. Also known as European Common Market. *See also* European Community, Treaty of Rome.

European Equity Fund: one of the 31 Canadian categories developed by the Investment Funds Standards Committee. Mutual funds in this category must have a minimum of 50 percent of the total assets, and 75 percent of the non-cash assets, of the portfolio in equities or equity equivalents of European companies or derivative-based exposure to developed European equity markets. More than one country must be represented in the portfolio at all times. The calculations to determine whether a mutual fund fits this definition are based on median values from fund data over three years, unless otherwise noted. The derivatives are weighted on an extended value basis. Each of the categories may be refined by the fund manager (e.g., a Canadian Large Cap Equity Fund might be described as "growth" or "value" to reflect the manager's style). *See also* Extended Value, Mutual Fund – Category.

European Federation of Financial Analysts' Societies (EFFAS): an organization of more than 13,000 European financial analysts and investment managers.

European Free Trade Association (EFTA): an association comprising Iceland, Liechtenstein, Norway and Switzerland.

European Monetary Institute (EMI): the organization that was forerunner to the European Central Bank. The EMI was an advisory body that coordinated the monetary policies of the European central

banks and administered the European Monetary System. *See also* European Central Bank, European Monetary System.

European Monetary System (EMS): since March 13, 1979, the organization responsible for creating monetary stability in Europe. All members of the European Community are members of the EMS.

European Monetary Union (EMU): a reference to the eleven countries that initially adopted the Euro: Austria, Belgium, Finland, France, Germany, Ireland, Italy, Luxembourg, Netherlands, Portugal and Spain. Also known as the Euro - 11. *See also* Euro.

European Parliament: an elected body of the European Union (EU), with legislative and budgetary power. It approves the president and members of the EU and retains the ability to force their resignations.

European Plan: a term used to describe hotel rates that include accommodations but not meals.

European-Style Option: the European form of option that must be exercised within five days of the expiration date. *See also* American-Style Option, Option.

European System of Central Banks (ESCB): a system designed to allow the national central banks of the European Community to implement the policy of the European Cental Bank. Also known as the Eurofed. *See also* European Central Bank, National Central Bank.

European Terms: the amount of foreign currency needed to buy one U.S. dollar (e.g., if it requires six French francs to buy one U.S. dollar, the franc is said to be "six in European terms").

European Union (EU): an all encompassing term that includes the countries of the European Community, the provisions for a common foreign and security policy and cooperation on justice and domestic affairs.

Eurostat: *see* Statistical Office of the European Communities.

Euro Zone: *see* Euro Area.

EV: *see* Enterprise Value.

Euthenics: the science of improving human well-being by improving living conditions.

Evaluate: to analyze with a view to establishing or estimating an accurate value.

Evergreen Loan: a loan with an extended due date because the borrower is unable to repay.

Evergreen Prospectus: in the U.S., a prospectus used for an offering of securities for a period of up to one year (e.g., by an open-end mutual fund). *See also* Mutual Fund.

Event Risk: the risk of a reduction in a bond rating because of an event related to a takeover (e.g., a large amount of new debt is issued to finance a takeover). *See also* Company Specific Risk, Industry Specific Risk, Non-Systematic Risk, Risk, Systematic Risk.

Exact Interest: simple interest charges calculated using a 365-day year. *See also* Ordinary Interest.

Examination for Discovery: a pre-trial legal process where one party questions another party about the case being contested. Also known as Discovery.

Excess Contribution: *see* Registered Retirement Savings Plan – Over Contribution.

Excess Liability Coverage: liability insurance that provides coverage over and above the liability limits of homeowner's and automobile insurance.

Excess Margin: in a margin account, equity that is in excess of the lender's requirement. *See also* Margin Account.

Excess Return: the rate of return from owning an asset class in excess of the expected rate of return based on risk, term to maturity and liquidity.

Exchange: 1. *see* Stock Exchange. **2.** to trade or turn in for a replacement. **3.** *see* Foreign Exchange. **4.** *see* Exchange Privilege.

Exchange Coffee House: the site of the first organized stock trading in Canada, in Montreal in 1832. It became the Montreal Stock Exchange in 1874. *See also* Montreal Stock Exchange.

Exchange Controls: regulations that restrict the movement of currency, or other financial instruments, in or out of a country.

Exchange Privilege: the ability of a mutual fund investor to switch from one fund to another within the same family of funds at little or no cost. *See also* Mutual Fund.

Exchange Rate: the ratio or value at which one currency can be converted into another. Also known as Rate of Exchange. *See also* Dirty Float.

Exchange Rate Mechanism (ERM): the system used by the European Community to control exchange rate movements of member currencies. The ERM ended on January 1, 1999. *See also* Exchange Rate Mechanism-2.

Exchange Rate Mechanism-2 (ERM-2): a system started on January 1, 1999, to control exchange rate movements of European countries not involved in the initial Euro.

Exchange Rate: the value of one currency in relation to another.

Exchange Risk: the risk of a possible loss of value as a result of changes in currency value. *See also* Risk.

Exchange Stock Portfolio (ESP): a single trade on the New York Stock Exchange to buy or sell the 500 stocks in the Standard & Poor's 500 Index in proportion to their weighting in the index. *See also* Basket,

Market Basket, Standard & Poor's 500.

Excise Tax: a tax on the manufacture, purchase or sale of goods or services.

Exclusive Listing: an agreement giving a real estate agent exclusive right to sell a property for a period, usually three months. *See also* Multiple Listing Service.

Exclusion: 1. an event defined in an insurance policy as not covered (e.g., earthquake damage). **2.** an item that is listed as not included under the terms of a contract.

Exculpate: to clear of blame.

Ex Dividend: the trading of shares when a declared dividend belongs to the seller rather than to the buyer. *See also* Cum Dividend, Dividend.

Ex Dividend Date: the date on which a declared dividend first belongs to the seller rather than to the buyer. *See also* Dividend.

Execution: the completion of a contract or agreement.

Executive: in a company, a person in a senior management position.

Executive Secretary: a secretary working for a senior executive. In addition to usual secretarial duties, an executive secretary may also handle an executive's appointments, travel arrangements and many other duties. *See also* Secretary.

Executive Stock Option: *see* Stock Option – Executive and/or Employee.

Executive Summary: a condensed version of a much longer report, often presented at the beginning of the latter.

Executor: a man designated in a will to execute the terms of the will. The responsibilities of an executor include making the funeral arrangements according to the deceased's wishes, locating the valid will, acting as trustee and managing the estate assets for the beneficiaries, settling the obligations of the estate, filing the final tax return of the deceased and distributing the assets according to the will. If the executor is a woman, the term is "executrix."

Executrix: *see* Executor.

Exempt: free from liability or obligation, as in "tax exempt."

Exempt Life Insurance: a life insurance contract with an investment component that remains non-taxable while the insurance is in force. *See also* Life Insurance.

Exempt List: a list of large institutional investors that are offered a participation in an underwriting on behalf of all members of the underwriting group. Investors on the exempt list are not subject to the same regulations as members of the public.

Exempt Purchaser: an institutional investor who can invest in a new issue of securities and for whom the issuer is not required to prepare or file a prospectus.

See also Prospectus.

Exercise: to carry out a right inherent in an option, right or warrant. *See also* Option.

Exercise Notice: notification from a broker to the Options Clearing Corporation that a client is exercising his/her right to buy the underlying stock of an option contract. *See also* Option.

Exercise Price: 1. the price at which shares can be bought or sold under a right or warrant. *See also* Right, Warrant. **2.** *see* Strike Price.

Ex Gratia: to do voluntarily (e.g., a voluntary payment made to settle a dispute and avoid litigation is done "ex gratia"; that is, without admitting liability or wrongdoing).

Exhaust Price: the price at which a broker sells a client's holdings if a margin call is not satisfied. *See also* Margin Account, Margin Call, Margin Sale.

Exit Fee: *see* Deferred Sales Charge.

Exit Options: the different ways an investor (often in a private business) can liquidate his/her investment. *See also* Exit Strategy.

Exit Strategy: the way in which a venture capital investor plans to get out of an investment. *See also* Exit Options.

Ex Officio: a right that exists by virtue of one's holding office.

Exogenous Event: in the financial markets, an event that is totally unpredictable and outside normal market factors (e.g., the assassination of President Kennedy would have caused a sharp drop in stock prices, so the New York Stock Exchange was closed when the news was reported).

Exonerate: to free from blame or responsibility.

Exoneration Clause: in a will, a clause that provides for an estate's debts, expenses and taxes to be paid out of the estate. *See also* Will.

Expansion: 1. the stage in a business or industry life cycle when the economy or industry grows. *See also* Business Cycle, Contraction, Cyclical, Economic Cycle, Industry Life Cycle, Peak, Trough. **2.** in computers, one resolution to the year 2000 problem in which the date field is increased from two digits to four.

Expansionary Monetary Policy: a central policy in which interest rates are relatively low and credit is easily accessible.

Expansion Stage Financing: financing provided to a business to facilitate growth in commercial sales or production. *See also* Stage of Development Financing.

Expectation: something that is considered likely to occur (often based on a calculation of probability).

Expected Life: the number of years an asset is expected to be in use as compared to the number of years over

which its value is depreciated. *See also* Effective Life.

Expected Return: a return, from a stock or portfolio, that is based on the sum of all possible returns multiplied by the probability of each.

Expediter: a job involved in facilitating or speeding up a process (e.g., the delivery of goods to a customer).

Expenditure: an outlay (usually of money).

Expense: money that must be spent to conduct business on a going-concern basis. *See also* Going Concern.

Expense Ratio: *see* Management Expense Ratio.

Experience Rating: 1. a method used by life insurance companies to estimate the amount that should be charged for life insurance by looking at their actual experience with a risk class (e.g., premiums for smokers). **2.** in general insurance, when the premium for the insurance is influenced by the claims experience of the individual.

Expiration: this occurs when a right under a financial agreement ceases to be valid.

Expiration Date: the date on which a financial option expires. *See also* Option.

Ex-Pit Transaction: a commodities trade that does not take place on a recognized exchange. *See also* Off-the-Board Trade.

Expiry: the end of something's term or validity (e.g., a credit card expiry date).

Exploitation: in oil and gas, drilling that is less risky than exploration but more risky than development.

Exploration Company: usually, a small company that is engaged in exploration and not the development or production of resources. *See also* Development, Integrated Oil Company, Oil Company, Production Company, Refining and Marketing.

Exploration Drilling: the act of drilling for a resource in a region in which it was not previously known to exist.

Explore: to search systematically in order to discover something (especially resources).

Export: 1. in trade, a transaction in which goods and services flow out and financial settlement flows in. *See also* Import. **2.** in computers, the act of sending data from one computer to another. *See also* Computer.

Exportation: the act of exporting. *See also* Computer.

Export Credit Insurance: insurance for some of the financial risks of selling into foreign markets. *See also* Export Development Credit Corporation.

Export Development Credit Corporation (EDCC): a Crown corporation that provides guarantees on foreign transactions.

Export Financing: a wide range of financial products and services available to companies expanding into foreign markets (e.g., letters of credit, loans, insurance).

Ex Post Facto: in law, after the fact.

Expropriate: an act whereby the Crown takes away a person's property rights against his/her will. *See also* Eminent Domain.

Ex Rights: in trading shares, rights that belong to the seller rather than to the buyer. Also known as Rights Off. *See also* Cum Rights, Right.

Extendable: 1. *see* Extendable Bond. **2.** *see* Extendable Preferred Share.

Extendable Bond: a bond issued with a term to maturity that can be extended to a longer period at the option of the holder. Also known as Extendable. *See also* Bond, Extension Clause, Retractable Bond.

Extendable Preferred Share: a preferred share that is issued with a maturity date that can be extended at the option of the shareholder at a specified date. Also known as Extendable. *See also* Extension Clause, Retractable Preferred Share.

Extended Health Care Insurance: insurance that covers health care needs beyond those covered by most government plans (e.g., ambulance services). Also known as Major Medical Insurance.

Extended Term Insurance: an option with cash value life insurance that, if premiums are not paid, enables the cash surrender value to be used to buy additional term insurance. *See also* Annual Renewable Term Insurance, Cash Surrender Value, Decreasing Term Insurance, Level Term Insurance, Life Insurance, Non-Forfeiture Options, Renewable Term Insurance, Term Insurance, Term to Age 100, Whole Life Insurance.

Extended Value: the value of the underlying securities represented by financial options rather than the value of the options themselves. Extended values are often used to calculate a portfolio's exposure to various economic sectors. *See also* Option.

Extend Term: to sell bonds with a shorter term to maturity to buy bonds with a longer term to maturity. This is an aggressive strategy because long-term bonds have more price volatility than do short-term bonds. Also known as Lengthening Term. *See also* Bond, Shorten Term.

Extension Clause: a term in a security offering (usually a bond or preferred share) that gives the owner the option of lengthening the maturity beyond the date specified. *See also* Extendable Bond, Extendable Preferred Share.

External Financial Statements: financial statements that have been reviewed or audited by an independent, external accountant.

External Funds: capital that does not come from a

company's own sources (e.g., bank loans).

Extortion: the act of taking something (usually money) by the threat of exposing something criminal or embarrassing.

Extradition: this occurs when one country gives up a person to another country, often because the latter has accused him/her of a crime.

Extralegal: outside the law.

Extranet: the extension of a corporation's Internet facilities to improve communication with its clients and suppliers and so to enhance the speed and efficiency of their business relationship. *See also* Internet.

Extraordinary Expense: a one-time expense that, due to its unusual nature, is not included in calculating net income. *See also* Expense.

Extraordinary Income: one-time income that, due to its unusual nature, is not included in calculating net income. *See also* Income.

Extrapolation: a method of forecasting that projects past trends in a straight line into the future.

Extraprovincial: 1. located outside a specific province. **2.** across all provinces.

Extraterritoriality: a country's attempt to extend laws in order to cover activities that take place in another country.

EXW (Ex Works): a transaction in which the buyer assumes all costs and risks when the goods leave the seller's facilities. *See also* CFR, CIF, FAS, FOB, FOR, FOT.

Ex Warrants: in trading shares, when a warrant that has been declared but not distributed belongs to the seller rather than to the buyer. *See also* Cum Warrants, Warrants.

Ex Works: *see* EXW.

Eyewitness: one who has personally seen an act and can testify to it.

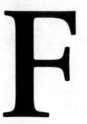

Face Amount: *see* Par Value.

Facet: a flat surface cut on a gemstone.

Face Value: *see* Par Value.

Facilitation Order: a client order that is filled by a cross with the brokerage firm's own account. *See also* Order.

Facilitator: a person with the function of ensuring that a meeting moves toward a conclusion in a timely manner.

Facility Insurance: auto insurance that may be available to drivers who cannot purchase regular insurance because of poor driving records. *See also* Automotive Insurance.

Facs: *see* Facsimile.

Facsimile: an electronic or electro-mechanical transmission of written communication. Also known as Facs, Fax.

Facsimile Machine: a machine that transmits written communication electronically or electro-mechanically. Also known as Fax.

Facsimile Signature: a mechanically reproduced signature.

Fact Finder: 1. a form used by financial planners to gather personal information required to develop a financial plan. **2.** in law, the party responsible for determining the facts.

Factoring: purchasing another's receivables for less than face value for the purpose of sale or collection.

Factoring Accounts Receivable: to purchase another's receivables as principal and not agent. Factoring is most common in the garment industry. *See also* Borrowing Factoring, Non-Borrowing Factoring, Non-Notification Basis, Notification Basis.

Factory Default Settings: in computers, the standard settings on a computer when delivered from the factory. *See also* Computer, Default Settings.

FAF: *see* Financial Analysts Federation.

Fahrenheit: a measure of temperature in which water boils at 212 degrees and freezes at 32 degrees. *See also* Celsius.

Fail: to be unable to settle a trade or obligation on time. *See also* Bad Delivery, Good Delivery.

Failsafe: an automatic safeguard built into a system (often used with reference to computers). *See also* Computer.

Failure of Issue: a condition pursuant to a will or deed where the deceased has no surviving children. Also known as Die Without Issue. *See also* Will.

Fair Market Value (FMV): 1. a value established by a buyer and a seller who are at arm's-length from one another and who are each in possession of all available information. **2.** a value established by a pattern of open-market trading in the same or similar assets.

Fairness Opinion: an independent opinion on the adequacy of an offer to take over a company or assets.

Fair Shake: a reasonable chance for success.

Fair Trade: an agreement by which retailers sell an item at no less than the manufacturer's minimum price.

Fair Value: a value based on sound assumptions. *See also* Fair Market Value.

Fair Weather Fund: a mutual fund that performs well during favourable economic conditions. *See also* All Weather Fund, Foul Weather Fund, Mutual Fund – Other.

Fairy Tale: 1. a fanciful description of an event. **2.** an overly optimistic forecast.

Fait Accompli: a done deal.

Fall: to decline sharply, usually in price.

Fallen Angel: 1. a bond of investment grade when issued that has declined below investment grade (BB or lower). *See also* Angel. **2.** in general investment terms, a once-popular security that has lost investor favour and has declined in value. *See also* Broken Story, Orphan Stock, Wallflower.

Fall Guy: a scapegoat. One who is forced or tricked into taking the blame. One could argue Michael De Guzman, a chief geologist of Bre-X Minerals, was a fall guy. De Guzman died under mysterious circumstances and was later tied into salting the cores, while the other principals including David Walsh, president (now deceased), and John Felderhof, chief geologist, were exonerated or there was insufficient evidence to bring charges.

Fallout: the result of, or response to, an event with mildly negative overtones.

Fall Out of Bed: a sharp drop in the price of a security or the level of a financial market.

Falter: to stumble or experience unsteadiness, as when a stock price that has been rising flattens out.

Family Allowance: *see* Child Tax Benefit.

Family Income: the total earnings of both spouses in a family.

Family Law: generally, the body of law dealing with marriage, separation, divorce and related matters (e.g., financial support and child custody).

Family of Funds: a group of mutual funds managed and/or marketed by the same company. *See also* Mutual Fund – Other.

Family Trust: a trust used to achieve income splitting in order to provide for the maintenance and education of children and to preserve assets.

Fannie Mae: *see* Federal National Mortgage Association.

FAQ: *see* Frequently Asked Questions.

Far East Common Stock Fund: *see* Far East Equity Fund.

Far East Equity Fund: 1. *see* Asia-Ex Japan Equity Fund. **2.** *see* Asia/Pacific Rim Equity Fund. **3.** *see* Japanese Equity Fund. **4.** *see* Mutual Fund – Category.

Farm Improvement and Marketing Cooperatives Loans Act (FIMCLA): a federal program to guarantee loans to farmers and cooperatives.

Farmer Mac: *see* Federal Agricultural Mortgage Corporation.

Farmer's Home Administration (FHA): a U.S. government agency that makes loans to those who wish to purchase real estate in rural areas.

Farm Roll Over: in Canada, if a taxpayer dies owning land or property that was used for farming immediately before his/her death, the adjusted cost base, capital cost and undepreciated capital cost will roll over to a person or persons who is his/her spouse, child, grandchild, great-grandchild or a person under 19 years of age who was under the custody of, and dependent on, the deceased.

Farsighted: in investing, to have the ability to envision the future.

Farther In: an option contract that has an earlier expiry date than does the one now owned or being considered. *See also* Option.

Farther Out: an option contract that has a later expiry date than does the one now owned or being considered. *See also* Option.

FAS (Free Alongside Ship): a transaction in which the seller assumes all costs and risks to the port and the buyer assumes all costs and risks thereafter. *See also* CFR, CIF, EXW, FOB, FOR, FOT.

FASB: *see* Financial Accounting Standards Board.

Fascism: a system in which a dictatorial, right-wing and internationally belligerent government controls economic and personal freedom (e.g., Germany under Adolph Hitler and the National Socialist Party [Nazis] during the Second World War).

Fast Buck: *see* Quick Buck.

Fast Track: 1. the quickest way to achieve a goal. **2.** a status that the U.S. Congress can confer on the president to negotiate a trade agreement with a foreign country without requiring subsequent approval from Congress.

Fat Cat: a wealthy person.

Fault: in mining, a disturbance or large crack below the surface of the Earth. It is often where mineralization occurs and where mines are located.

Favourable Balance of Trade: a situation where exports of merchandise exceeds imports or merchandise in a given period. A favourable balance of trade puts upward pressure on a country's currency. Also known as Trade Surplus. *See also* Trade Balance, Unfavourable Balance of Trade.

Favoured Beneficiary: one who has been bequeathed more than have those who have an equal claim to an estate.

Favourite Son: a man favoured, by the delegates of his state, for nomination as a U.S. presidential candidate.

Fax: 1. *see* Facsimile. **2.** *see* Facsimile Machine.

FBDB: *see* Business Development Bank of Canada.

FBE: *see* European Banking Federation.

FBSE: *see* Bulgarian Stock Exchange.

FCSI: *see* Fellow of the Canadian Securities Institute.

FDIC: *see* Federal Deposit Insurance Corporation.

Feasibility Study: a detailed study of how a mine will be brought into commercial production. It is essential for arranging the necessary financing. *See also* Prefeasibility Stage, Prefeasibility Study.

Featherbedding: the act of employing more workers than are needed to do a job.

Feather Your Own Nest: to make decisions based on what will result in one's personal benefit.

Fed: *see* Federal Reserve Board.

Federal Agricultural Mortgage Corporation (Farmer Mac): a U.S. agency that makes and promotes a market for the buying and selling of farm mortgage loans.

Federal Budget: a series of financial statements that details federal government spending plans for the ensuing year (including how they will be financed). *See also* Federal Budget Deficit, Federal Budget Surplus, Provincial Budget.

Federal Budget Deficit: the budget of the federal government when incoming revenue is less than what it is spending. *See also* Federal Budget, Federal Budget Surplus.

Federal Budget Surplus: the budget of the federal government when incoming revenue is more than what it is spending. *See also* Federal Budget, Federal Budget Deficit.

Federal Business Development Bank (FBDB): the predecessor (up until 1995) of the Business Development Bank of Canada. *See also* Business Develpoment Bank of Canada.

Federal Court: made up of trial and appeal divisions, the federal court presides over suits against the Crown in right of Canada, patents, trademarks, copyrights, Admiralty and appeals from federal boards and tribunals.

Federal Debt: *see* National Debt.

Federal Deposit Insurance Corporation (FDIC): the U.S. federal agency that guarantees deposits within limits of member banks. In 1989, FDIC was reorganized into the Bank Insurance Fund and the Savings Association Insurance Fund. *See also* Bank Insurance Fund, Canada Deposit Insurance Corporation, Savings Association Insurance Fund.

Federal Funds: 1. funds of U.S. banks that is in excess of reserve requirements that are held on deposit with the Federal Reserve Banks. *See also* Federal Funds Rate. **2.** money used by the Federal Reserve to pay for purchases of government securities.

Federal Funds Rate: the closely watched U.S. interest rate, considered a key indicator of Federal Reserve policy and the future direction of interest rates. It is the interest rate charged when a bank lends money it has in excess of bank reserve requirements loans to a bank with a reserve shortfall. Also known as Fed Funds Rate.

Federal Government Debt: *see* National Debt.

Federal Home Loan Mortgage Corporation (FHLMC): a U.S. federal agency that buys residential mortgages from lenders, packages the mortgages into a new security, provides certain guarantees and then resells the new securities on the open market. Also known as Freddie Mac.

Federal Housing Administration (FHA): the U.S. government-sponsored agency that insures lenders against loss on residential mortgages.

Federalism: a form of government in which a union of provinces or states recognizes a central authority while retaining some powers at the local level.

Federally Incorporated Company: 1. a company incorporated under the laws of Canada. *See also* Provincially Incorporated Company. **2.** an insurance company registered with the Department of Insurance in Ottawa and subject to federal regulation. *See also* Provincially Incorporated Company.

Federally Registered Company: *see* Federally Incorporated Company.

Federal National Mortgage Association (Fannie Mae): a U.S. company that buys mortgages from lenders and resells them to investors. Fannie Mae is publicly owned and trades on the New York Stock Exchange.

Federal Open Market Committee (FOMC): the committee of the Federal Reserve Board that establishes short-term monetary policy in the U.S. Members of the FOMC are the chairman of the Federal Reserve Board and the presidents of six Federal Reserve banks. *See also* Beige Book.

Federal Reserve Banks: the 12 banks that make up the U.S. Federal Reserve System. They are owned by member banks in Atlanta, Boston, Chicago, Cleveland, Dallas, Kansas City, Minneapolis, New York, Philadelphia, Richmond, St. Louis and San Francisco.

Federal Reserve Board (FRB): in conjunction with the 12 Federal Reserve Banks, the FRB sets U.S. monetary policy. It is administered by a board of governors appointed by the president and confirmed by the senate for 14-year terms.

Federal Reserve Note: U.S. paper money.

Federal Reserve System: created by the U.S. Federal Reserve Act, 1913, the Federal Reserve System includes the 12 Federal Reserve Banks, their 24 branches and their member banks. *See also* Reserve Bank.

Federal Savings and Loan Insurance Corporation (FSLIC): a U.S. federal deposit insurance company replaced by the Savings Association Insurance Fund in 1989. *See also* Savings Association Insurance Fund.

Fédération Bancaire de l'Union Européenne (FBE): *see* European Banking Federation.

Fed Funds Rate: *see* Federal Funds Rate.

Fed Watcher: someone who analyzes the U.S. Federal Reserve Board for clues as to the future direction of the American economy, interest rates, inflation and the stock market. *See also* Federal Reserve Board.

Fee: 1. a payment for a service. **2.** in real estate, an interest in a property that can be inherited or devised. *See also* Fee Simple.

Fee and Commission: a financial planner or investment advisor compensated by both fees paid by a client and the commissions charged on transactions in recommended securities. *See also* Commission Only, Fee Only, Financial Planner, Investment Advisor.

Feeler: an inquiry, often indirect, designed to elicit the intentions of others.

Fee Only: a financial planner or investment advisor compensated only by fees paid by a client. *See also* Commission Only, Fee and Commission, Financial Planner, Investment Advisor.

Fees and Disbursements: a lawyer's bill.

Fee Simple: outright and absolute ownership of a property. *See also* Fee.

Fee Tail: an estate created by deed or will that leaves property to a person and the heirs of his/her body. *See also* Tenant in Tail, Will.

Fellow of the Canadian Securities Institute (FCSI): the highest designation awarded by the Canadian Securities Institute, requiring education and five years' securities industry experience.

Fellow of the Credit Union Institute of Canada (FCUIC): a standing attained by credit union employees who have completed course work offered by the Credit Union Institute of Canada to prepare entry level to middle management employees.

Felon: someone convicted of a serious crime.

Felony: a serious crime.

Feminist: an advocate for the social, political, legal and economic rights of women.

Fence Sitter: someone who is unable to make an investment decision and so does nothing.

FHA: 1. *see* Farmer's Home Administration. **2.** *see* Federal Housing Administration.

FHLMC: *see* Federal Home Loan Mortgage Corporation.

Fiat: an authoritative pronouncement or decree.

Fibonacci, Leonardo (c.1170-c.1250): the Italian mathematician who did significant work on Euclidean geometry and developed the Fibonacci Series. *See also* Fibonacci Series.

Fibonacci Series: a series of numbers in which each number is the sum of the two preceding numbers (e.g., 1, 1, 2, 3, 5, 8, etc.). Some technical analysts have attempted to use this sequence as the basis for stock market forecasts. *See also* Fibonacci, Leonardo.

Fibre Optic Cable: a glass line that can transmit data 21,000 times faster than can copper wire. Also known as Optical Fibre.

Fibre Optics: the study of the transmission of information or images by internal reflection through glass or other fibres.

Fictitious Order: an order to buy shares placed by an unscrupulous stock promoter who has no intention of making payment. The buy order is designed to push the price of the stock higher and/or to create the illusion of trading activity.

Fiduciary: a person or firm entrusted with the assets of another.

Fiduciary Responsibility: the responsibility of a person or firm entrusted with the assets of another to act in the latter's best interest. *See also* Breach of Duty.

Field Test: *see* Beta Test.

Field Trial: *see* Beta Test.

Field Trip: a visit to a company or facility, often to conduct research or as a matter of due diligence prior to making an investment.

Fieldwork: work conducted under actual, as opposed to artificial, conditions.

FIEX 35: a market capitalization weighted index of 35 of the most liquid Spanish stocks traded on Spanish Continuous Market or Mercado Continuo, launched in 1989. The Interconnected Spanish Stock Exchange System (SIBE) is gradually consolidating all the trading on four Spanish exchanges into one automated exchange. Also known as IBEX 35.

FIFO: *see* First In, First Out.

Fifth Column: a secret organization, within a country or another organization, whose purpose is sabotage.

50/50: being equally likely and unlikely. Divided into two equal parts.

Fight the Tape: to trade against the trend. A trader fights the tape by continuing to buy in a falling market or by continuing to sell in a rising market. *See* Don't Fight the Tape.

Figurehead: a person who is in a prominent position but who lacks actual authority.

Fijian Stock Exchange: *see* Suva Stock Exchange.

File: 1. a cabinet or container for keeping written records in order. **2.** a collection of data or records in a computer. *See also* Computer.

File Server: a computer that keeps a centralized store of files to which other computers (clients) may gain access. *See also* Computer.

File Transfer: in computers, sending or receiving files. *See also* Computer.

Filibuster: a prolonged speech, the purpose of which is to delay legislative action on the part of government.

Fill: to complete an order to buy or sell a security. *See also* Fill or Kill.

Fill or Kill: an order to buy or sell a security that must be satisfied or cancelled. *See also* All or None Order.

FIMCLA: *see* Farm Improvement and Marketing Cooperatives Loans Act.

Finagle: to obtain something through deceit.

Final Order: a court order intended to last until changed by the court.

Final Prospectus: a completed prospectus, approved by the regulatory authority, that replaces the preliminary prospectus and must be delivered to each purchaser of the securities being underwritten. *See also* Preliminary Prospectus, Prospectus.

Final Tax Return: *see* Terminal Income Tax Return.

Finance: anything to do with money, credit, investment or banking. Also known as Financial.

Finance Company: a non-deposit-taking financial institution that makes loans to individuals and businesses.

Finance Paper: credit issued by a company to its own customers (e.g., credit from an automobile manufacturer to the buyer of one of its cars).

Financial: *see* Finance.

Financial Accounting Standards Board (FASB): in the U.S., a panel of certified public accountants that standardizes accounting practices.

Financial Advisor: *see* Financial Planner.

Financial Analyst: a professional who evaluates the investment merits, quality and risk of securities. Financial analysts make buy, hold or sell recommendations. Also known as Analyst, Securities Analyst.

Financial Analysts Federation (FAF): an affiliate of the Institute of Chartered Financial Analysts and a subsidiary of the Association for Investment Management and Research in the U.S. *See also* Association for Investment Management and Research, Institute of Chartered Financial Analysts.

Financial Asset: generally, an asset that derives its value from a contractual claim as compared with a real asset (e.g., a gold certificate is a financial asset but gold bullion is a real asset). Also known as Paper Asset. *See also* Real Asset.

Financial Centre: a city in which considerable financial activity takes place. The major world financial centres include New York, London and Tokyo. Canada's financial centres include Toronto, Montreal and Vancouver.

Financial Fire Drill: a regular review of a financial or investment plan.

Financial Futures Contract: a futures contract on a financial security. *See also* Interest Rate Future.

Financial Incentive: a financial benefit that motivates a desired behaviour (e.g., a sales quota to earn a bonus).

Financial Independence: in financial planning, the basic retirement objective. It means having the capital to provide the desired level of purchasing power at retirement.

Financial Institution: a company engaged in the financial services industry, often including banks, trust companies, life insurance companies and credit unions.

Financial Instrument: any contract or document having monetary value.

Financial Intermediary: a financial institution that attracts excess capital from individual investors or firms by offering a rate of return and making the funds raised available to other individual investors or firms with a capital shortfall. The financial intermediary earns the difference between the interest paid and the interest earned. *See also* Spread.

Financial Lease: a lease under which the service provided by the lessor to the lessee is limited to financing the purchase of machinery and/or equipment. *See also* Capital Lease, Graduated Lease, Ground Lease, Lease, Open-End Lease, Operating Lease.

Financial Leverage: 1. in business, the use of debt to increase profit and return on investment. *See also* Leverage. **2.** in investment, the use of borrowed funds. *See also* Leverage, Margin.

Financial Market: a market for the trading of financial instruments (e.g., a stock market). *See also* Bond Market, Commodity Exchange, Futures Exchange, Money Market, Stock Market.

Financial Markets Association: the largest international foreign exchange association for wholesale markets. Established in 1955, it is one of the sponsors of EONIA and EURIBOR. Also known as Association Cambiste Internationale (ACI). *See* EONIA, EURIBOR.

Financial Needs Approach: a method used to estimate the appropriate amount of life insurance required. Under this method, an individual estimates the capital needed by survivors to maintain their existing lifestyles. This amount is then covered by various forms of life insurance. *See also* Life Insurance.

Financial Neophyte: a beginner with regard to anything related to money, credit, investment or banking).

Financial Option: *see* Option.

Financial Planner: a person who provides financial, investment and retirement planning advice. Also known as Financial Advisor. *See also* Financial Planning, Money In, Money Out, Personal Financial Planning.

Financial Planners Standards Council (FPSC): a group founded in 1995 by the Canadian Association of Financial Planners, the Canadian Association of Insurance and Financial Advisors and the Canadian Institute of Financial Planners to standardize professional designations in the financial planning industry and, eventually, to become the self-regulatory organization for Canadian financial planners. By 1997, the Canadian Institute of Chartered Accountants, the Canadian Securities Institute, Certified General Accountants Association of Canada, Credit Union Institute of Canada, Institute of Canadian Bankers and Society of Management Accountants of Canada had also joined. In April 1998, the Canadian Securities Institute and the Institute of Canadian Bankers left the group.

Financial Planning: 1. generally, the business process involving financial forecasting and budgeting in preparation for a specific project. **2.** for a family, the process of planning a financial future through retirement to estate planning. *See also* Financial Planner; Money In, Money Out; Personal Financial Planning.

Financial Position: the status of a firm's assets, liabilities and equity at a given time. The balance sheet is sometimes called the Statement of Financial Position. *See also* Balance Sheet.

Financial Product: any contract or document that has monetary value or that confers monetary benefit as an investment.

Financial Public Relations: *see* Investor Relations.

Financial Ratio: the relationship in financial amount between two or more figures, expressed as one number divided by another (e.g., the Quick Ratio is a company's cash, cash equivalents and accounts receivable divided by current liabilities). *See also* Ratio, Quick Ratio.

Financial Ratio Analysis: the analysis, study, comparison and interpretation of financial ratios to make an investment decision. Also known as Ratio Analysis.

Financial Services: any business activity relating to lending, preserving, safekeeping or investing money.

Financial Supermarket: an institution that offers a wide range of financial products and services.

Financier: one who deals in large-scale money matters.

Finder's Fee: a fee paid to a party that introduces an investor(s) to an investee.

Finding: 1. a conclusion reached after investigation. **2.** the verdict of a judge or jury. **3.** a document containing an authoritative decision (e.g., from the president of the U.S.).

Fineness: a standard used to measure the precious metal content of a bar of metal. A fineness of .999 means that the metal is 99.9 percent pure. *See also* Triple Nine.

Fine Ounce: *see* Triple Nine.

Fine Print: the part of a contract that contains details rendered in small type and obscure language.

Finger: an Internet program that summarizes information on all users currently logged on. *See also* Internet.

Fingerprint: 1. in technical analysis, the unique way a particular stock trades. **2.** in law, a distinctive mark left by the ridges on a fingertip.

Finite: having bounds.

Finnish Stock Exchange: *see* Helsinki Stock Exchange.

Fire Insurance: insurance that covers the risk of loss from fire and related perils.

Fire Sale: 1. a condition in financial markets when securities prices are exceptionally low. **2.** in retailing, the sale of goods at a very low price.

Firewall: 1. an invisible barrier between an investment firm's corporate finance department and the research and trading areas. A firewall prevents the flow and misuse of inside information. Also known as Chinese Wall. *See also* Over the Wall. **2.** in computers, a system controlling the flow of data between parts of an internal network. A firewall is intended to filter unauthorized traffic to enhance a network's security. *See also* Access Control, Authentication, Biometric Authentication, Challenge-Response Token, Computer, Password, Public Key, Secret Key.

Firing Line: 1. the forefront of activity. **2.** where a sale is closed or a deal is concluded.

Firm: 1. the condition of a sure agreement, bid or offer. **2.** a description of the price of a security as

---

Financial Planning

In its simplest form, financial planning is managing a family's MIMO, that is, Money In, Money Out. Financial planning attempts to maximize the income coming in, make spending more efficient and minimize income taxes paid.

On the "money in" side of the equation, there is employment income such as salary, wages and commissions and investment income including interest, dividends and capital gains. There is also "other income" such as self employment income, pension income, money from RRIFs, disability pensions, and so on.

Depending on a family's income flexibility it may be possible to change income to increase the after tax amount retained. A simple example is to focus interest income in RRSPs and dividend income outside of RRSPs. This can increase the net after tax income of the family.

On the money out side, there are more planning opportunities. Most planners will ensure the basics such as home and mortgage, retirement savings, disability and life insurance, investment and Wills are in place. Depending on the family's circumstances, there may be advantageous tax and estate planning strategies to put into effect as well.

Financial planning is dependent on some knowledge blended with common sense. From a practical perspective, everyone knows they have a need for life insurance. A professional will refine the amount needed, the most suitable type and ensure the price is right.

It has been calculated most Canadian families spend more time watching television in one night than they spend planning their financial future in a year. Financial planning is important to all families. Don't overlook these opportunities.

solid. **3.** a non-legal description of a business, such as a law firm.

Firm Commitment: *see* Bought Deal.

Firming: this describes a security price or market level that is stabilizing and moving higher.

Firm Offer: an offer to buy an asset that will be concluded if the seller accepts. *See also* Conditional Offer, Order, Subject Offer.

Firm Prices: prices not subject to easy negotiation. *See also* Hard Prices, Soft Prices.

Firmware: instructions stored in the read-only memory of a computer. *See also* Computer, Freeware, Hardware, Shareware, Software.

First Base: the most preliminary step in a transaction.

First Board: in futures, delivery dates established by the Chicago Board of Trade.

First Bulgarian Stock Exchange (FBSE): *see* Bulgarian Stock Exchange.

First Devisee: the first person to receive an estate created by a will. *See also* Heir Apparent, Next Devisee, Ultimate Beneficiary, Will.

First Fixed and Floating Charge: a claim registered against certain specific assets and generally against all other assets. *See also* Fixed Charge, Floating Charge.

First Generation: in computers, the first commercial model or version of a product. *See also* Computer.

First Growth: in forestry, trees that have not been grown after harvesting.

First In, First Out (FIFO): an accounting method for valuing inventory in which items are considered to be taken out of inventory in the same order as they went in. *See also* Last In, First Out (LIFO).

First Loss, Best Loss: *see* Cut Losses, Let Profits Run.

First Market: in securities, the recognized stock exchanges.

First Mortgage: the mortgage that takes precedence over all others. *See also* Mortgage, Second Mortgage, Third Mortgage.

First Mortgage Bond: a long-term bond secured by a first mortgage on the issuer's property. *See also* Bond, Mortgage.

First Preferred Share: the preferred share with the first claim on dividends and assets.

First Quarter: the first three months of a fiscal year (often January, February and March).

First Quartile: a ranking in the top 25 percentile of a peer group, that is between the top zero and 25 percent. The upper half of the top 50 percent. *See also* Fourth Quartile, Second Quartile, Third Quartile.

First Refusal: *see* Right of First Refusal.

First Round Financing: 1. usually, the earliest stage of financing for a new business. **2.** the seed capital or venture capital stage of funding. *See also* Go Public, Second Round Financing.

First Section: the section in Japan's largest securities exchanges where blue-chip securities are traded.

First Stock Exchange: *see* Amsterdam Stock Exchange.

First-to-Die: life insurance based on two lives, it pays when the first insured dies. This insurance is often used to cover taxes payable when the first spouse dies. *See also* Joint and Last Survivor, Joint First-to-Die, Joint Second-to-Die, Second-to-Die.

First Year Republican Jinx: in the U.S., the theory that the stock market will fall in the first year of a Republican president's second term.

Fiscal: 1. originally, a term used to describe matters relating to government funds. **2.** in modern usage, a reference to all financial matters or money.

Fiscal Agent: a party appointed to advise or manage the financial affairs of a government or company.

Fiscal Dividend: money saved by a government through reduced spending and elimination of budget deficits that is available for other priority programs or to be passed along as a tax reduction. *See also* Peace Dividend.

Fiscal Policy: in government, financial activities that involve spending funds on various programs and raising revenue through taxation. *See also* Monetary Policy.

Fiscal Year: the accounting period for a business made up of 12 consecutive months, 52 weeks, 13 four-week periods or 365 days. At the end of a fiscal year, the books are closed so no further changes can be made and the profit or loss is calculated. *See also* Calendar Year.

Fiscal Year End: the final day of the financial reporting year.

Fish: a person who can be easily fooled with promises.

Fish Farm: a facility that commercially cultivates fish and/or shellfish for food. *See also* Aquaculture.

Fish or Cut Bait: an instruction to either act or to stand aside so that others can act.

Fit: 1. a condition in which a security fulfills an investor's portfolio needs, as in "That's a fit." **2.** a condition in which a merger meets the needs of both companies.

Five and Ten: a retail store that sells inexpensive articles. The equivalent of the modern dollar store.

Fixed Annuity: an annuity for which the regular payments are set at the time the annuity is purchased. *See also* Annuity, Variable Annuity.

Fixed Asset: in business, a tangible asset that is used for at least one year.

Fixed Capital: investment in fixed assets.

Fixed Charge: a claim registered against a certain asset. *See also* Floating Charge, First Fixed and Floating Charge.

Fixed Charges Coverage: a measure of the margin of safety for a supplier of capital, calculated by dividing the issuer's net income by interest charges plus preferred dividends. *See also* Times Interest Earned.

Fixed Cost: 1. an expense that is not sensitive to the volume of business (e.g., rental expense is a fixed cost that must be paid each month regardless of the level of business). Also known as Fixed Expense. *See also* Variable Costs. **2.** a contract under which the payment for work is a fixed dollar amount. *See also* Cost Plus.

Fixed Disk: *see* Hard Disk.

Fixed Dollar Withdrawal Plan: a plan that enables a mutual fund investor to redeem and receive a fixed dollar payment at regular intervals. Fixed dollar plans are commonly used for Registered Retirement Income Funds. *See also* Fixed Period Withdrawal Plan, Life Expectancy Adjusted Withdrawal Plan, Mutual Fund, Ratio Withdrawal Plan, Systematic Withdrawal Plan.

Fixed Exchange Rate: a rate of exchange between two currencies that does not change according to supply and demand in international currency markets. *See also* Floating Exchange Rate.

Fixed Expense: *see* Fixed Cost.

Fixed Income: a financial security that provides a fixed level of annual income (e.g., a bond). *See also* Bond.

Fixed Income Fund: a mutual fund investing primarily in fixed income investments. *See also* Mutual Fund – Other.

Fixed Interest Rate: an interest rate that is fixed for the term of an agreement. *See also* Floating Interest Rate.

Fixed Period Withdrawal Plan: a plan that enables a mutual fund investor to redeem and receive the total value of his/her holdings at regular intervals over a set period. *See also* Fixed Dollar Withdrawal Plan, Life Expectancy Adjusted Withdrawal Plan, Mutual Fund, Ratio Withdrawal Plan, Systematic Withdrawal Plan.

Fixed Rate Debt: a debt in which the interest rate is fixed until maturity. Also known as Fixed Rate Loan. *See also* Floating Rate Debt.

Fixed Rate Loan: *see* Fixed Rate Debt.

Fixed Rate Mortgage (FRM): a mortgage in which the interest rate is fixed until maturity. *See also* Mortgage.

Fixture: an improvement to a property that is permanent and is considered part of the real estate. As a rule of thumb, a fixture is something that would create damage if removed (e.g., built-in lighting is a fixture but a table lamp is not). Fixtures are sold as part of a property.

Flag: a technical stock price formation in which the price on a chart forms a rectangle by making successive peaks at the same price and troughs at the same price in a relatively short period. *See also* Pennant.

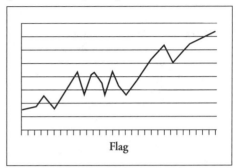

Flag

Flag of Convenience: describes the circumstance of a ship registered in a country (e.g., Liberia) for the sole purpose of avoiding certain duties, charges and taxes that would be payable if the ship were registered in the country of its owner.

Flame: on the Internet, a highly charged e-mail, often in response to poor "netiquette," that contains vicious, personal attacks. *See also* Internet.

Flameout: in the stock market, a term used to describe a company that has disappointed investors in some manner and has thus caused the share price to fall drastically.

Flat: 1. a term used to describe a brokerage firm's own account with a zero net position. *See also* Zero Net Position. **2.** *see* Selling Flat.

Flat Tax: a tax, favoured for its simplicity, that is levied at the same rate across all income levels. Also known as Proportionate Tax. *See also* Taxes.

Flavour of the Month: the current short-term fad in the securities market.

Flea Market: a market, often held outdoors, where used goods and curios are sold.

Fleece: to swindle or defraud.

Flexible Exchange Rate: *see* Floating Exchange Rate.

Flexible Mutual Fund: *see* Asset Allocation Fund.

Flextime: an arrangement that allows employees to set their own work schedules.

Flier: an investment in a highly speculative security.

Flight of Capital: the movement of capital from one jurisdiction to another (often referred to as a safe haven) due to political, currency or economic uncertainty. Also known as Capital Flight, Capital Outflow.

Flight to Quality: the tendency of investors during certain times to seek the safety offered by top-grade securities.

Flim-Flam: a swindle or deception.

Flip: *see* Flipping.

Flip-In Poison Pill: an entitlement to shareholders giving them the right to purchase additional shares of their company at a bargain price in the event of a takeover. *See also* Poison Pill.

Flip-Over Poison Pill: an entitlement to shareholders giving them the right to purchase shares of an acquiring company's stock at a bargain price or to convert the company's preferred shares into common shares. *See also* Poison Pill.

Flipper: an investor who buys and sells within a short period.

Flipping: 1. in investment, this term describes the practice of buying new issue securities and immediately selling in the after market. Also known as a Flip. *See also* After Market. **2.** in real estate, the unethical practice in which a real estate agent purchases a property that is about to be offered for sale, marks the price up and immediately offers it for sale. Also known as a Flip.

FLIRB: *see* Front Loaded Interest Reduction Bond.

Float: 1. the cash on hand for day-to day-operations. **2.** *see* Underwriting. **3.** *see* Share Float.

Floater: 1. *see* Floating Rate Debt, Floating Rate Mortgage. **2.** *see* Rider.

Floating an Issue: *see* Underwriting.

Floating Charge: a claim registered against all assets and not any specific asset. A floating charge ranks behind a fixed charge. *See also* Fixed Charge, First Fixed and Floating Charge.

Floating Exchange Rate: a rate of exchange (between two currencies) which changes according to supply and demand in international currency markets. Also known as Flexible Exchange Rate. *See also* Fixed Exchange Rate, Revaluation.

Floating Interest Rate: an interest rate that may change with market conditions (e.g., with changes in the prime lending rate) during the term of an agreement. Also known as Variable Interest Rate. *See also* Fixed Interest Rate.

Floating Rate: an interest or dividend rate that changes as market conditions change. Also known as Floater, Variable Rate. *See also* Cap, Drop Lock.

Floating Rate Debt: a debt for which the interest rate changes as market conditions change. Also known as Floater, Variable Rate Debt. *See also* Cap, Fixed Rate Debt.

Floating Rate Mortgage: a mortgage for which the interest rate changes as market conditions change.

Also known as Variable Rate Mortgage. *See also* Mortgage, Cap, Fixed Rate Debt.

Floating Rate Preferred Share: a preferred share for which the dividend rate is not fixed (e.g., the payment may be related to changes in the prime rate). Also known as Adjustable Rate Preferred Share, Variable Rate Preferred Share. *See also* Cap, Preferred Share.

Flood the Market: to offer a large number of securities for sale so that supply exceeds demand and prices fall.

Floor: 1. the physical area of a stock exchange where securities are traded. *See also* Pit. **2.** the lowest rate a variable rate security will pay. *See also* Cap, Collar.

Floor Broker: 1. an employee of a brokerage firm who executes orders on the floor of the exchange on behalf of his/her employer's clients. **2.** in common usage, floor broker and floor trader are synonymous. *See also* Floor Trader.

Floor Financing: a loan made to purchase items displayed on a showroom floor (e.g., furniture in a furniture store). *See also* Inventory Financing.

Floor Official: an employee of a stock market or other exchange who is stationed on the trading floor to make rulings and settle disputes. *See also* Stock Exchange.

Floor Trader: 1. an exchange member who executes trades on the floor of the stock exchange as principal. **2.** in common usage, floor trader and floor broker are synonymous. *See also* Floor Broker.

Floorwalker: a retail store employee who supervises personnel and assists customers.

Floppy: *see* Floppy Disk.

Floppy Disk: a flexible disk coated with magnetic material and used to store computer data. Also known as Floppy. *See also* Computer, Computer Disk, Disk, Hard Disk, Magnetic Disk.

Florida Land Boom: a major U.S. real estate swindle during the 1920s in which con men advertised and sold "tropical resort and retirement" developments in Florida. At the peak in 1925-1926, it is estimated that $7 billion of real estate was sold, an extremely large value for the times. Of course, most of the land proved to be under water or otherwise worthless. *See also* Moose Pasture, Swamp Land.

Flow Chart: a schematic representation of a sequence of operations.

Flow Through Share: a share that entitles its owner to claim certain deductions or credits that would otherwise be available to the issuing company. This arrangement is designed for non-taxable companies and taxable investors. *See also* Conduit Theory, Pass-Through Security.

Fluctuation: the ups and downs, over time, in security prices, the financial markets or the economy.

Fluff: a quality attributed to goods or services that are of little use or value.

Flurry: a sudden interest in a security or financial market.

Fly-by-Night: an unreliable, shady person, especially one who neglects his/her debts.

Flying Five: *see* Dow Five.

FMAN: short for February, March, August and November, the months of one of the option cycles. *See also* Option Cycle.

FMV: *see* Fair Market Value.

FOAF: Internet acronym for "friend of a friend."

FOB (Free on Board): a transaction in which the seller assumes all costs and risks until the goods are aboard ship at a specific location and the buyer assumes all costs and risks thereafter. *See also* CFR, CIF, EXW, FAS, FOR, FOT.

Focus Group: a small group gathered to provide independent responses to new products and services. Often used to assess new advertising campaigns. Depending on the responses, changes may be made in the product before it is put into general distribution.

Foil: a thin leaf or sheet of metal.

Foist: to pass off as genuine or valuable.

Follow the Herd: in investment, to do what everyone else is doing. To follow conventional wisdom. *See also* Herd Mentality, Lemming.

FOMC: *see* Federal Open Market Committee.

Food Stamp: a coupon redeemable for food purchases, it is issued to low-income individuals.

Foolproof: infallible, as in "a foolproof investment."

Fool's Gold: *see* Iron Pyrite.

Foot: a measure of length equal to 12 inches, or 30.48 centimetres. *See also* Yard.

Footsie: the nickname for the Financial Times – Stock Exchange 100-Share Index of the London Stock Exchange. Also known as FTSE (pronounced "footsie").

FOR (Free on Rail): a transaction in which the seller assumes all costs and risks until the goods are aboard a train at a specific location and the buyer assumes all costs and risks thereafter. *See also* CFR, CIF, EXW, FAS, FOB, FOT.

Forbearance: a method, utilized by a taxpayer, of effecting gifts or exercising change of control through purposeful action and/or inaction (e.g., a parent and child each own 50 percent of the voting shares of a company. They pass a corporate resolution allowing shareholders to acquire new shares for a nominal payment. The child acquires new shares and the parent does not).

Forbes 500: the annual list, published in *Forbes* magazine, of the 500 largest companies in the U.S.

Forced Conversion: this occurs when an issuer redeems a convertible security that is trading above redemption price because the value of underlying security has appreciated. Since the investor will realize more by converting and selling the underlying security, he/she is forced to convert. *See also* Convertible, Redeem, Redemption Price, Underlying Security.

Forced Sale: the non-voluntary sale of an asset.

Force Majeure: 1. a clause in an underwriting agreement that allows the underwriter to rescind the agreement if there is a monumental change in conditions (e.g., a stock market crash during the offering period). Also known as Disaster Out Clause, Market Out Clause. **2.** in general, any clause in a contract that provides for the agreement to be rescinded under specific, dire circumstances (e.g., war).

Forebear: the person from whom one is descended.

Forecast: to estimate or calculate about the future, often based on current trends. Forecasts are often made by economists, financial planners and securities analysts about financial matters. Also known as Projection.

Foreclose: to take action under the laws of foreclosure. *See also* Mortgage.

Foreclosure: in law, the process of a mortgagor taking back a property used to secure a loan because the loan is in default.

Foreign Bond Fund: one of the 31 Canadian categories developed by the Investment Funds Standards Committee. Mutual funds in this category must have a minimum of 75 percent of the market value of the portfolio in debt instruments that are denominated in foreign currency and have a dollar-weighted term to maturity of over one year. The calculations to determine whether a mutual fund fits this definition are based on median values from fund data over three years, unless otherwise noted. The derivatives are weighted on an extended value basis. Each of the categories may be refined by the fund manager (e.g., a Canadian Large Cap Equity Fund might be described as "growth" or "value" to reflect the manager's style). Also known as American Bond Fund. *See also* Extended Value, Mutual Fund – Category.

Foreign Currency: the currency of a foreign country.

Foreign Direct Investment: investment into Canadian businesses by foreign investors.

Foreign Exchange: any financial instrument used to settle payments between countries. Also known as Exchange, Forex.

Foreign Fund: a mutual fund that invests outside of Canada or in securities denominated in foreign currencies. *See also* Mutual Fund – Other.

Foreign Investment: 1. the act of investing money in a foreign country. **2.** the money invested in a foreign country.

Foreign Money Market Fund: one of the 31 Canadian categories developed by the Investment Funds Standards Committee. This definition makes reference to the statutory definition of money market funds. In summary, mutual funds in this category must invest in government obligations maturing in 25 months or less or high-quality corporate securities maturing in 13 months or less. The portfolio must have a weighted average term to maturity of not more than 180 days and 95 percent of the portfolio must be invested in assets denominated in the same currency as the units of the mutual fund. The calculations to determine whether a mutual fund fits this definition are based on median values from fund data over three years, unless otherwise noted. The derivatives are weighted on an extended value basis. Each of the categories may be refined by the fund manager (e.g., a Canadian Large Cap Equity Fund might be described as "growth" or "value" to reflect the manager's style). Also known as American Money Market Fund, U.S. Money Market Fund. *See also* Extended Value, Mutual Fund – Category.

Foreign Property Rule (FPR): *see* Registered Retirement Savings Plan – Foreign Content.

Foreign Security: a security issued by a foreign government or company.

Foreman: *see* Foreperson.

Forensic: used in connection with the law, especially in relation to crime detection (e.g., forensic medicine).

Foreperson: a person in charge of a group of workers, normally in a factory or plant. Also known as Foreman.

Forestry: the science of cultivating, maintaining and developing the forests, often for commercial purposes.

Forex: *see* Foreign Exchange.

Forint: the prime currency of Hungary.

Forfeit: in law, a punishment that entails the loss of some or all of an interest in a property.

Forgery: a crime in which a document or signature is altered or faked with the intent to defraud.

Form 8-K: in the U.S., a form required by the Securities and Exchange Commission in which a public company must report, within a month, any event that might affect its financial condition or share value.

Form Letter: a standardized letter sent to many people.

Form 10-K: in the U.S., an annual report required by all issuers of registered securities, all companies listed on a stock exchange and any company with 500 or more employees or $1 million in gross profit.

Form 10-Q: a quarterly report required of all companies listed on the U.S. stock exchange.

Formalized Line of Credit: a contractual agreement under which a financial institution agrees to provide a loan to a specified borrower to a maximum amount, usually for one year. *See also* Line of Credit, Temporary Line of Credit.

Formula: 1. a mathematical arrangement of values. **2.** a set of rules or procedures that is usually successful.

Formula Investing: *see* Formula Plan.

Formula Plan: to invest in a predetermined way, as in dollar cost averaging. Also known as Formula Investing.

For-Profit Organization: an organization that operates with the intent to earn profits. The term is often used in conjunction with a non-profit organization changing its structure (e.g., the New York Stock Exchange is considering becoming a For-Profit Organization. *See also* Non-Profit Organization.

Forswear: to renounce under oath.

Fortnight: a period of 14 days or two weeks.

FORTRAN: an early mathematical computer programming language. The term is derived from FORmula TRANslation. *See also* ALGOL, Computer, Machine Language.

Fortune 500: the annual list, published in *Fortune* magazine, of the 500 largest companies in the U.S.

Fortune 500 Company: 1. a company that is included on the Fortune 500 list. **2.** generally, any large company.

For Valuation Only (FVO): security quotes given for the purposes of valuing a portfolio and not for the purpose of participating in a trade. Such quotes will be marked FVO.

Forward Buying: buying a commodity or other asset at today's price for future delivery. Forward buying is done in the expectation that prices will rise. *See also* Forward Selling.

Forward Contract: an agreement to buy or sell an asset, at its current price, for future delivery.

Forward-Forward: a contract that becomes effective in the future dealing with an asset with an even further future date.

Forward-Looking Statements: *see* Future-Oriented Financial Information.

Forward Margin: the difference between the current market price of a currency and its cost on the futures market.

Forward Rate: the dollar amount a commodity, currency or other asset will cost for future delivery.

Forward Selling: selling a commodity or other asset at today's price for future delivery. Forward selling is done in the expectation that prices will fall. *See also* Forward Buying.

Fossil Fuel: hydrocarbons, such as oil or gas, believed to be derived from living matter over geologic time.

FOT (Free on Truck): a transaction in which the seller assumes all costs and risks for the goods until they are on a truck at a specified location and the buyer assumes all costs and risks thereafter. *See also* CFR, CIF, EXW, FAS, FOB, FOR.

Foul Play: unfair or unethical activities.

Foul Weather Fund: a mutual fund that performs well during unfavourable economic conditions. *See also* All Weather Fund, Fair Weather Fund, Mutual Fund – Other.

Foundation: a nonprofit, tax-free organization that raises money to help fund charitable or other worthwhile causes.

Founder: someone who is actively involved in starting up a new venture.

Founder's Stock: 1. shares owned by the founder(s) of a business venture. **2.** a formal category of shares provided as an incentive to management.

Four Bagger: in investment, an asset that quadruples in value. The term is derived from baseball, in which a home run is called a four bagger. The term is used with any number (e.g., five bagger, ten bagger). *See also* Home Run, Three Bagger, Two Bagger.

Four Cs: the main determinants of a diamond's value: carat, clarity, colour and cut. *See also* Diamond, Uncut.

Four Dragons of Asia: *see* Four Tigers of Asia.

Four-Flusher: in negotiation, someone who is bluffing or being misleading.

Four Pillars: in Canada, the financial services industry was separated into four distinct functions, called the Four Pillars. These were banking, life insurance, stock brokerage and trust operations. Over the years, legislation has been changed to allow each of these industries to compete with each other. Today, one can buy life insurance through a bank, buy investments at a trust company, pay bills from a brokerage account and invest in one's life insurance.

Fourth Estate: journalists. The media.

Fourth Market: a market for securities in which large investors bypass exchanges and trade directly among themselves. *See also* Institutional Network, Corporation.

Fourth Quarter: the last three months of a fiscal year (often October, November and December).

Fourth Quartile: a ranking in the bottom 25 percentile of a peer group; that is, between the top 75 and 100 percent. The lower half of the bottom 50 percent. Also known as Bottom Quartile. *See also* Decile, First Quartile, Second Quartile, Third Quartile.

Four Tigers of Asia: Hong Kong, Republic of Korea (South Korea), Singapore and Taiwan. Also known as Four Dragons of Asia. *See also* Big Tigers of Asia, Eight Tigers of Asia, Mini Tigers of Asia.

Fox: a person whose success is based on experience and guile.

FPR: *see* Foreign Property Rule.

FPSC: *see* Financial Planners Standards Council.

Fraction: less than a single unit.

Fractional Discretion Order: an order to buy or sell that gives the broker discretion within a specific fraction of one dollar (e.g., the order "buy at $10.00 with $.25 discretion" allows the broker to fill the order between $10.00 and $10.25 per share). *See also* Order.

Fractional Share: less than one share, often pertaining to dividend reinvestment plans and stock dividends.

Franc: the prime currency of Andorra, Belgium, Benin, Burundi, Coromos, Djibouti, France, French Guiana, French Pacific Islands, Gabon, Guadaloupe, Guinea, Ivory Coast, Liechtenstein, Luxembourg, Madagascar, Mali Republic, Martinique, Miquelon, Monaco, Niger Republic, Rwanda, Senegal, St. Pierre, Switzerland and Togo Republic.

Franchise: the right, subject to certain terms and conditions, to sell a particular product or service in a specified area.

Franchised Monopoly: a monopoly granted to a company by a government.

Franchisee: the recipient of a franchise.

Franchiser: *see* Franchisor.

Franchisor: the issuer of a franchise. Also known as Franchiser.

Francophone: 1. a French-speaking person. **2.** in Canada, usually a French-speaking person of French descent. *See also* Anglophone.

Frankfurt Five: the five Rothschild brothers – Amschel, Carl, James, Nathan and Salomon – who dominated European banking in the mid-1800s.

Frankfurter Wertpapier Bourse: *see* Frankfurt Stock Exchange.

Frankfurt Stock Exchange: a major stock exchange of Germany, located in Frankfurt. Also known as Frankfurter Wertpapier Bourse. Web site: www. exchange.de/

Frank Russell Company: a well-known pension-consulting company headquartered in Tacoma, Washington, and creator of the Russell group of indexes. The Russell indexes are widely followed by pension fund managers who use appropriate indexes as benchmarks for performance. Also known as Russell (Frank) Company. *See also* Russell 1000 Index, Russell 2000 Index, Russell 3000 Index.

Fraser Institute: an independent Canadian economic and social research organization. Its objective is to redirect public attention to the role of competitive markets in providing for the well-being of Canadians.

Fraud: an illegal act, involving misrepresentation or falsehoods, the purpose of which is to take or receive assets.

Fraudulent: a reference to gains made by illegal means.

Fraudulent Conveyance: the improper transfer of an asset for the purpose of protecting it from the claims of a creditor.

FRB: *see* Federal Reserve Board.

Freddie Mac: *see* Federal Home Loan Mortgage Corporation.

Free: 1. costing nothing. **2.** not subject to an obligation. **3.** exempt. **4.** not being used.

Free Alongside Ship: *see* FAS.

Free and Clear: without obligation.

Free and Open Market: any market in which prices are set by the unencumbered forces of supply and demand. Also known as Free Market.

Freebie: something given or received free of charge.

Free Credit Balance: the amount of money in a person's brokerage account that is held as a cash balance.

Free Crowd: the group that actively trades bonds on the New York Stock Exchange.

Freedom of Contract: the ability of parties to agree, without interference from the government or the court, upon the most advantageous bargain.

Free Enterprise: an economic system consisting of privately owned businesses that operate competitively, for a profit and with minimal government intervention.

Free Fall: a stock price or financial market that drops virtually straight down.

Freehold: a property title indicating that an asset can be inherited or devised. *See also* Devise, Seisin.

Freelance: a condition of employment, especially for writers and artists, in which services are sold, as needed, to a variety of employers.

Freeload: to take advantage of the generosity of others, often the government, rather than to work for a living.

Free Lunch: something acquired without apparent effort or cost.

Free-Mail: on the Internet, e-mail addresses that are provided free of charge in return for demographic information provided by the applicant. *See also* E-Mail, Internet.

Free Market Economy: an economy that operates with substantially free competition and minimal government regulation. *See also* Capitalism, Centrally Planned Economy, Communism, Free Enterprise, Market Economy, Socialism.

Free Market: *see* Free and Open Market.

Free on Board: *see* FOB.

Free on Rail: *see* FOR.

Free on Truck: *see* FOT.

Freeport: a port where imports are not subject to duties prior to re-export.

Free Riding: the illegal activity of buying a stock and selling it before paying for the purchase.

Free Speech: the right to express an opinion in public without being censored.

Free Stock: *see* Unlettered Stock.

Free Trade: trade between countries without protective tariffs. *See also* North American Free Trade Agreement.

Free Trade Area of the Americas: a proposed free trade area made up of the 34 countries of North, South and Central America. Current plans call for all commercial trade barriers to be removed by 2005. *See also* European Community, Mercosur, North American Free Trade Agreement. arge

Free Trading: *see* Unlettered.

Freeware: copyrighted software that is freely distributed and that can be used free of charge. *See also* Computer, Firmware, Hardware, Shareware, Software.

Freewheel: the market action of a stock that breaks above a resistance level and continues to rise. *See also* Resistance Level.

Freeze: in investment, a condition in which, due to uncertainty, investors are unable either to act or to react.

Freeze Out: a term used to describe any method of putting pressure on minority shareholders to sell their shares to the majority owner.

French Leave: an unauthorized departure.

French Stock Exchange: *see* Paris Stock Exchange.

Frequently Asked Questions (FAQ): a list of common questions and answers established to assist in the troubleshooting of particular computer software programs and/or hardware devices. Usually found in the product's user manual or posted in the technical support section of the manufacturer's Web site. *See also* Internet.

Fresh Start Accounting: an accounting method used following reorganization, it enables one to adjust certain historical costs in order to make them current.

Friedman, Milton (1912-): a well-known, award-winning economist most closely associated with the view that monetary policy has a most important impact on economic performance. Milton Friedman is a senior research fellow at Stanford University and a professor emeritus at the University of Chicago.

Friendly Takeover: the acquisition of a firm with the approval of its management, board of directors and shareholders. *See also* Unfriendly Takeover.

Fringe Benefit: *see* Perquisite.

Frivolity Theory: a theory stating that if Americans are spending more than 36 percent or less than 33 percent of household income on food and drink, the stock market will decline because they are either too frivolous or not frivolous enough. *See also* Aspirin Count Theory, Boston Snow Indicator, Hemline Indicator, SuperBowl Indicator, Tie Theory, Yellow Market Indicator.

FRM: *see* Fixed Rate Mortgage.

Frontage: a property line that faces a street or a waterfront.

Front End Fee: 1. generally, any fee payable at the beginning of a transaction. **2.** in lending, a fee payable to a financial institution at the time a loan is arranged. *See also* Funding Costs.

Front-Ending: this occurs when a broker agrees to buy part of a block order provided he/she is allowed to act as agent for the entire block.

Front End Load: 1. for mutual funds, a sales charge levied at the time of initial purchase. *See also* Back End Load, Deferred Commissions, Deferred Declining Redemption Fee – At Cost, Deferred Declining Redemption Fee – At Market Value, Deferred Sales Charge, Exit Fee, Life Insurance, Load, Loading Charge, Mutual Fund, No Load, Rear End Load, Sales Charge. **2.** in life insurance, the practice of using the initial premium payments to cover sales commissions and other costs.

Frontier Area: an area in which resources are known to exist but lack of infrastructure makes it uneconomic to extract them. (e.g., in Canada, the Beaufort Sea is a frontier area)

Front Loaded Interest Reduction Bond (FLIRB): a bond that pays a below market rate of interest in the early years. The interest rate rises at an agreed upon schedule for a period of five to seven years, after which it pays a floating rate until maturity.

Front Money: money paid in advance, usually with the expectation that additional money will follow.

Front Office: a reference to the area that houses a company's executive or policy-makers. *See also* Back Office.

Front Running: an improper activity in which an investment professional places a personal order to buy or sell a security just ahead of a client order that is expected to influence the price. Also known as Going

Ahead, Running Ahead, Tape Racing. *See also* Boiler Room, Bucketing, Bucketing Shop, Confidence Man, Dialling for Dollars, Salting, Scam, Tailgating.

Froth: in investment, the amount investors are willing to overpay for unsubstantial or trivial developments.

Frothy Market: a market (generally high) in which investors exhibit many signs of speculation.

Frozen Account: an account in which transactions are not allowed, usually for a disciplinary reason, such as non-payment of amounts owing.

FSLIC: *see* Federal Savings and Loan Insurance Corporation.

FTA: *see* Canada-U.S. Free Trade Agreement of 1989.

FTAA: *see* Free Trade Area of the Americas.

FTF: Internet acronym for "face to face."

FTSE: *see* Footsie.

FTTT: Internet acronym for "from time to time."

F2F: Internet acronym for "face to face."

Fuel: material (such as oil, gas, wood and coal) consumed to produce energy.

Fuel Cell: a power source in which a fuel and an oxidant react to produce electricity.

Full-Bodied Money: a commodity currency (e.g., gold) that is worth its full face value.

Full Credit Period: the term for which a supplier gives a customer trade credit. *See also* Dating, Trade Credit.

Full Disclosure: a regulatory requirement that issuers must provide all pertinent facts when offering a security for sale. *See also* Disclosure, Public Disclosure, Selective Disclosure, Soft Disclosure, Structured Disclosure, Timely Disclosure.

Full Faith and Credit: the pledge by a government borrower that the payment of interest and principal of any debt is supported by its full taxing and borrowing power.

Full Service Broker: a broker who provides a wide variety of financial services and charges a higher rate of commission than a discount broker, who provides fewer services.

Full Service Mutual Fund: a mutual fund that offers investors a broad range of services but especially the ability to automatically reinvest dividends. *See also* Mutual Fund.

Full Stock: any form of equity security with a par value of $100.

Full Trading Authorization: an authorization given to a person, other than the owner of the account, to make trades in an investment account. *See also* Discretionary Account, Discretionary Trading, Trading Authorization..

Fully Circled: a term used to describe a new issue of securities matched by clients' commitments to purchase it. *See also* Circle.

Fully Diluted: a calculation of the number of out-standing shares of a company, including shares issued and shares that will be issued if convertible securities are converted and any rights, warrants and manage-ment and employee stock options are exercised.

Fully Invested: an investor or portfolio that is hold-ing the minimum amount of uninvested cash.

Fully Managed Mutual Fund: *see* Asset Allocation Fund.

Fully Registered Bond: *see* Registered Bond.

Fully Valued: a stock price that accurately reflects the true worth of the underlying company.

Function Key: on a computer keyboard, a key that gives the computer an instruction rather than input data. *See also* Computer.

Fund: 1. short for mutual fund. *See also* Mutual Fund, Mutual Fund – Category, Mutual Fund – Other. **2.** a sum of money set aside for a specific pur-pose. **3.** to supply money.

Fundamental Analysis: a method of determining the relative attractiveness of a security through analyzing financial and related information. *See also* Technical Analysis.

Fundamental Analyst: an analyst who employs fun-damental analysis. *See also* Financial Analyst, Fundamental Analysis, Technical Analyst.

Fundamentalist: an investor or analyst who employs fundamental analysis.

Fund Category: *see* Mutual Fund – Category.

Funded Debt: 1. money raised through the issuance of long-term bonds. *See also* Bond, Unfunded Debt. **2.** bonds that will be retired by a sinking fund.

Fund Group: *see* Family of Funds.

Funding: capital provided for a future commitment.

Funding Costs: the costs associated with raising capi-tal. *See also* Front End Fee, Participation Fee.

Fund of Funds: 1. a mutual fund that invests in other mutual funds. *See also* Mutual Fund – Other. **2.** a term used to describe asset allocation services, espe-cially those that use mutual funds managed by one company. *See also* Asset Allocation, Family of Funds.

Fungible: a term used to describe interchangeable assets of identical quality. Securities and options are fungible assets. *See also* Option.

Fun Money: money that is available for speculative purposes because it is not needed for necessities. *See also* Drop Dead Money, Nest Egg.

Furthest Out: in futures and options trading, the contract month with the most distant delivery or expiry date. Also known as Back Month. *See also* Option.

Future Interest: an interest, in existing real or personal property, that will commence in the future.

Future-Oriented Financial Information: 1. informa-tion, forecasts or projections made by management about the prospects for its company. **2.** a special note in a prospectus to alert potential investors not to rely too heavily on management's forward-looking state-ments. Also known as Forward-Looking Statements.

Future(s): an asset sold today for delivery in the future. *See also* Futures Contract, Futures Market.

Futures Contract: an agreement to buy or sell a spe-cific amount of an asset at a specific price and time. *See also* Futures, Futures Market.

Futures Exchange: where futures contracts trade. Also known as Futures Market. *See also* Bond Market, Commodity Exchange, Financial Market, Futures, Futures Contract, Money Market, Stock Market.

Futures Market: *see* Futures Exchange.

Futures Spread: buying one commodities contract and selling another to take advantage of a discrepancy in pricing. *See also* Arbitrage.

Future Value: the value of an income stream at a spe-cific date in the future that reflects the fact that money can be invested and increase in value over time (e.g., if interest rates are 10 percent, $1.00 today is worth $1.10 in one year and $1.21 in two years). The concept of future value is the opposite of present value. *See also* Present Value, Time Value of Money.

Future Value Table: a financial table, in book form, that provides the future value of $1.00 (or $1.00 per annum) for a given number of years at a given rate of interest. *See also* Future Value, Present Value Table.

Futurology: the study of potential developments based on current trends.

FVO: *see* For Valuation Only.

FYA: Internet acronym for "for your amusement."

FYI: short form of "for your information."

G7: *see* Group of Seven.

G8: *see* Group of Eight.

G10: *see* Group of Ten.

G11: *see* Group of Eleven.

GAAP: *see* Generally Accepted Accounting Principles.

Gadfly: an irritating, persistent corporate critic.

Gage: something deposited as security.

Gag Order: an order that prevents the disclosure of proceedings pertaining to a case currently before the court.

Gag Rule: in some legislatures, a rule that limits debate on an issue.

Gaijin: a term used to describe non-Japanese in Japan. The term is often applied to major non-international brokerage firms with operations in Japan.

Gain: any capital appreciation on an investment.

Gainful: providing a profit.

Gain on Sale: any capital appreciation realized upon sale of an investment.

Gale Date: the date on which mortgage interest is payable. *See also* Mortgage.

Gallon: a measure of capacity equal to four quarts or 3.785 litres.

Galloping Inflation: a condition in which inflation is accelerating out of control. *See also* Inflation.

Gambit: a strategic manoeuvre, plan or comment meant to initiate a negotiation.

Gambler: one who makes high-risk investments. *See also* Conservative Investor, Investor, Nervous Nellie, Speculator.

Game: 1. an activity providing amusement with a procedure, set or rules and outcome. **2.** a term used to describe a business or profession, as in "the investment game."

Gamesmanship: use of marginally ethical activities in an attempt to improve one's competitive position.

Gamma Stock: in the London Stock Exchange's former system of ranking stocks, Gamma stocks were those that ranked lowest in terms of size and trading volume. Alpha, Beta and Delta were other rankings. *See also* Alpha Stock, Beta Stock and Delta Stock.

Gap: a term referring to a stock price moving sharply up or down without any trading (e.g., the price of a stock moves from $15 to $20 a share without trading at prices between $15 and $20 per share). So called because when the price is plotted over time, the line does not connect between the two prices (e.g., $15 and $20) because there is a gap. Also known as Price Gap. *See also* Breakaway Gap.

Garage: a nickname for the annex floor north of the New York Stock Exchange floor.

Garage Sale: a sale of used household items (so termed because it is often conducted in a residential garage). Also known as Yard Sale.

Garbage In, Garbage Out (GIGO): in computers, a phrase meaning that the integrity of computer output is dependent upon the integrity of its input. *See also* Computer.

Garbatrage: this occurs when stocks participate in a major market play even though their involvement is insignificant. (e.g., garbatrage occurred in 1998 and 1999 when the Internet stocks moved sharply higher and companies with minor involvement in the Internet also rose in price.) *See also* Rumourtrage.

Garnish: to bring a proceeding to claim a debtor's wages or other property in order to satisfy an obligation.

Garnishee: a person who receives notice to retain custody of the assets of another person until further instructions are received from the court.

Garnishment: a legal process whereby a first person's property, which is under the control of a second person, is put toward the payment of the former's debt to a third person.

GARP: *see* Growth at a Reasonable Price.

Gasohol: a blend of unleaded gasoline and ethyl alcohol to create a substance used as fuel.

Gasoline: a mixture of liquid hydrocarbons derived from crude petroleum and used as fuel.

Gates, William (Bill) H.: (1955-) a founder and now chairman and chief executive officer of computer software giant Microsoft and the wealthiest person in the world. By 1999, Gates' personal wealth was estimated to be approaching $100 billion. Adjusted to current dollars, Gates would be the second wealthiest American in history behind John D. Rockefeller, founder of Standard Oil Company. Gates' net worth is equal to the annual economic output of Israel or nearly 20 percent of the annual economic output of Canada.

Gateway: software that translates data from one system to another.

Gather in the Stops: a trading tactic in which shares are sold to reduce the price enough to trigger stop sell orders. The stop sell orders push the price down further, triggering other stop sell orders. This creates a snowball effect of prices being pushed lower and lower. *See also* Running in the Shorts, Stop Sell Order.

GATT: *see* General Agreement on Tariffs and Trade.

Gauge: a standard of measurement.

GDP: *see* Gross Domestic Product.

GDR: *see* Global Depository Receipt.

GDS Ratio: *see* Gross Debt Service Ratio.

Gedung Bursa Efek Jakarta: *see* Jakarta Stock Exchange.

Geek: *see* Computer Geek.

Geeking Out: bringing out a computer at an inappropriate time, such as at a formal dinner.

Geisha: a foreign company-issued, non-Yen security sold in Japan.

Gem: 1. a stone, such as a diamond or ruby, that can be cut and polished for ornamental purposes. **2.** anything of great value.

Gemology: the study of precious and semiprecious stones.

Gemstone: *see* Gem.

Generalist: a broker, financial analyst or other investment professional whose knowledge is not specialized.

Generally Accepted Accounting Principles (GAAP): the rules and procedures that govern accounting practices. Different accounting principles can produce different financial results, even under GAAP. *See also* Quality of Earnings.

General Agreement on Tariffs and Trade: *see* World Trade Organization.

General Insurance: insurance protecting property, financial arrangements and third party liability.

General Ledger: a reference to the central accounting records of a business, derived from the time such records were kept in a ledger. *See also* Ledger Posting.

General Lien: *see* Lien.

General Motors Indicator: a theory that the trend in GM's stock price is indicative of the direction in the overall market. The indicator has become less valid as GM's importance to the U.S. economy has declined. *See also* Bellwether Stock, Stock Market Barometer.

General Partner: 1. in a Limited Partnership, the party responsible for management and administration. *See also* Limited Partner, Limited Partnership. **2.** two or more partners who are jointly and severally responsible for the liabilities of the partnership. *See also* Partnership, Joint and Several.

Generation X: the children of the baby boomers. People born in the 1960s and 1970s. *See also* Baby Boomer, Echo Generation, Generation Y, Sandwich Generation.

Generation Y: people born in the 1980s. *See also* Baby Boomer, Echo Generation, Generation X, Sandwich Generation.

Generic: descriptive of a whole group (e.g., an unbranded commodity such as ASA is a generic form of the branded product Aspirin).

Genetic Engineering: to scientifically alter the structure of genes to reproduce desirable qualities.

Geochronology: the Earth's history as recorded by geologic events.

Geographical Domain: the part of an e-mail address that denotes country (e.g., .ca denotes Canada).

Geometric Progression: a sequence such as one, two, four, eight, et cetera, in which each number is multiplied by the same factor (in this case, two) to produce the next value.

Geometric Stock Market Index: a stock market index calculated to give all components an equal weighting period so that a 5 percent change in a high-priced share has the same effect on the index as a 5 percent change in a low-priced share. *See also* Stock Market Index.

Geophysical Anomaly: in mining, an abnormality identified by geophysical means (such as magnetics).

Geopolitics: the study of the relationship between geography and politics.

Geriojurisprudence: the study of how the law affects older people.

German Stock Exchange: *see* Berlin Stock Exchange.

Gerontocracy: government based on rule by elders. Most common in African tribes.

Gerrymander: to arrange the boundaries of electoral districts for the sole purpose of winning an election.

Get in the Game: to make an investment so as to participate in a market or in market play.

Ghana GSE All Share Index: a stock price index for the Ghana Stock Exchange.

Ghosting: an illegal activity that involves two or more market makers acting in a cooperative manner to influence stock prices up or down. Market makers are required to operate in a competitive fashion. *See also* Market Maker.

GIC Refugee: an investor who usually holds guaranteed investment certificates but now owns other assets because of the sharp decline in interest rates. A GIC refugee feels forced into other investments but is not comfortable with such investments.

Gielda Papierow Wartosclowych w Warszawle SA: *see* Warsaw Stock Exchange.

Gift: a voluntary transfer of an asset, without compensation, from one person to another person. *See also* Inter Vivos Gift.

Gifting: the act of giving.

Gift Tax: a tax charged on the value of a gift. There is no gift tax in Canada.

Gigabyte: in computers, approximately one billion bytes of memory. *See also* Bit, Byte, Computer, Kilobyte, Megabyte.

GIGO: *see* Garbage In, Garbage Out.

Gilt: a British term for a United Kingdom bond. *See also* Bond, Dragon Bond, Eurobond, Samurai Bond, Shogun Bond, Yankee Bond.

Gimmick: any device used to make an investment seem more attractive than it really is.

Ginnie Mae: *see* Government National Mortgage Association.

Girl Friday: a dated term for a woman whose job entails a variety of clerical and secretarial tasks.

Glamour Stock: a stock that receives favourable publicity in the press and enjoys popularity with investors.

Glasnost: a policy instituted in the former Soviet Union by Premier Gorbachev. It allows for the candid discussion of problems in government and for the wide dissemination of information.

Glass Ceiling: in the corporate setting, an unacknowledged level above which a minority group, such as women, will not be promoted.

Glass-Steagall Act: a 1933 U.S. act that prohibits commercial banks from undertaking such investment activities as underwriting the shares of private corporations. U.S. banks can now underwrite bonds and shares.

Global: in computers, the entire program or document. *See also* Computer.

Global Balanced and Asset Allocation Fund: one of the 31 Canadian categories developed by the Investment Funds Standards Committee. Mutual funds in this category must have a portfolio invested in a combination of equity, fixed income investments and cash and cash equivalents with 25 percent or more being non-Canadian. The calculations to determine whether a mutual fund fits this definition are based on median values from fund data over three years unless otherwise noted. The derivatives are weighted on an extended value basis. Each of the categories may be refined by the fund manager (e.g., a Canadian Large Cap Equity Fund might be described as "growth" or "value" to reflect the manager's style). Also known as International Balanced Fund. *See also* Extended Value, Mutual Fund – Category.

Global Bond Fund: 1. *see* Foreign Bond Fund. **2.** *see* Mutual Fund – Category.

Global Bonds: bonds issued in different countries and currencies around the world. *See also* Bond.

Global Common Stock Fund: *see* Global Equity Fund.

Global Depository Receipt (GDR): a certificate issued by a bank representing foreign securities it holds in a branch in the country where the securities are issued. Global depository receipts trade as domestic shares in a different country in which the issuing bank branch is located and enable companies in many countries to offer their securities for sale globally. *See also* American Depository Receipt, International Depository Receipt.

Global Equity Fund: one of the 31 Canadian categories developed by the Investment Funds Standards Committee. Mutual funds in this category must have a minimum of 50 percent of the total assets, and 75 percent of the non-cash assets, of the portfolio in equities or equity equivalents of companies located in each of the three geographical regions: Asia, the Americas and Europe, or derivative-based exposure to such markets. The calculations to determine whether a mutual fund fits this definition are based on median values from fund data over three years, unless otherwise noted. The derivatives are weighted on an extended value basis. Each of the categories may be refined by the fund manager (e.g., a Canadian Large Cap Equity Fund might be described as "growth" or "value" to reflect the manager's style). Also known as Global Common Stock Fund. *See also* Extended Value, Mutual Fund – Category.

Global Government Bond: a bond issued by a foreign government in a foreign currency.

Global Government Bond Fund: *see* Foreign Bond Fund.

Global Money Market Fund: *see* Foreign Money Market Fund.

Global Natural Resources Fund: one of the 31 Canadian categories developed by the Investment Funds Standards Committee. Mutual funds in this category must have a minimum of 50 percent of the total assets, and 75 percent of the non-cash assets, of the portfolio in firms whose primary business is related to the exploration, extraction or production of natural resources with no geographic restrictions. The calculations to determine whether a mutual fund fits this definition are based on median values from fund data over three years, unless otherwise noted. The derivatives are weighted on an extended value basis. Each of the categories may be refined by the fund manager (e.g., a Canadian Large Cap Equity Fund might be described as "growth" or "value" to reflect the manager's style). *See also* Extended Value, Mutual Fund – Category.

Global Positioning System (GPS): an electronic system using satellites to provide information on one's physical location or to monitor movements.

Global Precious Metals Fund: one of the 31 Canadian categories developed by the Investment Funds Standards Committee. Mutual funds in this category must have a minimum of 50 percent of the total assets, and 75 percent of the non-cash assets, of the portfolio in firms whose primary business is related to the exploration, extraction or production of precious metals with no geographic restrictions. The calculations to determine whether a mutual fund fits this definition are based on median values from fund data over three years, unless otherwise noted. The derivatives are weighted on an extended value basis. Each of the categories may be refined by the fund manager (e.g., a Canadian Large Cap Equity Fund might be described as "growth" or "value" to reflect the manager's style). Also known as Gold Mutual Fund, Precious Metals Fund. *See also* Extended Value, Mutual Fund – Category.

Global Science and Technology Fund: one of the 31 Canadian categories developed by the Investment Funds Standards Committee. Mutual funds in this category must have a minimum of 50 percent of the total assets, and 75 percent of the non-cash assets, of the portfolio in equities or equity equivalents of companies primarily engaged in some aspect of science or technology. The calculations to determine whether a mutual fund fits this definition are based on median values from fund data over three years, unless otherwise noted. The derivatives are weighted on an extended value basis. Each of the categories may be refined by the fund manager (e.g., a Canadian Large Cap Equity Fund might be described as "growth" or "value" to reflect the manager's style). *See also* Extended Value, Mutual Fund – Category.

Glory-Hole: 1. a large opening into a mine. **2.** in mining exploration, a drill core with outstanding results.

Glut: an oversupply.

GNE: *see* Gross National Expenditure.

GNI: *see* Gross National Income.

GNMA: *see* Government National Mortgage Association.

Gnomes of Zurich: 1. a nickname for Swiss bankers, arising from the 1964 sterling crisis. **2.** a mythical expert on gold and gold pricing. *See also* Smart Money.

GNP: *see* Gross National Product.

GNP Deflator: *see* Gross National Product Deflator.

Godfather Offer: a takeover offer that is so generous, the target company cannot refuse it.

Gofer: 1. a mildly derogatory term for a job that involves running errands (especially in an office). **2.** refers to the person who has such a job.

Go-Getter: an enterprising person, especially in business.

Go-Go Fund: a mutual fund that invests aggressively in speculative securities. Also known as Performance Fund. *See also* Mutual Fund.

Going Ahead: *see* Front Running.

Going Concern: a company operated under the assumption it will continue to exist permanently. *See also* Company.

Going Concern Opinion: an auditor's report that provides a qualified opinion as to the company in question being able to continue operations. In a going concern opinion, the auditor will point out issues such as, "Continuing operating losses raise substantial doubt about the company's ability to stay in business." *See also* Auditor's Report, Qualified Opinion.

Going Concern Value: the value that an acquired firm has to the acquiring company.

Going Private: *see* Go Private.

Going Public: *see* Go Public.

Going Short: *see* Short Sale.

Gold (Au): a metallic element used as currency and as a store of value, it has other commercial uses, especially in jewelry and electronics. Gold is a precious metal. *See* Black Gold, Precious Metal, White Gold.

Gold Account: in measuring the balance of payments, the gold account measures the flow of gold in and out of a country. *See also* Balance of Payments, Capital Account, Current Account.

Gold-Backed: currency or securities whose value is supported by gold bullion.

Gold Bar: *see* Gold Bullion.

Gold Bond: a bond backed by gold. These bonds are issued by gold producers and the interest rate is often related to the price of gold. *See also* Bond.

Gold Bug: a person partial to investment in gold.

Gold Bullion: gold in physical form. Also known as Gold Bar. *See also* Triple Nine.

Gold Certificate: legal tender or security that is convertible into gold on demand. Also known as Gold Note.

Gold Coin: a coin minted in gold that derives its value from the value of the gold. Popular gold coins include the Canadian Maple Leaf and the American Eagle. *See also* Bullion Coin, Numismatic Coin.

Gold Currency: currency that is either made out of gold or is convertible into gold.

Gold Digger: one who develops a relationship with another for the sole purpose of personal financial benefit.

Golden Boot: a financial incentive given to an employee to take early retirement. Golden Boots are often used to avoid lawsuits related to age discrimination. *See also* Golden Handshake.

Golden Handcuffs: a lucrative offer made to retain the services of an employee.

Golden Handshake: a financial incentive given to an executive to encourage him/her to leave his/her position. Golden handshakes are often used to avoid lawsuits related to wrongful dismissal or breach of contract. *See also* Golden Boot.

Golden Hello: a bonus paid to induce an employee to leave his/her current employer to accept a position with a new company.

Golden Mean: a course between two extreme choices.

Golden Parachute: a lucrative payment made to a senior executive who loses his/her job as a result of his/her company being taken over, merged or restructured. *See also* Pension Parachute.

Golden Wednesday: a term used by those who wanted the pound sterling out of the Exchange Rate Mechanism (ERM) to refer to September 16, 1992, when the Bank of England was forced to withdraw the currency from the European ERM. *See also* Black Wednesday.

Golden Years: retirement years.

Gold Fever: 1. a passion for gold prospecting. **2.** the emotional rush for gold or gold securities.

Gold Fixing: the price of gold established each day by bankers and specialists in London, Paris and Zurich.

Gold Fund: *see* Gold Mutual Fund.

Goldilocks Economy: an economy growing at a stable rate, as in "not too hot, not too cold, but just right."

Goldilocks Stock Market: a stock market that has been rising appropriately, as in "not too hot, not too cold, but just right."

Gold Leaf: gold beaten into extremely thin sheets.

Gold Market: a market specializing in trading gold.

Gold Mine: 1. a source of gold-bearing ore. **2.** informally, any highly profitable venture.

Gold Mutual Fund: 1. *see* Global Precious Metals Fund. **2.** *see* Specialty/Miscellaneous Fund. Also known as Gold Fund.

Gold Note: *see* Gold Certificate.

Gold Pool: the central banks of Belgium, Germany, Italy, the Netherlands, Switzerland, the U.K. and the U.S. These banks cooperate in trying to stabilize the market price of gold.

Gold Price: the price of gold, often in U.S. dollars per ounce. A widely followed financial indicator.

Gold Shares: *see* Gold Stock.

Gold Standard: a currency system based on gold reserves.

Gold Stock: 1. stock issued by a gold-mining company. Also known as Gold Shares. **2.** the amount of gold owned, often by a nation's central bank. **3.** the shares of companies engaged in the exploration, development and/or production of gold.

Go Long: to buy a security for investment purposes. *See also* Short Sale.

Goodbye Kiss: *see* Greenmail.

Good Debt: 1. slang for loans with tax deductible interest. **2.** debt to finance capital items rather than consumable items. *See also* Bad Debt, Tax Deductible Interest Expense.

Good Delivery: shares that are properly endorsed, presented and then delivered in order to complete a transaction. *See also* Bad Delivery, Dirty Stock.

Good Faith: the absence of an intent to mislead another or to purposefully neglect an obligation. *See also* Bad Faith.

Good Faith Deposit: a sum of money required of a new client when he/she places an initial order with a brokerage firm.

Goods: a material thing. An economic term for any basic product.

Goods and Chattels: generally, a reference to all personal property. *See also* Chattel, Personal Property.

Good Samaritan Legislation: U.S. statutes that protect would-be rescuers from liability if their efforts to provide assistance during an emergency lead to further injury or damage.

Goods & Services Tax (GST): a Canadian tax, currently 7 percent, added to a product at each stage of its production and on the end selling price. *See also* Harmonized Sales Tax, Provincial Sales Tax, Sales Tax, Value-Added Tax.

Good 'Til Cancelled Order (GTC Order): *see* Good Until Cancelled Order.

Good Times Virus: an Internet hoax which began in November, 1994 and which has reappeared in much the same form from time to time since then. The story is that if you receive and open e-mail with the words Good Times in the subject line, you will import a virus that will erase your hard drive. In more extreme versions, the story is that it will destroy your processor. *See also* Computer, Internet, Michelangelo Virus, Urban Legend, Virus.

Good Title: *see* Clear Title.

Good Until Cancelled Order: an order to buy or sell securities that is in effect unless cancelled. Also known as Good 'Til Cancelled Order, Open Order. *See also* Order.

Goodwill: 1. an intangible positive value such as the difference between the price at which a company is acquired and its book value. **2.** a positive feeling attributed to goods, service or brand name.

GOP: *see* Grand Old Party.

Gopher: in computers, an old system of finding textual information on the Internet. *See also* Internet, Veronica.

Gopherspace: all the information on the Internet that is available through gopher. *See also* Internet.

Go Private: the process of changing a company from public to private ownership. Also known as Going Private. *See also* Go Public.

Go Public: the process of changing a company from private to public ownership. This usually involves the sale of shares by an underwriter. Also known as Going Public. *See also* Go Private.

Go Short: *see* Short Sale.

Gossan: in mining exploration, a valueless, rusted decomposed rock visible at the Earth's surface which may be an indicator of valuable minerals, such as copper or tin, in the area.

Go To Bat: to move from a neutral position and take action (e.g., an investor who has been holding cash waiting for a stock market decline is said to "go to bat" when shares are finally purchased).

Gouge: to overcharge. To extort. To swindle.

Gourde: the prime currency of Haiti.

.gov: an appendage to an e-mail or Internet address that identifies a government location. *See also* .com, .edu, Internet, .mil, .net, .org.

Government: 1. the system used to administer the public policy of a country. **2.** in general, all levels of government, its departments, agencies and crown corporations. *See also* Crown Corporation.

Government Bond: a bond, usually long-term, issued by a government. *See also* Bond, Canadas, Corporate Bond, Municipal Bond, Provincial Bond.

Government Debt: *see* Public Debt.

Government Guaranteed Bond: a bond guaranteed as to interest and principal by a government. *See also* Bond.

Government National Mortgage Association (GNMA): a U.S. government corporation that supports housing by buying mortgages from the Veteran's Administration, the Farmer's Home Administration and the Federal Housing Administration and then issues bonds secured by those mortgages. Also known as Ginnie Mae.

Government Sponsored Retirement Arrangement: in Canada, an unregistered retirement plan paid for by the federal government.

Governor General: in Canada, the head of state and the personal representative of the Queen.

GPS: *see* Global Positioning System.

Grace Period: 1. the period between the date a payment is due and the date the borrower is in default. **2.** the length of time during which loan payments are not required (usually at the beginning of a loan). **3.** in life insurance, the period after which the premium payment was due and the insurance stays in force. *See also* Lapse, Reinstatement, Surrendered Policy. **4.** with credit cards, the number of days until payment is due without incurring an interest charge.

Grade: in mining, the amount of mineral contained in host rock, often expressed as a percentage or a physical amount per tonne.

Graduated Income Tax: *see* Progressive Income Tax.

Graduated Lease: a long-term lease under which payments are adjusted periodically based on an appraised value of the asset being leased. *See also* Capital Lease, Financial Lease, Ground Lease, Lease, Open-End Lease, Operating Lease.

Graduated Payment Mortgage (GPM): a mortgage in which payments begin at a lower level and increase for a few years before levelling off. A GPM is designed to assist young people to buy homes by matching the mortgage payments to expected increases in earnings. *See also* Mortgage.

Graft: to fraudulently obtain public funds by corrupting public officials.

Graham and Dodd: *see* Security Analysis.

Graham, Benjamin (1894-1976): a famous value investor and co-author of the book, *Security Analysis,* Graham is considered the father of financial analysis. *See also* Security Analysis.

Grain: .002285 of an ounce.

Gram: .035 of an ounce.

Gramm-Rudman Act: U.S. legislation passed in 1985, it required the elimination of the federal budget deficit by 1991.

Grandfather Clause: a clause that accompanies many new government regulations or laws when activities that were previously permitted become prohibited or restricted under the new legislation. The grandfather clause protects those already engaged in the now-prohibited or now-restricted activity. *See also* Grandfathering.

Grandfathering: the process of being granted relief by a grandfather clause. *See also* Grandfather Clause.

Grand Jury: in the U.S., a jury that evaluates criminal accusations and evidence in order to determine whether charges are justified.

Grand Old Party (GOP): in U.S. politics, the Republican Party.

Grant: 1. a property transfer by written instrument. **2.** the allocation of money or an asset of value for a specified purpose.

Grantee: one who, under a grant, receives the legal transfer of property. *See also* Grantor.

Grant of Letter Probate: *see* Letters Probate.

Grant of Probate Certificate: *see* Letters Probate.

Grantor: 1. one who gives property to another under a grant (e.g., a person who sets up and places assets into a trust). Also known as Settlor. *See also* Grantee, Trust. **2.** *see* Option Writer.

Grapevine: the system for transmitting informal information and rumour.

Graph: a diagrammatic representation of the relationship between two or more sets of numbers.

Grass Roots: 1. in mining, a very early stage of exploration. **2.** in politics, people at the local level.

Gratis: free.

Gratuity: an extra payment for goods or services, often in a bar or restaurant. Also known as Tip.

Graveyard Market: a point near the end of a severe bear market in which most investors have unrealized capital losses and new investors are unwilling to buy so trading volume is very thin. So termed because, like a graveyard, those who are in, can't get out, and those who are out, don't want to get in. *See also* Bear Market.

Graveyard Shift: hours of work from approximately midnight to eight in the morning.

Gravy: money earned easily.

Gravy Train: a position that requires very little work and pays exceptionally well. The term is often used to describe political appointments.

Gray Market: *see* Grey Market.

Gray Monday: *see* Grey Monday.

Grease: generally, to offer compensation, extravagant benefits or outright bribes.

Grease the Skids: to do whatever is required in order to facilitate the completion of a project (sometimes including the offer of compensation, extravagant benefits or outright bribes).

Grease the Wheel: to offer compensation, extravagant benefits or outright bribes in order to accomplish a specific objective.

Great Crash: *see* Crash of '29.

Great Depression: the severe economic contraction that followed the stock market crash of 1929 and lasted until the onset of the Second World War. *See also* Depression, Dirty Thirties.

Greater Fool Theory: the theory that one often makes an investment in the belief that someone else (in this case, "the greater fool") will pay more for it.

Greece ASE Composite Index: a stock price index for the Athens Stock Exchange.

Greed Index: a system for evaluating portfolio managers. A low index indicates a relatively conservative approach. A high index indicates a more aggressive management style.

Greek Stock Exchange: *see* Athens Stock Exchange.

Greenback: 1. paper money, especially U.S. paper money in which all denominations are green in colour. **2.** formerly, a reference to a Canadian $1 bill, which was green.

Green Card: the card the American government issues to aliens in order to allow them to work in the U.S.

Green Field: the basics. Green field investment is an investment in a company's basic business.

Green Gold: a gold and silver alloy.

Green Light: informally, permission to go ahead.

Greenmail: in an unfriendly takeover, greenmail occurs when the target company agrees to buy (at a high price) the shares already accumulated by the acquirer in return for the promise to halt takeover proceedings. Also known as Goodbye Kiss. *See also* Bankmail, Blackmail, Whitemail.

Green Sheet: a summary, prepared by an underwriter, that includes a comparison between securities offered and those similar to them in order to justify the pricing of a new issue.

Green Shoe: in an underwriting, the ability of the syndicate to purchase additional shares from the issuer at the offering price if demand is high.

Gregorian Calendar: the solar calendar used most widely today, it was introduced by Pope Gregory XIII in 1582. The year is divided into 12 months, 52 weeks and 365 days (or 366 days every fourth year, which is known as a leap year).

Grey Hairs: 1. a term used to describe an individual with vast experience, as in "that broker has some grey hairs." **2.** a tongue-in-cheek reference to the result of stress and aggravation.

Grey Knight: a second, unsolicited bidder in a corporate takeover who plans to take advantage of any problems between the first bidder and the target company.

Grey Market: 1. for a newly issued security, an informal market indicating the price at which trading may begin. **2.** a Eurobond market where new issues are traded on a "when issued" basis. **3.** consumer goods sold by unauthorized dealers.

Grey Monday: Monday, October 27, 1997, when the Dow-Jones Average dropped 554.26 points or 7.2 percent. *See also* Black Friday, Black Monday, Black Thursday, Black Tuesday, Black Wednesday, Golden Wednesday.

Grid: a network of electrical power lines.

Gridlock: a term used to describe government's inability to institute change because of complex and sometimes conflicting administrative procedures.

Grid: a network of electrical power lines.

Grievance: in management/labour disputes, a complaint that is considered to be justifiable.

Gross: 1. the total amount before deductions. **2.** an amount of 12 dozen or 144 items.

Gross Debt Service (GDS) Ratio: the percentage of family gross income before income taxes required to cover mortgage payments. Most lenders use a maximum 32 percent GDS ratio as a rule of thumb. *See also* Mortgage, Total Debt Service Ratio.

Gross Domestic Product (GDP): gross national product, excluding income from outside its borders.

Gross Earnings: *see* Gross Income.

Gross Income: a company's revenue less cost of goods sold. Also known as Gross Earnings. *See also* Net Income.

Gross Lease: usually, a short-term lease in which the property owner pays all related expenses. *See also* Net Lease.

Gross Margin: net sales less cost of goods sold expressed in dollars or percent. *See also* Margin, Net Margin.

Gross National Expenditure (GNE): *see* Net National Expenditure.

Gross National Income (GNI): income that accrues to a country as a result of its productive activity. GNI attempts to measure the income effect of a country's economic activity in contrast to Gross National Product, which measures the value of the output of a country's economic activity. *See also* National Income, Net National Income.

Gross National Product (GNP): the total output of goods and services for a country, including revenue from outside its borders. This is a broad measure of a country's economic size and growth. *See also* Net National Product.

Gross National Product Deflator: a broadly based price index used to remove the effect of inflation from the reported Gross National Product. *See also* Consumer Price Index.

Gross Proceeds: the sum of money received before deductions. *See also* Net Proceeds.

Gross Profit: 1. in business, net sales less cost of goods sold. *See also* Net Profit, Profit. **2.** in investment, the gain on sale of investment before deducting income taxes and commissions. *See also* Net Profit, Profit.

Gross Profit Margin: net sales less cost of goods sold expressed as a percentage of net sales. *See also* Net Profit Margin, Profit Margin.

Gross Sales: total sales before deducting returns, discounts or other allowances. *See also* Net Sales.

Gross Spread: *see* Gross Underwriting Spread.

Gross Underwriting Spread: the difference between the price an underwriter pays to the issuer (seller) of securities and the price charged to the investor (buyer) of those securities. Also known as Gross Spread.

Gross-Up: in calculating the income tax payable on dividends received from taxable Canadian corporations, the first step is to increase the amount of dividends received by 25 percent. This additional amount is called the gross-up.

Gross Yield: the yield on an investment before the deduction of income taxes.

Groundbreaking: a ceremony to mark the start of a major construction project.

Ground Floor: the earliest stage of a new venture.

Ground Lease: a lease on land. *See also* Capital Lease, Financial Lease, Graduated Lease, Lease, Open-End Lease, Operating Lease.

Ground Rent: an interest in the rent from a property or properties received through an inheritance. This is separate from the ownership of the property.

Ground Rule: a basic rule (e.g., a ground rule in a brokerage firm is the Know Your Client rule).

Groundswell: a broad gathering of momentum, as in "a groundswell of political opinion."

Group Averages: 1. stock price indexes representing industry groups or sectors. **2.** certain stock market statistical averages such as price earnings ratio and earnings per share for stocks in an industry or sector.

Group Benefits: *see* Employee Benefit Plan.

Group Bet: this occurs when a portfolio manager maintains a greatly overweighted or underweighted position in a particular group of stocks in a portfolio. The overweighting or underweighting is compared with the weighting in a stock market index or benchmark (e.g., a portfolio manager holding 20 percent of a portfolio in the oil and gas industry compared with 10 percent in the Toronto Stock Exchange 300 Index is said to be "making a group bet on the oils").

Group Insurance: an insurance program and other financial benefits normally offered by employers to employees. *See also* Creditor's Group Insurance, Life Insurance, Ordinary Life Insurance.

Group Insurance Plan: *see* Employee Benefit Plan.

Group of Eight (G8): the Group of Seven plus Russia. *See also* Group of Eleven, Group of Seven, Group of Ten, Group of Twenty-Two.

Group of Eleven (G11): the Group of Ten plus Russia. *See also* Group of Eight, Group of Seven, Group of Ten, Group of Twenty-Two.

Group of Five (G5): the inner circle of the Group of Ten made up of France, Germany, Japan, the United Kingdom and the U.S. The G5 sets the agenda for meetings of the G10.

Group of Seven (G7): an international organization of the seven leading industrialized economies: Canada, France, Germany, Italy, Japan, the United Kingdom and the U.S. *See also* Group of Eight, Group of Eleven, Group of Ten, Group of Twenty-Two.

Group of Ten (G10): an international organization of the 10 leading industrialized economies: Belgium, Canada, France, Germany, Italy, Japan, the Netherlands, Sweden, the United Kingdom and the U.S. *See also* Group of Eight, Group of Eleven, Group of Seven, Group of Twenty-Two.

Group of Twenty-Two: a group of 22 industrialized and developing nations convened by the U.S. Treasury to deal with the problems facing the global economy in the second half of 1988. The group consists of Argentina, Australia, Brazil, Canada, China, France, Germany, Hong Kong, India, Indonesia, Italy, Japan, Korea, Malaysia, Mexico, Poland, Russia, Singapore, South Africa, Thailand, the United Kingdom and the U.S. *See also* Group of Eight, Group of Eleven, Group of Seven, Group of Ten.

Growth: 1. an increase in size over time. **2.** *see* Capital Appreciation. **3.** *see* Growth Investor.

Growth and Income Fund: a mutual fund investing with an objective of capital appreciation and income. *See also* Mutual Fund – Other.

Growth at a Reasonable Price (GARP): an investment strategy that attempts to buy stocks with a high growth rate in earnings per share and a low price/earnings ratio.

Growth Driven: a security or investment for which growth is the primary attraction.

Growth Fund: *see* Growth Mutual Fund.

Growth Industry: an industry in which sales and earnings grow faster than does the overall economy.

Growth Investor: a portfolio management style that focuses on investment in growth stocks. Also referred to as Growth. *See also* Bottom-Up, Growth Stock, Portfolio Management Style, Top Down, Value Investor.

Growth Mutual Fund: a mutual fund with an objective of long-term growth. Also known as Growth Fund. *See also* Mutual Fund – Other.

Growth Portfolio: a securities portfolio made up of growth assets.

Growth Recession: a period of slow economic growth as well as high (and perhaps rising) unemployment.

Growth Stock: a share of a company in a growth industry. Growth stocks often trade at above-average price to earnings ratios.

Grubstake: the money put up to start a new business.

GST: *see* Goods & Services Tax.

GTC Order: *see* Good 'Til Cancelled Order.

Guarani: the prime currency of Paraguay.

Guarantee: 1. a contractual promise to assume liability for a debt if the primary debtor defaults. **2.** a promise to make full or partial restitution for a product or service in case of a manufacturer's defect or breakage under normal use.

Guaranteed Income Supplement (GIS): a means-tested pension supplement for Canadians on Old Age Security. The GIS is paid only to persons with minimal levels of income who are resident in Canada; it is not taxable. *See also* Old Age Supplement.

Guaranteed Insurability: an option with a cash value life insurance policy that enables the policy holder to purchase more insurance (at standard rates) without evidence of insurability. *See also* Life Insurance.

Guaranteed Investment Certificate (GIC): a money market instrument issued by a Canadian trust company that usually pays a fixed rate of interest. GICs are often available for terms of up to five years and are insured, within limits, by the Canada Deposit Insurance Corporation.

Guaranteed Investment Certificates &Term Deposits

A Guaranteed Investment Certificate (GIC) is a deposit investment offered by Canadian trust companies. An equivalent security from a bank or credit union is a term deposit.

GICs and term deposits are very safe, reflecting the financial strength of Canadian financial institutions. The interest paid on GICs tends to be on the low side: usually higher than treasury bills and Canada Savings Bonds but lower than Government of Canada bonds. The interest rate is normally fixed for the term of the GIC, although more recent innovations offer variable returns linked to the stock market as well as options to cash in early subject to an interest-rate penalty.

GICs and term deposits are often available for terms of up to five years. They can also be held in unregistered form, as RRSPs or within a self-directed RRSP.

A shortcoming of GICs is liquidity. The investment cannot be cashed prior to maturity, except in rare circumstances (such as severe financial hardship or death). Some GICs and term deposits are available in cashable form.

GICs and term deposits appeal to very conservative investors and savers. If the after-tax return exceeds the inflation rate, then purchasing power can be built over time.

Guaranteed Renewal Rates: a clause in term insurance contracts that enables the holder to renew the policy at a specified premium without evidence of insurability. *See also* Life Insurance.

Guarantee of Signature: *see* Signature Guarantee.

Guarantor: one who is bound by a contract to pay the debt of another, should the latter default on his/her loan.

Guardian: a person appointed to take care of another person, including his/her affairs and property.

Guesstimate: an estimate based on a combination of knowledge and supposition.

Guideline: a general rule of policy or procedure.

Guild: a trade organization formed in order to protect common interests and to maintain certain standards of training and work.

Guilder: the prime currency of the Netherlands.

Guinea Pig: a person upon whom research or experimental testing is conducted.

Guns and Butter Curve: the classic economic example of a trade-off. The curve illustrates that if an economy produces more guns (military spending), it must reduce its production of butter (basic necessities), and vice versa. Also known as Butter and Guns Curve. *See also* Trade-Off.

Gunslinger: a person whose method of investment is highly aggressive and speculative.

Guru: in financial markets, a recognized leader.

Gusher: a dated term for a successful oil well.

Gypsy Swap: this occurs when management or other insiders sell their free-trading shares to investors and reinvest the proceeds in a new issue of shares that cannot be sold for a specified period.

Habeas Corpus: a writ issued in order to bring a party before the court.

Hacker: a highly skilled programmer who investigates and modifies the codes of computer programs, occasionally for illegal purposes. *See also* Chiphead, Computer, Computer Geek, Cracker.

Haggle: to argue while bargaining.

Hail Mary: a term denoting that something has very little chance of success. A Hail Mary investment is one that will only be profitable if one's prayers are answered.

Haircut: 1. the amount by which a class of security must be reduced for purposes of valuation in calculating a broker-dealer's capital. *See also* Broker-Dealer. **2.** taking a loss, especially on those securities that constitute the required capital of a regulated company (such as a brokerage firm). *See also* Shave.

Haircut Finance: a term used to describe the process of borrowing money using securities as collateral.

Half Dollar: a coin valued at 50 cents.

Half-Life: the length of time before half the principal on a debt will be repaid through sinking fund payments. *See also* Sinking Fund.

Half Stock: a share with a $50 par value.

Hallmark: a sign of excellence.

Halo Effect: the effect that a general stock market trend has on the price of an individual stock (e.g., if technology stocks are in favour, any company that has a technology component will benefit from the halo effect).

Halted: *see* Trading Halt.

Hamanaka, Yasuo (1948-): *see* Mr. Copper.

Hammering: the intense selling of securities.

Handle: the whole number part of a price (e.g., if the price is $12¾, the handle is $12). Professional traders often omit the handle in their dealings. If the bid is $12¼ and the offer is $12½, traders will call the market ¼ - ½ because each assumes the other knows the handle is 12.

Hand-Off: the act of a cellular telephone call being transferred from one base station (e.g., where the call

was placed) to another base station (e.g., where the call is received).

Handshaking: a process whereby two modems determine a common ground upon which to communicate.

Hand Signal: a method of communicating prices and trades by traders on the floor of a securities exchange. *See also* Open Outcry.

Hands-Off Investor: *see* Passive Investor.

Hands-On Investor: *see* Active Investor.

Hang: in computers, this refers to a situation in which activity stops and does not resume (as in a program crash or a communications breakdown). *See also* Computer.

Hang Seng Index (HSI): a market capitalization weighted stock price index of 33 stocks on the Stock Exchange of Hong Kong.

Hard Asset: *see* Real Asset.

Hard Copy: *see* Printout.

Hard Currency: a currency that international investors and businesspeople view as having a stable or rising value. Also known as Hard Money. *See also* Soft Currency.

Hard Disk: in computers, a permanent data-storage device. Also known as a Fixed Disk, Hard Drive. *See also* Computer, Computer Disk, Disk, Floppy Disk, Magnetic Disk.

Hard Dollars: actual cash used to pay expenses. *See also* Soft Dollars.

Hard Drive: *see* Hard Disk.

Hard Money: 1. gold bullion or gold coins. *See also* Soft Money. **2.** *see* Hard Currency.

Hard Price: a price that is not subject to negotiation. *See* Firm Prices, Soft Prices.

Hard Rock Mining: a form of mining in which the ore is removed by way of shafts sunk into the ground.

Hard Sell: a high-pressure selling tactic.

Hardware: in computers and other forms of technology, a reference to equipment. *See also* Computer, Firmware, Freeware, Shareware, Software.

Hardwired: in electronics and computers, a reference to circuits that are permanently connected and cannot be changed. *See also* Computer.

Harmonized Sales Tax (HST): in Nova Scotia, New Brunswick, Newfoundland and Labrador, a 15 percent tax combining the Goods & Services Tax and the provincial sales tax. *See also* Goods & Services Tax, Provincial Sales Tax, Sales Tax.

Hash Function: in computers, an attachment to a message verifying that it has not been altered during transmission. *See also* Computer.

HASI: *see* Home Adaptations for Seniors' Independence.

Hatchet Man: a person who carries out unpleasant assignments (e.g., firing an employee).

Have: a slang reference to a person of some wealth and income. *See also* Have-Not.

Have-Not: a slang reference to a person of little wealth and income. *See also* Have.

HDTV: *see* High Definition Television.

Head: a leader. A senior executive.

Head and Shoulders: a stock price pattern on a graph that indicates a trend reversal. A head and shoulders is made up of a small peak on the left, a higher peak in the centre and a small peak on the right. *See also* Technical Analysis.

Headed North: rising in price or value.

Headed South: falling in price or value.

Headhunter: a person who, for a fee, recruits personnel. *See also* Body Shopping.

Head Office: the office that houses a company's senior executives. Routine functions, such as accounting and payroll, are performed here. *See also* Headquarters.

Headquarters: the main offices of a company, usually the head office. Also known as Home Base. *See also* Head Office.

Heads Up: a friendly warning or alert (e.g., a heads up on a disappointing earnings report).

Head Tax: *see* Poll Tax.

Health-Care Directive: instruction given by an individual, often in a living will, concerning his/her desire to have his/her life maintained through the use of aggressive medical procedures. *See also* Living Will, Will.

Healthy Clip: an above-average rate of growth, as in "the stock is growing at a healthy clip."

Health Maintenance Organization (HMO): in the U.S., a company that provides preventative and curative medical services to its members.

Heap Leaching: a mining method in which ore is piled into "heaps" through which cyanide is run in order to extract the desired mineral. The cyanide is then collected and the metal, (e.g., gold) is removed from it. Also known as Leaching.

Hearing: in law, an administrative tribunal that determines questions of law and fact.

Hearsay: information heard indirectly.

Heart Attack Market: a reference to the 6.5 percent market decline that occurred on September 26, 1955, following President Eisenhower's heart attack.

Heart Bond: a bond issued by a nonprofit organization (e.g., a religious organization or private school).

Heavy: *see* Heavy Market.

Heavy Industry: an industry that manufactures basic commodities or products (e.g., the steel industry).

Heavy Market: a securities market that demonstrates more difficulty in rising than it does in falling. Also known as Heavy.

Hecto: in the metric system, the prefix denoting a factor of 100 times, as in a hectolitre (i.e., 100 litres).

Hectare: a metric unit of area equal to 2.471 acres.

Hedge: a strategy using futures contracts that lessens the chances of future losses or locks in present gains. *See also* Commercial Hedge, Direct Hedge, Futures, Neutral Hedge.

Hedge Clause: *see* Disclaimer.

Hedge Fund: an aggressively managed portfolio that takes large positions on speculative opportunities, using stocks, options, short selling and any other strategy that might provide a very high rate of return. *See also* Mutual Fund – Other.

Hegemony: the dominance of one state over others.

Heir: a child, relative, devisee or legatee by will, or a person designated by statute to inherit part or all of

---

Hedge Fund

A hedge fund is an aggressively managed investment portfolio that may buy and sell quickly, go long or short, use options or speculate in commodities or real estate. The fund may take large positions relative to the size of the portfolio or the market capitalization of a target company. The professional manager is paid to make large bets in the quest for high returns.

The key to a hedge fund (other than the manager) is the shareholders, who are usually made up of relatively few, very high net-worth individuals. Because it is a private venture, the normal regulations constraining a mutual fund manager do not apply to the management of hedge funds. In such cases, there is no prospectus, and there are virtually no restrictions on what a manager can do.

It is estimated that in the U.S. in 1997 there were 1,200 hedge funds with total assets of $200 billion. The best known and largest hedge fund is managed by George Soros and Soros Fund Management. The second largest fund is managed by Julian Robertson of Tiger Management.

The problems experienced by Long-Term Capital Management LP in 1998 heightened investor awareness of the risks related to hedge fund investing.

an estate upon the owner's death. *See also* Beneficiary, Devisee, Heir Apparent, Heiress, Ultimate Beneficiary, Will.

Heir Apparent: the person who will become an heir should a particular person die. In business, the senior executive who is generally expected to be promoted to a higher position. *See also* Beneficiary, Devisee, Heir, Heiress, First Devisee, Ultimate Beneficiary, Will.

Heiress: a female heir. *See also* Beneficiary, Devisee, Heir, Heir Apparent, Ultimate Beneficiary, Will.

Heirloom: a valued family possession passed down through successive generations.

Heir Presumptive: an heir whose claim can be defeated by the birth of a relative closer to the estate's owner (as occurs in Royalty).

Helsingin Arvopaperiporssi: *see* Helsinki Stock Exchange.

Helsinki Stock Exchange: Finland's major stock exchange, located in its capital, Helsinki. Also known as Helsingin Arvopaperiporssi. Web site: www.hse.fi/

Hemline Indicator: a tongue-in-cheek theory holding that stock prices rise with the popularity of short skirts and fall with the popularity of long skirts. *See also* Aspirin Count Theory, Boston Snow Indicator, Frivolity Theory, SuperBowl Indicator, Tie Theory, Yellow Market Indicator.

Herd Mentality: a mildly derogatory term used to describe investors who are unable, or afraid, to make creative decisions. Such people are only capable of doing what everyone else (i.e., "the herd") is doing. *See also* Follow the Herd, Lemming.

Hereditament: a property that may be inherited.

HEX General Index: a market capitalization weighted index of the Helsinki Stock Exchange.

Heyday: a peak period of success.

HHOK: Internet acronym for "ha, ha, only kidding."

Hiccup: in the market, a very quick drop followed by a very quick recovery.

Hidden Agenda: the secret motive behind one's attempt to influence a decision.

Hidden Tax: *see* Indirect Tax.

Hidden Values: the undervalued and hence over-looked assets that appear on a company's financial statement.

Hierarchy: an arrangement structured according to rank or ability (e.g., a company's human resources are usually arranged according to a hierarchy, from upper management, to middle management, to support staff, and so on).

High Alpha: *see* Positive Alpha.

High Beta: high-risk.

High Close: a term used to refer to the improper tactic of manipulating stock prices to ensure the final

trade of the day is at a high price, in order to give the impression that trading was strong when it was not.

High Cost Producer: the least efficient manufacturer. *See also* Low Cost Producer.

High Definition Television (HDTV): television that uses between 1,125 and 1,250 lines (as opposed to the 525 horizontal lines used by the National Television System Committee [NTSC] standards in North America and the 625 lines dictated by the Phase Alternate Lines [PAL] and Sequential Couleur Avec Memoire [SECAM] systems in Asia and Europe). HDTV pictures are approaching the equivalent of 35 mm film.

Higher-Up: a person of superior rank or standing.

Highflown: inflated.

High Flyer: a speculative security that rises sharply in price over a short period.

High Frequency: radio frequency of three to 30 megahertz. *See also* Low Frequency, Ultra-High Frequency, Very High Frequency, Very Low Frequency.

High Grade: 1. high-quality investment or ranking. *See also* Low Grade. **2.** in mining, ore containing above average levels of mineralization. *See also* Low Grade. **3.** in mining, to extract high grade ore. High grading may be done in the early years of a mine or during periods of depressed prices.

High-Grade Bond: a high-quality bond (e.g., with a rating equivalent to AAA, AA or A on the Canadian Bond Rating Service rating system). Also known as Quality Bond. *See also* Bond, Low-Grade Bond.

High/Low Index: a stock market indicator that, over time, compares the number of new highs with the number of new lows.

High Net Worth Individual (HNWI): a person with substantial assets, generally over $1 million.

High-Pressure: above-average aggression, as in "high-pressure sales."

High-Profile: well-known or publicized, as in "high-profile portfolio manager."

High Quality: generally, a term describing securities of minimal risk.

High Ratio Loan: a loan that represents a high percentage of the value of the assets that were put up as security.

High Ratio Mortgage: a loan that exceeds 75 percent of the appraised value of the real estate. *See also* Mortgage.

High-Risk Stock: 1. a stock with a high beta factor or high volatility. Also known as High Beta. **2.** a stock that might rise or fall significantly in price depending on near-term developments. **3.** a speculative stock.

High Tech: relating to highly advanced computers or other technology. *See also* High Tech Stock, Technology.

High Tech Stock: the shares of a company engaged in the development, manufacture or production of highly advanced technology. *See also* High Tech, Technology.

High Ticket Items: personal belongings with a relatively high value (e.g., jewelry). Most homeowners' insurance policies restrict total coverage for high ticket items. Also known as Valuables. *See also* Homeowner's Insurance.

Hike: to raise, as in "hike prices."

Hilt: to the maximum, as in "I'm invested to the hilt."

Hindsight: 1. a look back. **2.** a second guessing of a decision, as in "I was going to buy that stock."

Hire: to engage, in return for financial compensation, the services of an individual or individuals.

Histogram: a bar graph of a frequency distribution in which the size of the bars is in proportion to the frequency of the item it represents.

Historical Alpha: the alpha value for a portfolio based on a historical period based on a comparison with a market portfolio of similar risk. *See also* Alpha.

Historical Beta: the beta factor calculated on the basis of five or more years of historical data. *See also* Beta.

Historical Cost: the original cost of an asset. Historical cost is often the basis for calculating capital gains and losses.

Historical Trading: the trading price pattern of a security over a number of years.

Hit: 1. the process of a security encountering unexpected selling. **2.** *see* Hit the Bid. **3.** to take a loss on an investment, as in "Investors will take a hit on ABC Company."

Hit a Home Run: *see* Home Run.

Hit List: often, a list of a project's prospective investors.

Hit on All Cylinders: to work as efficiently as possible.

Hits: a term used to describe the number of visits made to an Internet Web site. *See also* Internet, Web Site.

Hit the Bid: to fill a sell order by selling at the bid price, an action that usually pushes down the stock price. Also known as Hit.

Hit the Bricks: to go on strike.

Hit the Headlines: to be involved in significant news.

Hit the Silk: to drop out. Quit.

Hit Up: to ask for something, often for charity or a personal loan.

HMO: *see* Health Management Organization

HNWI: *see* High Net Worth Individual.

Hobnob: to associate with in a familiar manner (usually used with regard either to one's business seniors or to those of a higher social standing).

Hobson's Choice: a "lose-lose" choice offered on a take-it-or-leave-it basis. No choice at all.

Hock: to pawn an item; that is, to use an asset in order to secure a small loan. Also, "in hock"; that is, in debt.

Hold: 1. in banking, to retain an asset subject to collection (e.g., if a cheque is deposited, the bank may hold funds until the deposited cheque has cleared). **2.** in securities, a recommendation to retain an existing position in a certain security, as in "A hold recommendation." A recommendation that is not to buy or sell. **3.** to maintain an ownership position (e.g., to hold mutual funds).

Holdco: *see* Holding Company.

Holder in Due Course: the holder of a cheque, bank draft or note who was not a party to the original transaction.

Holder of Record: the person on record as owner of a security. *See also* Shareholder of Record.

Holding: an investment position.

Holding Company (Holdco): a company with no operations but often substantial portfolio investments. *See also* Operating Company.

Holding the Market: buying or selling shares in order to maintain a price level, usually during a common share underwriting period.

Holdout: 1. to not accept an offer for one's shares. **2.** an investor who does this.

Hold Period: the time during which certain issues, such as private placements, cannot be sold. *See also* Private Placement.

Hold Ticket: a reference to a recommendation to hold a stock, that is, not to buy or sell. A buy ticket generates a commission and a sell ticket generates a commission but "there are no hold tickets." *See also* Ticket.

Holographic Will: a will written, dated and signed entirely by hand. (A "fill-in-the-blanks" will does not qualify as a holographic will because it is not written entirely by hand.) The signature on a holographic will does not have to be witnessed, but it does have to be verified. *See also* English Form Will, International Will, Living Will, Notarial Will, Oral Will, Other Wills, Will.

Home: a term used by a seller of securities to describe a buyer, as in "looking for a home for 100,000 shares."

Home Adaptations for Seniors' Independence (HASI): a federal program to help low-income seniors adapt their homes to meet their special needs.

Home Banking: a service that allows the user to perform many banking functions from home by telephone, computer or the Internet.

Home Base: *see* Headquarters.

Home Buyers' Plan: *see* Registered Retirement Savings Plan – Home Buyers' Plan.

Homemaker: the person whose primary occupation is to manage the household for his/her family.

Homeowner's Insurance: a packaged policy that covers various risks, including those to a house and its contents.

Homeowner's Loan: a line of credit from a lending institution secured by the equity in the borrower's home.

Home Run: a single investment that proves to be a major success. Also known as Hit a Home Run. *See also* Four Bagger, Three Bagger, Two Bagger.

Home Stretch: the final stages of a project that it has taken some time to complete.

Home Turf: an area with which one is familiar and in which one has authority.

Honcho: a leader. The person in charge.

Honeymoon: a period, usually occurring when a party/politician is newly elected to office or when an executive assumes a new position, during which negative criticism is withheld.

Hong Kong Stock Exchange: *see* Stock Exchange of Hong Kong.

Honorarium: the payment for a service that is usually performed without remuneration (e.g., a speech).

Horizontal Analysis: a method of analysis that entails comparing an item in a financial statement with the same item in a financial statement for a different period (e.g., 1999 sales compared with 1988 sales). *See also* Vertical Analysis.

Horizontal Drilling: a method in which a well is drilled into a structure containing hydrocarbons horizontally or approximately parallel to the surface. Often used to raise production from a nearly depleted or slow-producing field. *See also* Directional Drilling.

Horizontal Integration: the act of expanding a company's operations into businesses that are similar to the ones owned and operated at present (e.g., a car company expanding into truck manufacturing). *See also* Vertical Integration.

Horizontal Merger: a merger of firms with similar products or services (e.g., a men's clothing retailer with a women's clothing retailer). *See also* Vertical Merger.

Horizontal Spread: *see* Calendar Spread.

Horizontal Trade: the selling of one security to buy a similar security.

Horsepower: a measure of power equal to 745.7 watts or 33,000 foot-pounds per minute.

Host Computer: 1. a main computer that provides services to a system of computers. **2.** the computer that one reaches when dialling into the Internet or a bulletin board system. *See also* Internet.

Hostile Takeover: a takeover that is resisted by the target company. *See also* Poison Pill.

Hostile Takeover Offer: an offer to purchase a company's shares that remains on the table even after management and/or the directors of the target firm have indicated opposition to the offer or formally recommended its rejection.

Host Rock: in mining, the rocks in which minerals are contained.

Host System: a bulletin board system into which callers may dial to read and send electronic mail, upload and download files and chat with other callers.

Hot: generally related to a trade union dispute. A work site is designated hot as a notification to other unionized persons to avoid providing services to the location. A product is designated as hot to notify unionized persons to avoid handling the goods.

Hot Buttons: key areas to watch as indicators of change or things to do to motivate change (e.g., during the 1990s, two hot buttons for the financial markets were inflation and interest rates).

Hot Issue: a newly issued security for which the demand for shares exceeds the supply and for which the market price is expected to be much higher than the offering price. Also known as Hot New Issue. *See also* Out the Window.

Hot Money: money that moves quickly from one aggressive investment opportunity to another.

Hot New Issue: *see* Hot Issue.

Hot Stock: 1. a stock having large price gains on very heavy volume. **2.** a stolen stock certificate.

Hot Story: an investment outlook that is in favour and is being followed by many investors.

Hot Tip: advice to buy a stock, often with the implication that it is based on inside information.

House: 1. a term applied to an investment firm or company (e.g., a brokerage house). **2.** *see* International Stock Exchange of the U.K. and the Republic of Ireland.

House Account: the account used by a financial institution for its own transactions.

Household: a domestic unit consisting of people who live together in a single dwelling.

Household Insurance: insurance for householders to provide against damage to buildings or contents.

House of Commons: 1. in Canada and the U.K., the lower house of Parliament, which is composed of elected members. **2.** the building in which the lower house of Parliament meets. *See also* Senate.

House Organ: a newsletter or periodical that an organization publishes for its employees or members.

House Paper: a bill of exchange or credit written by a parent company to a subsidiary. *See also* Parent Company, Subsidiary.

House Poor: a term used to describe a person or family that is short of discretionary income because most of its income is directed toward home ownership. Also known as Land Poor.

House Rules: a financial institution's regulations regarding customer accounts and practices. House rules can also cover activities of employees.

Housing Affordability Index: *see* Affordability Index.

Housing and Urban Development (HUD): a U.S. federal government agency established in 1965 in order to stimulate the residential housing market through the issuing of loan guarantees.

Housing Permits: the number of permits issued, in a given period, for new residential construction. Often used in conjunction with, and as a leading indicator of, housing starts. *See also* Housing Starts.

Housing Starts: the number of new residential units on which construction was started in a given period. One of the leading economic indicators. *See also* Housing Permits.

Howe Street: the main financial district of Vancouver. *See also* Bay Street, Main Street, Threadneedle Street, Wall Street.

HR: *see* Human Resources.

Hryvna: the primary currency of the Ukraine.

HSI: *see* Hang Seng Index.

HST: *see* Harmonized Sales Tax.

HTML: *see* Hypertext Markup Language.

HTTP: *see* Hypertext Transfer Protocol.

Huckster: one who peddles or hawks goods of questionable quality.

HUD: *see* Housing and Urban Development.

Human Capital: job skills derived from education, training or experience that increase a person's earning power.

Human Resources (HR): 1. the employees of an organization. **2.** the department responsible for hiring, training and overseeing of employees.

Hungarian Stock Exchange: *see* Budapest Stock Exchange.

Hung Jury: a jury whose members are unable to agree on a verdict.

Hurdle Rate: the minimum rate of return needed in order to justify investment.

Hustler: one who sells through the use of questionable and mainly aggressive means.

Hybrid Annuity: an annuity that combines the features of two or more types of annuity (e.g., a fixed annuity and a variable annuity). Also known as Combination Annuity. *See also* Annuity, Fixed Annuity, Variable Annuity.

Hybrid Security: a single security that has the features of two or more securities (e.g., a convertible bond).

Hydroelectricity: electricity generated by converting the energy of running water.

Hydroponics: a method of cultivation that entails growing plants in a nutrient solution rather than in soil. Illegal substances, such as marijuana, are often grown via hydroponics.

Hype: excessive publicity, especially in advertising.

Hyper-Inflation: exceedingly high inflation running out of control (usually at a rate of 100 percent a year or higher). Also known as Runaway Inflation.

Hyperlink: a "hot" link embedded into the text or graphics of a Web page. By clicking on a hyperlink one can go directly to a related page or Web site.

Hypertext: text documents that contain hyperlinks. *See also* Internet.

Hypertext Markup Language (HTML): a series of codes that format documents for display on the World Wide Web. *See also* Internet.

Hypertext Transfer Protocol (HTTP): a protocol used by computers in order to exchange information on the Internet. When an Internet address starts with "http://" it is accessing a Web page. *See also* Internet.

Hypothecate: to pledge a property in order to secure a loan. The title to the property does not change, but the lender has the right to sell it if the borrower defaults on the loan. *See also* Hypothecation.

Hypothecation: a pledge of property to secure a loan where the title to the property does not change but the lender has the right to sell the property if necessary if the borrower defaults. *See also* Hypothecate.

Hypothesis: a proposed explanation for a set of facts, a hypothesis must be amenable to being tested through experimentation.

I: 1. in Roman numerals, the number one. **2.** a symbol that, when used in combination with another word, describes an Internet relationship (e.g., I-commerce is business done on or through the Internet). *See also* Internet.

IA: *see* Investment Advisor.

IAE: Internet acronym for "in any event."

IBES: *see* Institutional Broker's Estimate System.

IBEX 35 Index: a market capitalization weighted index of 35 of the most liquid Spanish stocks traded on Spanish Continuous Market or Mercado Continuo, launched in 1989. The Interconnected Spanish Stock Exchange System (SIBE) is gradually consolidating all the trading on four Spanish exchanges into one automated exchange.

IBM: *see* International Business Machines Corporation.

IBRD: *see* International Bank for Reconstruction and Development.

IC: Internet acronym for "I see."

ICB: *see* Institute of Canadian Bankers.

Iceland Stock Exchange: the major stock exchange of Iceland, located in its capital, Reykjavik. E-mail: vi@vi.is

Iceland Stock Exchange Index: a market capitalization weighted stock price index for the Iceland Stock Exchange.

ICFA: *see* Institute of Chartered Financial Analysts.

ICFP: *see* Institute of Certified Financial Planners.

Icon: in computers, a small symbol used to indicate a specific command (e.g., a command to print can be initiated by clicking on an icon that symbolizes a printer). Also known as Ikon. *See also* Computer.

IDA: *see* Investment Dealers Association of Canada.

i.e.: that is to say. From the Latin *id est*.

IFIC: *see* Investment Funds Institute of Canada.

IFSC: *see* Investment Funds Standards Committee.

IFX Option: *see* International Option.

IGC: *see* Inter-Governmental Conferences.

IGPA: *see* Indice General de Precious de Acciones.

Ikon: *see* Icon.

Illegal Suite: a suite, usually located in a single-family residence, that is rented to a tenant without approval from the municipal government. *See also* In-Law Suite.

Ill-Gotten: obtained dishonestly or unlawfully, as in "ill-gotten gains."

Illicit: prohibited both by custom and by law.

Illiquid: difficult to convert into cash.

ILY: Internet acronym for "I love you."

Imbalance: lack of balance, especially with regard to demand, supply or distribution.

Imbalance of Orders: a stock market term used to describe a condition when there are far more orders to buy a stock than to sell it, or vice versa. Under these conditions, an exchange may halt trading until additional orders come in to enable an orderly market to continue. Order imbalances usually happen after a major event is announced. *See also* Trading Halt.

IMF: *see* International Monetary Fund.

IMHO: Internet acronym for "in my humble opinion."

Immediate Annuity: an annuity in which payments are to begin soon after the contract goes into effect. Also known as Immediate Payment Annuity. *See also* Annuity.

Immediate Family: close relatives by birth or marriage, including siblings, parents, children, in-laws and financial dependents. Members of the immediate family are sometimes included under regulatory restrictions (e.g., Pro Trading).

Immediate Payment Annuity: *see* Immediate Annuity.

Immigrant: one who moves into a foreign country with the intention of taking up permanent residence. *See also* Emigrant, Immigrate, Immigration.

Immigrate: to move into a foreign country in order to take up permanent residence. *See also* Emigrate, Immigrant, Immigration.

Immigration: the act of moving into a foreign country in order to take up permanent residence. *See also* Emigration, Immigrant, Immigrate.

Immunity: exemption from a duty or penalty.

Immunization: a portfolio management strategy in which the maturing of assets is matched by the maturing of portfolio obligations. *See also* Immunize, Mismatch.

Immunize: to invest in assets with a maturity rate and a return rate that exactly offset a liability (e.g., an obligation to pay $1,000,000 in 10 years can be immunized by investing $508,350 worth of government bonds yielding 7 percent). *See also* Immunization, Mismatch.

IMO: Internet acronym for "in my opinion."

Impact: to affect, as in "that news will negatively impact the stock market."

Impairment: a reduction, resulting from distribution or loss, in a regulated firm's required capital.

Impeach: to charge a public official with misconduct, often with the threat of loss of office.

Impecunious: lacking money.

Imperialism: 1. the extension, through political, economic and/or military means, of one country's authority over another. **2.** a form of government in which the head of state is an emperor.

Imperial Measure: a system of weights and measures used in the United Kingdom. *See also* Metric System.

Implicit Return: an implied or assumed rate of return.

Implicit Tax: *see* Indirect Tax.

Implied Cost: a cost based on a best estimate in the absence of an actual, measurable cost. *See also* All-In Cost.

Import: 1. in trade, to bring goods from one country into another. *See also* Export. **2.** in computers, to transfer data from one system into another. *See also* Computer.

Import Duty: a tax on imported items, usually levied in order to protect a domestic industry from foreign competition.

Impose: to force on others, as in "to impose a tax."

Impost: a tax, fee or duty.

Impound: to legally seize and hold.

Impoverish: to reduce to poverty.

Imprest Account: an account established between a branch office and head office against which the branch office can charge authorized expenditures and be refunded by head office.

Imprimatur: official permission to do something (often to publish).

Improvements Insurance: a form of insurance that a tenant can purchase to protect leasehold improvements. *See also* Leasehold Improvement.

Imputed Value: an implicit, calculated value used as an estimate for data that are not available (e.g., if the figure for 1996 is 28 and the figure for 1998 is 30, the imputed value for 1997 is 29). *See also* Interpolation.

In Absentia: in law, while not present, as in "tried in absentia."

Inactive Account: a client account in which, for an extended period of time, there have been no transactions.

Inactive Market: a market in which the volume of trading is below average.

Inactive Security: a security or stock with relatively low trading volume.

Inadmissible: something that cannot be admitted or allowed, as in "inadmissible evidence."

Inalienable: something that cannot be transferred to another, as in "inalienable rights."

In-and-Out: a security purchase followed by an immediate sale.

Inappropriate: in investment, an unsuitable recommendation given by an advisor to a client. This is a serious breach of fiduciary responsibility.

Inc.: abbreviation for "incorporated." Often used in conjunction with a company name, as in "ABC Inc."

In Camera: courtroom or government proceedings that are not open to the public.

Incapacity: a lack of legal, physical or intellectual ability. *See also* Competent, Incompetent, Legal Capacity, Non Compos Mentis.

Incarcerate: to imprison.

Incentive: something, usually a reward rather than a punishment, that induces action. *See also* Negative Incentive.

Incentive Fee: *see* Success Fee.

Incentive Stock Option: a stock option granted, on behalf of the shareholders of a public company, to management and employees in order to allow them to share in the success of their efforts. *See also* Stock Option – Executive and/or Employee.

Inch: a measure of length equal to one-twelfth of a foot, or 2.54 centimetres.

Inchoate Interest: a future right to a property.

Income: 1. *see* Safety of Income. **2.** the value received, often in periodical monetary terms, in exchange for work, the sale of goods and interest, dividends or other return on investment. *See also* Dividend, Interest, Salary, Wage.

Income Attribution Rules: in the Canadian Income Tax Act, rules that are designed to prevent income splitting. *See also* Income Splitting.

Income Averaging: the act of smoothing out highly variable personal income when calculating income taxes. A writer's income might fluctuate greatly from year to year and not reflect how it was earned (e.g., writing for three years and being paid in the year of publication). Under Canada's progressive income tax system, he/she would pay more tax because the rate of tax in the one income year would be very high. As a result, such income can be averaged out over the years.

Income Bond: a bond that pays interest in relation to a variable, such as the issuer's yearly earnings. *See also* Bond.

Income Bracket: *see* Income Group.

Income Deferral: the postponement of reporting income and, therefore, paying the taxes on that income, until a future taxation year.

Income Driven: a security or investment whose primary attraction is income rather than capital gains.

Income Earning: a reference to an asset or investment that generates net revenue or earnings.

Income Fund: *see* Income Mutual Fund.

Income Group: a portion of the population determined by level of income, as in "middle income group." Also known as Income Bracket.

Income Investment: an investment whose primary attraction is income rather than capital gains. Also known as Income Producing.

Income Mutual Fund: a mutual fund whose primary objective is income rather than capital gains. Also known as Income Fund. *See also* Canadian Dividend Fund, Canadian High Income Balanced Fund, Mutual Fund – Other.

Income Portfolio: an investment portfolio whose primary objective is income rather than capital gains. Also known as Income Account.

Income Producing: *see* Income Investment.

Income Property: real estate whose major return is in the form of rental income.

Income Share: the share of a dual purpose mutual fund that is entitled to the income generated by the portfolio. *See also* Capital Share, Dual Purpose Mutual Fund.

Income Shifting: the process of moving some income from an otherwise high income and taxation period to a lower income and taxation period.

Income Splitting: the process of reducing the total amount of income tax paid by members of a family by diverting income from a person in a higher tax bracket to a person in a lower tax bracket. *See also* Taxes.

Income Statement: *see* Profit and Loss Statement. Also known as Operating Statement, Statement of Income.

Income Stock: a common stock that is more attractive for its dividend prospects than for its capital appreciation.

Income Tax: a tax on income as defined by the Income Tax Act. *See also* Taxes.

Income Tax Act: the federal act governing all matters dealing with income taxes. As a general rule, changes to the Income Tax Act are announced in the federal budget and necessary legislative changes occur in the ensuing months. The current Income Tax Act has its roots in the War Debt Income Tax Act of 1917, which was not intended to be permanent. The Income Tax Act today is such a complex document that professional accountants and lawyers specialize in particular parts of the legislation. *See also* Taxes.

Income Tax Return: the forms filled out to report income and income taxes payable. Also known as Tax Return. *See also* Average Tax Rate, Effective Tax Rate, Income Tax, Negative Income Tax, Progressive Income Tax, T4, Taxable Income, Tax Bracket, Taxes.

Income Trust: a form of investment designed to provide investors with high regular income. The investment base of income trusts varies but may be a business or a resource-based commodity.

Incompatible: in computers, a term for hardware or software systems that cannot interact with each other. *See also* Computer.

Incompetent: in law, a lack of ability, qualification, fitness or capacity to perform duties. *See also* Competent, Incapacity, Legal Capacity, Non Compos Mentis.

Inconclusive: something that is not decisive, as in "inconclusive evidence."

Incontestability Clause: a clause in an insurance contract stating that the insurer cannot contest a claim (unless it is fraudulent) after a specified time period – usually two years. *See also* Life Insurance.

Incontestable: in law, something beyond dispute.

Incorporate: to set up a company.

Incorporation: one of the three basic forms of business organization, it involves setting up a legal entity known as a company or corporation. The main features of incorporation are that a company can have many of the legal rights and obligations of a person, and investors in the common stock of the company have limited liability. *See also* Partnership, Proprietorship.

Incorporeal: in law, having no material form but connected, as a right, to something that is actual (e.g., a house is corporeal, but the annual rent to live in the house is incorporeal). *See also* Corporeal.

INCOTERMS: standard definitions for terms of delivery developed by the International Chamber of Commerce (e.g., CIF, EXW or FOB).

"In" Country: a member of the European Community that participates in the single currency. *See also* Euro, European Community, "Out" Country, "Pre-In" Country.

Increasing Annuity: an annuity in which the amount of the payment increases over time. *See also* Annuity.

Increment: the amount added to a previous amount, often on a regular basis and over a specific period of time.

Incremental Cost: the change that occurs in a company's total outlay if one additional unit of output is produced.

Incriminate: to implicate in a crime or wrongful act.

Inculpable: in law, free of blame.

Incumbent: in politics, a person who currently holds office.

Indebted: 1. obligated. 2. owing something, such as money, to another.

Indefeasible: in law, a right that cannot be altered or defeated.

Indemnify: to secure against future loss.

Indemnity Agreement: an agreement between Party A and Party C such that Party C will make the payments required by party A if party B defaults.

Indemnity Clause: a clause that protects the purchaser from any liability (past or future) that may be caused by the seller.

Indenture: a formal, detailed contract between a bond issuer and investors that outlines the specific terms and conditions of the bond including matters such as when and how much interest is to be paid, what assets secure the loan and when and how the loan is to be repaid. *See also* Bond, Funded Debt, Unfunded Debt.

Independent Agent: a life insurance agent who sells the products of more than one insurance company. An independent agent has the advantage of being able to assess the different products of a variety of companies and offer the most appropriate ones to his/her clients. *See also* Captive Agent.

Independent Audit: a financial review conducted by a qualified, arm's-length party. *See also* Internal Audit.

Independent Board Member: *see* Outside Director.

Independent Broker: *see* Broker. Also known as Registered Representative.

Independent Financial Advisor: a financial advisor who is not affiliated with a bank, brokerage firm, mutual fund company or insurance company. *See also* Independent Agent.

Independent Life Insurance: life insurance that provides for a death benefit in the event of the death of the spouse or child of the policy holder. *See also* Life Insurance.

Independent Variable: in a correlation between two variables, the one that forms the basis for explaining the change in the other (i.e., the dependent variable). *See also* Dependent Variable, Multiple Regression Analysis.

Index: *see* Stock Market Index.

Indexed Annuity: an annuity in which payments increase each year by a fixed amount. The amount of the increase is not related to a change in inflation, but such an annuity does afford some cost of living protection during periods of inflation. Also known as Inflation Indexed Annuity. *See also* Annuity.

Indexed Fund: *see* Index Fund.

Indexed Portfolio: a portfolio that duplicates a stock market index. The objective of such a portfolio is to provide, over a long period of time, the same return as does the index. Also known as Index Portfolio.

Index Fund: a fund, often a pension or mutual fund, that duplicates a stock market index. The objective of such a fund is to provide, over a long period of time, the same return as does the index. Also known as Indexed Fund, Passive Fund. *See also* Mutual Fund – Other, Standard & Poor's Effect.

Indexing: 1. the process of tying wage increases or other payments directly to changes in inflation. **2.** a portfolio management strategy in which the portfolio duplicates or replicates an index such as the Dow-Jones Average or Toronto Stock Exchange Index. This strategy is employed by investors who wish to pay low portfolio management fees and are satisfied with average rates of return. The lower fees arise because such portfolios simply copy an existing index and are not actively managed. *See also* Active Management, Passive Management, Passive Portfolio Management.

Index of Coincident Economic Indicators: an index consisting of several economic variables that move at the same time, and in the same direction, as the economy.

Index of Industrial Production: in the U.S., an index that measures changes in industrial, mining and utility production.

Index of Lagging Economic Indicators: an index consisting of several economic variables that lag behind, but move in the same direction, as the economy. *See also* Index of Coincident Economic Indicators, Index of Leading Economic Indicators.

Index of Leading Economic Indicators: an index consisting of several economic variables that move ahead of, and in the same direction as, the economy. *See also* Index of Coincident Economic Indicators, Index of Lagging Economic Indicators.

Index of Economic Freedom: a ranking of 161 countries by the degree of capitalism in each's economy. It uses factors such as the degree of taxation, property rights and the ability to move investment capital freely. The index is published annually by the Heritage Foundation in Washington, D.C.

Index Option: *see* Stock Index Option.

Index Participation Unit (IPU): a basket of securities held in trust, designed to enable investors to buy a single security that duplicates or replicates a stock market index. *See also* Diamonds, Spiders, TIPs.

Index Portfolio: *see* Indexed Portfolio.

Index Tracking: a portfolio management approach that attempts to produce investment returns in line with a specific index without duplicating the index.

Index Weighting: 1. the proportion of a total index represented by each of its components. **2.** in a portfolio, positions with weightings similar to an index.

India NSE 50 30 Index: the National Stock Exchange index for India, calculated on the basis of market capitalization and liquidity.

India Sensex 30 Index: a market capitalization weighted index for the National Stock Exchange of India.

India Stock Exchange: *see* National Stock Exchange.

Indicated Order: *see* Indication of Interest.

Indication of Interest: an expression of willingness, but not a firm order, to buy or sell interest in a security. Also known as Indicated Order. *See also* Circle, Order.

Indicators: anything used to predict future financial or economic trends. *See also* Index of Lagging Economic Indicators, Index of Leading Economic Indicators.

Indice General de Precious de Acciones (IGPA): a stock price index for the Santiago Stock Exchange.

Indice Nacional de Precios y Cotizaciones del Mercado Ecuatoriano: a market capitalization weighted stock price index for the Quito Stock Exchange.

Indict: in law, to charge with a crime or to accuse of wrongdoing.

Indictment: in law, the process of laying a formal charge or accusation.

Indigent: needy. Poor.

Indirect Cost: *see* Indirect Expense.

Indirect Expense: a business expense that is not attributable to a specific department (e.g., a corporate president's salary). *See also* Direct Expense.

Indirect Holding: an individual or corporate interest in an asset that is owned through another company rather than directly. If Company A owns a 50 percent interest in Company B, which owns a 50 percent interest in Company C, Company A has a 50 percent direct holding in Company B and a 25 percent indirect holding in Company C. *See also* Direct Holding.

Indirect Labour Cost: wages paid to employees who are not involved in the actual production of a product (e.g., a secretary). *See also* Direct Labour Cost.

Indirect Lease: a third-party lease arranged by the seller of a product (e.g., an auto dealer). The purchaser of the product pays the lease company. *See also* Direct Lease, Leveraged Lease.

Indirect Tax: usually, a tax that is not visible to the party paying it (e.g., of a $20 bottle of liquor, more than $16 of the price are indirect taxes). Also known as Hidden Tax, Implicit Tax.

Individual Investor: a person who invests his/her own money. *See also* Institutional Investor.

Individualism: the belief that the interests of the individual should take precedence, whenever possible, over the interests of the state.

Individual Retirement Account (IRA): the U.S. equivalent of a Registered Retirement Savings Plan,

in this account, contributions are tax deductible within limits and income on investment is tax sheltered while residing in the plan. *See also* Registered Retirement Savings Plan, Roth IRA.

Indonesian Stock Exchange: *see* Jakarta Stock Exchange.

Induct: to place formally in office.

Induction: the process of being put formally in office.

Industrial: generally, a term describing the production of goods and services that are not in the utility, transportation or financial sectors.

Industrial Espionage: the use of unethical and/or illegal methods to steal trade secrets from a competitor. *See also* Industrial Spy.

Industrialist: one who owns, or has an interest in, an industrial enterprise.

Industrialize: to make an economy or region industrial.

Industrial Park: a closed area, often located in the outskirts of a city, within which industrial businesses are located.

Industrial Production: a monthly estimate of the total U.S. output from mining, manufacturing and utilities.

Industrial Spy: a person paid to steal trade secrets from a competitor. *See also* Industrial Espionage.

Industrial Stocks: shares of an industrial company.

Industry: a sector of the economy made up of a single or related business(es) (e.g., the automobile industry). *See also* Industry Analyst.

Industry Analyst: a financial analyst who specializes in appraising the investment merits of companies in a specific industry. Also known as Industry Specialist. *See also* Financial Analyst, Industry, Industry Forecast.

Industry Bet: a strategy in which a portfolio manager owns more (or fewer) shares in a paricular industry than is represented in a stock market index. *See also* Market Bet, Stock Bet, Stock Market Bet.

Industry Forecast: an outlook that takes into consideration an entire industry rather than the individual companies of which it is comprised. *See also* Industry Analyst.

Industry Fund: *see* Industry Mutual Fund.

Industry Life Cycle: the stages of evolution through which an industry progresses as it moves from its start-up through expansion, maturity and decline. Also known as Life Cycle. *See also* Decline, Expansion, Maturity, Startup.

Industry Mutual Fund: *see* Specialty/Miscellaneous Fund. Also known as Industry Fund.

Industry Sector Concentration (ISC): a measure developed by the Investment Funds Standards Committee to gauge the differences between a mutual

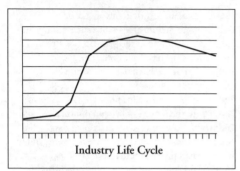

Industry Life Cycle

fund portfolio industry weightings and the weightings of the Toronto Stock Exchange 300 Sub-Indexes. The ISC is the cumulative difference between the industry weightings in the mutual fund portfolio and the weightings of the index. If the portfolio is exactly the same as the index, the ISC will equal zero. A high ISC indicates a portfolio that is concentrated in a few industries. *See also* Investment Funds Standards Committee, Toronto Stock Exchange 300 Sub-Index (Communications and Media Index)-(Utilities Index), Industry Weighting.

Industry Segment: a component of a business that is identified by product line, geographic region or division.

Industry Specialist: *see* Industry Analyst.

Industry Specific Risk: an influence on the price of a security that stems from industry factors (e.g., the price of shares of auto manufacturers drop when tougher emission standards are announced). *See also* Company Specific Risk, Event Risk, Non-Systematic Risk, Risk, Specific Risk, Systematic Risk.

Industry Weighting: the percentage of a portfolio that is held in securities of a specific industry group (e.g., financial services).

Inelasticity of Demand: a measure of how much demand changes for a given change in price. Demand is inelastic if large price changes result in small demand changes. *See also* Elasticity of Demand.

Inelasticity of Supply: a measure of how much supply changes for a given change in price. Supply is inelastic if large price changes produce small supply changes. *See also* Elasticity of Supply.

In Extremis: at the point of death.

Infancy: the early stages in the development of something (e.g., a new company).

Infant: *see* Minor.

Infant Industry Theory: the argument that domestic industries need protection until they are mature. This argument is used to justify tariffs and other forms of protection from international competition.

Infect: in computers, to contaminate with a virus. *See also* Computer, Virus.

Infighting: a disruptive or destructive rivalry within an organization.

Infill Drilling: the drilling of exploration holes between successful holes already drilled.

Inflation: 1. a period during which the Consumer Price Index and similar price indexes are rising. *See also* Deflation, Disinflation. **2.** a time of generally rising prices for consumer goods and services. Also known as Price Inflation. *See also* Deflation, Disinflation.

Inflation Accounting: accounting that reflects the effect of inflation on company financial statements. *See also* Inflation Profit, Inventory Profit.

Inflationary: causing inflation.

Inflationary Psychology: the expectation of inflation and the effect it has on individual behaviour (e.g., it makes consumers more likely to borrow in order to buy).

Inflation Hedge: an investment whose value will rise more quickly than will the rate of inflation.

Inflation Indexed Annuity: *see* Indexed Annuity.

Inflation Premium: the part of an investment return that compensates for expected inflation.

Inflation Profit: profit derived solely from the effect of rising prices because of inflation. Such profits are illusory because they cannot be repeated unless inflation continues. *See also* Inflation Accounting, Inventory Profit.

Inflation-Proofing: the act of protecting investments from loss of purchasing power due to inflation.

Inflation Rate: the percentage rate at which the price of consumer goods and services is rising (usually over a one-year period) or at which the purchasing power of currency is declining. *See also* Consumer Price Index.

Inflation Risk: the chance that the purchasing power of income and real value of assets will decline because of inflation, especially after retirement. Also known as Purchasing Power Risk. *See also* Inflation, Purchasing Power of a Dollar.

Info: short for information.

Infomercial: a television commercial made to look like a regular program in order to disguise that it is a bought-and-paid-for advertisement involved in direct-response marketing. *See also* Advertorial, Advocacy Advertising, Direct Response Marketing, Infotainment, Institutional Advertising, Situmercial.

Information Circular: a document sent to shareholders that provides information on matters to come before the annual general meeting. *See also* Annual General Meeting.

Information Package: material assembled by receivers in order to assist those interested in buying the assets of a party that has gone into receivership. Also used for underwriting securities.

Information Superhighway: another term for the Internet, first popularized in U.S. government circles by Vice-President Al Gore. The idea behind the Internet was that interconnected computers from around the world could use digital technology to move more information while involving less infrastructure. The Internet has expanded this concept into an international information infrastructure. *See also* Internet, World Wide Web.

Information Super Hypeway: a derogatory term applied to the Information Superhighway when initial optimistic forecasts were not achieved.

Information Technology (IT): a reference to a wide range of hardware and software products designed to process information, usually within a corporate setting. *See also* Chief Information Officer.

Infotainment: one of many television programs engaged in direct-response marketing, infotainment presents what appears to be entertainment but what is, in fact, a bought-and-paid-for commercial message. *See also* Advertorial, Advocacy Advertising, Direct Response Marketing, Infomercial, Institutional Advertising, Situmercial.

Infraction: a violation.

Infrastructure: 1. the economic foundation of a country, including roads, power, transportation and communications. **2.** the underlying base of an organization or structure.

Ingot: a bar of a precious metal.

Ingress: a means of entering a property. *See also* Egress, Ingress and Egress.

Ingress and Egress: the right of a lessee to enter and to leave a leasehold property. *See also* Egress.

Inherent Value: a notional concept of an asset's value that is actual or correct. Also known as Real Value or True Value.

Inherit: to possess, as an heir, either through descent or through a will. *See also* Will.

Inheritance: something that is inherited. *See also* Will.

Inheritance Tax: a tax levied on the estate of a deceased person.

In-House: in a company, something conducted or produced internally.

Initialize: 1. in computers, to assign a starting value to a variable. **2.** to prepare a computer disk for use. **3.** to start up a computer. *See also* Computer.

Initial Public Offering (IPO): the first offering of a company's shares to the public. An IPO is always a primary offering, but a primary offering is only an

IPO when it is the first time a company sells its shares to the public. *See also* Primary Offering, Second Round Financing.

Injunction: in law, a court order that prohibits an activity.

Injury: in law, any wrong or damage done to another.

In Kind: payment or satisfaction of an obligation using goods and/or services instead of money.

In-Law Suite: a suite, often located in a single-family residence, used or rented by a relative of the occupant/owner. The occupant/owner often contends that he/she has the right to house a relative, even though municipal bylaws prohibit him/her from renting to other individuals. *See also* Illegal Suite.

In Line: according to expectations. Earnings "in line" with estimates are actual earnings that are close to forecasts.

In-Migration: the movement of people into one region of a country from another region of the same country. *See also* Out-Migration.

Inner City: the central, usually older, part of a city.

Innocent: in law, a verdict of not guilty.

In Perpetuity: forever.

In Play: used with reference to a company that has been, or is widely rumoured to be, the target of a takeover attempt.

Input: information that is entered into a computer. *See also* Computer, Output.

Input/Output Device (IO Device): equipment used to move information into or out of a computer. A keyboard is an input device; a printer is an output device. *See also* Cathode-Ray Tube, Computer, Computer Screen, Disk Drive, Interactive Terminal, Joystick, Keyboard, Keypad, Laser Printer, Line Printer, Monitor, Optical Character Reader, Peripheral, Printer, Printout, Readout, Remote Access, Terminal.

Input/Output Unit (I/O Unit): concerned with one of the four basic functions of a computer, this unit controls the flow of data and instructions into and out of the machine. *See also* Computer, Control Unit, Logic Unit, Memory Unit.

Inquest: a judicial inquiry into an unexplained or suspicious death.

In Re: in the matter of.

Inside Buildup: cash value increases in a life insurance policy. *See also* Whole Life Insurance.

Inside Director: a director of a company who is also an employee and/or major shareholder. *See also* Board of Directors, Director, Interlocking Director, Outside Director.

Inside Information: company information that is not widely disseminated and that, if it were, would have a material effect on the price of company securities. It is not illegal to possess inside information, but using it to realize profits from stock trading may result in sanctions by a securities commission. Also known as Nonpublic Information. *See* Insider Trading, Material Information, Mosaic Theory, Tippee, Tipper.

Inside Market: 1. a market that involves security trades among and between investment dealers. **2.** a quote made up of the highest bid price and lowest offering price from market makers. *See also* Market Maker.

Inside Track: an advantageous position.

Insider: anyone with inside information. A senior management person may be an insider by virtue of his/her job. *See also* Insider Trading.

Insider Buying: a pattern of stock purchases by a company's management. Insider buying is generally interpreted as a positive sign for the stock in question. This form of insider buying is legitimate and must be reported to the regulators in a timely fashion. *See also* Insider Trading.

Insider Report: a report by all persons considered insiders, detailing all buying and selling activity. The report must be filed monthly with the provincial securities commission. *See also* Insider Buying, Insider Selling.

Insider Selling: a pattern of stock sales by a company's management. Insider selling is generally interpreted as a negative sign for the stock in question. This form of insider buying is legitimate and must be reported to the regulators in a timely fashion. *See also* Insider Trading.

Insider Trading: 1. an unethical and improper activity that entails a person taking advantage of inside information in order to earn profits by trading the securities in question. *See also* Self-Dealing, Tippee, Tipper. **2.** a legitimate activity that entails an insider buying or selling shares in his/her company while at the same time reporting trading as required by regulators. *See* Inside Information, Insider, Mosaic Theory.

In Situ: in the resource industries, a term that describes reserves that are in the ground in a natural, undisturbed state.

Insolvent: the condition of being unable to meet one's financial obligations. *See also* Bankrupt, Solvent.

Issuing Bank: in a transaction involving a letter of credit, the bank that acts on behalf of the buyer of goods and issues a letter credit for payment. Also known as Opening Bank. *See also* Advising Bank, Negotiating Bank.

Installed Base: in reference to computer hardware or software, the number of systems in commercial use. *See also* Computer.

Installment: one of a series of successive payments.

Installment Accounting: the act of accounting for income from the sale of an asset purchased on installments so that profits are recognized in proportion to the percentage of the sale price collected within a given period.

Installment Payments: 1. payments made when something is purchased subject to an installment sales contract. **2.** in income taxes, the requirement to make quarterly payments to Canada Customs and Revenue Agency.

Installment Receipt: a form of new issue, popular with income trusts, in which the investor pays part of the purchase price today and the balance (often half) in the future.

Installment Sale: 1. the sale of goods or services with a contractual obligation to make payments in agreed-upon amounts over time. **2.** the sale of a security through an installment receipt. *See also* Installment Receipt.

Installment Sales Contact: an agreement giving the buyer possession of, but not title to, an asset purchased under an installment sale.

INSTINET: *see* Institutional Networks Corporation.

Institute of Canadian Bankers (ICB): a body formed in 1967 to provide additional education and training courses for bank employees at universities across Canada.

Institute of Certified Financial Planners (ICFP): a U.S. financial-planning organization that issues the Certified Financial Planner designation.

Institute of Chartered Financial Analysts (ICFA): an affiliate of the Financial Analysts Federation and a subsidiary of the Association for Investment Management and Research in the U.S. that administers examinations and awards the professional designation of Chartered Financial Analyst.

Institution: an organization, often having to do with financial services.

Institutional Account: the account of an institutional investor at a brokerage firm. *See also* Retail Account.

Institutional Advertising: advertising that promotes a general product or industry rather than a specific brand. *See also* Advertorial, Advocacy Advertising, Direct Response Marketing, Infomercial, Infotainment, Institutional Advertising, Situmercial.

Institutional Broker: a broker specializing in servicing the needs of institutional investors such as banks, mutual funds and pension funds. *See also* Retail Broker.

Institutional Broker's Estimate System (IBES): a compilation of analysts' estimates of earnings of public companies. IBES is run by Lynch, Jones & Ryan, a New York–based specialist in institutional research and trading.

Institutional Buying: the buying of a security by institutional investors.

Institutional Department: in a brokerage firm, the group of brokers that deals with institutional investors.

Institutional Investor: a large investment organization (e.g., a mutual fund or pension fund manager) or a financial institution (e.g., a bank, insurance or trust company) that engages in the management of large pools of capital. *See also* Individual Investor.

Institutionalize: to raise to the status of an institution, as in "Wall Street has institutionalized the chairman of the Federal Reserve Board, Alan Greenspan."

Institutional Networks Corporation (INSTINET): a computerized system in the U.S. that facilitates fourth market trading for subscribers. *See also* Fourth Market.

Institutional Selling: the selling of a security by institutional investors.

Instrument: a legal document that provides evidence of a contractual agreement.

Insurability: the extent to which a person is or is not an acceptable insurance risk. *See also* Life Insurance.

Insurable Interest: in property, any title or interest that can be insured.

Insurance: a system in which one party seeks protection from an event by paying premiums to a second party (who will reimburse the first party should the event occur). *See also* Self-Insurance.

Insurance Age: a person's age as it pertains to the calculation of life insurance premiums. Some companies use the person's last birthday to determine his/her age; others use his/her nearest birthday. *See also* Life Insurance.

Insurance Agent: *see* Life Insurance Agent.

Insurance Broker: *see* Broker.

Insurance Company: a company licensed to underwrite and sell insurance to the public.

Insurance Dividend: a sum of money paid (often annually) to holders of cash value, participating life insurance. The amount of the dividend is based on the insurance company's mortality experience, administrative expenses and investment returns. *See also* Life Insurance.

Insurance Policy: the printed legal document stating the terms and conditions of an insurance contract. *See also* Life Insurance Policy.

Insurance Premium: payment made for insurance coverage. *See also* Life Insurance Premium.

Insurance Settlement: the payment of a claim made under the terms of an insurance contract.

Insure: to cover with insurance. *See also* Insurance, Insured, Insurer.

Insured: the person whose life is insured. Not always the policy holder. *See also* Insurance, Insure, Insurer.

Insurer: the company that accepts the risk and issues an insurance policy. Also known as Underwriter. *See also* Insurance, Insure, Insured.

IT: *see* Information Technology.

Intangible Asset: an asset that has value but not a physical presence (e.g., patents, trademarks and copyrights). *See also* Real Asset.

Integer: one of any of the positive whole numbers (1, 2, 3, etc.), negative whole numbers (-1, -2, -3, etc.) or zero (0).

Integrated Circuit: a tiny piece of semiconducting material containing miniaturized circuit elements. Also known as Microchip.

Integrated Oil Company: a company engaged in all aspects of the oil and gas industry, including exploration and development, production and refining and marketing. *See also* Development, Exploration Company, Oil Company, Production Company, Refining and Marketing.

Integrated Services Digital Network (ISDN): a worldwide digital communications network evolving from existing telephone services. The goal of ISDN is to enable the high-speed digital communication of data over regular telephone lines, which will provide users with faster, more extensive communications services.

Integration: a term used to describe the processes used by Canada Customs and Revenue Agency to equalize the amount of income tax paid on income by an individual, whether the income is derived from a corporate or personal structure. *See also* Taxes.

Intellectual Property: generally, intangible assets, such as patents, trademarks and copyrights, that are the product of invention or creativity.

Intelligence Quotient (IQ): a number designed to indicate a person's intelligence in relation to the average for his/her age group, which is set at 100.

Interac: an association of financial institutions to provide banking machine and direct payment services.

Interactive: having the ability to act upon each other or influence each other. An interactive program is one where the observer has a means to question and receive answers from the presenters.

Interactive Terminal: a computer terminal capable of providing a two-way flow of communication between the user and the system. *See also* Cathode-Ray Tube, Computer, Computer Screen, Disk Drive, Input/Output Device, Joystick, Keyboard, Keypad, Laser Printer, Line Printer, Monitor, Optical

Character Recognition, Peripheral, Printer, Printout, Readout, Remote Access, Terminal.

Inter Alia: among other things.

Inter Alia Mortgage: a mortgage against two or more properties. Also known as Blanket Mortgage. *See also* Mortgage.

Interconnected Spanish Stock Exchange System (SIBE): *see* IBEX 35.

Intercorporate Freeze: an estate-planning strategy in which the intended beneficiaries become share-holders of a new company, and the existing operating company engages in a tax-free rollover of its business and assets, which move to the new company. This transaction enables the beneficiaries to become share-holders in the existing company without triggering income tax consequences for the previous owners of the existing company. Also known as Reverse Freeze.

Interest: 1. a share in, or title to, an asset. **2.** *see* Interest Rate.

Interest Bearing: a security that pays interest.

Interest Coverage: *see* Time Interest Earned.

Interest Deduction: the amount of interest expense that can be used to reduce taxable income.

Interest Differential: 1. the difference between the interest rate paid by two different securities. **2.** the difference between the interest rate paid by similar financial securities issued by different countries.

Interest Equivalent: often, the amount of interest income needed to yield the same after tax return as dividends. In 1998, the interest equivalent of 3.75 percent dividend yield was 5.00 percent interest. In other words, a dividend yield of 3.75 percent and an interest yield of approximately 5.00 percent leave a taxable investor with the same amount of income after income taxes are paid. *See also* Interest Equivalent Ratio.

Interest Equivalent Ratio: the ratio that converts a dividend yield into the interest rate yield that will provide the same after tax return. In 1998, the ratio was 1.33. In other words, a dividend yield multiplied by 1.33 gives the approximate interest return needed to have the same after tax income (e.g., 3.75 per cent dividend yield times 1.33 equals 5.00 per cent inter-est equivalent). *See also* Interest Equivalent.

Interest Equalization Tax: a 15% tax on interest that used to be paid by foreign borrowers of U.S. capital. The tax was a major factor in the development of the Eurobond market, which enabled foreigners to bor-row U.S. dollars without paying the tax.

Interest Group: a group that supports a common cause.

Interest Letter: a letter from a lender to a borrower that is used to show Canada Customs and Revenue

Agency the amount of tax-deductible interest paid on a loan during a given taxation period. *See also* Taxes.

Interest on Interest: *see* Compound Interest.

Interest-Only: a loan payment that covers only the interest portion and does not reduce the principal amount outstanding.

Interest Option: in insurance, the right of a policy holder to reinvest insurance dividends at a fixed rate of interest. *See also* Life Insurance.

Interest Rate: 1. the cost of borrowing money expressed as a percentage of the amount borrowed for a given time period (usually a year). **2.** the return paid to a lender of money expressed as a percentage of the amount lent for a given time period (usually a year). *See also* Income.

Interest Rate Differential Penalty: a penalty often charged when a mortgage is prepaid to take advan-tage of lower interest rates. In effect, the borrower makes up the difference between the rate of interest that was being charged and the new rate of interest over the remaining term of the previous loan. *See also* Mortgage, Mortgage Prepayment, Penalty, Prepayment Penalty, Prepayment Privilege.

Interest Rate Future: futures contracts on financial assets, such as government securities and commercial paper. *See also* Financial Futures Contract, Futures.

Interest Rate Option: an option on a financial instrument with a market price sensitive to changes in interest rates (e.g., a call option on a bond). *See also* Option.

Interest Rate Risk: 1. the risk stemming from a rise in interest rates that may result in capital losses. This may occur because the value of bonds and other fixed income securities declines as interest rates rise. *See also* Bond, Risk. **2.** in a business, the risk that higher interest rates can raise costs and lower profits. *See also* Business Risk, Risk.

Interest Rate Swap: an exchange of different interest rate exposure between two financial portfolios. In an interest rate swap, the portfolios do not exchange the actual value of bonds but agree on an amount called the notional principal amount. The periodic interest payments (which are actually swapped) is calculated on the notional periodic amount. The transaction amounts to a reduction of risk for both portfolios. *See also* Asset Swap, Notional Principal Amount.

Interest Sensitive: a tendency to change in price as interest rates move up and down.

Interest Sensitive Security: a security, such as a bond, whose price changes conversely with interest rates. *See also* Interest Sensitive Stock.

Interest Sensitive Stock: a common stock with a share price that is sensitive to changes in interest rates. A public utility stock is considered interest sensitive. *See also* Interest Sensitive Security.

Interface: a piece of equipment that enables interaction between two or more computer systems. *See also* Computer.

Inter-Governmental Conferences (IGC): a forum for members of the European Union to negotiate treaty revisions.

Interim Dividend: usually, the first three dividend payments during any given year. The fourth and final payment is based on the relative success or failure of the financial year and may, as a result, be higher or lower than previous payouts.

Interim Financial Statement: a financial report covering part of a fiscal year, usually one quarter. Also known as Interim Report, Interim Statement.

Interim Financing: temporary short-term financing that is put in place while one is awaiting permanent, long-term financing.

Interim Insurance Certificate: evidence that, once the life insurance application is signed and the initial premium is paid, one's life insurance is in effect within certain limits. The interim insurance certificate is in effect until a contract is issued. *See also* Life Insurance.

Interim Order: in law, a temporary order.

Interim Report: *see* Interim Financial Statement.

Interim Statement: *see* Interim Financial Statement.

Interlocking Director: a director who serves on more than one board (often, directors serve on each other's boards). *See also* Board of Directors, Director, Inside Director, Outside Director.

Interlocutory Decree: a temporary decree made during the course of a trial.

Intermediary: an individual (or financial institution) who accepts excess capital from other individuals (or firms) and moves it to those who have a shortfall (e.g., a credit union takes deposits from members with excess capital and issues mortgages to members who have a shortfall).

Intermediate Term: *see* Medium Term.

Intermediate Trend: a short-term trend that occurs within the boundaries of, and in a different direction to, a long-term trend.

Intermediation: 1. the addition of various levels of activity between the product and the consumer. **2.** in finance, the process of funds flowing from a financial institution to investors and borrowers.

Internal Audit: an audit conducted by people who are employed by the company being audited. *See also* Independent Audit.

Internal Controls: the system used for placing restrictions on employees throughout the various levels of any organization (e.g., the size of loan that can be approved by a loans officer).

Internal Efficiency: *see* Internal Market Efficiency.

Internal Financing: the process of meeting financial requirements through the use of internally generated earnings and cash flow.

Internal Growth: *see* Organic Growth.

Internal Market Efficiency: the extent to which trading costs are minimized. The factors determining internal market efficiency include liquidity, minimum trading costs, equal treatment of all participants and close supervision to prevent trading abuses. Also known as Internal Efficiency.

Internal Rate of Return: the interest rate that, when used to discount an investment's future cash flow, results in a present value equal to the cost of investment. *See also* Discount, Future Value, Present Value, Time Value of Money.

Internal Revenue Service (IRS): the U.S. government agency responsible for the collection of income taxes. *See also* Canada Customs and Revenue Agency.

International Balanced Fund: *see* Global Balanced and Asset Allocation Fund.

International Bank for Reconstruction and Development (IBRD): *see* World Bank.

International Bond Fund: 1. *see* Foreign Bond Fund. **2.** *see* Mutual Fund – Category.

International Business Machines Corporation (IBM): one of the founding companies of the computer hardware industry. IBM produces computers and related technology, software, systems and services. IBM is one of the 30 stocks in the Dow-Jones Average. Also known as Big Blue. Web site: www.ibm.com *See also* Computer.

International Chamber of Commerce: an international group that promotes international trade. *See also* INCOTERMS.

International Common Stock Fund: *see* International Equity Fund.

International Copyright: the protection of literary and artistic property through international agreement.

International Court of Justice: *see* World Court.

International Depository Receipt: a bank-issued receipt for a foreign company's share certificate. *See also* American Depository Receipt, Global Depository Receipt.

International Equity Fund: one of the 31 Canadian categories developed by the Investment Funds Standards Committee. Mutual funds in this category must have a minimum of 50 percent of the total assets, and 75 percent of the non-cash assets, of the portfolio in equities or equity equivalents of companies located outside Canada and the U.S. or derivative-based exposure to such markets. The calculations to determine whether a mutual fund fits this definition are based on median values from fund data over three years, unless otherwise noted. The derivatives are weighted on an extended value basis. Each of the categories may be refined by the fund manager (e.g., a Canadian Large Cap Equity Fund might be described as "growth" or "value" to reflect the manager's style). Also known as International Common Stock Fund, International Stock Fund. *See also* Extended Value, Mutual Fund – Category.

International Financial Centre: under federal and provincial legislation implemented in 1987, Vancouver and Montreal were designated as international financial centres. Canadian and non-Canadian financial institutions with offices in Vancouver and/or Montreal with this designation receive income tax rebates and regulatory relief for financial transactions with non-resident investors.

International Fund: *see* International Mutual Fund.

International Government Bond Fund: 1. *see* Foreign Bond Fund. **2.** *see* Mutual Fund – Category.

International Law: a set of rules accepted as binding by those nations that have agreed to it.

International Monetary Fund (IMF): a United Nations agency whose goal is to help developing countries pay debts, lower inflation and promote domestic growth while generally trying to lower barriers to trade and stabilize currency values. Special drawing rights are used to help countries with a shortage of foreign exchange. *See also* Special Drawing Rights.

International Monetary Reserves: reserves of foreign currency, gold and International Monetary Fund (IMF) reserves held by countries. In early 1999, Canada's international monetary reserves were made up of U.S. dollars, other international currencies, gold, special drawing rights and reserves with the IMF. *See also* International Monetary Fund, Special Drawing Rights.

International Money Market Fund: 1. *see* Foreign Money Market Fund. **2.** *see* Mutual Fund – Category.

International Mutual Fund: a mutual fund that invests in securities of countries other than Canada. Also known as International Fund. *See also* Mutual Fund – Other.

International Option: a transferrable foreign currency option traded on the International Stock Exchange of the U.K. and the Republic of Ireland and Philadelphia Stock Exchange and cleared by the Options Clearing Corporation. Also known as an IFX Option. *See also* International Stock Exchange of

the U.K. and the Republic of Ireland, Options Clearing Corporation, Philadelphia Stock Exchange.

International Options Clearing Corporation (IOCC): an options clearing organization whose members are the Amsterdam, Montreal, Vancouver and Sydney stock exchanges. *See also* Amsterdam Stock Exchange, Montreal Exchange, Vancouver Stock Exchange, Stock Exchange Automated Trading System.

International Organization for Standardization (ISO): a federation of national standards bodies from approximately 90 countries. Promotes standardization in order to facilitate trade as well as intellectual, scientific, technical and economic activity. *See also* CSA International.

International Securities Exchange (ISE): subject to regulatory approval, this will be the first electronic options market in the United States. Web site: www.iseoptions.com/html/aeover.htm

International Securities Identification Numbering System (ISIN): a uniform code for identifying securities made up of 12 alpha-numeric characters. The first 2 identify the country, the following 9 are the security's local number and the final character is a check digit. The ISIN is issued by a National Numbering Agency. *See also* Committee on Uniform Security Identification Procedures, National Numbering Agency.

International Securities Market Association (ISMA): an association of investment and financial professionals active in international securities markets. The ISMA provides information and guidance to participants in international capital markets.

International Stock Exchange of the U.K. and the Republic of Ireland (ISE): the organization formed to replace the London Stock Exchange following the Big Bang in 1986. The ISE is still commonly referred to as the London Stock Exchange or by its nickname, "The House." Web site: www.stockex.co.uk

International Stock Fund: 1. *see* International Equity Fund. **2.** *see* Mutual Fund – Category.

International Will: an English form will that requires an additional witness who is defined as an "authorized person" (e.g., a lawyer). *See also* English Form Will, Holographic Will, Living Will, Notarial Will, Oral Will, Other Wills, Will.

Internaut: an active Internet user. *See also* Internet.

Internet: interconnected computers, located around the world, that can be accessed from remote locations for the purpose of data retrieval. The Internet is the world's largest computer network and is not owned by any one person or organization. Also known as The Net. *See also* Carpet Bomb, Chat

Room, .com, Corporate Web Site, Cybernaut, Cyberserf, Cybrarian, e-, .edu, Electronic Business, Electronic Mail, E-mail Address, Encrypt, Extranet, Finger, Flame, Free Mail, Frequently Asked Questions, Gopher, Goperspace, .gov, Hits, Host Computer, Hyperlink, Hypertext, Hypertext Markup Language, Hypertext Transfer Protocol, I-, Information Super Highway, Internaut, Internet2, Internet Acronym, Internet Appliance, Internet Service Provider, Interpreneur, Intranet, IT Department, Joint Photographic Experts Group, Linux, .mil, .net, .org, Search Engine, Universal Resource Language, Usenet, Viral Marketing, World Wide Web.

Internet

The Internet is a worldwide collection of inter-connected computers located primarily in corpo-rate, educational, government, military and research facilities.

It is estimated that, as of 1996, the Internet con-nected 25 million computers in 180 countries and was used by 15 million people every day. The "Net" is the world's largest computer network and is not owned by any one person or organization. It refers to all computer and communications equipment, which form the backbone of the network, and is linked by a common network language.

Internet Service Providers (ISP) offer gateway access to the Internet by, for example, providing a local telephone number that one can call with one's computer modem.

Important components of the Internet are the Hypertext Markup Language (HTML) and the Hypertext Transfer Protocol (HTTP). Files of infor-mation from many sources are formatted in HTML and are moved among computers via the rules that make up HTTP. These files are joined through hyperlinks and comprise the World Wide Web, or WWW.

Browsers, or Web browsers, are programs that use HTTP in order to find and access WWW files.

Internet2: a worldwide network of academic and research facilities. Internet2 is intended to enable sci-entists and others to work together over a computer network. Initially, Internet2 will not be available to the public. *See also* Internet.

Internet Acronyms: words formed by the first letters of a phrase (e.g., AAMOF, meaning **As a Matter of Fact**), acronyms are frequently used on the Internet because data entry is most often through a keyboard and using acronyms saves time. *See also* Internet.

Internet Appliance: a box that converts a cable signal so as to allow an Internet connection with a standard television set. *See also* Internet.

Internet Protocol: part of the common network lan-guage used by computers in order to communicate on the Internet. *See also* Internet.

Internet Protocol (IP) Telephony: an Internet sys-tem that converts a voice signal to a data packet that is then reconverted to voice. IP telephony facilitates telephone communication over the Internet. *See also* Internet.

Internet Service Provider (ISP): a business that pro-vides individuals, companies and other organizations with Internet access through the telephone. Also known as Service Provider. *See also* Internet.

Internet Stock: one of the public companies deriving revenues from business conducted through the Internet. These stocks were investor favourites and, in 1999, traded at extremely high multiples of sales and earnings. Also known as Dot.Com Stock.

Internet Telephony: the act of using the Internet, rather than long-distance telephone services, in order to reduce communication costs. *See also* Internet.

InterNIC: a group responsible for the provision of organizational services, such as network names, on the Internet. *See also* Internet.

Interoffice: something that occurs between offices (usually those belonging to the same organization).

Interpolation: the estimation of an unknown value that lies between two known values by assuming that the unknown value lies on a straight line that con-nects the two known values. *See also* Imputed Value.

Interpreneur: an independent businessperson who earns a living by using the Internet specifically and modern technology and electronic information gen-erally. *See also* Internet.

Interprovincial: between provinces.

Interstate: between states.

Interurban: between cities.

Interview: a face-to-face meeting, often conducted in order to enable one party to assess another as a potential employee.

Inter Vivos Gift: a gift from one living person to another. *See also* Gift.

Inter Vivos Trust: a trust that passes assets from one living person to another. Also known as Living Trust. *See also* Life Insurance Trust, Testamentary Trust, Trust.

Intestacy: *see* Intestate.

Intestate: the condition of being without a will. Also known as Intestacy. *See also* Will.

Intestate Succession: disposition of property accord-ing to the laws of descent upon the death of a person who did not leave a valid will. *See also* Statutory Next-of-Kin, Will.

In the Black: profitable. *See also* In the Red.

In the Hole: in a loss position.

In the Market: to be actively involved in the buying and/or selling of securities.

In the Money: a condition in which the strike price of a put option is above or the strike price of a call option is below the price of the underlying security. *See also* At the Money, Deep in the Money, Deep Out of the Money, Option, Out of the Money.

In the Penalty Box: a term used to describe a company that, for a specific reason (e.g., a poor earnings report) has a low stock price and/or low stock valuation.

In the Pink: in a healthy position.

In the Red: unprofitable. *See also* In the Black.

In the Tank: a security or market that is rapidly falling in value.

In Toto: completely.

Intraday: something that occurs within one day (e.g., an intraday high is the market high reached during one particular day but not necessarily at the close).

Intranet: a system that uses Internet-style e-mail and web browsers but that connects only the offices and/or branches of an individual company and/or organization. The offices/branches may connect with each other on the Internet but share data and proprietary programs only on the Intranet. *See also* Internet.

Intraprovincial: within a province.

Intra Vires: within the law.

Intrinsic Value: 1. the essential worth of something. **2.** in options, the difference between the market price of the underlying security and the strike price of the option. *See also* Option.

Intrusion: in mining, any rock formed initially by flowing magma that has now cooled.

In Trust For (ITF): an expression that denotes an account opened by an adult on behalf of a minor.

Inure: in law, to come into effect or to be operative.

Invalid: not legally binding. Void.

Invasion Power: a provision in a trust that permits the trustee to encroach upon the principal of the trust should the income be considered insufficient to satisfy the beneficiary's needs.

Inventory: 1. a balance sheet entry that represents the value of raw materials and finished goods. **2.** for a brokerage firm, the net position of securities owned for its own account.

Inventory Financing: financing the inventory of sellers of consumer or capital goods. The loan is secured by the value of the inventory. Also known as Wholesale Financing. *See also* Floor Financing.

Inventory Profit: profit derived from the selling price of a manufactured item rising while the cost of components that go into making the product are fixed at historical purchase prices. Inventory profits are considered illusory if inflation causes prices to rise. *See also* Inflation Accounting, Inflation Profit.

Inventory Risk: the chance that the value of inventory will decline. *See also* Business Risk.

Inventory Turnover: in a business, annual sales expressed in dollars divided by the average inventory expressed in dollars, for a given period. A high inventory turnover can be an indication of efficiency because it implies the cost of financing inventory is being kept at minimum levels. Also known as Turnover.

Inverse: reversed in order or effect, as in the inverse relationship between bond yields and bond prices; that is, when yields go up, prices go down and vice versa.

Inverted Market: in futures or options trading, this occurs when short-term contracts have a higher price than do long-term contracts. *See also* Backwardation, Contango, Futures, Option.

Inverted Yield Curve: *see* Negative Yield Curve.

Invest: to place capital with a view to securing income and/or capital gains.

Investigate, then Invest: the conservative practice of not investing until all the facts are known. *See also* Invest, then Investigate.

Investiture: the ceremony of conferring a high office (particularly in politics).

Investment: a lower risk venture that uses money to make money. It is more conservative in nature than speculation. *See also* Speculation.

Investment Advisor (IA): 1. in practice, this term is used as a self-descriptor by anyone who gives advice on investment or financial planning. Such persons may differ greatly in experience and qualifications. **2.** *see* Broker. **3.** *see* Investment Counsellor.

Investment Advisory: a person (or company) who provides investment advice and guidance, often in a newsletter.

Investment Bank: *see* Merchant Bank.

Investment Banker: an intermediary between a corporate or government issuer of securities and institutional or individual investors. Services include structuring financings and managing underwritings.

Investment Banking: *see* Merchant Banking.

Investment Boutique: a relatively small, specialized brokerage company.

Investment Business: an active business engaged in providing investment services. This is different from a person who simply places investments in a company in the expectation of benefiting from a lower income tax rate. *See also* Active Business, Personal Service Business.

Investment Climate: the general economic and monetary conditions that impact the financial markets.

Investment Club: a small group whose members pool money for investment, often with an objective as much educational and social as it is financial. Information on setting up an investment club is available from the Canadian Shareowner's Association Web site: www.shareowner.ca

Investment Company: a corporation, trust or partnership that pools the capital of a large number of investors (who have the same investment objectives) to purchase a professionally managed, diversified portfolio of investments. Closed end and open end mutual funds are the most common investment companies. *See also* Mutual Fund.

Investment Counsellor: a person or company licensed to invest money for others for a fee. Also known as Investment Manager.

Investment Dealer: *see* Broker.

Investment Dealers Association of Canada (IDA): in Canada, an industry association and self-regulatory organization for stockbrokers.

Investment Funds Institute of Canada (IFIC): in Canada, the trade industry association for mutual funds established to serve its members, work with regulators on behalf of members and protect the public investing in mutual funds. Members include representatives of mutual fund managers, mutual fund distributors and others involved in the mutual fund industry. Web site: www.ific.ca *See also* Mutual Fund, Mutual Fund – Category, Mutual Fund – Other.

Investment Funds Standards Committee (IFSC): an independent group that represents all of Canada's major providers of third-party mutual fund data and research. IFSC has a self-imposed mandate to develop standard classifications for Canadian domiciled mutual funds. The initial results were published in the fall of 1998. *See also* Mutual Fund – Category.

Investment Grade: medium to high quality. For Canadian bonds, a Dominion Bond Rating Service rating of Triple-B (low) or better. Also known as Bank Quality.

Investment Income: any periodic income from an investment (e.g., interest, dividends, rent).

Investment Letter: a newsletter that offers investment advice, often circulated to subscribers by mail, fax or e-mail. Also known as Advisory Letter.

Investment Management Company: *see* Management Company.

Investment Manager: *see* Investment Counsellor.

Investment Objectives: goals established for investing. Such goals often fall into the categories of safety, income, capital appreciation and income tax reduction.

Investment Philosophy: the general concepts and beliefs that guide the decisions of an investor or investment manager.

Investment Policy: a written statement that, within the accepted guidelines for investment objectives, outlines how money will be invested.

Investment Portfolio: a grouping of securities owned by a person or company.

Investment Property: real estate purchased with the objective of earning an investment return.

Investment Representative (IR): a person licensed to deal with members of the public on investment matters, including buying and selling securities.

Investment Services Bearish: a poll, published by Investors Intelligence, of the number of investment advisory services that rate the U.S. stock market outlook as negative. As a contrary market indicator, the higher the number of pessimistic services, the better the stock market outlook. Also known as Services Bearish. *See also* Contrarian, Contrary Market Indicator, Contrary Opinion, Investment Services Bullish, Investors Intelligence, Theory of Contrary Opinion.

Investment Services Bullish: a poll, published by Investors Intelligence, of the number of investment advisory services that rate the U.S. stock market outlook as positive. As a contrary market indicator, the higher the number of optimistic services, the worse the stock market outlook. Also known as Services Bullish. *See also* Contrarian, Contrary Market Indicator, Contrary Opinion, Investment Services Bearish, Investors Intelligence, Theory of Contrary Opinion.

Investment Strategy: a long-term approach used to produce high returns for a portfolio (e.g., investing in growth stocks). *See also* Investment Style, Investment Tactics.

Investment Style: a term used to describe an approach to investment that does not change with economic and market conditions (e.g., using an economic forecast as the basis for identifying attractive industries for investment is an investment style known as top down investing). *See also* Investment Strategy, Investment Tactics.

Investment Tactics: short-term methods used to accomplish a long-term investment strategy (e.g., purchasing computer manufacturing company shares may be an investment tactic used to accomplish the strategy of investing in growth stocks). *See also* Investment Strategy, Investment Style.

Investment Universe: *see* Market Portfolio.

Investment Vehicle: a specific investment (e.g., bonds, common stocks, annuities and collectibles).

Investor: a party with funds to commit for long-term returns and average risk. *See also* Conservative Investor, Gambler, Nervous Nellie, Speculator.

Investor Relations (IR): for large companies, an individual (or department) who communicates information to the investing public in a timely fashion. Also known as Financial Public Relations. *See also* Promotion. **2.** For small companies, an individual who promotes investor interest in the shares of the company. *See also* Stock Promoter.

Investors Intelligence: an organization that polls stock market advisory services in an attempt to forecast the outlook for the stock market. *See also* Investment Services Bearish, Investment Services Bullish.

Invest, then Investigate: the speculative practice of investing before all the facts are known. *See also* Investigate, then Invest.

Invoice: a written bill from the seller of goods or services to the buyer.

Involuntary Bailment: a situation that occurs when a landlord, mortgage lender or purchaser takes control of a property and finds a tenant, borrower or previous owner has left goods behind. Under such circumstances, the landlord, lender or purchaser has certain responsibilities for the goods left behind.

Involuntary Lien: *see* Lien.

IOCC: *see* International Options Clearing Corporation.

I/O Devices: *see* Input/Output Devices.

IOU: informal, but legal, evidence of a loan or indebtedness. *See also* Scrip.

I/O Unit: *see* Input/Output Unit.

IPO: *see* Initial Public Offering.

IPU: *see* Index Participation Unit.

Ipso Facto: by the very fact.

Ipso Jure: by the law.

IP Telephony: *see* Internet Protocol (IP) Telephony.

IQ: *see* Intelligence Quotient.

IR: 1. *see* Investor Relations. **2.** *see* Investment Representative.

IRA: *see* Individual Retirement Account.

Iridium: an extremely corrosion-resistant metallic element, used to harden platinum and in wear-resistant bearings. It is a precious metal. *See also* Precious Metal.

Irish Stock Exchange: *see* The Stock Exchange.

Irish Stock Exchange Overall Index: a market capitalization weighted stock market index of all stocks listed on the Irish Stock Exchange, excluding United Kingdom registered companies.

Ironclad: fixed and unchangeable, as in "an ironclad regulation."

Iron Curtain: the political, economic, ideological and military barrier that, between 1945 and 1990, divided the Soviet bloc from the rest of the world.

Iron Pyrite: a gold-coloured mineral commonly referred to as fool's gold.

Ironworker: generally, a construction worker who builds steel high-rise structures.

Irredeemable: something that cannot be bought back or paid off (e.g., a perpetual bond).

Irrefutable: something that is impossible to disprove (e.g., fingerprint evidence is irrefutable).

Irrevocable Beneficiary: a beneficiary whose interest in a life insurance policy cannot be changed without his/her permission. *See also* Beneficiary, Named Beneficiary.

Irrevocable Letter of Credit: a letter of credit that cannot be revoked or cancelled. *See also* Letter of Credit.

Irrevocable Trust: a trust that, once it is set up, cannot be changed.

IRS: *see* Internal Revenue Service.

ISC: *see* Industry Sector Concentration.

ISDN: *see* Integrated Services Digital Network.

ISE: *see* International Stock Exchange of the U.K. and the Republic of Ireland.

ISE National – 100: *see* Istanbul Stock Exchange National – 100.

ISIN: *see* International Securities Identification Numbering System.

ISO: *see* International Organization for Standardization.

Iso: a prefix meaning "equal" (e.g., an isobar, a line on a weather map that connects points of equal barometric pressure).

Isolationism: a national policy that espouses the avoidance of political or economic involvement with other countries.

ISP: *see* Internet Service Provider.

Israeli Stock Exchange: *see* Tel Aviv Stock Exchange.

Israel Stock Market General: a weighted average stock market index for the Tel Aviv Stock Exchange.

Issue: 1. an amount of new securities to be sold to the public. **2.** the process of selling new securities. **3.** in estate law, a person's descendants. *See also* Failure of Issue.

Issued Capital: *see* Issued and Outstanding.

Issued and Outstanding: shares of a company that have been issued and are owned by the public, as opposed to shares that are authorized to be issued but have not yet been distributed. Also known as Shares Issued, Shares Outstanding, Outstanding Shares. *See also* Authorized Capital.

Issue Price: the price at which new securities are sold to the public.

Issuer: a company or government that sells securities to the public.

Issuer Bid: *see* Normal Course Issuer Bid.

Issuing Company: a company that has issued the securities in question.

Istanbul Menkul Kiymetier Borsasi: *see* Istanbul Stock Exchange.

Istanbul Stock Exchange: the major stock exchange of Turkey, located in Istanbul. Also known as Istanbul Menkul Kiymetier Borsasi. Web site: www.ise.org/

Istanbul Stock Exchange National - 100: a market value based index for the Istanbul Stock Exchange in Turkey. This index replaced the Turkey Stock Market Indices National 100 on January 2, 1997. Also known as the ISE National - 100.

IT: *see* Information Technology.

Italian Stock Exchange: a major stock exchange of Italy, located in Milan. Also known as Borsa Valori di Milano, Milan Stock Exchange. Web site: www. borsaitalia.it/

IT Department: in a company, the department responsible for managing Internet activities and projects. *See also* Internet.

Iteration: an estimation method that involves a computer repeatedly trying slightly different variables until the desired answer is attained. *See also* Computer.

ITF: *see* In Trust For.

Itinerant: travelling from place to place to work. *See also* Migrant Worker.

Ivory Tower: a place removed from the ordinary world (generally used with reference to academic institutions).

Ivy League: a group of eastern U.S. universities renowned for their scholastic and social prestige, including Brown, Columbia, Cornell, Dartmouth, Harvard, Pennsylvania State, Princeton and Yale.

Jackpot: informally, a large profit from an investment.

JAJO: short for January, April, July and October, the months in which many companies pay quarterly dividends and one of the option cycles. *See also* Option Cycle.

Jakarta Stock Exchange: the major stock exchange of Indonesia, located in its capital, Jakarta. Also known as Gedung Bursa Efek Jakarta. Web site: www.dbc.com

Jakarta Stock Price Index: a market capitalization weighted index for the Jakarta Stock Exchange.

Jam: to force a security into an account when the appropriateness of so doing is questionable.

Jamaica Stock Exchange: the major stock exchange of Jamaica, located in its capital, Kingston. Web site: www.jamstockex.com

Jamaica Stock Market Index Main: a stock market index for the Jamaica Stock Exchange.

James Bond: a bond that matures in 2007.

Jane Doe: a reference to an anonymous or average female person. Also known as Jane Q. Public. *See also* John Doe.

Jane Q. Public: *see* Jane Doe.

January Barometer: an indicator stating that the direction of the U.S. stock market throughout the year will be the same as the direction set by Standard & Poor's in the month of January.

January Effect: the tendency of the U.S. stock market to be strong from December 31 through the first four trading days of the new year.

Japanese Equity Fund: one of the 31 Canadian categories developed by the Investment Funds Standards Committee. Mutual funds in this category must have a minimum of 50 percent of the total assets, and 75 percent of the non-cash assets, of the portfolio in equities or equity equivalents of Japanese companies or derivative-based exposure to Japanese equity markets. The calculations to determine whether a mutual fund fits this definition are based on median values from fund data over three years, unless otherwise noted. The derivatives are weighted on an extended value basis. Each of the categories may be refined by the fund manager (e.g., a Canadian Large Cap Equity Fund might be described as "growth" or "value" to reflect the manager's style). *See also* Extended Value, Mutual Fund – Category.

Japanese Stock Exchange: *see* Tokyo Stock Exchange.

Japan, Inc.: in the 1980s and early 1990s, a general reference to Japan's economic and business power.

Jargon: the technical language of a trade or profession.

Java: a programming language that can run on any operating platform. This makes it popular for creating small programs, called applets, for use on the World Wide Web.

Jawboning: *see* Moral Suasion.

JCP: *see* Junior Capital Pool.

J-Curve: a technical price pattern that, when plotted on a chart, looks like the letter "J." The term "J-Curve" is often used to describe the effect of a currency devaluation on a country's balance of trade.

Jelly Roll Spread: an option strategy made up of a put option and a call option on the same stock market index with different expiration dates. *See also* Option.

Jeopardy: in law, the risk of being convicted for a criminal offense.

Jerry-Build: to build in a shoddy manner.

Jewel: 1. a precious stone or gemstone. **2.** a general reference to something ornamental and of some value.

Jingoism: extreme nationalism, often accompanied by militaristic foreign policy.

Jitney: in investment, the process by which a broker with a direct access to a particular stock exchange performs trades for a broker who does not have such access.

Job: 1. a position of employment. **2.** to act as a jobber.

Job Action: a temporary strategy by unionized employees (e.g., rotating strikes) to support their contract demands.

Jobber: a person who buys merchandise from a manufacturer and resells it to retailers.

Job Lot: 1. a unit of trading that is less than a full contract amount. On the Winnipeg Commodity Exchange, for instance, a full contract for grain is 5,000 bushels and a job lot is 1,000 bushels. **2.** a variety of unrelated goods sold as one unit.

Johannesburg All Market Index: a market capitalization weighted index for the Johannesburg Stock Exchange.

Johannesburg Stock Exchange: a major stock exchange of South Africa, located in its capital, Johannesburg. Web site: www.jse.co.za

John Doe: a reference to an anonymous or average male person. Also known as John Q. Public. *See also* Jane Doe.

John Q. Public: *see* John Doe.

Joint: in mining, a disturbance or break below the surface of the Earth in which no rock movement has occurred. Often the source of mineralization and, thus, the location of mines.

Joint Account: an account held by two or more people who have equal rights and privileges to it. A joint account cannot be attacked by a creditor with a legal claim unless it applies to all joint owners.

Joint and Last Survivor: a term used in the insurance industry, often in reference to life insurance or an annuity, in which a benefit is contracted for as long as the two beneficiaries (usually a husband and wife) or one of the two beneficiaries is living. *See also* Annuity, Life Insurance.

Joint and Last Survivor Annuity: an annuity that continues to pay as long as the two beneficiaries (usually a husband and wife) or one of the beneficiaries is living. *See also* Annuity.

Joint and Several: a condition in which a guarantee is provided by a number of guarantors, all of whom, either together or individually, are responsible for the entire obligation. Also known as Jointly and Severally.

Joint Bond: a bond that either has more than one issuer or that is guaranteed by another party. *See also* Bond.

Joint Custody: a court order whereby both parents are awarded legal guardianship of a child (or children) after separation or divorce.

Joint Endorsement: this occurs when a financial instrument has more than one payee and when the signature of all payees is needed in order to negotiate it. *See also* Endorse, Qualified Endorsement, Restricted Endorsement.

Joint First-to-Die: insurance based on two lives (usually those of a husband and wife) and that pays when the first insured dies. This insurance is often used to cover taxes triggered by the death of the first spouse. *See also* Life Insurance.

Joint Liability: a shared liability, under the terms of which if any one party is sued, then he/she can insist that everyone else be sued as well.

Joint Life Annuity: an annuity based on two lives (usually those of a husband and a wife) and that pays until one person dies. *See also* Annuity, Life Insurance.

Jointly and Severally: *see* Joint and Several.

Joint Petition: an application for divorce made by two spouses, both of whom wish it to be uncontested. *See also* Contested Divorce, Uncontested Divorce.

Joint Photographic Experts Group (JPEG): JPEG is a common graphics file format that is used on the Internet. *See also* Internet.

Joint Second-to-Die: insurance based on two lives (usually those of a husband and a wife) and that pays when the second insured dies. This insurance is often used to cover taxes triggered by the death of the second spouse. *See also* Life Insurance.

Joint Stock Company: a company, somewhere between a partnership and a corporation, in which investors remain liable for all company obligations.

Joint Tenancy: *see* Tenants in Common.

Joint Tenancy with Right of Survival (JTWROS): a form of ownership in which each tenant has equal interests and survivor(s) automatically receive an equal share of a deceased tenant's interests through the "right of survivorship" (e.g, five joint tenants each own one-fifth or 20 percent of a bank account; if one owner dies, that interest disappears and the four surviving joint tenants each own one-fourth or 25 percent). *See also* Right of Survivorship, Tenant, Tenants in Common.

Joint Venture (JV): a business or project formed by two or more parties who agree to share profits, losses and control.

Jonestown Defence: a defence against a takeover that is so extreme, it appears to be suicidal (e.g., selling all the company's major assets). Also known as Suicide Pill. *See also* Poison Pill.

Jordanian Stock Exchange: *see* Amman Financial Market.

Joule: the energy produced when one ampere flows through one ohm for one second. *See also* Watt.

Journal: an official record of proceedings, often of commercial transactions, that forms the basis for official corporate documents such as financial statements.

Journal Entry: on official input of data, often an accounting entry, into a journal.

Journeyman: 1. one who has apprenticed in a trade and who works for someone else. **2.** a competent, low-profile worker.

Joystick: a popular input control device used mainly for computer games. *See also* Cathode-Ray Tube, Computer, Computer Screen, Disk Drive, Input/Output Device, Interactive Terminal, Keyboard, Keypad, Laser Printer, Line Printer, Monitor, Optical Character Reconition, Peripheral, Printer, Printout, Readout, Remote Access, Terminal.

JPEG: *see* Joint Photographic Experts Group.

JTWROS: *see* Joint Tenancy with Right of Survival.

Judge: an official who presides over cases brought before a court of law.

Judgement: a court order that requires an individual or company to pay a specified sum.

Judgemental Alpha: a prediction of extraordinary return from a common stock. *See also* Alpha.

Judgement Creditor: a creditor who has obtained a judgement against a debtor.

Judgement Debtor: a debtor who has had a judgement entered against him/her by a creditor.

Judicial: anything done by a court of law.

Jughead: an Internet search tool designed to locate Gopher menus and files within a restricted space (e.g., at a university or organization). *See also* Internet.

Juice: informally, a bribe or other payment made in order to have something done.

Jumbo Certificate of Deposit: a certificate of deposit that has a denomination of $100,000 or more

Jump: in financial markets, this term describes security prices suddenly moving higher.

Jump the Gun: to act too soon (e.g., a broker who solicits orders before a new issue has been given regulatory clearance has "jumped the gun").

Jungle: a slang term to describe a place of extreme competition.

Junior: *see* Subordinated.

Junior Capital Pool (JCP): a corporate structure started in Alberta to finance start-up ventures. A JCP can sell shares to the public before establishing its major line of business. Also known as Blank Cheque Offering, Blind Pool.

Junior Mortgage: a mortgage that is subordinate to another mortgage on the same property (e.g., a second or third mortgage). *See also* Mortgage, Subordinated.

Junior Preferred Share: a preferred share that is subordinate to other preferred shares issued by a company. *See also* Preferred Share.

Junior Producer: among resource companies, a small producer.

Junior Security: *see* Junior.

Junior Stock Plan: in the U.S., an employee benefit whereby an employee receives a right to specially issued shares that, after a period, can be exchanged for common shares.

Junk Bond: a speculative bond rated below Triple-B (low) by the Dominion Bond Rating Service. A U.S. junk bond is one rated below BAA3 by Moody's Investors Services or below BBB by Standard & Poor's. Junk bonds are often used to finance aggressive acquisitions and management buyouts. *See also* Bond, Bond Rating Agency, Noninvestment Grade.

Junket: a trip taken by a politician or businessperson at someone else's expense.

Junk Financing: financing with low-grade securities, often junk bonds. *See also* Junk Bond.

Junk Mail: unsolicited, third-class mail (usually advertising material).

Junta: a group of military leaders that rules a country after a revolution or coup.

Jurisdiction: the extent of legal or other authority.

Jurisprudence: the science or philosophy of law.

Jurist: one knowledgeable about the law (e.g., a judge).

Jury: a panel summoned by law and sworn to hear and issue a verdict on a case in law presented to them. The obligation and eligibility to serve as a juror and the process of jury selection is determined by provincial legislation in Canada. Generally, the process is to select a number of people from the community, assemble them in court at the start of a trial, select names at random to form a line and have the lawyers either accept or challenge each person in sequence. If a person is chosen, he/she enters the jury box. The process continues until a full jury is selected. *See also* Juror, Jury Box, Jury Panel.

Jungle

The world of business and investment is a jungle. Consider this sampling of the different forms of life that must be dealt with daily.

Asian Tigers	Dog and Pony Show	Kangaroo	Porcupine Provision
Bear	Double Eagle	Killer Bees	RAM
Bug	Dragon	Kitty	Shark Repellent
Bulldog Bond	Elephant	Lame Duck	Snail Mail
Bum Steer	ELKS	Lemming	Snake
Butterfly Spread	Fat Cat	Lion	Snowbird
Cash Cow	Fish	Lobster Trap	Spider
CATS	Four Tigers	Loon	Stag
Cats and Dogs	Fox	Mouse	Swan
Chicken	Gold Bug	Panda	SWIFT
Cougar	Gopher	Pig	Tigr
Dog	Guinea Pig	Piggyback	Wolf

Jury Box: the area in courtroom where the jury sits during a trail.

Jury of Executive Opinion: *see* Delphi Forecast.

Jury Panel: the group of eligible persons selected from the community from which a jury is then selected.

Justice of the Peace: a judge appointed by the provincial lieutenant-governor to perform functions such as issuing summonses and warrants, granting bail, performing marriage ceremonies, and so on.

Just-in-Time Inventory: an inventory management system that, by having on hand only what is needed, reduces the amount of capital invested in raw materials inventory.

Just Title: *see* Clear Title.

JV: *see* Joint Venture.

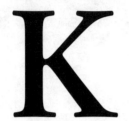

K: abbreviation for 1,000 (e.g., 64k stands for 64,000).

Kaffir: South African gold mining company shares traded in the U.S.

Kamikaze Economics: a decision that is made in spite of potentially disastrous economic consequences.

Kangaroo: a bond denominated in Australian dollars and sold in the U.S.

Kangaroo Court: an improperly constituted court, generally run for the sole purpose of finding the defendant guilty.

Kaput: slang for bankrupt.

Karachi Exchange – 100 Index: a stock price index for the Karachi Stock Exchange.

Karachi Stock Exchange: the major stock exchange of Pakistan, located in Karachi.

Karat: a measure of the gold content of an alloy where 24 karats is 100 percent gold.

24 karats = 24/24 = 100 percent gold of .999 fineness
22 karats = 22/24 = 91 percent gold of .999 fineness
14 karats = 14/24 = 58 percent gold of .999 fineness
10 karats = 10/24 = 41 percent gold of .999 fineness
In North America, "Carat" is used as a measure of the weight of gemstones. In other regions, "Carat" and "Karat" are interchangeable. *See also* Carat.

Kassenobligation: a German government bond with two to four years to maturity.

KC: *see* King's Counsel.

Keep Well Agreement: an agreement between companies involved in a merger or takeover that stipulates certain minimum financial ratios that must be maintained for the transaction to proceed.

Kelly Blue Book Official Guide: in the U.S., a widely followed reference guide to new and used car prices. Also known as Blue Book.

Kelvin: a measure of temperature in which absolute zero is set at zero and the value intervals correspond to the Celsius scale. In Kelvin, water boils at 373.15 degrees and freezes at 273.15 degrees.

Kennedy's Assassination: U.S. President John F. Kennedy was assassinated on November 22, 1963; it was one of the few times in which the New York Stock Exchange has halted trading during the day. Another time was in 1981, when U.S. President Ronald Reagan was shot, and again in October 1997, when the Dow crashed more than 500 points.

Kenyan Stock Exchange: *see* Nairobi Stock Exchange.

Keogh Plan: a U.S. retirement plan for self-employed people or employees of unincorporated businesses. Persons may put up to 25 percent of earned income into such plans, in which taxes on investment income are deferred until the funds are withdrawn.

Kerb Trade: a commodities transaction that takes place after the commodities exchange is closed.

Keyboard: in computers, a set of switches that is organized like a typewriter keyboard and offers the most common means of inputting data. *See also* Cathode-Ray Tube, Computer, Computer Screen, Disk Drive, Input/Output Device, Interactive Terminal, Joystick, Keypad, Laser Printer, Line Printer, Monitor, Optical Character Recognition, Peripheral, Printer, Printout, Readout, Remote Access, Terminal.

Keycard: a coded card that provides access to systems such as security locks and automated banking machines. *See also* Automated Banking Machine.

Key Indicator Operational Report: a weekly report on important financial ratios, it is filed by New York Stock Exchange members who are responsible for clearing customer accounts. The report is intended to alert the stock exchange to any financial difficulties that might affect the operation of member firms.

Key Industry: an industry of vital importance to a country or region.

Key Man Insurance: *see* Key Person Insurance.

Keynesian Economics: the economic theories of John Maynard Keynes (1883-1946), which were popular throughout the 1970s. Keynes, an English economist, laid the foundations of modern macroeconomics with *The General Theory of Employment: Interest and Money* (1936). The central theme of Keynesian economics argues that the only way a successful private-enterprise system (i.e., one that will lead to long-term, full employment) can be maintained is through active government involvement in the establishment of fiscal policy. *See also* Economic Theory, Multiplier Effect.

Keynes, John Maynard (1883-1946): *see* Keynesian Economics.

Keynesian Multiplier: *see* Multiplier Effect.

Keypad: a computer input device that consists of number and function keys, usually located on the right side of a keyboard. *See also* Cathode-Ray Tube, Computer, Computer Screen, Disk Drive, Input/Output Device, Interactive Terminal, Joystick,

Keyboard, Laser Printer, Line Printer, Monitor, Optical Character Recognition, Peripheral, Printer, Printout, Readout, Remote Access, Terminal.

Key Person Insurance: life insurance on the lives of principal shareholders or key employees, often in a small business. Also known as Key Man Insurance.

Keypunch: an obsolete keyboard-activated device that punched holes in paper cards in order to code data. The information was read according to the pattern of holes in the cards.

Keystroke: the pressing of a key on a keyboard.

KFX Index: a market capitalization weighted index of the Copenhagen Stock Exchange.

Kickback: 1. a secret payment, often illegal, to someone who helped secure the awarding of a contract, licence, sale or bring about a similar event. **2.** an illegal practice that occurs when employers, as a condition of employment, require people to return part of their wages as established under a union contract.

Kicker: a feature added to a security or offering in order to make it more attractive. *See also* Equity Kicker.

Kiddie Tax: a tax change proposed in the 1999 federal budget that would have the effect of taxing dividend income from private companies paid to children under 18 years old at the highest marginal tax rate in Canada. *See also* Taxes.

Kill: to cancel an order to buy or sell a security.

Killer Bee: an individual (or organization) who assists a firm in repelling a takeover attempt, especially by devising defensive strategies. *See also* Poison Pill.

Killing: a very large profit in the financial market.

Kilo: in the metric system, the prefix denoting a factor of 1,000 (as in a kilometre, or 1,000 metres). *See also* Metric System.

Kilobyte: a unit of computer memory equal to 1,000 bytes. *See also* Bit, Byte, Computer, Gigabyte, Megabyte.

Kina: the primary currency of Papua New Guinea.

Kind Arbitrage: buying and selling the same securities on the same market at about the same time in order to make a profit.

Kinetic Energy: the energy possessed by a body by virtue of its being in motion.

King's Counsel (KC): *see* Queen's Counsel.

Kiosk: a small, freestanding booth from which newspapers, tickets and so on are sold or from which information is circulated.

KISS: acronym for "keep it simple, stupid."

Kite: 1. to pass a bad cheque. **2.** to sell worthless securities.

Kitty: a pool of money, often to which many people have contributed.

Knock Down: to reduce in price, or a price that has been reduced.

Knock-Off: a product that is a cheap copy, often infringing on copyrights and/or brand names. Also known as Pirated Copy.

Knowbot: an artificial-intelligence program that performs certain automatic functions, such as seeking information from a database or responding to e-mail.

Knowledge Employee: a person with the knowledge and skill to be successful in the economy of the future.

Know Your Client Rule: the cardinal rule for investment advisors: know a client's investment objectives and risk aversion so that you can make appropriate recommendations. *See also* Know Your Customer, Suitability.

Know Your Customer: U.S. equivalent of the Know Your Client Rule. Also known as Rule 405. *See also* Know Your Client Rule.

Kobenhavns Fondsbors: *see* Copenhagen Stock Exchange.

Kondratieff Wave: the theory that capitalist economies move in 54-year supercycles, named after Nikolai Kondratieff (1892-1938), a Russian economist who made important studies of long-term cycles during the 1920s. *See also* Bear Market, Bull Market, Elliott Wave Theory, Peak, Presidential Election Cycle, Stock Market Cycle, Trough.

KOPSI: *see* Korea Stock Price Index.

Korea Stock Exchange: the major stock exchange of South Korea, located in its capital, Seoul. Web site: www.kse.or.kr/

Korea Stock Price Index: a market capitalization weighted stock price index for the Korea Stock Exchange. Also known as KOPSI.

Koruna: the prime currency of the Czech Republic and Slovakia.

Krona: the prime currency of Iceland, Sweden.

Krone: the prime currency of the Bouvet Islands, Denmark, Dronning Maudland, Faroe Islands, Greenland, Norway.

Kroon: the prime currency of Estonia.

Krugerrand: a one-ounce gold coin minted in South Africa. *See also* Maple Leaf.

Kuala Lumpur Composite Index: a market capitalization weighted index of the Kuala Lumpur Stock Exchange.

Kuala Lumpur Stock Exchange: the major stock exchange of Malaysia, located in its capital, Kuala Lumpur. Web site: www.klse.com.my/

Kuna: the prime currency of Croatia.

Kuwait Stock Exchange: the major stock exchange of Kuwait, located in Safat. Web site: www.kse.com.kw/en

Kuwait Stock Exchange Index: a stock price index
for the Kuwait Stock Exchange.
Kwacha: the primary currency of Malawi and
Zambia.
Kwanza: the primary currency of Angola.
Kyat: the primary currency of Myanmar.

L: in Roman numerals, the number 50.

Label: in computers, a symbol or name that identifies the contents of a file or other stored information. *See also* Computer.

La Bolsa de Valores de Lima: *see* Lima Stock Exchange.

La Bolsa de Valores de Lima General Sector Index: a stock price index for the Lima Stock Exchange.

Labour Day: a holiday to honour working people, observed in Canada and the U.S. on the first Monday of each September and observed elsewhere on May 1.

Labour Intensive: describes a company or industry that requires a relatively high labour content compared with capital (e.g., the construction industry is considered labour intensive).

Labour Productivity: the output of goods and services per unit of labour or labour cost (e.g., volume of output per person-hour). *See also* Productivity, Productivity of Capital.

Labour Relations: a function that requires maintaining a sound relationship between employer and employees.

Labour Sponsored Investment Fund (LSIF): *See* Labour Sponsored Venture Capital Corporation.

Labour Sponsored Venture Capital Corporation (LSVCC): one of the 31 Canadian categories developed by the Investment Funds Standards Committee. Mutual funds in this category are defined by federal and provincial statutes. In general, however, it is a labour-organization-sponsored investment that entitles investors to a tax credit; the shares purchased may be used as an RRSP investment. The tax credits are a combination of federal and provincial and differ from province to province. Also known as Labour Sponsored Investment Fund (LSIF), Venture Capital Corporation. *See also* Mutual Fund – Category, Venture Capital Corporation.

Labour Union: an organization of workers formed to promote the interests of its members, especially regarding income and working conditions. Also known as Trade Union, Union.

Ladder: 1. *see* Staggered Bond Portfolio. **2.** a series of ranked stages, or levels, as in "climbing the corporate ladder."

Laddering: *see* Staggered Bond Portfolio.

Lade: to load and ship goods as cargo.

Lady Macbeth Strategy: a takeover strategy in which a third party poses as a white knight before joining forces with the unfriendly bidder. *See also* Poison Pill, White Knight.

Laffer Curve: an theory put forward by U.S. economist Arthur Laffer (1940-) while a member of U.S. President Reagan's Economic Policy Advisory Board that holds that a tax reduction will be more than offset by the investment and economic growth it will stimulate. Also known as Supply Side Economics. *See also* Reaganomics.

Lag: in computers, the time between when data are sent and when they are received. *See also* Computer.

Lagging Economic Indicator: an economic variable that changes after, but in the same direction as, the overall economy. *See also* Coincident Economic Indicator, Leading Economic Indicator.

Lagging Indicator: a variable that changes after, but in the same direction as, another variable being forecast. *See also* Coincident Indicator, Leading Indicator.

Laissez-Faire: the theory, developed by 18th-century free trade French economists, that markets should be allowed to function without government intervention or involvement.

Lame Duck: 1. an office holder who has been defeated in an election but has not yet been replaced from the U.S. prior to 1934 when newly elected Senators and Representatives did not take office until December of the year following their November election. **2.** a second term U.S. President in his final months of office because a president is restricted to two terms in office.

LAN: *see* Local Area Network.

Landed: 1. owning land. *See also* Landed Property. **2.** in Canada, official recognition of immigration.

Landed Property: having an interest in, and pertaining to, the land. *See also* Landed.

Landholder: one who owns land.

Landlady: a woman who rents out or supervises a rental property. A lessor. *See also* Landlord.

Land Line: a standard telecommunication system that uses cables and wires over land.

Landlord: a man who rents or supervises a rental property. A lessor. *See also* Absentee Landlord, Landlady, Slum Landlord.

Land-Office Business: a thriving business.

Land-Poor: *see* House Poor.

Land Registry Office: the government office in which records of real estate ownership (current and historical) are kept. Also known as Land Titles Office. *See also* Abstract of Title.

Landscape Mode: in computers, a printer setting that will print documents across the longer side of the page. *See also* Portrait Mode.

Landslide: an overwhelming election victory.

Land Titles Office: *see* Land Registry Office.

Lapidary: one who polishes, cuts or engraves gemstones.

Lapping: *see* Ponzi Scheme.

Lapse: 1. generally, the expiry of a right or privilege resulting from the failure of one party to an agreement. **2.** the termination of a life insurance contract for non-payment of premiums. *See also* Life Insurance.

Lapsed Option: an option that has passed its expiry date without being exercised. A lapsed option has no value. *See also* Option.

Laptop Computer: a small, portable computer weighing three to 12 pounds. *See also* Computer, Mainframe Computer, Microcomputer, Minicomputer, Notebook, Personal Computer.

Larceny: the theft of another's personal property.

Large Cap: 1. a company with a relatively large stock market capitalization. **2.** a slang term that refers to larger or higher quality stocks. Also known as Macro Cap. *See also* Micro Cap, Mid Cap, Small Cap.

Lari: the primary currency of Georgia.

Laser Printer: a printer popular in desktop publishing because of its relatively low-cost, high-quality printing capabilities. *See also* Cathode-Ray Tube, Computer, Computer Screen, Disk Drive, Input/Output Device, Interactive Terminal, Joystick, Keyboard, Keypad, Line Printer, Monitor, Optical Character Recognition, Peripheral, Printer, Printout, Readout, Remote Access, Terminal.

Last In, First Out (LIFO): an accounting method in which items are recorded as if they are taken out of inventory in the opposite order to which they are put in. *See also* First In, First Out.

Last Sale: the price of a security at its most recent trade of not less than a board lot.

Last Trading Day: the final day on which a futures contract can be settled.

Last Twelve Months (LTM): a term used to indicate financial results are for the most recent 12-month period (e.g., July to June). Also known as Trailing, as in Trailing Earnings.

Lat: the prime currency of Latvia.

Late Charge: a fee charged to a borrower who fails to make a payment on time.

Latin America Common Stock Fund: *see* Latin America Equity Fund.

Latin American Equity Fund: one of the 31 Canadian categories developed by the Investment Funds Standards Committee. Mutual funds in this category must have a minimum of 50 percent of the total assets, and 75 percent of the non-cash assets, of the portfolio in equities or equity equivalents of Latin American companies or derivative-based exposure to such markets. The calculations to determine whether a mutual fund fits this definition are based on median values from fund data over three years, unless otherwise noted. The derivatives are weighted on an extended value basis. Each of the categories may be refined by the fund manager (e.g., a Canadian Large Cap Equity Fund might be described as "growth" or "value" to reflect the manager's style). Also known as Latin America Common Stock Fund. *See also* Extended Value, Mutual Fund – Category.

Latvia Dow-Jones Stock Exchange Index: a market capitalization weighted stock price index for the Riga Stock Exchange.

Latvian Stock Exchange: *see* Riga Stock Exchange.

Laundering: *see* Money Laundering.

Law: the aggregate of rules and principles of conduct established by legislative authority, court decisions or custom.

Law of Diminishing Returns: a principle of economics holding that beyond a certain point, one additional unit of labour or capital does not result in a proportionate increase in production.

Law of Large Numbers: a statistical concept that states that the larger the number of actual results included in a sample, the less important each result becomes. This means the sample becomes more and more like the actual. When all results are included in the sample, the sample and the actual are the same. This concept is the basis for life insurance: The more life insurance contracts an insurance company issues, the more likely its experience will match the average experience on which its premiums are based. This lowers the insurance company's risk (e.g., all the lives they have insured will be shorter than average). *See also* Antiselection, Life Insurance.

Law School Admission Test (LSAT): a standard written exam taken by candidates for law school in Canada and the U.S.

Lawyer: a barrister or solicitor. In Canada, a lawyer is both. *See also* Barrister, Solicitor.

Lawyer-Client Privilege: the right of a lawyer and client to have their professional communications remain confidential. Also known as Solicitor-Client Privilege.

Layaway Plan: a payment plan in which merchandise is held with a downpayment and reserved until the balance is paid in full.

Layman's Language: simple, concise and easily understood verbal communication.

Lay Off: 1. the removal of an employee to reduce costs. **2.** to reduce the risk of an obligation by sharing it with others, as in "lay off risk."

LBO: *see* Leveraged Buyout.

LC: *see* Letter of Credit.

LDC: *see* Less Developed Country.

Leaching: *see* Heap Leaching.

Leader: a stock or group of stocks at the front of a market trend.

Leading Economic Indicator: an economic variable that changes ahead of, but in the same direction as, the overall economy. *See also* Coincident Economic Indicator, Lagging Economic Indicator.

Leading Edge: at or near the forefront of change, especially in technology.

Leading Indicator: a variable that changes ahead of, but in the same direction as, another variable being forecast. *See also* Coincident Economic Indicator, Lagging Economic Indicator.

Lead Order: in the underwriting of a security, a sizeable order that is in hand when the offering commences.

Lead Time: the time between the initial stage of a project and its first tangible output.

Lead Underwriter: 1. the first underwriter to accept a share of an insurance risk. **2.** *see* Syndicate Manager.

Leaf: a very thin piece of metal, as in "gold leaf."

LEAPS: *see* Long-Term Equity Anticipation Securities.

Leap Year Bug: an additional problem for computers in the year 2000, in that it is the first change in century leap year since 1600. The year 2000 must be programmed for 366 days instead of 365 to avoid further potential problems. *See also* Bug, Computer, Year 2000 Problem, Year 2000 Conversion.

Learning Curve: a theoretical graph that plots a rapid improvement in productivity in the early stages of a new activity (e.g., a new manufacturing process). Eventually, the curve levels off and productivity stabilizes.

Lease: a contract that confers the use of a fixed asset in return for rent. *See also* Capital Lease, Financial Lease, Graduated Lease, Ground Lease, Open-End Lease, Operating Lease.

Leaseback: *see* Sale and Leaseback.

Leasehold: rights granted under a lease.

Leaseholder: a tenant under a lease. *See also* Lessee, Tenant.

Leasehold Improvement: the upgrading of a leased property, with the cost added to the value of the fixed assets and written off over the life of the improvement. *See also* Improvements Insurance.

Leasehold Interest: the specific rights in a property held through a lease. *See also* Lease.

Lease to Own: a contract that apportions part of each lease payment toward the purchase of the leased property. Also known as Lease to Purchase.

Lease to Purchase: *see* Lease to Own.

Lease Up: the renting of a commercial or multiresidential property to paying tenants.

Lebanese Arab Finance Corporation Lebanese Internationally Traded Stock Index: a market capitalization weighted stock price index for the Beirut Stock Exchange that includes very few stocks.

Lebanese Stock Exchange: *see* Beirut Stock Exchange.

LED: *see* Light Emitting Diode.

Ledger: an accounting or bookkeeping record. *See also* General Ledger.

Leeson, Nick (1967-): the derivatives trader whose $1.4 billion in trading losses resulted in the collapse of Barings Bank in early 1995. Barings Bank was 233 years old at the time. *See also* Barings Bank.

Left: *see* Left Wing.

Left Wing: a political position that generally favours socialism and the welfare state. Often referred to as the Left.

Leg: 1. a sustained trend in a security or financial market. **2.** in a spread transaction that has two parts (e.g., a spread involving both call options and put options), each part is called a leg. *See also* Lifting a Leg, Option.

Legacy: *see* Bequest.

Legacy Currency: the original currency that a security was issued in before conversion to the Euro.

Legacy System: an older computer system that remains in use after a more modern system is installed. *See also* Computer.

Legal Capacity: the ability to make legally binding decisions and enter into contracts. To have legal capacity, one must be of sound mind; that is, one must be able to know what one is doing, why one is doing it and to do it of one's own free will. *See also* Competent, Incapacity, Incompetent, Non Compos Mentis.

Legal Entity: in law, an organization or structure that can do things a person can do (e.g., enter into a contract). A company is a legal entity. *See also* Company.

Legalese: the law as written in legal documents (e.g., contracts), combining old-style wording with legal jargon.

Legal for Life: an investment that can be made by a Canadian life insurance company because it meets the regulated standards. *See also* Approved List.

Legal Liability: 1. the obligation to act responsibly. **2.** a financial obligation.

Legal Monopoly: a company (e.g., an electric utility) that is given the exclusive right to provide a service in an area. Such companies are also closely regulated.

Legal Opinion: a written expression, prepared by a lawyer, of the legal aspects of a new issue of securities. A legal opinion is often included in a prospectus to affirm the securities offered are legal for investment by various categories of investors.

Legal Tender: 1. currency. **2.** money.

Legal Transfer: in investment, a transfer that requires more documentation than a simple power of attorney (e.g., a security registered to a deceased person). *See also* Transfer.

Legate: 1. to bequeath. **2.** to give.

Legatee: the recipient of a legacy. *See also* Bequest, Heir.

Legislate: to create or pass laws.

Legislation: a proposed or enacted law in written form.

Legislative Assembly: *see* Legislature.

Legislature: the body of people empowered to make laws. Also known as Legislative Assembly.

Legwork: behind-the-scenes work that involves collecting information, asking questions, and so on.

Lehman Investment Opportunity Note (LION): a security marketed by the U.S. investment firm Lehman Brothers Kuhn Loeb, it represents ownership in the future interest and principal payments from a portfolio of U.S. government securities.

Lei: the primary currency of Moldova.

Lek: the primary currency of Albania.

Lemming: in investment, one who mindlessly follows the crowd toward impending disaster. *See also* Follow the Herd, Herd Mentality.

Lemon: 1. a malfunctioning product, often used to refer to a malfunctioning automobile. **2.** a disappointing investment.

Lempira: the primary currency of Honduras.

Lender: of the two parties to a loan agreement, the one who provides the money.

Lender of Last Resort: a support or guarantee position in which a government or financial institution agrees to provide a loan if no other lender will do so.

Lending Agreement: a document under which a client authorizes a brokerage firm to lend out securities held in his/her account.

Lending Policy: general guidelines adopted by a financial institution to govern decisions about the making of loans.

Lending Securities: *see* Security Lending.

Lengthening Term: *see* Extending Term.

Leone: the primary currency of Sierra Leone.

Leonine Contract: a contract that totally favours one party over the other.

Less Developed Country (LDC): a country with an underdeveloped economy, usually characterized by a low level of gross domestic product per capita. *See also* Emerging Markets, Gross Domestic Product.

Lessee: of the two parties to a lease, the one who pays the rent. *See also* Leaseholder, Tenant.

Lesser Developed Country (LDC): a country with an underdeveloped economy.

Lessor: of the two parties to a lease, the one who receives the rent. *See also* Landlady, Landlord.

Let: to rent or to lease.

Lettered: describes common shares, often issued on a private placement, that cannot be traded until a specified date in the future. *See also* Private Placement, Unlettered.

Letterhead: stationery with a printed heading that features corporate, business or personal information.

Letter of Credit (LC): a written undertaking by a bank, often on international transactions, that guarantees a buyer's payment to the seller up to a stipulated amount and within a set period. LCs are generally negotiable and irrevocable. As well, generally, the sum can be confirmed by the issuing bank in advance and payment can be as a sight draft or term draft. Also known as Documentary Credit, Documentary Letter of Credit.

Letter of Deficiency: *see* Deficiency Letter.

Letter of Intent: a document that outlines an intention to act.

Letter Quality: a term used to describe a printer feature that produces characters of high quality (i.e., crisp and dark).

Letters of Administration: a court grant that appoints an estate administrator.

Letters Probate: a court grant that confirms both the executor named in a will and the latter's validity. Also known as Grant of Letter Probate, Grant of Probate Certificate. *See also* Probate, Will.

Leu: the prime currency of Romania.

Lev: the prime currency of Bulgaria.

Level: the approximate price, as in "it's quoted at $99 for a level."

Level 1 Service of NASDAQ: *see* National Association of Securities Dealers Automated Quotations – Level 1 Service.

Level 2 Service of NASDAQ: *see* National Association of Securities Dealers Automated Quotations – Level 2 Service.

Level 3 Service of NASDAQ: *see* National Association of Securities Dealers Automated Quotations – Level 3 Service.

Level Playing Field: a business environment in which all competitors operate under the same rules.

Level Premium Life Insurance: an insurance contract that requires equal premiums until the policy runs its course. *See also* Life Insurance.

Level Term Insurance: term insurance in which the death benefit is fixed, usually for a period of five years. The premium may also remain level for longer terms. *See also* Life Insurance.

Leverage: 1. in general terms, an investment arrangement in which a smaller amount of money controls a larger value of assets (e.g., the use of options such as puts and calls). *See also* Call Option, Option, Put Option. **2.** the use of borrowed funds to invest. *See also* Financial Leverage, Reverse Leverage. **3.** in business, the extent to which additional revenue increases profits. *See also* Operating Leverage.

Leveraged: the condition of having borrowed money to invest. *See also* Leverage, Unleveraged.

Leveraged Buyout (LBO): the purchase of a company using borrowed money. In an LBO, the purchaser often uses credit available to the target company to fund the acquisition and uses the target company's future cash flow to repay the loans. *See also* Busted Takeover.

Leveraged Recapitalization: a strategy used to ward off an unfriendly bidder, it involves the target company borrowing a large amount of money and distributing the proceeds to shareholders. This increases the amount of debt and reduces the book value of the company, making it less attractive to the potential acquirer. *See also* Poison Pill.

Leverage Fund: a mutual fund that borrows money in an attempt to raise returns. *See also* Mutual Fund – Other.

Leveraged Lease: a lease in which a meaningful amount of the purchase price (e.g., 25 percent to 50 percent) is paid in cash and the balance is lease financed. *See also* Direct Lease, Indirect Lease.

Liability: any debt or obligation.

Liability Insurance: insurance to protect the policy holder from court-awarded settlements relating to property damage, bodily injury, libel, etc.

Libel: a written, printed or pictured statement that maliciously damages a person's reputation. *See also* Defame, Slander.

Libertarian: Someone who supports individual rights and freedoms before government regulations.

LIBOR: *see* London Interbank Offer Rate.

Licence: permission or authority to own or use something (e.g., a gun) or do something (e.g., drive a car).

Licensee: one to whom a licence has been granted.

Licenser: one who grants a licence.

LICO: *see* Low-Income Cut-Offs.

Lien: a charge or claim on a property that is registered under various provincial laws. A lien gives the creditor the right to sell mortgaged assets when the debtor is unable or unwilling to meet the obligations of the loan. Also known as General Lien. *See also* Discharge of Lien, Mortgage.

Lieutenant-Governor: in Canada, the Queen's representative in each province.

LIF: *see* Life Income Fund.

Life Annuity: an annuity that provides an income stream as long as the annuitant is living. Also known as Life Annuity without Guarantee. *See also* Annuity.

Life Annuity with Guarantee: an annuity that provides an income stream for whichever is longer: the annuitant's life or the guarantee period. Also known as Life with Guaranteed Term Annuity. *See also* Annuity.

Life Annuity without Guarantee: *see* Life Annuity.

Life Cycle: *see* Industry Life Cycle.

Life Estate: an estate whose duration is measured by the life of the person holding it.

Life Expectancy: the age to which half of the people of the same age group and gender will live.

Life Expectancy Adjusted Withdrawal Plan: a plan through which a mutual fund investor's holdings are fully depleted while providing maximum income over their lifetime. *See also* Fixed Dollar Withdrawal Plan, Fixed Period Withdrawal Plan, Mutual Fund, Ratio Withdrawal Plan, Systematic Withdrawal Plan.

Life Expectancy Table: a table that provides life expectancies.

Life Expectancy Table		
Age	**Females**	**Males**
10	68.7 yrs	61.6 yrs
20	59.0 yrs	52.1 yrs
30	49.3 yrs	43.0 yrs
40	39.7 yrs	33.6 yrs
50	30.5 yrs	24.9 yrs
60	22.0 yrs	17.2 yrs
70	14.3 yrs	11.1 yrs
80	8.1 yrs	6.4 yrs

Life in Being: a life relevant to a Trust.

Life Income Fund (LIF): an income option that allows individuals to gain access to locked-in pensions. *See also* Life Retirement Income Fund, Locked-In Pension Fund.

Life Insurance: a contract that agrees to pay a fixed amount of money to a beneficiary upon the death of the insured or, in some cases, cancellation of the policy in return for a payment or series of payments. *See also* Accidental Death Benefit, Accident, Death and Dismemberment Insurance, Accident Year, Actuarial Risk, Annual Renewable Term Insurance, Antiselection, Application, Assignment, Automatic Premium Loan, Beneficiary, Best (A.M.) Company, Inc., Best's Financial Performance Ratings, Best's Ratings, Binder, Broker, Canadian Association of Insurance and Financial Advisors, Canadian Life and Health Association, Canadian Life and Health Insurance Compensation Corporation, Captive Agent, Cash Surrender Value, Central Limit Theorem, Chartered Financial Consultant, Claim, Co-Insurance, Collateral Term Insurance, Commuted Value, Contingent Beneficiary, Contribution Holiday, Conversion, Conversion Clause, Convertible Term Insurance, Corporate Owned Insurance, Creditor's Group Insurance, Criss-Cross Insurance, Critical Illness Insurance, Death Benefit, Declination, Decreasing Term Insurance, Disability Benefit, Dividend, Dividend Options, Double Indemnity, Dread Disease Rider, Duff & Phelps Credit Rating Co., Employee Benefit Plan, Endowment Insurance, Estate Creation, Estate Liquidity, Estate Preservation, Exempt Life Insurance, Experience Rating, Extended Term Insurance, Financial Needs Approach, Financial Planners Standards Council, Financial Planning, First-to-Die, Front End Load, Grace Period, Group Insurance, Guaranteed Insurability, Guaranteed Renewable Rates, Incontestability Clause, Independent Agent, Independent Life Insurance, Inside Buildup, Insurability, Insurance Age, Insurance Company, Insurance Dividend, Insurance Policy, Insurance Premium, Insurance Settlement, Insure, Insured, Insurer, Interest Option, Interim Insurance Certificate, Irrevocable Beneficiary, Joint and Last Survivor, Joint First-to-Die, Joint Second-to-Die, Key Person Insurance, Lapse, Law of Large Numbers, Level Premium Life Insurance, Level Term Insurance, Life Insurance Policy, Life Insurance Policy Conditions, Life Insurance Policy Fee, Life Insurance Policy Holder, Life Insurance Policy Limit, Life Insurance Policy Loan, Life Insurance Policy Reserves, Life Insurance Premium, Life Insurance Settlement, Life Insurance Trust, Life Insured, Life Underwriter, Living Benefit, Load, Loading, Master Contract, Medical Information Bureau, Mortality, Mortgagee Clause, Mortgage Life Insurance, Mutual Life Insurance Company, Named Beneficiary, Non-Disclosure, Non-Forfeiture Options, Non-Participating Life Insurance, Ordinary Life Insurance, Overcharge, Paid-Up Bonus Addition, Paid-Up Life Insurance Policy, Partial Payment, Participating Life Insurance, Persistency, Plan Member, Planned Giving, Preauthorized Payment Plan, Preferred Lives, Preferred Premium Class, Rated Insurance, Rebating, Reduced Paid-Up Insurance, Registered Employee Benefits Consultant, Registered Health Underwriter, Reinstatement, Reinsurance,

Life Insurance

Life insurance is a contract that pays a death benefit to a beneficiary upon the death of the insured in return for one or more payments. This feature makes life insurance a financial planning essential.

Life insurance works because the average life expectancy of a large group of people is predictable. If an insurance company issues contracts to a large number of people and estimates its costs on the basis of average life expectancies, the statistical averages will prevail overall. For every person an insurance company has insured who dies too soon, someone else in the group will live long enough to bring up the average.

There are three primary reasons to have life insurance. When younger, it is for estate creation in the event of premature death. For this reason, it is used by young couples, especially as they begin to have children. Later, insurance provides estate liquidity. Although an estate may have many valuable assets, it may be short of cash to cover immediate expenses. Third, it preserves the value of an estate by providing funds to pay taxes triggered by death. Without life insurance, estate asset may have to be sold to pay taxes.

Cash value or permanent life insurance that combines insurance with a saving/investment component is less popular today.

Term insurance which provides only life insurance is an effective alternative.

Universal life insurance which combines life insurance and effective investment can hedge investment income from income tax.

Modern life insurance is an important financial planning product. It is inexpensive, flexible and affords tax benefits as well. Life insurance can play an important role in most financial plans.

Renewable Term Insurance, Rider, Sales Charge, Savings Element, Second-to-Die, Segregated Fund, Self-Insurance, Settlement Options, Single Premium Life Insurance, Split-Dollar Insurance, Standard Class, Stock Life Insurance Company, Sum Insured, Surrender, Surrendered Policy, Survivor's Benefit, Terminal Dividend, Term Insurance, Term to Age 100, Twisting, Uberrima Fides, Ultimate Beneficiary, Underwriting, Universal Life, Variable Life Insurance, Variable Premium Life Insurance, Viatical Contract, Waiver of Premium, Whole Life Insurance.

Life Insurance Agent: person licensed to give advice on and to sell life insurance. To be a life insurance agent, a person must pass the required tests and be registered with the province in which he/she works. Also known as Agent, Life Insurance Representative. Many Financial Planners are licensed as Life Insurance and Mutual Fund Agents. *See also* Broker, Chartered Financial Consultant, Chartered Life Underwriter, Financial Planner, Independent Agent, Mutual Fund Agent.

Life Insurance Broker: *see* Broker.

Life Insurance Policy: the printed legal document stating the terms and conditions of a life insurance contract. *See also* Insurance Policy, Life Insurance.

Life Insurance Policy Conditions: specific clauses in an insurance contract covering such important matters as exclusions, options and definitions. *See also* Life Insurance.

Life Insurance Policy Fee: a flat charge added to all life insurance premiums regardless of the size of the policy. *See also* Life Insurance.

Life Insurance Policy Holder: the person who owns the life insurance contract. This may or may not be the same as the life insured. *See also* Life Insurance.

Life Insurance Policy Limit: the maximum benefit payable under a life insurance contract. For life insurance on individuals, the limit is generally $1 million. *See* Life Insurance.

Life Insurance Policy Loan: a low-interest loan allowed by some life insurance companies using the cash surrender value of a life insurance contract as collateral. *See also* Life Insurance.

Life Insurance Policy Reserves: an amount insurance companies are required to keep in reserves to meet obligations. *See also* Life Insurance.

Life Insurance Premium: a payment made for life insurance coverage. The amount of the premium is based on the insurance company's risk of loss. In general, the cost of life insurance increases with the age of the insured. *See also* Life Insurance.

Life Insurance Representative: *see* Life Insurance Agent.

Life Insurance Settlement: the payment of a claim made under the terms of a life insurance contract. *See also* Life Insurance.

Life Insurance Trust: an inter vivos trust created in order to hold life insurance. *See also* Inter Vivos Trust.

Life Insured: the person whose life is insured under the life insurance contract.

Life Interest: in real estate, the right to use a property during one's lifetime. A life interest does not confer other rights of ownership (e.g., the right to sell the property).

Life Retirement Income Fund: an alternative to a life income fund established by some provinces (e.g., Alberta, Saskatchewan) under which an annuity does not need to be purchased at age 80. The plan holder can continue to withdraw funds according to the same formula used for registered retirement income funds. *See also* Life Income Fund, Registered Retirement Income Fund.

Lifetime Capital Gains Exemption: in Canada, an exemption under the Income Tax Act that allowed each individual to earn $100,000 in capital gains free of tax. This exemption was repealed on February 22, 1994. There is still a lifetime capital gains exemption on the shares of a Canadian-controlled private corporation and farmland.

Lifetime Reverse Mortgage: *see* Reverse Mortgage.

Life Underwriter: a life insurance sales agent.

Life Underwriters Association of Canada (LUAC): *see* Canadian Association of Insurance and Financial Advisors.

Life With Guaranteed Term Annuity: *see* Life Annuity With Guarantee.

LIFFE: *see* London International Financial Futures and Options Exchange.

LIFO: *see* Last In, First Out.

Lift: a rise in the price of an investment between purchase and resale.

Lifting a Leg: in a spread transaction involving two legs, lifting a leg occurs when one of the legs is offset (e.g., call options that were purchased are sold). *See also* Leg, Option.

Light Emitting Diode (LED): a semiconductor diode that emits light when electricity is applied to it. Frequently used for the digital display in calculators.

Lighten Up: to reduce, but not eliminate, an investment.

Lilangeni: the primary currency of Swaziland.

Lima Stock Exchange: the major stock exchange of Peru, located in its capital, Lima. Also known as La Bolsa de Valores de Lima. Web site: www.bvl.com.pe

Limit: 1. the boundaries of an order to buy or sell a security. *See also* Limit Order. **2.** *see* Price Limit.

Limitation: a time restriction imposed by law.

Limited (Ltd.): after a company name, "Limited" denotes a legal structure that provides shareholders with limited liability. *See also* Limited Liability, Limited Liability Company.

Limited Company: *see* Company.

Limited Liability: a term used to describe the legal restriction under corporate law whereby the financial loss of a company shareholder is limited to the amount he/she invested. *See also* Company, Limited, Limited Liability Company, Limited Partnership.

Limited Liability Company: a legal structure that provides shareholders with limited liability.

Limited Partner: a passive investor who is not involved in management and administration. *See also* General Partner.

Limited Partnership: a legal structure that combines a partnership with limited liability. *See also* Limited Liability, Oil & Gas Limited Partnership.

Limited Warranty: a warranty with certain restrictions (e.g., it covers parts but not labour).

Limit Order: an order to buy or sell a security at a fixed price. With a limit order, the purchase or sale can only occur at the stipulated price or better. *See also* Order.

Limit Up, Limit Down: the range in which a commodity price is allowed to fluctuate in one trading session. *See also* Limit.

Linchpin: a cohesive factor that helps to keep a group or project from falling apart.

Line: 1. a trade or occupation. **2.** an official policy, as in "the party line." **3.** merchandise of a similar nature, as in "a line of clothing."

Lineage: the line of direct descent from an ancestor.

Lineal: to be in the line of direct descent from an ancestor.

Line Chart: a graph that displays data, often over time, connected by a line.

Line of Credit: an agreement between a lender and borrower whereby the latter can draw funds to a specified limit. A line of credit is not a legal commitment and can be withdrawn at any time. Also known as Bank Line. *See also* Formalized Line of Credit, Temporary Line of Credit.

Line Printer: a high-speed printer, often used with mainframe computers, that prints one line at a time rather than one character at a time. *See also* Cathode-Ray Tube, Computer, Computer Screen, Disk Drive, Input/Output Device, Interactive Terminal, Joystick, Keyboard, Keypad, Laser Printer, Monitor, Optical Character Recognition, Peripheral, Printer, Printout, Readout, Remote Access, Terminal.

Linux: a disk operating system that competes with Microsoft Windows. Developed by Linus Torvalds in 1991 while a student at the University of Helsinki, Linux is distributed free through the Internet. *See also* Internet, Windows.

LION: *see* Lehman Investment Opportunity Note.

Liquefied Natural Gas (LNG): natural gas in a liquid state at -260 degrees Fahrenheit.

Liquid: easily converted into cash.

Liquid Assets: assets that are easily converted into cash. Also known as Liquid Securities.

Liquidate: 1. to convert assets into cash. **2.** to pay off a debt.

Liquidating Dividend: the final payout to shareholders from a company going out of business.

Liquidation: 1. the sale of an asset or closing down of a business by selling all remaining assets. **2.** the sale of all securities in a portfolio.

Liquidity: the ease with which a security or asset can be bought or sold. *See also* Liquidity Driven.

Liquidity Crisis: 1. in the economy, a period during which short-term interest rates are very high and credit is restricted under a tight money policy. During a liquidity crisis, both bonds and stocks will be falling in value and a recession is likely. **2.** in a company, a period when cash is insufficient to pay bills. This can force the company out of business.

Liquidity Driven: a security or asset whose primary attraction is its liquidity. *See also* Liquidity.

Liquidity Risk: the risk that an investment cannot be bought or sold quickly enough to prevent or minimize a loss. *See also* Risk.

Liquid Market: a market in which buying and selling is easily accomplished due to large volume and active trading.

Liquid Securities: *see* Liquid Assets.

Liquid Yield Option Notes (LYON): callable stripped coupon bonds created by Merrill Lynch & Co., a global financial management and advisory company. *See also* Merrill Lynch & Co.

Lira: the prime currency of Italy, Malta, San Marino, Turkey and Vatican City.

LIRA: *see* Locked-In Retirement Account.

Lisbon BVL General Index: a market capitalization weighted index of all stocks traded on the official market of the Lisbon Stock Exchange.

Lisbon Stock Exchange: the major stock exchange of Portugal, located in its capital, Lisbon. Also known as Bolsa de Valores de Lisboa. Web site: www.bvl.pt/

Lis Pendens: 1. notice of a court action recorded against title of a property. **2.** a suspended lawsuit or a pending lawsuit.

Listed Security: a security traded on a recognized exchange. *See also* Unlisted Security.

Listed Stock: a common share traded on a recognized stock exchange. *See also* Unlisted Stock.

Listing: 1. the formal offering of real estate for sale. **2.** admitting a stock for trade on a recognized stock exchange.

Listing Agent: the real estate agent responsible for listing a property and providing other services to the property owner. If the agent is a member of a Multiple Listing Service, he/she may share commissions with a selling agent. *See also* Multiple Listing Service, Selling Agent.

Listing Requirements: rules and regulations that must be met before a security can be listed on an exchange.

Listing Statement: a document that provides basic information on a company newly listed on an exchange. The listing statement is published by the exchange.

List Price: the published price, often subject to discounting.

Lit: the prime currency of Lithuania.

Lita: the prime currency of Lithuania.

Lithuania Litin Indices Official List: a market capitalization weighted stock price index for the Lithuanian National Stock Exchange.

Lithuanian Stock Exchange: *see* National Stock Exchange of Lithuania.

Litigants: the parties actively involved in a lawsuit.

Litigate: to engage in legal proceedings.

Litigation: the process of engaging in legal proceedings.

Litmus Test: a figurative test, the results of which are conclusive enough to lead to a decision.

Litre: a metric unit of capacity equal to 1 cubic decimetre or 1.76 pints.

Little Board: *see* American Stock Exchange.

Little Dragons of Asia: *see* Mini Tigers of Asia.

Little Tigers of Asia: *see* Mini Tigers of Asia.

Live Account: *see* Active Account.

Living Benefit: benefits from a life insurance policy that can be used while the insured is still living (e.g., in the event of terminal illness). Also known as Accelerated Benefit. *See also* Viatical Contract.

Living Dead: *see* Zombies.

Living Trust: *see* Inter Vivos Trust.

Living Will: a will in which the signer states that, in the event of severe terminal illness or brain death, he/she does not wish to be kept alive through the use of life support systems. Also known as Advance Directive. *See also* Will.

Ljubljana Stock Exchange: the major stock exchange of Slovenia, located in its capital, Ljubljana. Web site: www.ljse.si/

LL.B.: Bachelor of Laws degree.

LL.D.: Doctor of Laws degree.

LL.M.: Master of Laws degree.

Lloyd's of London: a long-established insurance organization with its roots in maritime insurance but with a reputation for insuring unusual risks. In the 1980s and 1990s, many investors in Lloyd's insurance syndicates experienced severe financial hardship because of unlimited liability. *See also* Name.

LME: *see* London Metal Exchange.

LNG: *see* Liquefied Natural Gas.

Load: 1. a commission payable on the purchase of mutual fund shares. Also known as Loading Charge. *See also* Back End Load, Deferred Commissions, Deferred Declining Redemption Fee – At Cost, Deferred Declining Redemption Fee – At Market Value, Deferred Sales Charge, Exit Fee, Front End Load, Loading Charge, Mutual Fund, No Load, Rear End Load, Sales Charge. **2.** a commission paid at the time of purchasing life insurance. *See also* Life Insurance.

Load factor: the ratio of the actual amount of a variable to the total amount available (e.g., in the airline industry, one measure of load factor is the number of fare-paying passengers divided by the number of seats available).

Loading: in life insurance, the practice of using initial premium payments to cover upfront sales commissions and other costs.

Loading Charge: *see* Load.

Load Up: to aggressively purchase a security.

Loan: money or goods given by one person to another for temporary use. *See also* Loan Agreement.

Loan Agreement: a written document recording the terms and conditions of a loan; both borrower and lender will have a copy. A loan agreement will state, among other things, the amount of the loan, the rate of interest to be paid to the lender, when the loan will be repaid and what assets, if any, are pledged as security for the loan. *See also* Loan.

Loan Crowd: members of the stock exchange who lend or borrow securities (e.g., to facilitate short selling). *See also* Short Sale.

Loan-to-Value Ratio: a ratio calculated by dividing the amount of a mortgage or loan by the appraised value of a property. Lenders will typically go to a 75 percent loan-to-value ratio on a conventional mortgage. *See also* Mortgage.

Loan Value: the maximum amount of credit available in a margin account for the purchase of securities. *See also* Margin Account.

Lobby: to engage in persuading legislators to enact, defeat or amend legislation to suit one's interests or those of one's clients. *See also* Lobbyist.

Lobbyist: one engaged in lobbying. *See also* Lobby.

Lobster Trap: a strategy to discourage unfriendly corporate takeovers. A lobster trap prevents anyone holding more than 10 percent of a company's voting shares from converting convertible securities into common shares. *See also* Poison Pill.

Local Area Network (LAN): a group of computers, typically in an office building, connected by a communications link that enables them to gain access to the same programs, files and printers. *See also* Computer.

Locked-In: a position wherein an investor is unable to sell or convert his/her investment(s).

Locked-In Registered Retirement Savings Plan: *see* Registered Retirement Savings Plan – Locked-In.

Locked-In Fund: a fund that facilitates pension portability. When an employee leaves his/her job, the employer deposits the value of the accumulated contributions of both the employer and employee into a locked-in fund (e.g., a locked-in Registered Retirement Savings Plan or a locked-in retirement account). *See also* Locked-In Retirement Account, Pension Portability, Registered Retirement Savings Plan – Locked-In.

Locked-In Retirement Account (LIRA): a retirement savings account created with money transferred out of a registered pension plan. Funds in a LIRA can be transferred only to a life income fund, a locked-in retirement income fund or a life annuity. *See also* Life Income Fund, Locked-In Retirement Income Fund, Life Annuity, Registered Pension Plan.

Locked Market: a term used to describe a situation that may arise in an active market when the bid and the offer prices are the same.

Lock-In: to buy or sell a security in order to fix the amount of profit or loss.

Locking In: generally, to convert a financial variable into a fixed amount for a long period of time (e.g., fixing a mortgage interest rate for five years may be referred to as "locking-in" the interest rate). *See also* Mortgage.

Lockout: the closing of a place of employment by management for the purpose of exerting pressure on employees, or a trade union, engaged in collective bargaining.

Lock-Up: an arrangement wherein members of the media are allowed to review a document, such as a budget or budget speech, before it is brought down in the legislature. The term alludes to the media's inability to leave the premises or report their findings until the information has been disseminated.

Lock-Up Agreement: a contractual offer of valuable assets or shares, made by a company targeted for takeover, to the most acceptable suitor. This is done to avoid a hostile takeover. Also known as Lock-Up Option. *See also* Poison Pill.

Lock-Up Option: *see* Lock-Up Agreement.

Lode: a vein of mineral ore.

Lodge: to deposit an asset for security, as in "Those securities are lodged as collateral."

Log: on a computer system, the record of activities that have taken place. *See also* Computer.

Logarithmic Scale: a graph with a vertical scale such that plotting a constant rate of change produces a straight line. *See also* Ratio Scale.

Logic Unit: one of the four main functions of a computer, the logic unit performs arithmetic tasks. *See also* Computer, Control Unit, Input-Output Unit, Memory Unit.

Log In: *see* Log On.

Logistics: the procurement, maintenance, delivery and replacement of materials and personnel.

Logo: a company's or product's distinctive symbol or trademark. *See also* Copyright, Symbol, Trademark.

Log Off: to terminate a session with a local or remote computer system. Also known as Log Out. *See also* Computer, Log On.

Log On: to identify oneself to a local or remote computer system, often by inputting one's user name and password. Also known as Log In. *See also* Computer, Log Off.

Log Out: *see* Log Off.

LOL: Internet acronym for "laughing out loud."

Lombard Rate: a key interest rate set by the central bank in Germany.

Lombard Street: the financial district of England, located in London. The area was originally occupied by German bankers from Lombard; hence, the name. *See also* Rue des Lombards.

London Commodity Exchange: a commodity exchange located in London that trades certain agricultural commodity futures. Formerly the London Futures and Options Exchange.

London Futures and Options Exchange: *see* London Commodity Exchange.

London Interbank Offer Rate (LIBOR): the interest rate London banks charge each other on short-term money in the Eurodollar market.

London International Financial Futures and Options Exchange (LIFFE): a major financial futures exchange located in London.

London Metal Exchange (LME): an exchange, established in 1876, for trading spot and forward contracts in metals. Web site: www.lme.co.uk *See also* Forward Contract, Spot Contract.

London Metal Exchange Gold Fixing: the gold price set once in the morning and once in the afternoon by members of the London Metal Exchange at a price that facilitates completion of trades on hand.

London Stock Exchange: *see* International Stock Exchange of the U.K. and the Republic of Ireland.

Long: 1. a securities transaction is profitable if an investor buys low and sells high. In a long transaction, the investor attempts to buy low first and later sell high. *See also* Short. **2.** an abbreviation for long-term, as in "That's a long bond."

Long Bond: *see* Long-Term Bond.

Long Coupon: 1. when a bond is first issued, the initial interest payment may represent a longer period than the remaining coupons. Such a payment is called a long coupon. *See also* Short Coupon. **2.** an interest-bearing bond that matures in more than 10 years. *See also* Short Coupon.

Long End (of the market): bonds with long terms to maturity (e.g., 10 years or more). *See also* Short End (of the market).

Long Hedge: 1. a futures or derivative purchased in the expectation that interest rates will decline. **2.** a futures contract purchased to protect against an increase in the cost of honouring a future commitment (e.g., delivery of wheat).

Long Side: a reference to the practice of investing long as opposed to investing short. *See also* Long, Short Side.

Long Term: an extended, but not specific, period. In investment, often a period of 10 years or longer. *See also* Medium Term, Near Term, Short Term.

Long-Term Asset: 1. in an investment portfolio, assets with a maturity exceeding 10 years, including common stocks. **2.** on the balance sheet, an asset with an indefinite useful life but in excess of one year. Also known as Long-Term Fixed Asset.

Long-Term Beta: a long-term (e.g., five years or longer) forecast of a security's volatility. *See also* Beta.

Long-Term Bond: a bond with a term to maturity of greater than 10 years. Also known as Long Bond. *See also* Bond.

Long-Term Capital: 1. long-term debt plus shareholder's equity. *See also* Long-Term Debt, Shareholder's Equity. **2.** the capital used to finance capital assets. *See also* Operating Capital.

Long-Term Capital Gain: 1. for U.S. income tax purposes, capital gains on shares held for longer than one year. **2.** generally, capital gains earned by a long-term investor. *See also* Long-Term Capital Loss.

Long-Term Capital Loss: for U.S. income tax purposes, capital losses on shares held for longer than one year. *See also* Long-Term Capital Gain.

Long-Term Debt: 1. a bond that matures in a long period of time, usually defined as more than ten years. *See also* Short-Term Debt. **2.** a corporate liability on the balance sheet that falls due in more than one year. *See also* Short-Term Debt.

Long-Term Disability: an accident or illness that prevents a person from working for an extended period. *See also* Short-Term Disability.

Long-Term Disability Insurance: insurance against loss of income caused by an accident or illness that prevents a person from working for an extended period.

Long-Term Equity AnticiPation Securities (LEAPS): long-term options that do not expire for two or three years. LEAPS are available on many stocks traded on the Toronto, New York and American stock exchanges and the NASDAQ. *See also* Option.

Long-Term Financing: an obligation that will not be due for at least one year.

Long-Term Fixed Asset: *see* Long-Term Asset.

Long-Term Goal: a financial planning goal that extends beyond five years (e.g., pay off the mortgage). *See also* Financial Planning, Long-Term Planning.

Long-Term Investment: an investment that the investor intends to hold for several years.

Long-Term Investor: someone who invests for the long term, usually for longer than five years. Also known as Patient Money.

Long-Term Liability: an obligation that will last for more than 10 years.

Long-Term Planning: the financial plans used to accomplish long-term goals. *See also* Financial Planning, Long-Term Goal.

Long-Term Trend: the general direction of financial assets or the economy over a five- to 10-year period.

Long Ton: a unit of weight equal to 2,240 pounds or 1,016.05 kilograms.

Look-Back Option: a put or call option on a commodity that allows the holder to buy or sell at the best available price during the term of the option. *See also* Option.

Loon: a nickname for the Canadian one-dollar coin, so termed because it features a loon on one side. Also known as Loonie.

Loonie: *see* Loon.

Loopback: in computers, a diagnostic test that compares the integrity of the signal returned with that of the signal sent out. *See also* Computer.

Loophole: a tax exemption that carries with it the strong implication that tax regulations are not being used as intended.

Lose-Lose: an agreement, transaction or settlement in which there is no favourable outcome. *See also* Win-Win.

Loss of Income Insurance: 1. *see* Business Interruption Insurance. **2.** *see* Disability Income Insurance.

Loser: 1. a security that has fallen in price. **2.** an investor who is habitually unsuccessful.

Loss Leader: an item offered for sale at a very low price in order to attract customers to a place of business.

Loss Reserve: an account that makes provision for losses such as bad debts or uncollectable accounts receivable.

Lot: a piece of land within identifiable boundaries.

Loti: the primary currency of Lesotho.

Lottery: 1. a game of chance, usually involving the sale of tickets, in which the winner(s) is selected by a random draw. In Canada, gambling (excluding horse racing) is managed by the provinces, with annual compensatory payments to the federal government. Gaming revenues in Canada increased from $4.3 billion in 1992/93 to $7.1 billion in 1995/96 and an estimated $10 billion in 1999. Of these amounts, lotteries generate more revenue than any other form of gaming. **2.** a method used to make selections when supply and demand are unbalanced. *See also* Oil and Gas Lottery, Partial Call.

Love Money: capital provided by an individual's family and friends to finance a start-up business. *See also* Seed Stock.

Low: 1. the lowest price of a security or financial market in a given period. **2.** generally, a depressed level.

Lowball: to make an offer that is significantly below market value.

Low Balance Method: *see* Minimum Monthly Balance.

Low Beta Stock: a stable or low-risk stock. *See also* Beta.

Low Cost Producer: the most efficient manufacturer. *See also* High Cost Producer.

Low Coupon Bond: a bond that pays a low rate of interest relative to par value. *See also* Bond.

Lower of Cost or Market: an accounting method that involves reporting an asset value at either the original cost or the current market value, whichever is lower.

Low Frequency: radio wave frequency of 30 to 300 kilohertz. *See also* High Frequency, Ultra-High Frequency, Very High Frequency, Very Low Frequency.

Low Grade: 1. a security that presents an investor with significant risk of failure to meet financial obligations, especially under adverse economic conditions. *See also* High Grade. **2.** in mining, ore with little mineral content. *See also* High Grade.

Low-Grade Bond: a bond that carries with it a significant risk of failure to pay interest and/or repay the loan at maturity, particularly under adverse economic conditions. A Canadian Bond Rating Service of BBB or lower. *See also* High-Grade Bond.

Low Hanging Fruit: the easiest profit to make.

Low-Income Cut-Offs (LICO): the standard used by Statistics Canada to measure poverty. In 1997, the poverty income level for different circumstances in a major metropolitan area was:

One person	$16,318
Two persons	$22,117
Three persons	$28,115
Four persons	$32,372

Low Priced Stocks: stocks with low prices, generally under $10 per share.

LSAT : *see* Law School Admission Test.

LSI: *see* Lump Sum Investment.

LSIF: *see* Labour Sponsored Investment Fund.

LSVCC: *see* Labour Sponsored Venture Capital Corporation.

Ltd.: *see* Limited.

LTM: *see* Last Twelve Months.

LUAC: Life Underwriters Association of Canada.

Lucre: slang for money or profits.

Lump Sum: a single large payment, often made in lieu of many smaller payments.

Lump Sum Investment (LSI): an investment made with one large payment in contrast to many smaller payments.

Luncheon Club: *see* Breakfast Club.

Lusaka Stock Exchange: the major stock exchange of Zambia located in its capital, Lusaka.

Luxembourg Stock Exchange Index: a stock price index for the Luxembourg Stock Exchange.

Luxembourg Domestic Share Price Index: a stock market index for the Luxembourg Stock Exchange.

Luxembourg Stock Exchange: the major stock exchange of Luxembourg, located in its capital, Luxembourg. Web site: www.bourse.lu

Luxury tax: a tax on non-essential items, such as theatre tickets. *See also* Progressive Tax.

Lynch, Peter, S. (1944-): renowned American portfolio manager, investment author and vice-chairman of Fidelity Management, one the largest investment management firms in the U.S. Former manager of the Magellan Fund, a flagship Fidelity mutual fund.

LYON: *see* Liquid Yield Option Notes.

M: 1. in Roman numerals, the number 1,000. **2.** thousand (e.g., 5M is 5,000).

M1: one of the main (and most narrow) definitions of money supply. Essentially, currency in circulation and demand deposits.

M2: one of the main definitions of money supply. M1 plus personal savings deposits and non-personal notice deposits.

M3: one of the main definitions of money supply. M2 plus other non-personal fixed term deposits plus foreign currency deposits of residents booked in Canada.

M4: the broadest definition of money supply. M3 plus banker's acceptances, commercial paper, savings bonds, treasury bills and certain offshore currency holdings.

Maastricht Treaty: *see* Treaty on European Union.

Mac: *see* Apple Computer, Inc.

Macaroni Defence: under this approach, a company that does not want to be taken over issues a large number of bonds with the requirement that the bonds must be redeemed at a high price if the company is taken over. The name refers to the way, when a company is threatened, the redemption price of the bonds expands like cooked macaroni. *See also* Chastity Bonds, Poison Pill.

Machine Language: this consists of sequences of 1s and 0s and is the only form of coded instructions a computer can use directly without additional translation. *See also* ALGOL, Computer, FORTRAN.

Macintosh: *see* Apple Computer, Inc.

Macro: 1. the big picture (e.g., macroeconomics is the study of the overall workings of the economy). *See also* Macroeconomics. **2.** in computers, a short key code or name that, when used, triggers a program to perform a certain function (e.g., a keystroke macro is a small program that records and executes a sequence of keystrokes in order to eliminate repetition). *See also* Computer.

Macro Cap: *see* Large Cap.

Macroeconomics: the study of the overall economy and such variables as gross national product,

inflation, unemployment and so on. *See also* Micro-economics.

Made-to-Order: manufactured according to individual specifications.

Madrid Stock Exchange: the major stock exchange of Spain, located in its capital, Madrid. Also known as Bolsa de Madrid, Spanish Stock Exchange. Web site: www/bolsamadrid.es

Madrid Stock Exchange General Index: a market capitalization weighted index for the Madrid Stock Exchange.

Maelstrom: a term used to describe unsettled financial and economic conditions.

Magic Sixes: a value investor's term, this refers to a stock that trades at less than six times its earnings, yields more than 6 percent and trades at less than 60 percent of its book value. *See also* Value Investment, Value Investor.

Magistrate: a judicial officer appointed by a provincial court, he/she presides over matters of a criminal nature.

Magnate: a powerful or influential person, especially in business.

Magnetic Disk: a computer disk coated with a magnetic material. *See also* Computer, Computer Disk, Disk, Floppy Disk, Hard Disk.

Magnetic Ink Character Recognition: the magnetic characters on the bottom of a cheque that facilitates automated clearing systems used by financial institutions.

MAI: *see* Multilateral Agreement on Investment.

Mailbox: in computers, a directory or folder that stores incoming and outgoing e-mail messages. *See also* Computer.

Mail Box Rule: in contract law, the mail box rule asserts that, unless otherwise stated, an offer is accepted by the offeree (and that such acceptance has been received by the offeror) once he/she places it in the mail box.

Mail Order: 1. a business operated by orders received and filled through the mail. **2.** to order goods through the mail.

Mail Server: a computer, usually at an Internet service provider, that collects, stores and fowards one's incoming and outgoing e-mail. One retrieves e-mail by dialling into the Internet service provider and checking the mail server for any new mail. *See also* Internet.

Mainframe Computer: a powerful computer used to store and process large volumes of data, to which many simple user terminals are connected. *See also* Computer, Laptop Computer, Microcomputer, Minicomputer, Notebook, Personal Computer.

Main Street: a reference to the general public as opposed to stock market professionals, as in "It's bigger news on Bay Street than it is on Main Street." *See also* Bay Street, Howe Street, Threadneedle Street, Wall Street.

Maintenance Order: a direction by the court for one spouse to support the other with fixed, regular payments for a period following a marriage breakup. *See also* Separation Agreement, Support Payment.

Major Bottom: a significant market low.

Majority: a number greater than half of a total.

Majority Shareholder: in a company, the person with the most voting shares. In widely held companies, a majority shareholder may own less than half the shares.

Major Market Index: an index of 20 bellwether stocks (19 of which are also in the Dow-Jones Industrial Average), used primarily by program traders. *See also* Program Trading.

Major Medical Insurance: *see* Extended Health Care Insurance.

Major Top: a significant market peak.

Major Trend: the overall direction of a market or economy.

Major Turning Point: a significant change in an intermediate or long-term trend.

Make a Market: to continually buy and sell round lots of a security in order to provide liquidity. *See also* Board Lot, Market Maker.

Make Whole Clause: a clause in a loan agreement stating that if the borrower chooses to prepay before maturity, then a penalty must be paid to protect the lender against loss of interest income should interest rates have declined.

Malawi Share Index: a stock price index for the Malawi Stock Exchange.

Malawi Stock Exchange: the major stock exchange of Malawi, located in its capital, Blantyre.

Malaysian Stock Exchange: *see* Kuala Lumpur Stock Exchange.

Malfeasance: a clearly illegal act.

Malicious Prosecution: a prosecution that is conducted without reasonable and probable cause.

Malta Stock Exchange: the major stock exchange of Malta, located in its capital, Valletta. Stocks only trade once per week (on Wednesdays).

Malta Stock Exchange Index: a market capitalization weighted stock price index for the Malta Stock Exchange.

Malthusian: of or pertaining to the best-known doctrine originated by English economist Thomas R. Malthus (1766-1834), which asserts that, in order to prevent catastrophe, population must be controlled if

and when growth begins to exceed the rate of increase in food production.

Managed Account: an account for which buy and sell decisions are made by a licensed portfolio manager in return for a fee.

Management: the person or persons who manage a business or organization.

Management Audit: a detailed audit that concentrates on the analysis and evaluation of procedures and performance.

Management Buyin: the purchase of control of a company by an investor group that retains the services of existing management. *See also* Management Buyout.

Management Buyout (MBO): the purchase of control of a company by its management.

Management by Objectives (MBO): a management style that involves a subordinate setting employment-related goals in consultation with his/her superior. At the end of a year, bonuses and compensation are based on attainment of the goals. *See also* Management Buyin.

Management Company: 1. a company that manages the assets of other investors for a fee. A management company often manages the assets of an investment company. *See also* Investment Company. **2.** the company engaged to manage the assets of a mutual fund. *See also* Mutual Fund.

Management Expense Ratio (MER): the total management fee (including expenses), expressed as a percentage of net assets, paid to investment managers for handling mutual funds. Also known as Expense Ratio. *See also* Management Fee, Mutual Fund.

Management Fee: a charge, usually expressed as a percentage of assets, paid to investment managers for handling portfolios, mutual funds or other accounts. *See also* Management Expense Ratio, Mutual Fund.

Management Information System (MIS): a corporate or business system that provides regular information and data in order to assist in management.

Management Style: *see* Portfolio Management Style.

Manager Diversification: the allocation of a portfolio among several investment managers. *See also* Dependence Adjustment Factor.

Managing Underwriter: *see* Syndicate Manager.

Manat: the primary currency of Turkmenistan.

M&A: *see* Mergers and Acquisitions.

Mandatory Redemption: the requirement that a security issuer must redeem a security in whole or in part prior to maturity. *See also* Redemption.

Man-Hour: *see* Person-Hour.

Mania: a fad that becomes a powerful trend in the financial markets. Manias can lead to securities being overpriced and, hence, subject to sharp declines. *See also* Tulipomania.

Manipulation: *see* Market Rigging.

Manitoba: *see* Canada's Provinces and Territories.

Manpower: 1. the total supply of people available for work. **2.** the power generated by workers as opposed to by machines.

Manslaughter: the unlawful killing of one person by another without either intent or premeditation.

Manual: something that involves work with one's hands, as in "manual labour."

Manufacture: to make or process from raw materials.

Manufactured Housing: generally, a residential structure that is substantially constructed off-site and then moved to a permanent location. *See also* Prefabricated Housing.

Manufacturer's Cycle: the time between when a new product is approved for manufacture and when it is available for sale.

Man-Year: *see* Person-Year.

Maple Leaf: a coin minted in Canada, available in gold, silver or platinum. Maple Leafs are available in various weights (one-twentieth of an ounce to one ounce) and usually sells at a modest premium to metal value. *See also* Krugerrand.

Margin: 1. in investment, the amount of cash or securities that must be deposited in a margin account (as a form of collateral) in order to borrow money from a brokerage firm to buy more securities. *See also* Excess Margin, Loan Value, Marginable Securities, Margin Account, Margin Agreement, Margin Buying, Margin Call, Margin Requirement, On Margin, Over Margin, Overmargined Account, Pyramiding, Under Margin, Undermargined Account. **2.** the amount of equity in a margin account. *See also* Excess Margin, Margin Account. **3.** in business, the difference between the selling price and the cost of goods sold. *See also* Gross Margin, Net Margin.

Marginable Security: a security acceptable to a brokerage firm as collateral in a margin account. *See also* Margin, Margin Account, Unmarginable Security.

Margin Account: in a brokerage firm, an account that facilitates borrowing money in order to buy securities. *See also* Buying Power, Cash Account, Concentration, Excess Margin, Loan Value, Margin, Marginable Securities, Margin Agreement, Margin Buying, Margin Call, Margin Requirement, On Margin, Over Margin, Overmargined Account, Pyramiding, Restricted Account, Under Margin, Undermargined Account.

Margin Agreement: the document that sets out the terms and conditions of a margin account. *See also* Margin Account.

Marginal Analysis: 1. this involves analyzing the change in one variable as a result of a one unit change in another (e.g., how much would earnings change if oil prices were to rise by one dollar?). **2.** an approach to making capital spending decisions that states a project should be approved if the marginal (additional) benefit exceeds the marginal cost.

Marginal Buyer: the hypothetical investor who will purchase the next lot of shares at a given price. *See also* Marginal Seller.

Marginal Cost: the change in a company's total cost when one additional unit of output is produced.

Marginal Efficiency of Capital: the calculation of the percentage cost of a company's next unit of capital. In theory, if the marginal efficiency of capital is 10 percent, then a new project that returns less than 10 percent should be turned down.

Marginal Seller: the hypothetical investor who will sell the next lot of shares at a given price. *See also* Marginal Buyer.

Marginal Tax Rate: the percentage of tax payable on the next dollar of taxable income. In 1998, British Columbia had the highest marginal tax rate in Canada at 54.17 percent (federal and provincial taxes combined), while the Northwest Territories was the lowest at 44.37 percent. *See also* Average Tax Rate, Effective Tax Rate, Taxes.

Margin Buying: to use money borrowed in a margin account in order to buy securities. *See also* Margin Account.

Margin Call: the request from a brokerage firm for additional cash or securities to maintain the required margin in an investor's account. *See also* Margin Account, Margin Sale.

Margin of Profit: *see* Profit Margin.

Margin of Safety: in any situation in which a required financial minimum is specified (e.g., the margin requirement in a margin account), the difference between the current level and the minimum required.

Margin Requirement: the minimum amount of cash and securities needed in order to secure a margin account. *See also* Exhaust Price, Margin Account, Margin Call.

Maritime Law: the traditional body of rules and practices that relate to commerce and navigation.

Mark: *see* Deutschemark.

Mark Down: to reduce a price in order to stimulate sales.

Market: 1. a place where goods and services are bought and sold. **2.** to promote goods and services for sale. **3.** an informal term used to describe the stock market or other financial market.

Marketability: 1. the ability of a security to be bought or sold in sizeable volume without impacting its price. **2.** the ability of an item (e.g., a new product or service) to be sold.

Marketable Securities: securities that are easily bought and sold.

Market Analysis: in investment, the study of factors that lead to a forecast of the future direction of a financial market. In business, the analysis of supply and demand factors for a company's products or services in order to identify opportunities for improvement.

Market Average: technically, an indicator of market direction calculated as a price average (e.g., Dow Jones Industrial Average). In everyday use, the term may be applied to any indicator of a market's direction. *See also* Stock Market Index.

Market Basket: 1. an order to buy or sell a group of 15 or more securities at once. Often used in program trading or by large institutional investors. Also known as Portfolio Basket. **2.** a single trade on the Chicago Board Options Exchange to buy or sell the 500 stocks in the Standard & Poor's 500 Index in proportion to their weighting in the index. *See also* Exchange Stock Portfolio, Standard & Poor's 500.

Market Bet: this occurs when a portfolio manager takes a position that will benefit a portfolio if a particular market (e.g., bond market, stock market) performs well. Also known as a Bet. *See also* Stock Bet, Stock Market Bet.

Market Bottom: the low point, occurring within a short specified time period, in a financial market.

Market Breadth: a reference to the number of individual securities participating in a market trend. If many securities are involved, then the market is said to "move broadly." Also known as Breadth. *See also* Advance/Decline Line.

Market Break: a sudden drop in securities prices.

Market Cap: *see* Stock Market Capitalization.

Market Capitalization: *see* Stock Market Capitalization.

Market Cycle: *see* Stock Market Cycle.

Market Discipline: the heightened awareness of competitive forces that comes with being a public company that is compared with other public companies.

Market Economy: an economy that operates with substantially free competition and minimal government regulation. *See also* Capitalism, Centrally Planned Economy, Communism, Free Market Economy, Socialism.

Market Equilibrium: the price at which supply and demand are equal.

Market Float: the number of shares held for investment, rather than control purposes, that is, shares held by a controlling shareholder are not part of the float.

Market High: 1. a high point in a financial market. *See also* Market Low. **2.** the point from which a downturn begins. *See also* Market Low.

Market if Touched Order: an order to buy or sell a security or commodity as soon as the price reaches a predetermined level, at which time it becomes a market order. *See also* Order.

Market Index: *see* Stock Market Index.

Market Indicator: a sign that indicates future market trends (e.g., lower interest rates indicates the stock market will rise).

Marketing: all activities involved in motivating or facilitating the sale of goods and services.

Marketing and Refining: *see* Refining and Marketing.

Marketing Board: an organization, often made up of agricultural producers, that establish production quotas and, by so doing, influences or controls the price of its commodity. Also known as Agricultural Cooperative. *See also* Cooperative.

Marketing Channel: *see* Distribution Channel.

Market Is Down: a phrase meaning the market has been closed during normal business hours (often because of a computer failure).

Market Is Off: a phrase meaning the market is lower than it was at the previous day's close. *See also* Market Is Up.

Market Is Up: a phrase meaning the market is higher than it was at the previous day's close. *See also* Market Is Off.

Market Jitters: a term used to describe a time when investors are nervous. This fear is often translated into sharp downward price movements.

Market Leader: a stock (or group of stocks) that appears to be significant with regard to establishing a short-term trend in prices.

Market Leadership: stocks that dominate trading volume during a given period of time.

Market Letter: a newsletter that comments on a market and market trends.

Market Low: 1. a low point in a financial market. *See also* Market High. **2.** the point from which an upturn begins. *See also* Market High.

Market Maker: a member of the National Association of Securities Dealers (NASD) who buys and sells securities listed on the National Association of Securities Dealers Automated Quotations (NASDAQ) for his/her own account. A market maker displays a bid and offering price for a guaranteed number of shares. There are more than 500 NASDAQ market makers. *See also* National Association of Securities Dealers, National Association of Securities Dealers Automated Quotations.

Market Multiple: 1. a price-to-earnings ratio based on all the stocks in a particular market average. **2.** a benchmark for valuing a stock, as in "This stock trades at less than the market multiple."

Market Myopia: the effect of the desire for short-term performance which causes investors to make decisions based on short-term (and often incorrect) factors.

Market-Neutral Fund: a mutual fund that attempts to profit despite the overall direction of the financial markets. A market-neutral fund buys long and sells short at the same time. In addition, it earns interest on the proceeds from selling short. *See also* Buy, Short Sale, Mutual Fund.

Market on Close Order: in options and futures trading, an order to be executed during the closing period. *See also* Closing Period, Market on Open Order, Option.

Market on Open Order: in options and futures trading, an order to be executed at the opening of the market. *See also* At Close Order, Closing Period, Option.

Market Opening: the first transaction in a stock during a new trading session.

Market Order: an order to buy or sell securities that will be executed at the next available price by purchasing at the lowest available offering price or selling at the highest available bid price. Also known as At the Market Order, On the Market Order. *See also* Order.

Market Order Trading System: a computer trading system for dual-listed stocks between the Toronto Stock Exchange and the American Stock Exchange.

Market-on-the-Close Order: an order to buy or sell a security as close as possible to the end of the trading session. *See also* Order.

Market-on-the-Opening Order: an order to buy or sell a security as close as possible to the opening of the trading session. *See also* Order.

Market Out Clause: *see* Force Majeure.

Market Penetration Rate: the proportion of a market that a product or service has reached (e.g., in 1996, personal computers had penetrated 41 percent of households). Also known as Penetration Rate.

Marketplace: the world of business and commerce.

Market Portfolio: 1. all the investments available to an investor. Also known as Investment Universe. **2.** all the investments available to an advisor to offer his/her clients.

Market Price: 1. on the stock market, usually the last trade. **2.** the price at which a buyer and seller who

are at arm's-length from one another agree to trade an asset.

Market Quote: the bid and offer price for a stock at a point during the trading session.

Market Report: 1. a report of a completed a trade. **2.** a news report on the stock market.

Market Research: 1. in investment, the examination of a financial market for the purpose of making a forecast. **2.** in general, a study to assess the potential demand for a new product or service.

Market Rigging: the illegal practice of causing an artificial price (through artificial buying and selling) to exist on a securities exchange. Markets are rigged to attract unsuspecting investors to buy stock at inflated prices. Also known as Manipulation, Rigged Market.

Market Risk: *see* Systematic Risk.

Market Sentiment: the prevailing attitude (either optimistic or pessimistic) toward a financial market. Also known as Market Tone.

Market Share: the proportion of total sales of a product or service held by one company or brand.

Marketspace: the world of shopping on the Internet. *See also* Internet.

Market Specific: an influence on the price of a stock that stems entirely from the stock market.

Market Specific Risk: an influence on the price of a security that stems entirely from the financial market (e.g., in the absence of any company or industry specific news, a stock declines in price because the overall stock market is falling). *See also* Company Specific Risk, Industry Specific Risk, Specific Risk.

Market Stance: a portfolio strategy that takes advantage of an expected trend in securities prices.

Market Sweep: this occurs after a buyer has accumulated a significant interest in a company pursuant to a formal offer to shareholders. In a market sweep, the investor canvasses remaining large shareholders in an effort to buy additional shares. The price offered may be slightly higher than the original offer.

Market Swing: a shift in the level of the stock market.

Market Timing: an attempt to shift a portfolio on the basis of an expectation that a financial market will rise or fall in the near future.

Market Tone: *see* Market Sentiment.

Market Top: the high point, occurring within a short specified time period, in a financial market.

Market Trend: the general direction of a market.

Market Uncertainty: a general lack of consensus about the future direction of a market.

Market Value: the value of an asset as established through trade on an open market. *See also* Face Value, Par Value, Stated Value.

Market Value of Trading: *see* Value of Trading.

Market Value Weighted Stock Market Index: a stock market index based on changes in the market value of companies (e.g., the Toronto Stock Exchange 300 Index).

Market versus Quote: a security's price at the last trade compared with the current bid and offer. The distinction is made when the two differ significantly.

Market Volume of Trading: *see* Volume of Trading.

Market Weighting: a stock (or group of stocks) held in a portfolio in the same proportion as they are in a widely followed stock market index.

Marking Time: a phrase used to describe a market that remains trendless.

Markka: the primary currency of Finland.

Mark to Market: to revalue a securities portfolio (or other assets) to reflect current market value. Most mutual funds mark to market at the close of each day.

Markup: an amount that the seller adds to the price of goods.

Marquee Asset: 1. the most attractive asset owned by a company. Also known as Trophy Asset. **2.** the asset that contributes most to a company's market value. Also known as Trophy Asset.

Marriage Breakdown: the termination of a marriage. The grounds for legally ending a marriage in Canada are evidence of adultery, physical or mental cruelty, and/or living separate and apart for one year. *See also* Adultery, Mental Cruelty.

Marriage Contract: *see* Prenuptial Agreement.

Married: for income tax purposes, one is married if (1) one has conjugally cohabited with a person of the opposite sex for a continuous period of 12 months ending in the taxation year or (2) if one is a parent of a child of whom the taxpayer is also a parent. As of mid-1999, the "opposite sex" wording may be subject to change, removing any gender-specific language.

Married Put and Stock: a put option and the underlying stock that is purchased so as to hedge a decline in the price of the stock owned. *See also* Option, Put Option.

Marry a Stock: to continue to hold a stock regardless of indications that it should be sold.

Martial Law: a system of arbitrary laws exercised by officers of the Crown or the military in case of war or other serious domestic disruption (e.g., the War Measures Act in Canada).

Massacre: in the stock market, a time of particularly severe losses (e.g., the stock market declines of October 1978 and October 1979, respectively, are sometimes referred to as the October Massacres).

Massage the Numbers: in investment, the process by which a securities analyst makes minor adjustments to financial forecasts.

Mass Marketing: a term used to describe any of the marketing approaches designed to appeal to the maximum number of customers (e.g., selling clothing through department stores rather than boutiques).

Mass Production: manufacturing in large volumes, especially through the assembly line technique.

Master Contract: 1. a life insurance policy, issued to an employer or trustee, that establishes group insurance for a number of associated persons. **2.** in labour, an overall agreement between a union and an industry.

Master of Business Administration: a post-graduate degree in business.

Matched: owning assets that mature at the same time and in the same amount as do one's liabilities. Also known as Asset/Liability Management. *See also* Mismatched.

Matched Orders: *see* Wash Trading.

Material: 1. in law, something or someone important enough to significantly affect the outcome of a judgement, as in "a material witness." **2.** *see* Material News.

Material Change: *see* Material News.

Material News: information about a public company that will likely affect the market price of its securities or influence investors' decisions. *See also* Inside Information.

Materialism: the belief that life is dominated by the desire to own worldly goods.

Mathematical Expectation: the probability of "winning," often expressed as an amount per dollar wagered or invested (e.g., the mathematical expectation when you buy a Lotto 649 is to get back approximately $.50 for every $1.00 spent).

Matrimonial Home: 1. the residence occupied by the married spouses as their family home. **2.** in estate law, the surviving spouse may have the right to occupy the matrimonial home for the rest of his/her life. *See also* Possessory Right.

Matrimonial Property: property that is to be divided between divorced spouses.

Matrix: 1. a rectangular arrangement of data in horizontal rows and vertical columns. **2.** in computer applications, the arrangement of data in table form (as in spreadsheets), where the values in one row or column interact with the values in another row or column. *See also* Computer, Spreadsheet.

Matrix Trading: a bond trading technique in which historical yield spreads trigger buying and selling (e.g., if the traditional spread between Government of Canada bonds and Ontario bonds widen, the trader will sell Canada bonds and buy Ontario bonds.

Matured: a contract, obligation, bond or other arrangement that has met all of its requirements and is no longer in effect.

Mature Industry: an industry with limited growth prospects.

Maturity: 1. the process of a loan coming due for repayment. *See also* Maturity Date. **2.** the stage at which a company, industry or economic life cycle is fully developed and at which a slower rate of growth begins. *See also* Decline, Expansion, Industry Life Cycle, Mature Industry, Start-Up.

Maturity Date: the repayment date of a loan or bond. Also known as Date of Maturity.

Mauritius Stock Exchange: the major stock exchange of Mauritius, located in its capital, Port Louis. Web site: lynx.intnet.mu/sem

Mauritius Stock Exchange Index: a market capitalization weighted stock price index for the Mauritius Stock Exchange. Also known as SEMDEX Index.

May Day: May 1, 1975, marking the date when the U.S. changed from fixed to negotiated commissions charged on stock trading. *See also* Big Bang.

Mayor: the head of a municipal government.

M.B.A.: Master of Business Administration.

MBO: 1. *see* Management Buyout. **2.** *see* Management by Objectives.

MBS: *see* Mortgage Backed Security.

MCI: *see* Monetary Conditions Index.

ME: *see* Montreal Exchange.

Mean: the arithmetic average value of a set of numbers. *See* Arithmetic Average, Median, Mode.

Mean Deviation: in a set of numbers, the average difference between each number and the mean.

Mean Return: the average of all expected returns from a set of securities.

Mean Reversion: the tendency for a statistic to return to its average (e.g., if mining stocks provide below-average returns for a period, then, according to mean reversion, they will provide above-average returns in order to get back to the long-term average).

Means Test: a test that establishes a person's need for financial assistance and, therefore, his/her eligibility for government benefits.

Mechanic's Lien: a lien on a property for labour or materials supplied to improve it. *See also* Lien.

Median: in a set of numbers, the point where half the values are greater and half the values are less. *See also* Arithmetic Average, Mean, Mode.

Mediator: one who facilitates an agreement between two or more parties (e.g., union and management).

Medical Information Bureau: an organization that keeps records on the insurability of life insurance applicants and those already insured.

Medium of Exchange: 1. any financial instrument that is widely accepted as a form of payment. The medium of exchange is taken as having value in its own right without consideration to other factors such as the bearer's credit rating. **2.** money (e.g., Canadian currency). *See also* Medium Other Than Cash.

Medium Other Than Cash: a medium of exchange other than currency (e.g., credit card, cash). *See also* Medium of Exchange.

Medium Term: an intermediate, but not specific, period. In investment, often a period of three to 10 years. Also known as Intermediate Term. *See also* Long Term, Near Term, Short Term.

Medium Term Bond: a bond with a maturity of greater than one year and less than 10 years. Also known as Mid-Term Bond. *See also* Bond.

Mega-: one million.

Megabyte: in computers, 1,024 kilobytes or 1,048,576 bytes. *See also* Bit, Byte, Computer, Gigabyte, Kilobyte.

Meltdown: a substantial decline in a financial market.

Member Firm: a brokerage firm that is a member of a recognized stock exchange or self-regulatory body.

Member of Parliament (MP): a person elected to the federal government of Canada. Members of Parliament serve in the House of Commons. *See also* House of Commons.

Member of the European Parliament (MEP): a member elected to the European Parliament in European Community-wide elections held every five years. *See also* European Community, European Parliament.

Member of the Legislative Assembly (MLA): a person elected to a provincial government of Canada.

Memory: *see* Memory Unit.

Memory Unit: one of the four main units of a computer, the memory unit stores instructions and data. *See also* Compression, Computer, Conventional Memory, Data, Data Bank, Database, Datawarehouse, Primary Memory, Random Access Memory, Read-Only Memory, Save, Secondary Memory.

Mental Cruelty: one of the grounds for divorce in Canada, this occurs when one spouse behaves in a manner that endangers the other spouse's mental or physical health to such an extent that the marriage is no longer tolerable. *See also* Adultery, Marriage Breakdown.

Mentally Infirm: with regard to the Canadian Income Tax Act, this refers to being unable to be gainfully employed for a considerable period of time due to a mental problem.

Mentor: a personal contact held in high esteem who can help a person achieve his/her goals.

Menu: in computers, a list of available options. *See also* Pull-Down Menu.

MEP: *see* Member of the European Parliament.

MER: *see* Management Expense Ratio.

Mercantile Agency: a business that supplies businesses with credit ratings and reports on customers or prospective customers.

Mercantile Law: the law relating to merchandising and trading.

Merchandise: 1. goods bought and sold for profit. **2.** to buy and sell in business or to promote goods etc. for sale.

Merchandise Trade Balance: the net amount of a nation's imported and exported goods (not including services).

Merchant Bank: a bank, or that part of a bank, engaged in investment banking, mergers, acquisitions, portfolio management, venture capital and other financial services. Also known as Investment Bank.

Merchant Banking: the activities relating to mergers, acquisitions, portfolio management and venture capital. Also known as Investment Banking.

Merchant Credit: *see* Merchant Letter of Credit.

Merchant Letter of Credit: a letter of credit issued without the guarantee or involvement of a bank. Also known as Merchant Credit.

Mercosur: as of 1998, a trade union with Argentina, Brazil, Paraguay and Uruguay as members and Chile and Bolivia as associate members. Lower tariffs prevail between members and associates which together maintain common tariffs with non-members. *See also* European Community, Free Trade Area of the Americas, North American Free Trade Agreement.

Merger: the combining of companies through the pooling of interests or the purchase of one company by another. *See also* Pooling of Interests, Purchase Method.

Mergers and Acquisitions (M&A): the activity and/or department in a brokerage firm or merchant bank that involves facilitating mergers and acquisitions.

Merit: in law, a person's legal rights.

Merit Increase: term used to describe an increase in pay given in recognition of a specific and measurable accomplishment instead of simply an adjustment to reflect inflation or greater seniority.

Merrill Lynch & Co.: a well-known global management and advisory company with offices in more than 40 countries. Merrill Lynch provides a wide range of services to individual and institutional investors. Also known as the "Thundering Herd" because of its dominant position and advertising campaigns featuring bulls. Web site: www.ml.com

Metallurgy: the science that deals with the extraction of metals from ores.

Metical: the primary currency of Mozambique.

Metre: a metric unit of length equal to 39.37 inches, 1.094 yards or the distance light travels (in a vacuum) in 1/299,792,458 of a second.

Metrication: to change to the metric system of weights and measures.

Metric Conversion: to change to or from the metric system of weights and measures.

Metric System: a decimal system of weights and measures used in Canada. The metric system is based on the metre, litre and gram as units of length, volume and mass. *See also* Centi, Deca, Deci, Gram, Hecto, Imperial Measure, Kilo, Litre, Metre, Metrication, Metric Conversion, Metric Ton, Milli.

Metric Ton: a unit of weight equal to 1,000 kilograms, or approximately 2,205 pounds. Also known as Tonne.

Metric Conversion Table

Linear Measure:
1 millimetre	.039 inch
1 centimetre	.390 inch
1 metre	1.094 yards
1 kilometre	.621 miles

Capacity Measure:
1 millilitre	.002 pint
1 litre	1.760 pint

Area Measure:
1 hectare	2.470 acres

Weight Measure:
1 kilogram	2.205 pounds
1 tonne	.984 ton

Temperature Measure:
100° Celsius	212° Fahrenheit
zero Celsius	32° Fahrenheit

Mexican Stock Exchange: the major stock exchange of Mexico, located in its capital, Mexico City. Also known as Bolsa Mexicana de Valores. Web site: www.bmv.com.mx

Mexico Bolsa Index: a market capitalization weighted index of the Mexican Stock Exchange.

Mezzanine Bracket: in a tombstone, the mezzanine bracket contains the list of underwriters who rank below the lead underwriters. *See also* Bulge Bracket, Tombstone.

Mezzanine: *see* Mezzanine Level.

Mezzanine Debt: debt used in a mezzanine financing. Mezzanine debt is riskier than conventional debt but not as risky as the common stock. *See also* Mezzanine Financing.

Mezzanine Financing: often used in takeovers, a form of quasi-equity financing that uses preferred and convertible securities in order to expand a target company's equity (often for the purpose of convincing creditors that the new owner is committed to the business). *See also* Mezzanine Debt.

Mezzanine Level: the stage of corporate growth just before going public. Some investors prefer this stage because the high-risk startup stage is over and the profit from going public may be near. Also known as the Mezzanine. *See also* Seed Financing, Venture Capital.

MFDA: *see* Mutual Fund Dealers Association of Canada.

MFN: *see* Most Favoured Nation.

Michelangelo Virus: a computer virus that threatened computer users on March 6, 1992, the Renaissance genius' birthday. In the end, concerns proved to be overblown. *See also* Virus.

Micro: the small picture (e.g., microeconomics is the study of the economy's individual parts) *See also* Microeconomics.

Micro Cap: a company with an extremely small market capitalization; that is, a very small company. *See also* Large Cap, Mid Cap, Small Cap.

Microchip: *see* Integrated Circuit.

Microcircuit: an electronic circuit composed of miniaturized components.

Microcomputer: a very small computer that uses a single-chip microprocessor. *See also* Computer, Laptop Computer, Mainframe Computer, Minicomputer, Notebook, Personal Computer.

Microeconomics: the study of the economy by examining such small-scale factors as producers, consumers and households. *See also* Macroeconomics.

Microfiche: a sheet of microfilm containing microphotographs of printed material.

Microfilm: a thin strip of film containing microphotographs of printed material.

Microprocessor: the central processing unit that controls most of the core functions of a computer. *See also* Computer.

Mid Cap: 1. a company with a medium-sized stock market capitalization. **2.** a slang term that refers to medium-sized or average-quality stocks. *See also* Large Cap, Micro Cap, Small Cap.

Mid Cap Common Stock Fund: *see* Mid Cap Equity Fund.

Mid Cap Equity Fund: 1. *see* Canadian Small to Mid Cap Equity Fund. **2.** *see* Mutual Fund – Category. **3.** *see* U.S. Small to Mid Cap Equity Fund. Also known as Mid Cap Common Stock Fund.

Middle Income: *see* Average Income.

Middleman: an individual who buys products from manufacturers and producers and sells them to retailers and consumers.

Middle Management: a category made up of individuals who occupy an intermediate managerial position. *See also* Top Management.

Middle Price: a price that falls between the bid price and the offering price for a security.

Mid-Term Bond: *see* Medium-Term Bond.

Midyear: the midpoint of a calendar or fiscal year.

Migrant Worker: a person who follows work from one place to another. *See also* Itinerant.

Migration: in computers, the process of making existing applications work on different computers or operating systems. *See also* Computer.

.mil: an appendage to an e-mail or Internet address that identifies a military location. *See also* .com, .edu, .gov, Internet, .net, .org.

Milan MIB Telematico Index: a market capitalization weighted index of the Italian Stock Exchange.

Milan Stock Exchange: *see* Italian Stock Exchange.

Mile: a measure of distance equal to 1,760 yards or 5,280 feet. *See also* Metric Conversion.

Milestone: a significant point in a project, a developing country's economy, and so on.

Milk: to take advantage of (especially financially), as in "milk it for all it's worth."

Mill: *see* Mill Rate.

Millennium: 1,000 years. *See also* New Millennium.

Millennium Bug: *see* Year 2000 Problem.

Milli: in the decimal system, the prefix denoting one part in 1,000, as in millimetre, which is one one-thousandth of a metre. *See also* Metric System.

Millionaire: an individual whose personal wealth exceeds one million or more units of currency. *See also* Billionaire.

Mill Rate: the rate at which tax is applied, generally by a municipality. One mill is one-tenth of one per cent or one part in one thousand (e.g., a tax rate of 15 mills on a $200,000 home equates to a tax of $3,000). Also known as Mill. *See also* Assessed Value.

MIME: *see* Multipurpose Internet Mail Extensions.

MIMO: *see* Money In, Money Out.

Minefield: a term used to describe an economic or financial forecast that includes many things that could go wrong.

Mineral: an element such as gold or silver (often obtained by mining).

Minicomputer: a computer with more capacity than a microcomputer but less than a mainframe computer. *See also* Computer, Laptop Computer, Mainframe Computer, Microcomputer, Notebook, Personal Computer.

Mini-Manipulation: an illegal activity that involves manipulating a security underlying an option so as to influence the latter's market value. *See also* Option.

Minimum Fluctuation: the smallest possible price movement in a security (e.g., one-eighth of a dollar for Toronto Stock Exchange stocks). On the stock market, also known as a Price Tick.

Minimum Monthly Balance (MMB): the lowest amount of funds in an account at the end of a business day during a calendar month. The MMB is sometimes used to determine the amount of interest earned on an account or the level of service charge that applies to an account. Also known as Low Balance Method. *See also* Adjusted Balance Method, Average Daily Balance Method, Past Due Balance Method.

Minimum Payment: the smallest payment required to keep a borrowing facility (e.g., a credit card) in good standing.

Minimum Wage: by law or contract, the lowest wage that can be paid for a specific job or job category. The minimum wage varies from province to province.

Minister: the head of a government department (e.g., the Minister of Finance).

Ministry: a government department headed by a minister (e.g., the Department of Finance).

Mini Tigers of Asia: Indonesia, Malaysia, the Philippines and Thailand. Also known as Little Dragons of Asia, Little Tigers of Asia. *See also* Big Tiger of Asia, Eight Tigers, Four Tigers.

Minor: 1. a person who has not attained the age of majority. **2.** in law, the same as an infant. *See also* Age of Majority.

Minority Interest: a significant but non-controlling interest in a company, often owned by another company. In calculating net income, the proportion of earnings that accrue to the minority interest is deducted.

Minority Shareholders: all the non-controlling shareholders in a company that is controlled by a major shareholder(s). In the event of a takeover, the acquiring company may be willing to pay more for the controlling block of shares than for the non-controlling shares. In many jurisdictions, regulators have taken steps to protect the rights of minority shareholders. *See also* Strike Suit.

Minor Trend: a trend that is considered insignificant because it is relatively recent and not clearly established.

Mint: a place where the government manufactures money.

Mint Par of Exchange: the ratio of one country's reserves of gold and silver divided by another's.

Mint Price of Gold: the price paid for gold delivered to a mint.

Minus Tick: this occurs when the last trade in a stock takes place at a lower price than the previous trade. Also known as Downtick. *See also* Closing Tick, Plus Tick, Tick, Zero-Minus Tick, Zero-Plus Tick.

Minute Book: the official record of a company's annual meetings and board meetings.

MIP: *see* Monthly Investment Plan.

MIS: *see* Management Information System.

Misery Index: *see* Discomfort Index

Mismatched: a circumstance when assets and liabilities are not matched as to dollar amounts and terms to maturity. *See also* Immunization, Immunize, Matched.

Mission: a diplomatic office in a foreign country.

Mission Critical: a computer system that is critical to the functioning of a business. *See also* Computer.

Mission Statement: a brief, concise statement describing the goals and objectives of a company, organization or group.

Missouri Market: a term used to refer to a climate in which the possibility of a favourable future event is not enough to cause investors to buy. Also known as Show Me Market. *See also* On the Come.

Miss the Market: 1. this occurs if one does not hold investments, or is not fully invested, when a financial market moves up. **2.** a broker's failure to execute a client order at an available favourable price.

Mistrial: a trial that, often due to some procedural error, is invalid.

Mixed: a market that goes up and down and ends up flat or is made up of securities that are up and down.

MJSD: short for March, June, September and December, the months in which many fiscal quarters end and one of the option cycles. *See also* Option Cycle.

MLA: *see* Member of the Legislative Assembly.

MLS: *see* Multiple Listing Service.

MM: one million. 2MM is two million.

Mobile Telephony: a wireless telephone service provided mainly through a cellular system.

Mode: the value that, in a set of numbers, occurs most often. *See also* Arithmetic Average, Mean, Median.

Model: in computers, a series of formulae designed to replicate or forecast a real-world situation or structure, such as an economy or a company. Different variables are plugged into the computer in order to see how a real-world situation might be affected by changing conditions. *See also* Simulation.

Modem: short for "modulator/demodulator," a device used to connect one's computer to a remote computer through phone lines. *See also* Computer.

Moderator: one who presides over a meeting or an assembly.

Modern Portfolio: a portfolio managed to meet the objectives outlined by the Modern Portfolio Theory. Also known as Portfolio Theory. *See also* Efficient Frontier, Efficient Portfolio, Modern Portfolio Theory, Portfolio Optimization.

Modern Portfolio Theory: a theory that holds a portfolio should be managed so as to maximize expected return for a given level of risk or minimize risk for a given level of expected return. Diversification is a key to attaining this result. *See also* Diversification, Efficient Frontier, Efficient Portfolio, Modern Portfolio, Portfolio Optimization Prudent Investor Rule.

Modified Duration: a measure of bond price changes for given changes in yield. *See also* Duration.

Modified Retirement Income Fund: a maturity option for a locked-in RRSP that specifies both a minimum and maximum amount that must be withdrawn each year. *See also* Registered Retirement Savings Plan – Locked-In.

Modus Operandi: a manner of operation.

Mom-and-Pop Shop: a very small, often family-run, independent business.

Momentum: the inherent strength of a movement in price. It is implied that the higher its momentum, the more likely it is that a price trend will persist.

Momentum Investor: an investor who selects stocks to purchase based on momentum. *See also* Earnings Momentum, Momentum.

Monetarism: an economic theory, associated with U.S. economist Milton Friedman, that argues that economic performance depends on the supply of money. In other words, inflation control, economic growth and job creation depend primarily on monetary policy. *See also* Friedman, Milton.

Monetary Aggregates: any one of the various definitions of money supply, the main ones being M1, M2, M3 and M4. *See also* M1, M2, M3, M4.

Monetary Base: the money in circulation plus the reserve deposits held by central banks.

Monetary Conditions Index (MCI): a gauge of the economic impact of interest rate and currency changes used by the Bank of Canada. The MCI indicates that a 3 percent rise in the value of the Canadian dollar has the same negative impact on the economy as a 1 percent rise in interest rates.

Monetary Inflation: inflation caused by excessive growth in the money supply. In monetary inflation, rising prices are the economic adjustment for less valuable currency.

Monetary Policy: the policy by which the central bank manages the supply of money (e.g., by buying and selling securities, changing bank reserve requirements and adjusting interest rates). *See also* Fiscal Policy.

Monetize: to establish as, or convert into, legal tender.

Monetize the Debt: to convert government debt from interest-bearing securities into money. Both are considered government debt, but money can be used for purchasing goods and services.

Money: 1. in law, a commodity established as an exchangeable equivalent for other commodities. **2.** the official currency of a country issued by its government.

Money Centre Bank: a major bank located in a world financial centre (such as New York, Tokyo or London).

Money In, Money Out (MIMO): a reference to a person's or family's cash flow and savings pattern. *See also* Financial Planner, Financial Planning, Personal Financial Planning.

Money Laundering: hiding illegal profits by running money through legitimate enterprises. Also known as Laundering.

Money Lender: a person or company that lends money at interest.

Moneymaker: a person who earns, or a thing that produces, much profit.

Money Management: 1. any of the services relating to money provided by a financial planner, including banking, budgeting and credit. **2.** *see* Portfolio Management.

Money Market: a market in which short-term government and corporate financial instruments (such as treasury bills, commercial paper) are traded. *See also* Bond Market, Commodity Exchange, Financial Market, Futures Exchange, Stock Market.

Money Market Account: a savings account that often offers a higher rate of interest for larger deposits.

Money Market Fund: *see* Canadian Money Market Fund.

Money Market Instrument: a security normally traded on the money market. Also known as Money Market Paper, Money Market Security.

Money Market Paper: *see* Money Market Instrument.

Money Market Rate: the current yield on money market instruments.

Money Market Security: *see* Money Market Instrument.

Money Market Trader: a brokerage firm employee engaged in buying and selling money market instruments.

Money Purchase Pension Plan: a pension plan in which the accumulated value of contributions by and on behalf of an employee is used to provide pension income. Also known as a Defined

Contribution Pension Plan, because the amount contributed is fixed but the retirement benefit is not. *See also* Defined Benefit Plan, Unit Benefit Pension Plan.

Money Supply: the total amount of money in an economy, including currency and near-cash securities. *See also* M1, M2, M3, M4.

Money Talks: in a business transaction, an expression that suggests that the person with the most money holds the most influence.

Monitor: an output device similar to a television screen, it is connected to one's computer by a cable.

Monopoly: a market in which there is only one producer but many buyers of a particular product or service. The opposite of a Monopsony. Also known as Seller's Monopoly. *See also* Duopoly, Monopsony, Natural Monopoly, Oligopoly, Oligopsony, Price Control.

Monopsony: a market in which there is only one buyer but many producers for a particular product or service. Opposite of Monopoly. Also known as Buyer's Monopoly. *See also* Duopoly, Monopoly, Natural Monopoly, Oligopoly, Oligopsony.

Montage Quote: a quote for a security in the local currency of each international stock market on which it is traded.

Month-End: the final securities exchange trading day for settlement each month, sometimes marked by weakness in thinly traded stocks (which must be sold to cover amounts owing in brokerage accounts).

Monthly Income Securities: any security that pays monthly income.

Monthly Investment Plan (MIP): 1. a New York Stock Exchange plan that allows small amounts of money to be invested in stocks each month. **2.** any plan involving regular monthly investments. *See also* Dollar Cost Averaging.

Monthly Statement: 1. a monthly report of activity sent by brokerage firms to clients. **2.** any monthly report of activity (e.g., bank account, credit card).

Month to Month: the change in results in the current month compared with the preceding month (e.g., mutual fund performance summaries).

Montreal Curb Market: founded in 1926 to trade speculative securities, it became the Canadian Stock Exchange and then merged with the Montreal Stock Exchange in 1974. *See also* Montreal Exchange.

Montreal Exchange (ME): a stock exchange located in Montreal, Quebec, it is Canada's oldest stock exchange, incorporated in 1874. The name Montreal Stock Exchange is often used in reference to the Montreal Exchange. Under an agreement in princi-

ple announced in March 1999, the Montreal Exchange will focus exclusively on futures and derivatives trading. The Alberta Stock Exchange will merge with the Vancouver Stock Exchange to form a national junior equities market. The Toronto Stock Exchange will become the senior securities market. Under the terms of the revised agreement in November, 1999, the ME will provide listing and regulatory services for small cap Quebec-based companies under rules identical to those of the proposed Canadian Venture Exchange. Also known as Bourse de Montreal. Web site: www.me.org *See also* Alberta Stock Exchange, Canadian Venture Exchange, Exchange Coffee House, Montreal Curb Market, Toronto Stock Exchange, Vancouver Stock Exchange.

Montreal Exchange Canadian Banking Index Official: a price weighted index of banking companies with the largest market capitalizations listed on the Montreal Exchange and at least one other Canadian stock exchange.

Montreal Exchange Canadian Forest Products Index Official: a price weighted index of forestry companies with the largest market capitalizations listed on the Montreal Exchange and at least one other Canadian stock exchange.

Montreal Exchange Canadian Industrial Products Index Official: a price weighted index of industrial companies with the largest market capitalizations listed on the Montreal Exchange and at least one other Canadian stock exchange.

Montreal Exchange Canadian Market Portfolio Index Official: a price weighted index of 25 companies with the largest market capitalizations listed on the Montreal Exchange and at least one other Canadian stock exchange.

Montreal Exchange Canadian Mining and Minerals Index Official: a price weighted index of mining companies with the largest market capitalizations listed on the Montreal Exchange and at least one other Canadian stock exchange.

Montreal Exchange Canadian Oil and Gas Index Official: a price weighted index of oil and gas companies with the largest market capitalizations listed on the Montreal Exchange and at least one other Canadian stock exchange.

Montreal Exchange Canadian Utilities Index Official: a price weighted index of public utility companies with the largest market capitalizations listed on the Montreal Exchange and at least one other Canadian stock exchange.

Montreal Stock Exchange: *see* Montreal Exchange.

Moody's Investors Service: a company that rates

corporate bonds and other securities. For bonds, AAA is the highest rating and C is the lowest. Moody's is a subsidiary of Dun & Bradstreet Corporation. *See also* Bond Rating, Bond Rating Agency, Canadian Bond Rating Service, Dominion Bond Rating Service, Dun & Bradstreet Corporation, Rating, Rating Agencies, Standard & Poor's Corporation.

Moose Pasture: in investment, worthless land owned or explored by a resource exploration company that is promoted as having value but does not. *See also* Florida Land Boom, Swamp Land.

Moral Suasion: the government's and/or central bank's ability to influence, rather than to mandate, actions. Also known as Jawboning. *See also* Talk Down, Talk Up.

Moratorium: in law, a suspension or delay of an expected action or activity (e.g., additional time a court allows a debtor to make a required payment).

Morbidity: the rate of incidence of a disease in a population. It is one way of measuring the health of a population.

MORF: Internet acronym for "male or female?"

Morphing: in computers, the process by which one image is gradually transformed, or metamorphosed, into another. *See also* Computer.

Mortality: the amount of a life insurance premium relating directly to the risk that the insured may die. *See also* Life Insurance.

Mortality Table: a summary of the statistical probability of death at any given age. *See also* Life Expec-tancy Table.

Mortgage: a loan secured by property. Often a loan for the purchase of property, with the property itself being used as security for the loan. *See also* Adjustable Rate Mortgage, After Acquired Clause, Amortization, Amortization Period, Anniversary, Anticipation, Anticipation Rate, Appraisal, Assumable Mortgage, Assumption Agreement, Blended Payment, Buy Down, Canada Mortgage and Housing Corporation, Canada Mortgage and Housing Corporation Chattel Loan Insurance Program, Canadian Mortgage Fund, Capped Rate Mortgage, Certificate of Charge, Chattel Mortgage, Closed Mortgage, Collateral Mortgage, Commercial Mortgage, Commercial Mortgage Backed Security, Construction Loan, Covenantee, Covenantor, Conventional Mortgage, Direct Reduction Mortgage, Due-on-Sale Clause, Encumbered, First Mortgage, First Mortgage Bond, Fixed Rate Mortgage, Floating Rate Mortgage, Foreclosure, Gale Date, Graduated Payment Mortgage, Gross Debt Service Ratio, High Ratio Mortgage, Inter Alia Mortgage, Interest Rate Differential Penalty, Junior Mortgage, Lien, Loan-to-Value Ratio, Locking-In, Mortgage Backed Security, Mortgage Banker, Mortgage Broker, Mortgage Department, Mortgaged Out, Mortgagee, Mortgagee Clause, Mortgage Lender, Mortgage Lien, Mortgage Life Insurance, Mortgage Loan Insurance, Mortgage in Possession, Mortgage Investor, Mortgage Portfolio, Mortgage Prepayment, Mortgager, National Housing Act, Non-Assumable Mortgage, Open Mortgage, Participating Mortgage, Participation Mortgage, Penalty, Pre-Approved Mortgage, Prepayment Clause, Prepayment Penalty, Prepayment Privilege, Redline, Refinance, Registered Retirement Savings Plan – Mortgages, Release Clause, Residential Mortgage, Right of Redemption, Second Mortgage, Shared Appreciation Mortgage, Skip Payment Privilege, Straight Loan, Subordination Clause, Third Mortgage, Timely Payment Guarantee, Twenty/ Twenty Mortgage, Underlying Mortgage, Variable Rate Mortgage, Vendor Financing, Walk Away Mortgage, Wrap-Around Mortgage.

Mortgage Assumption: *see* Assumption Agreement.

Mortgage Backed Security (MBS): a financial asset secured by mortgages, often on residential properties. *See also* Asset Backed Security, Commercial Mortgage Backed Security, Mortgage, Securitization.

Mortgage Banker: the intermediary between a mortgage issuer wanting to sell mortgages and an investor wanting to buy them. *See also* Mortgage.

Mortgage Broker: an agent (or firm) who arranges loans between those with money to lend as mortgages and those seeking to borrow. *See also* Mortgage.

Mortgage Department: the area of a lending institution that makes and administers mortgage loans. *See also* Mortgage.

Mortgaged Out: this occurs when one's total mortgage debt equals or exceeds the market value of one's property. *See also* Mortgage.

Mortgagee: in a mortgage transaction, the party that lends the money. *See also* Mortgage, Mortgager.

Mortgagee Clause: a clause in an insurance contract that directs death benefits be paid to the mortgagee. *See also* Mortgage.

Mortgage in a Registered Retirement Savings Plan: *see* Registered Retirement Savings Plan – Mortgages.

Mortgage in Possession: a mortgage that has been taken over by a creditor. *See also* Mortgage, Mortgage Life Insurance.

Mortgage Insurance: 1. *see* Mortgage Life Insurance. **2.** *see* Mortgage Loan Insurance.

Mortgage Investor: a person or company who owns mortgages as an investment for security and income. *See also* Mortgage.

Mortgage Lender: an institution (or individual) that lends money in the form of mortgages. *See also* Mortgage.

Mortgage Lien: a claim against a mortgage that has been used to secure a loan. *See also* Lien.

Mortgage Life Insurance: life insurance obtained to cover the amount owing under a mortgage should the borrower die. Also known as Mortgage Insurance. *See also* Mortgagee Clause, Mortgage Loan Insurance.

Mortgage Loan Insurance: insurance that is required on a high-ratio mortgage to protect the lender if the borrower fails to repay the loan. Also known as Mortgage Insurance. *See also* Mortgage Life Insurance.

Mortgage Portfolio: all the mortgage loans held by a mortgage lender or investor. *See also* Mortgage.

Mortgage Prepayment: the repaying of a mortgage loan before it is due. Prepayment is often motivated by the lower interest rates available on new mortgages. *See also* Anticipation, Anticipation Rate, Mortgage, Penalty, Prepayment, Prepayment Clause, Prepayment Penalty, Prepayment Privilege.

Mortgager: the party to the mortgage transaction that borrows the money. Also known as Mortgagor. *See also* Mortgage.

Mortgagor: *see* Mortgager.

Mortmain: perpetual ownership of real estate by an institution (e.g., a church). Such real estate cannot be transferred or sold.

Mosaic Theory: the theory that a financial analyst can reach conclusions and recommendations based on public and non-material inside information even if those conclusions and recommendations would have been material inside information if communicated to the analyst directly from the company. *See* Insider Information, Insider Trading, Material Information, Tippee, Tipper.

Moscow International Stock Exchange: the major stock exchange of Russia, located in its capital, Moscow. Web site: www.fe.msk.ru/infomarket/rinacoplus/overview.html

Most Active: a list of securities on an exchange that, for a given period, have the highest volume of trading.

Most Favoured Nation (MFN): 1. a standing awarded by the U.S. to indicate a country is entitled to the most attractive terms of trade. **2.** *see* Normal Trading Relations.

Motion: a formal request, put to a court and filed with an affidavit, for a particular order. *See also* Affidavit.

MOTOS: Internet acronym for "member of the opposite sex."

Mouse: 1. a timid, risk-averse investor. **2.** a hand-manoeuvred computer pointing device that, when placed on a mouse pad, controls an on-screen cursor.

See also Computer.

Mouthpiece: slang for a spokesperson or lawyer.

Movement: a change in price.

Moving Average: a single number representing the average of a stated number of previous numbers, it is updated by adding a new number and dropping the oldest one (e.g., a 10-day moving average is the closing price of a stock for the previous 10 trading days divided by 10. When one day passes, the new day's closing price is added, the oldest day's closing price is dropped and the new total is divided by 10). Technical analysts use moving averages to describe trends in variables such as stock prices. *See also* One Hundred Day Moving Average, Two Hundred Day Moving Average.

MP: *see* Member of Parliament.

Mr. Copper: Yasuo Hamanaka (1948-), former metals trader with Sumitomo Corporation. Hamanaka controlled the copper market through unauthorized trading from roughly 1985 to 1996. He was also known as Mr. 5 Percent because it is estimated that he controlled 5 percent of the world copper market at the height of the scandal. He lost his employer $2.6 billion U.S. and subsequently went to jail.

Mr. 5 Percent: *see* Mr. Copper.

MS-DOS: a common but aging disk operating system developed and sold by Microsoft. *See also* Disk Operating System, PC-DOS.

MSE: *see* Montreal Exchange.

MUD: *see* Multiuser Dungeon.

Multi-Family Residential Housing: 1. usually, a reference to apartment buildings. **2.** generally, any form of housing intended for use by more than one family. *See also* Duplex., Single-Family Residence, Triplex.

Multilateral: an agreement, treaty, conference, etc., that involves more than two countries or groups.

Multilateral Agreement on Investment (MAI): an agreement on investment under discussion that involves 29 of the world's richest countries, including Canada.

Multi-Level Marketing: a term to describe a marketing approach that focuses as much on recruiting additional sales representatives as it does on selling products. Also known as Network Marketing. *See also* Pyramid Selling.

Multi-Manager Approach: *see* Manager Diversification.

Multinational Corporation: a company that does business around the world and has facilities in one or more foreign countries.

Multiple: *see* Price/Earnings Ratio.

Multiple Currency Security: a security for which the holder can select the currency for interest or dividend payments.

Multiple Listing Service (MLS): an organization of real estate brokers who work cooperatively in selling property. A listing with an MLS agent will be communicated to all MLS agents, which exposes the property to a wider list of potential buyers. *See also* Exclusive Listing, Listing Broker, Selling Agent.

Multiple Regression Analysis: a statistical method for testing the historical relationship between a dependent variable and one or more independent variables. *See also* Dependent Variable, Independent Variable.

Multiplier Effect: an economic theory that argues that expenditures have a ripple effect throughout the economy (e.g., as one dollar's worth of activity moves through the economy it results in more than one dollar's worth of economic activity). John Maynard Keynes, an English economist, used the multiplier effect in the 1930s, and it has since become an important tool of economic management and analysis. Also known as Keynesian Multiplier. *See also* Keynesian Economics, Keynes, John Maynard, Trickle-Down Theory. **2.** the way in which bank deposits have a magnified impact on the money supply. Because banks are required to keep only part of a deposit as reserves, the balance can be loaned to other customers. When a loan is granted to a customer, the funds are put on deposit and the bank is again required to hold a reserve, but the balance can be lent to a customer. If the reserve requirement is 20 percent, a $1 deposit can support as much as $5 in credit and $4 in loans.

Multipurpose Internet Mail Extensions (MIME): an Internet standard for the e-mail transfer of such non-text information as graphics and sounds. *See also* Internet.

Multitasking: in computers, the ability to switch back and forth between one or more programs. *See also* Task Switching.

Multiuser Dungeon (MUD): a virtual role-playing game environment (located on the Internet), within which many people may interact. *See also* Internet.

Muni: *see* Municipal Bond.

Municipal Bond: 1. a bond issued by a municipality. **2.** in the U.S., a bond issued by a municipality, state or other subdivision (e.g., a hospital), that is popular because interest earned on it is exempt from tax. Also known as Muni. *See also* Bond.

Municipal Court: a lower court of limited jurisdiction, it deals with municipal bylaws.

Municipality: a city, town or district with a local government.

Murder: in law, the unlawful killing of one person by another, especially with malice and premeditation.

Muscat Securities Market: the major stock exchange of Oman. Also known as Oman Stock Exchange.

Mutilated Security: a stock or bond certificate that is damaged and cannot be used to settle a trade.

Mutual Company: a company whose ownership and profits are divided among its member/owners according to the amount of business each does with the company. A common structure in the insurance business. *See also* Demutualization, Mutual Life Insurance Company.

Mutual Fund: a fund in which the investments of many individuals are pooled and managed by a professional. Some mutual funds are mutual fund trusts. *See also* Accumulation Plan, Acquisition Cost, Automatic Investment Program, Automatic Withdrawal Program, Clone, Closed Up Mutual Fund, Condensed Prospectus, Contractual Plan, Custodian, Deferred Declining Redemption Fee – At Cost, Deferred Declining Redemption Fee – At Market Value, Deferred Sales Charge, Distribution, Evergreen Prospectus, Exchange Privilege, Fixed Dollar Withdrawal Plan, Fixed Period Withdrawal Plan, Front End Load, Fund, Investment Company, Investment Funds Institute of Canada, Investment Funds Standards Committee, Life Expectancy Adjusted Withdrawal Plan, Load, Management Company, Management Expense Ratio, Management Fee, Market-Neutral Fund, Mutual Fund Cash Position, Mutual Fund – Category, Mutual Fund – Type, Net Asset Value, Net Asset Value Per Share, No Load Fund, Periodic Payment Plan, Ratio Withdrawal Plan, Redemption Fee, Registered Mutual Fund, Reinvestment Plan, Right of Rescission, Road Show, Sales Charge, Simplified Prospectus, Star System, Summary Prospectus, Systematic Savings Plan, Systematic Withdrawal Plan, Tied Selling, Unit, Unitholder, Unit Trust, Voluntary Accumulation Plan, Wholesaler.

Mutual Fund Agent: a person who is licensed to give advice on and sell mutual funds to the investing public. To be a mutual fund agent, a person must pass the required tests and be registered with the province in which he/she works. Many financial planners are licensed as mutual fund and life insurance agents. *See also* Broker, Financial Planner, Life Insurance Agent.

Mutual Fund Cash Position: the amount of cash held in one or all mutual funds as a percentage of total assets. Cash of zero percent to 10 percent is normal; higher than 10 percent is defensive; and higher than 20 percent is very defensive. *See also* Mutual Fund.

Mutual Fund – Category: there are 31 Canadian categories developed by the Investment Funds Standards Committee. Each of the categories may be refined by the fund manager (e.g., to Canadian Large Cap Equity Fund might be added the term "growth" or "value" to reflect the manager's style). Each can be referred to for a specific definition. The categories are: Asia/Pacific Rim Equity Fund, Asia-Ex Japan Equity Fund, Canadian Asset Allocation Fund, Canadian Balanced Fund, Canadian Bond Fund, Canadian Dividend Income Fund, Canadian Equity Fund, Canadian High Income Balanced Fund, Canadian Large Cap Equity Fund, Canadian Money Market Fund, Canadian Mortgage Fund, Canadian Short-Term Bond Fund, Canadian Small to Mid Cap Equity Fund, Country Specific Fund, Emerging Markets Equity Fund, European Equity Fund, Foreign Bond Fund, Foreign Money Market Fund, Global Balanced and Asset Allocation Fund, Global Equity Fund, Global Natural Resources Fund, Global Precious Metals Fund, Global Science and Technology, International Equity Fund, Japanese Equity Fund, Labour Sponsored Venture Capital Fund, Latin American Equity Fund, Mutual Fund – Other, North American Equity Fund, Specialty or Miscellaneous, U.S. Equity Fund, U.S. Small to Mid Cap Equity Fund.

Mutual Fund Custodian: *see* Custodian.

Mutual Fund Dealers Association of Canada (MFDA): a self-regulatory body for mutual fund distributors. The MFDA will initially address issues such as supervision of sales staff, record keeping, sales practices and other consumer protection issues. The MFDA covers mutual fund distributors of firms that are members of the Investment Dealers Association of Canada and the Investment Funds Institute of Canada. It has no jurisdiction over other mutual fund distributors (e.g., those employed by the life insurance industry). *See also* Investment Dealers Association of Canada, Investment Funds Institute of Canada, Self-Regulatory Organization.

Mutual Fund – Other: *see* Aggressive Growth Fund, All Weather Fund, Asset Allocation Fund, Balanced Mutual Fund, Bond Mutual Fund, Closed End Mutual Fund, Dual Purpose Mutual Fund, Equity Mutual Fund, Ethical Mutual Fund, Fair Weather Fund, Family of Funds, Fixed Income Fund, Foreign Fund, Foul Weather Fund, Fund of Funds, Go-Go Fund, Growth and Income Fund, Growth Fund, Hedge Fund, Income Mutual Fund, Index Fund, International Government Bond Fund, International Stock Fund, Leverage Fund, Money Market Fund, Mortgage Fund, Mutual Fund – Category, Offshore Mutual Fund, Open End Mutual Fund, Real Estate Mutual Fund, Sector Fund, Segregated Mutual Fund, Socially Responsible Mutual Fund, Venture Capital Fund, Vulture Fund.

Mutual Life Insurance Company: a life insurance company without shareholders. In theory, a mutual life insurance company is owned by its policy holders. *See also* Demutualization, Stock Life Insurance Company.

Mutual Fund Trust: *see* Unit Trust.

Myth-Information: in financial markets, incorrect information that is nonetheless believed to be correct

---

Mutual Funds

A mutual fund is a fund in which the investments of many individuals are pooled and managed by a professional.

Not all mutual funds invest the same way. A money market mutual fund is a conservative portfolio that focuses on high-quality, short-term money market investments; a bond fund focuses on a variety of government and corporate bonds; a common stock fund focuses on common shares that are riskier than bonds or money market instruments; and an aggressive growth fund focuses on very high risk investments in a variety of different securities.

Mutual funds are offered by prospectus; that is, by a legal document that describes the investment. Most investors refer to a simplified prospectus that summarizes the investment's highlights.

When mutual funds are purchased, there is usually a sales charge. A front end load is a commission paid at the time the investment is made, while a back end load is a commission that is paid at the time the investment is cashed in (if the mutual fund has been owned for a long time, this commission is usually low). A no load fund is for sophisticated investors who need neither advice nor service.

Certain costs are charged to the mutual fund investor: normal business expenses are included in the expense ratio and a management fee is also paid to the portfolio manager. These two costs comprise the management expense ratio.

When one enters uncharted areas, it is a good idea to go with a group and to take a professional guide. And, indeed, this is what less experienced investors do when they venture into new markets, whether it is through an asset allocation fund, an international money market fund or a socially responsible mutual fund. However, mutual funds also offer significant benefits for experienced investors. Under current conditions, mutual funds comprise the most attractive investment vehicle for the majority of investors.

Nabob: a person of wealth and position.

Nader, Ralph (1934-): a well-known American consumer advocate, he has been instrumental in bringing forth legislation concerning automobile safety standards, radiation hazards, insecticide use and more.

Nairobi Stock Exchange: the major stock exchange of Kenya, located in its capital, Nairobi.

Nairobi Stock Exchange Index (NSE20): a market capitalization weighted stock price index for the Nairobi Stock Exchange.

Nakfa: the primary currency of Eritrea.

NAFTA: *see* North American Free Trade Agreement.

NAFTZ: *see* North American Free Trade Agreement.

Naked Call Option: *see* Uncovered Call Option.

Naked Option: *see* Uncovered Option.

Naked Put Option: *see* Uncovered Put Option.

Naked Position: *see* Uncovered Position.

Naked Transaction: *see* Uncovered Transaction.

Naked Writer: *see* Uncovered Writer.

Naked Writing: *see* Uncovered Writing.

Naira: the primary currency of Nigeria.

Name: 1. an investor in a Lloyd's of London insurance syndicate. Lloyd's experienced $12.4 billion U.S. in losses in the five years ended 1992 because of claims for asbestos related illness and hurricane and earthquake damage. Because "Names" have unlimited liability, this resulted in severe financial difficulty for many people, including Canadians. Legal actions are ongoing. The primary source of capital for Lloyd's today is limited liability corporations. *See also* Lloyd's of London. **2.** a reference to a person's reputation.

Named Beneficiary: in a life insurance contract or RRSP, the person who is listed as the recipient of a benefit in case of the contract holder's death. *See also* Beneficiary, Irrevocable Beneficiary, Life Insurance.

Named Peril Insurance: a form of property insurance that covers a specific peril, such as fire or theft.

Namibian Stock Exchange: the major stock exchange of Namibia, located in its capital, Windhoek. Web site: www.nse.com.na/

Namibian Stock Exchange Overall Index: a market capitalization weighted stock price index for the Namibian Stock Exchange. This index includes stocks also listed on the Johannesburg Stock Exchange.

Nanosecond: 1. one-billionth of one second. **2.** in computers, a time measure used to represent computing speed.

Narrowcast: the delivery of a message to a very focused, qualified audience. Opposite of broadcast. *See also* Broadcast.

Narrow Market: a market undergoing light trading.

Narrow the Spread: to reduce the difference between the bid and offer price for a security. *See also* Bid Price, Offer Price.

Nascent: just emerging (e.g., a nascent economic recovery is a turnaround that is just beginning).

NASD: *see* National Association of Securities Dealers.

NASDAQ: *see* National Association of Securities Dealers Automated Quotations.

NASDAQ Composite Index: a broadly based market capitalization weighted index of all NASDAQ listed stocks. The base value was 100 on February 5, 1971, when this index was first published.

NASDAQ National Market: the market tier that lists larger companies on the NASDAQ system. *See also* NASDAQ Small Cap Market, NASDAQ Stock Market.

NASDAQ Small Cap Market: the market tier that lists smaller companies on the NASDAQ system. Companies listed on the NASDAQ small cap market must have the sponsorship of a market maker. *See also* Market Maker, NASDAQ National Market, NASDAQ Stock Market.

NASDAQ Stock Market: a market listing service consisting of the NASDAQ National Market and the NASDAQ Small Cap Market. In early 1998, the NASDAQ Stock Market and the American Stock Exchange agreed to merge. Web site: www.nasdaq.com *See also* American Stock Exchange, NASDAQ National Market, NASDAQ Small Cap Market.

National Association of Investment Clubs: a U.S. organization that helps investors set up investment clubs. *See also* Canadian Shareowner's Association.

National Association of Securities Dealers (NASD): a U.S. organization of brokers and dealers that regulates all over-the-counter brokers. The NASD is supervised by the Securities and Exchange Commission. Web site: www.nasdaq.com

National Association of Securities Dealers Automated Quotations - Level 1 Service: a computerized subscription service available to brokerage firms that provides the highest bid prices and the lowest offer prices of NASDAQ listed stocks. *See also* NASDAQ.

National Association of Securities Dealers Automated Quotations - Level 2 Service: a computerized subscription service available to institutional investors and traders that provides the names of market makers and their bids for NASDAQ listed stocks. *See also* Market Makers, NASDAQ.

National Association of Securities Dealers Automated Quotations - Level 3 Service: a computerized subscription service available to market makers that provides the names of market makers and their bids for NASDAQ listed stocks. *See also* Market Makers, NASDAQ.

National Central Bank (NCB): the central bank of a country (e.g., the Bank of Canada is a national central bank). *See also* Bank for International Settlements.

National Contingency Fund: *see* Canadian Investor Protection Fund.

National Currency Unit (NCU): the national currency of countries participating in the Euro. NCUs will continue to be in use until they are phased out (between January 1, 2002, and July 1, 2002). *See also* Euro.

National Debt: the debt of the federal government and its agencies, including bonds, the debts of Crown corporations and drawings from foreign central banks and the International Monetary Fund. Also referred to as Federal Debt, Federal Government Debt. *See Also* Public Debt.

National Energy Board (NEB): a federal agency created in 1959 to monitor Canada's supply of, demand for and reserves of oil and natural gas. The NEB determines whether Canada has a surplus of electricity, oil and/or gas and administers the export programs and licences. In addition, the NEB conducts hearings on the construction of energy delivery systems and, in the case of pipelines, the allowable tariffs that can be charged to carry oil and/or gas.

National Housing Act (NHA): 1. federal legislation designed to maintain an adequate flow of mortgage funds at reasonable interest rates in Canada. This is accomplished by insuring mortgages on new housing, financing rental housing construction for low-income persons and promoting special housing needs (e.g., for seniors). The NHA is administered by Canada Mortgage and Housing Corporation. *See also* Mortgage. **2.** in the U.S., the law that established the Federal Housing Administration. *See also* Federal Housing Administration.

National Income: *see* Gross National Income.

Nationality: the status of belonging to a particular nation by origin, birth or naturalization. *See also* Naturalize.

Nationalization: the transfer of privately owned assets into government hands. *See also* Naturalize, Privatization.

Nationalize: to convert from private ownership to government ownership. *See also* Naturalize, Privatization.

National Market Advisory Board: in the U.S., a panel appointed by the Securities and Exchange Commission to advise on securities market regulation.

National Numbering Agency (NNA): the agency responsible for issuing International Securities Identification Numbering System codes for securities in a country. Also known as Société Interprofessionnelle pour la Compensation des Valeurs Mobilières.

National Quotation Bureau: a U.S. interdealer network that facilitates the trading of over-the-counter stocks.

National Securities Legislation: to streamline the sale and distribution of securities in Canada, there has been an effort to change securities legislation from provincial to federal. Although changes have been made in various provinces to coordinate rules and regulations, a national securities act is not yet in place. *See also* Securities Act.

National Stock Exchange (NSE): a third stock exchange in New York City founded in 1960.

National Stock Exchange of Lithuania: the major stock exchange of Lithuania located in its capital, Vilnius. Web site: www.nse.lt/

National Stock Exchange of India: the major stock exchange of India, located in Bombay. Also known as Bombay Stock Exchange. Web site: www.nseindia.com

National Television System Committee (NTSC): the committee responsible for setting the communications standards for television and video in North America. *See also* High Definition Television, Phase Alternate Lines, Sequential Couleur Avec Memoire, Standard Definition Television.

NATO: *see* North Atlantic Treaty Organization.

Natural Corner: to corner a market or a security without manipulation. *See also* Corner the Market.

Natural Gas: a mixture of gaseous hydrocarbons.

Natural Gas Liquids (NGL): liquids, extracted or recovered from natural gas, that are included in reserve and production figures for oil and gas companies.

Natural Interest Rate: the interest rate that prevails when the current supply of funds to lend equals the current demand for loans.

Naturalize: to grant full citizenship to a person of foreign birth.

Natural Monopoly: this occurs when a company has a monopoly because unusual circumstances prevent any other company from competing with it (e.g., a farm growing produce that will not grow anywhere else has a natural monopoly over that commodity). *See also* Duopoly, Monopoly, Oligopoly, Oligopsony, Price Control.

Natural Resource: a source of wealth that occurs in a natural state (e.g., minerals, timber, oil and gas).

Nautical Mile: a unit of length equal to one minute of the great circle of the Earth, a distance that is different by some 62 feet between the equator and the pole. By convention, the accepted distance is 1,853 metres or about 6,080 feet. Also known as Air Mile, Sea Mile.

NAV: *see* Net Asset Value.

Navigate: in computers, to move around the Internet. *See also* Internet.

NAV per Share: *see* Net Asset Value per Share.

NB: *see* Nota Bene.

NCB: *see* National Central Bank.

NCU: *see* National Currency Unit.

Nearbys: in commodities and options, the contracts that are nearest to delivery or expiry. *See also* Option.

Near Cash Security: a financial security that is liquid enough to be considered the same as cash. Also known as Near Money Security.

Near Money Security: *see* Near Cash Security.

Near Term: occurring in the immediate future, that is, in a few weeks or months (e.g., "The outlook for the stock market is positive in the near term"). *See also* Long Term, Medium Term, Short Term.

NEB: *see* National Energy Board.

Negative Balance: the debit balance in an account due to an excess of debits over credits. *See also* Credit, Debit.

Negative Carry: this occurs when the interest earned on an investment is less than the interest charged on the money borrowed to make the investment. *See also* Positive Carry.

Negative Covenant: in a bond indenture, a clause to prevent a company from making changes that will benefit shareholders at the expense of bondholders (e.g., payment of an extraordinary cash dividend). Also known as Restrictive Covenant. *See also* Negative Pledge.

Negative Incentive: a punishment that induces action (e.g., anyone who does not meet their sales quota will be fired). *See also* Incentive.

Negative Income Tax: an income tax system in which low-income individuals file a tax return and receive a payment if their income is below a prescribed level. *See also* Taxes.

Negative Interest Rate: a rare condition in which a depositor pays interest to a financial institution to accept a deposit. Negative interest rates have prevailed during periods of deflation when the annual increase in purchasing power exceeds the negative interest paid. It has also occurred (e.g., in Switzerland) when the currency is so strong that currency gains exceed the negative interest rate paid.

Negative Option Billing: a sales technique in which the seller bills for a service unless and until the buyer indicates that he/she does not want it. This practice is banned in many jurisdictions and is generally considered to be unethical.

Negative Option Marketing: a sales technique in which the seller assumes that, unless the buyer indicates otherwise, a purchase has been made. This practice is banned in many jurisdictions and is generally considered to be unethical.

Negative Pledge: a guarantee not to pledge assets if such an action would decrease a bondholder's security. Also known as Restrictive Covenant. *See also* Negative Covenant, Pledge.

Negative Real Interest Rate: an interest rate that is less than the rate of inflation. *See also* Real Interest Rate

Negative Working Capital: this occurs when current liabilities exceed current assets. *See also* Working Capital.

Negative Yield Curve: a situation in which interest rates on securities with shorter terms to maturity are higher than yields on securities with longer terms to maturity. Also known as Downsloping Yield Curve, Inverted Yield Curve. *See also* Positive Yield Curve, Yield Curve.

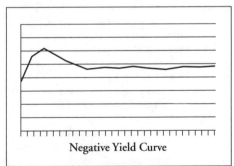

Negative Yield Curve

Negligence: in law, the failure to exercise the level of care considered reasonable under a given set of circumstances.

Negotiable: a term used to describe the feature of a financial instrument that means it can be sold or transferred. *See also* Transferable.

Negotiable Instrument: a financial asset that can be transferred without notifying the issuer. *See also* Transferable.

Negotiable Security: a security that is easy to transfer. *See also* Negotiated Scale.

Negotiated Bid: a term used to describe a price established for a security issue that is determined by discussion rather than competitive bidding.

Negotiated Sale: a term used to describe a securities transaction that is completed at a price determined by discussion rather than competitive bidding. *See also* Negotiated Bid.

Negotiated Underwriting: a term used to describe a new issue of securities in which the main variables (e.g., price, commission) are determined by discussion rather than competitive bidding. *See also* Underwriting.

Negotiating Bank: in a transaction involving a letter of credit, the bank that acts on behalf of the buyer of goods and arranges for settlement according to the terms of the draft. *See also* Advising Bank, Issuing Bank.

Negotiation: 1. in computers, the process that takes place between two modems when handshaking occurs. *See also* Computer, Handshaking. **2.** the process of coming to terms on an agreement, especially between management and labour. *See also* Binding Arbitration.

Neocolonialism: a policy on the part of a major power to use economic and political means to perpetuate or extend its influence over other nations.

Nepotism: a practice that involves bestowing favouritism or patronage upon relatives.

Nerd: an excessively studious person, particularly with computers and technology, who is socially inept. *See also* Computer, Computer Geek.

Nervous Nellie: an investor who is not comfortable with investment and who may change his/her mind at any given moment. *See also* Conservative Investor, Gambler, Investor, Speculator.

Nest Egg: conservative investments that a person sets aside (usually for emergencies or retirement). *See also* Drop Dead Money, Fun Money.

Net: the amount left after expenses or deductions, as in "net income" or "net profit." *See also* Gross. Also, an abbreviation for Internet. *See also* Internet.

.net: an appendage to an e-mail or Internet address that identifies a networking company. *See also* .com, .edu, .gov, Internet, mil, Networking, .org.

Net Assets: a company's assets less liabilities.

Net Asset Value (NAV): 1. in mutual fund valuations, the total value of the portfolio less liabilities. **2.** in corporate valuations, the book value of assets less liabilities. *See also* Mutual Fund, Net Asset Value Per Share.

Net Asset Value Per Share (NAV per Share): 1. in mutual fund valuations, the net asset value divided by the number of shares or units outstanding. **2.** in corporate valuations, the net asset value divided by number of shares outstanding. *See also* Mutual Fund, Net Asset Value.

Net Change: the difference between a stock's current price and its previous close.

Net Current Assets: a company's current assets less current liabilities. Also known as Working Capital. *See also* Negative Working Capital.

Net Earnings: *see* Net Income.

Net Income: a company's revenue less all expenses, including income taxes. Also known as Net Earnings. *See also* Gross Income.

Net Investment Income: the profit from an investment less all costs, including any interest on money borrowed to make the investment, commissions and income taxes.

Netiquette: an informal code of etiquette observed on the Internet. *See also* Internet.

Net Lease: a lease whereby the tenant is responsible for all costs relating to the asset being leased. Most commercial property leases are net leases. Also known as Net, Net, Net Lease or Triple Net Lease. *See also* Gross Lease.

Netmail: 1. a message sent over a network. **2.** a private e-mail using a bulletin board.

Net Margin: net sales less all costs, expressed in dollars or as a percentage. *See also* Gross Margin, Margin.

Net National Expenditure: *see* Gross National Expenditure.

Net National Income (NNI): income earned by labour, capital and land in a country. NNI attempts to measure the income effect of a country's economic activity, in contrast to Gross National Product, which measures the value of the output of a country's economic activity. *See also* Gross National Product.

Net National Product (NNP): Gross National Product less depreciation. *See also* Gross National Product.

Net, Net, Net Lease: *see* Net Lease.

Net New Highs: an indicator based on the cumulative number of stocks with a closing price that is a new high less the number of new stocks with a closing price that is a new low for a given period. A rising index is a favourable trend, and a falling index is an unfavourable trend.

Net Operating Income: operating income after minority interest and income taxes. *See also* Gross Operating Income, Minority Interest.

Net Order: *see* Contingent Order.

Net Present Value (NPV): all future cash inflows less all future cash outflows discounted at an interest rate that reflects the investment risk and duration. *See also* Present Value, Time Value of Money.

Net Proceeds: the sum of money received after all deductions. *See also* Gross Proceeds.

Net Profit: 1. in business, net sales less all costs, expressed in dollars. *See also* Gross Profit, Profit. **2.** in investment, the gain on sale of investment after deducting income taxes and commissions. *See also* Gross Profit, Profit.

Net Profit Margin: in business, net sales less all costs, expressed as a percent of net sales. *See also* Gross Profit Margin, Profit Margin.

Net Realizable Value: the value of an asset assuming it is sold at current fair market value less all costs of making the sale. *See also* Fair Market Value.

Net Sales: in business, gross sales less returns, discounts and other allowances. *See also* Gross Sales, Returns.

Net Tangible Assets: total assets less intangible assets (e.g., goodwill) less liabilities. Also known as Tangible Net Worth.

Network: 1. a term used to describe the process of meeting new people, often within a business context (e.g., to identify potential clients or customers). *See also* Networking. **2.** computers and related equipment that are connected together in a way that allows users to share programs, databases and input/output devices. *See also* Computer Network.

Network A: a service that reports New York Stock Exchange trading information for the consolidated tape. *See also* Consolidated Tape.

Network B: an organization that reports American Stock Exchange trading information for the consolidated tape. *See also* Consolidated Tape.

Network Computer: any computer that has the software and hardware necessary for it to be hooked up to a network. Also known as Workstation. *See also* Network.

Network Congestion: a state that exists when network volume is so high that communication rates slow down. *See also* Network.

Network Information Centre (NIC): an administrative support group for a network.

Networking: 1. the process of meeting new people, often within a business context (e.g., to identify potential clients or customers). Also known as Bridge Building. *See also* Network. **2.** connecting computers together to share programs, databases and input/output devices. *See also* Computer.

Network Marketing: *see* Multi-Level Marketing.

Net Worth: the difference between total assets and total liabilities (usually with reference to individuals).

Neutral Hedge: a portfolio hedging strategy that will provide a maximum portfolio return, assuming a particular investment in the portfolio does not change in value. *See also* Hedge.

Neutral Spread: an options strategy combining one call at a lower price and a long expiration date with two calls at a higher price a short expiration dates. *See also* Option.

Neutral Trend: a lateral price movement over time.

New Age Technology: 1. in general, computer technology. **2.** any modern, leading-edge technology.

Newbie: a mildly derogatory term used to describe someone new to the Internet. *See also* Internet, RTFM.

New Brunswick: *see* Canada's Provinces and Territories.

New Economy: that part of the economy likely to prosper because it contains a relatively high number of knowledge employees. *See also* Knowledge Employee.

New Economy

New economy refers to that part of the economy likely to prosper because it contains a relatively high number of knowledge employees. Today's new economy is the technological economy. It is the result of a natural progression that began with the manufacturing economy typified by Henry Ford's mass production.

The clearest explanation of the transition from a manufacturing economy to a technological economy may be found by comparing Microsoft and the Big Three automobile companies. In November 1998 just before the merger of Chrysler and Daimler-Benz, the combined market capitalization of General Motors, Ford and Chrysler was around $170 billion U.S. or around one-third less than that of Microsoft. To sound an ominous note, Microsoft had only 20 percent of the number of employees the Big Three had in total.

In a manufacturing economy, the key variables are industrial production, capacity utilization and new car sales. In a technological economy, the important factors are microchip production, telecommunications and computer sales.

The message to future employees is critical: manual labour has given way to intellectual capability; production is not as important as productivity; and the most important commodity is no longer steel or oil, it is information.

Newfoundland: *see* Canada's Provinces and Territories.

New High: a stock on an exchange that closes at its highest price for a given calendar year. *See also* New Low.

New Issue: a security offered for sale to the public for the first time. If this is the first time a company has offered any security for sale to the public, it is referred to as an Initial Public Offering or IPO. *See also* Initial Public Offering.

New Issue Market: a time when new issues are well received by investors. *See also* New Issue.

New Kip: the primary currency of Laos.

New Low: a stock on an exchange that closes at its lowest price for a given calendar year. *See also* New High.

Newly Industrialized Countries (NICS): countries with free-market economies that seek trade with and investment from Western industrialized nations and are growing rapidly (e.g., Mexico).

New Millennium: the next 1,000 years, which most people believe begins on January 1, 2000, but which really begins on January 1, 2001. Also known as Next Millennium. *See also* Millennium.

New Money: 1. capital available to an investment manager from new clients or existing clients. **2.** in a corporate or government debt refinancing, the amount by which the par value of new securities exceeds the par value of the securities being refunded.

Newsgroup: a single-topic discussion forum on the Internet (usually consisting of articles, opinions, questions and follow-up postings). *See also* Internet.

Newsletter: a printed report providing information of interest to a specific group (often consisting of investors). Newsletter delivery options now commonly include regular mail, fax or e-mail. *See also* Market Letter.

New Sol: the prime currency of Peru.

News Wire: 1. in investment, the services delivering financial news, including Bloomberg, Dow Jones and Reuters. **2.** in general, any service that provides news bulletins or reports, such as Associated Press.

Newton: the force needed to accelerate a mass of one kilogram one metre per second every second.

New York Curb Exchange: *see* American Stock Exchange.

New York Futures Exchange (NYFE): a wholly owned subsidiary of the New York Stock Exchange, it trades financial futures. *See also* New York Stock Exchange.

New York Mercantile Exchange (NYMEX): an exchange in New York trading futures contracts on agricultural products, currency, oil and precious metals. Web site: www.nymex.com *See also* Commodity Exchange of New York.

New York Stock Exchange (NYSE): a major U.S. stock exchange headquartered in New York City at the junction of Wall Street and Broad Street. The NYSE was founded in 1792 by 24 brokers who met under a buttonwood tree at what is now 68 Wall Street. The NYSE lists the common shares of most of the largest companies in the U.S.. Web site: www.nyse.com *See also* Buttonwood Tree Agreement.

New York Stock Exchange Composite Index: a market capitalization weighted index based on all stocks listed on the NYSE. The base value was 50 on December 31, 1965, when this index was introduced. *See also* New York Stock Exchange Financials Index, New York Stock Exchange Industrials Index, New York Stock Exchange Transportation Index, New York Stock Exchange Utilities Index.

New York Stock Exchange Financials Index: a market capitalization weighted index based on all financial stocks listed on the NYSE. The base value was 50 on December 31, 1965, when this index was introduced. *See also* New York Stock Exchange Composite Index, New York Stock Exchange Industrials Index, New York Stock Exchange Transportation Index, New York Stock Exchange Utilities Index.

New York Stock Exchange Industrials Index: a market capitalization weighted index based on all industrial stocks listed on the NYSE. The base value was 50 on December 31, 1965, when this index was introduced. *See also* New York Stock Exchange Composite Index, New York Stock Exchange Financials Index, New York Stock Exchange Transportation Index, New York Stock Exchange Utilities Index.

New York Stock Exchange Transportation Index: a market capitalization weighted index based on all transportation stocks listed on the NYSE. The base value was 50 on December 31, 1965, when this index was introduced. *See also* New York Stock Exchange Composite Index, New York Stock Exchange Financials Index, New York Stock Exchange Industrials Index, New York Stock Exchange Utilities Index.

New York Stock Exchange Utilities Index: a market capitalization weighted index based on all utility stocks listed on the NYSE. The base value was 50 on December 31, 1965, when this index was introduced. *See also* New York Stock Exchange Composite Index, New York Stock Exchange Financials Index, New York Stock Exchange Industrials Index, New York Stock Exchange Transportation Index.

New Zealand Stock Exchange: the major stock exchange of New Zealand, located in its capital, Wellington. Web site: www.nzse.co.nz

New Zealand Stock Exchange 40 Index: a market capitalization weighted index of the New Zealand Stock Exchange.

Next Day Settlement: a term used to refer to a transaction requiring settlement one business day following the trade (e.g., options).

Next Devisee: the person(s) who receives the rest of an estate after the first devisee. *See also* Will.

Next Millennium: *see* New Millennium.

Next of Kin: the closest living blood relative.

NGL: *see* Natural Gas Liquids.

Ngultrum: the primary currency of Bhutan.

NHA: *see* National Housing Act.

NIC: *see* Network Information Centre.

Niche Market: a smaller, specialized market.

Nickel: 1. a five-cent coin. **2.** a five-cent change in a security price. **3.** five basis points.

Nickel and Dime: 1. in negotiation, to be overly concerned about small amounts of money or unimportant details. **2.** to place a financial strain on someone by levying small charges for minor services.

NICS: *see* Newly Industrialized Countries.

Nifty-Fifty: 1. the largest 50 companies listed on the New York Stock Exchange. **2.** the 50 stocks most popular with institutions. **3.** when the market is focused on a very narrow list of stocks, a reference to one of those stocks.

Nigerian Stock Exchange: the major stock exchange of Nigeria, located in Lagos.

Nigerian Stock Exchange Common Stocks Index: a stock price index of all stocks listed on the Nigerian Stock Exchange.

Nihilism: the belief that all existing political and social institutions must be destroyed before improvements can be made.

Nikkei 225 Index: a price weighted index of 225 top Japanese companies on the Tokyo Stock Exchange.

Nil: nothing. Zero.

Nimble: often, a term used to describe an investor who is quick or clever.

NNA: *see* National Numbering Agency.

NNI: *see* Net National Income.

NNP: *see* Net National Product.

Nobel Prize: an international award bestowed upon individuals for their exceptional achievements in the categories of physics, chemistry, physiology/medicine, literature, economics and world peace.

No-Brainer: an investment analysis where the final decision is obvious.

No Contest: *see* Nolo Contendere.

No-Fault: 1. motor vehicle insurance in which insurance compensation occurs without assignment of blame. **2.** a divorce in which blame is not assigned to either party. *See also* Condonation. **3.** a system in which blame is not required to apply for and receive a divorce. *See also* Condonation.

Noise: 1. in physics and statistics, information that obscures rather than clarifies the message. **2.** in computers, any interference in a signal that results in an error or inefficient operation of a device. *See also* Computer.

No Load Fund: a mutual fund with no sales charge. *See also* Back End Load, Deferred Commissions, Deferred Declining Redemption Fee – At Cost, Deferred Declining Redemption Fee – At Market Value, Deferred Sales Charge, Exit Fee, Front End Load, Life Insurance, Load, Loading Charge, Mutual Fund, Rear End Load, Sales Charge.

Nolo Contendere: in law, a plea that is similar to a plea of guilty but that permits the denial of some of the alleged facts. Latin for "I do not wish to contend," commonly interpreted as "No contest."

Nominal: 1. an amount at a point in time not adjusted for factors such as inflation or interest rates. **2.** a very small amount or an amount substantially below actual value (e.g., "a nominal amount").

Nominal Dollars: dollars not adjusted for inflation.

Nominal Interest Rate: the annual coupon rate of a bond or interest rate on a loan without any adjustment.

Nominal Value: the face or par value of a bond. *See also* Par Value.

Nominee: a person appointed to represent or replace the beneficial owner of a stock certificate. *See also* Beneficial Owner.

Nominee Name: a name used by a brokerage firm to register client securities in street form. Also known as Street Name. *See also* Street Certificate, Street Form.

Nonage: the condition of being under full legal age.

Non-Apportionable Annuity: an annuity that makes no final payment to the annuitant's estate. *See also* Annuity.

Non-Arm's-Length Transaction: a contract or agreement made by related parties in a position of conflict of interest. *See also* Arm's-Length Transaction, Conflict of Interest, Self-Dealing.

Non-Assumable Mortgage: a mortgage that cannot be taken over from the vendor of a property by the buyer. *See also* Assumable Mortgage, Mortgage.

Non-Borrowing Factoring: when accounts receivable are not purchased by a third party and the third party provides only a collection service. *See also* Factoring.

Noncallable: a security that cannot be called before maturity.

Non Compos Mentis: in law, not legally responsible due to being of unsound mind. Latin for "not in control of one's mind." *See also* Competent, Incapacity, Incompetent, Legal Capacity.

Non-Conforming Use: the use of land or buildings that existed before a change in zoning and does not conform to the new bylaw. Such land or buildings may continue to be used as "non-conforming." *See also* Conforming Use, Zoning.

Noncontributory Pension Plan: a pension plan that does not entail an employee paying into it. *See also* Contributory Pension Plan.

Noncontributory Plan: an employee benefit plan that does not entail an employee contributing to the cost. Also known as Noncontributory. *See also* Contributory Plan, Employee Benefit Plan.

Noncumulative Dividend: a dividend that does not accrue if a payment is missed.

Noncumulative Preferred Share: a preferred share in which unpaid dividends do not accrue. *See also* Cumulative Preferred Share, Preferred Share.

Non-Deductible Interest Expense: interest paid on money that does not qualify as an income tax deduction. *See also* Bad Debt.

Non-Disclosure: in insurance law, the failure of the insured to provide insurers with material information as required.

Non-Disclosure Agreement: *see* Confidentiality Agreement.

Nonfeasance: in law, the failure to perform an official duty or legal requirement.

Non-Forfeiture Option: an alternative to forfeiting a life insurance policy in return for the cash surrender value (e.g., purchasing a reduced face value cash value policy or buying extended term insurance).

Noninterest Bearing: a security that does not pay interest. Usually such securities trade below, and mature at, face value.

Nonintervention: failure or refusal to intervene, usually in the affairs of another nation.

Noninvestment Grade: low quality. For Canadian bonds, a Canadian Bond Rating Service rating below Triple-B (low). *See also* Investment Grade, Junk Bond.

Nonlegal Investment: an investment that is not qualified for investment in certain types of regulated accounts (e.g., pension plans or Registered Retirement Savings Plans).

Nonmarketable Securities: securities that either cannot be sold or are difficult to sell.

Non-Market Risk: *see* Non-Systematic Risk.

Non-Member Firm: a brokerage firm that is not a member of a recognized stock exchange or other self-regulatory organization. Individual accounts at a non-member firm are not insured by the Canadian Investor Protection Fund. *See also* Canadian Investor Protection Fund.

Non-Negotiable: a security that, in its present form, cannot be sold or transferred.

Non-Notification Basis: in factoring, when the purchaser of the accounts receivable assumes the collection function. *See also* Factoring, Notification Basis.

Non-Participating Life Insurance: a form of life insurance in which the insurer guarantees the death benefit and retains excess premium payments (should there be any). *See also* Life Insurance, Overcharge, Participating Life Insurance.

Non-Performance: failure to honour a contract.

Non-Performing Loan: a bank loan in which the borrower is behind in his/her payments. As a rule, a commercial loan 90 days past due and a consumer loan 180 days past due is considered non-performing.

Non-Profit Organization: an organization that does not operate with the intent to earn profits. Also known as Not for Profit.

Non-Proliferation: a call for an end to the expanded use (or storage) of something, especially nuclear weapons.

Nonpublic Information: *see* Inside Information.

Nonrecourse Debt: a loan secured by a particular property. In case of default, the lender can seize the property but nothing else.

Nonrecurring Charge: *see* Nonrecurring Expense.

Nonrecurring Expense: a one-time expense. Also known as Nonrecurring Charge.

Nonrecurring Income: one-time income.

Non-Refundable: not repayable (e.g., a "nonrefundable deposit").

Non-Refundable Tax Credit for Dependent Children: *see* Child Tax Benefit.

Nonresident: a person who does not permanently reside in a particular country.

Nonresident Withholding Tax: a withholding tax applied to the income of nonresidents (e.g., taxes on investment income, gambling winnings). *See also* Withholding Tax.

Non-Revolving Line of Credit: a loan made for a specific purpose that is repaid once that purpose has been served (e.g., a loan to purchase a specific investment).

Non-Starter: something that is not worth getting involved with because it is clearly unlikely to succeed.

Nonsuit: in law, a judgement against a plaintiff for failure to present sufficient evidence.

Nonsupport: failure to provide for the maintenance of dependents.

Non-Systematic Risk: risk that is specific to an individual security (e.g., a poor earnings report). Also known as Non-Market Risk, Security Specific Risk, Unique Risk, Unsystematic Risk. *See also* Beta Risk, Company Specific Risk, Event Risk, Industry Specific Risk, Risk, Specific Risk, Systematic Risk.

Nonunion: not organized into a union. Not recognizing a labour union.

Nonviolence: the practice of using civil disobedience in order to gain political ends.

Non-Voting Shares: shares that carry no voting rights. *See also* Voting Shares.

No Par Value (NPV): securities having no face value or stated value. Par value is of little significance today. At one time, par value represented the original investment in a company by its owners, but this is no longer the case.

Norm: a standard, as in "Two car families are the norm."

Normal Beta: the desired level of risk targeted for a portfolio. *See also* Beta.

Normal Course Issuer Bid: the process used by a company to purchase some of its own outstanding shares in order to cancel them. The terms are approved by the stock exchange, which specifies the maximum number of shares that may be purchased and retired when the approval period ends. Also known as Buyback, Issuer Bid, Repurchase, Stock Buyback, Share Repurchase, Stock Repurchase.

Normal Distribution: a distribution of factors in a bell curve such that two-thirds of all outcomes fall into a confidence interval of one standard deviation of error, while 95 percent of all outcomes fall into a confidence interval of two standard deviations of error. *See also* Bell Curve, Confidence Coefficient, Probability Distribution, Standard Deviation, Standard Deviation of Error.

Normalized Earnings: 1. a company's earnings adjusted to remove unusual or temporary influences (e.g., if a company sold a building and realized a substantial capital gain, this gain would be removed to calculate normalized earnings). **2.** earnings adjusted to reflect more normal conditions (e.g., in a recession, mining stocks will be valued on the basis of what earnings will be during the next recovery).

Normal Retirement: the earliest date at which an employee can retire without any reduction in retirement benefits.

Normal Return: an investment's typical return.

Normal Settlement: to settle a securities trade on a regular settlement date without special conditions.

Normal Trading Relations: a term used to describe the most attractive trading arrangements offered by one country to another. Also known as Most Favoured Nation.

Normal Yield Curve: *see* Positive Yield Curve.

North American Common Stock Fund: *see* North American Equity Fund.

North American Equity Fund: one of the 31 Canadian categories developed by the Investment Funds Standards Committee. Mutual funds in this category must have a minimum of 50 percent of the total assets, and 75 percent of the non-cash assets, of the portfolio in equities or equity equivalents of companies located in the U.S. and Canada or derivative-based exposure to these markets. The U.S. equity component must represent a minimum of 25 percent of the non-cash assets of the portfolio. Unlike Canadian equity funds with U.S. exposure, these funds are typically not eligible as Canadian content for Registered Retirement Savings Plans and Registered Retirement Income Funds. The calculations to determine whether a mutual fund fits this definition are based on median values from fund data over three years, unless otherwise noted. The derivatives are weighted on an extended value basis. Each of the categories may be refined by the fund manager (e.g., a Canadian Large Cap Equity Fund might be described as "growth" or "value" to reflect the manager's style). Also known as North American Common Stock Fund. *See also* Extended Value, Mutual Fund – Category.

North American Free Trade Agreement (NAFTA): a multilateral free trade agreement between Canada, Mexico and the U.S. The goals of NAFTA are to phase out all import tariffs, eliminate all non-tariff barriers to trade, protect intellectual property rights and provide a method to settle disputes. NAFTA effectively extended the Canada-U.S. Free Trade Agreement of 1989 to include Mexico. Also known as North American Free Trade Zone (NAFTZ). *See also* Canada-U.S. Free Trade Agreement of 1989, European Community, Free Trade Area of the Americas, Mercosur.

North American Free Trade Zone (NAFTZ): *see* North American Free Trade Agreement.

North Atlantic Treaty Organization (NATO): formed in 1949 after the Second World War, NATO is a military alliance of Western countries against the perceived threat from the USSR.

North of: higher or better than (e.g., if a stock is headed "north of $20," then its price will rise above $20). *See also* South of.

Northwest Territories: *see* Canada's Provinces and Territories.

Nosedive: a very sharp drop in a financial market.

No Strings Attached: unconditional. If an agreement has "no strings attached," then there are no other terms or conditions to the settlement.

Nota Bene (NB): observe what follows. Indicates important information in a written document. Latin for "note well."

Notarial Copy: a true copy of an original document, as attested by a lawyer or notary public.

Notarial Will: valid only in Quebec, a will executed by the testator before two notaries and a witness or before two witnesses and a notary. The executed will must be left with a notary. *See also* Will.

Notarized: certified or attested by a notary public.

Notary: *see* Notary Public.

Notary Public: a person empowered to witness and certify documents and take affidavits and depositions. Also known as Notary.

Note: a legal certificate, usually to evidence a loan.

Notebook: in computers, a personal computer smaller than a laptop. *See also* Computer, Laptop Computer, Mainframe Computer, Microcomputer, Minicomputer, Personal Computer.

Not for Profit Organization: *see* Non-Profit Organization.

Not Held Order: an order to buy or sell securities that gives the trader discretion as to price and timing. *See also* Order.

Notice Day: any day that notification of the intention to make physical delivery of the commodity underlying a futures contract can be given. *See also* Futures Contract.

Notice Deposit: a deposit with a financial institution from which a withdrawal can be made only by providing advance notice as required.

Notice Disputing Petition: a document that a party resisting bankruptcy uses to provide an opportunity to put his/her case before the courts. *See also* Bankruptcy.

Notice of Assessment: notification from Canada Customs and Revenue Agency that an income tax return has been assessed. The assessed return may or may not have changes, and Canada Customs and Revenue Agency has the right to make (further) changes at a later date. *See also* Notice of Objection.

Notice of Garnishment: the document used by a creditor with a judgment against a debtor to enforce and recover the judgement amount. *See also* Garnishment.

Notice of Objection: formal notification to Canada Customs and Revenue Agency that a taxpayer disputes a Notice of Assessment. A Notice of Objection is filed with Form T400A. *See also* Notice of Assessment, T400A.

Notification Basis: in factoring, when the seller of the accounts receivable retains the collection function. *See also* Factoring, Non-Notification Basis.

Notifying Bank: *see* Advising Bank.

Notional Principal Amount: the par value on which an interest rate swap is based. *See also* Interest Rate Swap, Swap.

Not Rated: a term pertaining to fixed-income securities that have not been rated by an agency such as the Canadian Bond Rating Service. It does not necessarily have negative connotations.

Not Sufficient Funds Cheque (NSF Cheque): a cheque that, due to there being insufficient funds in the pertinent account, is not honoured by the bank upon which it is written. Also known as a Rubber Cheque because it bounces. *See also* Bounce.

Nouveau Riche: 1. one who has recently become wealthy. *See also* Old Money. **2.** the class of people in a society that has recently become wealthy. *See also* Old Money.

Nova Scotia: *see* Canada's Provinces and Territories.

Novation: 1. the substitution of one debt for another. **2.** an agreement to replace one party to a contract with another. This usually requires the consent of all parties.

NPV: 1. *see* Net Present Value. **2.** *see* No Par Value.

NRN: Internet acronym for "no response necessary."

NSE: *see* National Stock Exchange.

NSE20: *see* Nairobi Stock Exchange Index.

NSF Cheque: *see* Not Sufficient Funds Cheque.

Nth: the highest, or an indefinitely large, number, as in "the nth degree."

NTSC: *see* National Television Standards Committee.

Nuclear Family: a family that consists of a working father, a full-time stay-at-home mother and their children. Considered a basic social unit.

Nuclear Reactor: a device within which a controlled nuclear fission reaction generates energy.

Nugget: a small, solid lump, as in a "nugget of gold."

Null: having no legal force, as in "null and void."

Null Character: in computers, a control character used as a filler between data blocks. *See also* Computer.

Nullify: to invalidate.

Number: one of a set of positive integers.

Numerator: in a fraction, the number above the line. *See also* Denominator.

Numismatic Coin: a coin that has a value greater than its metal content because of its rarity. *See also* Gold Coin.

Numismatics: the study or collection of coins, money and other currency.

Nunavut: a Canadian territory created by legislation effective April 1, 1999. With an area of 2,254,402 square kilometres, it represents 25 percent of Canada's land mass. The population of 24,665 is 83 percent Inuit and the Inuktituk language predominates. *See also* Canada's Provinces and Territories.

Nuncupative Will: a will made verbally before witnesses. The circumstances of a nuncupative will is important in determining its validity (e.g., if the person was dying and writing it down was not practical). Also known as Oral Will, Verbal Will. *See also* Will.

NYFE: *see* New York Futures Exchange.

NYMEX: *see* New York Mercantile Exchange.

NYSE: *see* New York Stock Exchange.

OAS: *see* Old Age Security.

Oath: a formal pledge that often calls upon God as a witness to the truth of what one says or to the truth of one's stated intent to do something.

OATS: *see* Options Automated Trading System.

Object Linking and Embedding (OLE): a way to place one kind of Windows document (e.g., a spreadsheet) inside another (e.g., a word processing program). *See also* Computer.

Obligation: 1. a debt such as a bank loan. **2.** a constraint such as a negative pledge. *See also* Negative Pledge. **3.** a promise such as the terms of a contract.

Obligee: a person to whom another person is obligated. *See also* Obligor.

Obligor: a person who has an obligation to another person. *See also* Obligee.

OBO: a tag that means "or best offer." It is added when a price is negotiable, as in "asking $350 OBO."

Obsolescence: declining in usefulness due to becoming outmoded or being surpassed by new, superior products. *See also* Planned Obsolescence.

OBX Stock Index: *see* Oslo Stock Exchange Index.

OCC: *see* Options Clearing Corporation.

Occasional Employment Income: income that neither employers or employees are required to report to Canada Customs and Revenue Agency (e.g., income from babysitting). *See also* Taxes.

Occupancy: the act or condition of dwelling or residing (e.g., in an apartment). *See also* Vacancy.

Occupancy Rate: the extent to which a rental property is rented. The occupancy rate may apply to one building or several buildings in a specific region. Calculated as 100 percent less the vacancy rate. *See also* Vacancy Rate.

Occupation: the activity that provides one's regular source of income. *See also* Avocation.

Occurrence: in mining, the presence of minerals in a sampling that has not been tested by drilling.

OCR: *see* Optical Character Recognition.

October Massacres: the stock market declines of October 1978 and 1979 and the subsequent crash of October 1987. *See also* Stock Market Crash.

Odd Job: a temporary, unskilled task.

Odd Lot: a quantity of common stocks that constitute less than 100 shares. *See also* Odd Lotter.

Odd Lot Dealer: a dealer who purchases shares in board lots and breaks them into odd lots for sale to buyers. Such dealers will also buy odd lots and put them back into board lots.

Odd Lot Order: an order to a broker to buy or sell less than 100 shares. *See also* Order.

Odd Lot Sales to Purchase Ratio: a ratio calculated by dividing the number of odd lot shares sold by the number of odd lot shares purchased (unlike board lot trading, the number of odd lot shares sold does not need to equal the number of odd lot shares purchased). This ratio is used to measure the market sentiment of small investors who trade in odd lots. The indicator is a contrary opinion indicator; in other words, if odd lot selling is high, the market outlook is positive, and vice versa. *See also* Odd Lot Dealer, Odd Lot Theory.

Odd Lot Short Sales: shares sold short in odd lots. *See also* Odd Lot Theory, Short Sale.

Odd Lot Short Sales Ratio: this is calculated by dividing odd lot short sales by odd lot sales. Investors sometimes use this as a measure of market sentiment. The indicator is a contrary opinion indicator; in other words, if the ratio is high, then the market outlook is positive (and vice versa). *See also* Odd Lot Theory.

Odd Lotter: 1. an investor who buys and sells in odd lots. *See also* Board Lotter. **2.** a term, sometimes used in a derogatory manner, applied to a small investor.

Odd Lot Theory: a theory that, because small investors are always wrong, when odd lot buying is high relative to odd lot selling, the stock market is about to fall, and that when odd lot buying is low relative to odd lot selling, the stock market is about to rise. For the same reasons, when odd lot short selling is high, the market is about to rise, and when odd lot short selling is low, the market is about to fall. *See also* Odd Lot Sales to Purchase Ratio, Odd Lot Short Sales, Odd Lot Short Sales Ratio.

Odds: the statistical probability of an event occurring, expressed mathematically (e.g., 75:25 or one in four or 90 percent).

OECD: *see* Organization for Economic Cooperation and Development.

OEM: *see* Original Equipment Manufacturer.

OEX: *see* Standard & Poor's 100 Index.

OFEX: an unregulated exchange based in London, England, that allows trading in certain securities not listed on other exchanges. So termed because the trading takes place "Off Exchange."

Off: lower in price, as in "the stock is off $1."

Off Balance Sheet Financing: corporate borrowing that does not appear on the financial statements (e.g., lease obligations).

Off-Board Trade: *see* Off-the-Board Trade.

Offence: a crime or the commission of a crime.

Offer: the price quote for a security is comprised of a bid and offer. The offer is the price at which a seller will sell a security. When the bid equals the offer, then a trade occurs. Also known as Ask, Ask Price, Offering Price. *See also* Bid.

Offered Down: securities offered for sale at a price lower than the last trade.

Offered Without: a market in which there is an offer but no bid. *See also* Bid Without, Bid Wanted.

Offeree: the party to whom an offer is addressed and who may be bound by acceptance. *See also* Offeror.

Offering: something offered, often a new issue of securities. *See also* Offering Circular, Offering Memorandum, Offering Period, Offering Price.

Offering Circular: an abbreviated document that describes a new issue of securities. *See also* Offering, Offering Memorandum, Offering Period, Offering Price.

Offering Memorandum (OM): a document that describes a company's past and present and provides an indication of future prospects. The OM is usually used under the prospectus exemption for seed capital and private placement financing. *See also* Prospectus.

Offering Price: 1. *see* Offer. **2.** the price at which a new issue of securities is offered for sale.

Offeror: the party that makes an offer and indicates a willingness to enter into a contract. *See also* Offeree.

Offer Price: *see* Offer.

Offer Wanted: when there are no offers, a notice given by a broker who is interested in purchasing a security. *See also* Bid Wanted, Bid Without.

Office of Internet Enforcement: a new office of the U.S. Securities and Exchange Commission responsible for uncovering illegal investment practices on the Internet. *See also* Internet.

Officer: a member of senior corporate management, usually the president, vice-president, corporate secretary or treasurer. *See also* Chief Executive Officer, Chief Operating Officer, President, Vice-President.

Official: relating to an office of authority or to one who holds such an office.

Official Rate: in foreign exchange trading, the lawful rate at which an exchange rate is set.

Offing: selling securities.

Offline: the state of not being connected to a network or a dial-up network such as the Internet. It is common practice to work offline and then to make

an online connection in order to transfer one's work. *See also* Internet, Online.

Off-Load: 1. to get rid of a poor investment by selling. **2.** in computers, to transfer data to a peripheral device. *See also* Computer.

Off-Season: 1. a time of year when business is quiet (e.g., summer at a ski resort). *See also* Shoulder Season. **2.** a reference to unseasonable merchandise (e.g., beach towels in winter).

Offset: something that balances or compensates (e.g., the loss on one stock in a portfolio is offset by the gain in another). *See also* Right of Offset.

Offshore: 1. outside of Canada. **2.** business conducted in a tax haven jurisdiction (e.g., Bermuda, the Bahamas, the Turks & Caicos Islands) and not subject to Canadian taxation or securities law.

Offshore Account: 1. an investor domicile in a foreign country, usually other than the U.S. **2.** an account in a tax haven. *See also* Tax Haven.

Offshore Fund: *see* Offshore Mutual Fund.

Offshore Investment: an investment held in a tax haven jurisdiction, with the intention of making sure that the income derived from it is sheltered from taxes. *See also* Offshore.

Offshore Mutual Fund: a mutual fund domicile in a foreign country, usually other than the U.S. Also known as Offshore Fund. *See also* Mutual Fund – Other.

Offshore Protection Trust: a trust set up to hold assets offshore in order to protect them from creditors. *See also* Offshore Trust.

Offshore Trust: a trust domicile in a foreign country, usually one that has preferential tax treatment for trusts. *See also* Offshore Protection Trust.

Offside: in investment, a loss position. *See also* Onside.

Off-the-Board Trade: 1. trading between a buyer and seller without using the facilities of a stock exchange. Also known as Off-Board Trade. *See also* Ex-Pit Transaction, Third Market. **2.** trading done on the over-the-counter market. *See also* Over-the-Counter.

Off-the-Run Stock: a stock that is of little interest and that is thinly traded.

Off Year: 1. in business, an unsuccessful year. **2.** in the U.S., a year in which no major elections are held.

Of Record: a term that denotes a record on the official company books (e.g., a shareholder of record is a shareholder recorded on the company's books). *See also* Holder of Record, Shareholder of Record.

Ohm: a unit of electrical resistance.

OIC: Internet acronym for "Oh, I see."

Oil & Gas Limited Partnership: a limited partnership investing in oil and gas. Unless recourse debt is being used, partners are only responsible for the amount invested. *See also* Limited Partnership, Recourse Debt.

Oil and Gas Lottery: the granting of rights to explore prospective oil and gas producing properties by a random draw. *See also* Lottery.

Oil Baron: a person whose wealth and influence is based on ownership of, or is otherwise related to, oil and gas.

Oil Bearing: relating to a natural structure that contains oil and/or gas.

Oil Company: a company engaged in activities related to oil, gas or other petroleum products. The major activities are usually described as: exploration, development and production, and refining and marketing. A company active in all areas is known as an integrated oil company. The top three companies in the Toronto Stock Exchange Oil & Gas Index in late 1999 were Suncor Energy Inc., Talisman Energy Inc. and Alberta Energy Company Ltd. *See also* Development, Exploration Company, Integrated Oil Company, Refining and Marketing, Production Company.

Oil Derrick: the structure that supports the drill used in oil exploration.

Oil Drum: a metal barrel for holding oil.

Oil Embargo: *see* Arab Oil Embargo.

Oil Field: an area that produces oil and gas.

Oil Patch: 1. a general reference to a place where oil and gas are found (or produced) **2.** where oil and gas companies are based.

Oil Platform: a platform, supported on the open sea by legs or floatation devices, from which oil exploration or production activities are conducted. Also known as Production Platform.

Oil Refinery: a facility in which crude oil is broken down into end products.

Oil Sand: sand soaked in bitumen, a thick, oil-based material.

Oil Shale: shale from which oil can be extracted.

Oil Sheik: an Arab whose great wealth and influence stems from oil and gas.

Oil Sheikdom: an Arab or Middle East nation that generates substantial economic activity and wealth from the sale of oil and gas products.

Oil Slick: a layer of oil on water, often the result of an oil spill.

Oil Spill: a release of oil, usually because of an oil tanker accident or break in a pipeline.

Oily: a term used to describe an area that produces oil and gas.

Okun's Law: an economic theory put forward by Arthur M. Okun (1928 -), Professor of Economics at Yale University, it states that U.S. growth of three percent above the economy's long-term potential is consistent with a one percent decline in unemployment. The general theory is that to avoid the waste of unemployment, an economy must continue to grow. *See also* Discomfort Index.

Old Age Security (OAS): a guaranteed minimum income for Canadians resident in Canada who are age 65 or over. OAS does not require an employment history although certain residency requirements must be met. Also known as Old Age Security Pension. *See also* Guaranteed Income Supplement, Resident, Social Safety Net.

Old Age Security - Guaranteed Income Supplement: an amount payable to those who receive Old Age Security and have little other income. *See also* Old Age Security.

Old Age Security Pension: *see* Old Age Security.

Old Age Security - Spouse's Allowance: payable to a spouse of a person receiving Old Age Security or a widow or widower. Certain residency and income guidelines apply. *See also* Old Age Security.

Old Age Security - Widowed Spouse's Allowance: a payment to a low-income senior whose spouse has died.

Old Money: wealth that has been in a family for many generations. *See also* Nouveau Riche.

OLE: *see* Object Linking and Embedding.

Oligarchy: government by a few.

Oligopoly: a market condition in which a small group of companies control the total supply of a good or service. *See also* Duopoly, Monopoly, Monopsony, Natural Monopoly, Oligopsony, Price Control.

Oligopsony: a market condition in which only a small number of buyers exists for a good or service. *See also* Duopoly, Monopoly, Monopsony, Natural Monopoly, Oligopoly, Price Control.

Olive Branch: a conciliatory action; something designed to end a dispute.

OM: *see* Offering Memorandum.

Oman Stock Exchange: *see* Muscat Securities Market, Muskat Securities Exchange.

Oman Stock Exchange Market Index: a stock price index for the Muscat Securities Market.

Ombudsman: *see* Ombudsperson.

Ombudsperson: 1. a government official appointed to receive, investigate and report on public grievances against the government. **2.** a position in an institution responsible for investigating complaints from employees. Also known as Ombudsman.

Omission: in law, the act of neglecting or failing to do something.

On Account: 1. in partial payment of an obligation. **2.** on credit. In this sense, the term implies an ongoing relationship between the buyer and seller.

On Balance: the difference between the amount of a security bought and sold by one party within a short period of time (e.g., a person who buys 4,000 shares and sells 2,000 shares the same day is said to have purchased 2,000 shares, on balance).

On-Balance Volume: a comparison of the volume on common stock trades on upticks with the volume on common stock trades on downticks. Technically high volume on common stock trades on upticks is bullish while high volume on common stock trades on downticks is bearish. *See also* Bearish, Bullish, Downtick, Uptick.

One Cancels the Other Order: *see* Alternative Order.

One Decision Stock: a high-quality stock that is appropriate for a buy and hold strategy. Hence, only the buy decision is needed. *See also* Buy and Hold.

One Hundred Day Moving Average: a price chart that averages the previous 100 days' closing prices. Each day, the current price is added and the price from 101 days ago is subtracted. Technical analysts believe that if the current price rises above this average, then it is a positive sign and that if it falls below this average, then it is a negative sign. *See also* Moving Average, Two Hundred Day Moving Average.

One-Off: 1. a single model of a product. **2.** a prototype.

One-Share-One-Voting: *see* Statutory Voting.

One-Shot: offering a single opportunity, as in "a one-shot deal."

One-Sided Market: a market for a security in which either a bid or an offer (but not both) is quoted.

One-Size-Fits-All: a term used to describe financial approaches that do not take into account differences among individuals (e.g., a recommendation to buy a stock directed to all investors without regard to their investment objectives).

One-Stop Shopping: a facility that offers many related services under one roof or in one branch (e.g., a facility that offers banking, investment and insurance services offers one-stop shopping).

One-Trick Pony: 1. a person who is successful in one area but cannot replicate that success in other areas. **2.** a company whose business is restricted to one area.

Online: the state of being connected to a network or a dial-up network (such as the Internet). *See also* Internet, Offline.

Online Banking: gaining access to one's bank account(s) through a personal computer. *See also* Electronic Commerce.

Online Brokerage: a stock brokerage account operated through the Internet. *See also* Electronic Commerce, Internet.

Online Shopping: the process of reviewing goods and services, and placing purchase orders for them, on the Internet. *See also* Electronic Commerce, Internet.

On Margin: securities bought by borrowing all or part of the amount needed from a broker. *See also* Margin Account.

Onside: in investment, a profit position. *See also* Offside.

Ontario: *see* Canada's Provinces and Territories.

On the Carpet: to be given a reprimand by one's supervisor.

On the Come: to justify an investment decision by relying on the future occurrence of a favourable event. Also known as Buy on the Come. *See also* Missouri Market.

On the Cuff: a term used to suggest that payment is being made by charging it to one's account. *See also* On Account.

On the House: free of charge.

On the Market Order: *see* Market Order.

On the Money: *see* At the Money.

On the Shelf: describes a financial product that can be offered to clients over a fairly long period of time (e.g., several months). *See also* Shelf Life.

On the Sidelines: *see* Sideline.

On Title: to be listed as a legal owner of an asset. *See also* Title, Title Deed, Title Defect, Title Search.

Opco: *see* Operating Company.

OPEC: *see* Organization of Petroleum Exporting Countries.

Open: an unexecuted order that is still valid.

Open-and-Shut: obvious and easily settled, as in "an open-and-shut case."

Open Contract: a commodities or futures contract to buy or sell that has not been closed out by a delivery or repurchase.

Open Court: a public court of justice.

Open Credit: a credit free of restrictions.

Open-End Credit: *see* Revolving Line of Credit.

Open-End Lease: a lease contract that requires one final payment at the end of the lease to adjust for changes in the value of the asset leased. *See also* Capital Lease, Financial Lease, Graduated Lease, Ground Lease, Lease, Operating Lease.

Open End Mutual Fund: a mutual fund in which shares or units purchased by investors are continuously bought from the fund while shares or units sold by investors are continuously repurchased by the fund. *See also* Mutual Fund – Other.

Open House: 1. a general-invitation social event usually hosted by an institution that allows customers, clients or visitors access to its place of business. **2.** an opportunity for prospective buyers to inspect a home offered for sale.

Opening: 1. generally, the start of a trading day on a securities market. *See also* Opening Bell. **2.** the price of a security at the start of a trading day on a securities market. *See also* Opening Price, Opening Trade.

Opening Bank: *see* Issuing Bank.

Opening Bell: the start of a trading session on a securities exchange, so termed because of the ringing of a bell to announce the start of each day's trading on the New York Stock Exchange. Also known as the Bell. *See also* Closing Bell.

Opening Price: on any given day, the price of a security at the first trade. *See also* Closing Price.

Opening Purchase: the initial transaction that creates an investor's long position, most often in a financial option.

Opening Quote: the first posted bid and offer of a security when a trading session begins. *See also* Closing Quote.

Opening Sale: the initial transaction that creates an investor's short position, most often in a financial option.

Opening Trade: 1. on any given day, the first transaction in a security. *See also* Closing Trade. **2.** the first trade in a series of trades. *See also* Opening Transaction.

Opening Transaction: the trade that opens a position in which another trade is usually required (e.g., selling shares short). *See also* Closing Transaction, Opening Trade.

Open Interest: in options and futures, the total number of contracts not closed, liquidated or delivered.

Open Market: a market (e.g., a stock market) open to all buyers and sellers.

Open Market Operations: the buying or selling of securities on the open market, often related to the action of central banks.

Open Market Purchase: the buying of stocks and bonds in the securities markets, often for the purpose of sinking funds or buying shares during a takeover offer. *See also* Sinking Fund.

Open Market Rates: interest rates set on the basis of the supply and demand for debt securities. *See also* Fixed Income.

Open Mortgage: a mortgage that can be prepaid at any time without penalty. *See also* Mortgage, Prepayment Clause, Prepayment Penalty.

Open Order: *see* Good Until Cancelled Order.

Open Outcry: 1. the system of trading on the floor of an exchange, where orders are shouted out. *See also* Trading Floor. **2.** a term used to describe the general method of trading in financial markets. *See also* Auction.

Open Pit Mining: a method for mining in which the ore is removed starting at the surface of the ground, the result being that a large hole, or pit, develops over time. Also known as Strip Mining, a term that is often restricted to the mining of coal seams just below the surface. *See also* Placer Mining, Seam, Strip Ratio, Underground Mining.

Open Position: an option or futures contract that has been bought or sold but that has not yet been offset or settled through delivery. *See also* Futures, Option.

Open Prospectus: a prospectus that does not detail the intended use of funds. *See also* Prospectus.

Open Shop: a business that employs both union and nonunion employees. *See also* Closed Shop.

Open Space: a large area of undeveloped land.

Open System: 1. in computer systems, one that is not proprietary. **2.** a system that will operate using different hardware, operating systems and software. *See also* Computer, Proprietary.

Open Trade: an order that is neither filled nor cancelled.

Operating Asset: an asset that is used in generating the day-to-day income of a business (e.g., cash, inventories). *See also* Capital Asset.

Operating Budget: a budget that itemizes the day-to-day operating expenses of a business (e.g., office rent, salaries). *See also* Capital Budget.

Operating Capital: the money a company uses to finance its day-to-day operations. *See also* Long-Term Capital.

Operating Company (Opco): a company that carries on a business activity, as opposed to a holding company, which mainly makes investments. *See also* Holding Company, Active Investor.

Operating Costs: the things a company must pay for because they are essential to maintaining its business. *See also* Operating Surplus.

Operating Income: the amount of revenue a company makes through its usual business. Also known as Operating Profit. *See also* Operating Loss.

Operating Lease: a lease in which the benefits and risks of ownership remain with the lessor. *See also* Capital Lease, Financial Lease, Graduated Lease, Ground Lease, Lease.

Operating Leverage: the extent to which additional production increases net income. This is a function of the respective position of fixed costs and variable costs. A business with substantial fixed costs and minimal variable costs has high operating leverage. This occurs because one additional unit of output does not increase costs significantly. Conversely, a business with few fixed costs and substantial variable costs has little operating leverage. *See also* Leverage.

Operating Line of Credit: a commitment from a lender to make loans to a specific borrower to a specified limit, usually for one year. Also referred to as an Operating Line. *See also* Formalized Line of Credit, Operating Loan.

Operating Loan: a loan under an operating line of credit. *See also* Operating Line of Credit.

Operating Loss: the amount of money a company loses though its usual business. *See also* Operating Income.

Operating Margin: a company's operating costs divided by revenues.

Operating Platform: in computers, a general reference to the software (e.g., UNIX) that facilitates operation of the computer. *See also* Computer.

Operating Profit: *see* Operating Income.

Operating Rate: a statistic that measures the percentage of the production capacity of an industry or company that is in use. For brief periods, a company may be able to operate at over 100 percent of capacity, but eventually problems will arise (e.g., equipment will break down). *See also* Capacity Utilization Rate.

Operating Statement: *see* Income Statement.

Operating Surplus: a business's revenue less operating costs. *See also* Operating Costs.

Operating System: 1. software designed to control the hardware of a computer system and so to enable its effective use. **2.** the control program that runs a computer. *See also* Computer, Control Unit.

Operations Department: 1. the department in a brokerage firm responsible for clearing, settling and recording transactions. **2.** the department of any company responsible for the planning and operating functions.

Opinion Shopping: a term used to describe what occurs when a company seeks an auditor solely on the basis of the auditor's willingness to provide an unqualified opinion on the financial statements. *See also* Auditor's Report, Going Concern Opinion, Qualified Opinion.

OPM: *see* Other People's Money.

Opportunist: one who, without regard for principles, takes advantage of opportunities.

Opportunity Cost: 1. the difference in return when one investment is passed up in favour of another. At a minimum, the opportunity cost is the interest to be earned on a one-month treasury bill. *See also* All-In

Cost. **2.** in general, the next highest return that would be available from an alternative course of action.

Optical Character Recognition (OCR): in computers, a device that reads printed characters and converts them into a format that can be edited with a text editor or a word processor. *See also* Computer.

Optical Disc: *see* Compact Disc.

Optical Fibre: *see* Fibre Optical Cable.

Optimize: a statistical process for combining two or more variables in the most efficient manner (e.g., a portfolio optimizer takes many individual stocks and combines them in order to maximize potential return and minimize potential risk). *See also* Portfolio Optimization.

Optimum Capacity: the level of a company's output that results in the lowest cost per unit.

Optimum Portfolio: *see* Efficient Portfolio.

Opting Out: a decision to leave or exit a plan (e.g., an employee leaving a pension plan while remaining employed or a doctor leaving a government-sponsored billing plan while continuing to practise).

Option: 1. a financial security deriving value based on the value of another financial security. Also known as a Financial Option. *See also* Alligator Spread, American Style Option, Arbitrage Trading Program, Assignment, At the Money, Bear Spread, Bear Straddle, Black-Scholes Option Pricing Model, Box Spread, Bull Spread, Bull Straddle, Butterfly Spread, Buy and Write, Call, Call Option, Chicago Board Options Exchange (CBOE), Closing Out, Contract Month, Contract Size, Covered Call Option, Covered Option, Covered Put Option, Covered Writer, Covered Writing, Daily Limit, Deep in the Money, Deep out of the Money, Delta, Delta Hedge, Derivative, Diagonal Spread, Double Witching Hour, European Style Option, Exercise, Expiration Date, Farther In, Farther Out, Furthest Out, Index Option, Interest Rate Option, In the Money, Intrinsic Value, Jelly Roll Spread, Lapsed Option, Leg, Lifting a Leg, Long-Term Equity Anticipation Securities (LEAPS), Look-back Option, Market on Close Order, Market on Open Order, Married Put and Stock, Mini Manipulation, Naked Call Option, Naked Option, Naked Put Option, Naked Position, Nearbys, Neutral Spread, Option Account, Option Premium, Options Clearing Corporation, Options Market, Option Cycle, Option-Eligible Security, Option Series, Option Writer, Out of the Money, Overwrite, Partial Covered Writing, Portfolio Insurance, Premium Income, Program Buying, Program Selling, Program Trading, Put, Put Option, Quanto Option, Ratio Spreading, Ratio Writer,

Registered Option Principal, Relationship Trading, Roll Backward, Roll Down, Roll Forward, Roll Up, Spread, Straddle, Strap, Strike Price, Strip, Synthetic Asset, Synthetic Portfolio, Time Value, Triple Witching Hour, Underlying Security, Underlying Stock, Uncovered Call Option, Uncovered Option, Uncovered Put Option, Uncovered Writer, Uncovered Writing, Witching Hour, Write. **2.** the right to purchase an asset in a fixed amount, for a fixed price by a fixed date. **3.** see Stock Option.

Option Account: an account with a brokerage firm approved to trade in financial options. *See also* Option.

Optional Dividend: a dividend that can be taken as either cash or additional shares. *See also* Dividend.

Option Contract: an agreement to buy or sell a specific amount of an asset at a specific price and time. *See also* Option, Option Market.

Option Cycle: the grouping of months in which options expire. The three most common cycles are (1) January, April, July, October (2) February, March, August, November and (3) March, June, September, December. Because of these cycles, there are eight times a year when options on two of the three cycles expire on the same day (Double Witching Hour) and four times a year when options in all three cycles expire on the same day (Triple Witching Hour). Also known as Series Month. *See also* Double Witching Hour, FMAN, JAJO, MJSD, Triple Witching Hour.

Option-Eligible Security: a security that meets the option exchange requirements to be an underlying security. *See also* Option, Underlying Security.

Option – Executive and/or Employee: *see* Stock Option – Executive and/or Employee.

Option Market: the market in which option contracts are bought and sold. *See also* Option.

Option Premium: the price in dollars per share that an option buyer pays an option writer. *See also* Option, Option Writer.

Options Automated Trading System (OATS): the automated trading system used on the Australian Options Market.

Options Clearing Corporation (OCC): an organization established in 1972 to process and guarantee option trading on organized exchanges. *See also* Clearing Corporation, Option.

Options – Executive and/or Employee: options, granted to executives and/or employees, that carry the right but not the obligation to buy shares of that company's stock at a predetermined price and before a predetermined date.

Option Series: all of the options of the same class

(i.e., put or call) that have the same underlying security, exercise price and maturity month. Also known as Series, Series of Option. *See also* Option.

Option Writer: an option seller who grants an option buyer the right to buy a security if it is a call option or the right to sell a security if it is a put option. Also known as Grantor. *See also* Option.

Opulent: possessing and demonstrating great wealth.

Oracle of Omaha: *see* Buffett, E. Warren.

Oral Contract: *see* Verbal Contract.

Oral Will:. *see* Nuncupative Will.

Order: 1. a client's instruction to a broker to buy or sell a security along with the necessary details (e.g., a market order). *See also* All or None Order, Alternative Order, Any or All Order, Block Order, Buy, Buy Minus Order, Contingent Order, Cross, Day Order, Discretionary Order, Facilitation Order, Firm Order, Fractional Discretionary Order, Good Until Cancelled Order, Indicated Order, Limit Order, Market If Touched Order, Market-on-the-Close Order, Market-on-the-Opening Order, Market Order, Not Held Order, Sell, Split Order, Stop Buy Order, Stop Sell Order, Stop Loss Order, Switch Order, Working Order. **2.** a court's decision on a matter it was asked to resolve.

Order Backlog: business that is booked but not completed. Usually a positive business indicator. Also known as Order Book.

Order Book: *see* Order Backlog.

Order Driven Market: an auction market, so termed because trading is motivated by traders with an order to buy or sell. *See also* Auction Market, Electronic Market, Quote Driven Market.

Order Entry System: the method used by a broker to enter client orders to buy or sell securities. This can be as basic as filling out a form and physically delivering it to an order desk or as sophisticated as a fully computerized, electronic system.

Orderly Market: a market in which supply and demand are never significantly out of balance and in which wild price changes are very infrequent.

Order of Magnitude: approximately, as in "I think their sales are around $50 million in order of magnitude."

Ordinary Annuity: an annuity that pays for the period just passed. In other words, the payment from an ordinary annuity at the start of the month is for the month just passed. *See also* Annuity, Annuity Due.

Ordinary Asset: an asset that a company buys and sells as a part of its usual business (e.g., books to a bookseller).

Ordinary Income: all income except income from capital gains.

Ordinary Interest: simple interest charges calculated using a 360-day year. *See also* Exact Interest.

Ordinary Life Insurance: life insurance issued to and owned by an individual. *See also* Life Insurance.

Ordinary Stock: *see* Common Share.

Ordinary Voting: *see* Statutory Voting.

Ore: mineral or rock with a valuable constituent that can be extracted commercially (e.g., copper).

.org: an appendage to an e-mail or Internet address identifying a non-profit organization. *See also* Internet.

Organic Growth: the growth of a business excluding the effects of mergers and acquisitions. *See also* Same Store Sales. Also known as Internal Growth.

Organization: a group of people that is structured for a particular purpose.

Organization Chart: a chart of an organization's positions as well as its levels of authority and responsibility.

Organization for Economic Co-operation and Development (OECD): an organization established in 1961 to foster economic growth among its members. Members are: Australia, Austria, Belgium, Canada, the Czech Republic, Denmark, Finland, France, Germany, Greece, Hungary, Iceland, Ireland, Italy, Japan, Luxembourg, Mexico, the Netherlands, New Zealand, Norway, Poland, Portugal, South Korea, Spain, Sweden, Switzerland, Turkey, the U.K. and the U.S.

Organization for Security and Cooperation in Europe (OSCE): a 54-nation group, including the U.S. and Canada, established pursuant to a meeting in Helsinki, Finland in 1975 and headquartered in Vienna, that performs such functions as supervising elections in Europe.

Organization of Arab Petroleum Exporting Countries: an association of Arabian oil producers that sets international oil prices and settles disputes among Arab nations. Members are Abu Dhabi, Algeria, Bahrain, Egypt, Iraq, Kuwait, Libya, Qatar, Saudi Arabia and Syria. *See also* Organization of Petroleum Exporting Countries.

Organization of Petroleum Exporting Countries (OPEC): an oil-producing cartel established in 1960. Members are Abu Dhabi, Algeria, Ecuador, Gabon, Indonesia, Iran, Iraq, Kuwait, Libya, Nigeria, Qatar, Saudi Arabia and Venezuela. OPEC produces about one-third of the world's oil. *See also* Organization of Arab Petroleum Exporting Countries.

Organization type: the appendage on an e-mail or Internet address identifying the type of organization (e.g., .com denotes a commercial organization). *See also* .com, .edu, Electronic Mail, .gov, Internet, .mil, .net, .org.

Original Cost: all costs, including the price, incurred in buying an asset.

Original Equipment Manufacturer (OEM): the manufacturer of a part that is included in a new product. *See also* After Market.

Original Issue: the first stock issued by a company.

Original Maturity: the term to maturity on a bond when it was issued. *See also* Term to Maturity.

Orphan Stock: a stock that has been ignored by financial analysts. *See also* Financial Analyst, Wallflower.

OS/2: in computers, an operating system originally designed by IBM and Microsoft but now owned solely by IBM. It features a multitasking, windowed environment, but a lack of software support has caused it to lose ground in the competition with Microsoft's Windows products.

OSCE: *see* Organization for Security and Cooperation in Europe.

Oslo Bors: *see* Oslo Stock Exchange.

Oslo Stock Exchange: the major stock exchange of Norway, located in its capital, Oslo. Also known as Oslo Bors. Web site: www.ose.no *See also* Oslo Stock Exchange Index.

Oslo Stock Exchange Index: a market capitalization weighted index of all stocks listed on the Oslo Stock Exchange. The OBX Index is a market capitalization weighted index of the 25 most actively traded issues.

OTC: *see* Over-the-Counter.

Other Income: income from nonrecurring sources.

Other People's Money (OPM): in investment, a reference to client monies.

Other Wills: as a rule, a person must have attained the age of majority to have a will. In some provinces, a person who is married can have a valid will regardless of age. In all provinces except Quebec, a person can have a valid will if she/he is in active service in the military or is a mariner "at sea." *See* Will.

OTOH: Internet acronym for "on the other hand."

Ouguiya: the primary currency of Mauritania.

Ounce: a unit of weight equal to one-sixteenth of a pound or 28.4 grams.

Out: 1. to have lost money, as in "I'm out $300." **2.** to be in error, as in "My chequing account is out $200."

Outbid: to bid higher than someone else. *See also* Underbid.

"Out" Country: 1. a member of the European Community that is not participating in the single currency. *See also* European Community, Euro, "In" Country, "Pre-In" Country. **2.** a country not participating in the European Community. *See also* European Community.

Outcrop: a protrusion of rock at the surface of the ground.

Outfit: 1. a business engaged in a particular activity (e.g., a construction outfit). **2.** the historical name given to the fiscal year of the Hudson's Bay Company.

Outgo: an expenditure of something, especially money.

Outlay: an expenditure of money.

Outlet: a shop for the sale of goods or services.

Out-Migration: the movement of people out of one region of a country and into another region of the same country. *See also* Emigration, In-Migration.

Out-of-Favour: *see* Underloved Security, Underloved Stock.

Out-of-Line: a term used to describe a security that is priced too high or too low in comparison to similar securities.

Out-of-Pocket: 1. paid out in cash (e.g., out-of-pocket expenses). **2.** lacking funds.

Out of the Money: in options, a condition in which the strike price of a put option is below the price of the underlying security or in which the strike price of a call option is above the price of the underlying security. Also known as Underwater Option. *See also* At the Money, Deep in the Money, Deep out of the Money, In the Money, Option.

Outperforming Asset: 1. in investment, a security in a portfolio that is providing a higher return than the rest of the portfolio or the portfolio benchmark. *See also* Underperforming Asset. **2.** a corporate asset earning a higher rate of return than the same asset owned by other companies. *See also* Underperforming Asset.

Output: the amount produced or manufactured in a specific period of time. *See also* Computer, Input.

Outright: 1. without qualification or restriction (e.g., the outright transfer of title). **2.** completely, entirely and not by degrees or installments (e.g., the outright sale of property).

Outsell: to surpass in sales.

Outside Director: a member of the board of directors who is neither an employee nor officer of the company in question and is not in a conflict of interest position. Also known as an Independent Board Member. *See also* Board of Directors, Inside Director, Interlocking Director.

Outsource: to employ the services of an external provider instead of making use of internal people and resources (e.g, sending material to an outside print shop instead of using an internal printing department). Outsourcing is done to reduce costs and is a major trend in North American manufacturing.

Outspend: 1. to spend more than one's resources allow. **2.** to spend more than another person.

Outstanding Shares: *see* Issued and Outstanding Capital.

Out the Back Door: an informal reference to theft by employees.

Out the Window: a term to describe a new issue of securities that is sold very quickly and easily. *See also* Hot Issue.

Overage: a surplus.

Over-Allotment Option: a number of shares, in excess of the number offered by an underwriter, that can be added to an offering to satisfy additional demand or to stabilize the market.

Overbid: to make a bid that is too high and results in a price higher than was necessary. *See also* Underbid.

Overbooked: *see* Oversubscribed.

Overbought: 1. a situation in which an investor has purchased more of a security or a category of securities than he/she had intended. *See also* Underbought. **2.** a term used to describe a security or financial market that has been bid up to an exceptionally high price. *See also* Oversold.

Overbuild: 1. to construct according to standards beyond what is needed or expected. **2.** to place so many buildings in a particular place or on a particular piece of land that vacancy rates rise and real estate prices decline. *See also* Underbuild, Vacancy Rate.

Overburden: the topsoil or other material that lies on top of ore that is to be extracted through open pit mining. *See also* Open Pit Mining.

Overcapitalized: a term used to describe the condition of a company with more capital than is required to conduct business. Such businesses may have a poor return on invested capital. *See also* Return on Invested Capital, Under Capitalized.

Overcharge: 1. the difference between the premiums for the same amount of participating and non-participating life insurance. *See also* Life Insurance, Non-Participating Life Insurance, Participating Life Insurance. **2.** to ask for too much payment or an amount beyond established guidelines. *See also* Undercharge.

Over Contribution: *see* Registered Retirement Savings Plan – Over Contribution.

Overdraft: a situation that occurs when the amount of money taken out of an account exceeds the amount of money on deposit. *See also* Overdraft Protection, Overdraft System, Overdraw, Personal Overdraft Facility.

Overdraft Protection: an agreement with a financial institution to cover overdrafts. Usually there is a limit to the amount that will be covered, and a fee is paid for this service. *See also* Overdraft, Overdraft System, Personal Overdraft Facility.

Overdraft System: an agreement with a financial institution to automatically extend a loan to cover an overdraft. *See also* Overdraft, Overdraft Protection, Personal Overdraft Facility.

Overdraw: to take out more money from an account than one's credit allows. *See also* Overdraft.

Overdue: unpaid when due.

Overemployment: a term used to describe the situation in which there is a severe labour shortage in an economy. Overemployment usually occurs when the economy has been very strong for an extended period. *See also* Employment, Underemployment.

Overestimate: to make too high an approximation or forecast. *See also* Underestimate.

Overfollowed Security: a security that is analyzed and reported on by too many financial analysts. Over followed securities are very efficiently priced, and it is difficult to make above-average returns on them. *See also* Underfollowed Security.

Overfollowed Stock: a stock analyzed and reported on by too many financial analysts. Overfollowed stocks are very efficiently priced, and it is difficult to make above-average returns on them. *See also* Underfollowed Stock.

Overfunded: a condition of having more capital than needed to complete a transaction.

Overhang: a large block of stock known to be for sale.

Overhead: 1. large numbers of shares known to be for sale at higher prices if the stock price moves up, as in "overhead supply." *See also* Stock Ahead. **2.** the fixed expenses of running a business. **3.** *see* Corporate Overhead.

Overheated: in business or the economy, a condition in which growth exceeds capacity and negative consequences (e.g., higher inflation in the economy or lower profit margins in a company) result.

Overinvested: to have too much invested in an individual security or single asset. *See also* Under Invested.

Overinvestment Theory: the economic concept that business will always make excess capital investments during favourable economic conditions and underinvest during unfavourable economic conditions.

Overline Lending: the process of extending credit beyond the amount of the usual credit line of the borrower.

Overlooked Security: *see* Underfollowed Security.

Overlooked Stock: *see* Underfollowed Stock.

Overloved Security: a security with overly optimistic investor expectations. *See also* Underloved Security.

Overloved Stock: a stock with overly optimistic investor expectations. *See also* Underloved Stock.

Over Margin: to have excess security for a margin account. *See also* Margin Account, Under Margin.

Overmargined Account: a margin account with above minimum security requirements *See also* Margin Account.

Overnight Inventory: a brokerage firm's security holdings for its own account at the end of the trading day.

Overowned Security: a security that is very widely followed and popular with investors. *See also* Underowned Security.

Overowned Stock: a stock that is very widely followed and very popular with investors to the point where its share price is overvalued. *See also* Overowned Security, Overpriced Security.

Overpriced Security: a security that is trading above its inherent value. Also known as Overvalued Security. *See also* Inherent Value, Underpriced Security.

Overpriced Stock: a stock that is trading above its inherent value. Also known as an Overvalued Stock. *See also* Inherent Value, Underpriced Stock.

Overrate: to evaluate too high. *See also* Underrate.

Overreach: in commercial law, a term that is synonymous with fraud. *See also* Fraud.

Overreaction: in financial markets, this occurs when price changes in response to an event are either too positive or too negative.

Override: 1. a share of another person's commission. **2.** to replace one computer command with another. **3.** to declare null and void.

Oversold: 1. a situation in which an investor has sold more of a security or a category of securities than he/she had intended. *See also* Overbought, Undersold. **2.** a term used to describe a security or financial market that has been sold down to an exceptionally low price. *See also* Overbought.

Overspeculation: a condition in which the amount of speculative buying and selling threatens the overall stability of the market. *See also* Speculation.

Overstay: to hold an investment too long, with the result that profit or rate of return is reduced.

Oversubscribed: this occurs when demand exceeds supply for a new issue of securities. Also known as Overbooked. *See also* Undersubscribed.

Over-the-Counter (OTC): a market for securities that are not listed on a recognized stock exchange. Also known as Second Market. *See also* Off-the-Board, Third Market.

Over-the-Counter Bulletin Board: *see* Bulletin Board.

Over-the-Counter Pink Sheets: *see* Pink Sheets.

Over the Wall: a term used to describe an analyst who is employed by a brokerage firm, assigned to work on a corporate finance project and becomes party to inside information that prevents him/her from fulfilling his/her research function. The "wall" is the firewall that is supposed to separate research and corporate finance. *See also* Firewall, Inside Information, Restricted.

Overtrading: 1. in investment, too much activity in a brokerage account. **2.** a situation that occurs when an underwriter agrees to purchase one security at a premium to enable an investor to raise capital to invest in a new issue. **3.** a situation that occurs when a broker agrees to purchase one security to enable an investor to purchase another security the broker is offering for sale. **4.** in banking, a term used to describe a company that maintains insufficient working capital relative to sales.

Overvalued Security: *see* Overpriced Security.

Overvalued Stock: *see* Overpriced Stock.

Overview: a broadly based, general review (e.g., an economic overview).

Overweighted: a stock or industry position that is much greater in a portfolio than it is in a benchmark. *See also* Underweighted.

Overwithholding: a situation that occurs when too much income tax is deducted each month, resulting in a taxpayer claim for a refund each year. Overwithholding can stem from either an overestimate of income or an underestimate of deductions. *See also* Tax Refund, Underwithholding.

Overwrite: 1. the process of an option writer selling more options of the underlying security than he/she owns. **2.** in computers, allowing one set of instructions or data to take the place of another. *See also* Option, Override.

Owe: to be indebted.

Owner: one who has title or a legal claim to something.

Own Occupation: *see* Same Occupation.

P

PA: 1. Pension Adjustment. *see* Registered Retirement Savings Plan – Pension Adjustment. **2.** *see* Power of Attorney.

p.a.: *see* Per Annum.

Pa'anga: the primary currency of Tonga.

PABX: *see* Private Automatic Branch Exchange.

Pacific Exchange: a regional U.S. stock exchange located in San Francisco, California. Web site: www.pacificex.com

Packet: a cluster of data transmitted as a unit on a computer network. *See also* Computer.

Pac Man Defence: in a hostile takeover, this occurs when the target tries to acquire the raider. *See also* Flip-In Poison Pill, Flip-Over Poison Pill, Jonestown Defence, Killer Bee, Lady Macbeth Strategy, Leveraged Recapitalization, Lobster Trap, Lock-up Agreement, Macaroni Defense, Pension Parachute, People Pill, Poison Pill, Poison Put Bond, Safe Harbour, Scorched Earth Policy, Suicide Pill, White Squire Defence.

Pact: a formal agreement, often between nations.

Pagination: in word processing, the numbering of pages.

Paid-In Capital: a balance sheet entry for the amount of money a company has received in exchange for its shares. Also known as Contributed Capital Share Capital, Share Capital. *See also* Paid-In Surplus, Paid-Up Capital, Paid-Up Stock.

Paid-In Surplus: a balance sheet entry that represents the difference between the par value of shares and the dollar amount actually received from the sale of those shares. *See also* Paid-In Capital, Paid-Up Capital, Paid-Up Stock.

Paid-Up Bonus Addition: additional life insurance purchased with dividends paid on an insurance policy. *See also* Life Insurance.

Paid-Up Capital: the total of the par value and the full payment received for any no par value stock that has been issued. *See also* No Par Value, Paid-In Capital, Paid-In Surplus, Paid-Up Stock, Par Value.

Paid-Up Life Insurance Policy: a life insurance policy in which all required payments have been made

and that will remain in force until surrendered or terminated by the death of the insured. *See also* Life Insurance, Reduced Paid-Up Life Insurance.

Paid-Up Stock: shares that have been issued for cash, goods or services with a value equal to or greater than the par value of the stock. *See also* Paid-In Capital, Paid-In Surplus, Paid-Up Capital.

Painting the Tape: 1. the unethical practice of changing large orders into many small orders to have more trades on the tape to attract investor interest. **2.** the illegal practice of trading a stock between members in a group to create the impression of market activity. *See also* Daisy Chain, Wash Trading. **3.** A term used to describe active trading of a stock because of its special interest to investors. In this sense, it is both legal and ethical.

Pakistanian Stock Exchange: *see* Karachi Stock Exchange.

PAL: *see* Phase Alternate Lines.

Palimony: an informal term for a court-ordered support payment from one spouse to the other after separation.

Palladium: a metallic element used in hydrogen purification, jewelry, watch parts and surgical instruments. Palladium is one of the precious metals. *See also* Precious Metal.

Pan: 1. to wash gravel in order to extract gold or other precious materials. **2.** the handheld instrument in which gravels are washed. *See also* Placer Mining, Sluice Box.

Panama Stock Exchange: the major stock market of Panama, located in its capital, Panama City. Also known as Bolsa de Valores de Panama.

Panama Stock Market General Index: a market capitalization weighted stock price index for the Panama Stock Exchange.

Panda: a gold coin minted in the People's Republic of China.

P&L: *see* Profit and Loss Statement.

Panic: in investment, a sudden, broadly based loss of confidence resulting in emotional rather than rational decisions. *See also* Bear Panic, Panic Buying, Panic Selling.

Panic Buying: a flurry of high-volume purchases brought about by sharp price increases. In panic buying, buyers do not evaluate fundamentals because their goal is to acquire securities before prices rise even more. *See also* Fundamental Analysis, Panic Selling.

Panic Selling: a flurry of high-volume selling brought about by sharp price declines. In panic selling, sellers do not evaluate fundamentals because their goal is to sell securities before prices fall even more. *See also* Fundamental Analysis, Panic Selling.

Paper: *see* Financial Asset.

Paper Asset: *see* Financial Asset.

Paper Company: 1. a corporation formed to perform a specific financial task rather than to produce a product or service. **2.** a company with no substance.

Paper Gold: *see* Special Drawing Rights.

Paper Hanger: any stock promoter, but especially one who actively encourages the buying of a stock he/she is selling. *See also* Stock Promoter.

Paper Investment: an investment that is a written claim or promise (e.g., government bonds).

Paperless: a term that indicates records are kept electronically (e.g., a computer record).

Paper Loss: an investment loss (or losses) that is not yet realized or one that has not been triggered by a sale or disposition. Also known as Book Loss. *See also* Paper Profit, Unrealized Capital Loss.

Paper Money: paper currency or the equivalent (e.g., money held in a chequing account).

Paper Profit: an investment profit(s) that is not yet realized or one that has not been triggered by a sale or disposition. Also known as Book Profit. *See also* Paper Loss, Unrealized Capital Loss.

Paper Tiger: an investment person who seems powerful and important but is not.

Paper Trail: the hard-copy record that enables one to trace financial transactions to their source.

Par: 1. Par Value. **2.** Pension Adjustment Reversal. *see* Registered Retirement Savings Plan – Pension Adjustment Reversal.

Parachute: the process of filling a corporate position from outside rather than from inside, as in "parachute in a new president."

Paralegal: a person who is specially trained to assist a lawyer.

Parallel: in computers, the simultaneous flow of data side by side along multiple data lines (e.g., one byte would be transmitted by sending eight bits down eight data lines at the same time). *See also* Serial.

Parallel Port: the input/output device on a computer, this is where data are transmitted in a parallel fashion to an external device, usually a printer. *See also* Computer, Serial Port.

Parallel Processing: the ability of a computer to execute two instructions simultaneously, allowing it to complete more than one process at once. For this to be done, the computer must have more than one microprocessor. *See also* Computer, Microprocessor.

Paramount Title: the one title to a property that prevails over all others. *See also* Title.

Pardon: 1. in law, the forgiveness of the legal consequences of a crime. **2.** the remission of an obligation (e.g., a payment, a debt, a penalty).

Parent Company: a company that owns or controls other companies. *See also* Affiliated Companies, Subsidiary Company.

Pareto's Law: the theory of Italian-Swiss economist, mathematician and sociologist Vilfredo Pareto (1848-1923). Pareto stated that changing taxation policies do not help the poor because 80 percent of a country's income benefits only 20 percent of its people. In general, this has become known as the law of the trivial many and the critical few or the Eighty/Twenty Rule (e.g., the majority of a company's sales come from a minority of its customers). *See also* Pareto Optimum.

Pareto Optimum: a theoretical economic state in which no one can be made better off without making someone else worse off. *See also* Pareto's Law.

Pari passu: a Latin term meaning "without partiality." It is used to mean ranking equally (e.g., secured creditors during the liquidation of assets).

Paris Stock Exchange: the major stock exchange of France, located in its capital, Paris. Also known as Société des Bourses Francaises or, simply, Bourse. Web site: www.bourse-de-paris.fr *See also* CAC-40 Index, SAF-250 Index.

Parity: equal in amount, status or value.

Parking: putting money or securities in a safe, highly liquid asset while looking for the next investment.

Parkinson's Laws: a set of humorous (but often accurate) observations set down by C. Northcote Parkinson (1909-1993) in his book *Parkinson's Law* (1957). Some of these laws include the following. "Work expands so as to fill the time available for its completion." "Expenditures rise to meet income." "The time spent on any item of a committee's agenda will be in inverse proportion to the sum of money involved." *See also* Peter Principle.

Parliament: the federal legislature of Canada, made up of the Queen, the Senate and the House of Commons. *See also* Senate.

Parole: the conditional release of a prisoner before serving his/her full sentence. The conditions include good behaviour and reporting regularly to a parole officer. *See also* Probation.

Partial Call: a security called by the issuer but not for the entire issue. A partial call can be conducted proportionately for all securities tendered or by lottery. Also known as Partial Redemption. *See also* Call, Lottery.

Partial Covered Writing: an option position made up of both covered and uncovered calls written on the same stock. *See also* Option.

Partially Amortized Loan: *see* Balloon Loan.

Partial Payment: when an insurance company pays

part of a claim and the balance of the claim, if any, remains open until final settlement.

Partial Redemption: *see* Partial Call.

Participating Lease: a lease that pays the lessor a share in the lessee's sales (or some other participation, such as a share of net income) in addition to fixed payments. Also known as Percentage Lease, Percentage Rent.

Participating Life Insurance: a form of whole life insurance that returns excess premium payments. *See also* Life Insurance, Non-Participating Life Insurance, Overcharge.

Participating Mortgage: a mortgage that receives a participation in future income or some other participation in addition to regular interest. *See also* Mortgage.

Participating Preferred Share: a preferred share that may be entitled to additional dividends after common stock dividends have been paid.

Participating Rent: rent that gives the landlord an interest in a commercial renter's sales (or some other participation, such as a share of net income) in addition to fixed payments. *See also* Participating Lease.

Participation Fee: a fee charged by a lender for taking part in arranging and providing a loan. *See also* Funding Costs.

Participation Loan: a loan made by more than one lender. Participation loans make it possible for a borrower to obtain a very large bank loan when the amount of the loan exceeds the lending limit of an individual bank.

Participation Mortgage: a mortgage loan made by more than one lender. *See also* Mortgage.

Participation Rate: the proportion of people over age 15 who are employed or actively looking for work.

Partner: one who is associated with another in a common interest, often a business. *See also* Copartner, Partnership.

Partnership: a form of ownership involving two or more parties, with each owner being involved in the management of operations and accepting liability for obligations. *See also* Incorporation, Partner, Proprietorship, Silent Partner.

Party: a person or persons directly interested or involved in an arrangement, agreement or contract.

Party at Interest: a person with a financial interest in a company.

Party in Interest: a person who provides investment advice and services.

Par Value: the face value of a bond or other security. Also known as Face Amount, Face Value, Par. *See also* Above Par, At Par, Bond, Market Value, Nominal Value, Stated Value.

Par Value – Bonds: the face value of a bond. Usually, the amount paid back to investors at maturity. A bond trades "at par" if its market price equals its par value. *See also* No Par Value, Paid-Up Capital.

Par Value – Common Stocks: before 1917, all Canadian companies had a par value or stated value that represented the value contributed for each share in cash or goods. Over time, par value lost its relevance as par value and market value grew farther apart. Most common shares today are No Par Value (NPV) or have a par value that is relevant only for accounting purposes.

Pass: 1. to decide not to participate in a trade or new issue. **2.** to not pay a dividend.

Passbook: *see* Bankbook.

Passed Dividend: a fixed or regular dividend that was not paid. This usually occurs when the issuer is in financial difficulty and cannot afford to pay. Also known as Dividend Omission. *See also* Dividend.

Passive Bond: a bond that does not pay interest. Passive bonds are often issued by charitable institutions. *See also* Bond.

Passive Fund: *see* Index Fund.

Passive Investor: an investor who is not involved in the operations or management of the business he/she has invested in. Also known as Hands-Off Investor. *See also* Active Investor.

Passive Management: *see* Passive Portfolio Management.

Passive Portfolio Management: a portfolio management technique in which a portfolio replicates an index such as the Dow-Jones Average or Toronto Stock Exchange Index. This is done to lower management fees and provide average rates of return. Generally, passive portfolio management is the management style used for index funds. Also known as Passive Management. *See also* Active Management, Index Fund.

Pass the Book: the process of moving responsibility of a brokerage firm's own trading account to different offices because financial markets are now traded 24 hours a day. The book may start in New York and at the end of the business day be passed to Los Angeles, Tokyo, Singapore, London and then back to New York the following day.

Pass-Through Security: a security that acts as a conduit (e.g., a mortgage-backed security that collects interest and principal payments and passes the amounts through to its investors). *See also* Conduit Theory, Flow Through Share.

Password: in computers, a security code needed to gain access to a system or file. *See also* Access

Control, Authentication, Biometric Authentication, Challenge-Response Token, Computer, Fire Wall, Public Key, Secret Key.

Past Due Balance Method: the calculation of finance costs or interest payable based on the amount owing that is past due. This method is used by general purpose credit cards that offer a "grace period" (e.g., 30 days), during which interest is not charged. *See also* Adjusted Balance Method, Average Daily Balance Method, Minimum Monthly Balance and Previous Balance Method.

Past-Service Pension Adjustment (PSPA): a reduction in allowable RRSP contributions to reflect improved pension benefits for a past period or additional years of employment after 1989.

Pataca: the prime currency of Macau.

Patch: 1. a temporary solution to a computer systems problem. **2.** a specific solution created for a specific problem. *See also* Computer.

Patent: a government licence that provides exclusive use of a new design, invention or process for a specific period. The patent is issued to enable the inventor time to benefit financially from his/her efforts and usually is in effect for 17 years.

Patent Pending (Pat. Pend.): a patent applied for but not yet issued.

Pathfinder Minerals: in resource exploration, related minerals indicating the presence of the actual mineral being sought.

Patient Money: *see* Long-Term Investor.

Pat. Pend.: *see* Patent Pending.

Patron: one who provides support, often financial, for a specific cause.

Pawn: an expensive form of financing in which personal property is used as security for a loan. *See also* Pawnbroker, Pawnshop.

Pawnbroker: the operator of a pawnshop. *See also* Pawn, Pawnshop.

Pawnshop: a facility that grants loans when personal property is turned over as security. *See also* Pawn, Pawnbroker.

Pay: to settle a debt or obligation.

Payables: trade or other liabilities evidenced by an invoice or other document.

Pay As You Go: a financial arrangement in which current revenues are used to pay current expenses.

Payback: the time, usually in years, when invested capital will be recouped from investment income. *See also* Unfunded Pension Plan.

Pay-As-You-Go Pension Plan: *see* Unfunded Pension Plan.

Pay Cheque: a cheque issued as payment of salary or wages.

Pay Date: the date on which an interest or dividend payment is made.

Pay Dirt: 1. an economic orebody. **2.** any profitable activity.

Paydown: a partial repayment of the principal on a debt.

Payee: in a financial transaction, the party receiving payment. *See also* Payer.

Pay Equity: the general concept that there should be equal compensation for equal work performed.

Payer: in a financial transaction, the party making or dispensing payment. *See also* Payee.

Payer Swapation: an option that gives the owner the right (but not the obligation) to enter into an interest rate swap at a predetermined interest rate and within a set period. *See also* Interest Rate Swap, Receiver Swapation, Swapation.

Paying Agent: the party named in a bond indenture as responsible for making payments to the bondholders.

Paymaster: the person in charge of paying wages.

Payment Date: 1. the date a dividend or interest payment is to be made. **2.** the settlement date for a securities trade. **3.** the date on which a loan or credit card payment is due.

Payment Holiday: an allowance, often in a loan agreement or mortgage, that allows the borrower to miss a specified number of regular payments during the term of the loan. *See also* Contribution Holiday.

Payment in Kind (PIK): use of the same or similar good or service as an alternative for money in payment for a good or service (e.g., a payment in kind to a Registered Retirement Savings Plan involves depositing a security instead of cash). Payment in Kind differs from barter because the latter involves the exchange of a good or service for a different good or service. *See also* Barter, Payment in Kind Bond, Payment in Kind Security, Registered Retirement Savings Plan.

Payment in Kind Bond: a bond that pays interest in the form of additional bonds instead of cash. *See also* Payment in Kind, Payment in Kind Security.

Payment in Kind Security: a financial security that pays income (e.g., interest, dividends) in the form of additional securities instead of cash. *See also* Payment in Kind, Payment in Kind Bond.

Payoff: 1. full payment of an obligation. **2.** a bribe.

Payola: a bribe offered to promote a commercial product or service. *See also* Bribe, Baksheesh.

Payout: the amount paid out to shareholders as dividends. *See also* Retention Rate.

Payout Rate: *see* Payout Ratio.

Payout Ratio: after taxes, the percentage of corporate profits paid out to shareholders as dividends. It is 1 minus the Retention Rate. Also known as Payout Rate. *See also* Retention Rate.

Payroll: 1. a list of people entitled to wages for a particular pay period. **2.** the personnel costs of a business.

Payroll Deduction: a deduction from an employee's pay cheque to pay for income taxes, an employee benefit or related item. *See also* Payroll Deduction Plan, Source Deduction.

Payroll Deduction Plan: a plan that allows employees to make investments by having the employer deduct regular amounts from their pay cheques (e.g., to purchase Canada Savings Bonds).*See also* Payroll Deduction, Source Deduction.

Pay Scale: the rate of pay for a particular type of employee or work. Also known as Scale.

Pay Through the Nose: to pay an excessively high price for a product or service.

Pay to Order: an instruction in a negotiable instrument that names the person to whom it is payable.

Pay to Play: 1. a term that describes the now forbidden U.S. practice of underwriting firms contributing to the election campaigns of politicians to help win state and local bond underwriting business. **2.** generally, any situation in which a business makes an indirect outlay to win a contract or business. The term "Pay to Play" does not necessarily imply an illegal activity.

Pay Up: 1. this occurs when an anxious buyer pays the offering price. **2.** to settle a debt or obligation.

Pay Yourself First: the financial planning adage that states that the first commitment from one's pay cheque is to saving or investment.

PBX: *see* Private Branch Exchange.

PC: *see* Personal Computer.

PC-DOS: a disk operating system developed and sold by International Business Machines. *See also* Computer, Disk Operating System, MS-DOS.

PCMCIA: *see* Personal Computer Memory Card International Association.

PCO: *see* Privy Council Office.

PCS: *see* Personal Communications Services.

PDI: *see* Personal Disposable Income.

P/E: *see* Price/Earnings Ratio.

Peace Dividend: a term used to refer to funds available for domestic priorities following a war. *See also* Fiscal Dividend.

Peak: the high point in an economic or financial market cycle, often before a contraction or decline. *See also* Bottom, Bull Market, Business Cycle, Contraction, Cyclical, Economic Cycle, Elliott Wave Theory, Expansion, Kondratieff Wave, Market Cycle, Presidential Election Cycle, Stock Market Cycle, Top.

Pecking Order: the social or business hierarchy of a group, class or nation.

Pecuniary: relating to money or monetary matters.

Peer Group: in valuing a stock, comparisons are made with shares of similar companies; that is, they are made within a peer group.

Peg: 1. to fix the price of a new security issue during the issuance period. **2.** to fix the foreign exchange rate between currencies.

PEG Ratio: *see* Price/Earnings to Growth Ratio.

Penalty: a clause in an agreement that imposes a financial payment if certain conditions are not met (e.g., a mortgage prepayment penalty is the additional amount that must be paid in order to repay a mortgage before maturity). *See also* Anticipation, Anticipation Rate, Mortgage Prepayment, Prepayment, Prepayment Clause, Prepayment Penalty, Prepayment Privilege, Right of Anticipation.

Pending: not yet decided or completed, as in "patent pending." *See also* Patent Pending.

Penetration Rate: *see* Market Penetration Rate.

Pennant: a technical stock price formation in which the price on a chart forms a triangle by making successively lower peaks and higher troughs in a relatively short period. *See also* Flag.

Penny: a one-cent coin.

Penny Dreadful: *see* Penny Stock.

Penny Stock: 1. a common stock that trades for less than a dollar a share, indicating a low quality, speculation. Also known as Penny Dreadful. **2.** generally, any low-priced, high-risk common stock.

Penny-Wise and Pound Foolish: this refers to situations in which actions taken to save a small expenditure in the short run result in the need to make a very large expenditure in the long run (e.g., preparing one's own contract saves legal fees in the short run but can result in costly litigation in the long run).

Pension: retirement income received from a pension plan or a registered retirement income fund. *See also* Pension Plan, Registered Retirement Income Fund.

Pension Adjustment (PA): *see* Registered Retirement Savings Plan – Pension Adjustment.

Pension Adjustment Reversal (PAR): *see* Registered Retirement Savings Plan – Pension Adjustment Reversal.

Pension Benefits Standards Act: Canadian legislation governing investment and related policies for registered pension funds. *See also* Registered Pension Plan.

Pensioner: one who receives a pension.

Pension Fund: *see* Registered Pension Plan.

Pension Fund Trustee: an individual appointed or elected to monitor the processes of a pension fund that has been established as a trust. *See also* Trusteed Pension Plan.

Pension Parachute: a pension agreement that, in the event of an unfriendly takeover of a company, allows any surplus pension assets to increase pension benefits *See also* Poison Pill.

Pension Plan: *see* Registered Pension Plan.

Pension Plan Administrator: the individual responsible for the administrative aspects of a pension plan.

Pension Portability: the ability to take benefits from one pension plan to another (or to an RRSP) when changing jobs. Also known as Portability. *See also* Locked-In Pension Fund.

Pentad: a five-year period. *See also* Quinquennial.

Pentaphilia Theory: 1. the theory that stock prices rise in years divisible by five. **2.** the theory that stock prices rise in years ending in five.

People Pill: an agreement that in the event a company is successfully taken over, all members of management will resign at once. *See also* Flip-In Poison Pill, Flip-Over Poison Pill, Jonestown Defence, Killer Bee, Lady Macbeth Strategy, Leveraged Recapitalization, Lobster Trap, Lock-up Agreement, Macaroni Defense, Pac Man Defense, Pension Parachute, Poison Pill, Poison Put Bond, Safe Harbour, Scorched Earth Policy, Suicide Pill, White Squire Defence.

Per: for each, as in "10 dollars per person."

Per Annum (p.a.): each year. *See also* Per Mensum.

Per Capita: literally, for each head (e.g., a country's income per capita is the total national income divided by the population).

Per Capita Debt: *see* Per Capita Government Debt.

Per Capita Gift: a gift shared equally by all its beneficiaries.

Per Capita Government Debt: a government's debt divided by the population. Also known as Per Capita Debt.

Per Capita Income: for a country, the net national income divided by the population. *See also* Net National Income.

Per Capita Tax: *see* Poll Tax.

Percent: one part in every 100.

Percentage: a ratio with a denominator of 100.

Percentage Lease: *see* Participating Lease.

Percentage of Completion: an accounting method that records income and expenses based on the stage of a project's completion.

Percentage Rent: *see* Participating Lease.

Percentile: each set of values derived by dividing a number of quantities into 100 equal groups. Each percentile indicates the number of groups that do not exceed it (e.g., the tenth percentile is exceeded by 90 of the 100 groups).

Per Diem: 1. by the day. Often used in reference to compensation. **2.** daily expenses that stipulate the allowance or the maximum amount that can be billed. Such charges (e.g., for meals on a business trip) are often a fixed amount that can be claimed whether the actual expenditure was more or less than the per diem amount.

Peremptory: in law, not open to appeal or challenge.

Perfect Competition: a theoretical state in which buyers and sellers compete with equal knowledge and have no special ability to influence production, pricing, supply or demand of the product or service. *See also* Free and Open Market.

Perfect Hedge: a hedge in which the change in the value of the hedge exactly offsets the change in value of the item being hedged. *See also* Hedge.

Perfect Lien: a creditor's claim to an asset held in security of a loan that is legally binding. *See also* Lien.

Perfidy: deliberate breach of faith.

Performance: the rate of return earned on investment over a specific period of time, usually measured against a benchmark. *See also* Benchmark.

Performance Bond: a security to protect one against failure of another party to fulfill a contract or obligation. Also known as Bond, Surety Bond.

Performance Fee: in investment management, a management fee that increases with good performance and decreases with poor performance. *See also* Contingency Fee, Management Fee, Success Fee.

Performance Fund: *see* Go-Go Fund.

Performance Stock: a stock with a history of appreciating in value – a history that is expected to continue.

Peril: the event or cause of an insurance claim.

Period Certain Annuity: *see* Annuity Certain.

Periodic Payment Plan: a plan whereby regular contributions are deposited at regular intervals to build an investment in a mutual fund. *See also* Accumulation Plan, Contractual Plan, Mutual Fund, Systematic Savings Plan, Voluntary Accumulation Plan.

Periodic Purchase Deferred Annuity: an annuity that is purchased with fixed payments over time. The payments from the annuity do not begin until a future date. *See also* Annuity.

Peripheral: in computers, a device connected to the outside of a computer, such as a monitor or keyboard. *See also* Computer.

Perjure: to deliberately lie under oath.

Perk: *see* Perquisite.

Permanent Capital: the capital needed at all times to operate a business. Permanent capital is the total of long-term capital and net current assets. *See also* Long-Term Capital, Net Current Assets.

Permanent Financing: long-term financing.

Permanent Life Insurance: *see* Whole Life Insurance.

Per Mensem: every month. *See also* Per Annum.

Permit: 1. in real estate, a document that is required to undertake a stage of development (e.g., a building permit). **2.** in general, any document giving approval to take an action.

Perpetual: a security or agreement without a maturity date. *See also* Perpetual Bond.

Perpetual Bond: a bond without a maturity date. *See also* Bond, Perpetual.

Perpetual Inventory: *see* Continuous Inventory.

Perq: *see* Perquisite.

Perquisite: something in addition to regular income (e.g., a company car). Also known as Fringe Benefit, Perk, Perq.

Per Se: by or in itself.

Persistency: a reference to the number of insurance contracts that are renewed instead of lapsing.

Persona Grata: a person who is welcome, especially to a government. *See also* Persona Non Grata.

Personal Article Floater: *see* Rider.

Personal Assets: assets owned in the name of an individual.

Personal Bankruptcy: this occurs when an individual cannot meet his or her financial obligations and so legally renounces them. *See also* Bankrupt, Bankruptcy.

Personal Communications Service (PCS): a generation of wireless telephone service similar to cell phones but smaller, cheaper and with a shorter roaming range. *See also* Cellular Telephone.

Personal Computer (PC): a computer specifically designed to be used by one person at a time, usually consisting of a central processing unit, keyboard and monitor. The term "PC" was originally used to describe the IBM personal computer but later became synonymous with any computer that could run DOS or Windows-based programs. *See also* Computer.

Personal Computer Memory Card International Association (PCMCIA): the international association that establishes the standards and protocols for PC card-based peripherals and the slot designed to hold them. The PCMCIA slot has become a common industry standard for laptops and notebooks. *See also* Computer.

Personal Consumption: the purchase of goods and services by individuals calculated as the difference between personal disposable income and personal savings. *See also* Personal Disposable Income, Personal Savings.

Personal Disposable Income: after-tax income of

individuals and unincorporated businesses. PDI is the economic equivalent of take-home pay. *See also* Take-Home Pay.

Personal Effects: privately owned items.

Personal Financial Planner (PFP): a designation issued by the Institute of Canadian Bankers to industry professionals working with clients in wealth management. *See also* Institute of Canadian Bankers.

Personal Financial Planning: for a family, the process of planning a financial future through retirement to estate planning. *See also* Financial Planner, Financial Planning, Money In, Money Out.

Personal Financial Statement: a summary of a person's financial status, including assets, liabilities, income, expenses and contingent liabilities (such as loans guaranteed for another party).

Personal Guarantee: a legal undertaking by an individual to assume responsibility for the repayment of debt or other obligation if the primary party fails. In many cases, a loan to a small business will require a personal guarantee from the owner/operator.

Personal Holding Company: a company, owned by one person or a small number of people, that derives most of its income from investments.

Personal Identification Number (PIN): a number used in conjunction with credit cards, debit cards and automated banking machines to provide secure access.

Personal Income: the pretax income of individuals and unincorporated businesses.

Personal Income Tax: a tax paid by individuals based on income. *See also* Taxes.

Personal Inflation Rate: the rate of inflation as it effects a specific individual (e.g., a person who owns his/her home without a mortgage is not effected by rising mortgage rates, which push up the Consumer Price Index). As a rule, young families have much higher personal inflation rates than older, retired families. *See also* Consumer Price Index, Inflation.

Personalized Cheque: a cheque with an individual's name and other information printed on it.

Personal Line (of Credit): a prearranged amount of credit, usually unsecured, that can be borrowed for any purpose. *See also* Line of Credit.

Personal Loan: a loan granted by a financial institution to a private person specifically for his/her personal needs.

Personal Overdraft Facility: a loan arrangement that allows a customer to overdraw his/her bank account, subject to certain restrictions. *See also* Overdraft, Overdraft Protection, Overdraft System.

Personal Property: all of one's rights and ownership in chattels and chattel interests except the chattel interests that pass to heirs upon the owner's death. Also known as Personalty or Property. *See also* Chattel, Chattel Interest, Goods and Chattels, Private Property.

Personal Property Record: a central registry of liens on all personal property except land and buildings. The personal property record should be checked before any major private purchase. The record is available from any Motor Vehicles Office. *See also* Lien.

Personal Property Security Act: legislation governing the law and practice of secured transactions in personal property. Where individual provinces have acts, they are coordinated to ensure an agreement of interest.

Personal Savings: the difference between personal disposable income and personal consumption. *See also* Personal Consumption, Personal Disposable Income.

Personal Service Business: for income tax purposes, a company that has been put in the place of an employee in what would normally be an employer-employee relationship. This is often done in the expectation that the earnings reported as corporate rather than personal income will result in the payment of less income tax. In such cases, income taxes will not be reduced. *See also* Active Business, Investment Business.

Personalty: *see* Personal Property.

Persona Non Grata: a person who is unwelcome, especially to a government. *See also* Persona Grata.

Person-Day: the time worked by one person, full time during one day. Government and other large organizations manage staffing budgets in terms of person-days, person-hours and person-years. Still sometimes referred to as Man-Day. *See also* Person-Hour, Person-Year.

Person-Hour: the time worked by one person for one hour. Government and other large organizations manage staffing budgets in terms of person-days, person-hours and person-years. Still sometimes referred to as Man-Hour. *See also* Person-Day, Person-Year.

Personnel: all the people employed by an organization or business.

Person-Year: the time worked by one person, full time during one year. Government and other large organizations manage staffing budgets in terms of person-days, person-hours and person-years. Still sometimes referred to as Man-Year. *See also* Person-Hour, Person-Day.

Per Stirpes: by the number of families.

Per Stirpes Gift: the division of assets so that if one of the people to receive a share is deceased, then the children of that person divide that share.

Peruvian Stock Exchange: *see* Lima Stock Exchange.

Peseta: the prime currency of Andorra, Balearic Islands, Canary Islands, Spain.

Peso: the prime currency of Argentina, Chile, Columbia, Cuba, Dominican Republic, Guinea-Bissau, Mexico, Philippines, Uruguay.

Peter Principle: the principle that, "In a hierarchy, every employee tends to rise to his/her level of incompetence." That is, people are promoted, and if they continue to excel, they continue to be promoted. Eventually, they attain a position that they cannot handle and the promotions stop. From the book, *The Peter Principle* (1969), by Laurence J. Peter (1919-1990) and Raymond Hull (1919-1985). *See also* Parkinson's Law.

Petition: 1. in law, an application to the court for something it has jurisdiction over (e.g., a bankruptcy order) or other judicial action pertaining to a suit. *See also* Petition for Divorce. **2.** in general, any request to a party to exercise his/her authority to redress a wrong.

Petition for Divorce: the formal document used by one spouse to ask the court to dissolve his/her marriage. *See also* Petition.

Petrochemicals: chemicals made from crude oil and natural gas.

Petrodollars: money deposited by oil-producing countries with financial institutions around the world.

Petroleum: in general, all hydrocarbons. Most often, crude oil.

Petty Cash: cash, often held in small amounts and in currency form, to be used to settle small, day-to-day transactions.

Phantom Stock Plan: a financial incentive plan for senior corporate management based on a certain number of the company's shares. The shares are not actually owned by the individuals in the plan. Share performance is used as a measure to determine the amount of the incentive to be paid. It is similar to having a call option on the shares without having to pay for the option. Also known as Shadow Stock. *See also* Bonus, Bonus Plan, Call Option, Compensation, Perquisite.

Phase Alternate Lines (PAL): a television broadcasting standard common in Asia. *See also* High Definition Television, National Television Standards Committee, Sequential Couleur Avec Memoire, Standard Definition Television.

Philadelphia Lawyer: a very clever lawyer who knows the finer points of the law. Also known as Wall Street Lawyer.

Philadelphia Stock Exchange: a regional U.S. stock exchange located in Philadelphia, Pennsylvania. Web site: www.libertynet.org

Philippines Stock Exchange: the major stock exchange of the Philippines, located in its capital, Manila. Web site: www.pse.com.ph

Philippines Stock Exchange Composite Index: a market capitalization weighted stock price index for the Philippines Stock Exchange.

Phosphor: a solid material, used especially in cathode-ray tubes, that emits visible light when excited by an external energy source such as ultraviolet light. *See also* Cathode-Ray Tube.

Photocell: *see* Photoelectric Cell.

Photoelectric Cell: an electronic device that has an electrical output that varies directly with the incidence of illumination. Also known as Photocell.

Photovoltaic Cell: *see* Solar Cell.

Physical Commodity: the actual commodity, such as copper or coffee, that a seller delivers to the buyer of a commodities contract.

Physical Delivery: the settlement of a commodities contract by the delivery of the physical commodity.

Physically Infirm: in the context of the Canadian Income Tax Act, the condition of a person who, because of a physical problem, is unable to be gainfully employed for a considerable period.

PI: *see* Principal and Interest.

Picket Line: a procession of people staging a public protest, especially union workers on strike. *See also* Strike.

Pickup: *see* Yield Pickup.

Picture: the bid and ask price at which a dealer is willing to buy or sell a security.

Piecework: work paid for by the number of units produced.

Pie Chart: a graph in which a circle, representing the total, is divided into sectors used to represent quantities. *See also* Bar Graph, Point and Figure Chart.

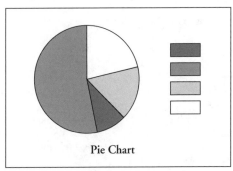

Pie Chart

Pierce the Corporate Veil: to disregard the offending corporate entity and to impose liability on a person (or entity) behind the scenes.

Pig: a greedy investor, as in the old saw, "Bulls make money. Bears make money. Pigs get slaughtered."

Piggyback: a clause that allows one party the same rights as another if certain actions are taken by the latter.

PIK: *see* Payment in Kind.

Pilot Plant: a small-scale plant set up to test the potential for a full-sized plant.

PIN: *see* Personal Identification Number.

Pink Sheets: a publication offered by the National Quotation Bureau, it lists quotes on over-the-counter securities and the market maker's name. Bids on the pink sheets are not firm. Also known as Over-the-Counter Pink Sheets. *See also* Market Maker, National Quotation Bureau, White Sheets, Yellow Sheets.

Pink Slip: notification of dismissal from employment. *See also* Walking Papers.

Pin Money: money for incidental expenses.

Pint: a measure of volume equal to one-half a quart or .47 litres.

Pipeline: 1. a delivery system for crude oil, natural gas and similar products. **2.** all the underwriting procedures that must occur before a public offering of securities. **3.** any long process, as in "It's in the pipeline."

Pirate: someone who makes a profit by infringing on another person's rights (e.g., a copyright or patent).

Pirated Copy: *see* Knock-Off.

PIT: *see* Principal, Interest and Taxes.

Pit: the trading area on the floor of a commodities or stock exchange. Also known as a Ring, especially on a stock exchange floor. *See also* Floor.

Pitch: a line of talk designed to persuade or sell.

Pitfall: a trap that can ensnare an unsuspecting or inexperienced investor or businessperson.

PITI: *see* Principal, Interest, Taxes and Insurance.

Pixel: in computers, the smallest image-forming unit of a video display. *See also* Computer.

Place: to sell a security, often as a new issue.

Placee: the investor buying a security as a new issue.

Placement: the distribution of a security, often as a new issue.

Placer: the sand or gravel left by a river or glacier, it can contain valuable minerals (e.g., gold) in its particles. *See also* Placer Mining.

Placer Mining: mining that involves washing placer with water and allowing the heavier minerals to sink to the bottom of the pan or sluice box. *See also* Open Pit Mining, Pan, Place, Sluice Box, Underground Mining.

Placing Power: a broker's or distributor's ability to sell a security, often as a new issue.

Plaintiff: in law, the party that initiates a legal action. *See also* Defendant.

Plan A: the initial or primary plan. *See also* Plan B.

Plan B: a secondary or emergency plan put into effect when Plan A fails. *See also* Plan A.

Plan Member: a participant in a pension or group insurance plan. *See also* Group Insurance Plan, Registered Pension Plan.

Planned Giving: a method for making charitable donations by prearranging a gift through one's estate. A planned gift is often funded by life insurance taken out by the donor with a charity as the named beneficiary. *See also* Trust.

Planned Obsolescence: a product, such as a car, built so as to experience a change in design or decline in usefulness. Planned obsolescence induces consumers to constantly replace old products with new ones. *See also* Obsolescence.

Plastic: slang for a credit card.

Plant: a company's fixed assets, especially real estate and equipment.

Plateau: a flat, sideways movement in price that occurs after a period of rising prices. The term "plateau" often implies a high point in prices with a decline to come.

Platform: *see* Operating Platform.

Platinum: a metallic element used as a catalyst, in electronics, jewelry and electroplating. Platinum is one of the precious metals. *See also* Precious Metal.

Play: 1. a speculative investment. **2.** the reason for making a speculative investment.

Play the Market: to invest in common stocks or other asset classes.

Plaza Accord: the October 1995 agreement by the finance ministers of France, Germany, Japan, the U.K. and the U.S. to devalue the U.S. dollar. Held at the Plaza Hotel in New York City, the accord is important because Canada's and Italy's objections to being left out of this decision-making process led to their addition and the creation of the Group of Seven. *See also* Group of Seven.

PLC: *see* Public Limited Company.

Plea: in law, a defendant's response to a charge.

Plea Bargain: the act of giving up the right to a trial in order to obtain a reduced charge and/or sentence.

Pleadings: in family law, the written description of each person's claims.

Plebiscite: an election poll that indicates the popular view of the people regarding a particular issue.

Pledge: to put up an asset as security for a loan or obligation. *See also* Negative Pledge.

Pledging Accounts Receivable: *see* Discounting Accounts Receivable.

Plenipotentiary: a diplomat fully authorized to represent his or her government.

Plow Back: to invest money back into a business or project rather than to pay it out as dividends.

Plug and Play: an innovation, developed by Intel, in which hardware is automatically configured to run properly upon being installed in a Windows-based computer. *See also* Computer.

Plug-In: a small software program that is added to a larger application for increased functionality (e.g., on a Web browser such as Netscape Navigator, an audio plug-in accesses and executes the audio playback available from certain Web pages). *See also* Computer.

Plum: a particularly attractive opportunity for a profit.

Plummet: to fall virtually straight down, as in "the market plummeted."

Plunge: a sudden, sharp decline in prices.

Plunger: a person who makes impulsive, speculative investment decisions.

Plurality: in a vote for more than two contestants, the number of votes for the winner if the total is less than half of the total votes cast. *See also* Simple Majority.

Plus Accrued: *see* Price Plus Accrued.

Plus Tick: this occurs when the last trade in a stock takes place at a higher price than the previous trade. Also known as Uptick. *See also* Closing Tick, Minus Tick, Tick, Zero-Minus Tick, Zero-Plus Tick.

Plus-Tick Rule: *see* Rule 10a – 1.

Plutocracy: government by the rich.

Pluton: in mining, a massive intrusion of plutonic rock, sometimes several kilometres in size. *See also* Craton, Plutonic, Volcanic.

Plutonic: pertaining to rocks formed by heat, fusion and crystallization at great depth before coming to the surface. Generally, the opposite of Volcanic. *See also* Volcanic.

PMV: *see* Private Market Value.

PO: *see* Purchase Order.

Point: 1. one dollar on the price of a common stock, as in "It's up a point." **2.** one percent on the amount of a loan, as in "A mortgage free of one point." *See also* Basis Point. **3.** one percent of the par value of a bond (e.g., for a $1,000 par value bond, a point is $10). *See also* Basis Point. **4.** for a stock market index, a point is one unit (e.g., for the Toronto Stock Exchange 300 Index, a rise from 6,900 to 6,950 is a rise of 50 points).

Point and Figure Chart: a chart that plots day-to-day price increases as a rising stack of X's and that plots day-to-day price declines as a declining stack of O's. *See also* Bar Graph, Pie Chart.

Point of Presence: the location from which an Internet service provider provides local Internet access. *See also* Internet, Internet Service Provider.

Point of Sale Technology (POST): equipment, such as highly integrated cash registers, that records sales, changes to inventory and inventory ordering when a sale is made.

Point-to-Point Protocol (PPP): a communications protocol for dial-up networking (e.g., gaining access to the Internet by connecting a computer's modem to an Internet service provider's system). *See also* Internet, Internet Service Provider.

Poison Pill: an arrangement made by a company to discourage an unwanted takeover bid (e.g., the issuing of a convertible preferred stock that shareholders would ordinarily hold for the dividend but would convert in the event of a takeover attempt thus making the acquirer have to purchase many more shares in order to complete the acquisition). Also known as Porcupine Provision, Shark Repellent. *See also* Flip-In Poison Pill, Flip-Over Poison Pill, Jonestown Defense, Killer Bee, Lady Macbeth Strategy, Leveraged Recapitalization, Lobster Trap, Lock-Up Agreement, Macaroni Defense, Pac Man Defense, Pension Parachute, People Pill, Poison Put Bond, Safe Harbour, Scorched Earth Policy, Suicide Pill, White Squire Defence.

Poison Put Bond: a bond that can be cashed in if the issuing company becomes a takeover target. The poison put bond makes a company less attractive to takeover because the bond must be repaid at the same time. This is an attractive feature for the bondholder because it can prevent the issuer from being taken over by a financially weak company. *See also* Poison Pill.

Police State: a state or country whose government applies rigid and repressive controls on its citizenry.

Policy: 1. a general guideline to which corporate behaviour must conform (e.g., family members may not be hired). **2.** *see* Life Insurance Policy.

Policy Conditions: *see* Life Insurance Policy Conditions.

Policy Fee: *see* Life Insurance Policy Fee.

Policy Holder: *see* Life Insurance Policy Holder.

Policy Limit: *see* Life Insurance Policy Limit.

Policy Loan: *see* Life Insurance Policy Loan.

Policy Reserves: *see* Life Insurance Policy Reserves.

Political Risk: an investment risk related to changing government policies. *See also* Country Risk, Risk, Sovereign Risk.

Poll Tax: a fixed amount of tax charged to individuals without reference to income or wealth. Also known as Capitation, Head Tax or Per Capita Tax.

Pony Up: to pay an amount owed.

Ponzi Scheme: a fraud in which money from new investors is used to provide a return to previous investors. The scheme eventually collapses when money owed to former investors exceeds the amount that can be raised from new investors. Named after Charles Ponzi, a con man who perpetrated several such frauds in the 1920s. Also known as Lapping, Pyramid Scheme. *See also* Bre-X Minerals Ltd., Equity Funding Corporation, Prime Bank Note, Salad Oil Scandal, ZZZZ Best.

Pool: a group of people who combine their resources for a common purpose.

Pooling of Interest: an accounting method used when two companies merge by combining assets and liabilities. *See also* Merger, Purchase Method.

Poop: slang for inside information.

Poor-Mouth: to plead poverty in order either to receive funds or avoid giving them.

POP: *see* Post Office Protocol.

Porcupine Provision: *see* Poison Pill.

Pork Barrel: a government project that benefits the proposing legislator's constituents.

Pork Belly: a commodity. Pork bellies are the source of bacon.

Port: in computers, a connection point for a device. *See also* Computer.

Portability: *see* Pension Portability.

Portfolio: 1. most commonly, the financial investments held by an investor (e.g., cash, bonds, common stocks and mutual funds). **2.** a reference to all investments held by an investor.

Portfolio Basket: *see* Market Basket.

Portfolio Beta: the volatility of a portfolio as measured by the beta coefficients of the stocks held. A beta of 1.0 means volatility equal to the overall market. A higher beta means greater volatility; a lower beta means lower volatility. *See also* Beta.

Portfolio Dedication: the act of synchronizing returns on a portfolio with known future liabilities. Also known as Dedicated Portfolio.

Portfolio Dressing: *see* Window Dressing.

Portfolio Effect: a reduction in the variation of returns when assets are combined. The portfolio effect reduces risk below the average risk of the individual assets. *See also* Diversification.

Portfolio Insurance: the use of options or other financial derivatives to hedge a portfolio. *See also* Option.

Portfolio Management: the activities performed by a licensed portfolio manager, including making decisions on buying and selling securities owned. Also known as Money Management.

Portfolio Management Style: the general approach used by a portfolio manager. Also known as Management Style. *See also* Bottom-Up, Growth Investor, Sector Rotation, Top Down, Value Investor.

Portfolio Manager: a professional advisor licensed to make discretionary investment decisions on behalf of another individual or individuals. Also known as Professional Portfolio Manager.

Portfolio Optimization: maximizing the expected portfolio return for a given level of risk or minimizing the risk for a given level of expected return. *See also* Efficient Frontier, Efficient Portfolio, Modern Portfolio, Modern Portfolio Theory.

Portfolio Rebalancing: as prices for individual securities change over time, so do the respective percentage positions in a portfolio for a stock or industry grouping. If the objective is, for example, to hold 5 percent of the portfolio in Stock A or Industry B, and the position varies, then the process of restoring the holding to 5 percent by buying or selling shares is called portfolio rebalancing. Also known as Rebalancing.

Portfolio Tab: *see* Portfolio Tabulation.

Portfolio Tabulation: a current statement of a portfolio, including up-to-date prices, interest and dividends. Also known as Portfolio Tab.

Portfolio Theory: *see* Modern Portfolio.

Portfolio Turnover: a measure of how frequently securities in a portfolio are bought and sold. A portfolio turnover of 25 percent means one-quarter of the portfolio is bought and sold each year. This implies an average holding period of four years for a position in the portfolio. Also known as Turnover.

Portrait Mode: in computers, a printer setting that will print documents across the shorter side of the page. *See also* Landscape Mode.

Position: 1. to expose a person or portfolio to a desired outcome, as in "Position the portfolio for a higher gold price." **2.** the extent to which an investor is exposed to a market, as in "He has taken a position in gold."

Position Building: *see* Scale In.

Positioning: the act of taking or building a position.

Position Trader: in commodities, an investor who buys a position for the long term. In commodities, the long term is generally six months to one year.

Positive Alpha: a security or portfolio that is providing or is expected to provide a higher return than the average return from stocks or portfolios of similar risk. Also known as High Alpha.

Positive Carry: this occurs when the interest earned on an investment exceeds the interest owed on the money borrowed to make the investment. *See also* Negative Carry.

Positive Covenant: a contractual clause to do something. *See also* Negative Covenant.

Positive Yield Curve: a situation in which interest rates on securities with shorter terms to maturity are lower than are yields on securities with longer terms to maturity. Also known as Normal Yield Curve, Upsloping Yield Curve. *See also* Negative Yield Curve, Yield Curve.

Possessory Right: a right that gives each spouse equal entitlement to the matrimonial home. *See also* Matrimonial Home.

Possible Reserves: in mining, the lowest category of measurable reserves (i.e., behind proven and probable). *See also* Probable Reserves, Proven Reserves, Resource, Three P's.

Post: 1. in accounting, the act of entering a transaction to the ledger. **2.** *see* Trading Post. **3.** *see* Point of Sale Technology.

Post 30: a special New York Stock Exchange trading post for inactive stocks and odd lots.

Postdate: to date a financial instrument or document, especially a cheque, later than the date on which it was signed or issued (e.g., a postdated cheque). *See also* Antedate.

Posting: in accounting, the transfer of data to the general ledger. *See also* General Ledger.

Post Office Protocol (POP): a standard that enables servers on the Internet to function as post offices for e-mail users. *See also* Internet, Server.

Pot: securities from a new issue that are returned to the syndicate manager by syndicate members are said to be "back in the pot." *See also* Pot is Clean, Syndicate, Syndicate Manager.

Potential Dilution: the decrease that occurs in the proportional equity position when additional authorized shares are issued.

Pot Is Clean: an indication from the syndicate manager of a new issue that no securities have been returned or that those that have been returned have been sold. *See also* Pot, Syndicate, Syndicate Manager.

Pound: 1. the prime currency of Britain, Canton & Enderbury Islands, Cyprus, Egypt, Falkland Islands, Gibraltar, Lebanon, St. Helena, Sudan, Syria. **2.** a unit of weight equal to 16 ounces or .45 kilograms.

Poverty: the state of being poor. In 1997, the Statistics Canada poverty income levels for a major metropolitan area were:

One person	$16,318
Two people	$22,117
Three people	$28,115
Four people	$32,372

Power of Attorney (PA): a document authorizing a person to sign a legal document, vote or generally act on behalf of another. *See also* Durable Power of Attorney, Stock Power, Testamentary Capacity, Trading Authorization.

Powwow: a conference or meeting, usually of senior management.

PPI: *see* Producers' Price Index.

PPP: *see* Point-to-Point Protocol.

PR: *see* Public Relations.

Practice: the work or business of a professional person (e.g., an accountant or doctor).

Practice Insurance: general and liability insurance for dentists, doctors, lawyers and other professionals. Also known as Professional Indemnity Insurance, Professional Liability Insurance.

Prague Stock Exchange (PSE): the major stock exchange of the Czech Republic, located in its capital, Prague. Web site: www.pse.cz *See also* PX50.

Pre-Approved Mortgage: preliminary approval from a lender for a mortgage at a set interest rate and maximum amount subject to certain terms and conditions. *See also* Mortgage.

Preauthorized Cheque (PAC): a voided cheque used to set up a preauthorized payment plan through which an individual allows a stated amount of money to be automatically withdrawn from his/her account on a regular basis. PACs are popular in the mutual fund industry for investors who wish to invest a fixed amount each month. *See also* Preauthorized Payment Plan.

Preauthorized Payment Plan: a plan in which an individual allows a fixed amount of money to be withdrawn from his/her account on a regular basis. Preauthorized payment plans are popular for dollar cost averaging mutual funds or to pay regular insurance premiums. *See also* Dollar Cost Averaging, Preauthorized Cheque.

Precedence of Order: the rules governing the priority sequence of orders to buy or sell a security. In general, the rules give higher bids precedence over lower bids, lower offerings have precedence over higher offerings, first bids and offerings have precedence over others at the same price and large orders have precedence over small orders. Also known as Priority. *See also* Order.

Precedent: in law, a previous judicial decision used as an authoritative rule in similar subsequent cases.

Precious Metal: generally, any of the metals gold, iridium, palladium, platinum and silver. *See also* Gold, Iridium, Palladium, Platinum, Silver.

Precious Metals Fund: *see* Global Precious Metals Fund.

Predate: *see* Antedate.

Predatory Practice: the action by a firm or firms with the intention to drive a competitor out of business.

A common predatory practice is predatory pricing. *See also* Predatory Pricing.

Predatory Pricing: the setting of artificially low prices by a firm or firms with the intention of driving a competitor out of business. Once the competitor has been eliminated, prices are allowed to move back up. *See also* Predatory Practice.

Pre-Empt: to settle on public land in order to acquire the right to buy ahead of others.

Pre-Emptive Right: a shareholder's ability to maintain a proportionate interest in the ownership of a company when the latter offers additional shares for sale (e.g., a shareholder owning 10 percent of a company has a pre-emptive right to buy 10 percent of any new offering of shares in order to maintain a 10 percent interest). In most public companies, shareholders waive their pre-emptive right at the annual general meeting.

Prefabricate: to manufacture (e.g., a building or its parts) ahead of time so that construction consists mainly of assembly.

Prefabricated Housing: to manufacture a building or its parts ahead of time so that construction consists of assembly. *See also* Manufactured Home.

Prefeasibility Stage: in mine development, the period after extensive, successful exploration but before the commissioning of a formal feasibility study. *See also* Feasibility Study, Prefeasibility Study.

Prefeasibility Study: a study that is less detailed and less expensive than a feasibility study. A prefeasibility study is often used to raise the money needed to carry operations though to the feasibility report. *See also* Feasibility Study, Prefeasibility Stage.

Preference: the improper satisfaction of one creditor's claim over another's.

Preference Share: *see* Preferred Share.

Preferred Creditor: a creditor who has prior claims over others. *See also* Secured Creditor.

Preferred Dividend Coverage: a financial ratio indicating the level of security of a preferred dividend. It is calculated as net income divided by the dollar amount of preferred dividends. *See also* Preferred Share.

Preferred Lives: persons in exceptionally good health who may be eligible to pay lower premiums for insurance. *See also* Life Insurance.

Preferred Preferred Share: a preferred share with priority over all other preferred shares issued by a company. Also known as Preferred Prior Share. *See also* Preferred Share, Prior Preferred Share.

Preferred Premium Class: in life insurance, a better than normal risk class (e.g., nonsmokers). *See also* Life Insurance.

Preferred Prior Share: *see* Preferred Preferred Share.

Preferred Share: a class of share capital. Preferred shares are usually issued with a par value and a fixed dividend rate. Preferred shares have a prior or preferred claim over common shares as to dividends. This means the dividends on preferred shares must be paid before any dividends can be paid on common shares. Preferred shares also have a prior claim over common shares if a company is being wound up. Usually, the par value of the preferred must be distributed to holders before any distribution can be made to common shareholders. *See also* Common Share, Convertible Preferred Share, Cumulative Preferred Share, Dividend Enhanced Convertible Stock, Extendable Preferred Share, First Preferred Share, Floating Rate Preferred Share, Junior, Noncumulative Preferred Share, Participating Preferred Share, Redeemable Preferred Share, Retractable Preferred Share, Second Preferred Share.

Preferred Shareholder: an owner of preferred shares.

"Pre-In" Country: a member of the European Community that did not initially participate in the single currency. Also known as "Out" Country. *See also* Euro, European Community, "In" Country, "Out" Country.

Preliminary Prospectus: the initial form of a prospectus, which underwriters often use to judge investor interest in a new issue. It does not include pricing and does not offer securities for sale. Also known as Red Herring. *See also* Final Prospectus, Prospectus.

Premier: in Canada, the first minister of a province or territory. *See also* Member of the Legislative Assembly.

Premium: 1. in bonds, the amount by which the market price or redemption price is above the par value. *See also* Above Par, Bond. **2.** in insurance, the amount paid for coverage. *See also* Insurance Premium, Life Insurance Premium. **3.** in options, the amount paid for a put or call. *See also* Call Option, Option, Option Premium, Put Option. **4.** *see* Time Value. **5.** for convertibles, the amount by which the market price exceeds the conversion value. **6.** in new issues, the amount by which the market price is above the offering price. *See also* Offering Price.

Premium Bond: a bond that trades above par value.

Premium Income: the proceeds from the sale of either a put or a call option. *See also* Option.

Premium Over Bond Value: the amount by which the market price of a convertible bond of a company exceeds the price that such a bond would sell for without the conversion privilege. *See also* Convertible Bond.

Premium Over Conversion Value: *see* Conversion Premium.

Premium Raid: an attempt to gain control of a company by offering to purchase common shares at a price higher than the market price.

Prenup: *see* Prenuptial Agreement.

Prenuptial Agreement: a written contract providing for the rights and obligations of spouses during marriage and upon separation, divorce or death. Prenuptial agreements may not stand up to a legal challenge. Also known as Marriage Contract, Prenup.

Pre-Owned: a term often applied instead of "used" with regard to high-end consumer products (e.g., expensive cars).

Prepackage: to package a product before retail.

Prepaid Expense: an asset representing amounts paid in advance (e.g., fire insurance).

Prepayment: 1. payment of an obligation before it is due. **2.** payment for a future benefit. The amount of the prepayment creates an asset on the balance sheet which is reduced in value as the benefit is realized. *See also* Prepaid Expense. **3.** *see* Prepayment Penalty.

Prepayment Charge: *see* Prepayment Penalty.

Prepayment Clause: 1. a clause granting the right, without penalty, to make additional principal payments on a mortgage. *See also* Anticipation, Anticipation Rate, Mortgage, Mortgage Prepayment, Penalty, Prepayment, Prepayment Penalty, Prepayment Privilege, Right of Anticipation. **2.** a clause that describes the penalties that will be charged if a mortgage is prepaid. *See also* Mortgage, Mortgage Prepayment.

Prepayment Penalty: a penalty charged when a mortgage is paid off early. A standard prepayment penalty for a mortgage is three months' interest. Also known as Prepayment Charge. *See also* Anticipation, Anticipation Rate, Interest Rate Differential Penalty, Mortgage, Mortgage Prepayment, Penalty, Prepayment, Prepayment Clause, Prepayment Privilege, Right of Anticipation.

Prepayment Privilege: the mortgage clause that gives a borrower the right to prepay some or all of the mortgage without penalty. Also known as Right of Anticipation. *See also* Anticipation, Anticipation Rate, Mortgage, Mortgage Prepayment, Penalty, Prepayment, Prepayment Clause, Prepayment Penalty.

Presale Estimate: an auctioneer's estimate of the selling value of an item or items for sale. *See also* Auction, Reserve Bid.

Presentment: 1. delivery of a negotiable instrument for payment. **2.** in law, the act of presenting a statement with respect to an issue before the court.

Present Value: the lump sum today that is equal to an income stream in the future at a given rate of investment return (e.g., if interest rates are 10 percent, $1.00 due in one year is worth $.909 today because $.909 can be invested at 10 percent, to be worth $1.00 in one year. For the same reason, $1.00 in two years has a present value of $.8264, and the present value of $1,000 a year for the next 10 years is $6,000). *See also* Net Present Value, Time Value of Money.

Present Value Table: a financial table, in book form, that provides the present value of $1.00 (and $1.00 per annum) for a given number of years at different rates of interest. *See also* Future Value Table, Present Value.

Preservation of Capital: an investment objective in which not losing money takes priority over making high profits. *See also* Capital Appreciation, Income.

Preservation of Purchasing Power: one of the principal investment objectives. The likelihood that an investment will at least offset the effect of inflation. *See also* Purchasing Power, Safety of Capital, Safety of Income.

Preside: to be in a position of authority, especially as the chair of a meeting.

President: a senior officer of a company, this person is appointed by the board of directors. *See also* Chief Executive Officer, Chief Operating Officer, Vice-President.

Presidential Election Cycle: a theory put forward by Yale Hirsch, editor of *Stock Trader's Almanac*. It states that the stock market is weakest in the year following the election of a new U.S. president. After that, the market improves until the next election. The strongest year is the third year of the four-year cycle. *See also* Bear Market, Bull Market, Elliott Wave Theory, Kondratieff Wave, Peak, Stock Market Cycle, Stock Trader's Almanac.

Presold: 1. a new security issue that is sold out before all its specifics have been announced. **2.** in real estate, the sale of property before construction is completed.

Press Release: a formal announcement of a newsworthy event, issued by an official source. Companies use press releases to disseminate information in a timely fashion. *See also* Disseminate Information, Timely Dissemination.

Pretax: before taxes, as in "pretax income."

Pretax Income: income before payment of taxes. *See also* After Tax Income.

Pretax Return: the rate of return on investment before taking into account payment of income. Also known as Pretax Yield. *See also* After Tax Return.

Pretax Yield: *see* Pretax Return.

Previous Balance Method: the calculation of finance costs or interest payable based on the amount owing at the end of the last payment period. This method is used by many general-purpose credit cards. *See also* Adjusted Balance Method, Average Daily Balance Method, Minimum Monthly Balance, Past Due Balance Method.

Price: 1. the amount of money for which a thing is bought or sold. **2.** in economics, the value per unit that prevails when supply equals demand. **3.** to establish the price at which a new issue of securities will be sold, as in "Price the new issue." **4.** the amount of money needed to induce a person to do something (e.g., change jobs), as in "We met his price."

Price Alert: in technical analysis, when a stock rises or falls in price to a resistance point. A price alert warns investors that action may be called for soon. *See also* Resistance Level, Technical Analysis.

Price Averaging: *see* Averaging.

Price Change: the difference in the price of a security at the close of a trading session from the price at the close of a previous trading session.

Price Conscious: sensitive to price when buying or selling. *See also* Elasticity of Demand.

Price Control: 1. the ability to set artificial prices, often by a business in a monopoly or oligopoly position. *See also* Monopoly, Natural Monopoly, Oligopoly, Oligopsony. **2.** *see* Wage and Price Controls.

Priced In: expectations reflected in current security prices, as in "the stock has priced in higher earnings."

Priced Out: a price that is so high, no one will pay it.

Price/Earnings Ratio (P/E): a statistic calculated by dividing the price of a common share by its earnings per share. The higher the price/earnings ratio, the more that is being paid for each dollar of earnings. High P/E stocks are generally expected to grow faster. The P/E ratio is a basic stock valuation measure. Also known as Multiple, Price to Earnings Ratio. *See also* Price to Sales Ratio.

Price/Earnings to Growth Ratio (PEG Ratio): a ratio calculated as a price earnings ratio divided by the rate of growth in sales or earnings. Generally, a ratio of one or less means the stock is not overvalued.

Price Fixing: an illegal activity in which competing manufacturers conspire to set the price of a product or service higher than it would be under normal competitive conditions.

Price Freeze: an artificial restraint usually set by a government or government body that prevents the price of a good or service from being raised. A price freeze differs from wage and price controls in that the former is used selectively while the latter is applied generally. *See* Wage and Price Controls.

Price Gap: *see* Gap.

Price Hike: an increase in price.

Price History: for a security, the prices it has sold for in the past.

Price Index: *see* Consumer Price Index.

Price Inflation: *see* Inflation.

Price Leader: a dominant supplier of a product or service, it has the power to set or influence prices.

Price Limit: 1. the highest price a broker may pay for a security or the lowest price a broker may sell a security on behalf of a client. **2.** the maximum price change allowed for a commodity price during a trading session. Also known as Limit. *See also* Limit Down, Limit Up.

Price Plus Accrued: a common pricing method in bond trading, in which the buyer pays the price plus interest accrued to the date of purchase. At the next interest payment date, the buyer receives the entire interest payment. Because interest accrued to the date of purchase was paid, the net interest received is the correct amount for the balance of the period. The bond is said to trade "price plus accrued." Also known as And Interest, Plus Accrued. *See also* Dirty Price, Selling Flat.

Price Range: within a given period, the prices that fall between the highest price and lowest price. Also known as Range. *See also* Trading Range.

Price Sensitive: a term used to describe a person (or decision) for whom price is a very important variable.

Price Spread: 1. *see* Spread.

Price Support: a policy by which government establishes a price minimum, or support price, for certain products (usually agricultural). If the price falls below the minimum, then the government buys at the support price or pays the difference to the producer. *See also* Support Price.

Price Taker: an investor whose transactions are so small they do not influence the market.

Price Target: *see* Target Price.

Price Tick: *see* Minimum Fluctuation.

Price to Book Value: a measure of the value of a stock that compares the market price per share to the book value per share. The lower the ratio, the better the value. *See also* Book Value, Book Value Per Share.

Price to Earnings Ratio: *see* Price/Earnings Ratio.

Price to Sales Ratio: a statistic calculated by dividing a company's price per share by sales per share. This if often used to evaluate companies that do not have earnings, which makes the price/earnings ratio meaningless. The higher the price to sales ratio, the more being paid for each dollar of sales, and vice versa.

The lower the ratio, the better the value. *See also* Price/Earnings Ratio.

Price War: a period of intense competition in which prices are reduced even if it means selling at a loss.

Price Weighted Stock Market Index: an index based on the change in the prices of the component stocks. The higher the price of the stock, the larger the impact on such indexes. The Dow-Jones Industrial Average is price weighted. *See also* Dow-Jones Industrial Average.

Pricey: a term used mainly to describe an offer to sell that is too high. Used occasionally to describe an offer to buy that is too low.

Prima Facie Case: a case based on prima facie evidence. *See also* Prima Facie Evidence.

Prima Facie Evidence: evidence that proves a fact at issue, unless it is overcome by other evidence; that is, evidence that is obvious or accepted. *See also* Prima Facie Case.

Primary: *see* Primary Offering.

Primary Distribution: *see* Primary Offering.

Primary Earnings Per Share: net income after taxes and preferred dividends divided by the number of common shares outstanding.

Primary Issue: *see* Primary Offering.

Primary Market: the market in which underwriters sell newly issued securities. This stands in contrast to the secondary market, in which previously issued securities are traded. In the primary market, the proceeds from the sale of securities accrue to the treasury of the company. In Canada, the primary market represents about 2 percent of total trading. *See also* Aftermarket, Secondary Market.

Primary Memory: the section of a computer's memory in which frequently used instructions and data are stored. *See also* Compression, Computer, Conventional Memory, Data, Data Bank, Database, Datawarehouse, Memory, Memory Unit, Random Access Memory, Read-Only Memory, Save, Secondary Memory.

Primary Offering: the first time a company sells a particular security to the public. Also known as Primary, Primary Distribution, Primary Issue, Public Offering. *See also* Initial Public Offering, Secondary Offering, Second Round Financing.

Primary Trend: the overriding trend, ignoring small, short-term fluctuations. *See also* Trend.

Prime Bank Note: a non-existent security that has been offered for sale in financial frauds both on and off the Internet during the late 1990s. *See also* Bre-X Minerals, Equity Funding Corporation, Salad Oil Scandal, ZZZZ Best.

Prime Lending Rate: *see* Prime Rate.

Prime Minister: the chief executive of a parliamentary democracy. *See also* House of Commons, Member of Parliament, Senate, Senator.

Prime Paper: the highest quality commercial paper. *See also* Commercial Paper.

Prime Plus: a rate of interest calculated off the prime rate (e.g., prime plus one is the prime rate plus one percent). *See also* Prime Rate.

Prime Rate: the rate of interest that chartered banks charge most credit-worthy customers. Everyone else is charged higher interest, which is expressed as "prime plus" (e.g., prime rate of interest plus one percent). The prime rate is important because it is sensitive to changes in the Bank of Canada's monetary policy (e.g., a rise in the bank rate will often result in a similar rise in the prime rate, which will then push up lending rates throughout the banking and financial sector). Also known as Prime Lending Rate. *See also* Bank Rate, Bank of Canada, Prime Plus.

Prince Edward Island: *see* Canada's Provinces and Territories.

Principal: 1. the party an agent represents. *See also* Agent. **2.** *see* Principal Amount. **3.** a broker-dealer when purchasing for his/her own account. *See also* Broker-Dealer. **4.** any major party to a transaction that is buying or selling for his/her own account.

Principal Amount: 1. the par value of a bond. **2.** the original sum of money invested or lent. Also known as Principal.

Principal and Interest (PI): a term used to denote that a mortgage payment covers principal and interest but not taxes or insurance. *See also* Principal, Interest and Taxes; Principal, Interest, Taxes and Insurance.

Principal, Interest and Taxes (PIT): a term used to denote that a mortgage payment covers principal, interest and taxes but not insurance. *See also* Principal and Interest; Principal, Interest, Taxes and Insurance.

Principal, Interest, Taxes and Insurance (PITI): a term used to denote that a mortgage payment covers principal, interest, taxes and insurance. *See also* Principal and Interest; Principal, Interest and Taxes.

Principal Residence: the one property per household where an individual or family usually resides. Also known as Residence. *See also* Principal Residence Exemption, Recreational Property, Retirement Property.

Principal Residence Exemption: an exemption under the Canadian Income Tax Act by which individual taxpayers or a family can designate a property as a principal residence in order to be exempt from tax on capital gains. A principal residence is generally the home and up to one-half a hectare of land. For income tax purposes, a principal residence does not have to be in Canada. *See also* Taxes.

Principals: major shareholders, investors or owners.

Principal Shareholder: a shareholder owning more than 10 percent of a company's shares, or the shareholder with the largest single ownership position.

Print: 1. in the stock market, a confirmation that an order has been filled, as in "That's a print." **2.** in computers, the function that activates a printing device. *See also* Computer, Printer.

Printed Circuit Board: an insulated board on which chips and other electronic components are mounted. *See also* Chip.

Printer: a common output device for computers, it converts electronic data into words or images and prints them on paper or another medium (e.g., transparency film). *See also* Cathode-Ray Tube, Computer, Computer Screen, Disk Drive, Input/Output Device, Interactive Terminal, Joystick, Keyboard, Keypad, Laser Printer, Line Printer, Monitor, Optical Character Recognition, Peripheral, Printout, Readout, Remote Access, Terminal.

Printer Driver: in computers, the software that controls printers. *See also* Computer, Printer.

Printout: in computers, any printed output. Also known as Hard Copy. *See also* Computer.

Priority: *see* Precedence of Order.

Prior Lien: a mortgage or debt that has a prior claim over other mortgages or obligations. *See also* Lien.

Prior Preferred Share: a preferred share that is issued and will remain senior to any subsequent preferred and common shares issued. *See also* Preferred Preferred Share, Preferred Share.

Private Automatic Branch Exchange (PABX): a private telephone exchange installed on the user's premises that transmits from the public telephone system throughout the PABX or from the PABX to the public telephone system. *See also* Private Branch Exchange.

Private Branch Exchange (PBX): a telephone switching system on the user's premises that allows private telephones on the PBX to connect directly to each other and also the public telephone network. *See also* Private Automatic Branch Exchange.

Private Company: a company that has not sold ownership shares to the public. *See also* Public Company.

Private Distribution: the distribution of a company's securities to a small group of investors.

Private Enterprise: business activities owned and operated with minimal input or interference from government.

Private Key: one of the two keys in public key encryption. The user keeps the private key secret and uses it to encrypt digital signatures and decrypt messages. Also known as Secret Key. *See also* Access Control, Authentication, Biometric Authentication, Challenge-Response Token, Computer, Encryption, Fire Wall, Password, Public Key.

Private Label: a generic product (e.g., potato chips) manufactured specifically for a retailer and bearing the retailer's name.

Privately Held: describes the ownership of a company that has never sold shares to the public. *See also* Private Company.

Private Market Value (PMV): an estimate of a company's value if each of its operations was a separate company with its own shares traded on a stock exchange. Also known as Break-Up Value, Takeover Value.

Private Placement: a sale of securities by a company directly to investors. Prior registration with a stock exchange or securities commission is usually not required, though investors may have to attest to having a certain degree of investment sophistication and the securities purchased may be subject to a hold period. *See also* Hold Period, Sophisticated Investor.

Private Property: the right of ownership or use that is protected and limited by law. *See also* Personal Property, Property, Public Domain, Public Property.

Private Sector: the part of the economy owned and controlled by individuals as opposed to the government. *See also* Public Sector.

Privatization: the transfer of government-owned assets into private hands. *See also* Nationalization.

Privy: in law, a party to or one having an interest in an action or matter, including a contract.

Privy Council: a council appointed by the governor general to advise the government of Canada and, by convention, the federal cabinet.

Privy Council Office (PCO): a federal government department that serves the prime minister. The main functions include coordinating the cabinet and its committees, preparing material for the prime minister and working with government departments on cabinet matters.

Privy Purse: the allocation from a budget to fund the private expenses of a monarch.

Pro: a term applied to registered representatives or employees of investment firms. In any activity involving the buying and selling of securities, client orders have priority over pro orders. *See also* Pro Order, Pro Trading.

Probability: the likelihood, expressed as a percentage, that an event will occur.

Probability Distribution: the distribution of possible outcomes to an event, illustrated in terms of the probability of each. *See also* Confidence Coefficient, Normal Distribution, Standard Error.

Probable Reserves: in mining, the middle category of measurable reserves (i.e., behind proven and ahead of possible). *See also* Possible Reserves, Proven Reserves, Resource, Three P's.

Probate: a legal process whereby a deceased person's will is presented to the court and an executor is designated to carry out its terms. *See also* Disclosure Statement, Letters Probate, Will.

Probate Division of the Supreme Court: the court responsible for resolving problems arising during the administration of estates. *See also* Letters Probate, Will.

Probate Filing Fee: a fee of $14 per $1,000, it is charged in British Columbia on assets passing through an estate. *See also* Letters Probate, Will.

Probation: in law, a system of dealing with offenders (usually young or first-time offenders convicted of less serious crimes) who are released on condition of good behaviour and under the supervision of a probation officer rather than being imprisoned. *See also* Parole.

Pro Bono: for the public good. If a lawyer works "pro bono," he/she does not charge a fee.

Proceeds: 1. the amount received after selling an asset and paying all fees and commissions. **2.** the amount of money a borrower receives from a loan after deducting costs (e.g., underwriting fee).

Processor: *see* Central Processing Unit.

Producer: 1. a broker who generates large commissions for a brokerage firm. **2.** *see* Production Company.

Producers' Price Index (PPI): a measure of the change in U.S. wholesale prices. Formerly called the Wholesale Price Index.

Product: something that is grown or produced, usually for sale.

Product Liability Insurance: insurance to protect a business from customers harmed by their products.

Production Company: 1. in resources, a company engaged in production, usually in large amounts. Also known as Producer. **2.** in the film industry, a company that produces movies. *See also* Development, Exploration Company, Integrated Oil Company, Oil Company, Refining and Marketing.

Production Platform: *see* Oil Platform.

Productivity: the output of goods and services per unit of input (e.g., the number of person-hours of labour it takes to assemble one automobile). *See also* Labour Productivity, Person-Hour, Productivity of Capital.

Productivity of Capital: the physical output of the economy, industry or business unit divided by the value of capital stock (i.e., buildings, machinery and equipment and technology. *See also* Labour Productivity, Productivity.

Product Mix: the composition of goods and services produced and/or sold by a firm.

Product Pipeline: the process by which a company produces and introduces new products.

Profession: an occupation (usually white-collar), especially one that requires study and training (e.g., accounting, teaching, law). *See also* White-Collar.

Professional: 1. a person duly licensed to buy and sell securities for clients. **2.** a qualified advisor. **3.** a person working in a profession. *See also* Profession.

Professional Corporation: a company that provides professional services, such as dental care, architectural services or legal advice.

Professional Fees: fees paid to a professional group (e.g., Canadian Institute of Chartered Accountants). Normally, annual professional fees are deductible for income tax purposes. *See also* Deductible Expense.

Professional Indemnity Insurance: *see* Practice Insurance.

Professional Liability Insurance: *see* Practice Insurance.

Professional Portfolio Manager: *see* Portfolio Manager.

Professional Trading: *see* Pro Trading.

Proffer: in law, to put forward a proposal for acceptance.

Profit: 1. the amount by which, through its normal business activities, a company's revenues exceed its expenses. *See also* Gross Profit, Net Profit, Profitability. **2.** the amount earned on an investment. *See also* Gross Profit, Net Profit.

Profitability: the ability to generate profit, as measured relative to a particular standard (e.g., shareholder's equity). *See also* Profit.

Profit and Loss Statement (P&L): a financial statement that calculates profit or loss for a fixed period. Also known as Earnings Statement, Income Statement. *See also* Balance Sheet, Statement of Changes in Financial Position, Statement of Retained Earnings, Source and Application of Funds Statement.

Profit Centre: any department, division, branch, region or identifiable part of a company that is responsible for its own profit. Usually, profit will be calculated as the revenue less expenses less an allocation of indirect expenses. *See also* Indirect Expense, Profit.

Profit Margin: 1. the difference between the total cost of buying or producing something and the pro-

ceeds from selling it. Also known as Margin of Profit. **2.** the net income of a business as a percentage of sales. *See also* Gross Profit Margin, Net Profit Margin.

Profit Motive: the idea that the primary motivating force in a free market economy is the ability to realize a profit in return for one's efforts.

Profit Sharing Plan: a plan in which employees are paid bonuses by participating in a business' net profit, the level of participation being in accordance with their contribution to the generation of the profit in question. *See also* Bonus, Deferred Profit Sharing Plan.

Profit Squeeze: a reduction in earnings that results from a poor business climate, increased competition or rising costs. *See also* Profit Taking.

Profit Taker: an investor who is easily induced to sell a security as it begins to rise in price. *See also* Profit Taking.

Profit Taking: the selling of a stock in order to realize a profit, often shortly after an increase in prices. A drop in prices after a rally is often attributed to profit taking. *See also* Profit Taker, Rally, Reaction.

Pro Forma: 1. provided in advance of goods supplied (e.g., pro forma invoice). **2.** *see* Pro Forma Financial Statement. **3.** a fininical statement that does not reflect the write-off of goodwill as required under generally accepted accounting principles. *See also* Generally Accepted Accounting Principles, Goodwill.

Pro Forma Financial Statement: a financial statement put together to reflect a proposed or planned change.

Program: a set of instructions that can be executed by a computer. *See also* Computer.

Program Buying: the buying of shares, often triggered automatically by a computer program, that occurs when spreads widen between stock and option prices. *See also* Arbitrage Trading Program, Option, Program Selling, Program Trading.

Programmer: one who writes computer programs. *See also* Computer, Cracker, Hacker.

Program Selling: the selling of shares, often triggered automatically by a computer program, that occurs when spreads narrow between stock and option prices. *See also* Arbitrage Trading Program, Option, Program Buying, Program Trading.

Program Trading: the buying and selling of large numbers of shares, often triggered automatically by a computer program, that occurs according to the spreads between stock and option prices. Program trading is blamed for the stock market crash of October 19, 1987. *See also* Arbitrage Trading, Crash of '87, Major Market Index, Program, Option, Program Buying, Program Selling.

Progressive Income Tax: a system that takes a larger share of income tax from those who report higher amounts of reported income. Canada's income tax is a progressive tax. Also known as Graduated Income Tax. *See also* Ability to Pay, Effective Tax Rate, Income Tax, Negative Income Tax, Progressive Tax, Regressive Tax.

Progressive Tax: a system in which a larger share of tax is taken from high-income individuals than from individuals with moderate or low income. *See also* Ability to Pay, Luxury Tax, Progressive Income Tax, Regressive Tax.

Progress Payments: payments made at fixed intervals as a job moves toward completion. Progress payments are common in the construction industry.

Project Financing: the arrangement of debt (usually non-recourse) from lending institutions for the development and construction of a new project.

Projection: *see* Forecast.

Prolific: producing in abundance, often used in the context of oil and gas production.

Promissory Note: a written commitment to pay the holder of the note a specific sum of money on a specific date.

Promoter: 1. an intermediary who represents ventures to develop business. **2.** *see* Stock Promoter.

Promotion: in the stock market, a program that includes mailing information, advertising and/or conducting a series of seminars with potential investors in order to generate interest in a stock. *See also* Investor Relations. **2.** in business, an appointment to a more senior or better paying position than the one currently held.

Prompt: 1. in computers, a symbol on the monitor that indicates where to enter commands. In MS-DOS, the prompt usually follows a letter that identifies the drive being used. The hard drive prompt is usually "c:>" *See also* MS-DOS. **2.** in computers, text that indicates, sometimes in the form of a question, that the computer is waiting for further input from the user. *See also* Computer.

Pro Order: an order to buy or sell a security for a registered representative or employee of a brokerage firm. Client orders have priority over pro orders. *See also* Pro, Pro Trading.

Propane: a colourless, paraffinic gas occuring in petroleum.

Property: 1. *see* Personal Property. **2.** *see* Private Property. **3.** *see* Real Estate.

Property Assessment: an estimate of a property's value for the purpose of calculating taxes payable. *See also* Assessed Value, Mill Rate, Property Tax.

Property Inventory: in financial planning, a list of personal property including both the cost and market value. For insurance and tax purposes, pictures of the more valuable items should be kept on file. *See also* Financial Planning.

Property Tax: a municipal tax levied on the value of land and buildings. *See also* Ad Valorem Tax, Appraisal, Assessed Value, Mill Rate, Property Assessment.

Property Transfer Tax: a provincial tax in British Columbia charged when ownership of a property changes.

Proportional Representation: *see* Cumulative Voting.

Proportional Tax: *see* Flat Tax.

Proposal: a formal plan put forward by a debtor under the laws of bankruptcy. The debtor gives notice and then must put forward a plan within 30 days. If the plan is approved by half the creditors representing two-thirds of the debt, the plan is accepted and is binding on all creditors. *See also* Bankrupt, Bankruptcy, Creditor's Committee.

Proprietary: an exclusive right to something.

Proprietary Drug: a drug that a company owns exclusively under a trademark or patent.

Proprietary Process: an exclusively owned process or method of doing something.

Proprietary Product: a product owned exclusively by a person or company (e.g., a proprietary drug).

Proprietor: the sole owner of an unincorporated business. *See also* Sole Proprietorship.

Proprietorship: *see* Sole Proprietorship.

Pro Rata: a proportionate allocation.

Prosecute: 1. to initiate a court action. **2.** to represent those who initiate a court action.

Prosecutor: a public official who prosecutes those accused of a crime.

Prospect: 1. a potential customer or client. *See also* Cold Call, Suspect. **2.** to try to find new customers or clients. *See also* Prospecting.

Prospecting: 1. looking for potential customers or clients. **2.** looking for undiscovered natural resources.

Prospectus: a securities disclosure document that provides full, true and plain disclosure of all facts that may materially affect the market price of an issuer's securities (including the securities proposed to be issued). A prospectus must be prepared in accordance with governing securities legislation and disclose all required information. *See also* Condensed Prospectus, Final Prospectus, Offering Memorandum, Preliminary Prospectus, Right of Rescission, Simplified Prospectus, Summary Prospectus.

Protected Strategy: an investment strategy whose goal is to limit risk.

Protectionism: a government policy of administering high tariffs on imports in order to protect domestic producers. *See also* Tariff.

Pro Tem: for the time being.

Protocol: 1. in computers, a set of rules governing the way data are transmitted. *See also* Computer. **2.** a code of conduct, especially one followed by diplomats. *See also* Diplomat.

Protocol Amending the Canada-U.S. Tax Treaty: a new section of the Canada-U.S. Tax Convention, which became effective January 1, 1996. *See also* Convention Between the United States of America and Canada with Respect to Taxes on Income and Capital.

Prototype: the original model, after which copies are patterned.

Pro Trading: the buying and selling of securities for the account of a registered representative. Such orders must be clearly indicated because client orders to buy and sell have priority. Also known as Professional Trading. *See also* Pro, Pro Order.

Proven Reserves: in mining, the highest category of measurable reserves (i.e., ahead of probable and possible). *See also* Possible Reserves, Probable Reserves, Resource, Three P's.

Provincial Bond: a bond issued by a province in Canada. *See also* Bond Yield Average, Canadas, Corporate Bond, Government Bond, Municipal Bond.

Provincial Budget: a series of financial statements that detail a provincial government's spending plans for the ensuing year, it shows where the money will come from to finance planned activities. *See also* Federal Budget, Provincial Budget Deficit, Provincial Budget Surplus.

Provincial Budget Deficit: the budget of a provincial government whose incoming revenue is less than its expenditures. *See also* Provincial Budget, Provincial Budget Surplus.

Provincial Budget Surplus: the budget of a provincial government whose incoming revenue is more than its expenditures. *See also* Provincial Budget, Provincial Budget Deficit.

Provincially Incorporated Company: 1. a company incorporated under the laws of a province of Canada. Also known as Provincially Registered Company. *See also* Federally Incorporated Company. **2.** an insurance company incorporated and registered with a province in Canada. *See also* Federally Incorporated Company.

Provincially Registered Company: *see* Provincially Incorporated Company.

Provincial Sales Tax (PST): a tax on consumer purchases levied by a provincial government. *See also* Goods & Services Tax, Harmonized Sales Tax, Sales Tax.

Proving Ground: a place for testing new devices.

Provisional Rating: a bond rating that is conditional upon the completion of a project or the fulfillment of a condition.

Proviso: a clause in a document that sets a condition or restriction.

Proxy: the method by which one person grants to another person the right to vote or act on his/her behalf. *See also* Proxy Battle, Proxy Statement.

Proxy Battle: a situation in which a person or a group attempts to gather enough shareholder proxies to win a corporate vote (usually related to changing management). Also known as Proxy Fight. *See also* Proxy.

Proxy Fight: *see* Proxy Battle.

Proxy Statement: a formal document sent to shareholders in advance of the annual general meeting, it explains the issues to be voted on. *See also* Proxy.

Prudent Expert Rule: a U.S. standard that holds a person in a fiduciary position responsible for acting not only as a prudent person but also to the standard of a person familiar with all relevent matters. In other words, a fiduciary must be prudent within his/her area of expertise. *See also* Fiduciary, Prudent Investor Rule, Prudent Man, Prudent Man Rule.

Prudent Investor Rule: a U.S. standard that holds an investment fiduciary responsible for an entire portfolio and not individual positions within the portfolio. This is consistent with the Modern Portfolio Theory, which holds diversification into speculative stocks, for example, may be a positive investment decision even if the speculative stocks decline in value. *See also* Fiduciary, Modern Portfolio Theory, Prudent Expert Rule, Prudent Man, Prudent Man Rule.

Prudent Man: in law, an imaginary person who possesses and uses the careful, intelligent judgement required of anyone who is expected to be able to protect his/her own interest or the interests of others. This standard is used to measure the performance of fiduciaries. Also known as Reasonable Person. *See also* Fiduciary, Prudent Expert Rule, Prudent Investor Rule, Prudent Man Rule.

Prudent Man Rule: an investment standard in certain jurisdictions of Canada and the U.S. that a fiduciary is required to act as a prudent man or woman when investing other people's money. *See also* Fiduciary, Prudent Expert Rule, Prudent Investor Rule, Prudent Man.

PS: abbreviation for "postscript," a note added after a letter writer's signature. From the Latin *postscriptum*, meaning "after writing."

PSE: *see* Prague Stock Exchange.

PSPA: *see* Past-Service Pension Adjustment.

PST: *see* Provincial Sales Tax.

PTB: Internet acronym for "powers that be."

Public: a term used to refer to individual investors as opposed to institutional investors or insiders. *See also* Individual Investors, Institutional Investors, Insider.

Public Company: a company that has sold ownership shares to the public. *See also* Private Company.

Public Debt: the debt of all levels of government and their related agencies, including bonds, the debts of Crown corporations and drawings from foreign central banks and the International Monetary Fund. Also referred to as Government Debt. *See also* International Monetary Fund, National Debt.

Public Defender: a lawyer hired by the state to represent individuals who cannot afford to employ their own legal representative. *See also* Public Prosecutor.

Public Disclosure: the announcement of material information or events by a company. Public disclosure must be made electronically (e.g., through news services) and through national and local media (e.g., newspapers). *See also* Disclosure, Full Disclosure, Selective Disclosure, Soft Disclosure, Structured Disclosure, Timely Disclosure.

Public Domain: 1. any work, including books, music or software, that has never been copyrighted, or whose title and copyright has expired, so that it may be freely reproduced, altered or otherwise used in any manner for any purpose. **2.** land owned or controlled by the government. *See also* Private Property, Public Ownership, Public Property.

Public Easement: a public right of way. *See also* Easement.

Public Key: in computers, an encryption key for a specific person that is available to the public. *See also* Access Control, Authentication, Biometric Authentication, Challenge-Response Token, Computer, Fire Wall, Password, Private Key.

Public Holiday: *see* Statutory Holiday.

Public Limted Company (PLC or plc): in the United Kingdom, an indication that the business in question is a limited liability company (e.g., British Telecom PLC).

Publicly Traded: a company whose securities are traded on the public markets. *See also* Public Company.

Public Market: a securities market available to the public.

Public Offering: 1. the offer to sell a company's shares to the public at large. *See also* Go Public. **2.** *see* Primary Offering. **3.** *see* Secondary Offering.

Public Office: generally, a government position (either elected or appointed).

Public Ownership: 1. the shares of a company owned by the public. *See also* Public Company. **2.** the ownership of any asset by the government. *See also* Public Domain.

Public Property: lands owned by a government. *See also* Government.

Public Prosecutor: a law officer appointed to conduct prosecutions on behalf of the Crown. *See also* Public Defender.

Public Relations (PR): the process of developing and maintaining a good relationship between an organization and the general public. *See also* Investor Relations

Public Sector: the part of the economy owned and controlled by the government. *See also* Private Sector.

Public Service: service to the community, often under government direction.

Public Utility: a company or organization that provides a public service under government ownership and/or regulation (e.g., an electricity power company). Also known as Utility.

Public Utility Stock: shares in a public utility, these are generally high-quality, income-oriented investments. *See also* Public Utility.

Puff: to publicize or advertise with exaggerated claims.

Pula: the primary currency of Botswana.

Pull Back: *see* Reaction.

Pull-Down Menu: in computers, a menu that is "pulled down" when the user clicks on the menu bar. *See also* Computer, Menu.

Pull in Their Horns: a term used to describe the actions of investors as they become more cautious.

Pull Strings: to work behind the scenes to make something happen.

Pull Technology: on the Internet, software that requires a subscriber to request data rather than have the server deliver it automatically. *See also* Internet, Push Technology.

Pull the Plug: to withdraw supporting bids for a stock.

Pull Up Stakes: to move from one's present location.

Pulp: a mixture of cellulose material (such as wood) ground up to make paper.

Pulse Dialling: in computers, a form of dialling associated with rotary telephones, in which the computer sends pulses to represent the telephone number being being dialled. *See also* Automatic Dial Pulse, Computer, Tone Dialling.

Punitive Damages: a financial award to a plaintiff to compensate for wrong doing, injury or other non-financial losses in addition to actual financial loss. *See also* Damages.

Punt: the prime currency of Ireland.

Puppet: often, a government or head of a small state that is controlled by another power, as in "a puppet state."

Purchase Accounting: *see* Purchase Method.

Purchase Acquisition: *see* Purchase Method.

Purchase Fund: a provision in some issues of bonds and preferred shares, it requires the issuer to use its best efforts to repurchase a certain number of securities each year. Unlike a redemption requirement, a purchase fund is not required to buy securities. *See also* Redeem, Sinking Fund.

Purchase Method: an accounting method used for a merger in which one firm is considered to have purchased the assets of another firm. If the price of the acquired company exceeds the market value of its assets, the difference is recorded as goodwill, which is written off over a period of years. Also known as Purchase Acquisition. *See also* Pooling of Interest.

Purchase Order (PO): a written order authorizing the purchase of a certain number of goods or services at a certain price.

Purchasing Power: the amount of goods and services that one unit of money can buy. *See also* Inflation Risk, Purchasing Power of a Dollar, Real Income.

Purchasing Power of a Dollar: the amount of goods and services one dollar can buy. Usually, a comparison of the purchasing power is made over time. *See also* Inflation Risk, Purchasing Power, Real Income.

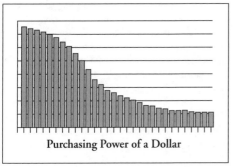

Purchasing Power of a Dollar

Purchasing Power Parity: the exchange rate between two currencies that will equalize the price for equivalent goods and services in both countries in either currency. *See also* Big Mac Index.

Purchasing Power Risk: *see* Inflation Risk.

Pure Play: investment in a company that is in one line of business. *See also* Conglomerate.

Push Technology: on the Internet, the capability of a server to deliver data to subscribers automatically rather than have them request it. *See also* Internet, Pull Technology.

Put: 1. *see* Put Option. **2.** to sell a security back to the former owner under the terms of an agreement made at the time of purchase. *See also* Put Bond.

Put All Your Eggs in One Basket and Watch the Basket: investment advice offered as an alternative to diversification. *See also* Diversification, Don't Put All Your Eggs in One Basket.

Put Bond: a bond that can be sold back to the issuer at specified times before maturity. If the bond can be sold back at only one date, it is a retractable bond. *See also* Put, Retractable Bond.

Put-Call Agreement: *see* Shotgun Clause.

Put Option: a stock option that gives the holder the right to sell a fixed number of shares at a fixed price by a fixed date. Also known as Put. *See also* Call Option, Option.

PX50: a market capitalization weighted index of the Prague Stock Exchange. *See also* Prague Stock Exchange.

Pyramiding: 1. to use profits derived (with borrowed money) from a security position in order to acquire an even larger investment position. **2.** an investment process whereby additional shares are purchased on maximum margin. As long as the price of the shares rises, more margin becomes available and more buying can be conducted. The risk involved is that a small reversal will trigger margin calls and shares must then be sold. *See also* Margin, Margin Call. **3.** *see* Pyramid Selling.

Pyramid Selling: a form of marketing that is often dubious, sometimes fraudulent and restricted by law in some jurisdictions. In such enterprises, income is generated mainly by recruiting new representatives, who are required to buy goods themselves. In other words, income is generated by sales to "representatives" or by receiving a commission on the sales of recruits. *See also* Multi-Level Marketing.

QC: *see* Queen's Counsel.

QDIB: *see* Quebec Deposit Insurance Board.

QED: short for "proven," it is taken from the Latin *quod erat demonstrandum* (literally, "which was to be demonstrated").

Q Factor: often used as an abbreviation for "quality" or "qualitative" factor, it refers to the subjective part of a decision-making process.

QPP: *see* Quebec Pension Plan.

Q-Ratio: the ratio of the stock market value of a company's assets as compared with their replacement value. *See also* Replacement Value.

QS: an internationally recognized quality management standard used to control the design, testing, documentation, manufacture and delivery of products and services in the automobile industry (e.g., QS9000).

Q-Tip Trust: *see* Spousal Trust.

Quadrant: 1. one-quarter of a circle's circumference. **2.** In general, any area representing about one-quarter.

Quadrennial: recurring every four years.

Qualification: a criterion that must be fulfilled before an office or position can be held.

Qualification Period: *see* Elimination Period.

Qualified Endorsement: an endorsement on a negotiable instrument intended to limit the endorsing party's liability. An endorsement on a third-party cheque may add the words "without recourse." This qualification is intended to restrict the endorser's liability if the cheque is not honoured. *See also* Endorse, Joint Endorsement, Negotiable Instrument, Restricted Endorsement.

Qualified Opinion: an auditor's report that is limited or restricted for the reasons provided (e.g., an outstanding lawsuit that represents a significant financial risk). Also known as Adverse Opinion, Disclaimer of Opinion. *See also* Auditor's Report, Going Concern Opinion, Opinion Shopping.

Qualifying Share: a share that is owned in order that a person may qualify to be a director of the issuing corporation. *See also* Director.

Qualitative Analysis: 1. a subjective analysis based on factors that cannot be measured precisely. *See also* Quantitative Analysis. **2.** in investment, an assessment of factors such as the calibre of management or employee loyalty. *See also* Quantitative Analysis.

Quality Bond: *see* High-Grade Bond.

Quality Control: an inspection process the purpose of which is to ensure that a product or service meets established standards. *See also* QS.

Quality of Earnings: the recognition that, within Generally Accepted Accounting Principles, reported earnings can be stated differently. As a rule, the more conservatively stated the earnings, the higher the quality. *See also* Generally Accepted Accounting Principles.

Quality Stock: *see* Blue Chip Stock.

Quant: 1. an analyst whose conclusions are based almost entirely on mathematical relationships. *See also* Quantitative Analysis. **2.** a person who has expertise in mathematics, computers and statistics.

Quantise: to denominate the value of something in a currency other than the one usually used.

Quantitative Analysis: 1. an analysis based on factors that can be measured precisely (e.g., length, weight, dollar value). **2.** in investment, an analysis based on financial information and other statistical/mathematical data. *See also* Qualitative Analysis.

Quanto Option: an option in one currency that pays out in another. If an investor was optimistic about Country A's stock market but pessimistic about its currency, an option on Country A's stock market index that paid out in Country B's currency would be a quanto option. *See also* Option.

Quart: a measure of volume equal to one-quarter of a U.S. gallon, or .946 litres.

Quarter: 1. a three-month period (often referred to in accounting). *See also* First Quarter, Second Quarter, Third Quarter, Fourth Quarter. **2.** an informal reference to the 25-cent coin. *See also* Two Bits.

Quarterly: recurring every three months (e.g., a dividend).

Quarter Stock: a stock with a $25 par value.

Quarter over Quarter: a comparison between results from a quarter in the current year and the same quarter in the previous year (e.g., second quarter of 1999 to second quarter of 1998). *See also* Quarter to Quarter, Year over Year.

Quarter to Quarter: a comparison between results from the current quarter and those from the previous quarter. *See also* Quarter over Quarter, Year over Year.

Quartile: a ranking into four equal groups, with the first quartile being the top 25 percent and the fourth quartile being the bottom 25 percent. *See also* Decile,

First Quartile, Fourth Quartile, Quintile, Second Quartile, Third Quartile.

Quash: to reject by judicial decision.

Quasi-Contract: a payment or action that, even though not recorded in written form, is legally enforced because failure to do so would be unjust.

Quasi-Equity: any part of a company's capital that is not paid-up capital or retained earnings (e.g., paid-in surplus). *See also* Paid-In Surplus, Paid-Up Capital, Retained Earnings.

Quasi-Money: any asset that has money qualities (e.g., a cheque).

Quasi-Public Corporation: a government-regulated, private company (e.g., a privately owned telephone company).

Quayle Bond: named after former Vice-President James Danforth (Dan) Quayle (1947-), this bond is said to have no principles, no interest and no maturity. Also known as a Clinton Bond, after President William (Bill) Jefferson Clinton (1946-).

Quebec: *see* Canada's Provinces and Territories.

Quebec Deposit Insurance Board (QDIB): the equivalent of the Canada Deposit Insurance Corporation in the province of Quebec. *See* Canada Deposit Insurance Corporation.

Quebec Pension Plan (QPP): similar to the Canada Pension Plan but administered by the government of Quebec specifically for Quebec residents. *See also* Canada Pension Plan.

Queen's Counsel (QC): in Canada, U.K., Australia and New Zealand, a title of distinction conferred on prominent lawyers by the Attorney General.

QUOTATION PAGE FOR MUTUAL FUNDS EXPLAINED

Fund Category	Assets	Rate of Return					Load	RSP	SD	MER
		1 mo	6 mo	1 yr	2 yr	5 yr				
Canadian Equity	$265.7	1.0%	6.0%	12.0%	10.5%	11.2%	Choice	Yes	1.2	2.75

The table above is a typical presentation of mutual fund quotes. Depending on the source, the headings and definitions may be different. Consult the detailed notes that explain each category.

Fund Category: a rose is a rose is a rose, but mutual funds are not all the same. The term "Fund Category" (also known as "Mutual Fund Category" or "Fund Group") provides a general description of the nature of the mutual fund portfolio. Sometimes the funds are grouped by the "family," or corporate, name. Definitions for the following fund categories can be found within the alphabetical listings: American Bond Fund, American Equity Fund, American Money Market Fund, Canadian Balanced Fund, Canadian Bond Fund, Canadian Equity Fund, Canadian Money Market Fund, Emerging Markets Equity Fund, Energy Mutual Fund, Equity Fund, European Equity Fund, Far East Equity Fund, Fund of Funds, Global Bond Fund, Global Equity Fund, Global Government Bond Fund, Global Money Market Fund, Industry Mutual Fund, International Balanced Fund, International Bond Fund, International Equity Fund, International Money Market Fund, Latin American Equity Fund, Mid Cap Equity Fund, North American Equity Fund, Small Cap Equity Fund, Specialty Fund, U.S. Bond Fund, U.S. Equity Fund, U.S. Money Market Fund, among others.

Assets: indicates the size of the mutual fund portfolio, usually in millions of dollars. Extremely large funds make the task of management more difficult, while extremely small funds tend to be more volatile.

Rate of Return: the presentation of returns is not consistent. Each table will have its own definition of how returns are calculated and over what period of time. Generally speaking, the returns for periods of one year or less are the absolute changes for the period. For longer terms, the returns are often compounded annual rates.

Load: refers to the commission options available. An entry such as "Choice" indicates that both front end and rear end loads are available. An entry such as "No Load" indicates that this is the only option available.

RSP: indicates whether the fund is eligible as Canadian content in a Registered Retirement Savings Plan (RRSP). If it is not, then it may still be held in an RRSP as foreign content.

SD: many tables also present a measure of volatility. As each may be different, refer to the notes in the table you use. In this case, SD refers to "Standard Deviation of Error." ("Beta" or "Risk" are also used in place of SD.) Standard deviation of error is a measure of volatility compared with an average, which is 1.0. A number above 1.0 indicates that the fund is more volatile than average, and a number below 1.0 indicates that the fund is less volatile than average.

MER: refers to "Management Expense Ratio." This is the total of a mutual fund's management fee (including expenses) expressed as a percentage of net assets. For a typical equity fund, an MER in the 2.50 percent to 2.75 percent range is normal. A mutual fund's returns are presented after subtracting the MER.

Privileges include the right to wear a silk gown and to argue cases from a position located near the judge. If the British monarch is a king, the title is King's Counsel (KC).

Quetzal: the prime currency of Guatemala.

Queue: in computers, a list of data items, commands and so on from which elements can only be removed in a specific order (usually the order in which they were inserted). *See also* Computer.

Quick Buck: money made, usually within a short period of time, through investment or speculation. Also known as Fast Buck.

Quick Ratio: a company's cash, cash equivalents and accounts receivable divided by its current liabilities. A high quick ratio indicates high liquidity. *See also* Cash Ratio.

Quick Turn: a transaction that involves the purchase and sale of the same security within a short period of time. *See also* Short Term Trading.

Quid pro quo: 1. Latin, meaning something of value in return for something of similar value (e.g., an institutional investor receives research from a broker. The quid pro quo is that any transactions based on the service will be conducted through the broker). **2.** a term used to describe a transaction involving a trade or barter of a good or service for another product or service.

Quiet Period: with regard to a distribution of securities, the time during which a broker may not publish or otherwise promote an underwritten company's securities. *See also* Restricted.

Quietus: the final discharge of a debt.

Quinquennial: recurring every five years. *See also* Pentad.

Quintile: a ranking into five equal groups, with the first quintile being the top 20 percent and the fifth quintile being the bottom 20 percent. *See also* Decile, Quartile.

Quitclaim: the full release of one's interest in a property.

Quito Stock Exchange: the major stock exchange of Ecuador, located in its capital, Quito. Also known as Bolsa de Valores de Quito. *See also* Indice Nacional de Precios y Cotizaciones del Mercado Equatoriano.

Quorum: the minimum number of people needed in order to validate the proceedings of a meeting or assembly.

Quota: a share that one is either obligated to contribute or entitled to receive.

Quotation: 1. in the stock market, one or all of a stock's bid, offer and last trade. **2.** an estimate (often written) of the cost of a product or service.

Quotation Page: a page, often in a newspaper, that summarizes statistical and other information about financial securities.

Quote: to state a price for a security.

Quote Driven Market: an electronic market, so termed because trading is motivated by posting bids and offers electronically. *See also* Auction Market, Electronic Market, Order Driven Market.

Quote Machine: an electronic system that provides real time securities bids and offers transaction summaries and other information. Quote machines are used by investment professionals (e.g., stockbrokers), but such services are now also used by sophisticated or active individual investors. *See also* Real Time.

Quo Warranto: in law, a procedure to determine the extent of a person's authority (e.g, in a company).

QWERTY Keyboard: a keyboard originally designed by Christopher Latham Sholes in order to minimize the clashing and locking of keys on mechanical typewriters. The QWERTY keyboard was first commercially produced in 1887. Named for the six left-most letters in the top row of letters on most keyboards: Q-W-E-R-T-Y. The original layout was modified by the makers of the Remington typewriter to include "R" so that the letters in the word "typewriter" would be located on one row. In France, an AZERTY keyboard is common, a QWERTZ keyboard is used in Germany, and the Italians have a QZERTY keyboard.

R1: *see* R Squared.

Rabbit: a quick, aggressive investor. An active trader.

Racketeer Influenced and Corrupt Organization Act (RICO): a U.S. federal law used to combat organized crime in the business world.

Radar Alert: a warning to corporate management that the shares of its company may be under accumulation for takeover purposes. *See also* Radar Screen.

Radar Screen: a computer or electronic news and stock quotation screen that a professional investor uses to watch for early warnings of changing conditions. Radar screens are often used by investors who look for signs of takeovers in the early stages. *See also* Radar Alert, Shark Watcher.

Radio: audio signals sent over the Internet that are comparable in quality to those broadcast by commercial radio stations.

Rag Stock: 1. the shares of a company engaged in the clothing manufacturing or distribution industries. **2.** a stock with a low price.

Raid: a move to manipulate stock prices so that they will either rise or decline. *See also* Bear Raid, Bull Raid.

Raider: a person or company that tries to take over another company by purchasing shares.

Rails: common shares of companies in the railroad industry. Rails were stock market leaders in the 1800s.

Rainmaker: an individual, usually an employee, who brings substantial business to a brokerage firm (e.g., wealthy individuals with large investment portfolios or corporate clients needing to raise capital).

Rainy Day Money: funds set aside for the purpose of taking advantage of unexpected investment opportunities.

Rake: to acquire in abundance, as in "rake in the money."

Rakeoff: a share of the profits, the implication being that this is the result of an illegal act (e.g., a bribe).

Rally: an advance in securities prices following a decline or a flat period. *See also* Bounce, Reaction, Run-Up.

RAM: *see* Random Access Memory.

Rampup: to expand operations in anticipation of a new contract or a substantially higher output.

Rand: the prime currency of South Africa.

R&D: *see* Research and Development.

Random Access Memory (RAM): in computers, memory that can directly access any piece of information without moving through previously stored data. *See also* Computer, Conventional Memory, Memory, Memory Unit, Primary Memory, Read-Only Memory, Secondary Memory.

Random Walk Theory: the theory that stock prices change randomly. This means that past stock price information is useless in forecasting future trends. It also implies that accurate predictions of future price levels for individual stocks or financial markets require accurate predictions for new data or developments regarding the stock or financial markets, respectively.

Range: *see* Price Range.

Rank and File: in organized labour, often used in reference to union members as opposed to union management.

Rank Exploration: high-risk exploration.

Ranking: for a specific period, the position of an investment manager's results (or a security's performance) in relation to those of other managers.

Rapine: the forcible seizure of property.

Rara Avis: something rare.

Ratable Distribution: a term used to describe an estate that has been distributed proportionately to all heirs. *See also* Will.

Rate Base: for a regulated industry, the base value on which the applicable regulatory authorities apply the rate of return the company is allowed to earn. *See also* Regulated Industry.

Rated Insurance: a life insurance policy issued at a higher than normal premium because of the health, lifestyle or occupation of the insured. Also known as Substandard Insurance. *See also* Life Insurance, Standard Class.

Rate of Change: the speed at which a financial or economic variable increases or decreases over a given period of time (normally, a year). A frequent measurement used in economics, business and financial markets.

Rate of Exchange: *see* Exchange Rate.

Rate of Return: the total income and capital gain on investments received during a one-year period divided by the amount of investment. Also known as Return. *See also* Abnormal Return, Annualized Rate of Return.

Ratification: the formal process of confirming a contract, treaty or other transaction, often in reference to a labour/management agreement.

Rating: an independent assessment of the investment quality of government bonds, money market securities, corporate bonds or preferred shares. The Canadian Bond Rating Service and Dominion Bond Rating Service are two well-known Canadian agencies. Standard & Poor's Corporation and Moody's Investors Service are two well-known U.S. agencies. *See also* Bond, Bond Rating, Bond Rating Agency, Canadian Bond Rating Service, Dominion Bond Rating Service, Moody's Investors Service, Rating Agencies, Standard & Poor's Corporation.

Rating Agency: *see* Bond Rating Agency.

Ratio: the relationship in quantity between two or more things expressed as one number divided by another. In financial analysis, ratios are an important measurement tool.

Ratio Analysis: *see* Financial Ratio Analysis.

Ratio Scale: a graph on which equal distances on the vertical scale represent equal percentage changes. *See also* Logarithmic Scale.

Ratio Spreading: buying and selling a different number of option contracts on the same security at the same time. *See also* Option.

Ratio Withdrawal Plan: a plan offered by mutual funds in which a regular withdrawal is made based on a percentage of the value of units held. *See also* Fixed Dollar Withdrawal Plan, Fixed Period Withdrawal Plan, Life Expectancy Adjusted Withdrawal Plan, Mutual Fund, Systematic Withdrawal Plan.

Ratio Writer: an investor who writes call options on more shares than he/she owns (e.g., a person who writes one covered option and one naked option is a two for one ratio writer°. *See also* Option.

Raw: 1. not changed, as in "raw data." **2.** in a natural condition, as in "raw materials."

Raw Material: material used in manufacturing a product.

RCA: *see* Retirement Compensation Arrangements.

RE: used at the beginning of a letter or memo, the abbreviation for "regarding." It states what the document is concerning, as in "RE Your Recent Proposal."

Reach Back Benefit: a term used to describe a situation in which an investor can participate in a tax shelter as if the investment were in place all year, even though it was in place for only part of the year.

Reaction: a brief decline in security prices during a prolonged period of rising security prices. Also known as Correction, Rally. *See also* Pull Back.

Reading the Tape: *see* Tape Reading.

Read-Only Memory (ROM): computer and related memory from which information can be taken but not inputted. It is for constantly used, unchanging information storage. *See also* Computer, Conventional Memory, Memory, Memory Unit, Primary Memory, Random Access Memory, Secondary Memory.

Readout: the presentation of computer data in an understandable form. *See also* Cathode-Ray Tube, Computer, Computer Screen, Disk Drive, Input/Output Device, Interactive Terminal, Joystick, Keyboard, Keypad, Laser Printer, Line Printer, Monitor, Optical Character Recognition, Peripheral, Printer, Printout, Remote Access, Terminal.

Reaganomics: the economic program put forward by President Ronald Reagan (1911-) that combined lower taxes, higher defence spending and stable spending on social programs. To the extent that lower taxes were expected to create sufficient economic growth to generate more tax revenue in total, the plan was also referred to as Supply Side Economics. *See also* Laffer Curve.

Real: 1. an amount in excess of the rate of inflation (e.g., Real Consumer Spending Gains). **2.** the prime currency of Brazil.

Real Asset: generally, a physical asset as compared with a financial asset (e.g., gold bullion is a real asset but a gold certificate is a financial asset). Also known as Real Property, Tangible Asset.

Real Consumer Spending Gains: consumer spending increases that are in excess of the rate of inflation.

Real Dollar: a reference to the U.S. dollar, which is so called because it has a much higher value than does the Canadian dollar. Also known as Real Money.

Real Economic Growth: growth in the economy that is in excess of the rate of inflation.

Real Estate: technically, land. However, in common usage it also refers to buildings. Also known as Property, Real Property, Realty.

Real Estate Agent: a person duly licensed to represent the seller of a property and to charge a commission upon the completion of a sale. Also known as Real Estate Broker. *See also* Broker.

Real Estate Appreciation Loan: a loan secured by real estate, with the lender entitled to receive regular interest plus a share of the increase in the value of the real estate.

Real Estate Broker: *see* Real Estate Agent.

Real Estate Investment Trust (REIT): a structure that enables a large number of investors to pool resources and to share the benefits of investment in various forms of real estate, often in the form of rental income.

Real Estate Limited Partnership: a partnership structure, with limited liability, formed to invest in real estate. The partnership is usually managed by a general partner. *See also* General Partner.

Real Estate Mutual Fund: a mutual fund that invests in some combination of industrial, commercial and residential real estate for the purpose of generating tax-preferred income and long-term capital gain. *See also* Mutual Fund – Other, Specialty/Miscellaneous Fund.

Real Income: income adjusted for inflation; that is, income expressed as purchasing power over time. *See also* Purchasing Power.

Real Interest Rate: the prevailing level of interest rates less the prevailing rate of inflation. *See also* Negative Real Interest Rate.

Realize: to initiate a transaction in order to create a cash profit or loss on investment. If the profit or loss is not realized, then it is a paper profit or loss. *See also* Paper Loss, Paper Profit.

Realized Capital Gain: for income tax purposes, an increase in value that results in a taxable capital gain. *See also* Realize, Realized Capital Losses, Unrealized Capital Gain.

Realized Capital Loss: for income tax purposes, a decrease in value that results in a taxable capital loss. *See also* Realize, Realized Capital Gains, Tax Loss Selling, Unrealized Capital Loss.

Realized Compound Yield: *see* Effective Yield.

Realized Yield: the yield on a bond based on the purchase price. *See also* Yield to Maturity.

Real Market: security quotes from a dealer who is willing to buy and sell in large volume.

Real Money: 1. coin and/or cash. **2.** *see* Real Dollar.

Realpolitik: politics based on practical, rather than on moral, considerations.

Real Property: 1. *see* Real Asset. **2.** *see* Real Estate.

Real Return: the rate of return on investment less the inflation rate.

Real Return Bond: a bond that pays a real rate of interest (e.g., the interest paid is equal to the rate of change in the Consumer Price Index plus 2 percent). *See also* Bond.

Real Time: 1. the actual moment in time that a process or event occurs. **2.** given the speed of computers, real time means that data analysis occurs as soon as the requisite information is input. **3.** in financial markets, quotes reflecting existing market conditions. *See also* Quote Machine.

Real Time Gross Settlement (RTGS): a system for financial settlement that treats each transaction separately and settles it in real time. RTGS is part of the European Central Bank Payment Mechanism. *See also* European Central Bank Payment Mechanism.

Realtor: a broker member of the Canadian Real Estate Association. *See also* Canadian Real Estate Association.

Realty: *see* Real Estate.

Real Value: *see* Inherent Value.

Real Wage Gains: increases in wages in excess of the rate of inflation (e.g., a 4 percent wage increase in a year of 2 percent inflation is a real wage gain of 2 percent).

Rear End Load: 1. *see* Back End Load.
2. *see* Deferred Sales Charge

Reasonable Person: *see* Prudent Man.

Reassessment: 1. the changing of a base value. **2.** in real estate, the changing of an appraised value or a former assessed value. **3.** in income tax, the changing of one's tax return by Canada Customs and Revenue Agency. *See also* Assessment.

Rebalancing: *see* Portfolio Rebalancing.

Rebate: upon meeting a specific condition, the return of a sum of money that has already been paid.

Rebating: a serious contravention of industry practice that entails returning part of the premium to the purchaser of life insurance. *See also* Kickback.

REBC: *see* Registered Employee Benefits Consultant.

Rebound: to bounce back, often referring to the stock market or the price of an individual stock.

Recall: to order back (e.g., in the auto industry, the process by which a particular model of cars is returned to the dealer so that a mechanical problem can be corrected).

Recapitalization: a change in a company's long-term financing mix (e.g., raising equity to reduce debt).

Recapture: 1. a stipulation that gives the seller of an asset the right to repurchase an ownership interest, either in whole or in part. **2.** *see* Recapture of Capital Cost Allowance.

Recapture of Capital Cost Allowance: if there is a disposition (or a deemed disposition) of real estate, and the proceeds exceed the undepreciated capital cost allowance, then the excess (up to the original capital cost allowance) is added back to the income. This latter amount is known as recaptured capital cost allowance. Also known as Recapture, Tax Recapture.

Receipt: a written acknowledgement that something has been received.

Receivables: *see* Accounts Receivable.

Receiver: a court-appointed party that oversees a bankrupt company until it is liquidated and creditors are paid or until new financing can be arranged to satisfy creditors. *See also* Bankruptcy, Receivership.

Receivership: the condition that exists when a business in financial difficulty has been put under a receiver. *See also* Receiver.

Receiver Swapation: an option that gives the owner the right (but not the obligation) to receive certain interest payments under an interest rate swap. *See also* Interest Rate Swap, Payer Swapation, Swapation.

Recession: 1. an official recession is usually a period of two or more consecutive quarters during which, after having been adjusted for inflation, economic output has declined. **2.** generally, a period in which economic activity is reduced and unemployment increases.

Recidivist: in law, a repeat offender.

Reciprocal Business: this occurs when Party A conducts business with Party B, partly in recognition of prior business conducted by the latter with the former.

Reciprocity: a mutual exchange of rights or privileges between nations or individuals.

Reclamation: 1. the right of either party to a securities transaction to recoup losses resulting from the other's failure to settle on time. **2.** returning polluted land to a productive condition.

Recompense: award compensation for damage or loss.

Reconciliation: *see* Account Reconciliation.

Reconveyance: this occurs when a property title is transferred back to the original owner. *See also* Conveyance.

Recordation: a written notice of a property lien.

Record Date: day on which a shareholder must own shares to be entitled to a dividend, attend an annual meeting or participate in any event as a shareholder. Also referred to as the Date of Record.

Recoup: 1. to enjoy a recovery sufficient to cover the original outlay on an investment. **2.** to offset a previous loss through a different investment.

Recourse: 1. in the event of a default on an obligation, the right of the obligee to seek full financial restitution from the obligor. **2.** in general, the right to apply for help, as in "recourse to the courts." *See also* Obligee, Obligor, Recourse Debt.

Recourse Debt: a secured loan. In case of default, if the security is insufficient, the lender can seize any or all other property of the borrower as repayment.

Recovery: 1. in investment, a period of advance in security prices following a decline. **2.** in economics, the stage during which a recession turns into the expansion phase. **3.** In business, realizing value on an asset that has been written off (e.g., collecting a bad debt).

Recreational Property: a second home, such as a cottage, used for recreational purposes. As a recreational property is not a principal residence, capital gains realized upon sale will be taxable. Under certain circumstances, a recreational property can be declared as a principal residence for income tax purposes. *See also* Principal Residence, Retirement Property.

Re-cycle Ratio: in oil and gas exploration, the net cashflow received from the sale of a barrel of oil equivalent (BOE) divided by the finding and development cost of a BOE. A re-cycle ratio of two means a company is able to add two BOE for every one BOE produced, that is, it is growing.

Red Clause: a clause in a letter of credit authorizing payment before shipping documents are ready. *See also* Letter of Credit.

Redeem: the process whereby an issuing company repurchases securities according to the terms and conditions laid out at the time they were issued. *See also* Purchase Fund, Redeemable, Redeemable Bond, Redeemable Preferred Share, Sinking Fund.

Redeemable: a security that can be repurchased. Also known as Callable. *See also* Purchase Fund, Redeem, Redeemable Bond, Redeemable Preferred Share, Redemption Notice, Redemption Price.

Redeemable Bond: a bond that gives the issuer the right to repurchase the bond at set prices and times in the future. Also known as Callable Bond. *See also* Redeem, Redeemable, Redeemable Preferred Share, Redemption Notice, Redemption Price.

Redeemable Preferred Share: a preferred share that gives the issuer the right to repurchase the preferred at set prices and times in the future. Also known as Callable Preferred Share. *See also* Redeem, Redeemable, Redeemable Bond, Redemption Notice, Redemption Price.

Redemption: this occurs when an issuer repurchases a security. *See also* Purchase Fund, Redeemable, Redeemable Bond, Redeemable Preferred Share, Redemption Notice, Redemption Price, Sinking Fund.

Redemption Fee: a fee charged by a mutual fund when an investor buys and sells shares in the mutual fund in a short period. The redemption fee is used to discourage short-term trading in mutual fund shares and is not related to deferred sales charges. *See also* Mutual Fund.

Redemption Notice: a formal document informing security holders that securities will be repurchased. *See also* Redeem.

Redemption Price: the price at which securities will be redeemed. *See also* Redeemable, Redeemable Bond, Redeemable Preferred Share, Redemption Notice.

Redemption Risk: *see* Call Risk.

Redenomination: the process of changing the denomination of securities from the currency of issue to the Euro. *See also* Euro.

Red Herring: 1. *see* Preliminary Prospectus. **2.** something used to take attention away from the real issue.
Red Hot: in great demand (e.g., a new issue of securities).
Red Ink: a reference to losses, as in "The income statement was awash in red ink."
Rediscount: to discount a negotiable instrument for a second time. *See also* Discount.
Redistribution of Income: the process involved when a government taxes high-income earners in order to provide services to low-income earners.
Redline: to refuse to grant mortgages or home insurance in high-risk areas. So termed because of the practice of circling high-risk areas in red ink. *See also* Mortgage.
Red Tape: the problems caused by excessive and strict adherence to official procedures and forms. So termed because of the red tape commonly used to secure legal documents.
Reduced Paid-Up Insurance: a non-forfeiture option of a cash value life insurance policy, in which the cash surrender value is used to purchase a lesser amount of paid-up insurance than the initial death benefit. *See also* Life Insurance.
Referendum: a method for obtaining the community view on an issue through a general vote (e.g., the Quebec Referendum).
Referral: a recommendation from a client of a professional to another person who may also need that professional's services. Canadian consumers express a high degree of confidence in advisors they meet by way of referral.
Refinancing: 1. a term used to describe the process when a borrower, often under a mortgage, takes out a new loan (e.g., for a larger amount of money) to repay an existing loan. *See also* Mortgage. **2.** to use a new issue of a security (e.g., a lower interest rate bond) to repay a former issue of a security (e.g., a higher interest rate bond).
Refined Oil: crude oil that has been purified into a finished product.
Refinery: 1. a facility that produces finished petroleum products from crude oil and other feedstock. *See also* Downstream. **2.** in general, any facility that purifies a crude substance.
Refining and Marketing: the segment of the oil industry that breaks down crude oil into its various component products and sells them to users. Refining and marketing are the downstream sectors of the oil and gas industry. *See also* Development, Downstream, Exploration Company, Integrated Oil Company, Oil Company, Production Company.

Reflation: the process of stimulating economic growth and inflation by increasing money supply after steps have been taken to reduce economic growth and inflation. Reflation is often a last ditch effort to avert an economic recession or depression. *See also* Deflation, Disinflation, Inflation.
Reflex Rally: a small price rise that is not sufficient to reverse an established downward trend. *See also* Rally, Reflex Reaction.
Reflex Reaction: a small price decline that is not sufficient to reverse an established upward trend. *See also* Reaction, Reflex Rally.
Refund: a repayment, especially part of a price.
Refundable Child Tax Credit: *see* Child Tax Benefit.
Refunding: *see* Refinancing.
Regime: a government or administration in power.
Regional Stock Exchanges: stock exchanges in a country outside the main financial centre. In the U.S., a stock exchange outside New York City (e.g., in Boston or Philadelphia). In Canada, a stock exchange outside Toronto (e.g., in Calgary or Vancouver).
Register: to formally record.
Registered: most often, a term used to refer to a security with ownership recorded in a specific name. *See also* Unregistered.
Registered Annuity: an annuity in which the interest portion of the payment is level for the life of the annuity.
Registered as to Interest: a bond in which interest payments are made to the registered holder but in which the face value may be payable to the bearer.
Registered as to Principal: a bond in which interest payments are made by coupons cashable by the bearer but in which the face value must be repaid to the registered holder.
Registered Bond: a bond registered, in the owner's name, with the issuing company or registrar. Also known as Fully Registered Bond. *See also* Bond.
Registered Charity: a charity that, because it is registered with Canada Customs and Revenue Agency, can issue an income tax receipt for donations received.
Registered Company: a company that has filed a registration statement with the Alberta, B.C., Ontario or Quebec securities commissions regarding a public offering of securities. Such a company must comply with the disclosure requirements of the appropriate province. *See also* Registration Statement.
Registered Education Savings Plan (RESP): a plan in which investment returns are allowed to compound tax free. If the accumulated income is used by a beneficiary for a post-secondary educational

purpose (e.g., tuition or the purchase of text books), such amounts are taxable in the hands of the student. Under certain circumstances, up to $40,000 can be transferred from an RESP to the contributor's RRSP. Effective January 1, 1998, there is a 20 percent Canada Education Savings Grant on the first $2,000 an individual contributes each year. Also referred to as an Education Savings Plan. *See also* Canada Education Savings Grant.

Registered Employee Benefits Consultant (REBC): a designation granted by the Canadian Association of Insurance and Financial Advisors to professionals who specialize in retirement planning.

Registered Financial Planner (RFP): a professional financial planning designation in Canada granted by the Canadian Association of Financial Planners. The RFP has been replaced by the Certified Financial Planner designation.

Registered Health Underwriter (RHU): a designation granted by the Canadian Association of Insurance and Financial Advisors to professionals specializing in disability income and health insurance.

Registered Mutual Fund: a fund that is duly registered and is eligible for investment as RRSPs. *See also* Mutual Fund.

Registered Options Principal (ROP): a brokerage firm employee who is responsible for the company's option trading. *See also* Option.

Registered Owner: the name of the owner of securities as it is recorded by the transfer agent of the issuer. *See also* Registered, Transfer Agent.

Registered Pension Plan (RPP): a plan, registered with regulatory authorities, often established by an employer for retired or disabled employees. Also known as Pension Fund, Pension Plan. *See also* Canada Pension Plan, Retirement Compensation Arrangement.

Registered Representative (RR): *see* Broker.

Registered Representative Rapid Response Program: a service of the New York Stock Exchange that enables member firms to receive information on executed trades before confirmation from the trading floor is received.

Registered Retirement Income Fund (RRIF): a maturity option for RRSPs. RRIFs are a continuation of RRSPs because the latter cannot continue after December 31 of the year in which the beneficiary turns age 69. RRIFs are simply one way to withdraw money accumulated in RRSPs. RRIFs specify an annual minimum amount that must be withdrawn each year. Before 1992, the withdrawal formula was designed to leave a zero value in a RRIF when the beneficiary attained age 90. Since 1992, the formula

is designed to maintain a RRIF value indefinitely. RRIFs created before 1992 may have different rules applied to them than RRIFs created after 1992. *See also* Registered Retirement Savings Plan – Maturity Options.

Registered Retirement Income Fund – Locked-In: a tax-sheltered savings plan that provides retirement income, this is a maturity option for a locked-in RRSP. Also known as Locked-In Registered Retirement Income Fund. *See also* Registered Retirement Savings Plan – Locked-In.

Registered Retirement Savings Plan (RRSP): a plan providing income tax incentives to encourage Canadians to save for retirement. *See also* Annuitant, Annuity, Commutation Payment, Earned Income, Income Splitting, Named Beneficiary, Past-Service Pension Adjustment, Payment in Kind, Pension Adjustment, Pension Adjustment Reversal, Registered Retirement Income Fund, Registered Retirement Savings Plan – Unused Contribution Room.

Registered Retirement Savings Plan – Administered or Directed: generally, an RRSP in which a contributor has minimal input into day-to-day investment management.

Registered Retirement Savings Plan – Contribution: RRSP contribution is limited to a maximum of 18 percent of the previous year's earned income, to a maximum of $13,500 as of 1999. If a person is a member of a Deferred Profit Sharing Plan or Pension Plan, the contribution is the same amount as above less the pension adjustment. To these amounts can be added any unused contribution room from previous years. If the maximum amount is not contributed, the balance may be carried forward to future years. *See also* Pension Adjustment, Registered Retirement Savings Plan – Unused Contribution Room.

Registered Retirement Savings Plan – Deregistration: to close out an RRSP. This may occur because the RRSP has been moved to a RRIF or because the contributor has withdrawn all his/her money.

Registered Retirement Savings Plan – Earned Income: for purposes of calculating the allowable RRSP contribution, the definition of earned income includes salary and wages less deductions (other than to a pension plan or retirement compensation arrangement), disability payments under the Canada or Quebec Pension Plans provided the individual was resident in Canada when payments were received, royalties from a work or invention, income from carrying on a business, net rental income, supplementary unemployment benefit plans, alimony or maintenance payments included in income for tax purposes and net research grants. From the above must be deducted losses from carrying on a business, net rental losses, deductible alimony or maintenance payments and certain other capital amounts.

Registered Retirement Savings Plan – Educational Leave Option: a tax-free withdrawal from an RRSP to cover the costs of going back to school in a full-time qualifying program. Generally, a qualifying program is one that requires full-time attendance for more than three months. Up to $10,000 per year may be withdrawn, to a maximum of $20,000 over four years. As a rule, the amounts must be repaid in equal installments over 10 years, starting no later than 60 days after the fifth year following the year of first withdrawal.

Registered Retirement Savings Plan – Eligible Investments: securities in which an RRSP can invest, including government securities, term deposits, guaranteed investment certificates, bonds, listed shares and mutual funds. *See also* Mutual Fund.

Registered Retirement Savings Plan – Foreign Content: the restriction on foreign property is 20 percent of the value of the RRSP at the time the investment is made. If the foreign content rises to a higher percentage of the RRSP value because of market value changes, the restriction does not apply. However, if a foreign investment is sold, the 20 percent restriction is once again in effect when the proceeds are reinvested. If an RRSP invests in mutual funds, the effective foreign content can be increased. The 80 percent invested in Canadian property can be mutual funds that are themselves 20 percent invested in foreign property. In this case, an RRSP can be 36 percent foreign content (20 percent foreign content plus 20 percent foreign content of the 80 percent Canadian content). Also known as Foreign Property Rule. *See also* Mutual Fund.

Registered Retirement Savings Plan – Homebuyer's Plan: an allowance that enables RRSP holders to withdraw up to $20,000 free of tax and to apply it toward the purchase of a first residence. The amount

Registered Retirement Savings Plans

The RRSP is the one financial and investment planning item that each Canadian should maximize. The benefit of the income tax deductibility of eligible contributions and the tax sheltering of investment returns within the plan enables a taxpayer to accumulate about four times as much capital for retirement as with non-registered savings.[1]

There are three income tax benefits to using an RRSP:

1. Deductibility of Contributions: within limits, amounts contributed to RRSPs are deductible for calculating taxable income. In other words, every $1.00 put into an RRSP can reduce income tax payable in that year by $.50 or more. This means that $500 saved outside an RRSP is the equivalent of $1,000 or more saved inside an RRSP. Deductions for a calendar taxation year must be made within 60 days following the year end.

2. Tax Sheltering of Interest, Dividends and Capital Gains: when money inside an RRSP earns an investment return, it is not taxable until the funds are taken out of the plan. This makes it possible to earn money by investing the money that would have been paid in income taxes if the investments had been outside an RRSP. This enables an RRSP to increase in value considerably faster than non-registered savings.

3. Income Splitting: the third tax benefit comes at retirement. Canada has a progressive income tax, which means that the higher the earnings, the higher the percentage rate of income tax. As a result, the income from two small RRSPs (one per spouse) is taxed less than the income from one large RRSP, even if the total amount of income is the same.

There are two main types of RRSPs:

1. Administered or Directed Plans: these RRSPs are popular with people who are just starting out, whose invested amounts are small, and who need more experience. Such plans, which require minimal decision making by the investor, are commonly offered through major financial institutions (e.g., banks, trust companies, credit unions, mutual funds and insurance companies).

2. Self-Administered or Self-Directed Plans: these RRSPs are popular with contributors who have accumulated more savings in RRSPs and/or are experienced investors who want to take a more active role in managing their investments. Such plans are normally offered through brokerage firms, many of which are subsidiaries of the banks, as well as through some mutual fund and life insurance agents.

Registered Retirement Savings Plans are the one tax shelter that every Canadian should view as an integral part of their financial and retirement plan.

[1] *Calculation based on an annual contribution of $5,000 per annum, earning 10 percent per annum for 25 years and assuming a 50 percent marginal income tax rate.*

must be repaid in equal installments over 15 years. If a repayment is missed, then the amount is added to the holder's taxable income.

Registered Retirement Savings Plan – Locked-In: one alternative for taking money out of an employee pension plan when employment has been terminated. Locked-In RRSPs are restrictive and usually only allow funds to be used to purchase an annuity at retirement. Also known as Locked-In Registered Retirement Savings Plan.

Registered Retirement Savings Plan – Matured: an RRSP that has been converted into a RRIF or an annuity that is paying retirement income. *See also* Registered Retirement Savings Plan – Maturity Options.

Registered Retirement Savings Plan – Maturity Options: RRSPs must be converted no later than December 31 of the year the taxpayer reaches age 69. Taxpayers may convert RRSPs to an annuity or a RRIF, or they may collapse the plan and take cash. *See also* Registered Retirement Savings Plan – Matured.

Registered Retirement Savings Plan – Mortgages: an RRSP can invest in National Housing Act – insured mortgages, including one issued to the RRSP holder. While the concept of putting one's own mortgage into an RRSP and paying oneself the interest is appealing, analysis shows this strategy is not all that attractive.

Registered Retirement Savings Plan – Over Contribution: an amount, currently $2,000, that can be contributed and held in an RRSP in excess of the amount that is based on 18 percent of one's earned income. Also known as Over Contribution. *See also* Registered Retirement Savings Plan – Contribution.

Registered Retirement Savings Plan – Pension Adjustment (PA): the reduction in allowable registered retirement income fund contributions for those contributing to a registered pension plan. *See also* Registered Retirement Savings Plan - Pension Adjustment Reversal, Registered Pension Plan, Registered Retirement Income Fund.

Registered Retirement Savings Plan - Pension Adjustment Reversal: an adjustment in allowable registered retirement savings plan contributions that occurs if a person leaves a registered pension plan or has pension benefits that are less than assumed in calculating the pension adjustment reversal. *See also* Registered Retirement Savings Plan - Pension Adjustment, Registered Pension Plan.

Registered Retirement Savings Plan – Retiring Allowance: an allowance that enables one to transfer,

tax free, up to $2,000 for each year of service prior to 1996. One can transfer, tax free, up to an additional $1,500 for each year of service prior to 1989 in which one did not have a vested interest in employer contributions to a Registered Pension Plan or a Deferred Profit Sharing Plan.

Registered Retirement Savings Plan – Self-Administered or Self-Directed: a plan in which the contributor makes day-to-day investment decisions for the RRSP. Also known as Self-Administered Registered Retirement Savings Plan, Self-Directed Registered Retirement Savings Plan.

Registered Retirement Savings Plan – Spousal: an RRSP in which one spouse makes a contribution for the other. The RRSP is the property of the non-contributing spouse. The attraction of a spousal RRSP is that it provides a second source of family retirement income. Under Canada's progressive income tax system, the total tax on two smaller incomes is less than the tax on one large income. Also known as Spousal RRSP. *See also* Progressive Income Tax.

Registered Retirement Savings Plan – Undeducted Contributions: contributions to an RRSP that have not been deducted for income tax purposes and are available for use in future years. Also known as Undeducted RRSP Contributions.

Registered Retirement Savings Plan – Unused Contribution Room: the cumulative amount of contributions to RRSPs that a person could have been made in prior years but that have not been used to date. *See also* Registered Retirement Savings Plan – Contribution.

Registered Security: 1. a security whose owner is recorded with the issuer or the issuer's transfer agent. **2.** a security issued with a provincial securities commission as a new issue.

Registered Tax Deferral Savings Plan: any government-approved plan with the characteristics of tax deductible contributions within annual limits, tax deferral of income earned on investments within the plan and taxation of money withdrawn from the plan (e.g., Registered Pension Plans, Registered Retirement Savings Plans).

Registrar: 1. in investment, usually a trust company that receives the cancelled certificate and the new certificate from the transfer agent. The registrar records and issues the new certificate. Usually, the registrar and transfer agent are the same trust company. *See also* Transfer Agent. **2.** in general, an official responsible for record keeping (e.g., in an educational facility).

Registration: registering a proposed new issue of securities in each province in which the securities will be offered for sale. Registration includes the filing of a prospectus that has been approved by the securities commission.

Registration Statement: a document file with a provincial securities commission that provides a minimum level of required information (e.g., current financial statements and the intended use of the funds raised). *See also* Registered Company.

Regression Analysis: a method of comparing the effect of an independent variable on a dependent variable (e.g., an analysis of housing starts [independent variable] and lumber prices [dependent variable] will provide an estimate of lumber prices for a given level of housing starts). *See also* Dependent Variable, Independent Variable.

Regression Coefficient: *see* Correlation Coefficient.

Regressive Tax: a tax system that takes a successively larger share of tax from lower-income individuals than it does from higher-income individuals. The goods & services tax is considered regressive because it takes a higher proportion of tax from lower-income Canadians than it does from higher-income Canadians. *See also* Progressive Income Tax, Progressive Tax, Taxes.

Regular Bond: a bond that pays interest (usually twice a year) at a fixed rate.

Regular Delivery: to deliver securities on the usual delivery date. *See also* Delivery Date.

Regular Lot: *see* Board Lot.

Regular Settlement: to pay for a securities trade on the normal due date without special conditions. *See also* Settlement Date.

Regulated Company: a company that operates in a regulated industry (e.g., an electric utility). *See also* Rate Base, Regulated Industry, Regulatory Climate.

Regulated Industry: an industry, such as utilities, whose operations are closely regulated by government or a government-appointed agency. *See also* Rate Base, Regulated Company, Regulatory Climate.

Regulation Q: in the U.S., a Federal Reserve System ceiling on interest rates that member banks pay.

Regulation T: a Federal Reserve Board regulation governing the amount of credit a broker or dealer may extend through a margin account. *See also* Margin Account.

Regulation U: a Federal Reserve Board regulation governing the amount of credit a bank may extend to customers to purchase securities on margin. *See also* Margin Account.

Regulation X: in the U.S., the regulations that restrict the type and amount of credit extended to individuals for buying securities.

Regulation Z: in the U.S., the provision that enforces the Truth in Lending Act.

Regulatory Climate: in decisions affecting a regulated company or industry, a recent trend that favours either companies or consumers. *See also* Regulated Company, Regulated Industry.

Rehypothecation: the circumstance when a broker takes client-owned securities that have been hypothecated to secure a margin account or short sale and uses them to secure a bank loan. *See also* Hypothecation

Reimburse: to pay back.

Reinstatement: the restoration of a lapsed insurance policy to premium paying status. *See also* Life Insurance.

Reinsurance: this occurs when an insurance company sells part of an insurance policy to another insurance company in order to diversify the risk.

Reintermediation: the reintroduction of layers, or levels, of activity between the product or service provider and consumer (e.g., an automobile insurance company that changed from selling through a sales force to direct sales goes back to using a sales force).

Reinvestment: the use of dividends to buy additional shares of a company. *See also* Dividend Reinvestment Plan.

Reinvestment Plan: 1. a program set up by mutual funds to allow investors to automatically reinvest distributions into additional shares or units of the mutual fund. *See also* Dividend Reinvestment Plan, Mutual Fund, Reinvestment Privilege. **2.** in general, any plan that allows for dividends to be used to purchase additional shares. *See also* Dividend Reinvestment Plan.

Reinvestment Privilege: the right granted to shareholders of certain companies or mutual funds to reinvest dividends to buy more shares or units, usually without commission. *See also* Dividend Reinvestment Plan, Mutual Fund, Reinvestment Plan.

Reinvestment Rate: the rate of return that will be earned from the reinvestment of future bond interest payments. *See also* Reinvestment Risk.

Reinvestment Risk: the risk that interest rates will decline below the yield on the original investment. In such cases, not only is the reinvestment rate lower but the yield on the original investment may be lower because the yield calculation often assumes a reinvestment rate equal to the current bond yield. *See also* Reinvestment Rate.

REIT: *see* Real Estate Investment Trust.

Rejection: 1. in investment, refusal by one broker to accept a security delivered by a customer or another broker. **2.** in insurance, refusal by an insurance company to insure the risk. **3.** in banking, refusal by a bank to make a loan.

Relationship Manager: a person in an investment counselling firm responsible for providing non-portfolio management services to clients and prospects.

Relationship Trading: taking simultaneous opposite positions between a security and an option contract on the security during periods of unusual price movements. *See also* Option.

Relative Downtrend: a price trend that does not perform as well as a benchmark. *See also* Relative Performance, Relative Performance Chart, Relative Trend, Relative Uptrend.

Relative Performance: the performance of a stock compared to a benchmark or stock market index. A stock that rises faster than average is expected to fall slower than average if the overall market turns down, and vice versa. Also known as Relative Strength. *See also* Relative Downtrend, Relative Performance Chart, Relative Trend, Relative Uptrend.

Relative Performance Chart: a chart plotting the price of a stock divided by a benchmark or stock market index over time. *See also* Relative Downtrend, Relative Performance, Relative Trend, Relative Uptrend.

Relative Strength: *see* Relative Performance.

Relative Trend: the general direction of a relative performance chart. *See also* Relative Downtrend, Relative Performance Chart, Relative Uptrend.

Relative Uptrend: a price trend that performs better than a benchmark. *See also* Relative Downtrend, Relative Performance, Relative Performance Chart, Relative Trend.

Relative Value: the value of one security in relation to another.

Release 1.0: a term that generally denotes the first commercial release of a version of software. Subsequent releases will increase by one-tenth (as in "Release 1.1") or by a full unit amount (as in "Release 2.0").

Release Clause: in a mortgage, a clause that provides for the freeing of the pledged property when a certain proportion of the mortgage has been repaid. *See also* Mortgage.

Relevance Feedback: an Internet technique used by search engines, it orders documents on the basis of their relevance to the search request. It uses a scoring system based on the number of matches with a search criterion. *See also* Internet, Search Engine.

Remainder: in law, the amount left in a trust (or estate) after expenses and prior beneficiaries have been paid. *See also* Remainderman.

Remainderman: the final beneficiary of a trust or estate. *See also* Remainder.

Remand: to send back to prison (or court) to await further proceedings.

Remargining: this occurs when an investor puts up additional cash or securities in order to meet a margin call. *See also* Margin Call.

Remit: to send in payment.

Remittance: credit or money sent to someone.

Remote Access: the ability to connect with a computer from outside the building in which it is located. *See also* Computer.

Remote Login: the ability to access the Internet from various locations. *See also* Internet.

Remove Subjects: this occurs when an offer subject to certain conditions is made binding. *See also* Subject, Subject To.

Remunerate: to pay for goods or services.

Remuneration: *see* Compensation.

Renege: to fail to carry out a promise or commitment, as in "I think he plans to renege on the deal."

Renewable Term Life Insurance: term insurance that is renewable at regular intervals. In some cases, the premium may be fixed for a number of years, after which payments increase with age. Many term policies carry an age limit, after which the insurance cannot be renewed. In most cases, the policy holder may renew without evidence of insurability. *See also* Life Insurance.

Renminbi: the primary currency of China.

Renounce: to surrender or abandon, usually by formal announcement.

Rent: a periodic payment from a tenant in return for the right to use a property.

Rental Income: income from a property that is rented or leased.

Rental Property: real estate owned for the purpose of generating rental income. *See also* Rental Income.

Rent Control: government regulations limiting the amount charged for rent.

Rentier: a person who lives off investment income.

Reorg: *see* Reorganization Department.

Reorganization: a method of saving a company from bankruptcy and liquidation by enabling it to change its financial structure (and perhaps its management) and to deal with other issues (such as unions).

Reorganization Bond: a bond sometimes issued to creditors as part of a reorganization plan. A reorganization bond often contains clauses to assist the company (e.g., a requirement to pay interest only if it is earned).

Reorganization Department: the department in a brokerage firm that handles security exchanges, execution of rights and completion of tender offers. Also known as Reorg.

Repairers' and Storers' Lien: a legal right that benefits the claims of those providing repair or storage services.

Reparation: the act of making amends.

Repatriation: the process of bringing back assets from a foreign country.

Repay: to pay back.

Repayment Terms: the terms and conditions agreed to by a borrower of a loan, including the interest charged, the timing and amount of payments and the date the loan will be retired.

Repeal: to revoke, especially by a formal act.

Replacement: *see* Twisting.

Replacement Cost: what it costs to replace an asset at current fair market prices.

Replacement Cost Accounting: an accounting system that values assets and liabilities at replacement cost rather than at historical cost.

Replacement Value: the value of an asset if it had to be replaced at current market value. A corporate balance sheet can contain many hidden values in the form of replacement value (e.g., a building purchased 15 years ago recorded at cost).

Repo: *see* Repurchase Agreement.

Repo Rate: the rate of interest charged on a repurchase agreement. *See also* Repurchase Agreement.

Report: *see* Research Report.

Reporting Limit: the maximum number of futures contracts one investor may own without having to report his/her position to the commodities exchange.

Repossess: to take back an asset, usually after it has been sold on credit and the buyer has failed to satisfy his/her financial obligation.

Representations and Warranties: in a contract, legal opinions and guarantees.

Representative: an agent (e.g., a stockbroker is a registered representative).

Representative Money: currency that is fully backed by gold or silver.

Republic: a country governed by elected officials and whose head of state is not a monarch.

Repurchase: 1. *see* Normal Course Issuer Bid. **2.** to purchase again any asset that was previously owned. Also known as Share Buyback, Stock Buyback.

Repurchase Agreement: an agreement enabling an investor who sells a security to buy it back at a certain price by a certain date. Also known as Repo.

Required Alpha: the Alpha that is targeted for a portfolio expressed as the additional risk necessary to attain the targeted return. *See also* Alpha.

Required Rate of Return: the minimum rate of return that an investment must be expected to provide in order to justify its acquisition.

Requite: to make repayment.

Rescind: to cancel a purchase or an offer, often under rights granted in a contract or prospectus.

Rescission: cancellation of a contract.

Research and Development (R&D): 1. the activity (often scientific or engineering) that leads to the development of a new product or process. **2.** a department of a company that looks for new and different ways to do things or new and different products or services to sell.

Research Department: the department in a brokerage firm or financial institution that analyzes securities, financial markets and the economy and that makes forecasts for the benefit of clients.

Research Report: often, a written study of a company or industry that analyses investment prospects. Also referred to as Report.

Research Universe: the total list of stocks followed by a research department or firm. *See also* Universe.

Reserve: 1. capital set aside for a future contingency (e.g., a fine from a lawsuit still being contested). **2.** an amount set aside to meet unpredictable but expected operating losses (e.g., a reserve for bad debts). *See also* Bad Debt. **3.** for a regulated company, an amount of capital that must be set aside in a certain form (e.g., the reserve requirement for chartered banks). *See also* Reserve Requirement. **4.** in mining and oil and gas, a measure of the amount of resources in the ground as attested by a qualified engineering report. *See also* Reserve Life Index.

Reserve Bank: a bank that is a member of the U.S. Federal Reserve System. *See also* Federal Reserve System.

Reserve Bid: a bid set by the owner of an item put up for sale at an auction, it represents the price below which he/she will not sell. Also known as Upset Price. *See also* As Is; As Is, Where Is; Auction; Presale Estimate; World Reserve.

Reserve City Bank: a bank that is a member of the U.S. Federal Reserve System and located in a city that has one of the Federal Reserve District Banks or one of its 24 branches.

Reserve Life Index: a calculation, especially in oil and gas, of the expected number of years a reserve will last at assumed recovery and production rates.

Reserve Requirement: the required percentage of deposits that banks and certain other financial institutions must hold in liquid reserves.

Reset Bond: a form of junk bond that stipulates the interest payable must be reset at a specified date in the future such that the bond trades at par. *See also* Bond.

Residence: *see* Principal Residence.

Resident: 1. a person who lives in a jurisdiction. **2.** a person who qualifies as a resident for income tax purposes even though he/she may reside elsewhere for substantial periods. *See also* Snowbird.

Residential Mortgage: a mortgage secured by a residential property. *See also* Commercial Mortgage, Mortgage.

Residential Property: any property zoned for individual or family living (e.g., an apartment, condominium, duplex, single-family home). *See also* Commercial Property.

Residential Rehabilitation Assistance Program (RRAP): a federal program that provides loans and grants to low-income homeowners and landlords of low-income housing to modernize properties to current health and safety standards.

Residual: the part of a stripped bond representing repayment of the principal amount. Also known as Residual Strip. *See also* Bond.

Residual Dividend Theory: the theory that companies pay cash dividends only if they lack a reasonable investment opportunity.

Residual Security: a security, such as a convertible, with the potential for diluting earnings per share. *See also* Convertible Bond, Convertible Debenture, Convertible Preferred Share.

Residual Strip: *see* Residual.

Residual Value: 1. the value of an asset based on original cost less depreciation. **2.** *See also* Salvage Value.

Residuary Beneficiary: the party that receives the residue of an estate. *See also* Beneficiary.

Residuary Estate: all the assets remaining in an estate after all debts and taxes have been paid. *See also* Estate.

Residuary Trust: a trust established to receive the assets of an estate after all debts and taxes have been paid. *See also* Trust.

Residue: the balance of an estate after payment of debts, taxes, probate fees, bequests and specified gifts. *See also* Residuary Beneficiary.

Resistance Level: in technical stock market analysis, a price level that a commodity, stock or index will have

difficulty rising through. In theory, passing through a resistance level is a sign of very positive momentum. *See also* Support Level, Test.

Resolution: 1. a clause in a contract that expresses an intention. **2.** *see* Corporate Resolution. **3.** *see* Director's Resolution.

Resolution Trust Corporation (RTC): a U.S. government agency created in the 1989 bailout of the savings and loan industry. A major function of the RTC was to take over and sell assets of bankrupt savings and loans companies.

Resource: 1. anything of value that can be used in exchange for something else. **2.** in mining, the total of proven, probable and possible reserves. *See also* Possible Reserves, Probable Reserves, Proven Reserves.

RESP: *see* Registered Education Savings Plan.

Respondeat Superior: the legal concept that a principal is responsible for the actions of his/her agent.

Respondent: one who responds, often as a defendant in a divorce or equity case. *See also* Co-respondent.

Restatement: the revised presentation of a portion (or all) of an earlier financial statement.

Resting Order: an order to buy or sell a security that remains in effect until it cannot be filled because prices have changed significantly.

Restitution: the act of giving something back to its rightful owner.

Restraining Order: 1. in general, a court order prohibiting or specifying the terms and conditions under which one person may come in contact with another. **2.** in family law, a court order prohibiting contact between two spouses and some cases, their children. Restraining orders may specify the terms and conditions under which contact may occur.

Restraint of Trade: in business, the organized interference with free competition through the restriction of production or through otherwise controlling the market. *See also* Combination in Restraint of Trade.

Restricted: describes a situation in which an analyst cannot publish a report on a company because the firm he /she works for is acting in an underwriting or other advisory role for that company. *See also* Over the Wall, Quiet Period, Underwriting.

Restricted Account: a margin account that is under margin. *See also* Margin Account, Under Margin.

Restricted Endorsement: an endorsement that applies only to a specific case (e.g., a cheque endorsed "For deposit only"). *See also* Endorse, Joint Endorsement, Qualified Endorsement.

Restricted List: a list, given by an employer to a stockbroker, of securities that may be traded only in response to an unsolicited order from a client. *See also* Unsolicited Order.

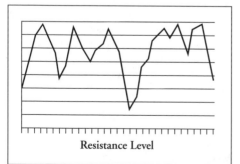

Resistance Level

Restricted Voting Shares: the shares of a company that rank equally with other shares except they have fewer votes per share. Also known as Differential Voting Shares, these are often used in family-founded firms to enable family members to retain control.

Restrictive Covenant: 1. generally, a contractual clause not to do something (e.g., a loan is made with the borrower agreeing not to allow the company's debt/equity ratio to rise above 50 percent. **2.** *see* Negative Covenant. **3.** *see* Negative Pledge.

Retail: 1. the sale of securities or mutual funds to individual investors. *See also* Mutual Fund, Wholesale. **2.** the sale of goods directly to consumers.

Retail Account: the account of an individual investor at a brokerage firm. *See also* Institutional Account.

Retail Buying: in the stock market, the buying of a security by individual investors. *See also* Institutional Buying, Retail Selling.

Retail Client: a client of a brokerage firm that is an individual investor. *See also* Institutional Client.

Retail Department: in a brokerage firm, the department of brokers that deals with individual investors. *See also* Institutional Department.

Retailer: *see* Retail House.

Retail House: a brokerage firm that specializes in dealing with individual investors. Also known as Retailer. *See also* Institutional Boutique.

Retail Investor: 1. *see* Individual Investor. **2.** an investor who buys and sells securities for his/her own account. *See also* Institutional Investor.

Retail Sales: the value of goods sold directly to the consumer. Retail sales make up more than 50 percent of the demand in the economy and is an important economic indicator.

Retail Selling: in the stock market, the selling of a security by individual investors. *See also* Institutional Buying, Retail Buying.

Retained Earnings: the corporate balance sheet account that accumulates reported earnings that have not been paid out to shareholders. Also known as Undistributed Profits.

Retained Earnings Statement: *see* Statement of Retained Earnings.

Retainer: a fee paid to retain the services of a professional advisor (e.g., a lawyer).

Retention Rate: after taxes, the percentage of corporate profits not paid out to shareholders as dividends. It is 1 minus the dividend payout rate. *See also* Payout Rate.

Retire: to cancel, redeem or repay a securities issue.

Retirement: 1. a period of no longer working, often later in life, to live on pension or investment income. **2.** cancellation of bonds or stocks that have been reacquired by the issuer. *See also* Normal Course Issuer Bid. **3.** repayment of a loan or other obligation. *See also* Maturity. **4.** removal of an asset from service after the end of its useful life.

Retirement Compensation Arrangement (RCA): a funded agreement that guarantees payments to a retiring employee. *See also* Registered Pension Plan.

Retirement Counsellor: a professional (e.g., an accountant, broker, financial advisor, financial planner or life insurance agent) who assists in planning all phases of one's life after retirement.

Retirement Property: usually, a smaller, less expensive property than one's previous property, where one lives upon retirement. *See also* Principal Residence, Recreational Property.

Retiring Allowance: in the Income Tax Act, an amount of compensation received upon or after retirement in recognition of long service or in respect of the loss of office. *See also* Registered Retirement Savings Plan – Retirement Allowance.

Retiring Allowance and RRSPs: *see* Registered Retirement Savings Plan – Retiring Allowance.

Retractable: 1. *see* Retractable Bond. **2.** *see* Retractable Preferred Share. **3.** *see* Retraction Clause.

Retractable Bond: a bond issued with a term to maturity that can be retracted to a shorter period at the option of the holder. Also known as Retractable. *See also* Bond, Extendable Bond, Put Bond, Retraction Clause.

Retractable Preferred Share: a preferred share that may be sold back to the issuer at the option of the shareholder at a specified price and date. Also known as Retractable. *See also* Retractable Bond, Retraction Clause.

Retraction Clause: a term in a security offering (usually a bond or preferred share) that gives the owner the option of selling the security back to the issuer at a specified price and date. *See also* Extension Clause, Retractable Bond, Retractable Preferred Share.

Retreat: a decline in securities prices.

Retrench: to cut expenses and to economize; this reflects a slowdown in business.

Retribution: something given or demanded in repayment.

Retroactive: a change that applies to a period before enactment (e.g., if a labour contract is negotiated on February 15 but is effective on February 1, the contract is "retroactive to February 1").

Retroactive Wage Increase: a wage increase that applies to previous pay periods (e.g., if a labour contract is negotiated on February 15 but is effective February 1, the wage increase is "retroactive to February 1").

Retrofit: to modify an existing product by incorporating subsequent improvements. *See also* After Market.

Return: 1. exchange of an item previously sold for a refund or credit. One of the items deducted from gross sales to calculate net sales. *See also* Gross Sales, Net Sales. **2.** *see* Income Tax Return. **3.** *see* Rate of Return.

Returned Item: a negotiable item forwarded for payment and sent back unpaid (e.g., a not sufficient funds cheque).

Return of Capital: a flow of cash or securities to the owner of an investment, it represents a return of all or part of the original investment.

Return on Assets: for a company, net income divided by total assets. It is common practice to use both net income before taxes and net income after taxes. Also known as Return on Investment.

Return on Capital: *see* Return on Invested Capital.

Return on Common Equity: *see* Return on Equity.

Return on Equity (ROE): a measure of corporate profitability calculated as net income divided by shareholder's equity. ROE is often used to compare the relative attractiveness of the shares of various companies. Also known as Return on Common Equity.

Return on Invested Capital: for a company, a percent figure calculated as net income minus dividends paid divided by the total of long-term debt plus preferred and common share equity. Also known as Return on Capital.

Return on Investment (ROI): 1. the relationship between the amount of income generated by an investment and the amount of money invested. The return is the income for a given period divided by the amount of investment. **2.** *see* Return on Assets.

Return on Sales: a ratio calculated by dividing net income before taxes by net sales. It is a ratio widely used to measure a company's operating efficiency.

Reuters Holdings Plc: a major international news and information service. Reuters provides economic and financial information to the business community and general news to the media. *See also* Bloomberg, L.P., Dow Jones & Co. Ltd.

Revaluation: a change in a country's exchange rate that is not made by the forces of supply and demand but as a decision of the government. *See also* Fixed Exchange Rate, Floating Exchange Rate.

Revenue: a company's or government's gross income.

Revenue Bond: a bond that is backed by a tax on a specific project (e.g., a bond is issued to raise money to build a new bridge and a toll on the bridge pays interest and principal to the bondholders).

Revenue Canada: *see* Canada Customs and Revenue Agency.

Revenue Neutral: a term used to describe a change to the tax system that does not increase the total amount of tax collected. *See also* Taxes.

Revenue Sharing: 1. the sharing of tax revenues collected by a senior level of government and passed down to a lower level government. **2.** in a limited partnership, the proportionate amount of income or distributions between the general partner and the limited partners.

Reversal: 1. a change in direction in a security's price from up to down or down to up. **2.** a change in fortunes, usually negative, as in "He has suffered a business reversal."

Reversal Pattern: in investments, a chart formation or other indicator that points to a long-term decline following a rise or a long-term rise following a decline.

Reverse Annuity Mortgage: *see* Reverse Mortgage.

Reverse Circulation Drilling: in mining, drilling that does not produce a core but that does force material to the surface under water pressure.

Reverse Conversion: the process by which a brokerage firm uses the assets held on behalf of clients to earn a profit (e.g., sell short the shares held on behalf of clients, hedge against a market rise by purchasing call options and invest the proceeds from short selling to earn interest). *See also* Call Option, Option, Short Sale.

Reverse Engineering: the examination of a finished product to study its makeup. Reverse engineering is often done in the hope that a product can be copied.

Reverse Freeze: *see* Intercorporate Freeze.

Reverse Hedge: the simultaneous purchase of common shares and a short sale of a security convertible into the same stock in the expectation that the conversion premium on the convertible will decline. *See also* Conversion Premium.

Reverse Leverage: this occurs when the interest that must be paid on borrowed funds exceeds the return on the investment the funds were borrowed to make. *See also* Leverage.

Reverse Mortgage: a loan based on part of the equity in an owner-occupied, residential, single-family dwelling. The money borrowed is generally used to purchase an annuity in order to give the homeowner more income. The loan payments are not made in cash but are added to the amount of the loan. The borrower's estate is responsible only for the amount of the loan up to a maximum of the total equity in the residential property. If there is more equity than the amount owing on the reverse mortgage, the rest is paid to the estate. Reverse mortgages have various terms and conditions. Some simply provide a line of credit based on the equity in the home. Others give ownership of the home to the lender upon the home-owner's death. Individuals considering a reverse mortgage should seek professional advice. Also known as Lifetime Reverse Mortgage, Reverse Annuity Mortgage. *See also* Mortgage.

Reverse Split: a share consolidation; that is, a change where one new share equals two old shares. Also known as Reverse Stock Split, Rollback, Scottish Dividend, Share Consolidation, Stock Consolidation. *See also* Stock Split.

Reverse Stock Split: *see* Reverse Split.

Reverse Takeover (RTO): a takeover of a larger company by a corporate shell or smaller company so that, afterward, the former owners of the larger entity have control. *See also* Corporate Shell, Shell Game.

Reversionary Annuity: an annuity that begins to pay after an event (e.g., when a person dies). Also known as Survivorship Annuity. *See also* Annuity.

Review: in law, a judicial reexamination.

Revisionary Trust: a trust that is irrevocable for a pre-determined period, after which it becomes revocable. *See also* Irrevocable Trust, Revocable Trust.

Revocable Trust: a trust, set up to hold an asset deeded to a beneficiary, that can be changed at any time.

Revocation by Destruction: revoking a will by a physical act (e.g., burning, tearing up or obliterating). *See also* Will.

Revocation by Marriage: in all provinces except Quebec, a will is automatically revoked by a subsequent marriage unless it was created in contemplation of the marriage. *See also* Will.

Revocation by Subsequent Testamentary Instrument: the revocation of a will by a later will or codicil. *See also* Will.

Revoke: to void or annul by recalling.

Revolving Credit: *see* Revolving Line of Credit.

Revolving Letter of Credit: a letter of credit used when a buyer does business continuously with a seller. The revolving letter of credit is valid for a specified period and eliminates the need for the buyer to apply for a new credit with each purchase.

Revolving Line: *see* Revolving Line of Credit.

Revolving Line of Credit: a loan for operating purposes, with the amount borrowed fluctuating below a stated upper limit. Revolving lines of credit are available to both corporate and personal customers. Also known as Open-End Credit, Revolving Credit, Revolving Line.

RFP: *see* Registered Financial Planner.

RHU: *see* Registered Health Underwriter.

Rial: the prime currency of Iran, Oman and Yemen.

Rich: 1. a price (often for a security) that is too high. **2.** wealthy.

RICO: *see* Racketeer Influenced and Corrupt Organization Act.

Rider: 1. in life insurance, an extra benefit added to the basic policy with an added charge. *See also* Dread Disease Rider. **2.** in household insurance, a written document that changes the basic policy (e.g., to cover a new piece of jewelry). Also known as Floater, Personal Article Floater. **3.** an amendment added to a piece of legislation.

Riding the Yield Curve: to purchase a security with a longer term to maturity in order to increase returns from the resultant higher yields. *See also* Yield Curve.

Riel: the prime currency of Cambodia.

Rifle Approach: a business technique that targets a narrowly defined market or audience. The rifle approach to marketing would be to target married women between the ages of 30 and 40 as compared with women of any age whether married or not. *See also* Shotgun Approach.

Rig: equipment used for a particular purpose, such as in oil and gas exploration (e.g., drill rig).

Rigged: the condition of a security or market being illegally manipulated.

Riga Stock Exchange: the major stock exchange of Latvia, located in its capital, Riga. Web site: www.rfb.lv *See also* Latvia Dow-Jones Stock Exchange Index.

Rigged Market: *see* Market Rigging.

Right: 1. *see* Share Purchase Right. **2.** a legal or moral due or justifiable claim. **3.** *see* Right Wing.

Right of Anticipation: *see* Prepayment Privilege.

Right of First Refusal: the right of a first party to purchase or otherwise acquire an asset at the same terms and conditions agreed to by a third party before ownership is transferred to a second party (e.g., Party A has the right of first refusal on a property owned by Party B. Party B receives [from Party C] a firm offer to buy the property. Party A has the right to buy the property from Party B under the same terms and conditions as agreed to by Party C.) Right of first refusal usually must be exercised within a relatively short, specified period. Also known as First Refusal.

Right of Offset: the legal right of a financial institution to seize a customer's funds on deposit to cover a loan to the same customer that is in default.

Right of Redemption: 1. the right to buy back a security at a given price within a given period. **2.** the right to take back or purchase a piece of property by paying off the mortgage. Also known as Equity of Redemption. *See also* Mortgage.

Right of Rescission: 1. a right, available in mutual funds offered by prospectus, to change one's mind about a purchase, often within two business days of receiving a copy of the prospectus or confirmation of purchase. In some provinces, there are additional remedies or damages (within certain time restrictions) if information in the prospectus is found to be misrepresented. *See also* Mutual Fund, Statutory Rights of Rescission. **2.** the right to change one's mind about a purchase of new securities within two business days of receiving a prospectus. Also known as Right of Withdrawal. In some provinces, there are additional remedies or damages (within certain time restrictions) if information in the prospectus is found to be misrepresented. *See also* Prospectus, Statutory Rights of Rescission. **3.** in the U.S., the right to cancel a contract within three business days without penalty, for a full refund.

Right of Survivorship: in a joint tenancy, when one tenant dies, the survivor(s) automatically receive an equal share of the deceased's interest in (e.g., in a building) through the "right of survivorship" (e.g., five joint tenants each own one-fifth, or 20 percent, of a building; if one owner dies, then that interest disappears and the four surviving joint tenants each own one-fourth, or 25 percent). Also known as Survivorship. *See also* Joint Tenancy, Joint Tenancy with Right of Survivorship, Tenant, Tenants in Common.

Rights Off: *see* Ex-Rights.

Rights Offering: the issue of rights to existing security holders to buy a proportionate number of additional securities at a given price within a fixed period. *See also* Right, Standby Commitment.

Right of Withdrawal: *see* Right of Rescission.

Rights On: *see* Cum Right.

Rights or Things: items to be included in a deceased person's tax return (e.g., matured but uncashed bond coupons; declared but unpaid dividends).

Right Wing: a political position that generally takes a conservative or reactionary stance. Also known as Right. *See also* Left Wing.

Ringgit: the prime currency of Malaysia.

Ring: *see* Pit.

Ring the Cash Register: to generate revenue.

Rio de Janeiro Stock Exchange: a major stock exchange of Brazil, located in Rio de Janeiro. Also known as Bolsa de Valores de Rio de Janeiro. Web site: www.bvrj.com.br

Rio Trade: a securities trade made in a desperate attempt to recover earlier losses, so termed because if the trade fails, the trader would have to move to Brazil to escape from his/her creditors.

Riparian Rights: rights of landowners on the banks of any natural waterway (e.g., to use of the water and to the use of land under the water).

Ripoff: in general, any purchase that is purposely not

fair value for the buyer.

Ripple Effect: the tendency of an event to cause numerous other changes in the economy or financial markets.

Rising Bottoms: a price pattern in which subsequent lows are at successively higher levels.

Risk: 1. in general, the measurable probability that an expected event will not occur. **2.** in financial markets, risk is equated with volatility because the greater the volatility in price, the more likely an unexpectedly poor return or result will be realized. *See also* Active Risk, At Risk, Beta Risk, Company Specific Risk, Country Risk, Credit Risk, Downside Risk, Equity Risk Premium, Event Risk, Industry Specific Risk, Inflation Risk, Market Specific Risk, Non-Systematic Risk, Risk Arbitrage, Risk Averse, Risk Capital, Risk Factor, Risk Free Asset, Risk Free Return, Risk Premium, Risk/Reward Ratio, Risk Tolerance, Safety, Sovereign Risk, Specific Risk, Systematic Risk, Unique Risk, Unsystematic Risk.

Risk Adjusted Return: the rate of return on investment, taking risk into account. A higher rate of return per unit of risk is more desirable than a lower rate of return per unit of risk. *See also* Sharpe Ratio.

Risk Arbitrage: a high-risk form of arbitrage in which the investor buys and/or sells short the shares of companies being acquired. The arbitrage involves speculation on whether an acquisition will be completed and if another bidder for the same company will make a higher bid. *See also* Arbitrage.

Risk Averse: a preference for less, rather than more, risk.

Risk Capital: money invested in securities that are characterized by a high level of risk.

Risk Factor: *see* Standard Deviation of Error.

Risk Free Asset: the return on a senior government-guaranteed, short-term security (e.g., a treasury bill). Also known as Riskless Investment.

Risk Free Return: the return on a risk free asset. Usually, the yield on treasury bills is used as a measure of the risk free return.

Riskless Investment: *see* Risk Free Asset.

Risk of Collection: *see* Collection Risk.

Risk of Redemption: *see* Call Risk.

Risk Premium: a high rate of return offered to compensate for high risk.

Risk/Return Ratio: *see* Risk/Reward Ratio.

Risk/Return Trade-Off: *see* Risk/Reward Trade-Off.

Risk/Reward Ratio: in an investment, a comparison of the maximum likely loss with the maximum likely profit. Also known as Risk/Return Ratio.

Risk/Reward Trade-Off: the concept that the potential return from an investment varies directly with the risk. In other words, to attain a higher rate of return, investors must accept greater risk. The concept is significant because it also means a low risk, high return investment does not exist. Also known as Risk/Return Trade-Off.

Risk Tolerance: an individual's comfort level with regard to risk. A person with high risk tolerance is comfortable making high risk investments and vice versa.

Risk Transfer: the act of managing risk by transferring it to others (e.g., purchasing insurance, factoring accounts receivable).

Riyal: the prime currency of Qatar and Saudi Arabia.

Road Show: travelling presentations made by underwriters (often with the assistance of company management), the purpose of which is to outline the prospects for a new issue of securities. Also held by mutual fund companies for the benefit of brokers and/or potential investors. *See also* Mutual Fund.

Roam: a cellular telephone feature that allows a subscriber of one wireless service to use another wireless carrier while in its service area. *See also* Cellular Telephone.

Roaring Twenties: the decade of the 1920s, so termed because of its buoyant economy and financial markets. *See also* Dirty Thirties.

Robot: a mechanical device, operated automatically or by remote control, that can perform human tasks. Robots are often used in manufacturing products such as cars and computers.

Robotics: the science and technology of creating and programming robots.

Rock: the natural mineral matter that makes up much of the Earth's crust.

Rock Bottom: the lowest possible level, as in "stock prices hit rock bottom."

Rocket: in financial markets, a very rapid price rise.

Rocket Science: something particularly difficult to understand or accomplish. Often expressed in the negative, as in "Successful investment isn't rocket science."

Rocky: a term used to describe economic and financial market conditions that are full of bumps and difficulties.

ROE: *see* Return on Equity.

ROI: *see* Return on Investment.

Rollback: 1. a reduction in wages. **2.** a reduction in prices. **3.** *see* Reverse Split.

Roll Backward: replacing a former options position with a new options position with an earlier expiration date. *See also* Option.

Roll Down: to replace a former options position with a new options position with a lower exercise price. *See also* Option, Roll Forward, Roll Up.

Roller Coaster Market: a stock market that has a series of ups and downs over a short period of time.

Roll Forward: to replace a former options position with a new options position with a later expiration date. *See also* Option, Roll Down, Roll Up.

Rolling Return: an annualized return for a period that is updated regularly (e.g., a three-year rolling return is the three-year return on an investment from June 1, 1995, to May 31, 1998. When another monthly result is known, the three-year rolling return is calculated from July 1, 1995, to June 30, 1998).

Rolling Stock: movable transportation equipment (e.g., automobiles, railroad cars and trucks).

Rollover: 1. the exchange of one asset for another in a way that does not trigger a capital gain for tax purposes. *See also* Spousal Rollover, Tax Free Rollover. **2.** the transfer of funds or assets from one account to another. **3.** to replace a maturing security to another with a longer term to maturity. **4.** in international finance, when a country that cannot make a loan repayment is allowed to renegotiate terms so that payment is deferred for many years.

Roll the Dice: in investment, to take a chance.

Roll Up: to replace a former options position with a new options position with a higher excercise price. *See also* Option, Roll Down, Roll Forward.

ROM: *see* Read-Only Memory.

Roman Numeral: the number system made up of the characters: I = 1, V = 5, X = 10, L = 50, C = 100, D = 500, M = 1,000.

ROP: *see* Registered Options Principal.

Roth Individual Retirement Account (Roth IRA): a U.S. retirement plan in which the annual contribution is not tax deductible but income is tax sheltered while in the plan. *See also* IRA.

Roth IRA: *see* Roth Individual Retirement Account.

Round Lot: *see* Board Lot.

Round Lotter: *see* Board Lotter.

Round Table: a conference or discussion that has several participants.

Round Trip: in securities, the transactions involved in opening and closing a position (e.g., buying shares and selling them is a round trip).

Roustabout: an unskilled oil field worker.

Rout: a sharp decline in financial markets.

Routine: in computers, a set of programming instructions. *See also* Computer, Subroutine.

Row: in a computer matrix, the horizontal lines. *See also* Column, Spreadsheet.

Royalty: 1. payment to the owner of a patent or copyright for the right to use the material. **2.** a form of tax charged by a government to a company for the extraction of natural resources. **3.** payment to a private owner of a mineral extraction right for the extraction of a resource from the property. **4.** payment to a composer or artist relating to the use or sale of his/her work.

RPP: *see* Registered Pension Plan.

RR: *see* Registered Representative.

RRAP: *see* Residential Rehabilitation Assistance Program.

RRIF: *see* Registered Retirement Income Fund.

RRSP: *see* Registered Retirement Savings Plan.

RS-232C: a standard for exchanging information between computers and modems.

R Squared (R²): a fraction of change in the dependent variable that is explained by the independent variable. The range is from zero to one, with one meaning that the independent variable explains all the change in the dependent variable.

RTC: *see* Resolution Trust Corporation.

RTFM: Internet acronym for "read the f******
manual." The message urges newbies to read a manual before bothering an Internet expert with a question. *See also* Newbie.

RTGS: *see* Real Time Gross Settlement.

RTO: *see* Reverse Takeover.

Rubber Cheque: *see* Not Sufficient Funds Cheque.

Ruble: the prime currency of Belarus, Russia and Tajikistan.

Rue des Lombards: the financial district of France, located in Paris, it is the equivalent of London's Lombard Street. The area was originally occupied by German bankers from Lombard; hence, the name. *See also* Lombard Street.

Rukeyser, Louis: host of the public television program *Wall $treet Week* since 1970. He is the author of *How to Make Money in Wall Street,* which won the Best Investment Book of the Year Award. Other awards he has received include Free Enterprise Man of the Year (1987) from Texas A&M University, the Annual Award from the New York Financial Writers Association and the George Washington Honor Medal. Web site: www.pbs.org/rukeyser

Rule 10a – 1: the U.S. Securities and Exchange Commission rule that prohibits a short sale at a price below the last price at which a security was traded. This rule prevents the short sale order from pushing

stock prices lower. Also known as Plus-Tick Rule. *See also* Minus Tick, Plus Tick, Short Sale, Zero-Minus Tick, Zero-Plus Tick.

Rule 80A: a reference to the New York Stock Exchange rule stating that if the Dow-Jones Average has fallen 50 points in one session, then computerized selling can only take place after prices have risen. This is to prevent a repeat of the October 19, 1987, disaster, when computerized selling led to a market decline of more than 500 points. In early 1998, the parameters were changed to a one-hour halt of all trading if the Dow-Jones Average falls 10 percent, to two hours if it falls 20 percent and for the balance of the day if it falls 30 percent.

Rule 80B: effective April 15, 1998, the circuit-breaker parameters were changed to refer to 10 percent, 20 percent and 30 percent declines in the Dow-Jones Industrial Average as indicated in the chart at the bottom of the page. Every calendar quarter, the percentage declines will be applied to the average closing value of the Dow-Jones Industrial Average for the previous month to determine how many points the decline must be to trigger the circuit breaker. In the first quarter of 1999, the values were 900, 1,800 and 2,700 points. *See also* Circuit Breaker, Rule 80A.

Rule 405: *see* Know Your Customer.

Rule of Eighteen: a rule stating that when the inflation rate is added to the Dow-Jones Average price/ earnings ratio, stocks will go higher if the total is under 18 and lower if the total is over 18. *See also* Rule of Twenty.

Rule of Five: *see* Dow Five.

Rule of Seven: a rule stating that a long-term return of 7 percent on the assets in a RRIF will enable the minimum required withdrawal to be taken from a RRIF for around 25 years before the capital is depleted.

Rule of Seventy-Eight: a method of approximating monthly interest payments for a loan that is to be repaid in one year. Since the numbers one through 12 add up to 78, the interest in the first month is 12/78, the interest in the second month is 11/78 and so on until the last month, when the interest is 1/78 and the debt is retired.

Rule of Seventy-Two: a rule stating that when the compound return on investment is divided into 72,

Rule 80B				
Decline	before 1:00 pm	1:00 – 1:59 pm	2:00 – 2:29 pm	2:30 pm or later
10%	1 hour halt	1 hour halt	1/2 hour halt	no halt
20%	2 hour halt	1 hour halt	← market closed for the day →	
30%	← market closed for the day →			

the result approximates the number of years it takes for money to double (e.g., at 10 percent interest, 72 divided by 10 equals seven and two-tenths. This means that at 10 percent, money will double every seven and two-tenths years.

Rule of Ten: *see* Dow Ten.

Rule of Twenty: the theory that the price/earnings ratio of the Dow-Jones Average and the U.S. inflation rate should add up to 20, that is, the price/earnings ratio should rise as inflation drops, and vice versa. *See also* Rule of Eighteen.

Ruling: an authoritative decision from a court or official body.

Rumourtrage: the arbitraging of the shares of companies rumoured to be acquired or merged. *See also* Garbatrage.

Run: 1. when a stock price moves up quickly, as in "the stock has had a good run." **2.** *see* Run on a Bank. **3.** to contest an election, as in "run for office." **4.** to manage or operate, as in "run a business." **5.** a list of stock offerings provided by a market maker, including bid and offer prices for stocks and also par values for bonds. *See also* Market Maker. **6.** in computers, to execute a program.

Runaway Inflation: *see* Hyper-Inflation.

Run in the Shorts: a trading tactic in which shares are purchased to push the price up. This causes short sellers to buy to cover positions, which pushes prices up further. This creates a snowball effect, pushing prices up even more. Also known as Running in the Shorts. *See also* Gather in the Stops.

Running Ahead: *see* Front Running.

Running in the Shorts: *see* Run in the Shorts.

Running Yield: the income from a portfolio calculated as a percentage of a changing market value over time.

Runoff: 1. to print a list of stocks listed on a stock exchange with closing prices at the end of the trading session. **2.** the vote to break a tie in an election. **3.** *see* Run on a Bank.

Run on a Bank: this occurs when depositors panic and withdraw deposits in large amounts. Because a bank maintains only a small fraction of the value of deposits in the form of cash, a run on a bank can put the bank in a position of not being able to meet all the requests for cash. This can result in a greater loss of customer confidence, resulting in more deposits being withdrawn. If the run continues, a bank may be forced to call in loans made to other customers. Eventually, the bank will be forced to close. Also referred to as a Runoff.

Run Rate: *see* Annualized Rate.

Run-Up: a sharp, short-term increase in the price of a stock or the stock market. *See also* Rally.

Rupee: the prime currency of India, Mauritius, Nepal, Pakistan, the Seychelles and Sri Lanka.

Rupiah: the prime currency of Indonesia.

Russell (Frank) Company: *see* Frank Russell Company.

Russell 1000 Index: a U.S. stock market index consisting of the 1,000 largest companies in the Russell 3000 Index. The Russell 1000 Index is a common benchmark for large cap investment fund managers. *See also* Frank Russell Company, Large Cap, Russell 2000 Index, Russell 3000 Index.

Russell 2000 Index: a U.S. stock market index consisting of the smallest 2,000 largest companies in the Russell 3000 Index. *See also* Frank Russell Company, Russell 1000 Index, Russell 3000 Index.

Russell 3000 Index: a U.S. stock market index consisting of the 3,000 companies with the largest market capitalizations in the U.S. The Russell 3000 Index is a widely used benchmark for investment fund managers. *See also* Frank Russell Company, Russell 1000 Index, Russell 2000 Index.

Russian Trading System: the major stock exchange of Russia, located in its capital, Moscow. Web site: www.rtsnet.ru *See also* ASP General Index.

Russian Trading System Index: a market capitalization weighted index in U.S. dollars for Russian stock prices.

Rust Bowl: any geographic area in which outmoded manufacturing plants are going out of business (e.g., certain areas of the American eastern seaboard and the Ruhr Valley in Germany).

Sack: slang for to fire from a job.

Safe: free of risk, as in "a safe investment." *See also* Safety.

Safe Deposit Box: *see* Safety Deposit Box.

Safe Harbour: a legal provision to reduce or eliminate liability when presenting material that includes forecasts and estimates together with factual information. *See also* Poison Pill.

Safe Haven: a jurisdiction favoured by international investors because of a combination of a stable political environment, a strong currency and favourable economic outlook. *See also* Flight of Capital.

Safekeeping: a service, offered by many financial institutions, that entails storing and protecting financial assets and other documents.

Safety: 1. *see* Safety of Capital, Safety of Income. **2.** a reference to low investment risk. *See also* Risk, Safe.

Safety Deposit Box: a metal box, kept in a bank vault, in which individuals store valuables. Also known as Safe Deposit Box.

Safety of Capital: one of the principal investment objectives relating to the likelihood that an investment will maintain or increase its value. Also known as Safety, Safety of Principal. *See also* Diversification, Preservation of Purchasing Power, Safety of Income.

Safety of Income: one of the principal investment objectives relating to the likelihood that an investment will continue to pay a dividend, interest or income. Also known as Safety. *See also* Diversification, Income.

Safety of Principal: *see* Safety of Capital.

Sag: a minor decline in prices. *See also* Reaction.

SAIF: *see* Savings Association Insurance Fund.

Salad Oil Scandal: a famous U.S. swindle based on false-bottomed tanks said to contain salad oil but that were filled mostly with water. The perpetrator was Antonio de Angelis and his Allied Vegetable Oil Company. When the scam was exposed in 1963, nearly two billion pounds of salad oil worth $175 million were missing. The scandal was particularly serious because the losses hit American Express, a public company, and several Wall Street brokerage firms. *See also* Bre-X Minerals Ltd, Equity Funding Corporation, Ponzi Scheme, Prime Bank Note, ZZZZ Best.

Salary: compensation for employment, usually at a fixed rate changed from time to time. Salary often implies payment for professional or clerical services. *See also* Compensation, Wage.

Sale: 1. this occurs when a buyer and seller agree to exchange a product or service for money. *See also* Barter. **2.** this occurs when a merchant reduces prices on goods to attract customers.

Sale and Lease Back: an agreement made when the owner sells an asset to another party and contracts back the use of that asset for payments over a fixed period. Also known as Leaseback. *See also* Lease.

Sales Agreement: a contract in which a seller agrees to provide a product or service and a buyer agrees to pay a specified price for it. *See also* Back End Load, Deferred Commissions, Deferred Declining Redemption Fee – At Cost, Deferred Declining Redemption Fee – At Market, Deferred Sales Charge, Exit Fee, Front End Load, Life Insurance, Load, Loading Charge, No Load, Rear End Load.

Salesman: *see* Salesperson.

Salesperson: someone who earns a living mainly from commissions charged on goods and services sold. Also known as Salesman, Saleswoman.

Sales Tax: a tax on purchases, usually calculated as a percentage of the amount spent. *See also* Goods & Services Tax, Harmonized Sales Tax, Provincial Sales Tax.

Saleswoman: *see* Salesperson.

Salting: the fraudulent activity of adding a valuable mineral to a sample in order to fake a mineral discovery. *See also* Bre-X Minerals Ltd.

Salvage Value: the value of an asset based on the value of the component commodities with zero value attributed to its usefulness (e.g., an old automobile that is no longer functional and has value only as scrap steel). Also known as Scrap Value.

SAM: *see* Shared Appreciation Mortgage.

Same Day Delivery: *see* Cash Delivery.

Same Day Settlement: *see* Cash Settlement.

Same Occupation: a stipulation in some disability income insurance contracts that benefits will continue until the insured is able to perform the occupation he/she was performing when he/she was disabled. Also known as Own Occupation. *See also* Any Occupation, Disability Income Insurance.

Same Store Sales: in retailing, a measure of the growth in sales only for outlets that were open in the current year and the previous year. *See also* Organic Growth.

Sample: 1. a small piece representing the whole. **2.** in statistics, a portion taken from a population that is analyzed to estimate the characteristics of the whole. **3.** in resource exploration, specimens collected in the field and brought to a laboratory for study.

Samurai Bond: a debt instrument denominated in Japanese Yen and sold in Japan but not issued by a Japanese government, agency or corporation. *See also* Bond, Shogun Bond.

Sanctions: coercive measures, usually undertaken by several countries at once, to force another country to comply with international law.

S&P: *see* Standard & Poor's Corporation.

S&P Effect: *see* Standard & Poor's Effect.

S&P Phenomenon: *see* Standard & Poor's Effect.

S&P 100: *see* Standard & Poor's 100 Index.

S&P 400: *see* Standard & Poor's Midcap 400.

S&P 500: *see* Standard & Poor's 500.

S&P 600: *see* Standard & Poor's Smallcap 600.

Sandwich Generation: middle-aged people who are squeezed by the financial demands of raising a family on the one side and the need to provide financial support to aging parents on the other. *See also* Baby Boomer, Echo Generation, Generation X, Generation Y.

Santa Claus Rally: *see* Year End Rally.

Santiago Stock Exchange: the major stock exchange of Chile, located in its capital, Santiago. Also known as Bolsa de Comercio de Santiago. Web site: www.bolsantiago.cl *See also* Indice General de Precious de Acciones.

Santiago Stock Exchange (IGPA) Index: *see* Indice General de Precious de Acciones.

São Paulo Stock Exchange: a major stock exchange of Brazil, located in São Paulo. Web site: www.bovespa.com.br/ *See also* Bovespa Index.

Saskatchewan: *see* Canada's Provinces and Territories.

Satellite: a country that is economically and politically dominated by another.

Saturated: the condition of a market that has absorbed such a large amount of selling that prices will fall if more selling takes place.

Saturday Night Special: a surprise attempt by one company to acquire another company. So named because the bids are often announced on weekends in order to avoid publicity.

Save: in computers, to store data for future use. *See also* Computer.

Save Harmless: a clause intended to protect a buyer from past or future liability brought on by the seller (e.g., when buying a business, the buyer will insist that the seller is responsible for any future lawsuits arising from actions predating the purchase).

Savings Account: a deposit account for funds intended to stay on deposit but not locked in. The cost of processing a cheque and the interest paid on cash balances is higher in a saving account than in a chequing account. Also known as Bank Account. *See also* Chequing Account, Combination Account, Demand Deposit, Deposit.

Savings and Loan: a U.S. financial institution whose primary business is to take deposits and make home mortgages. Also known as Thrift.

Savings Association Insurance Fund (SAIF): the unit of the U.S. Federal Deposit Insurance Corporation that provides deposit insurance for thrift institutions. *See also* Federal Deposit Insurance Corporation.

Savings Bond: *see* Canada Savings Bond.

Savings Element: the cash or investment value accumulated in an insurance contract. *See also* Cash Surrender Value, Cash Value Life Insurance, Life Insurance.

Savings Rate: an economic statistic calculated by dividing personal savings by personal disposable income. Savings rate comparisons between countries is controversial because of the different ways in which it is calculated.

Sawbuck: U.S. slang for a 10-dollar bill.

SBF – 250 Index: a market capitalization weighted index of French stocks on the Paris Stock Exchange. *See also* Paris Stock Exchange.

SBLA: *see* Small Business Loans Act.

Scab: slang for a non-unionized worker who replaces a striking unionized worker. Also known as Strike Breaker.

Scale: *see* Pay Scale.

Scale In: the act of buying a position in a security over time. Dollar Cost Averaging is a form of scaling in. Also known as Position Building. *See also* Dollar Cost Averaging, Scale Out.

Scale Out: the act of selling a position in a security over time. Systematic withdrawal is a form of scaling out. *See also* Scale In, Systematic Withdrawal.

Scaling: this occurs when an investor buys or sells a security position over time by placing a series of orders at various times and prices.

Scalper: 1. in general, a person involved in questionable activities in the hope of turning a quick profit (e.g., a person who buys several tickets to a sporting event and tries to sell them for more than his/her cost). **2.** a broker who buys a position in a security before recommending it to clients, in the expectation that his/her client's purchases will push the price higher. **3.** a market maker who charges an excessive amount for his/her service. *See also* Market Maker.

Scalping: trading for quick, small profits.

Scam: a fraudulent business or investment scheme. *See also* Bre-X Minerals Ltd., Equity Funding Corporation, Florida Land Boom, Ponzi Scheme, Salad Oil Scandal.

Scan: 1. in computers, to automatically search stored data for specific information. **2.** to digitize an image using a computer. *See also* Computer.

Scarcity: in economics, the condition in which all wants cannot be satisfied. It is this condition that creates the need for economics; that is, a system to ensure the orderly allocation of scarce resources (if there were totally unlimited resources, there would be no need for economics). *See also* Economics.

Scenario: a set of facts or assumptions forming the basis for a discussion or forecast, as in "The economic scenario in the federal budget assumes growth of 3 percent next year."

Schedule I Bank: this category of banks includes the widely held (public) Canadian banks, including the "Big Five" Canadian chartered banks. Formerly known as Schedule A Bank. *See also* Big Five Chartered Banks, Schedule II Bank, Widely Held.

Schedule II Bank: this category of banks includes foreign banks or banks controlled by one or a few shareholders (e.g., the Hongkong Bank of Canada may have many characteristics of a Schedule I bank, but it is a subsidiary of HSBC Holdings PLC, a U.K. company. Laurentian Bank of Canada used to be a Canadian Schedule II bank when it was controlled by Desjardins-Laurentian Financial Corporation). Formerly known as Schedule B Bank. *See also* Schedule I Bank.

Schedule A Bank: *see* Schedule I Bank.

Schedule B Bank: *see* Schedule II Bank.

Schilling: the prime currency of Austria, Kenya, Somalia, Tanzania and Uganda.

Scholarship: a grant to a student, it is based on academic achievement and is usually for the purpose of financing his/her further education.

Scorched Earth Policy: a strategy used to discourage a takeover attempt in which the company's most attractive assets are sold to other buyers. *See also* Poison Pill.

Score a Gain: to make a profit.

ScotiaMcLeod: *see* Bond Yield Average.

Scottish Dividend: *see* Reverse Split.

Scrap Value: *see* Salvage Value.

Screen: the act of using a computer to find items that meet certain criteria and to discard those that don't (e.g., screen for all companies trading under six times earnings, yielding over six per cent and trading at less than 60 per cent of book value). Also known as a Computer Screen. *See also* Magic Sixes.

Scrip: 1. a written document that acknowledges a debt. *See also* IOU. **2.** a document that represents a fraction of a share that is issued following a stock split. *See also* Stock Split. **3.** any provisional document recording ownership. **4.** paper money issued for temporary emergencies.

Scripophily: the hobby of collecting old stock certificates or other financial memorabilia. Literally, the love of paper.

SD: *see* Standard Deviation.

SDR: *see* Special Drawing Rights.

SDTV: *see* Standard Definition Television.

Seal: an impression made on a written document, it functions as a formal method of giving assent. A company must have a seal because it cannot sign. *See also* Signing Officer.

Seam: 1. in computers, an interface between different software systems. *See also* Computer, Seamless. **2.** a layer of mineralized rock under the ground, as in "coal seam." *See also* Open Pit Mining.

Sea Mile: *see* Nautical Mile.

Seamless: a term used to describe computer software that allows for the total access and exchange of information among systems. *See also* Computer.

Search: in computers, the process of looking for a particular file or set of data. In a search, the computer takes the name or data that is entered and compares it to the database to find a match. *See also* Computer.

Search Engine: 1. on the Internet, a program that searches for keywords or files located on the World Wide Web. *See also* Internet, Relevance Feedback, Search, World Wide Web. **2.** in computers, a program that conducts a search. *See also* Computer, Search.

Seasonal Dating: *see* Dating.

Seasonality: *see* Seasonal Trend.

Seasonally Adjusted: economic statistics that have been adjusted to offset the effect of seasonal trends (e.g., unemployment is usually higher in the winter months than in the summer months. Therefore, an unadjusted unemployment rate of 10 percent will be seasonally adjusted to a lower rate if it occurs in December and to a higher rate if it occurs in August).

Seasonal Trend: a trend in economic and financial markets, repeated in certain months of the year, forming a part of cyclical and secular trends. Also known as Seasonality. *See also* Cyclical Trend, Secular Trend, Summer Rally, Summer Valley, Year End Rally.

Seasoned: an investment that has successfully withstood the test of time, and indicative of high quality and low risk.

Seasoned Security: a security that has established a pattern or record of trading under various market conditions. The term suggests high quality and low risk. *See also* Unseasoned Security.

Seat: 1. to hold an elected position, or seat, in parliament. **2.** *see* Stock Exchange Seat.

SEATS: *see* Stock Exchange Automated Trading System.

SEC: *see* Securities and Exchange Commission.

SECAM: *see* Sequential Couleur Avec Memoire.

Secondary: *see* Secondary Offering.

Secondary Distribution: *see* Secondary Offering.

Secondary Issue: *see* Secondary Offering.

Secondary Market: the market in which previously issued securities trade. This is in contrast to the primary market, in which underwriters first sell newly issued securities. In Canada, the secondary market represents about 98 percent of total trading. *See also* Aftermarket, Primary Market.

Secondary Memory: in computers, where infrequently used instructions and data are stored, often externally (e.g., on a disc). *See also* Computer, Conventional Memory, Memory, Memory Unit, Primary Memory, Random Access Memory, Read-Only Memory.

Secondary Offering: an issue of securities, sometimes underwritten, that is the resale of securities already issued. Often, the shares are being sold by founding shareholders or venture capital investors. Also known as Secondary, Secondary Distribution, Secondary Issue. *See also* Primary Offering, Public Offering.

Secondary Reaction: a price move that is contrary to the primary trend. *See also* Rally, Reaction.

Secondary Stock: a stock that ranks below a stock in the Toronto Stock Exchange 300 or the Standard & Poor's 500 in terms of size, quality and risk. *See also* Blue Chip Stock.

Secondary Trade: a trade between two investors.

Second Market: *see* Over-the-Counter.

Second Mortgage: a loan secured by a property on which there is a mortgage with a prior claim. *See also* First Mortgage, Mortgage, Third Mortgage.

Second Preferred Share: a preferred share issued when there is another preferred share with a prior claim on dividends and assets. In the case of liquidation, the first preferred share claims are satisfied in full before the second preferred shares receive anything. Also known as Second Preferred Stock. *See also* First Preferred Share, Junior, Preferred Share.

Second Preferred Stock: *see* Second Preferred Share.

Second Quarter: the second three months of a fiscal year (often April, May and June). *See also* Quarter.

Second Quartile: a ranking in the second best 25 percentile of a peer group, that is between the top 25

and top 50 percent. The lower half of the top 50 percent. *See also* Decile, First Quartile, Fourth Quartile, Third Quartile.

Second Round Financing: usually, the level of funding that entails going public, after a company has progressed through the venture capital stage. *See also* First Round Financing, Go Public, Initial Public Offering, Primary Offering.

Second-to-Die: life insurance based on two lives, it pays when the second insured dies. This insurance is often used to pay taxes triggered when the second spouse dies. *See also* First-to-Die, Joint and Last Survivor, Joint First-to-Die, Joint Second-to-Die Life Insurance.

Secretary:. 1. *see* Corporate Secretary. **2.** a person employed by a company (or individual) to handle correspondence and clerical work. *See also* Executive Secretary.

Secret Ballot: a method of voting in which the votes cast by individuals is not made known to others. *See also* Vote.

Secret Key: *see* Private Key.

Section: an area equivalent to one square mile, used especially with reference to agricultural land and resource exploration claims. *See also* Township.

Sector: a distinct branch of the economy or financial market.

Sector Fund: a mutual fund that invests in a specific industry or sector of the economy, a country or region of the world. *See also* Mutual Fund – Other, Specialty/Miscellaneous Fund.

Sector Rotation: management of a portfolio by shifting assets from group to group according to the outlook for a particular group at a particular stage in the economic cycle. *See also* Bottom-Up, Growth Investor, Portfolio Management Style, Top Down, Value Investor.

Secular Trend: the long-term, dominant trend within which cyclical and seasonal trends take place. *See also* Cyclical Trend, Seasonal Trend.

Secured Bond: a bond backed by collateral. *See also* Bond.

Secured Creditor: a creditor protected by a specific asset or assets that have been pledged as collateral. *See also* Preferred Creditor, Unsecured Creditor.

Secured Debt: any obligation that has assets that have been identified as collateral for a loan. *See also* Unsecured Debt.

Secure Electronic Transaction (SET): the security standard agreed upon by MasterCard and Visa to secure electronic financial transactions. *See also* Credit Card.

Securities: *see* Security.

Securities Act: Provincial legislation that regulates the underwriting, distribution and sale of securities. Because it is provincial legislation, there may be differences from region to region. *See also* National Securities Legislation.

Securities Analyst: *see* Financial Analyst.

Securities and Exchange Commission (SEC): the major regulatory body for the U.S. investment industry.

Securities Cage: a physical location in a brokerage firm where clients can deliver securities or cheques to settle trades or pick up cheques paid from accounts. So termed because the original securities cages featured bars to prevent theft. Also known as Cage. *See also* Window Settlement.

Securities Exchange: a facility for the organized trading of securities. *See also* Stock Exchange, Stock Market.

Securities Industry Advisory Council: a group made up of representatives of the Investment Dealers Association of Canada and the Toronto, Montreal, Vancouver and Alberta stock exchanges. This group advises the Canadian Securities Institute with respect to proficiency standards for financial planners under its jurisdiction.

Securities Industry Association (SIA): a lobby group for the U.S. securities industry.

Securitization: this involves taking financial assets and creating a security to sell to investors (e.g., mortgage backed securities). *See also* Mortgage Backed Security.

Security: 1. a financial instrument giving evidence of ownership or an ownership right (e.g., common shares). Also known as Securities. **2.** anything pledged as collateral for a loan (e.g., property backing a mortgage).

Security Analysis: a book, for many years considered to be the bible of fundamental financial analysis, written by Benjamin Graham (1894-1976), often considered to be the "father of financial analysis," and David Dodd (1895-1988).

Security Deposit: 1. money deposited by a tenant with a landlord to insure compliance with the lease agreement. **2.** any consideration deposited to secure a contract.

Security Interest: an interest that allows a property to be sold or otherwise dealt with should the owner fail to meet an obligation to the holder.

Security Lending: 1. the practice of a brokerage firm whereby it lends client-owned securities (e.g., to a short seller) to generate additional revenue. *See also* Lending Agreement. **2.** the practice of an institutional investor (e.g., a pension fund) whereby it lends portfolio-owned securities to generate additional return.

Security Specific: an influence on the price of a stock that comes entirely from the security owned.

Security Specific Risk: *see* Non-Systematic Risk.

Security Value: a monetary value a lender is willing to assign an asset for the purposes of accepting it as security for a loan. Also known as Collateral Value. *See also* Collateral.

Sedition: language or actions that incite rebellion against a government.

Seed Capital: 1. the first, and generally a small, amount of equity capital put into a new venture, often at a conceptual stage. Because it is at the earliest stage of development, which is the time of highest risk, the price of the stock is very low and the potential is high. Also known as Seed Money. *See also* Equity Capital, Mezzanine Level, Seed Financing, Venture Capital. **2.** the initial funds invested by a venture capital firm. Such investment is generally in the form of a loan or convertible security.

Seed Financing: the raising of the first contribution of capital toward a new venture. If the security issued is common stock, it is known as a Seed Stock Offering. *See also* Seed Capital.

Seed Money: *see* Seed Capital.

Seed Stock: shares that provide early equity financing for a new business, normally before going public. The price is generally very low, reflecting a high level of risk. *See also* Seed Capital.

Seed Stock Offering: *see* Seed Financing.

Seek a Home: to look for a buyer for a block of stock. *See also* Seek a Market.

Seek a Market: this occurs when a seller seeks a buyer or a buyer seeks a seller of a block of stock. *See also* Seek a Home.

Seesaw: a term often applied to an up and down financial market.

Seg Fund: *see* Segregated Fund.

Segregated Fund (Seg Fund): an investment similar to a mutual fund but based on a variable deferred annuity. As an insurance product, it is offered only by insurance agents. It often guarantees between 75 percent and 100 percent return of capital over a specified period such as 10 years. It may have certain features of life insurance, such as creditorproofing. *See also* Creditorproofing, Life Insurance, Mutual Fund – Other, Variable Deferred Annuity.

Segregation: this involves separating the client's securities and cash from the brokerage firm's securities and cash.

Seisin: a legal term used to describe possession of title to a freehold estate. *See also* Freehold.

Seize: 1. to take into custody. **2.** to legally confiscate an asset to partially or fully satisfy an obligation.

Selective Disclosure: the announcement of information to a restricted group (e.g., securities analysts). Selective disclosure may or may not be Soft Disclosure. *See also* Disclosure, Full Disclosure, Public Disclosure, Soft Disclosure, Structured Disclosure, Timely Disclosure.

Self-Administered Registered Retirement Savings Plan: *see* Registered Retirement Savings Plan – Self-Administered or Self-Directed.

Self-Dealing: 1. a transaction between related or non-arm's-length parties, the terms and conditions of which may not reflect market conditions. *See also* Conflict of Interest, Non-Arm's-Length Transaction. **2.** a term more or less synonymous with insider trading. *See also* Insider Trading.

Self-Directed Registered Retirement Savings Plan: *see* Registered Retirement Savings Plan – Self-Administered or Self-Directed.

Self-Fulfilling Prophecy: something that happens as a consequence of having forecast that it will happen (e.g., if an influential advisor forecasts a stock price decline, then this creates selling, which, in turn, creates a price decline).

Self-Government: government by the inhabitants of a political unit rather than by an outside authority. *See also* Sovereignty.

Self-Insurance: a financial decision not to purchase insurance but, rather, to assume the risk. *See also* Insurance.

Self-Liquidating: an investment that will return the principal amount invested through regular income distributions over a relatively short period of time.

Self-Regulatory Organization (SRO): in investment, a major Canadian stock exchange or the Investment Dealers Association of Canada. In order to avoid government regulation, these organizations develop a set of rules to govern members. *See also* Investment Dealers Association, Sponsoring Self-Regulatory Organization.

Sell: 1. a recommendation to sell a security. Also known as Sell Recommendation. **2.** to liquidate an asset in return for money. **3.** a security for which liquidation is being recommended, as in "It's a sell." **4.** an order to sell. Also known as Sell Order.

Sell Away: 1. a situation in which a block of stock is being sold, but, before the sale is completed, the price falls below the minimum acceptable price. **2.** while selling securities, to falsely represent oneself as working for a brokerage firm.

Seller: in a transaction, the party that provides a product or service in return for payment.

Seller Financing: *see* Vendor Financing.

Seller's Market: a market in which demand exceeds supply, thus giving sellers the advantage. *See also* Buyer's Market.

Seller's Monopoly: *see* Monopoly.

Selling: in financial markets, trading that is initiated by orders to liquidate. *See also* Buying.

Selling Agent: the real estate agent responsible for selling a property. If the selling agent is different from the listing agent (e.g., under a multiple listing agreement), the two share the commission, often equally. *See also* Listing Agent, Multiple Listing Service.

Selling Away: this occurs when a broker sells securities that he/she has not been authorized by the firm to sell.

Selling Climax: a short period of panic selling, near the end of a long-term price decline, that pushes prices down sharply. This selling frenzy ends quickly and then prices rebound. *See also* Buying Climax.

Selling Concession: *see* Concession.

Selling Flat: this occurs when the buyer of a bond does not have to pay an additional amount for such items as accrued interest. Also known as Flat. *See also* Price Plus Accrued.

Selling, General and Administrative Expenses (SG&A): a corporate expense category that includes costs related to selling as well as to general and administrative expenses.

Selling Group: *see* Underwriting Group.

Selling Off: 1. in investment, a term that describes the sale of securities under some duress. **2.** a description of a market that is declining, as in "The market is selling off."

Selling Panic: a period of rapidly falling stock prices on high volume brought about by investors liquidating securities without regard to price. *See also* Bear Panic, Buying Panic.

Selling Pressure: this occurs when orders to sell a security outweigh orders to buy and, consequently, the price sags. *See also* Buying Pressure.

Selling Program: a policy, often instituted by a large institutional investor, to sell a stock (or stocks) over a period of time. *See also* Buying Program.

Selling Range: the price range in which a security is considered to be overpriced. *See also* Buying Range.

Selling the Crown Jewels: thwarting a takeover attempt by selling off valuable assets in order to make the target company less attractive *See also* Marquee Asset, Poison Pill.

Sell Off: a decline in prices.

Sell on News: *see* Buy on Mystery, Sell on History.

Sell Order: *see* Sell.

Sell Out: 1. this occurs when a buying broker or client fails to settle on time and the shares purchased are forcibly sold. *See also* Buy In. **2.** this occurs when a client is unable to meet a margin call and shares are forcibly sold until margin is restored. *See also* Buy In, Buy-In Notice, Margin Call, Sell-Out Notice.

Sell-Out Notice: notification from a broker to a client informing him/her of an amount that must be paid immediately or the broker will begin selling the client's securities to satisfy the debt. If the value of securities is not sufficient to repay the debt, the client is liable for any remaining balance. *See also* Buy-In Notice, Sell Out.

Sell Plus: an order to a broker to sell at a price above the current market. *See also* Buy Minus, Order.

Sell Recommendation: *see* Sell.

Sell Short: *see* Short Sale.

Sell Side (of the Street): the stock brokerage industry. *See also* Buy Side (of the Street).

Sell Signal: a financial market indicator that points to a drop in prices. *See also* Buy Signal.

Sell Stop Order: *see* Stop Sell Order.

Sell Ticket: the form used by a broker to enter a client's order to sell shares. Most order entry systems are now electronic. *See also* Buy Ticket.

SEMDEX Index: *see* Mauritius Stock Exchange Index.

Semiannual: twice a year. Also known as Biannual.

Semi-Annual Compound Return: a rate of return calculation in which interest is reinvested twice a year.

Seminar: a meeting at which an audience gathers to listen to an expert speaker. Seminars are often offered by financial institution employees in order to introduce services to the investing public.

Senate: in a legislature, the upper house. *See also* House of Commons, Senator, Triple E Senate.

Senator: a member of a senate. *See also* Senate.

Senile Dementia: a form of insanity that progresses with age until it deprives a person of testamentary capacity. *See also* Competent, Incompetent, Incapacity, Legal Capacity, Non Compos Mentis, Testamentary Capacity.

Senior: 1. *see* Senior Citizen. **2.** corporately, a position relatively high in the structure, as in a senior executive. **3.** in securities, a class of securities whose priority as to income and/or assets takes precedence over that of all other securities in the same class of the same issuer. Also known as Senior Bond, Senior Debt, Senior Security. *See also* Subordinated.

Senior Bond: *see* Senior.

Senior Citizen: generally, a person who is retired or is over the traditional age of retirement, usually 65.

The age is sometimes reduced to 55 and older for purposes of special prices for transit fares, theatre tickets, and so on. Also known as Senior, Seniors. *See also* Senior Seniors.

Senior Debt: *see* Senior.

Seniority: 1. the status of a security that has priority for the payment of income and the repayment of principal. *See also* Senior. **2.** in labour, a privileged status attained by length of service (e.g., in a company).

Senior Management: *see* Top Management.

Seniors: *see* Senior Citizen.

Seniors' Housing: most often gated or separate communities in which owner/occupants must be of a minimum age (e.g., 50 or 55 years old).

Senior Security: *see* Senior.

Senior Seniors: generally, those over age 75. *See also* Senior Citizen.

Sensitivity Analysis: an assessment of how much one variable changes given a change in another variable (e.g., the amount an oil company's earnings change given a $1 change in the price of oil).

Sentence: a court judgement regarding the punishment of someone (or some entity) who has been found guilty.

Sentiment: a reference to the optimism or pessimism prevailing among investors. Generally, sentiment is taken as a contrary indicator; that is, when optimism is high, the outlook is negative, and when pessimism is high, the outlook is positive.

Sentiment Indicator: an indicator that measures the mood of investors. *See also* Investment Services Bearish, Investment Services Bullish.

Separately Traded Residual and Interest Payment Bond (STRIP Bond): effectively, a zero coupon, long-term bond created by Canadian brokerage firms. They appeal to investors who want a guaranteed reinvestment rate, a fixed yield to maturity and a specific amount of money at a date well in the future. These securities are well suited for self-administered RRSPs of long-term investors. *See also* Bond.

Separation: in law, the state of being married but not living together. *See also* Separation Agreement.

Separation Agreement: an agreement between individuals no longer in a spousal relationship with regard to items such as maintenance and child support payments. *See also* Maintenance Order, Separation, Support Payment.

Sequential Couleur Avec Memoire (SECAM): the colour television broadcast standard invented in France and commonly used in Eastern Europe. *See also* High Definition Television, National Television System Committee, Phase Alternate Lines, Standard Definition Television.

Sequester: 1. in law, to hold a jury in seclusion. **2.** to confiscate property as security against legal claims.

Sergeant-at-Arms: an officer appointed to keep the peace (e.g., in a courtroom or legislature).

Serial: in computers, the consecutive flow of data, one bit at a time, along a single data line. *See also* Computer, Parallel.

Serial Bond: bonds that were issued at the same time but that were broken down into blocks with different maturity dates. *See also* Bond.

Serial Port: the input/output device on a computer, this is where data are transmitted to an external device in serial fashion; that is, one bit at a time along a single data line. *See also* Computer, Parallel Port.

Series: *see* Option Series.

Series Month: *see* Option Cycle.

Series of Option: *see* Option Series.

Serve: in law, to present a writ or summons.

Server: 1. in computers, an application that directs messages to different locations (e.g., an e-mail server distributes mail to different addresses). *See also* Computer, Post Office Protocol. **2.** *see* Process Server.

Service: 1. an economic term referring to employment (or work done for others) that does not result in the output of a physical product. **2.** payment of interest and principal on debt. **3.** the number of years of employment that count toward pension benefits. **4.** *see* Civil Service.

Service Charge: a fee for specific services (e.g., having a cheque certified).

Service Industries: in contrast to the so-called productive industries, service industries (e.g., accounting, administration, entertainment, law, finance, hotels, restaurants and retailing) do not produce a physical product. Mature economies, such as Canada, tend to have an increasing number of service jobs and a decreasing number of productive jobs.

Service Provider: *see* Internet Service Provider.

Services Bearish: *see* Investment Services Bearish.

Services Bullish: *see* Investment Services Bullish.

Servient Estate: in an easement, the party that surrenders a use to the dominant estate. *See also* Dominant Estate, Easement.

SES Singapore All Share Index: a market capitalization weighted index of the Stock Exchange of Singapore. *See also* Stock Exchange of Singapore.

Session: 1. a trading day on an exchange. **2.** a meeting of a legislative or judicial body.

SET: *see* Secure Electronic Transaction.

Setback: in real estate, the amount by which a building must be recessed from the property line.

Settle: 1. in investment, to finalize a securities trade by making the requisite payment and delivering the requisite securities. **2.** in law, to resolve a dispute prior to a court decision. **3.** to distribute the assets of an estate after all legal procedures have been completed.

Settle Away: the improper activity of making a private arrangement with a client in return for his/her promise to testify against his/her broker.

Settlement: 1. the finalizing of a securities trade. *See also* Cash Settlement, Settle, Three-Day Settlement. **2.** a term used to describe an agreement made with a creditor to satisfy an obligation in full with less than full payment, as in "make a settlement with the bank." **3.** *see* Termination Pay.

Settlement Date: the day on which settlement is due (e.g., three days after the trade date for stocks). *See also* Trade Date.

Settlement Options: the different ways in which a beneficiary of a life insurance contract can choose to receive a benefit. *See also* Claim, Coverage, Death Benefit, Policy.

Settlor: *see* Grantor.

Seven Sisters: seven international oil companies: British Petroleum Company PLC, Chevron Corporation, Exxon Corp., Gulf Oil Corp., Mobil Corporation, Royal Dutch Petroleum Company (Shell) and Texaco Inc. Only six "sisters" survive as independents. *See also* Six Sisters.

Several: where a guarantee is provided by a number of guarantors, "several" is the portion for which each guarantor is responsible.

Severally but Not Jointly: 1. any agreement in which a participant is responsible only for his/her obligation and not the obligation of others. *See also* Joint and Several. **2.** an underwriting agreement stating that each firm is responsible for selling the shares allotted to it but that it is not responsible for the activities of other members of the group.

Severalty: a legal individual right to ownership.

Severance: termination of employment, the implication being that it is non-voluntary. *See also* Constructive Dismissal, Dismissal for Cause, Severance Pay, Wrongful Dismissal.

Severance Package: *see* Severance Pay.

Severance Pay: additional pay (or benefits) given to an employee at the time he/she leaves employment. Severance pay is generally allotted when an employee leaves a job involuntarily and without cause. Also known as Severance Package. *See also* Constructive Dismissal, Dismissal for Cause, Wrongful Dismissal.

SFC: *see* Specialist in Financial Counselling.

SG&A: *see* Selling, General and Administrative Expenses.

Shadow: a term used in conjunction with another term to imply that something is hidden (e.g., shadow-vacancy means there is unused property that is not rented that may come on the market. Shadow-unemployment means there are jobs that will be lost at the first sign of a downturn).

Shadow Stock: *see* Phantom Stock Plan.

Shakedown: slang for extortion.

Shakeout: usually, a dip in prices that results in marginal holders selling their positions.

Shakeup: major corporate management changes.

Shallow Money: profits made by investing in existing trends such as a rising stock market. *See also* Deep Money.

Shanghai Stock Exchange: the major stock exchange of the People's Republic of China, located in Shanghai. Web site: www.comnex./can/stock/stocks.htm

Share: 1. *see* Common Share. **2.** *see* Preferred Share.

Share Buyback: *see* Normal Course Issuer Bid.

Share Capital: *see* Paid-In Capital.

Share Capital: capital provided by a company's shareholders.

Share Certificate: evidence of ownership of shares in a company. A share certificate will usually include the name of the issuer, the number of shares, the name of the registered owner and the par value. Also known as Certificate, Stock Certificate.

Share Consolidation: *see* Reverse Split.

Shared Appreciation: an arrangement in which a lender participates in the increase in value of an asset purchased with the money he/she has lent. *See also* Shared Appreciation Mortgage.

Shared Appreciation Mortgage (SAM): a non-conventional mortgage in which the lender receives a percentage of the equity in the property appreciation. Also known as Shared Equity Mortgage. *See also* Mortgage.

Shared Equity Mortgage: *see* Shared Appreciation Mortgage.

Share Float: the number of shares issued by a company that are available for public trading (e.g., shares held by a parent company would not be included in the share float). *See also* Parent Company.

Shareholder: an individual, corporation, institution or any other legal entity (e.g., a trust) that owns shares in a company. Also known as Stockholder.

Shareholder Activist: a person who aggressively challenges corporate management in order to defend individual shareholder rights.

Shareholder of Record: a shareholder whose name is recorded with the transfer agent of a company and who is eligible to receive dividends, vote at meetings and perform any other functions associated with a shareholder. *See also* Holder of Record, Of Record.

Shareholder's Equity: the residual value of total assets minus total liabilities. Also known as Capital.

Share Purchase Right: a security that gives the holder the option to purchase a fixed number of common shares from the issuer at a fixed price on or before a specified date. Rights are usually distributed to existing shareholders of a company on a per share basis but often trade on an exchange so investors can buy or sell them. As a rule, rights are distinguished from warrants by having a shorter time period within which they must be exercised. Also known as Rights, Stock Purchase Rights. *See also* Rights Offerings, Share Purchase Warrant.

Share Purchase Warrant: a security that gives the holder the option to purchase a fixed number of common shares from the issuer at a fixed price on or before a specified date. Warrants are usually distributed to existing shareholders of a company on a per share basis but often trade on an exchange so investors can buy or sell them. As a rule, warrants are distinguished from rights by having a longer time period within which they may be exercised. Also known as Stock Purchase Warrant, Warrant. *See also* Share Purchase Right.

Shares Authorized: *see* Authorized Capital.

Shares Issued: *see* Issued and Outstanding.

Shares Outstanding: *see* Issued and Outstanding.

Share Repurchase: *see* Normal Course Issuer Bid.

Share Rollback: *see* Reverse Split.

Share Split: this occurs when the number of outstanding shares are split into a larger number of shares. *See also* Reverse Split.

Shareware: software distributed freely, in the hope of compensation. *See also* Computer, Firmware, Freeware, Hardware, Software.

Shark: a company or person that preys on other companies by trying to take them over when they are vulnerable. *See also* Shark Watcher.

Shark Repellent: *see* Poison Pill.

Shark Watcher: a company that specializes in identifying early signs of corporate takeovers. *See also* Radar Screen, Shark.

Sharp: quick and steep, as in "A sharp market drop."

Sharpe Ratio: a ratio calculated by dividing the amount of a portfolio rate of return in excess of the risk free return and dividing it by the portfolio standard deviation. The ratio indicates whether a higher return was realized by shrewd investment or by taking higher risk. *See also* Risk Adjusted Return.

Shave: a relatively modest loss on the stock market, often across the board. *See also* Haircut.

Shear: often, to swindle or defraud.

Shed: in investing, to sell a small proportion of a holding, as in "Shed some stock."

Sheik: an Arab or Muslim leader.

Shekel: the prime currency of Israel.

Shelf Life: the period during which a financial offering may be sold. *See also* On the Shelf.

Shelf Prospectus: a form of prospectus that can be used to issue securities over an extended period (e.g., a mutual fund prospectus). *See also* Mutual Fund.

Shell: *see* Shell Company.

Shell Company: a stock exchange listed company with minimal assets and liabilities. Also known as Shell. *See also* Shell Game.

Shell Game: the activity of finding businesses to put into shell companies. *See also* Reverse Takeover, Shell Company.

Shell Shock: the condition of an investor who is unable to make decisions due to the stress caused by adverse financial developments.

Shelter: *see* Tax Shelter.

Sheriff: 1. a Crown-appointed official who, among other things, serves legal documents and subpoenas. **2.** in the U.S., the chief law enforcement officer in a county.

Shift: to gradually adjust a portfolio by moving certain investments from one area to another.

Shill: one who acts as a satisfied customer in order to induce others into a swindle.

Shingle: a public notice, or advertisement, pertaining to the business of a professional. *See also* Profession, Professional.

Shipment: the quantity of goods sent, delivered or received.

Shock Market: a term used to describe the stock market after a period of unexpected (and usually negative) events.

Shoestring: a term used to describe a small amount of money or capital used to start a new business. *See also* Bootstrap.

Shogun Bond: a foreign-company-issued, non-Yen security sold in Japan. *See also* Bond, Dragon Bond, Eurobond, Gilt, Samurai Bond, Yankee Bond.

Shop: 1. to contact a number of dealers in a security in order to obtain the best bid or ask price. **2.** an informal term for a firm, as in "brokerage shop." **3.** to survey a large number of buyers or sellers to determine the best possible price.

Shop Steward: a union member elected to represent co-workers in their negotiations with management. *See also* Labour Union.

Short: *see* Short Sale.

Short Against the Box: describes a condition of holding a long position and a short position in the same security in the same amount in the same account. *See also* Long Position, Short Position.

Short Bond: *see* Short-Term Bond.

Short Coupon: 1. when a bond is first issued, the initial interest payment may represent a shorter period of time than the remaining coupons. Such a payment is called a short coupon. *See also* Long Coupon. **2.** an interest-bearing bond that matures in less than two years. *See also* Long Coupon.

Short Covering: buying back shares previous sold short to complete the short sale transaction. Also known as Bear Covering, Buyback, Buying Back, Short Purchase.

Short End (of the market): bonds with short terms to maturity (e.g., two years or less). *See also* Long End (of the market).

Shorten Term: to sell bonds with a longer term to maturity and to buy bonds with a shorter term to maturity. This is a defensive strategy because short-term bonds have more price stability than do long-term bonds. *See also* Extend Term.

Shortfall: a condition in which supply or demand is less than either expected or needed.

Short Form Prospectus: an abbreviated prospectus that can be used in certain security underwritings. *See also* Prospectus, Simplified Prospectus.

Short-Handed: being short of workers, often because someone is ill (especially in a service business). Also known as Short-Staffed.

Short Hedge: a transaction that limits the risk of loss from owning an asset by owning a different asset (e.g., holding a stock position and gaining a short hedge by purchasing a put option). *See also* Long Hedge.

Short Interest: the total number of shares investors have sold short and not bought back. A high short interest indicates investors are pessimistic. Also known as Short Sale Interest. *See also* Short Sale.

Short Interest Indicator: a contrary market indicator. A high short interest ratio is a sign investors are pessimistic, which contrarians believe indicates that prices will rise, and vice versa. *See also* Contrary Market Indicator, Short Interest Ratio.

Short Interest Ratio: the short interest divided by the average trading volume. *See also* Short Interest, Short Interest Indicator, Short Sale.

Short Position: a net investment position in an individual portfolio in which securities have been borrowed and sold but not yet replaced. *See also* Short Sale.

Short Purchase: *see* Short Covering.

Short Sale: a securities transaction is profitable if an investor buys low and sells high. In a short sale, the investor attempts to sell high first and buy low later. This transaction is possible because specific securities are exactly the same and are interchangeable; that is, one common share of the Royal Bank is exactly the same as any other share of the Royal Bank. Brokers accommodate the trade by lending the investor shares for delivery to settle the short trade. The shares are replaced when the investor buys back. When the transaction is complete, that is, the sale and repurchase have been done, the investor's account is in balance. A short sale differs from buying long in one important way: when an investor buys long, his/her loss is limited to the sum invested; that is, the value can fall only to zero. When an investor sells short, his/her loss is unlimited because, in theory, the price of the stock can rise an infinite amount. Also known as Going Short, Go Short, Sell Short, Short. *See also* Long, Trap the Shorts, Uptick Rule.

Short Sale Interest: *see* Short Interest.

Short Sale Rule: *see* Uptick Rule.

Short Side: a reference to the practice of investing short as opposed to investing long. *See also* Short, Long Side.

Short Squeeze: pressure on short sellers to cover their positions as a result of price increases or difficulty in borrowing the required security. Also known as Bear Squeeze, Squeeze, Squeezing the Shorts.

Short-Staffed: *see* Short-Handed.

Short Term: in investment, generally a period of less than one year but possibly as many as three years depending on the asset class. *See also* Long Term, Medium Term, Near Term.

Short-Term Beta: a short-term (e.g., three months or less) forecast of a security's volatility. *See also* Beta.

Short-Term Bond: a bond with one year or less to maturity. Also known as Short Bond. *See also* Bond.

Short-Term Debt: 1. a bond that matures in a short period of time, sometimes defined as less than five years but more often defined as less than one year. **2.** a corporate liability on the balance sheet that falls due in less than one year. *See also* Long-Term Debt.

Short-Term Disability: an accident or illness that, for a relatively short period of time, prevents a person from working. *See also* Long-Term Disability.

Short-Term Disability Insurance: insurance against loss of income caused by an accident or illness that prevents a person from working for a short period.

Short-Term Trading: the buying and selling of a security within a short period. *See also* Day Trading, Quick Turn.

Short the Market: 1. in an active sense, selling short. *See also* Short Sale. **2.** in a passive sense, being in a short position. *See also* Short Position.

Short Ton: a unit of weight equal to 907.19 kilograms, or 2,000 pounds. Also known as Ton.

Shotgun Approach: a business technique that targets a very broad market or audience. The shotgun approach to marketing would be to target women of any age, as compared to targeting married women between the ages of 30 and 40. *See also* Rifle Approach.

Shotgun Clause: a contractual agreement stating that if the first party offers to buy out the second party, then the second party must either sell to the first party or buy him/her on the same terms and conditions. Also known as Put-Call Agreement. *See also* Buy-Sell Agreement.

Shoulder Season: the months just before and just after the busy season(s) (e.g., at a golf/ski resort, the shoulder seasons are spring (when skiing has ended but golf hasn't started) and fall (when golf has ended but skiing hasn't started). *See also* Off-Season.

Show Me Market: *see* Missouri Market.

Showstopper: 1. a disagreement in a negotiation that is serious enough to terminate discussions or to terminate a deal. Also known as Deal Breaker. **2.** a legal barrier to a takeover attempt that is virtually impossible for the buyer to overcome. Also known as Deal Breaker.

Shrinkage: loss of inventory (often to theft) encountered in the normal course of business.

Shyster: an unethical practitioner or a person practising with false credentials (especially in law).

SIA: *see* Securities Industry Association.

SIBE: *see* Spanish Stock Exchange System.

Sickout: a job action that involves employees staying away from work because, allegedly, they are ill.

Sicovam: *see* Société Interprofessionnelle pour la Compensation des Valeurs Mobilières. *See also* Sit-Down, Work-to-Rule.

Sidelines: a point from which one watches, rather than participates in, market trends. An investor on the sidelines watches the market but does not invest. Also known as On the Sidelines.

Sideways Market: *see* Trendless Market.

Sight Draft: a draft that is payable when presented with necessary documents, if any (e.g., a cheque). *See also* Demand Draft, Term Draft.

Sight Letter of Credit: a letter of credit that is payable when presented with the necessary documents. *See also* Letter of Credit.

Signal: an event that indicates the future (e.g., the U.S. Federal Reserve lowering the Federal Funds rate signals a willingness on the part of regulators to have interest rates decline.)

Signal to Noise Ratio: a slang term on the Internet, this is a reference to the amount of useful information that is received along with the useless information that cannot be avoided.

Signature Guarantee: a certificate issued by a bank or brokerage firm attesting to the authenticity of a person's signature. A signature guarantee is required for certain transactions (e.g., transferring securities registered in one person's name to another). Also known as Guarantee of Signature.

Signature Loan: an unsecured loan requiring only the borrower's signed promise to repay.

Signing Officer: a senior executive authorized to sign documents on behalf of a company. *See also* Seal.

Silent Partner: a partner in a business arrangement who maintains a low profile and, often, plays an inactive role. *See also* Partner.

Silicon Chip: a small piece of silicon on which very small electronic circuits are printed. A silicon chip can contain more than 100,000 transistors. Also known as Silicon Wafer.

Silicon Valley: the region of California south of San Francisco Bay (otherwise known as Santa Clara Valley), so termed because of its high concentration of electronics and computer research, development and manufacturing facilities.

Silicon Wafer: *see* Silicon Chip.

Sill: in mining, a horizontal dike. A structure formed by magma that flowed into a horizontal, rather than into a vertical, crack in the Earth. *See also* Dike.

Silver (Ag): a heavy metallic element, it has the highest thermal and electrical conductivity of all metals and is used in coins, photography and printed circuits. Silver is a precious metal. *See also* Precious Metal.

Silver Bullion: silver in its physical form. *See also* Triple Nine.

Silver Lining: some piece of good news gleaned from an otherwise negative event (e.g., when a company reports a decline in sales, the silver lining is that it will be easier to report a strong sales increase next year).

Silver Thursday: refers to March 27, 1980, when Nelson Hunt, Bunker Hunt and William Herbert Hunt ("the Hunt brothers") failed to meet a margin call of $100 million on their silver futures, sending the price of silver into a tailspin. *See also* Black Friday, Black Monday, Black Thursday, Black Tuesday, Black Wednesday, Golden Wednesday, Grey Monday.

Silviculture: relating to the growing of trees or forests.

Simple Interest: interest based on the original principal amount (i.e., without the effect of compounding). *See also* Compound Interest, Plurality, Straight Line Interest.

Simple Majority: a vote of 50 percent plus one.

Simplified Prospectus: a legal document in abbreviated form, describing an offering of mutual fund shares to the public. A simplified prospectus contains all the information that must be disclosed by securities regulations. Also known as Condensed Prospectus, Summary Prospectus. *See also* Mutual Fund, Prospectus.

Simulation: the process of building a mathematical computer model of a system, such as a company or an economy, and altering variables to observe their effects. *See also* Model.

Simultaneous Death Clause: *see* Common Disaster Clause.

SIN: *see* Social Insurance Number.

Sine Qua Non: an essential element or condition.

Singapore Stock Exchange: *see* Stock Exchange of Singapore.

Single Country Mutual Fund: *see* Country Specific Fund.

Single Family Residence: a unit designed to house one family. *See also* Duplex, Multi-Family Residential Housing, Triplex.

Single Life Annuity: an annuity that pays for the length of the beneficiary's life. *See also* Annuity, Beneficiary.

Single Premium Annuity: an annuity purchased with one lump-sum payment. *See also* Annuity.

Single Premium Life Insurance: a life insurance contract purchased with one up-front payment rather than with the promise of regular future payments. *See also* Life Insurance.

Sinker: *see* Sinking Fund Bond.

Sinking Fund: a financial reserve set aside by a company in order to satisfy a future obligation to redeem a bond or preferred share. The sinking fund assures investors that the obligation to redeem will be met. *See also* Half-Life, Purchase Fund.

Sinking Fund Bond: a bond with a sinking fund requirement. Also known as Sinker. *See also* Bond, Sinking Fund.

SIN: *see* Social Insurance Number.

Sin Tax: a tax levied on alcohol and/or cigarettes.

Sister Company: 1. a company that works closely with another company. **2.** a company that does many things in common with another but is not its exact replica.

Sit-Down: a labour protest in which workers refuse either to work or to leave their place of employment until their demands are met. *See also* Sickout, Work-to-Rule

Sit-In: a protest in which a disruption is caused by a number of people sitting down somewhere and refusing to leave.

Sitting on the Sidelines: a strategy that involves watching the market but not investing in it.

Situmercial: a television program that appears to be a comedy or light drama but is actually an advertisement. Also known as Storymercial. *See also* Advertorial, Advocacy Advertising, Direct Response Marketing, Infomercial, Infotainment, Institutional Advertising.

Six Sisters: the six oil companies which were members of the Seven Sisters that survive as international oil companies: BP Amoco PLC, Chevron Corporation, Exxon Corp., Mobil Corporation, Royal Dutch Petroleum Company (Shell) and Texaco Inc. *See also* Seven Sisters.

Size: 1. the number of shares available at the bid and offer prices. **2.** *see* Size the Market. **3.** a large number of shares, as in "I'm bidding for size."

Size the Market: to find out how many shares will be sold at the offering or purchased at the bid, as in "Please size the bid." Also known as Size.

Skate Onside: to move from a loss to a profit.

Skid: a slide, often downward, as in "the stock went for a skid."

Skim: to steal by taking small amounts of money over a long period of time.

Skin: to cheat. To swindle money from.

Skip Payment Privilege: the option, commonly on mortgages and credit cards, to skip or defer a regular payment.

Slack: 1. in business, a time of inactivity. **2.** a term used to indicate capacity for growth, as in "There's a lot of slack in the economy."

Slag: the material left after smelting ore.

Slam Dunk: an obvious or easy decision, as in "Buying the stock was a slam dunk." *See also* No-Brainer.

Slander: an oral statement that maliciously damages a person's reputation. *See also* Defame, Libel.

Sleeper: an underpriced, undiscovered stock.

Sleeping Beauty: an ideal corporate takeover target that has not yet been approached.

Sleep Mode: in computers, this occurs when a computer automatically shuts itself down after a period of inactivity. *See also* Computer.

Sleep Well, Eat Well: *see* Eat Well, Sleep Well.

Slide: a decline in prices.

Slide Rule: a mathematical calculating device consisting of logarithmically scaled rules that slide beside each other.

Sliding Scale: a situation in which one factor changes with another (e.g., the purchase price per unit declines as the number of units purchased increases).

Slovenian Equity Index: a market capitalization weighted stock price index for the Ljubljana Stock Exchange. *See also* Ljubljana Stock Exchange.

Slow: 1. a term used to describe a market with little volume and small price changes. **2.** an inactive economic period.

Slowdown: 1. a slackening of activity. **2.** *see* Work-to-Rule.

Sluggish: slow, as in "a sluggish economy."

Sluice Box: a long inclined trough over which sand and gravel is washed to allow gold flakes and nuggets to sink and be separated. *See also* Placer Mining.

Slum Landlord: one who owns and rents property in the poorest parts of town. *See also* Landlady, Landlord.

Slump: a temporary decline (sometimes of a sudden nature) in the economy or financial markets.

Slush Fund: a fund whose purposes are undesignated (and often unethical or illegal).

Small Business Corporation: a Canadian-controlled private corporation that uses substantially all of its assets to carry on an active business in Canada. *See also* Active Business, Canadian-Controlled Private Corporation.

Small Business Deduction: a federal tax credit to Canadian-controlled private corporations that has the effect of reducing the federal corporate tax rate on the first $200,000 of income. *See also* Taxes.

Small Business Loans Act (SBLA): a joint initiative of the federal government and private-sector lenders to make loans more accessible to small business. The program provides for certain government guarantees on loans to qualifying small businesses.

Small Cap: 1. a company with a relatively small stock market capitalization. *See also* Large Cap, Micro Cap, Mid Cap. **2.** a slang term used to refer to small or low-quality stocks.

Small Cap Common Stock Fund: *see* Small Cap Equity Fund.

Small Cap Effect: a term used to refer to the fact that, over the long term, the shares of small firms outperform the shares of large firms. Also known as Small Firm Effect. *See also* Small Cap.

Small Cap Equity Fund: 1. *see* Canadian Small to Mid Cap Equity Fund. **2.** *see* Mutual Fund – Category. **3.** *see* U.S. Small to Mid Cap Equity Fund. Also known as Small Cap Common Stock Fund.

Small Claims Court: a court designed to quickly dispense judgements on matters involving small amounts of money.

Small Firm Effect: *see* Small Cap Effect.

Small Investor: 1. an individual investor, usually with limited funds to invest. **2.** an investor who usually buys and sells in odd lots.

Small Office, Home Office (SOHO): a reference to the changes resulting from expanding electronic communications. SOHO means many business people can get by with small offices, working from home. *See also* Telecommute.

Small Print: in contracts, the legal terms and conditions that are in small type and so are often overlooked.

Smart Card: a bank card with a computer chip embedded in it. The chip contains information on the customer, thus allowing one card to offer a complete range of services: access to a bank machine, the ability to store cash electronically, credit, special price discounts (e.g., for travel) and so on. *See also* Smart Cash Card.

Smart Cash Card: a bank card with a computer chip embedded in it that allows the user to store cash electronically and to make everyday payments. Also known as Smart Money Card. *See also* Smart Card.

Smart Money: 1. an investor with above-average market experience and acumen. **2.** a mythical investor who knows what to do, as in "The smart money is moving into mutual funds." *See also* Gnomes of Zurich.

Smart Money Card: *see* Smart Cash Card.

Smell Test: a term used to explain why a technically legal activity may be deemed illegal, usually by Canada Customs and Revenue Agency or a regulatory authority (e.g., an activity is so offensive, it fails the "smell test").

Smiley: *see* Emoticon.

Smokestack Industry: a basic manufacturing industry, such as automobile or steel production, that has limited growth potential and high cyclicality. *See also* Cycle.

Snail Mail: a term that e-mail users employ to describe the regular postal system. *See also* Electronic Mail.

Snake: in April 1972, the European Community agreed to exchange rates between the currencies of each nation. These rates were to operate within a band of plus or minus 2.25 percent. This was known as the snake. *See also* Snake in the Tunnel.

Snake in the Tunnel: at the same time that the European Community agreed that exchange rates between the currencies of each nation would be held within a band of plus or minus 2.25 percent, they agreed that each currency would stay in a wider band of plus or minus 4.5 percent relative to the U.S. dollar. This was known as the snake in the tunnel. *See also* Snake.

Snake Oil: generally, anything of little value that is offered as something of great value.

Snowbird: a Canadian who spends a considerable amount of time each year in the U.S. Sunbelt but remains a resident of Canada for income tax purposes. *See also* Resident, Sojourner, Taxes.

SO: Internet acronym for "significant other."

Social Capital: the total resources of a society including land, natural resources, infrastructure (e.g., roads, hospitals) and the skills and abilities of the people. *See also* Capital.

Social Insurance Number (SIN): a nine-digit number issued by the Canadian government for the purposes of official identification (e.g., paying income tax).

Social Investing: *see* Socially Responsible Investing.

Socialism: an economic and political philosophy that advocates the public ownership of the means of production and distribution. In practice, socialist states offer significant government benefits funded by high rates of tax, which tends to minimize the disparity between high income and low income citizens. Since the 1980s, there has been a clear shift in world opinion away from socialism. *See also* Capitalism, Centrally Planned Economy, Communism, Free Market Economy, Market Economy, Private Property, Public Domain, Public Property.

Socialized Medicine: a system of public health care in which services are provided at no (or nominal) cost because they are paid for by government funds.

Socially Responsible Investing: an investment program focusing on social benefits (e.g., investing in a project that will produce high employment in a region). Compared with ethical investing, socially responsible investing is more likely to sacrifice rate of return to meet its goals. Also known as Social Investing. *See also* Ethical Investing.

Socially Responsible Mutual Fund: a mutual fund focusing on social benefits (e.g., investing in a project that provides low income housing). Compared with an Ethical Mutual Fund, a Socially Responsible Mutual Fund is more likely to sacrifice rate of return to meet its goals. *See also* Ethical Mutual Fund, Mutual Fund – Other.

Social Safety Net: government programs that are available to help people in time of need (e.g, unemployment insurance, welfare and old age security). *See also* Employment Insurance, Old Age Security, Welfare.

Société de la Bourses de Luxembourg: *see* Luxembourg Stock Exchange

Société des Bourses Francaises: *see* Paris Stock Exchange

Société Interprofessionnelle pour la Compensation des Valeurs Mobilières (Sicovam): *see* National Numbering Agency.

Society for Worldwide Interbank Financial Telecommunications (SWIFT): an international interbank electronic messaging system that forms part of the Trans-European Automated Real-Time Gross Settlement Express Transfer System. SWIFT is the clearing service provider for the Euro Banking Association. *See also* Euro Banking Association, Bank for International Settlements, Trans-European Automated Real-Time Gross Settlement Express Transfer.

Society of Management Accountants of Canada: an organization dedicated to accrediting, professional development and maintenance of standards of management accountants.

SOE: *see* State Owned Enterprise.

Soft: 1. something without much conviction (e.g., a soft order is one that is likely to be cancelled). **2.** a financial market or economic condition that is weak and could decline sharply at any time. *See also* Soft Market.

Soft Currency: a currency fixed at too high an exchange rate or not secured by gold and so difficult to exchange for hard currency. *See also* Hard Currency.

Soft Cyclical Stock: the common stock of a company engaged in a business that is affected greatly by the economy (e.g., banking). Soft cyclical stocks usually perform best in the early stages of an economic recovery. *See also* Cyclical.

Soft Disclosure: to provide information to securities analysts and/or investors of a non-material nature. Soft disclosure is used to help guide analysts and investors (e.g., to raise or lower earnings estimates). *See also* Disclosure, Full Disclosure, Insiders, Public Disclosure, Selective Disclosure, Structured Disclosure, Timely Disclosure.

Soft Dollars: a form of payment that does not involve cash (e.g., commissions). *See also* Hard Dollars.

Soft Landing: an economic slowdown that does not become a recession.

Soft Market: a market that, in response to a small amount of selling, will drop sharply in price. *See also* Soft.

Soft Money: paper currency. *See also* Hard Money.

Soft Pedal: *see* Soft Sell.

Soft Prices: prices subject to easy negotiation. *See also* Firm Prices, Hard Prices.

Softs: generally a reference to tropical commodities such as coffee, sugar and cocoa. In some cases, other agricultural products are included, but metals, financial futures and livestock are specifically excluded.

Soft Sell: to market without being aggressive. Also known as Soft Pedal.

Soft Spot: in an otherwise strong market, an industry or group of stocks that is weak.

Software: computer programs. The instructions that tell a computer what to do in order to perform tasks for the user. *See also* Computer, Firmware, Freeware, Hardware, Shareware.

SOHO: *see* Small Office, Home Office.

Sojourner: a person who may be resident elsewhere but who spends 183 days (or more) a year in Canada and is, therefore, deemed to be subject to Canadian tax law. *See also* Canada/U.S. Tax Convention of 1980, Protocol Amending the Canada-U.S. Tax Treaty, Snowbird, Taxes.

Solar Cell: a semiconductor device that converts solar energy into electricity. Also known as Photovoltaic Cell.

Sole Proprietorship: one of the three basic forms of business organization, it is an unincorporated business often owned by one person or family. Sole proprietorships are generally small and many do not have outside employees. Also known as Proprietorship, Unincorporated Business. *See also* Incorporation, Partnership.

Solicited Order: an order from a client to a stockbroker that was prompted by a recommendation from the stockbroker to the client. *See also* Unsolicited Order.

Solicitor: a member of the legal profession who is qualified to plead cases in the lower courts. Solicitors also deal with conveyancing and will preparation. In Canada, all solicitors are also barristers, except in Quebec. *See also* Barrister, Lawyer.

Solicitor-Client Privilege: *see* Lawyer-Client Privilege.

Solicitor General: a federal or provincial Cabinet member who is responsible for reformatories, prisons, penitentiaries, parole, the Royal Canadian Mounted Police and the Canadian Security Intelligence Service.

Solvent: the condition of being able to meet one's financial obligations. *See also* Bankrupt, Insolvent.

Som: the primary currency of Kyrgyzstan.

Son: a male child. With daughters, the next in line for an estate after a surviving spouse.

Sophisticated Investor: an experienced, high net worth investor who is eligible for an exemption that entitles him/her to invest in private placements. *See also* Private Property, Private Placement.

Sound: 1. financially secure, as in "A sound investment." **2.** in law, legally valid.

Sour Bond: a bond that is in default of payment of interest and/or principal. *See also* Bond.

Source and Application of Funds Statement: a financial statement that reconciles changes in assets and liabilities to changes in cash. *See also* Balance Sheet, Profit and Loss Statement, Statement of Retained Earnings.

Source Deduction: an automatic deduction from regular pay amounts used to pay for income tax, group benefits, a pension contribution or related item. *See also* Payroll Deduction.

South Korean Stock Exchange: *see* Korea Stock Exchange.

South of: lower or worse than (e.g., if a stock is headed "south of $20," its price will fall below $20). *See also* North of.

Sovereign Risk: the risk that a foreign investment will suffer a loss due to changes in government, government policy or foreign exchange rates. *See also* Country Risk, Exchange Risk, Political Risk.

Sovereignty: independence and self-government. *See also* Self-Government.

Spam: an unsolicited message sent to multiple newsgroups or users on the Internet. *See also* Internet.

Spanish Stock Exchange: *see* Madrid Stock Exchange.

SPDR: *see* Standard & Poor's 500 Depositary Receipt.

Special: a fund category describing mutual funds that invest in specific industry groups (e.g., high technology or biotechnology companies). *See also* Mutual Fund, Mutual Fund Category.

Special Fund: a fund category describing mutual funds that invest in specific industry groups (e.g., high technology or biotechnology companies). *See also* Mutual Fund, Specialty/Miscellaneous Fund.

Special Drawing Rights (SDR): a country's reserve account, held with the International Monetary Fund, to be used to support its currency. Special Drawing Rights were initially set up by the IMF in the 1960s because it felt the supply of gold and U.S. currency would not be sufficient to finance world trade. Also known as Paper Gold. *See also* Artificial Currency.

Specialist: 1. a person or securities firm that holds a seat on a national exchange and must maintain orderly markets for the select group of stocks over which it is given an exclusive franchise. **2.** often, a reference to a specialist on the New York Stock Exchange. **3.** a broker, financial analyst or other investment professional who devotes much time and effort to a specific area of expertise.

Specialist in Financial Counselling (SFC): a designation issued by the Institute of Canadian Bankers to industry employees engaged in retirement and estate planning.

Special Meeting of Shareholders: a meeting (other than the annual general meeting) that can be called if it is done so in accordance with the conditions set out in the articles of incorporation. *See also* Articles of Incorporation.

Special Situation: 1. an undervalued stock that can suddenly increase in value because of imminently favourable circumstances. **2.** a term used to describe a group of unrelated securities followed by a professional financial analyst.

Special Terms: the specific conditions under which an order to buy or sell a security is entered (e.g., an all or nothing bid). *See also* All or Nothing.

Specialty Fund: 1. *see* Mutual Fund – Category. **2.** *see* Specialty/Miscellaneous Fund.

Specialty/Miscellaneous Fund: one of the 31 Canadian categories developed by the Investment Funds Standards Committee. Mutual funds in this category must have a minimum of 50 percent of the total assets, and 75 percent of the non-cash assets, of the portfolio relating to the sector or geographic specialty as established in the fund's prospectus. The calculations to determine whether a mutual fund fits this definition are based on median values from fund data over three years, unless otherwise noted. The derivatives are weighted on an extended value basis. Each of the categories may be refined by the fund manager (e.g., a Canadian Large Cap Equity Fund may be described as "growth" or "value" to reflect the manager's style). Also known as Gold Mutual Fund, Industry Mutual Fund, Specialty Fund. *See also* Extended Value, Mutual Fund – Category.

Special Warrants Underwriting: a form of underwriting in which the shares issued may not be sold by the purchaser until subsequently cleared by a prospectus. The funds raised are sometimes put in trust until the prospectus is approved. If the clearing occurs as agreed, then the shares become free trading. If there is a delay in the clearing, then the issuer normally suffers a penalty in the form of added shares for the investor.

Specie: money made out of something of value (e.g., gold coins).

Specific Bequest: in wills, a gift of a specific item of personal property or a set amount of cash. *See also* Will.

Specific Devise: in wills, a gift of a specific item of real estate. *See also* Will.

Specific Risk: *see* Company Specific Risk.

Speculation: a very high-risk venture offering very high potential returns. A speculation often involves an untested, unproven investment. *See also* Investment.

Speculative: an untested, unproven, risky investment.

Speculator: a person who invests in high risk investments in the pursuit of above average gains. *See also* Conservative Investor, Gambler, Investor, Nervous Nellie.

Speed Bump: an event that slows or interrupts the upward trend in financial markets without altering its direction.

Spend: to pay out money.

Spendthrift Trust: an informal term referring to a trust that has been made restrictive so that its beneficiary cannot deplete it and so that it remains beyond the reach of his/her creditors. *See also* Trust.

Spider: *see* Standard & Poor's 500 Depositary Receipt.

Spiel: an extravagant speech (especially, a sales pitch).

Spike: a rapid and sharp rise in price.

Spin Doctor: a communications professional, usually hired by a politician to present his/her positions in the most favourable light.

Spinoff: a divestiture, sale or dividend whereby one company distributes assets, or makes a separate entity out of, a subsidiary.

Split: *see* Stock Split.

Split Coupon Bond: a bond that begins as a zero coupon bond but becomes an interest paying bond in the future. *See also* Bond.

Split Close: this occurs when one market index closes up on the day and another closes down on the day (e.g., June 25, 1998, when the Dow-Jones Average rose 11.71 points and the Standard & Poor's 500 fell 3.60 points). *See also* Split Opening.

Split-Dollar Insurance: in this case, each shareholder buys a cash value insurance policy on the other and assigns the cash value to the company. When a shareholder dies, the death benefit less the cash value goes to the surviving shareholder(s), who uses the money to buy the shares of the deceased. The company receives the cash value. This is a combination of Criss-Cross Insurance and Corporate-Owned Insurance. *See also* Criss-Cross Insurance, Corporate-Owned Insurance.

Split Down: an amendment to a company charter that reduces the number of issued shares and proportionately increases the par value of each share. *See also* Issued and Outstanding Capital, Par Value.

Split Off: an exchange of the stock of a subsidiary for shares in the parent company.

Split Opening: this occurs when an error is made and a stock opens trading at two different prices. *See also* Split Close.

Split Order: a large order to buy or sell securities that is split into smaller orders to minimize fluctuations in the price. *See also* Order.

Split Rating: this occurs when two or more bond rating services give the same issuer different ratings. *See also* Bond Rating, Bond Rating Agency.

Split-Schedule Loan: a loan (often a mortgage) that begins with an interest-only payment and later reverts to a normal amortization schedule. *See also* Amortization, Interest-Only.

Split Yield Security: a special investment set up to purchase a dividend paying common stock. One category of split yield security is entitled to all the dividends received. The second category of split yield security is entitled to all the capital gain realized. *See also* Toronto 35 Index Dividend Capital Receipt, Toronto 35 Index Secondary Warrant.

Spoiler: a posting to a newsgroup that reveals what is intended to be a surprise, such as the way a movie ends or the answer to a puzzle. According to netiquette, such postings should include "spoiler" in the title so that people can avoid them if they so choose. *See also* Netiquette, Newsgroup.

Sponsor: an influential investor who induces other investors to buy a particular stock. *See also* Sponsorship

Sponsoring Self-Regulatory Organization (SSRO): in Canada, the organizations that sponsor the Canadian Investor Protection Fund. These are the Alberta, Toronto and Vancouver Stock Exchanges, the Montreal Exchange and the Investment Dealers Association of Canada. *See also* Investor Protection Fund, Self-Regulatory Organization.

Sponsorship: the practice of an investor supporting a particular security. *See also* Sponsor.

Spoofing: in computers, making a transmission appear to come from an authorized user (e.g., to obtain access to a secured computer). *See also* Computer.

Spot Contract: a financial security to evidence the purchase or sale of a commodity or currency for immediate delivery. *See also* Forward Contract, London Metal Exchange, Spot Market.

Spot Commodity: a commodity traded in the expectation that it will be delivered.

Spot Market: 1. a transaction for immediate delivery and payment. *See also* Spot Contract. **2.** a futures transaction that will expire in one month or less. *See also* Cash Delivery, Cash Settlement, Spot Contract.

Spot Price: the price of something that is available for immediate delivery. *See also* Spot Contract, Spot Market.

Spotty Market: *see* Trendless Market.

Spousal Registered Retirement Savings Plan: *see* Registered Retirement Savings Plan – Spousal.

Spousal Rollover: the transfer (or bequeathing) of assets from the account of one spouse to another in such a way that income taxes otherwise payable are deferred to a future date. Also known as Spousal Transfer. *See also* Rollover, Tax Free Rollover.

Spousal Support: a payment by agreement or court order by one spouse to the other after they are separated or divorced. Also known as Alimony, Support Payment. *See also* Maintenance Order, Separation Agreement.

Spousal Transfer: *see* Spousal Roll Over.

Spousal Trust: in term used informally to refer to a trust set up to provide a life income for a spouse, with the capital passing to beneficiaries upon the latter's death. Also known as Q-Tip Trust. *See also* Sprinkling Trust, Trust.

Spread: 1. a historical differential between two or more financial variables (e.g., the difference between the yield on Government of Canada bonds and a provincial bond). *See also* Matrix Trading, Yield Spread. **2.** the difference between the quoted bid and the offer for a security. Also known as Price Spread. **3.** in options, the difference in premiums on a put and call for the same security. *See also* Option. **4.** in underwriting, the difference between the price an issue was purchased for by the underwriting syndicate and the price the security was sold for to the investing public. **5.** in foreign exchange, the difference between exchange rates on different exchanges. **6.** in banking, the difference between the rate a bank must pay to attract funds and the rate of interest the funds can earn when lent to others.

Spreadsheet: a computer program that consists of a large array of columns and rows into which data can be entered for easy manipulation. Data are placed in cells, and each cell can be programmed to behave like a small calculator. The spreadsheet is interconnected, so changing the value of one cell automatically changes the value of any associated cells. *See also* Array, Cell, Column, Row.

Sprinkling Trust: an informal term that refers to a trust, the income from which can be distributed among some or all family members at the trustee's discretion. *See also* Spousal Trust, Trust.

Spud: to begin to drill an oil or gas well.

Squawk Box: a telephone system, usually open during working hours, that stock traders use to communicate with all branches and offices.

Squeeze: 1. the effect on profit margins when cost increases cannot be passed along and profits decline. **2.** *see* Short Squeeze.

Squeeze-Out: the act of forcing stockholders to sell.

Squeezing the Shorts: *see* Short Squeeze.

Sri Lanka Stock Exchange: *see* Colombo Stock Exchange.

Sri Lanka Stock Market All Share Index: an index of shares traded in Sri Lanka.

SRO: *see* Self-Regulatory Organization.

Stabilization: the action of a central bank that buys or sells currencies in order to maintain an orderly market for its currency.

Stag: a speculator who buys and sells for quick profit.

Stage of Development Financing: an arrangement of loans sometimes used by financial institutions, according to the stage of development of borrowers. The categories are Early Stage Financing, Expansion Stage Financing, Acquisition Stage Financing and Turnaround Stage Financing. *See also* Acquisition Stage Financing, Early Stage Financing, Expansion Stage Financing, Turnaround Stage Financing.

Stagflation: the combination of an economic slowdown (or recession) and high inflation.

Staggered Board of Directors: a board of directors in which only a portion of the total board comes up for election each year. This is to make it more difficult for someone to takeover the company, since it takes much longer to gain control of the board of directors. *See also* Board of Directors.

Staggered Bond Portfolio: a bond portfolio with holdings evenly distributed among terms to maturity. Also known as Ladder, Laddering.

Stagnation: a period of economic slowdown.

Stake: in resource prospecting, the process of marking the limits or boundaries of an area to be explored.

Stand-Alone: a self-contained project or investment.

Standard & Poor's Corporation (S&P): a financial information and services company known for calculating stock market indexes and rating money market securities, bonds and preferred shares. *See also* Bond Rating, Bond Rating Agency, Canadian Bond Rating Service, Dominion Bond Rating Service, High-Grade Bond, Low-Grade Bond, Moody's Investors Services, Rating, Standard & Poor's Effect.

Standard & Poor's Effect (S&P Effect): the heavy buying or selling by index funds and indexed portfolios of a stock added to or removed from a Standard & Poor's index. Also known as S&P Phenomenon. *See also* Index Fund, Standard & Poor's Corporation.

Standard & Poor's 100: *see* OEX.

Standard & Poor's 100 Index: a market capitalization weighted index of 100 stocks for which options are listed on the Chicago Board Options Exchange. Also known as S&P 100, OEX.

Standard & Poor's 500 (S&P 500): a market capitalization weighted index of 500 large companies, representing all major industries. The index had a base value of 10 in the period between 1941 and 1943.

Standard & Poor's 500 Depositary Receipt (SPDRs): index participation units, offered by the American Stock Exchange, that replicate movements in the Standard & Poor's 500 Index. Spiders are a basket of securities that provides index-like returns and that investors can buy as a single common share. Also known as Spider. *See also* Diamonds, Index Participation Units.

Standard & Poor's Midcap 400 (S&P 400): a market capitalization weighted index of 400 middle sized companies. The index had a base value of 100 on December 31, 1990.

Standard & Poor's Smallcap 600 (S&P 600): a market capitalization weighted index of 600 small sized companies. The index had a base value of 100 on December 31, 1993.

Standard Bar Gold: standard sizes of gold bullion bars (e.g., 100 ounces of 99.9 percent pure).

Standard Bar Silver: standard sizes of silver bullion bars (e.g.,1,000 ounces of 99.9 percent pure).

Standard Class: in insurance, an average or normal risk class. *See also* Life Insurance, Rated Insurance.

Standard Definition Television (SDTV): television that uses 525 horizontal lines in North America and 625 horizontal lines in Asia and Europe. *See also* High Definition Television, National Television Standards Committee, Phase Alternate Lines, Sequential Couleur Avec Memoire.

Standard Deviation (SD): in statistics, a measure of the volatility of a set of observations by measuring the variance of each observation from the average. It is calculated as the square root of the average of the squares of the deviations. If the observations fall into a bell curve, it is a normal distribution. *See also* Historical Beta, Long-Term Beta, Normal Beta, Normal Distribution, Portfolio Beta, Short-Term Beta, Standard Error.

Standard Deviation of Error: a statistic measuring the accuracy of an estimate, it is equal to the standard deviation. *See also* Standard Deviation.

Standard of Living: in any given country, a measure of the output of goods and services per capita. For purposes of international comparisons, analysts now try to look at the quality of life using data on housing, education and employment opportunities.

Standard Stock and Mining Exchange: an exchange for the trading of mining stocks that merged with the Toronto Mining and Industrial Exchange before merging with the Toronto Stock Exchange in 1934. *See also* Toronto Stock Exchange.

Standby Charge: a fee charged for providing a stand-by loan, whether or not the loan is actually used. Also known as Standby Fee. *See also* Standby Loan.

Standby Commitment: 1. in underwriting, a commitment to purchase for resale any part of a rights offering that is not taken up by the rights holders. Also known as Underwriting Rights. *See also* Rights Offering. **2.** *see* Standby Loan.

Standby Fee: *see* Standby Charge.

Standby Letter of Credit: the guarantee of a letter of credit that will be called if the original payer defaults.

Standby Loan: a loan from a bank for a prescribed amount of money should certain events occur (e.g., if long-term mortgage financing falls short of the required amount). Also known as Standby Commitment. *See also* Standby Charge.

Standstill Agreement: an agreement between a securities issuer and a large investor, it stipulates that the investor will not buy or sell any more of the issuer's securities without prior approval.

Star System: the approach used by some Canadian mutual fund companies to feature the money management skills of an individual fund manager rather than the skills of the team or corporation. *See also* Mutual Fund.

Startup: 1. a new business in its early stages. **2.** a public company before it has significant sales or earnings. **3.** the preliminary (or initial) stage of an industry life cycle, usually followed by expansion, maturity and decline. *See also* Decline, Expansion, Industry Life Cycle, Maturity.

Stated Value: a value for a security used for accouting purposes. *See also* Face Value, Market Value, Par Value.

Stateless: without citizenship.

Statement: 1. in law, a written communication setting out allegations and/or facts. **2.** a financial summary or summary of transactions. *See also* Account Statement.

Statement of Changes in Financial Position: a financial statement that reconciles changes in a company's working capital. *See also* Balance Sheet, Profit and Loss Statement, Source and Application of Funds Statement, Statement of Retained Earnings.

Statement of Financial Position: *see* Balance Sheet.

Statement of Income: *see* Income Statement.

Statement of Material Facts: a document that provides basic information about a listed company when it is being underwritten.

Statement of Retained Earnings: a financial statement that reconciles the opening and closing balances in the retained earnings account. The general formula is the opening balance plus or minus net profit or loss minus dividends plus or minus other items. The statement of retained earnings must accompany the balance sheet and income statement under Generally Accepted Accounting Principals. Also known as Retained Earnings Statement. *See also* Balance Sheet, Profit and Loss Statement, Source and Application of Funds Statement.

State Owned Enterprise (SOE): a company or business owned by a government.

Statesman: *see* Statesperson.

Statesperson: a leader in national or international affairs who is often noted for public service. Also known as Statesman, Stateswoman.

Stateswoman: *see* Statesperson.

Statistical Office of the European Communities (Eurostat): one of the services of the European Commission, Eurostat provides up-to-date and accurate statistics for the European Community. *See also* European Commission, European Community.

Statistician: a person with expertise in the field of statistics.

Statistics: 1. a branch of mathematics that deals with collecting, organizing and analyzing numerical data. **2.** generally, any mathematical data.

Statistics Canada (StatsCan): a statistics gathering agency of the Canadian federal government, it gathers data on demographics, economics and finance. StatsCan is acknowledged as one of the finest organizations of its kind in the world.

StatsCan: *see* Statistics Canada.

Status Quo: things as they are.

Statute: a law or laws created by an act of the provincial legislature or the federal parliament.

Statute Mile: a distance of approximately 1,609 metres or 5,280 feet.

Statute of Limitations: in law, a period after which legal action cannot be taken.

Statutory Declaration: an oath.

Statutory Holiday: a holiday established by a federal or provincial statute (e.g., Christmas, Labour Day). Also known as Public Holiday.

Statutory Lien: a security interest deemed to exist by statute rather than private contract. The statute of limitations for Canada Customs and Revenue Agency is six years from the time a return is filed unless fraud is alleged.

Statutory Merger: this occurs when two companies merge into one and one of the companies retains its legal identity.

Statutory Next-of-Kin: the next of kin as specified by legislation. The statutory next-of-kin is used

when a person dies without a will. *See also* Intestate, Succession, Will.

Statutory Rights of Rescission: *see* Rights of Rescission.

Statutory Voting: generally, a shareholder's right to one vote for each share held, especially in the election of directors. Also known as One-Share-One-Voting, Ordinary Voting. *See also* Cumulative Voting.

Staying Power: the ability of an investor to hold onto an investment that has declined in value.

Steady: a market that is essentially flat.

Steep: 1. rapid change, as in "A steep decline in the stock market." **2.** expensive, as in "A steep price."

Stem the Tide: to stop a trend, most often a decline, or change its direction. Often used with respect to stopping an economic slump or a stock market decline. Also known as Stop the Bleeding.

Step, Step, Stumble Rule: a stock market rule that says the U.S. bond and stock markets will fall after the Federal Reserve raises the discount rate three times in succession. Also known as Three Steps and a Stumble Rule. *See also* Discount Rate, Federal Reserve Board.

Step-Up: a scheduled increase in the exercise or conversion price at which a warrant, an option or a convertible may acquire shares of common stock.

Step Up to the Plate: to move from a neutral position to an active one (e.g., an investor who has been holding cash waiting for a stock market decline, "steps up to the plate" when he/she finally purchases stocks).

Sterile Investment: an investment that does not pay interest or dividends (e.g., gold bullion).

Sticky: in the investment field, an issue that is hard to market.

Stipend: a fixed, regular payment received (often with the suggestion that the amount is small).

Stipulate: to put forward as a condition of an agreement.

Stochastic Model: a mathematical model that assumes the values of variables are unknown or random. *See also* Deterministic Model.

Stock: 1. a unit of ownership in a company. **2.** a reference to a business's inventory of goods.

Stock Ahead: 1. a term used to describe a number of limit orders to sell shares that were placed earlier and are still in effect. If the price rises to the limits, selling will be triggered. *See also* Limit, Limit Order, Overhead, Supply Area. **2.** this occurs when two orders to buy or sell at the same price are entered at the same time and the exchange rules for priority of orders takes effect.

Stock Appreciation Right: executive compensation of cash or stock that is equal to the amount by which the firm's stock price exceeds a specified base price. *See also* Stock Option – Executive and/or Employee.

Stock Average: *see* Stock Market Index.

Stock Bet: this occurs when a portfolio manager owns either more or fewer shares than are reflected in the stock's weighting in a stock market index or benchmark. Also known as Bet. *See also* Industry Bet, Market Bet, Stock Market Bet.

Stockbroker: *see* Broker.

Stock Brokerage Firm: a company engaged in the buying and selling of securities for clients.

Stock Buyback: 1. *see* Normal Course Issuer Bid. **2.** *see* Repurchase.

Stock Certificate: *see* Share Certificate.

Stock Company: a company that has issued shares to stockholders in order to raise capital. *See also* Company.

Stock Consolidation: *see* Reverse Split.

Stock Dividend: a dividend paid in shares rather than cash. *See also* Cash Dividend, Dividend, Optional Dividend.

Stock du Jour: the stock of the day. A derogatory reference to stock that investment advisors recommend simply in order to generate commissions.

Stock Exchange: *see* Stock Market.

Stock Exchange Seat: a membership in a commodities or stock exchange. Before computerized trading, a membership provided a location, or seat, on the stock exchange floor from which to conduct trading. Also known as Seat. *See also* Stock Exchange.

Stock Exchange Automated Trading System (SEATS): the automated trading system used on the Australian Stock Exchange that links the trading floors of Adelaide, Brisbane, Hobart, Melbourne, Perth and Sydney.

Stock Exchange of Hong Kong: the major stock exchange of Hong Kong. Also known as Hong Kong Stock Exchange. Web site: www.sehk.com.hk

Stock Exchange of Montevideo: the major stock exchange of Uruguay, located in its capital, Montevideo. Also known as Bolsa de Valores de Montevideo. Web site: www.bvm.com.uy

Stock Exchange of Singapore: the major stock exchange of Singapore, located in its capital, Singapore. Web site: www.ses.com

Stock Exchange of Singapore Straits Times Index: a market capitalization weighted index of the Stock Exchange of Singapore. Also known as Straits Times Index.

Stock Exchange of Thailand: the major stock exchange of Thailand, located in its capital, Bangkok. Web site: www.set.or.th/

Stock Exchange of Thailand SET Index: a market capitalization weighted stock price index for the Stock Exchange of Thailand.

Stockholder: *see* Shareholder.

Stockholm Fondbors: *see* Stockholm Stock Exchange.

Stockholm Stock Exchange: the major stock exchange of Sweden, located in its capital, Stockholm. Also known as Stockholm Fondbors. Web site: www.xsse.se *See also* Swedish General Index.

Stock Index: *see* Stock Market Index.

Stock Index Future: a futures contract that uses a stock index as its underlying asset and is settled by delivery of the underlying shares in the index.

Stock Index Option: a put or call option on a stock index, with profits and losses settled in cash. Also known as Index Option. *See also* Option.

Stock Jockey: an aggressive stockbroker who actively recommends buying and selling common stocks.

Stock Lending: *see* Security Lending.

Stock Life Insurance Company: a life insurance company whose management is directed by shareholders and participating life insurance policy holders. *See also* Mutual Life Insurance Company.

Stock Market: an organized institution for the trading of stocks. Some stock exchanges also list bonds and other financial instruments. Also known as Exchange, Stock Exchange. *See also* Bond Market, Commodity Exchange, Futures Exchange, Financial Market, Money Market.

Stock Market Average: *see* Stock Market Index.

Stock Market Barometer: usually, one stock that has a price pattern indicative of the overall market.

Stock Market Bet: a high portfolio holding in the stock market in the expectation of above-average rates of return. *See also* Industry Bet, Market Bet, Stock Bet.

Stock Market Capitalization: 1. for a company, the price of its shares times the number of common shares outstanding. Also known as Cap, Capitalization, Market Cap, Market Capitalization. **2.** for a market, the total stock market capitalization of all listed companies. Also known as Cap, Capitalization, Market Cap, Market Capitalization.

Stock Market Crash: a very large and rapid drop in stock prices (e.g., the 500+ point drops in the Dow-Jones Average on October 19, 1987). A crash is usually defined as a one-day drop of 10 percent or more. Also known as Crash. *See also* October Massacres.

Stock Market Cycle: the tendency for stock prices to move in a cyclical pattern from a trough, through a bull (or rising) market, to a peak, followed by a bear (or declining) market. Also known as Market Cycle.

See also Bear Market, Bull Market, Elliott Wave Theory, Kondratieff Wave, Peak, Presidential Election Cycle, Trough.

Stock Market Index: an index, based on the price movement of a sample of common stocks, that is used to provide a simple indication of the price changes in the overall market. The Dow-Jones Industrial Average is one of the oldest stock market indexes, first published on May 26, 1896. Because computers were not invented yet, calculations had to be kept simple. The Dow was simply the prices of 20 stocks added up and divided by 20. For this reason, stock market indexes are still sometimes referred to as stock market averages. Today, index calculations are made automatically by computers. The Toronto Stock Exchange 300 Index, for example, is based on the stock market capitalization of 300 companies. Modern stock market indexes are used to measure specific trends (e.g., the share prices of large companies, small companies, companies in specific industries). Also known as Average, Index, Market Average, Market Index, Stock Market Average, Stock Index. *See also* Dow-Jones Industrial Average, Geometric Stock Market Index, Stock Average, Stock Bet, Stock Market Capitalization, Toronto Stock Exchange 300 Index.

Stock Market Term Deposit: a variable rate term deposit that offers a low rate of guaranteed interest and additional return based on the performance of common stocks, as measured by a stock market index. *See also* Term Deposit.

Stock Option: 1. *see* Stock Option – Executive and/or Employee. **2.** *see* Option.

Stock Option – Executive and/or Employee: options, granted to executives and/or employees, that carry the right but not the obligation to buy shares of that company's stock at a predetermined price and before a set date. Also known as Employee Stock Option, Option – Executive and/or Employee, Stock Option. *See also* Incentive Stock Option, Option.

Stock/Bond Power: *see* Stock Power.

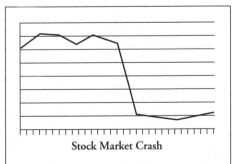

Stock Market Crash

Stock Power: a power of attorney form used to transfer ownership of registered securities from one person to another. The stock power is attached to the certificate when it is delivered or pledged as collateral. Also known as Stock/Bond Power. *See also* Power of Attorney.

Stock Promoter: a person who tries to induce investors to buy shares of a particular company. A stock promoter is often associated with very small, little-known companies and may use questionable, unethical or illegal methods to induce people to buy stock. Also known as Promoter. *See also* Promotion, Tout.

Stock Purchase Rights: *see* Share Purchase Rights.

Stock Purchase Warrants: *see* Share Purchase Warrants.

Stock Recommendation: advice to buy, hold or sell a stock.

Stock Repurchase: *see* Normal Course Issuer Bid.

Stock Split: an action by which a stock is divided into a larger number of shares. Also known as Split. *See also* Reverse Split, Scrip, Share Consolidation, Stock Consolidation.

Stocks Will Continue to Fluctuate: oft-quoted answer by legendary U.S.-financier J.P. Morgan (1837-1913), when asked for a stock market forecast.

Stock Symbol: a standardized abbreviated notation for a stock (e.g., the symbol for Royal Bank is RY; the symbol for International Business Machines is IBM). Stock symbols can be used for marketing purposes (e.g., professional golfer Jack Nicklaus' public company is Golden Bear Golf Inc., but the stock symbol is JACK). Also known as Symbol, Ticker Symbol.

Stock Ticker: *see* Ticker Tape.

Stock Trader: 1. an employee of a brokerage firm engaged in buying and selling common stocks based on client orders. *See also* Bond Trader, Trader. **2.** an employee of a financial institution engaged in buying and selling common stocks based on instructions from a portfolio manager. *See also* Bond Trader, Trader. **3.** an investor who actively buys and sells stocks for his/her own account. *See also* Bond Trader, Trader.

Stock Trader's Almanac: an annual publication edited by Yale Hirsch and focused on various ways to forecast the stock market (especially from a seasonal point of view). *See also* Presidential Election Cycle.

Stock Universe: the total list of companies followed by a research analyst or portfolio manager. *See also* Research Universe.

Stop-and-Go: a technique for deferring income to a future period and accelerating future expenses to the present.

Stop Buy Order: an order to buy securities at market but only after the price rises to a certain level. Also known as Buy Stop Order, Stop Order. *See also* Order, Stop Limit Order, Stop Price, Stop Sell Order.

Stop Limit Order: an order to buy or sell securities at a specified price or better but only after the stop limit price has been reached or exceeded. *See also* Stop Order.

Stop Loss Order: an order to sell a security if the price drops to a predetermined level. So termed because its purpose is to automatically limit losses. *See also* Order.

Stop Order: an order to buy or sell securities at the market but only after the stop order price has been reached or exceeded. *See also* Stop Buy Order, Stop Sell Order.

Stop Payment: an instruction from the issuer of a cheque to the bank to refuse to honour payment.

Stopped Out: the process of a stop loss order being executed and shares being sold as instructed. *See also* Stop Loss Order.

Stop Price: the price a security must reach to trigger a stop order. *See also* Stop Buy Order, Stop Order, Stop Sell Order.

Stop Sell Order: an order to sell securities at the market but only after the price falls to a certain level. Also known as Sell Stop Order, Stop Order. *See also* Gather in the Stops, Stop Buy Order, Stop Limit Order, Stop Price.

Stop the Bleeding: *see* Stem the Tide.

Story Bond: a bond so unique or complex that brokers are frequently called on to explain its intricacies. *See also* Bond.

Storymercial: *see* Situmercial.

Story Stock: a common stock with a value that reflects its potential rather than its real tangible assets and earnings.

Straddle: buy or own a put and call on the same security with the same exercise price and expiry date. *See also* Option, Strangle.

Straight Debt: a loan without special features.

Straight Life Annuity: an annuity that makes payments only for the duration of the annuitant's life. *See also* Annuity, Life Annuity, Life Annuity with Guarantee, Life Annuity without Guarantee.

Straight Life Insurance: *see* Whole Life Insurance.

Straight Line Depreciation: this occurs when the cost of an asset is written down in value by equal annual amounts over its useful life. *See also* Depreciation, Sum-of-the-Years' Digits Method.

Straight Line Interest: interest calculated annually as a percentage of the unpaid balance of a loan. *See also* Compound Interest, Simple Interest.

Straight Loan: a mortgage with interest-only payments. *See also* Mortgage.

Straits Times Index: *see* Stock Exchange of Singapore Straits Times Index.

Strangle: to sell or buy both a well out-of-the-money call and a well out-of-the-money put on the same security with the same expiry date. A strangle is cheaper than a straddle but requires a significant move in the price of the underlying security to produce a profit. *See also* Call Option, Option, Out of the Money, Put Option, Straddle.

Strap: an option consisting of two calls and one put. *See also* Call Option, Option, Put Option.

Strata Council: in a multifamily condominium, a group of owners elected to make decisions on matters of common interest to all owners. *See also* Condominium

Strategic Alliance: an agreement between Company A and Company B in which Company A provides an expertise that Company B is lacking, and vice versa. Generally, the term covers joint ventures and joint marketing or joint manufacturing agreements.

Strategic Asset Allocation: management of a portfolio by investing in a variety of asset classes such as treasury bills, bonds and common stocks and making very few changes in the amounts allocated to each asset class over time. *See also* Asset Allocation, Tactical Asset Allocation.

Strategic Plan: generally, the long-term, "big picture" plan as opposed to the short-term, "small picture" plan. *See also* Tactical Plan.

Straw Boss: a person temporarily in charge.

Straw Poll: *see* Straw Vote.

Straw Vote: an informal and unofficial vote, often taken by a show of hands or by voice, to test whether or not consensus is building on the issue being discussed. Also known as Straw Poll. *See also* Vote.

Street: a reference to the professionals in the investment industry who are engaged in buying and selling securities. Also known as The Street. *See also* Buy Side (of the Street), Sell Side (of the Street).

Street Broker: an over-the-counter broker who is not a member of a recognized stock exchange. *See also* Over-the-Counter.

Street Certificate: a security that can be transferred without a change having to be recorded on the issuing company's book. *See also* Nominee Name, Street Form.

Street Estimates: estimates made by professional securities analysts working in the investment industry. The term is usually applied to corporate earnings per shares.

Street Form: securities that are held in the name of a brokerage firm (or its nominee name) but that belong to a client. *See also* Nominee Name, Street Certificate, Unregistered.

Street Name: *see* Nominee Name.

Street Price: the price of a security that is not traded on a recognized exchange.

Street Side: an informal reference to the broker in a broker/client relationship. *See also* Buy Side (of the Street), Sell Side (of the Street).

Stretching Payables: this occurs when a company intentionally does not pay obligations until after due dates.

Strike: 1. an organized work stoppage on the part of unionized workers. When this occurs, it is almost always within the context of wage and benefit negotiations. *See also* Labour Union, Sickout, Sit-Down, Walkout, Work-to-Rule. **2.** to discover something, especially a resource. *See also* Strike Oil. **3.** *see* Strike Price.

Strike Breaker: *see* Scab.

Strike Oil: 1. literally, to discover oil. **2.** to do something that leads to wealth and affluence.

Strike Price: the price at which shares can be purchased under a call option or sold under a put option. Also known as Strike. *See also* Option.

Strike Suit: a lawsuit by a minority shareholder to convince a company to buy his/her shares. *See also* Minority Shareholder.

Stringency: this occurs when interest rates are rising and financing is difficult.

Strip: 1. an option consisting of two puts and one call. *See also* Option. **2.** a term for a stripped bond or coupon. *See also* Bond.

STRIP Bond: *see* Separately Traded Residual and Interest Payment Bond.

Strip Mining: *see* Open Pit Mining.

Stripped Bond: a bond from which the interest coupons have been removed and sold separately. *See also* Accretion Bond, Bond, Residual, Stripped Coupon, Zero Coupon Bond.

Stripped Coupon: an interest coupon that has been removed from a bond. *See also* Accretion Bond, Bond, Residual, Stripped Bond, Zero Coupon Bond.

Strip Ratio: in mining, the ratio of the amount of waste that must be removed for each ton of ore mined. *See also* Open Pit Mining.

Strong Hands: a person (or institution) who holds an investment for the long term that he/she cannot be forced to sell by (e.g., by a margin call). *See also* Weak Hands.

Strong Market: a market that consistently rises in value. *See also* Weak Market.

Struck from Register: the status of a company that has gone out of business.

Structured Disclosure: information released as required and in the form specified by a regulator (e.g., a prospectus). *See also* Disclosure, Full Disclosure, Public Disclosure, Selective Disclosure, Soft Disclosure, Timely Disclosure.

Stumble: a term used to describe a stock price that flounders, as in "the stock stumbled on a poor earnings report."

Stump: to go about making political speeches.

Sub-Assembly: in manufacturing, a unit made separately from, but eventually to be part of, a larger product.

Sub-Branch: typically, a small office separate from, but under the management and regulation of, a larger office.

Subclause: in a contract, a clause that is a subsidiary section of, or subordinate to, another clause.

Subcommittee: a subordinate committee, often made up of representatives of the main committee.

Subcontractor: an individual or company to whom the principal contractor sublets part of a contract.

Subdirectory: in computers, a subdivision of a directory. *See also* Computer.

Subdivide: in real estate, to split one property into two or more smaller properties. *See also* Zoning.

Sub-Index: an index made up of a smaller subset of the main index (e.g., the Toronto Stock Exchange 100 Index is an index made up of the 100 largest companies in the Toronto Stock Exchange 300 Index and reveals the performance of the largest companies on the Toronto Stock Exchange).

Subject: a condition that must be met in order to conclude an agreement (e.g., a real estate purchase might be subject to a building inspection). *See also* Remove Subjects, Subject To.

Subject Bid: an offer to buy a security that indicates an interest but is not binding. *See also* Subject Offer.

Subject Market: a term used to refer to a bid or offer price that must be confirmed before a transaction can be completed.

Subject Price: a non-binding bid or offer price.

Subject Offer: an offer to sell a security that indicates an interest but is not binding. *See also* Subject Bid.

Subject To: an order or offer to buy that is conditional on something happening. *See also* Remove Subjects, Subject.

Subject to Prior Sale: this pertains to filling a security purchase order when the seller still has shares to sell. The sale will be complete provided the seller still has available shares.

Sublease: an agreement in which a tenant grants an interest in his/her interest in a leasehold. Also known as Sublet. *See also* Lease, Lessee, Lessor Sublet, Tenant.

Sublet: *see* Sublease.

Subordinated: 1. a security that ranks below others within its class with regard to having a claim on earnings or assets (e.g., subordinated debenture). Also known as Junior, Junior Security. *See also* Subordinated Debenture. **2.** a class of security that ranks below other classes of security with regard to having a claim on earnings or assets (e.g., common shares are subordinated to bonds). Also known as Junior Security. *See also* Bond, Common Share, Senior.

Subordinated Debenture: a debenture that ranks below other debentures. *See also* Debenture, Subordinated.

Subordinated Debt: a loan ranking below that of other loans with regard to claims on earnings or assets. *See also* Subordinated.

Subordinated Interest: a financial interest whose claim is inferior to that of another financial interest.

Subordination Clause: a clause in a mortgage that allows for a future mortgage to have preference over the original mortgage. *See also* Mortgage.

Subpoena: 1. a writ issued by the court to compel a witness to appear. **2.** to summon with such a writ.

Subprogram: in computers, a self-contained program stored and called upon when operating other programs. *See also* Computer.

Subrogate: generally, to substitute, as in replacing one party with another as creditor.

Sub rosa: in secrecy or confidence.

Subroutine: in computers, a set of instructions that performs a specific task needed by the main program. *See also* Computer, Routine.

Subscriber: an investor who agrees to buy a specific amount of a new issue or who has completed a subscription form to apply for a new issue. *See also* New Issue, Subscription Agreement, Subscription Form.

Subscription Agreement: 1. an order to purchase a specific amount of a new issue. *See also* New Issue, Subscriber, Subscription Form. **2.** an application by an investor to join a limited partnership. *See also* Limited Partnership.

Subscription Form: a form required when an investor wishes to participate in a new issue of securities. *See also* New Issue, Subscriber, Subscription Agreement.

Subscription Price: the price at which rights or warrants give holders the right to buy additional shares. *See also* Right, Warrant.

Subsequent Event: a note in an annual report that provides information on a material event taking place after the period covered by the financial statements but before the statements were published (e.g., an acquisition).

Subsidiary: a company that has 50 percent or more of its voting shares owned by another company. *See also* Affiliated Companies, Parent Company.

Subsidy: financial assistance, generally given by a government.

Substandard Health Annuity: an annuity that pays a higher return than usual because the annuitant has demonstrated a diminished life expectancy. *See also* Annuity.

Substandard Insurance: *see* Rated Insurance.

Substantial Presence Test: a test applied by the Internal Revenue Sevice to Canadians who spend considerable time in the U.S. Generally, a Canadian who spends four months a year in the U.S. will, for tax purposes, be considered a U.S. resident. *See also* Canada/U.S. Tax Convention of 1980, Internal Revenue Service, Protocol Amending the Canada-U.S. Tax Treaty, Snowbird, Sojourner, Taxes.

Subtenant: one who leases all or part of a rented premises from a lessee. *See also* Lease, Lessee, Lessor, Sublease, Tenant

Subvention: 1. a subsidy. **2.** an endowment.

Success Fee: in corporate finance and underwriting, a fee that is payable only if the transaction is successful (e.g., an agreed-upon amount of capital is raised). Also known as Incentive Fee. *See also* Contingency Fee, Performance Fee.

Succession: the sequence of order with regard to inheriting an estate. *See also* Statutory Next-of-Kin, Will.

Succession Duty: *see* Estate Tax.

Succession Planning: formulating an orderly and well-conceived plan to replace senior executives or, in the case of a private company, new owners.

Succession Tax: *see* Estate Tax.

Sucre: the prime currency of Ecuador.

Sue: to institute legal proceedings in order to redress a grievance.

Suicide Pill: *see* Jonestown Defence.

Suit: in law, a proceeding to recover a claim.

Suitability: a very important guideline for investment advisors, it ensures that securities recommended to clients are appropriate (given their investment objectives). *See also* Know Your Client Rule.

Suite: 1. in computers, a set of related and interactive programs. *See also* Computer. **2.** in mining, a group of related minerals.

Suitor: a company that offers to purchase another company. *See also* Takeover, Target.

Sum: the prime currency of Uzbekistan.

Sum Insured: the amount payable to the beneficiary when the insured dies. *See also* Life Insurance.

Summary Conviction Offense: in law, a minor offense, less serious than a felony. *See also* Felony.

Summary Prospectus: *see* Simplified Prospectus.

Summation: a concluding statement made before a court of law.

Summer Market: an old saw about the unpredictability of seasonal stock price patterns, as in "Sum'er up and sum'er down."

Summer Rally: the supposed tendency of the stock market to rise during the summer months. *See also* Seasonal Trend, Summer Market, Summer Valley.

Summer Valley: the supposed tendency of the stock market to fall during the summer months. *See also* Seasonal Trend, Summer Market, Summer Rally.

Summit: *see* European Council.

Summons: a legal call to appear in court.

Sum-of-the-Year's Digits Method: a method for calculating depreciation. If an asset is to be written off over five years, then the numbers one, two, three, four and five are added together to make a total of 15. In the first year, 5/15ths is written off, in the second year 4/15ths is written off and so on until in the fifth year the final 1/15th is written off. *See also* Depreciation, Straight Line Depreciation.

Sunk Cost: a past expenditure or loss that cannot be altered by current actions.

Sunrise Industry: a relatively new industry that will be of future economic significance. *See also* Electronic Commerce, Sunset Industry.

Sunset Clause: a legal provision included to ensure that an agreement or contract will expire at a fixed date.

Sunset Industry: an old industry near the end of its productive life cycle. *See also* Sunrise Industry.

Sunshine Law: in the U.S., a reference to the law that opens government meetings to the public.

Superannuation Plan: generally, a retirement or pension fund.

Super Bowl Indicator: a tongue-in-cheek indicator, conceived by well-known U.S. investment advisor Robert H. Stovall (1925-) in 1979, which states that the stock market will rise in any year that a National Football League Team (or a team that was from the original NFL) wins the Super Bowl. This statistical oddity has worked 88 percent of the time since the Super Bowl began. *See also* Aspirin Count Theory, Boston Snow Indicator, Frivolity Theory, Hemline Indicator, Tie Theory, Yellow Market Indicator.

Superficial Loss: a Canadian income tax term that applies to a capital loss triggered by the sale of an asset followed by a repurchase of the same asset within 30 days. Such capital losses will be disallowed. In the U.S., this transaction is called Wash Trading.

Supermajority Provision: a corporate bylaw that, in certain situations such as a takeover offer, requires an abnormally high percentage (67 percent to 90 percent) of shareholder votes (e.g., a vote to approve a takeover offer). *See also* Board of Directors.

Superpower: a dominant international economic, political and military country.

Supervoting Stock: shares that carry more voting rights than do other classes of stock in the same company.

Supper Club: *see* Breakfast Club.

Supplier Credit: *see* Trade Credit.

Supplier Discount: *see* Trade Credit Discount.

Supply: the amount of a product, service or financial instrument that is available for sale at a given price. *See also* Demand, Equilibrium Price.

Supply Area: a price level at which a technical analyst believes share selling will increase and so provide resistance to future price increases.

Supply Curve: a chart, with prices on the vertical axis and units on the horizontal axis, that rises from left to right, indicating a lesser supply of units at lower prices. *See also* Demand Curve.

Supply Side Economics: *see* Laffer Curve.

Supporting the Market: entering buy orders, either to prevent the market price of a security from falling or to encourage it to go up.

Support Level: a price at which technical analysts believe buying will start to support the price of a stock. If a stock price falls through a support level, then the expectation is that the price will fall still further. *See also* Resistance Level, Test.

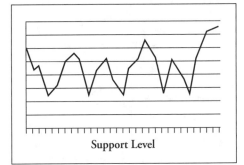

Support Level

Support Payment: *see* Spousal Support.

Support Price: a minimum price guarantee (e.g., to a farmer for wheat) that is maintained by government buying or subsidies. *See also* Price Support.

Supranational: extending beyond a nation's authority.

Supreme Court of Canada: in Canada, the final court of appeal for all civil and criminal cases.

Surcharge: a charge added to the original cost of something (e.g., a surtax is a form of surcharge). *See also* Surtax.

Surety: a guarantee or security that protects its holder in the event that a party owing money defaults (e.g., a performance bond). *See also* Performance Bond.

Surety Bond: *see* Performance Bond.

Surf: to move around the Internet in an exploratory manner, as in "Surf the Net." *See also* Internet.

Surface Rights: the right to use the surface of the land (e.g., to live on) or the flowing water. *See also* Underground Rights.

Surplus: something that is in excess of what is needed. *See also* Budget Surplus.

Surrender: when a policy holder gives up all rights under an insurance policy. *See also* Cash Surrender Value, Life Insurance, Surrendered Policy, Surrender Value.

Surrendered Policy: a cash value life insurance policy terminated for nonpayment of premiums. *See also* Cash Value Life Insurance, Grace Period, Lapse, Life Insurance, Reinstatement.

Surrender Value: *see* Cash Surrender Value.

Surrogate Court: the court to which an executor applies for letters probate. *See also* Executor, Letters Probate, Will.

Surtax: an additional income tax. Surtaxes are usually announced as temporary, but often they are not.

Surveillance Department: the division of a securities exchange that looks for unusual trading patterns that could indicate unethical or illegal activity. Also known as Compliance Department. *See also* Compliance, Daisy Chain, Wash Trading.

Survey: a report of the boundaries and quantity of land, the location of buildings and physical features.

Surviving Company: the company in control after a merger.

Surviving Spouse: the longer living of the spouses. Surviving spouses have certain rights to the deceased's estate, which varies from province to province.

Survivor's Benefit: financial compensation that is sometimes paid under an insurance contract or pension to the surviving spouse of the deceased. *See also* Canada Pension Plan Survivor's Benefit, Life Insurance, Registered Pension Plan.

Survivorship: *see* Right of Survivorship.

Survivorship Annuity: *see* Reversionary Annuity.

Suspect: in sales, a person that is considered closer to being a potential client than a cold call but not as close as a prospect. *See also* Cold Call, Prospect.

Suspended Trading: *see* Trading Halt.

Suspense Account: in accounting, an account used to record certain items until a permanent decision can be made on where it should be allocated.

Suspension: this occurs when a licensed investment advisor is temporarily or permanently prevented from dealing with the public due to securities regulations violations.

Sustainable Yield: in forestry, the volume of wood that can be harvested annually and still leave the total volume of available wood at a stable level.

Suva Stock Exchange: the primary stock exchange of Fiji, located in its capital, Suva. Web site: www.findat.com/fiji.htm

Swamp Land: any worthless or grossly overvalued real estate. *See also* Florida Land Boom, Moose Pasture.

SWAN: acronym for "sleep well at night," which results from a successful investment program.

Swap: *see* Asset Swap.

Swapation: an option to enter into an interest rate swap. *See also* Interest Rate Swap, Payer Swapation, Receiver Swapation.

Swap Order: *see* Contingent Order.

Swaziland Stockbrokers Ltd.: the major stock exchange of Swaziland located in its capital, Mbabane.

Swear: to make a solemn declaration, often a legal oath.

Sweat Equity: equity created in a business or asset by the hard work of the owner (e.g., sweat equity is the value added to a home because of renovations made by the owner).

Sweatshop: a shop or factory in which people (sometimes children) work long hours in poor conditions for little pay.

Swedish General Index: a market capitalization weighted index for the Stockholm Stock Exchange. *See also* Stockholm Stock Exchange.

Sweep Account: an investment account that allows an investor to transfer idle cash into an interest-paying account or money market mutual fund.

Sweet Crude: crude oil that has a low sulphur content.

Sweeten: to add a feature in order to make a transaction more attractive and so facilitate its completion. Often used to assist a new issue of securities that is not being well received (e.g., adding a warrant to a common share offering). *See also* Sweetener, Sweeten the Offering, Warrant.

Sweetener: the feature added to a transaction to make it more attractive and so facilitate its completion. *See also* Bells and Whistles, Sweeten.

Sweeten the Offering: *see* Sweeten.

Sweetheart Deal: an unethical transaction between two parties in which one gives the other excessively attractive terms and conditions.

SWIFT: *see* Society for Worldwide Interbank Financial Telecommunications.

Swindle: to defraud money or property.

Swing: a price movement, normally opposite to the previous trend.

Swing Loan: *see* Bridge Loan.

Swiss Exchange: the major stock exchange of Switzerland, located in Zurich. Web site: www.bourse.ch

Swiss Market Index: a market capitalization weighted stock price index of the largest stocks listed on the Electronic Bourse System in Switzerland. *See also* Electronic Bourse System.

Switch: 1. to sell a security and use the proceeds to buy another security. *See also* Trade. **2.** to move from one mutual fund to another. If the switch is done within the same family of funds, the decision is easier. If the switch involves moving to a totally different mutual fund, the investor may wish to consider the impact on the deferred sales charge, if any. *See also* Deferred Sales Charge, Mutual Fund.

Switch Order: an order to a broker to simultaneously buy one security and sell another. *See also* Order.

Symbol: 1. *see* Stock Symbol. **2.** something written and/or drawn which becomes an emblem representing something else. *See also* Copyright, Logo, Trademark.

Synchronous: in computers, occurring at the same time or at the same rate. *See also* Asynchronous, Autosynch.

Syndicate: 1. *see* Underwriting Syndicate. **2.** a group of Lloyd's names. *See also* Lloyd's of London, Name.

Syndicate Manager: the lead underwriter of the members of a syndicate, this firm is responsible for organizing the distribution of securities. Also known as Lead Underwriter, Managing Underwriter. *See also* Syndicate Member.

Syndicate Member: an underwriter that participates in the distribution of securities to the public. *See also* Syndicate Manager.

Synfuel: a fuel derived from another commodity through a conversion process (e.g., alcohol from grain).

Synthetic Asset: securities (such as options and futures) that have been combined so as to produce the same financial effect as does the ownership of a specific asset. *See also* Option, Synthetic Stock.

Synthetic Crude Oil: oil recovered from coal, oil shales or tar sands.

Synthetic Derivative: a term used to describe any one of a wide range of financial futures contracts.

Synthetic Portfolio: a portfolio that replicates or duplicates an actual holding of securities. A synthetic portfolio invest a substantial majority of the funds in treasury bills and a small minority of the funds in financial options. *See also* Option.

Synthetic Stock: this involves purchasing a call and selling a put on the same stock. By producing unlimited gains if the stock rises and unlimited losses if the stock falls, this combination replicates owning the underlying stock. *See also* Call Option, Option, Put Option, Synthetic Asset.

Sysop: in computers, the **sys**tem **op**erator of a bulletin board. The person who sets up and maintains a bulletin board system. *See also* Bulletin Board, Internet.

System: in computers, any group of hardware components and software that work together to perform a task. *See also* Computer.

Systematic Risk: 1. a risk that all assets, or all assets of the same category, share in common. *See also* Company Specific Risk, Event Risk, Industry Specific Risk, Non-Systematic Risk, Risk. **2.** a risk specific to a market. Also known as Market Risk.

Systematic Savings: a long-term savings plan that involves regular, fixed contributions for savings and investment.

Systematic Savings Plan: an investment option, offered by many mutual funds, that involves the investor depositing a fixed amount of money at regular intervals. *See also* Accumulation Plan, Contractual plan, Mutual Fund, Periodic Payment Plan, Voluntary Accumulation Plan.

Systematic Withdrawal Plan: an investment option, offered by many mutual funds, that involves the investor withdrawing a fixed amount or redeeming a fixed number of units and withdrawing the proceeds at regular intervals. The money may be from income or capital or both. *See also* Fixed Dollar Withdrawal Plan, Fixed Period Withdrawal Plan, Life Expectancy Adjusted Withdrawal Plan, Mutual Fund, Scale Out.

Systems Analysis: the study of a desired end and the most efficient way to attain it.

Systems Integrator: a service provider that offers a turnkey solution (i.e., that integrates all the hardware and software needed for a specific business or purpose). *See also* Turnkey.

10-K: a detailed annual report of a firm's operations filed by companies that have securities listed with the U.S. Securities and Exchange Commission. *See also* Securities and Exchange Commission.

10-Q: a quarterly unaudited financial report of a firm's operations filed by companies that have securities listed with the U.S. Securities and Exchange Commission. *See also* Securities and Exchange Commission.

12B-1 Mutual Fund: a no load mutual fund registered with the U.S. Securities and Exchange Commission. *See also* Securities and Exchange Commission.

24X7: *see* Twenty-Four by Seven.

T4: the basic required Canadian income tax form that summarizes information with respect to annual employment income and income taxes deducted at source. *See also* Income Tax, Taxes.

T400A: the form used to file a Notice of Objection to an income tax assessment. *See also* Notice of Objection.

Tab: *see* Tabulation.

Tabulation: an organization and listing in table form, as in a "monthly portfolio tabulation." Also known as Tab.

Tactical Asset Allocation: managing a portfolio by investing in a variety of asset classes such as treasury bills, bonds and common stocks and making changes in the amounts allocated to each asset class to take advantage of changing market conditions. *See also* Asset Allocation, Strategic Asset Allocation.

Tactical Plan: generally, the short-term, "small picture" plan as opposed to the long-term, "big picture" plan. *See also* Strategic Plan.

TAFN: Internet acronym for "that's all for now."

Tag Ends: small amounts of securities available when an underwriting or larger order is nearly competed.

Tailgating: this occurs when an investment advisor buys or sells a security for a client and then immediately does the same for him/herself Tailgating is not illegal but is considered unethical by some professionals. *See also* Front Running.

Tailings: the refuse or dross that remains after ore has been processed.

Taiwan Stock Exchange (TWSE): the major stock exchange of Taiwan, located in its capital, Taipei. Web site: www.tse.com.tw

Taiwan Stock Exchange Weighted Index: a market capitalization weighted stock price index for the Taiwan Stock Exchange.

Taka: the prime currency of Bangladesh.

Take a Bath: to experience a sizeable investment loss, as in the old saw, "In the stock market, it is hard to get your feet wet without taking a bath." Also known as Take a Hit.

Take a Flyer: to make a speculative investment.

Take a Hit: *see* Take a Bath.

Take a Plunge: to invest aggressively, often in a speculative security.

Take a Position: to purchase a holding in the shares of a company.

Take a Profit: to sell a stock to realize a gain, even though its price may continue to rise, as in the old saw, "You won't lose money taking a profit."

Take Delivery: to accept delivery of securities in order to complete a transaction. *See also* Delivery

Take Down: 1. the number of shares for which a member of an underwriting syndicate is financially responsible. **2.** buy a new offering of securities.

Take-Home Pay: the part of one's earnings that constitutes one's net pay after income tax and other deductions; that is, the amount one takes home.

Take It or Leave It: a final negotiating position that implies that one party is indifferent as to whether the terms of an agreement are accepted or rejected.

Take Losses, Let Profits Run: *see* Cut Losses, Let Profits Run.

Taken to the Cleaners: 1. to be defrauded **2.** to be wiped out in a business transaction.

Takeoff: a term used to describe the sharp rise in a security price.

Take-or-Pay: a contract that stipulates that the buyer must pay whether the goods or services are delivered or not (e.g., a business may sign a take-or-pay contract with an electric utility and guarantee to pay an amount whether the power is used or not).

Takeout: 1. this occurs when a buyer purchases a block of securities that has been offered for some time, as in "Take out the block." **2.** a bid for a seller's remaining position in a security, as in "Take out the position."

Takeover: this occurs when one company purchases control of another company. *See also* Suitor, Target.

Takeover Arbitrage: to buy shares of a company subject to a takeover bid if the prevailing market price is deemed too low compared to the takeover price or to sell such shares if the prevailing market price is deemed too high.

Takeover Artist: a person skilled in profiting from arranging takeovers of companies.

Takeover Bid: an offer to buy shares sufficient to provide the buyer with not less than 10 percent of the voting shares of a federally incorporated company or 20 percent of a provincially incorporated company. *See also* Federally Incorporated Company, Provincially Incorporated Company.

Takeover Target: a company that another company wants to acquire. Also known as Target. *See also* Suitor, Takeover.

Takeover Value: *see* Private Market Value.

Take Up: to pay any remaining amount due on a margined security so that full ownership is available free and clear. *See also* Margin Account.

Tala: the primary currency of Western Samoa.

Talk Down: the government's and/or central bank's ability to put downward pressure (e.g., on currency values) by stating that the exchange rate is too high. This causes investors to sell the currency in the belief that it will either fall or the authorities will take steps to make it fall. *See also* Moral Suasion, Talk Up.

Talking the Book: a term used to describe a major investor discussing trading plans ahead of the fact. Talking the book is frowned on because it can work against the best interest of the investor's portfolio value.

Talk the Talk: a real or implied threat, usually from a central banker or politician, to implement a policy change to counteract an economic trend. If the policy change follows, then it is referred to as Walk the Walk. *See also* Walk the Walk.

Talk Up: the government's and/or central bank's ability to put upward pressure (e.g., on currency values) by stating that the exchange rate is too low. This causes investors to buy the currency in the belief that it will either rise or the authorities will take steps to make it rise. *See also* Moral Suasion, Talk Down.

Tallinn Stock Exchange: the major stock exchange of Estonia, located in its capital, Tallinn. Web site: www.tse.ee

Talon: a certificate attached to another security that confers a set of rights or privileges to the owner (e.g., a warrant). *See also* Warrant.

Tangible Asset: *see* Real Asset.

Tangible Net Worth: *see* Net Tangible Assets.

Tank Farm: a storage facility for crude oil.

Tape: *see* Ticker Tape.

Tape Is Late: a term used to describe the situation that occurs when the volume of trading on the floor

of the stock exchange is so heavy, reporting of trades is delayed by more than one minute. *See also* Ticker Tape.

Tape Racing: *see* Front Running.

Tape Reader: a trader who watches stock price and volume patterns and uses the information to make stock trading decisions. *See also* Tape Reading.

Tape Reading: observing price and volume irregularities for use as signals for buying or selling securities. Also known as Reading the Tape.

Target: *see* Takeover Target.

TARGET: *see* Trans-European Automated Real-Time Gross Settlement Express Transfer System.

Target Price: the projected price of a security, usually stated by an investment professional to indicate potential return on investment (e.g., recommend purchase at $10 for a target price of $15 within a year). Also known as Price Target.

Target Rate: the interest rate the central bank has indicated is satisfactory. The target rate can also be a percent change (e.g., the target rate for money supply growth).

Tariff: 1. a tax on goods and services imported into a country, its purpose is to protect domestic companies from foreign competition. Also known as Duty. *See also* Protectionism. **2.** generally, a list of fees or charges.

Task Switching: in computers, the ability to change from one program to another without shutting down the first program. *See also* Computer, Multitasking.

Tax: *see* Taxes.

Taxable Benefits: usually, employment perks that Canada Customs and Revenue Agency has determined should, in some way, be included in taxable income. *See also* Taxes.

Taxable Capital Gains: the amount of capital gains that is taxable after taking into account all deductible costs, exemptions and net of capital losses. *See also* Taxes.

Taxable Event: an event that results in a tax liability (e.g., selling a stock at a profit).

Taxable Income: the amount of income that is subject to income tax. *See also* Income Tax, Taxes.

Tax Advantaged Investment: an investment that provides the investor with an income tax reduction. *See also* Taxes.

Tax and Spend: a term used to describe the tendency of liberal or left-wing governments to raise taxes in order to fund increased spending on social programs. *See also* Balanced Budget, Budget Deficit, Budget Surplus, Left Wing, Right Wing.

Tax Audit: a review by Canada Customs and Revenue Agency to ensure a taxpayer is paying the correct amount of tax. An audit may be triggered by unusual claims (e.g., very high claims deductions). A tax audit can also be initiated to review a company's procedures for collecting and paying tax.

Tax Avoidance: legal steps that can be taken to reduce income tax liability. *See also* Taxes, Tax Evasion.

Tax Base: the base on which taxes payable are calculated (e.g., adjusted cost base, historical cost). *See also* Adjusted Cost Base, Historical Cost.

Tax Bill: the amount of taxes (often income taxes) that must be paid. *See also* Taxes.

Tax Bite: an informal reference to the amount of income that is given over as taxes. *See also* Taxes.

Tax Bracket: generally, the range into which a person's taxable income falls. All income in a given tax bracket is taxed at the same rate. Under Canada's progressive income tax system, the higher a taxable income bracket, the more income tax payable. Also known as Bracket. *See also* Average Tax Rate, Effective Tax Rate, Income Tax, Progressive Income Tax, T4, Taxable Income, Taxes, Tax Return.

Tax Bracket Creep: *see* Bracket Creep.

Tax Break: any event or opportunity that results in a reduction of taxes payable. *See also* Taxes.

Tax Burden: a reference to the total amount of taxes payable, with the implication being that it is too much. *See also* Taxes.

Tax Cost: the cost of an asset for income tax purposes. This may differ from the actual purchase price. *See also* Taxes.

Tax Credit: a reduction in tax liabilities, either as a fixed amount of money or as a percentage calculation. *See also* Taxes.

Tax Deductible: a term used to describe an item that reduces the income base on which taxes are calculated. *See also* Taxes.

Tax Deductible Interest Expense: interest paid on money borrowed to make an investment for the purpose of generating income. *See also* Good Debt, Non-Deductible Interest Expense, Taxes.

Tax Deferral: a strategy that enables a taxpayer to put off taxes payable to a future period. *See also* Taxes.

Tax Dodge: a strategy to legally avoid taxes. *See also* Taxes.

Tax Effective: the structuring of income or investments in a way that lowers the amount of tax payable and increases the after-tax income. *See also* Taxes.

Taxes: an amount of money that people are required to pay to support government activities. The most common forms of tax are income tax and sales tax. *See also* Abatement, Ability to Pay, Adjusted Cost Base, Alternative Minimum Tax, Average Tax Rate, Bracket Creep, Canada/U.S. Tax Convention of 1980, Consumer Tax Index, Corporate Income Tax, Cumulative Net Investment Losses, Deductible Interest, Deduction, Deemed Disposition, Disposition, Dividend Tax Credit, Effective Tax Rate, Flat Tax, Goods & Services Tax, Income Tax, Integration, Interest Letter, Kiddie Tax, Negative Income Tax, Occasional Employment Income, Progressive Income Tax, Protocol Amending the Canada-U.S. Tax Treaty, Regressive Tax, Small Business Deduction, Sojourner, T4, Tax, Taxable Benefits, Taxable Capital Gains, Taxable Income, Underappreciated Capital Cost, Unearned Income, World Wide Income.

Tax Evasion: the illegal reduction of income tax liability. *See also* Tax Avoidance, Taxes.

Tax Exempt: not subject to tax (normally, income tax). *See also* Taxes.

Tax Exemption: under certain circumstances, a claim that provides freedom from paying taxes. *See also* Taxes.

Tax Exile: a person who resides in a jurisdiction because of its lower income tax regime. *See also* Taxes, Tax Haven.

Tax Freedom Day: a day calculated each year by the Fraser Institute as the point when Canadians have finished working to pay all their taxes and start

---

Taxes and Taxation

The Canadian income tax was to be a temporary measure according to the War Debt Income Tax Act of 1917. More than 80 years later, there is still no end to it in sight.

Canada has a progressive income tax. This means that as more income is earned, a larger proportion is taken as income tax. This is based on a notion called "ability to pay."

On the other hand, the controversial Goods & Services Tax is a regressive tax. It weighs more heavily on lower-income Canadians. The reason for this is that the GST is a consumption tax and so represents a larger cost to those who must consume more of their income each month.

The income tax and sales tax are the two main revenue sources of the federal government.

Since 1961, the Fraser Institute calculates that taxes in Canada have increased much faster than have individual incomes, inflation and the cost of food, clothing or shelter. In 1999, approximately half of the average Canadian's pay for the year went for taxes at all levels.

working for themselves. In 1999, Tax Freedom Day for Canada fell on July 1. *See also* Fraser Institute, Taxes.

Tax Free Income: income received that is not subject to taxes. *See also* Taxes.

Tax Free Rollover: the transfer of funds or assets from one account to another account – specifically, one in which income taxes otherwise payable are deferred to a future date. *See also* Rollover, Spousal Rollover, Taxes.

Tax Haven: a jurisdiction that attracts residents, corporations and financial institutions by offering low income taxes (e.g., Bermuda, Bahamas, Liechtenstein). *See also* Taxes, Tax Exile.

Tax Holiday: a period of zero or reduced taxes offered as an incentive to make an investment (e.g., starting a new business). *See also* Taxes.

Tax Lien: a lien on a property because the owner is delinquent in paying taxes. *See also* Lien, Taxes.

Tax Loophole: something that allows an unintended tax exemption. *See also* Taxes.

Tax Loss: a loss that can be used to offset other income and so reduce overall tax payable. *See also* Taxes, Tax Loss Carryback, Tax Loss Carryforward.

Tax Loss Carryback: for income tax purposes, the ability to use capital losses in the current year to claim back taxes paid on capital gains in the previous three years. *See also* Taxes, Tax Loss Carryforward.

Tax Loss Carryforward: for income tax purposes, the ability to use capital losses in the current year to offset taxes payable on capital gains indefinitely into the future. *See also* Taxes, Tax Loss Carryback.

Tax Loss Selling: a tax strategy to sell securities in the final few weeks of the year in order to trigger capital losses to offset taxes payable on capital gains realized earlier in the year. *See also* Realized Capital Gains, Realized Capital Losses, Taxes.

Tax Opinion: a professional opinion on a related income tax matter sometimes included as part of a prospectus. *See also* Prospectus, Taxes.

Taxpayer: one who pays taxes. *See also* Taxes.

Tax Planning: determining a strategy to minimize taxes payable. Tax planning usually involves the examination of different options available to a taxpayer. This is an integral part of the financial planning process. *See also* Financial Planning.

Tax Preparation Service: a service that prepares tax returns. All major accounting firms offer tax preparation services. There are also many firms specializing in this service. *See also* Taxes.

Tax Rate: the percentage of tax that is levied. *See also* Tax Bracket, Taxes.

Tax Recapture: *see* Capital Cost Allowance Recapture.

Tax Relief: something that reduces the tax payable or defers the payment of tax. *See also* Taxes.

Tax Refund: the return of taxes paid to the government in excess of the amount due. *See also* Overwithholding.

Tax Return: *see* Income Tax Return.

Tax Sale: 1. the sale of properties seized by a government to satisfy unpaid taxes. Tax sales are usually by tender or open auction. *See also* Taxes. **2.** any forced sale of assets to satisfy a tax liability. *See also* Taxes.

Tax Schedule: one of the schedules used to make up a tax return. Schedules are used to provide detailed information on deductions, interest and dividend income, investment income, profit or loss from a business, capital gains and losses, tax credits, medical expenses and charitable donations. *See also* Taxes.

Tax Shelter: an investment or business opportunity that offers income tax savings as well as economic benefits from a successful venture. Also known as Shelter. *See also* Taxes.

Tax Shift: this occurs when suppliers of goods or services are hit by a new tax or tax increase and it is passed along to their customers in the form of price increases. *See also* Taxes.

Tax System: in any given country, the collection of laws and regulations that outline all the important details of taxation. *See also* Taxes.

Tax Threshold: the point at which taxes become payable. *See also* Taxes.

Tax Treaty: a term that usually refers to the Convention Between the United States of America and Canada with Respect to Taxes on Income and Capital, also referred to as the Canada-U.S. Tax Convention. *See also* Taxes.

Tax Year: a 12-month reporting period for tax purposes. For individuals, this is usually the calendar year. *See also* Taxes.

T-Bill: *see* Treasury Bill.

TDS Ratio: *see* Total Debt Service (TDS) Ratio.

Techie: an individual with an active interest in technological development and change.

Technical Adjustment: a short-term change in the direction of security prices in reaction to changes in supply and demand rather than to changes in the underlying economic fundamentals. Also known as a Technical Move.

Technical Analysis: the process of examining the historical price patterns of various assets as the basis for predicting future prices. *See also* Fundamental Analysis.

Technical Analyst: an analyst who uses technical analysis. Also known as Technician. *See also* Chartist, Financial Analyst, Fundamental Analyst, Technical Analysis.

Technical Bankruptcy: a term used to describe the state of being in default on a financial obligation that would have the effect of bankruptcy if the creditor made a formal claim. *See also* Bankruptcy.

Technical Correction: a short-term decline in a rising stock price (or market) that does not represent a change in the overall trend (which remains upward). The decline in the price of the stock (or market) is caused by supply and demand factors related directly to the specific security (or market) rather than a change in the underlying economic fundamentals. Also known as Technical Decline, Technical Drop, Technical Reaction. *See also* Technical Rally.

Technical Decline: *see* Technical Correction.

Technical Divergence: this occurs when a stock market average does not move as might be expected given the movement in other similar averages.

Technical Drop: *see* Technical Correction.

Technical Indicators: indicators based more on supply and demand factors related to a specific security or market rather than the underlying company's operations or the economy as a whole.

Technical Insolvency: *see* Technical Bankruptcy.

Technicality: in law, the use of a legal precedent or statute (often in a way that is unrelated to the issues relating to the case at hand) to gain an acquittal.

Technically Strong Market: a market in which rising prices coincide with rising volume or in which falling prices coincide with falling volume. *See also* Technical Analysis.

Technically Weak Market: a market in which rising prices coincide with falling volume or falling prices coincide with rising volume. *See also* Technical Analysis.

Technical Move: *see* Technical Adjustment.

Technical Position: the potential strength or weakness in a market based on indicators related to a specific security or market rather than on the underlying company's fundamentals or the economy as a whole. *See also* Technical Analysis.

Technical Rally: a short-term rise in a falling stock price (or market) that does not represent a change in the overall trend (which remains downward). The rise in the price of the stock (or market) is caused by supply and demand factors related directly to the specific security (or market) rather than a change in the underlying economic fundamentals. *See also* Technical Correction.

Technical Reaction: *see* Technical Correction.

Technician: *see* Technical Analyst.

Technology: the application of science and scientific methods to industry and commerce. *See also* High Tech, High Tech Stock.

Tel Aviv Stock Exchange: the major stock exchange of Israel, located in Tel Aviv. Web site: www.tase.co.il/ *See also* Israel Stock Market General Index.

Telebanking: *see* Telephone Banking.

Telecommunications: the science of sending messages electronically. *See also* Teleconference.

Telecommute: to work from home using the telephone and other forms of electronic communication. *See also* Small Office, Home Office.

Teleconference: a meeting held with people in different locations through the use of audiovisual telecommunications. *See also* Telecommunication.

Telemarketing: any of the various ways the telephone is used to market goods and services.

Telephone Banking: banking that entails using a telephone and password to perform banking functions (e.g., bill payment, funds transfer, accessing account information). Also known as Telebanking.

Telephone Booth: one of the cubicles around the perimeter of the New York Stock Exchange trading floor used by member firms to receive orders. *See also* Floor, New York Stock Exchange.

Telephony: the process of transmitting sound by converting it into electrical signals (most commonly used in telephone technology).

Teller: a bank or other deposit-taking financial institution employee who interacts with the public (e.g., to receive cash on deposit, to dispense cash on withdrawal).

Telnet: a communications protocol that enables an Internet user to log on to, and to enter commands on, a remote computer linked to the Internet. *See also* Internet.

Temp: an employee hired as a short-term substitute. Short for temporary employee.

Templeton, Sir John Marks (1912 -): a well-known value manager and investment guru. In managing the Templeton Growth Fund, he was one of the first managers to practise international investment.

Temporary Line of Credit: a credit line that is established over and above a normal credit line and is used to handle seasonal or other short-term borrowing needs. Also known as Bulge Line of Credit. *See also* Formalized Line of Credit, Line of Credit.

Temporary Receipt: a receipt in evidence of security ownership until the permanent certificate is issued.

Ten: *see* Bo Derek.

Tenancy: possession, normally of land and/or buildings, by title, lease or rental.

Tenancy at Will: a tenancy under which a person occupies real estate with the permission of the owner for an unspecified time (e.g., while a lease is being negotiated).

Tenant: one who pays rent for the right to occupy land and/or buildings. *See also* Leaseholder, Lessee.

Tenant in Tail: one who has an interest in an estate that is limited to him/her and "the heirs of his/her body." *See also* Fee Tail.

Tenants in Common: a form of joint ownership that involves two or more tenants. If one of the tenants dies, then his or her interest in, for example, a building passes to his or her heirs and not to the other tenants. *See also* Co-Tenancy, Joint Tenancy, Right of Survivorship, Tenant, Undivided Interest.

Tender: 1. to accept a formal offer (e.g., a takeover bid). *See also* Tender Offer. **2.** the acceptable means of settlement in a financial transaction (e.g., legal tender). **3.** to make a bid to buy treasury bills.

Tender Offer: an offer to shareholders to buy their shares (usually as part of a takeover or buyout attempt).

Tenement: 1. property held by a tenant. **2.** generally, a reference to a run-down, low-rent facility that barely meets minimum standards.

Tenge: the prime currency of Kazakhstan.

Ten Percent Rule: an investment adage that states that if the stock market falls 10 percent from a recent high, then one should sell. If the stock market rises 10 percent from a recent low, then one should buy.

Ten Percent Solution: the financial planning adage that states that 10 percent of one's income should be saved or invested each month.

Ten Thousand by Two Thousand: a popular forecast (first made in the mid 1990s) that the Dow-Jones Average and/or the Toronto Stock Exchange 300 Index will reach a level of 10,000 by the year 2,000. The Dow Jones closed at 10,006.78 on March 29, 1999.

Tenure: 1. a form of title under which property (e.g., real estate) is held. **2.** the holding of an office or property.

Term: 1. the time between the issue date and the maturity date of a security (e.g., a bond). *See also* Term to Maturity. **2.** any limited or defined time period. **3.** a stipulation (e.g., the terms of the contract).

Term Certain Annuity: *see* Annuity Certain.

Term Deposit: a money market instrument issued by a financial institution in Canada, for a fixed term and interest rate, with Canada Deposit Insurance Corporation coverage. *See also* Guaranteed Investment Certificate, Stock Market Term Deposit.

Term Debt: any debt that matures in more than one year.

Term Draft: a draft that is payable on or after a specific date (e.g., a letter of credit). Also known as Time Draft. *See also* Demand Draft, Sight Draft.

Terminable Annuity: an annuity in which payments stop after a specified number of years. *See also* Annuity.

Terminal: in computers, usually a keyboard and monitor used to access a central computer. *See also* Computer.

Terminal Dividend: a final dividend paid by an insurance company when an insurance contract is surrendered. *See also* Life Insurance.

Terminal Income Tax Return: an income tax return filed for the year of a person's death by his/her personal representative. Also known as Final Tax Return, Terminal Return.

Terminal Market: a futures market.

Terminal Return: *see* Terminal Income Tax Return.

Terminal Year: in estate planning and income tax, a reference to the year of death. *See also* Terminal Income Tax Return.

Termination Pay: pay that arises when an employee is terminated from a job or position. Also known as Settlement.

Term Insurance: a form of life insurance in which there is no savings/investment element and the benefit is for a fixed period (as specified in the contract). Each time the insurance is renewed, the premium is higher because the insured person is older. Term insurance is popular with individuals who have an insurance need but prefer to handle their savings/investment directly. Also known as Term Insurance. *See also* Annual Renewable Term Insurance, Decreasing Term Insurance, Extended Term Insurance, Level Term Insurance, Life Insurance, Renewable Term Insurance, Term to Age 100.

Term Life Insurance: *see* Term Insurance.

Term Loan: a loan, generally with a fixed interest rate and repayment schedule.

Term Sheet: a listing of the main features of a proposed financing.

Term Structure (of Interest Rates): *see* Yield Curve.

Term to Age 90 Annuity: an annuity that pays a fixed amount each year until the year in which the annuitant turns age 90. Term to age 90 annuities were developed to meet the needs of RRIF holders when the regulations stipulated that RRIFs pay out fully at age 90. *See also* Annuity, Registered Retirement Income Fund.

Term to Age 100: term insurance that guarantees a fixed premium until age 100. *See also* Life Insurance.

Term to Maturity: the time between the present and the maturity date of a bond (i.e., the remaining term). *See also* Bond, Long-Term Bond, Original Maturity, Short-Term Bond, Term.

Test: 1. when a price is near a support or resistance level. If the support or resistance level holds, it is said to have passed the test. *See also* Resistance Level, Support Level. **2.** a formal evaluation of knowledge or ability.

Testacy: *see* Testate.

Testament: a legal document for the disposition of property after death. *See also* Testamentary Trust, Will.

Testamentary Capacity: the legal ability to make decisions about one's will. *See also* Power of Attorney, Will.

Testamentary Spousal Trust: a trust into which assets are transferred to a spouse according to the instructions of a deceased person's will. A testamentary spousal trust usually allows for the surviving spouse to receive the income from the trust while preserving the assets for children or others. *See also* Testamentary Trust.

Testamentary Trust: a trust into which assets are transferred according to the instructions of the deceased person's will. *See also* Inter Vivos Trust, Testamentary Spousal Trust, Trust, Will.

Testate: having made a valid will. Also referred to as Testacy. *See also* Will.

Testator: a person who has made a valid will. *See also* Intestate, Testate, Will.

Testatrix: a woman who has made a valid will. *See also* Intestate, Testate, Will.

Testify: to make a declaration under oath, often in court. *See also* Testimony.

Testimonial: the endorsement of a product or service.

Testimony: a declaration under oath, often in court. *See also* Testify.

Text File: a computer file made up of text characters. A text file can be a word-processing file or a file made up only of ASCII characters. *See also* American Standard Code for Information Interchange, Computer, Word Processing.

TFE: *see* Toronto Futures Exchange.

Thailand Stock Exchange: *see* Stock Exchange of Thailand.

The Dow: *see* Dow Jones.

The Euro/Dollar (TED) Spread: the difference in yield between a three-month U.S. treasury bill and a three-month Eurodollar future. The spread is used as an indicator of investor confidence in the U.S. market.

The Net: *see* Internet.

Theory of Contrary Opinion: based on the "Letters of Contrary Opinion" written by Humphrey B. Neill prior to the Second World War. The theory states that prevailing, widely held views of the stock market will be wrong and that, consequently, a successful investor must act on information not widely known.

This means a successful investor is always making decisions that run contrary to the prevailing view. *See also* Contrarian, Contrary Market Indicator, Contrary Opinion, Investment Services Bearish, Investment Services Bullish.

The Stock Exchange: the major stock exchange of the Republic of Ireland, located in its capital, Dublin. Also informally known as the Irish Stock Exchange. Web site: www.ise.ie/ *See also* Irish Stock Exchange Overall Index.

The Street: *see* Street.

The Tigers of Asia: *see* Eight Tigers of Asia.

Thin: a term used to describe minimal trading volume, as in "A thin market." *See also* Thinly Traded, Thinly Traded Stock.

Thin Company: a company with substantial debt relative to equity.

Think Tank: a research group, often government organized and funded, whose purpose is to solve complex problems.

Thinly Held: a term used to describe a security held by a small number of investors.

Thinly Traded: a term used to describe a security that has minimal trading volume. *See also* Thin, Trade by Appointment.

Thinly Traded Stock: an individual stock that consistently trades very little volume. Thinly traded stocks tend to be quite volatile because relatively small orders to buy or sell push prices up or down.

Thin Market: a market for a security (or securities) that trades inactively.

Third Market: the market in which an investment dealer (who is not a member of a recognized exchange) trades stocks listed on a recognized exchange. *See also* Off-the-Board, Over-the-Counter.

Third Mortgage: a loan secured by real estate that is subordinated to two senior mortgages (the first and second), each of which is secured by the same property. *See also* First Mortgage, Second Mortgage, Mortgage.

Third Party: an independent party to the two parties involved in a contract or agreement.

Third Party Cheque: a cheque endorsed by a third party (e.g., a cheque made out by A in favour of B. B endorses the cheque and gives it C. With C's endorsement, it becomes a third party cheque).

Third Quarter: the third three months of a fiscal year (often July, August and September). *See also* Quarter.

Third Quartile: a ranking in the third best 25 percentile of a peer group, that is, between the top 50 and 75 percent. The upper half of the lower 50 percent. *See also* Decile, First Quartile, Fourth Quartile, Second Quartile.

Third World: the developing countries of Africa, Asia and Latin America. *See also* Emerging Markets.

Threadneedle Street: the main financial district of London. *See also* Bay Street, Howe Street, Main Street, Wall Street.

Three Bagger: in investment, an asset that triples in value. The term is derived from baseball, in which a three-base hit is called a triple or three bagger. The term is used with any number (e.g., five bagger, ten bagger). *See also* Four Bagger, Home Run, Two Bagger.

Three-Day Settlement: the requirement to pay for common stocks purchased within three business days. *See also* Cash Settlement, Settlement, T-Plus-Three.

Three P's: a reference to the three categories of mining reserves: proven, probable and possible. *See also* Possible Reserves, Probable Reserves, Proven Reserves, Resource.

Three Steps and a Stumble Rule: *see* Step, Step, Stumble.

Thrift: 1. *see* Credit Union. **2.** *see* Savings and Loan.

Thundering Herd: an informal term for the U.S. brokerage firm Merrill Lynch & Co., in reference to the company's large size and advertising (which features a large bull). *See also* Merrill Lynch & Co.

TIA: Internet acronym for "Thanks in advance."

Tick: the upward or downward movement that accompanies each trade in a security. *See also* Closing Tick, Minus Tick, Plus Tick, Zero-Minus Tick, Zero-Plus Tick.

Ticker Symbol: *see* Stock Symbol.

Ticker Tape: an outmoded method for delivering stock exchange quotations, it consisted of a machine stamping the price and volume of trades on a narrow strip of paper. In the modern world, the system that delivers information about trading prices and volumes is still referred to as the ticker tape. Also known as Stock Ticker, Tape.

Tickets: usually, a reference to the form a broker uses to enter his/her clients' orders to buy and sell securities. Most order entry is now electronic.

Tick Index: the volume of trading on downticks from the volume of trading on upticks. *See also* Downtick, Downtick Volume, Uptick, Uptick Volume.

Tickle File: any form of calendar that provides reminders of significant market events (such as bond maturity dates).

Tied Selling: the provision of a product or service that is conditional upon the purchase of a product or service from a related company (e.g., an automobile company offers financing to buyers of its make of car). *See also* Mutual Fund, Tied House.

Tie Theory: a tongue-in-cheek theory holding that when neckties widen in style, the stock market declines, and that when they narrow, the stock market rises. *See also* Aspirin Count Theory, Boston Snow Indicator, Frivolity Theory, Hemline Indicator, SuperBowl Indicator, Yellow Market Indicator.

TIGER: *see* Treasury Investment Growth Receipt.

Tigers of Asia: *see* Asian Tigers.

Tight: a term used to describe a closely held stock.

Tight Market: an active and competitive market in which the spread between the bid and ask price for securities is very narrow.

Tight Money: a period of time during which interest rates are high and credit is difficult to get.

Tight Money Policy: this comes into effect when a central bank pushes up interest rates and restricts credit.

TIGR: *see* Treasury Investment Growth Receipt.

Till Money: cash held by a financial institution for cash payments to customers. The total cash held by an institution is till money plus vault cash. *See also* Vault Cash.

Time Draft: *see* Term Draft.

Timely Disclosure: the prompt release of material information. "Prompt" in this context is not defined, but factors such as evidence that investors with inside information are taking advantage of the situation or if the information represents a significant change in what is generally expected, need to be considered. Also known as Timely Dissemination of Information. *See also* Disclosure, Full Disclosure, Public Disclosure, Selective Disclosure, Soft Disclosure, Structured Disclosure.

Timely Dissemination of Information: *see* Timely Disclosure.

Timely Payment Guarantee: a guarantee, provided by the Canada Mortgage and Housing Corporation, to make interest payments on NHA mortgage-backed securities in the event that a mortgagor defaults. *See also* Canada Mortgage and Housing Corporation, Mortgage Backed Securities, National Housing Act.

Time-Share: 1. a form of property ownership or rights providing access for certain periods. **2.** in computers, the use of a central computer by more than one user at the same time. *See also* Computer.

Times Interest Earned: a measure of the margin of safety for interest on a loan, it is calculated by dividing the issuer's net income by interest charges. Also known as Interest Charges, Fixed Charges Coverage.

Time Value: the part of a stock option price that is over and above its intrinsic value. Time value is larger, the longer it is to its expiration date. Also known as Premium. *See also* Expiration Date, Intrinsic Value, Option.

Time Value of Money: an acknowledgment that money can earn interest over time and is, therefore, worth more in the future than it is today (e.g., if interest rates are 10 percent, $1.00 today is worth $1.10 in one year and $1.21 in two years). The concept of time value of money is the opposite of present value. *See also* Future Value, Net Present Value, Present Value.

Time Weighted Return: an accurate measure of a portfolio's return calculated as the return on the assets at the start of the period plus one-half of the return on the net of additions and subtractions of capital during the period.

Timing: the ability to buy securities as closely as possible to the start of a rise in value and to sell them as closely as possible to the start of a fall in value.

Tip: 1. advice to buy or sell a stock, with the implication being that such advice is based on inside information. Also known as Tipoff. *See also* Tippee, Tipper. **2.** *see* Gratuity.

Tipoff: *see* Tip.

Tipoff: a hint or warning. A tipoff regarding stock prices usually implies that inside information is being employed.

Tippee: a person receiving inside information. *See also* Insider Trading, Tip, Tipper, Tipster.

Tipper: a person who reveals inside information. *See also* Insider Trading, Tip, Tippee, Tipster.

Tipping: *see* Gratuity.

TIPS: *see* Treasury Inflation Protection Securities.

TIPs (Toronto Index Participation units): index participation units that replicate movements in various Toronto Stock Exchange indexes. A basket of securities providing index-like returns and that investors can buy as a single unit. *See also* Diamonds, Index Participation Units, Spider, TIPs35, TIPs100.

TIPs35 (Toronto 35 Index Participation Units): index participation units in a trust that holds the shares of the Toronto Stock Exchange 35 Index. A basket of securities providing index-like returns and that investors can buy as a single unit. *See also* Index Participation Units, TIPs, TIPs100, Toronto 35 Index Dividend Capital Receipt, Toronto 35 Index Secondary Warrant.

TIPs100 (Toronto 100 Index Participation Units): index participation units that replicate movements in the Toronto Stock Exchange 100 Index. A basket of securities providing index-like returns that investors can buy as a single unit. *See also* Index Participation Units, TIPs, TIPs35.

Tipster: a person who claims to have inside information that will impact a stock price but who most likely does not. *See also* Insider Trading, Tippee, Tipper.

Title: the instrument, such as a deed, that gives evidence of property ownership. *See also* Bad Title, Clear Title, Cloud on Title, Deed, Defective Title, On Title, Paramount Title, Title Deed, Title Defect, Title Search.

Title Deed: *see* Deed.

Title Defect: an issue that may invalidate a property title. *See also* Bad Title, Clear Title, Cloud on Title, Defective Title, On Title, Title, Title Deed, Title Search.

Title Search: a process that entails researching the history and chain of ownership of property recorded in the land titles office. *See also* Bad Title, Clear Title, Cloud on Title, Defective Title, On Title, Title, Title Deed, Title Defect.

Toehold Purchase: the purchase of less than 10 percent of a company. Once 10 percent or more is purchased, the buyer must file a report with regulatory authorities, the stock exchange and the company, and outline future intentions.

Toggle: in computers, to alternate back and forth between two modes. *See also* Computer.

Tokyo Stock Exchange: the major stock exchange of Japan, located in its capital, Tokyo. Web site: www.tse.or.jp/

Tolar: the primary currency of Slovenia.

Tombstone: a written advertisement for a securities issue that lists the security, some of the security's specifics and, in order of importance, the members of the syndicate who sell the issue. The underwriters are listed alphabetically in groups according to the amount of the issue sold. The tombstone is a public announcement of an issue that will be offered for sale but, in practice, the announcement is made after the issue has been sold. *See also* Bulge Bracket, Mezzanine Bracket.

Ton: 1. in bond trading, an amount of $100 million, as in "I want to buy a ton." **2.** *see* Short Ton.

Tone: the prevailing optimism or pessimism of a financial market, it is determined mainly by intuition.

Tone Dialling: in computers, a form of dialling associated with push-button telephones, in which the computer sends tones of various frequencies to represent the telephone number being dialled. *See also* Automatic Dial Tone, Computer, Pulse Dialling.

Tonnage: the total weight of goods handled through a port.

Tonne: *see* Metric Ton.

Toonie: the Canadian two-dollar coin, so termed as a take off on the one-dollar coin, which is called a loonie. Also known as Twoonie. *See also* Loonie.

Top: 1. in investment, the high point in the price for an individual security or market before a decline begins. *See also* Bottom. **2.** in economics, the high point in the economic cycle. *See also* Peak.

Top-Down: an investment strategy that uses an economic forecast to identify areas of expected strength and weakness. One makes investments in areas of strength and avoids areas of weakness. *See also* Bottom-Up, Growth Investor, Portfolio Management Style, Sector Rotation, Value Investor.

Top Hat Plan: an employee benefit plan through which selected employees receive additional benefits. Also known as Cadillac Plan.

Top Heavy: a term used to describe a security or financial market that shows signs of being overvalued and about to drop. Also known as Toppy.

Top Line: sales or revenue, in contrast to the bottom line, which is net income or net profit. *See also* Bottom Line.

Top Management: a category made up of individuals who occupy the highest ranking managerial positions in a company or business. Also known as Senior Management. *See also* Middle Management.

Topping Out: a security or market that is in the process of moving from a rising trend to a falling trend.

Toppy: *see* Top Heavy.

Top Quartile: *see* First Quartile.

TOPRS: *see* Trust Originated Preferred Securities.

Toronto Futures Exchange (TFE): an exchange located in Toronto, Ontario, that trades futures on the Toronto Stock Exchange Indexes.

Toronto 35 Index Dividend Capital Receipt: a security that, together with a transferable fixed term warrant, makes up a unit that can be exchanged for a Toronto 35 Index Participation unit. The dividend capital receipt entitles the holder to the dividend distributions from a Toronto 35 Index Participation unit. *See also* Split Yield Security, TIPs35, Toronto 35 Index Secondary Warrant.

Toronto 35 Index Participating Fund units: *see* TIPs35.

Toronto Index Participation units (TIPs): *see* TIPs.

Toronto 35 Index Secondary Warrant: a security that, together with an transferable dividend capital receipt, makes up a unit that can be exchanged for a Toronto 35 Index Participation unit. The secondary warrant entitles the holder to the capital appreciation from a Toronto 35 Index Participation unit. *See also* Split Yield Security, TIPs35, Toronto 35 Index

Dividend Capital Receipt.

Toronto Mining and Industrial Exchange: an exchange for trading mining and industrial stocks that merged with the Standard Stock and Mining Exchange and subsequently with the Toronto Stock Exchange, in 1934. *See also* Toronto Stock Exchange.

Toronto Stock Exchange (TSE): a major stock exchange headquartered in Toronto, Ontario. Under an agreement in principle announced in March 1999, the Toronto Stock Exchange will become the senior securities market in Canada. The Alberta Stock Exchange will merge with the Vancouver Stock Exchange to form a national junior equities market known as the Canadian Venture Exchange and the Montreal Exchange will focus exclusively on futures and derivatives trading. Web site: www.telenium.ca/tse *See also* Alberta Stock Exchange, Canadian Venture Exchange, Montreal Exchange, Standard Stock and Mining Exchange, Toronto Mining and Industrial Exchange, Vancouver Stock Exchange.

Toronto Stock Exchange 35 Index (TSE35): a stock price index of the 35 largest companies on the Toronto Stock Exchange. *See also* TIPs35, Toronto 35 Index Dividend Capital Receipt, Toronto 35 Index Secondary Warrant, Toronto Stock Exchange 35 Index, Toronto Stock Exchange 100 Index, Toronto Stock Exchange 200 Index, Toronto Stock Exchange 300 Index.

Toronto Stock Exchange 100 Index (TSE100): a stock price index of the 100 largest companies on the Toronto Stock Exchange. *See also* TIPs100, Toronto Stock Exchange 35 Index, Toronto Stock Exchange 100 Sub-Index (Consumer Index)-(Resource Index), Toronto Stock Exchange 200 Index, Toronto Stock Exchange 300 Index.

Toronto Stock Exchange 100 Sub-Index (Consumer Index): one of the four stock market capitalization weighted price sub-indexes of the Toronto Stock Exchange 100 Index made up of the companies in the consumer industries. *See also* Toronto Stock Exchange 100 Index.

Toronto Stock Exchange 100 Sub-Index (Interest Sensitive Index): one of the four stock market capitalization weighted price sub-indexes of the Toronto Stock Exchange 100 Index made up of the companies in the interest-rate-sensitive industries. *See also* Toronto Stock Exchange 100 Index.

Toronto Stock Exchange 100 Sub-Index (Industrial Index): one of the four stock market capitalization weighted price sub-indexes of the Toronto Stock Exchange 100 Index made up of the companies in the industrial and industrial service industries. *See also* Toronto Stock Exchange 100 Index.

Toronto Stock Exchange 100 Sub-Index (Resource Index): one of the four stock market capitalization weighted price sub-indexes of the Toronto Stock Exchange 100 Index made up of the companies in the resource industries. *See also* Toronto Stock Exchange 100 Index.

Toronto Stock Exchange 200 Index (TSE200): a stock price index of the 200 largest companies on the Toronto Stock Exchange. *See also* Toronto Stock Exchange 35 Index, Toronto Stock Exchange 100 Index, Toronto Stock Exchange 300 Index.

Toronto Stock Exchange 300 Index (TSE300): a stock price index of the 300 largest companies on the Toronto Stock Exchange. *See also* Toronto Stock Exchange 35 Index, Toronto Stock Exchange 100 Index, Toronto Stock Exchange 200 Index, Toronto Stock Exchange 300 Sub-Index (Communications and Media Index), Toronto Stock Exchange 300 Sub-Index (Utilities Index), Toronto Stock Exchange 300 Total Return Index.

Toronto Stock Exchange 300 Sub-Index (Communications and Media Index): one of the 14 stock market capitalization weighted price sub-indexes of the Toronto Stock Exchange 300 Index made up of the companies in the communications and media industries. *See also* Toronto Stock Exchange 300 Index.

Toronto Stock Exchange 300 Sub-Index (Conglomerates Index): one of the 14 stock market capitalization weighted price sub-indexes of the Toronto Stock Exchange 300 Index made up of the companies that are conglomerates. *See also* Toronto Stock Exchange 300 Index.

Toronto Stock Exchange 300 Sub-Index (Consumer Products Index): one of the 14 stock market capitalization weighted price sub-indexes of the Toronto Stock Exchange 300 Index made up of the companies in the consumer products industries. *See also* Toronto Stock Exchange 300 Index.

Toronto Stock Exchange 300 Sub-Index (Financial Services Index): one of the 14 stock market capitalization weighted price sub-indexes of the Toronto Stock Exchange 300 Index made up of the companies in the financial services industries. *See also* Toronto Stock Exchange 300 Index.

Toronto Stock Exchange 300 Sub-Index (Gold & Precious Minerals Index): one of the 14 stock market capitalization weighted price sub-indexes of the Toronto Stock Exchange 300 Index made up of the companies in the gold and silver industries. *See also* Toronto Stock Exchange 300 Index.

Toronto Stock Exchange 300 Sub-Index (Industrial Products Index): one of the 14 stock market capital-ization weighted price sub-indexes of the Toronto Stock Exchange 300 Index made up of the companies in the industrial products industries. *See also* Toronto Stock Exchange 300 Index.

Toronto Stock Exchange 300 Sub-Index (Merchandising Index): one of the 14 stock market capitalization weighted price sub-indexes of the Toronto Stock Exchange 300 Index made up of the companies in the merchandising industries. *See also* Toronto Stock Exchange 300 Index.

Toronto Stock Exchange 300 Sub-Index (Metal & Mineral Index): one of the 14 stock market capital-ization weighted price sub-indexes of the Toronto Stock Exchange 300 Index made up of the compa-nies in the metals and minerals industries. *See also* Toronto Stock Exchange 300 Index.

Toronto Stock Exchange 300 Sub-Index (Oil & Gas Index): one of the 14 stock market capitaliza-tion weighted price sub-indexes of the Toronto Stock Exchange 300 Index made up of the companies in the oil and gas industries. *See also* Toronto Stock Exchange 300 Index.

Toronto Stock Exchange 300 Sub-Index (Paper & Forest Index): one of the 14 stock market capitaliza-tion weighted price sub-indexes of the Toronto Stock Exchange 300 Index made up of the companies in the paper and forest products industries. *See also* Toronto Stock Exchange 300 Index.

Toronto Stock Exchange 300 Sub-Index (Pipelines Index): one of the 14 stock market capitalization weighted price sub-indexes of the Toronto Stock Exchange 300 Index made up of the companies in the pipelines industry. *See also* Toronto Stock Exchange 300 Index.

Toronto Stock Exchange 300 Sub-Index (Real Estate Index): one of the 14 stock market capitaliza-tion weighted price sub-indexes of the Toronto Stock Exchange 300 Index made up of the companies in the real estate industry. *See also* Toronto Stock Exchange 300 Index.

Toronto Stock Exchange 300 Sub-Index (Transportation and Environmental Services Index): one of the 14 stock market capitalization weighted price sub-indexes of the Toronto Stock Exchange 300 Index made up of the companies in the transportation and environmental services indus-tries. *See also* Toronto Stock Exchange 300 Index.

Toronto Stock Exchange 300 Sub-Index (Utilities Index): one of the 14 stock market capitalization weighted price sub-indexes of the Toronto Stock Exchange 300 Index made up of the companies in the utilities industries. *See also* Toronto Stock Exchange 300 Index.

Toronto Stock Exchange 300 Total Return Index: a stock price and dividend return index of the 300 largest companies on the Toronto Stock Exchange. *See also* Toronto Stock Exchange 300 Index, Total Return Index.

Torpedo: to take an action that either causes a stock drop or prevents a plan from being completed.

Torpedo Stock: a stock that has been declining for some time and that is continuing to decline.

Tort: in law, a wrongdoing for which a civil remedy is available.

Total Cost: the total amount it costs to buy something, including prices, fees, commissions and other costs.

Total Debt Service (TDS) Ratio: the percentage of family gross income before income taxes required to cover all debts and financing obligations. Most lenders use a maximum 40 percent TDS ratio as a rule of thumb. Also known as TDS Ratio. *See also* Gross Debt Service (GDS) Ratio.

Total Disability: an injury or illness that is so serious the person cannot perform any job for which he/she is qualified. Totally disabled workers may be entitled to financial benefits from a private plan, social security or workers' compensation. *See also* Disability Income Insurance.

Total Return: the cash income return (plus appreciation) on an investment.

Total Return Index: a stock market index that takes into account dividends and capital appreciation. *See also* Toronto Stock Exchange 300 Total Return Index.

Tout: 1. an individual who promotes the buying of a particular stock. The term has a more negative connotation than does the term "stock promoter." *See also* Stock Promoter. **2.** the process of promoting the buying of a particular stock. *See also* Promotion.

Township: a surveying unit of 36 square miles, often used in relation to resource exploration claims. *See also* Section.

T-Plus-Three: a reference to three-day settlement for securities: the trade date plus three business days. *See also* Three-Day Settlement.

TPTB: Internet acronym for "The powers that be."

Track Record: 1. a summary of historical returns generated by an investment class, a specific investment or a portfolio manager. **2.** the listing of sales and earnings of a company.

Trade: 1. a term used to describe the buying and selling of items (often securities), usually within a short period. *See also* Switch. **2.** a term applied to an occupation, especially one requiring training and skilled labour. *See also* Tradespeople.

Trade Association: an organization whose members are in the same or similar business and meet to share information and contacts.

Trade Balance: *see* Balance of Trade.

Trade by Appointment: a term used to describe a stock that trades very infrequently. *See also* Thinly Traded.

Trade Credit: credit offered by a supplier of a product or service to a customer. Trade credit terms are often expressed as, for example, "2 percent, 10 net 30," which means there is a 2 percent discount if the bill is paid within 10 days or the full amount is due in 30 days. Also known as Supplier Credit. *See also* Dating, Full Credit Period, Trade Creditor.

Trade Creditor: one who grants trade credit. *See also* Trade Credit.

Trade Date: in investment, the date on which a security trade takes place. *See also* Settlement Date.

Trade Deficit: *see* Unfavourable Balance of Trade.

Trade Discount: a discount offered by a supplier for early payment (e.g., a 2 percent discount if the bill is paid within 10 days). Also known as Supplier Discount. *See also* Full Credit Period, Trade Credit.

Trade-In: merchandise accepted as partial payment for a purchase (e.g., a used car may be used as a trade-in when purchasing a new car).

Trademark: a name, symbol or other identification, the use of which is legally restricted to the owner. *See also* Canadian Intellectual Property Office, Copyright, Logo, Symbol.

Trade Name: a name used to identify a commercial product or service.

Trade Off: to realize a reduced interest in one area for an increased interest in another area. *See also* Guns and Butter Curve.

Trader: 1. an employee of a brokerage firm engaged in buying and selling securities based on client orders. *See also* Bond Trader, Stock Trader. **2.** an employee of a financial institution engaged in buying and selling securities based on instructions from a portfolio manager. *See also* Bond Trader, Stock Trader. **3.** an investor who actively buys and sells securities for his/her own account. *See also* Bond Trader, Stock Trader.

Tradespeople: people (i.e., tradesmen and tradeswomen) engaged in a trade. *See also* Trade.

Trade Surplus: *see* Favourable Balance of Trade.

Trade Union: *see* Labour Union.

Trading Ahead: using knowledge of an impending event (such as the issuance of a research report) to buy or sell securities.

Trading Authorization: an agreement in which an account holder authorizes another person to buy and sell securities in the account. *See also* Discretionary Account, Discretionary Trading, Full Trading Authorization, Power of Attorney.

Trading Day: whenever the securities markets are open, usually Monday to Friday. Also known as Trading Session.

Trading Dollars: a term that describes a non-growth activity (e.g., an oil exploration company that spends as much to find and develop a barrel of oil as it receives from selling a barrel of oil is "trading dollars").

Trading Down: trading in such a manner as to reduce quality and to increase risk. *See also* Trading Up.

Trading Floor: the area of a stock exchange where trading takes place. With computer assisted trading, the floor is no longer needed. *See also* Open Outcry.

Trading Halt: a listed stock that is not being traded in order to allow significant news to be disseminated. A trading halt usually lasts less than a day but can last several days. If a trading halt is initiated by the company whose stock it is, it is called a Voluntary Trading Halt. Also known as Halted, Suspended Trading.

Trading Instructions: additional instructions that an investor may give when entering a buy or sell order (e.g., a limit order). *See also* Limit Order.

Trading Market: a market that exhibits short-term ups and downs but is relatively flat overall.

Trading Pattern: the characteristics associated with how a security trades over a given period of time.

Trading Post: the area on the floor of an exchange where specific securities are traded. Also known as Post.

Trading Range: the area between the highest and lowest prices at which a security trades within a given period of time. *See also* Price Range.

Trading Ring: the bond trading area of the New York Stock Exchange.

Trading Session: *see* Trading Day.

Trading Up: trading in such a manner as to increase quality and to decrease risk. *See also* Trading Down.

Trading Value: *see* Value of Trading.

Trading Volume: *see* Volume of Trading.

Trading Window: for a person whose buying and selling of securities is restricted, the period during which he/she can buy or sell (e.g., company management is sometimes allowed to buy or sell shares in their company only for a specific period following quarterly reports). *See also* Insider Trading.

Traffic: a reference to the commercial exchange of goods.

Trailing: *see* Last Twelve Months.

Train Wreck: a major financial loss experienced by an individual or a company, often due to illegal activity.

Famous Financial Train Wrecks
(1980-99)

Year	Company	Loss	Reason
1998	Long-Term Capital Mgmt	$4.0 bil.	Mismanagement
1996	Sumitomo Corp	$2.6 bil.	Unauthorized copper trading
1995	Barings PLC	$1.4 bil.	Unauthorized derivatives trading
1994	Daiwa Bank	$1.1 bil.	Unauthorized bond trading
1994	Orange County, California	$1.7 bil.	Derivatives speculation
1994	Hanwa	$1.1 bil.	Securities mismanagement
1993	Metallgesellschaft AG	$1.5 bil.	Oilfutures speculation
1992	Showa Shell	$1.1 bil.	Currency speculation

Tranche: one installment or quota of a securities issue that is to be done in several installments or quotas. Each tranche of the offering has different pricing and payment terms.

Transaction: 1. the execution of a securities trade. *See also* Trade. **2.** the completion of a deal in the course of business.

Transaction Cost: the cost associated with buying and selling an asset (usually securities) that is in addition to the price of the asset (e.g., commissions).

Transceiver: a hardware device that is both a transmitter and a receiver.

Trans-European Automated Real-Time Gross Settlement Express Transfer System (TARGET): the European System Central Bank central settlement system for wholesale Euro transactions, made up of the European Central Bank Payment Mechanism, consisting of the Real-Time Gross Settlement System and the Society for Worldwide Interbank Financial Telecommunications Interlinking Network. *See also* European Central Bank, Real-Time Gross Settlement System, Society for Worldwide Interbank Financial Telecommunications.

Transfer: 1. the act of conveying title to property.

See also Conveyance. **2.** generally, to transfer legal ownership in law. *See also* Legal Transfer.

Transferable: capable of being legally assigned from one person to another. *See also* Negotiable.

Transferable Notice: a document sent by the seller of a commodities future contract to the buyer of the contract. The buyer can transfer the notice to another party, who will take physical delivery of the commodity. *See also* Commodity.

Transferable Vote: in some voting systems, a vote that can be moved to another candidate if the original candidate for whom it was cast is eliminated or has more votes than are necessary for election.

Transfer Agent: the party, often a trust company, that records the owners of a company's shares, sends out dividends, cancels and issues certificates and deals with other issues such as lost certificates. *See also* Certificate, Registered Owner.

Transferee: the person to whom something is transferred. *See also* Transferor.

Transferor: the person who transfers something to someone else. *See also* Transferee.

Transfer Payment: taxes collected by the federal government and turned over to provincial governments.

Transfer Price: the price at which a company sells a product or service to a related company.

Transfer Tax: a tax levied on the transfer of documents (e.g., deeds, securities).

Transition Relief: *see* Transition Rule.

Transition Rule: an income tax rule designed to enable taxpayers to adjust to a change in the Income Tax Act. Also known as Transition Relief.

Transmission: the conveyance of a title to property, with the rights of the beneficiary taking effect upon the death of the donor.

Transmittal Letter: a letter sent with a document or package that describes the contents and the purpose of the transaction.

Trap the Shorts: to own sufficient shares of a security so that an investor who executes a short sale must borrow shares from you to settle the trade or must buy shares from you to cover the trade. *See also* Corner the Market, Short Covering, Short Sale.

Travel, Accident Insurance: insurance to cover the insured while he/she is travelling.

Traveller's Cheques: a cheque for a specific amount of money (e.g., $50, $100, $500) that can be cashed in most countries in payment for goods or services on the holder's endorsement against his/her original signature. Vacationers use traveller's cheques because they can be replaced if lost or stolen.

Treasurer: 1. a member of a company's top management, he/she is generally responsible for the banking and related functions of a company. *See also* Top Management. **2.** generally, the individual in charge of funds (e.g., in a club).

Treasury: 1. an informal reference to U.S. government securities such as treasury bills and bonds, as in "treasury bonds." **2.** a place where currency and financial documents are received and held. **3.** the government department responsible for processing public revenue, as in "U.S. Treasury."

Treasury Bill: a form of short-term government bond known as an accretive bond. T-bills do not pay interest but trade at one price and mature (in less than one year) at a higher price. The increase in price at maturity provides the return and is considered interest income for tax purposes. T-bills are very safe because the government guarantees payment and the term to maturity is very short, so prices do not decline significantly if interest rates rise. Also known as T-Bill. *See also* Accretion Bond, Residual, Stripped Bond, Stripped Coupon, Zero Coupon Bond, Zero.

Treasury Bill Auction: a regular sale of treasury bills conducted by the Bank of Canada.

Treasury Bond: a long-term bond that matures in 10 years or more and that is issued by the U.S. Treasury. *See also* Treasury, Treasury Receipts.

Treasury Certificate: a short-term security that matures in less than one year and that is issued by the U.S. Treasury. *See also* Treasury.

Treasury Inflation Protection Securities (TIPS): a note issued by the U.S. Treasury whose interest is related to the inflation rate. *See also* Treasury.

Treasury Investment Growth Receipt (TIGR): a stripped U.S. treasury bond created by Merrill Lynch & Co. *See also* Merrill Lynch & Co., Treasury Bond.

Treasury Note: a medium-term security that matures in one to 10 years and that is issued by the U.S. Treasury. *See also* Treasury.

Treasury Receipts: stripped treasury bonds. *See also* Stripped Bonds, Treasury Bonds, Treasury Investment Growth Receipt.

Treasury Stock: issued shares that have been repurchased by the issuer. Treasury stock is issued but not outstanding, cannot be voted and is not entitled to dividends.

Treaty: a pact between two or more sovereign countries with a view to public welfare.

Treaty of Brussels: a treaty that came into force in 1967, merging the executives of the three original European Communities: the European Coal and Steel Community, the European Economic

Community and the European Atomic Energy Community. Also known as Brussels Treaty, EC Treaty. *See also* the European Coal and Steel Community, the European Economic Community, the European Atomic Energy Community.

Treaty of Paris: a treaty signed in 1951 by Belgium, France, Italy, Luxembourg, the Netherlands and West Germany. It established the European Coal and Steel Community, one of the three original communities in Europe (the European Economic Community and the European Atomic Energy Community were the other two). *See also* European Coal and Steel Community, the European Economic Community, the European Atomic Energy Community.

Treaty of Rome: there were two Treaties of Rome, each signed in 1957 by Belgium, France, Italy, Luxembourg, the Netherlands and West Germany. The treaties established the European Economic Community and the European Atomic Energy Community, two of the three original communities in Europe (the European Coal and Steel Community was the other). *See also* European Coal and Steel Community, the European Economic Community, the European Atomic Energy Community.

Treaty on European Union: a treaty signed on February 7, 1992. It transformed the Common Market into a monetary union, established a timetable for European Monetary Union and the launch of the Euro. Also known as Maastricht Treaty, Union Treaty.

Trench: in mineral exploration, a form of soil sampling in which material is tested at regular intervals along a trench.

Trend: an extended financial pattern (such as a stock price) that goes in one direction for several months. *See also* Privacy Trend ,Trend Analysis.

Trend Analysis: analysis, usually statistical, used to locate, identify or interpret trends. *See also* Trend Line.

Trendless Market: a price movement that is constituted by a series of short ups and downs with no clear overall direction. Also known as Sideways Market, Spotty Market.

Trend Line: a line drawn through a set of data, it indicates a trend. *See also* Trend Analysis.

Trespass: unauthorized entry into land that is in the possession of another. *See also* Easement.

Trial: in law, an examination of evidence to determine the guilt or innocence of a party with regard to specified charges.

Trial Balloon: the disclosure of an idea, often by a politician, for the purpose of gauging public response.

Triangle: a price pattern that forms a triangle by going up, down, and then up again. *See also* Technical Analysis.

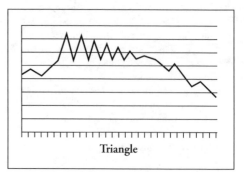

Triangle

Tribunal: an officer or body with the authority to adjudicate judicial or quasi-judicial matters.

Trickle-Down Theory: an economic theory stating that money invested in companies stimulates economic activity because it flows down through various levels of the economy. *See also* Multiplier Effect.

Triennial: occurring every three years. *See also* Annual, Biennial.

Trigger: *see* Crystallize.

Trinidad & Tobago Stock Exchange: the major stock exchange of Trinidad and Tobago, located in its capital, Port of Spain.

Tripartite: an agreement between three parties.

Triple A: *see* AAA.

Triple Bottom: a price pattern that recovers after falling to approximately the same low point three times within a relatively short period. *See also* Double Bottom.

Triple-E Senate: an idea introduced by Alberta premier Don Getty (1933-) in the late 1980s, it referred to a Canadian senate that would have more effective powers, would consist of elected members and would represent the provinces equally. Derived from the three Es: Equal, Elected and Effective. *See also* Senate, Senator.

Triple Net Lease: *see* Net Lease.

Triple Nine: the highest purity rating for gold or silver bullion equal to a fineness of .999 or purity of 99.9 percent. The European equivalent to triple nine is "fine ounce." Also known as Fine Ounce. *See also* Gold Bullion, Silver Bullion.

Triple Top: a price pattern that drops after rising to approximately the same high point three times within a relatively short period. *See also* Double Top.

Triple Witching Hour: the final hour of trading on the third Friday of March, June, September and December. On this day, equity options, index options and futures contracts on stock market indexes expire. *See also* Double Witching Hour, Option, Option Cycle, Witching Hour.

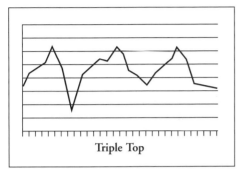

Triple Top

Triplex: a residential unit divided into or built as three separate living units. *See also* Duplex, Multi-Family Residential Housing, Single Family Residence.

Troika: a group made up of the present, immediate past and immediate future Presidents of the European Council. *See also* European Council.

Trophy Asset: *see* Marquee Asset.

Trophy Building: a distinctive, high-profile building with a higher investment value than most other buildings.

Trophy Director: a corporate director who may be selected more for celebrity than business acumen.

Trough: the low point in an economic or financial market cycle before an expansion or advance. *See also* Bottom, Business Cycle, Contraction, Cyclical, Economic Cycle, Expansion, Peak, Top.

Troy Weight: the system of weights (used for precious metals and gems) based on one pound equalling 12 ounces, or 5,760 grains.

Truck: to barter or trade.

True Value: *see* Inherent Value.

Trunk Line: a direct line between two switchboards.

Trust: an arrangement in which a person holds assets for the ultimate benefit of another person. The main reasons for setting up a trust include to facilitate the management of assets for someone who is not capable because of age, physical or mental disability; for tax planning; to protect assets from creditors; to provide an alternative to distributing assets through a will and for planned giving. A widely used trust in Canada is an RRSP. Also known as Trust Fund. *See also* Discretionary Trust, Inter Vivos Trust, Planned Giving, Registered Retirement Savings Plan, Spendthrift Trust, Spousal Trust, Sprinkling Trust, Testamentary Spousal Trust, Testamentary Trust, Trustee, Wasting Trust.

Trust Company: a Canadian financial institution

that acts as trustee for trusts and estates, provides custodial services and stock registration and transfers. Most trust companies also offer a full range of personal and corporate banking services.

Trustee: a formal party to a trust agreement, he/she is responsible for assets in the trust fund. *See also* Trust.

Trusteed Pension Plan: a pension plan in which the company contributes to a trust fund for employees. Those corporate individuals who are appointed or elected to monitor the process are pension fund trustees. *See also* Pension Fund Trustee.

Trustee Fee: a fee paid for the performance of trust services (e.g., the annual administration or trustee fee for an RRSP account). *See also* Administration Fee.

Trustee in Bankruptcy: a federally licensed person or company who receives and administers the property of a bankrupt party. *See also* Bankruptcy.

Trust Fund: *see* Trust.

Trustor: one who creates a trust.

Trust Originated Preferred Securities (TOPRS): securities issued to investors by a U.S. trust that remits proceeds to a U.S. parent company in return for notes.

TSE: *see* Toronto Stock Exchange.

TSE35: *see* Toronto Stock Exchange 35 Index.

TSE100: *see* Toronto Stock Exchange 100 Index.

TSE200: *see* Toronto Stock Exchange 200 Index.

TSE300: *see* Toronto Stock Exchange 300 Index.

TTYL: Internet acronym for "talk to you later."

Tuck-In Deal: a corporate acquisition that is so small and trouble free that it disappears into the larger entity with little noticeable effect. Also known as Tuck-Under Deal.

Tuck-Under Deal: *see* Tuck-In Deal.

Tugrik: the primary currency of Mongolia.

Tulipomania: a term used to describe the tulip craze in Holland during the 17th century, when the price of tulip bulbs became unbelievably overpriced. The term "tulipomania" is often used to refer to markets driven completely by emotional and irrational factors. *See also* Mania.

Tumble: to fall in a sudden and disorderly manner, as in "stock prices tumbled."

Tunisian Stock Exchange: the major stock exchange of Tunisia, located in its capital, Tunis. Also known as Bourse des Valeurs Mobilieres de Tunis. *See also* Bourse des Valeurs Mobilieres de Tunisie Index.

Turf War: a business circumstance in which people put their own interests ahead of the common good.

Turkey Stock Market Indices National 100: an index of stocks traded in Turkey.

Turn: this occurs when a price trend changes direction.

Turnaround: 1. generally, a term used to describe

what happens when a company that has been facing severe financial problems begins to recover. *See also* Turnaround Candidate. **2.** The condition of a stock (or financial market) that has been declining in price once it begins to recover.

Turnaround Candidate: a company that faces severe financial problems but that has the potential to recover from them. *See also* Company Doctor, Turnaround.

Turnaround Stage Financing: financing provided to a business in the expectation that sales and earnings will reverse and rescue the business from bankruptcy. *See also* Stage of Development Financing.

Turnkey: a product manufactured to completion, the result being that its user needs no expert knowledge to employ it. *See also* Turnkey Project.

Turnkey Project: often, a highly engineered project that is built to completion for a customer. *See also* Turnkey.

Turnover: 1. *see* Portfolio Turnover. **2.** *see* Trading Volume. **3.** *see* Inventory Turnover. **4.** *see* Employee Turnover. **5.** in the United Kingdom, the term is synonymous with "sales" or "revenue."

Twenty-Four by Seven (24x7): a reference to providing service for 24 hours per day, seven days per week.

Twenty/Twenty Mortgage: a mortgage that allows monthly payments to be increased by up to 20 percent and that allows for principal to be reduced by up to 20 percent once a year without a prepayment penalty. There are variations (e.g., a Fifteen/Twenty Mortgage allows 15 percent increases in monthly payments and a 20 percent reduction once a year). *See also* Mortgage, Prepayment Clause, Prepayment Penalty, Prepayment Privilege.

Twisting: in life insurance, the unethical action of an agent replacing one life insurance policy with another when the change is not in the best interests of the policy holder. Also known as Replacement. *See also* Rebating.

Two Bagger: in investment, an asset that doubles in value. The term is derived from baseball, in which a two-base hit is called a double or two bagger. The term is used with any number (e.g., five bagger, ten bagger). *See also* Four Bagger, Home Run, Three Bagger.

Two Bits: an informal reference to 25 cents, from the historical "pieces of eight," in which two pieces of eight, or two bits, represented one-quarter of the whole. *See also* Quarter.

Two-Dollar Broker: in the U.S., a broker who executes orders for other brokers who are too busy to do so themselves, so termed because in the past, such brokers were paid two dollars for each trade.

Two Hundred Day Moving Average: a price chart that averages the previous 200 days' closing prices. Each day, the current price is added and the price from 201 days ago is subtracted. Technical analysts believe that if the current price rises above this average, then it is a positive sign and that if it falls below this average, then it is a negative sign. *See also* Moving Average, One Hundred Day Moving Average, Technical Analysis.

TwoIC: second in command or authority.

Twoonie: *see* Toonie.

Two-Sided Market: this refers to a condition in which a broker has one order to buy and one order to sell a block of the same security. Also known as Either Way, Two Ways.

Two Tier Bid: *see* Two Tier Pricing.

Two Tier Pricing: 1. specifically, this occurs when a company making a takeover bid pays a higher price for the control block than for the rest of the shares. Also known as Two Tier Bid. *See also* Control Block, Cross. **2.** any pricing system with two levels of prices for the same product or service.

Two Ways: *see* Two-Sided Market.

TWSE: *see* Taiwan Stock Exchange.

Tycoon: a powerful businessperson.

U

Uberrima Fides: Latin for "utmost good faith," and the principle assumed to be in effect in all insurance agreements.

UHF: *see* Ultra-High Frequency.

UI: *see* Employment Insurance.

Ukrainian PFTS OTC Stock Index: a liquidity weighted stock market index of Ukrainian stocks.

Ukrainian Stock Exchange: the major stock exchange of the Ukraine, located in its capital, Kiev.

Ultimate Beneficiary: the beneficiary who will receive the principal amount of the final distribution of an estate or trust. *See also* Beneficiary, Devisee, Heir, Heir Apparent, Heiress, First Devisee, Life Insurance, Trust, Will.

Ultimo: the previous month.

Ultra-High Frequency (UHF): radio wave frequency of 300 to 3,000 megahertz. *See also* High Frequency, Low Frequency, Very High Frequency, Very Low Frequency.

Ultra Vires: 1. Latin for "outside the law." **2.** a government action, including legislating and regulating, that is unconstitutional under the British North America Act. Both federal and provincial governments have had such claims supported and rejected by the Supreme Court of Canada. *See also* British North America Act, Canadian Charter of Rights and Freedoms. **3.** actions of a company not authorized by its corporate charter. *See also* Articles of Incorporation.

Umbrella Coverage: liability insurance that provides additional coverage over and above the liability limits of homeowner's and automobile insurance.

UN: *see* United Nations.

Unaudited Financial Statement: a financial statement that is not subject to strict audit procedures and that does not come with an auditor's opinion. *See also* Audited Financial Statement.

Unauthorized Investment: an investment that is made without approval or that falls outside the bounds of approval.

Unbundle: to package products and/or services separately so the buyer can buy one without paying for them all. *See also* Bundle.

Uncontested Divorce: this occurs when neither spouse disputes the grounds for divorce, child care or support payments. *See also* Contested Divorce.

Uncovered Call Option: a call option on a stock written and sold when the seller does not own a sufficient amount of the underlying security to satisfy an exercise of the call option by the buyer. Also known as Naked Call Option. *See also* Covered Call Option, Option, Uncovered Option.

Uncovered Option: an option on a stock written and sold when the seller does not own a sufficient amount of the underlying security to satisfy an exercise of the option by the buyer. Also known as Naked Option. *See also* Covered Option, Option.

Uncovered Position: a term used to describe the circumstance of having written an uncovered option. Also known as Naked Position. *See also* Covered Position, Option.

Uncovered Put Option: a put option on a stock written and sold when the seller does not have sufficient collateral to take delivery of the security if the option is exercised. Also known as Naked Put Option. *See also* Covered Put Option, Option, Uncovered Option.

Uncovered Transaction: the act of buying or selling security while not holding an offsetting position. This leaves the investor with either a long or short position outstanding. Also known as Naked Transaction. *See also* Covered Transaction.

Uncovered Writer: a person who sells options against a security he/she does not own. An uncovered writer is exposed to significant risk because the theoretical potential loss is infinite. *See also* Covered Writer, Naked Writer, Option, Writing Naked.

Uncovered Writing: the process of writing options without owning the underlying security. Also known as Naked Writing, Writing Naked. *See also* Option, Covered Writing.

Uncut: a term used to describe a gemstone, especially a diamond, in its natural condition (i.e., not cut or shaped). *See also* Diamond, Four Cs.

Undeducted RRSP Contributions: *see* Registered Retirement Savings Plan – Undeducted Contributions.

Undepreciated Capital Cost: in income tax, the remaining value of an asset that can still be depreciated and charged to income to reduce income tax.

Underbid: 1. to make an offer that is too low. *See also* Overbid. **2.** to make an unsuccessful offer. *See also* Outbid.

Underbooked: *see* Undersubscribed.

Underbought: a situation in which an investor has purchased less of a security (or a category of securities) than he/she had intended. *See also* Overbought, Undersold.

Underbuild: 1. to construct according to standards below what is needed or expected. *See also* Overbuild. **2.** to place so few buildings in a particular place or on a particular piece of land that vacancy rates fall and real estate prices rise. *See also* Overbuild, Vacancy Rates.

Undercapitalized: a term used to describe the condition of a company with insufficient capital to conduct business. This is often the plight of new or small businesses. *See also* Overcapitalized.

Undercharge: to sell at a price less than the established guidelines. *See also* Overcharge.

Undercut: to sell at a lower price or to work for lower wages than a competitor.

Underemployment: a term used to describe the situation in which individuals are forced to accept jobs below their level of qualification. Underemployment usually occurs when unemployment is high. *See also* Employment, Overemployment.

Underestimate: to make too low an approximation or forecast. *See also* Overestimate.

Underfollowed Security: a security that is analyzed and reported on by very few financial analysts. Under followed securities are inefficiently priced and offer opportunities for above-average returns. *See also* Overfollowed Security, Underfollowed Stock.

Underfollowed Stock: a stock that is analysed and reported on by very few financial analysts. Underfollowed stocks are inefficiently priced and offer opportunities for above-average returns. *See also* Overfollowed Stock, Underfollowed Security.

Underfunded: the condition of not having enough capital to complete a transaction. *See also* Overfunded.

Underfunded Pension Plan: a defined benefit pension plan that does not have sufficient capital to satisfy its pension obligations. *See also* Defined Benefit Pension Plan, Pension Plan, Unfunded Pension Plan.

Underground: 1. hidden or clandestine. **2.** a part of society that operates illegally.

Underground Economy: business and financial activity not reported to the government. The underground economy is estimated to be 15 percent or more of the regular economy. A large underground economy stems from high and rising taxes. Also known as Unreported Economy.

Underground Mining: mining in which the ore is removed by sinking shafts into the ground. *See also* Open Pit Mining, Placer Mining.

Underground Rights: the legal ownership of mineral or petroleum rights beneath a property. *See also* Surface Rights.

Underinvested: the condition of not having enough invested in an individual security or single asset class. *See also* Overinvested.

Underloved Security: a security with prospects and potential not fully appreciated by investors. Also known as Out-of-Favour. *See also* Overloved Security.

Underloved Stock: a stock with prospects and potential not fully appreciated by investors. Also known as Out-of-Favour. *See also* Overloved Stock.

Underlying Mortgage: a mortgage with a prior claim over another mortgage. *See also* Mortgage.

Underlying Security: 1. the security or stock on which an options contract is written. *See also* Option, Option-Eligible Security. **2.** the security or stock into which a convertible may be converted. *See also* Convertible, Convertible Bond, Convertible Debenture, Convertible Preferred Share.

Underlying Stock: *see* Underlying Security.

Under Margin: to have insufficient security for a margin account. *See also* Margin Account, Over Margin, Restricted Account.

Undermargined Account: a margin account that has fallen below margin requirements. *See also* Margin Account, Overmargined Account.

Underowned Security: a security that is neither widely followed nor particularly popular with investors to the point that it is undervalued. *See also* Underowned Stock.

Underowned Stock: a stock that is neither widely followed nor particularly popular with investors to the point that it is undervalued. *See also* Underowned Security.

Underperforming Asset: 1. in investing, a security in a portfolio that is not providing as high a return as the rest of the portfolio or the portfolio benchmark. *See also* Outperforming Asset. **2.** a corporate asset earning a lower rate of return than the same asset owned by other companies. *See also* Outperforming Asset.

Underpriced Security: a security that is trading below its inherent value. Also known as Undervalued Security. *See also* Overpriced Security.

Underpriced Stock: a stock that is trading below its inherent value. Also known as an Undervalued Stock. *See also* Inherent Value, Overpriced Stock.

Underrate: to evaluate too low. *See also* Overrate.

Under Review: the announcement from a bond rating agency that a particular bond rating is being reviewed. The agency will sometimes indicate the reason for the review by adding a phrase such as "with negative implications" or "with positive implications."

Undersell: to sell at a lower price than a competitor.

Undersold: a situation in which an investor has sold less of a security or category of securities than he/she had intended. *See also* Oversold, Underbought.

Undersigned: a person whose signature appears at the bottom of a document.

Undersubscribed: this occurs when supply exceeds demand for a new issue of securities. Also known as Underbooked. *See also* Oversubscribed.

Undertaking: a brokerage firm's written promise to deliver a security in a timely fashion. The undertaking is usually accepted as being the same as the delivery of the security. *See also* Good Delivery.

Under-the-Counter: *see* Under the Table.

Under the Table: 1. traded or sold illegally. Also known as Under-the-Counter. **2.** money changing hands improperly (e.g., a bribe).

Undertone: a reference to the market's general state (i.e., whether it is optimistic or pessimistic).

Undervalued Security: *see* Underpriced Security.

Undervalued Stock: *see* Underpriced Stock.

Underwater Option: *see* Out of the Money.

Underweighted: a stock or industry position that is much lower in a portfolio than it is in a benchmark. *See also* Overweighted.

Underwithholding: this occurs when insufficient income tax is deducted each month, resulting in a taxpayer owing taxes each year. Underwithholding can stem from either an underestimate of income or an overestimate of deductions. *See also* Overwithholding, Tax Refund.

Underwriter: 1. a firm that engages in bringing new issues of securities to market. *See also* Underwriting Syndicate. **2.** *see* Insurer.

Underwriting: 1. the process of bringing new issues of securities to market. Also known as Floating an Issue. **2.** in life insurance, the process by which an insurer determines whether to accept an application for life insurance. *See also* Life Insurance.

Underwriting Agreement: the contract between an underwriter and the issuer of new securities. The underwriting agreement sets the specific terms and conditions of the underwriting. *See also* Underwriter.

Underwriting Fee: the fee that accrues to syndicate members in an underwriting. The syndicate manager is entitled to an additional fee. *See also* Funding Costs.

Underwriting Group: a group comprising the investment firms involved in underwriting an issue of securities. Also known as Selling Group. *See also* Syndicate.

Underwriting Rights: *see* Standby Commitment.

Underwriting Risk: the risk to an underwriter in a bought deal that the value of securities will decline sharply before being sold. *See also* Bought Deal, Risk.

Underwriting Spread: the difference between the price that investors pay for a newly issued security and the amount of money per share the issuer receives. *See also* Underwriter.

Underwriting Syndicate: a group of investment bankers that underwrites a new offering of securities. The underwriting syndicate assumes responsibility for the issue and manages the distribution and sale of the securities. Also known as Banking Group, Syndicate. *See also* Underwriter, Underwriting.

Undiluted: a financial statistic calculated using only shares issued and outstanding but excluding shares that may be issued as a result of conversion of convertible securities outstanding, any rights or warrants issued and employee and management stock options (e.g., undiluted earnings per share). *See also* Full Diluted.

Undistributed Profits: *see* Retained Earnings.

Undivided Interest: an interest in property that gives each tenant an equal right to use the entire property. *See also* Joint Tenancy, Tenant, Tenants in Common.

Undivided Right: a portion of ownership that cannot be separated from other portions of ownership (e.g., a joint tenancy interest). *See also* Joint Tenancy.

Unearned Income: an income tax term used to describe income gained through investments, interest payments and so on rather than through salaries, wages or fees. *See also* Taxes.

Unearned Interest: interest a lender has received but not recorded as income. *See also* Accrural Accounting.

Unemployment: the condition of being without a job. *See also* Employment.

Unemployment Insurance (UI): *see* Employment Insurance.

Unencumbered: a term used to describe an asset that has no liens against it and that has not been pledged as collateral. *See also* Encumbered.

Uneven Market: a market with fluctuating prices.

Unfavourable Balance of Trade: a situation in which imports of merchandise exceed exports of merchandise within a given period. An unfavourable balance of trade puts downward pressure on a country's currency. Also known as Trade Deficit. *See also* Balance of Trade, Favourable Balance of Trade.

Unfriendly Takeover: the acquisition of a firm in spite of resistance by its management and/or board of directors. *See also* Friendly Takeover.

Unfunded Debt: debt not secured by an indenture. *See also* Funded Debt.

Unfunded Pension Plan: a pension plan in which benefits are paid out of current income. The Canada Pension Plan is a substantially unfunded pension plan. Also known as Pay-As-You-Go Pension Plan. *See also* Canada Pension Plan, Current Disbursement Funding, Underfunded Pension Plan.

Uniform Resource Locator (URL): on the World Wide Web, an address that leads to a specific site. *See also* Address, Internet, Web Page, Web Site, World Wide Web.

Unilateral Contract: an agreement in which the promisor agrees to do or refrain from doing something if the promisee does or refrains from doing something. However, the promisee is not bound by an undertaking or promise.

Unincorporated Business: *see* Sole Proprietorship.

Union: *see* Labour Union.

Union Dues: fees paid to a union. Normal, annual union dues are deductible for income tax purposes. *See also* Labour Union.

Union Movement: the promotion of the principles, theory and systems favouring labour unions. *See also* Labour Union.

Union Shop: *see* Closed Shop.

Union Treaty: *see* Treaty on European Union.

Unique Risk: *see* Non-Systematic Risk.

Unissued Common Shares: common shares that are authorized to be issued but have not yet been distributed. *See also* Issued and Outstanding.

Unit: 1. a standard quantity. **2.** in unincorporated mutual funds, the basic investment quantity. *See also* Mutual Fund, Unit Trust.

Unit Benefit Pension Plan: *see* Defined Benefit Pension Plan.

United Nations (UN): an organization set up in 1945 to replace the League of Nations to promote inter-national peace and security. Its six primary bodies are the Security Council, the General Assembly, the Economic and Social Council, the Trusteeship Council, the International Court of Justice and the Secretariat.

Unitholder: an owner of a mutual fund structured as a unit trust. *See also* Mutual Fund, Unit Trust.

Unit Pricing: pricing, or showing the price of, goods on a price per unit of measure (e.g., $25 per milligram).

Unit Trust: an unincorporated structure used by some mutual funds to hold the assets and pass through income to the individual owners, called unitholders. Also known as Mutual Fund Trust. *See also* Unitholder, Mutual Fund.

Universal Life Insurance: a life insurance contract in which premiums are paid into an investment account. Deductions are made from this account to pay for insurance and related expenses. The policy holder can increase or decrease the amount of

insurance and make withdrawals from the deposit account. When the insured person dies, the life insurance death benefit and the value of the investment portfolio can, within limits, pass to beneficiaries tax free. *See also* Life Insurance, Variable Life Insurance.

Universal Product Code (UPC): a series of vertical bars of varying widths printed on consumer product packaging, used to record prices and monitor inventory.

UNIX: a multitasking, multiuser computer operating system developed in 1969. Its many versions are popular in the educational, business and scientific communities. *See also* Computer, Internet, Operating System.

Unlettered: describes common shares, usually once restricted from trading, which can now be freely traded. Also known as Free Stock, Free Trading. *See also* Lettered.

Unleveraged: without debt. *See also* Leverage, Leveraged.

Unlisted Security: a security that trades over-the-counter because it is not listed on a recognized stock exchange. *See also* Listed Security, Over-the-Counter, Unlisted Stock.

Unlisted Stock: a common share that trades over-the-counter because it is not listed on a recognized stock exchange. *See also* Listed Stock, Unlisted Security.

Unloading: the selling of securities, often in an undisciplined fashion.

Unmarginable Security: a security that is unacceptable for deposit in a margin account. *See also* Margin, Marginable Security, Margin Account.

Unorganized: not unionized.

Unpaid Dividend: a dividend that has been declared but not paid. *See also* Dividend.

Unparted Bullion: precious metal bullion that contains other metals as well. *See also* Bullion.

Unqualified Opinion: *see* Clean Opinion.

Unrealized Capital Gain: a capital gain on an investment, it is not taxable because it has not been triggered by a sale or disposition. *See also* Paper Profit, Realized Capital Gain.

Unrealized Capital Loss: a capital loss on an investment, it is not tax deductible because they have not been triggered by a sale or disposition. *See also* Paper Loss, Realized Capital Loss.

Unregistered: a term used to refer to a security with ownership not recorded in a specific name. *See also* Registered, Street Form.

Unreported Economy: *see* Underground Economy.

Unseasoned Security: a security that has recently started trading and has not established a pattern or record of trading under various market conditions. *See also* Seasoned Security.

Unsecured Creditor: a creditor with a claim for which no specific asset or assets have been pledged as collateral. *See also* Secured Creditor.

Unsecured Debt: debt supported by the issuer's creditworthiness and not by any collateral. *See also* Secured Debt.

Unsolicited Order: an order from a client to a stockbroker that was not prompted by a recommendation from the stockbroker to the client. *See also* Restricted List, Solicited Order.

Unsystematic Risk: *see* Non-Systematic Risk.

Unused RRSP Contribution Room: *see* Registered Retirement Savings Plan – Unused Contribution Room.

Unwind: 1. to undertake the transactions necessary to offset or void an investment position (e.g., to sell a security previously purchased). **2.** to rectify a transaction when a mistake has been made.

UPC: *see* Universal Product Code.

Updraft: a sudden rise in prices. *See also* Downdraft.

Upfront: payment in advance.

Upgrading: 1. the process of selling a lower quality security to buy a higher quality security. *See also* Downgrading. **2.** converting heavy oil into lighter oil products. *See also* Refinery. **3.** in computer software or hardware, the process of moving from one version to an improved version. *See also* Computer. **4.** this occurs when an investment professional raises an earnings estimate or a recommendation for a company. *See also* Downgrading.

Upload: the process of moving data files from one's own computer to a remote computer. *See also* Computer, Download.

Upset Price: *see* Reserve Bid.

Upside: the possible amount by which a market or stock could rise in value. *See also* Downside.

Upside Potential: an estimate of how far a market or security might rise in price under favourable conditions. *See also* Downside Risk.

Upsloping Yield Curve: *see* Positive Yield Curve.

Upstairs Trade: a trade in a listed security that is not completed through the stock exchange.

Upstream: 1. in the oil and gas industry, the functions of exploration and production. *See also* Downstream, Refining and Marketing. **2.** in general, a point in the manufacture or distribution of a product or service that is far removed from the ultimate consumer of the product or service.

Uptick: *see* Plus Tick.

Uptick Rule: a rule common in most securities markets, it holds that a short sale can be made only on

an plus tick or a zero-plus tick. Also known as Short Sale Rule. *See also* Short Sale, Plus Tick, Zero-Plus Tick.

Uptick Volume: the number of shares traded on upticks. *See also* Downtick Volume, Tick Index, Uptick.

Up Trend: a price trend in which successive peaks are higher than preceding peaks and successive troughs are higher than preceding troughs. *See also* Down Trend.

Urban Legend: on the Internet, a story that circulates and is widely believed by readers even though it is not true (e.g., the Good Times e-mail virus). *See also* Good Times Virus, Internet.

URL: *see* Universal Resource Locater.

U.S. Bond Fund: 1. *see* Foreign Bond Fund. **2.** *see* Mutual Fund – Category.

U.S.-Canada Free Trade Agreement: *see* Canada-U.S. Free Trade Agreement of 1989.

U.S. Common Stock Fund: *see* U.S. Equity Fund.

Useful Life: *see* Effective Life.

Usenet: an Internet bulletin board system made up of thousands of newsgroups that allow anyone to participate in their discussions. *See also* Internet.

U.S. Equity Fund: one of the 31 Canadian categories developed by the Investment Funds Standards Committee. Mutual funds in this category must have a minimum of 50 percent of the total assets, and 75 percent of the non-cash assets, of the portfolio in equities or equity equivalents of companies located in the U.S. or derivative-based exposure to Japanese equity markets. The calculations to determine whether a mutual fund fits this definition are based on median values from fund data over three years, unless otherwise noted. The derivatives are weighted on an extended value basis. Each of the categories may be refined by the fund manager (e.g., a Canadian Large Cap Equity Fund might be described as "growth" or "value" to reflect the manager's style). Also known as American Equity Fund, U.S. Common Stock Fund. *See also* Extended Value, Mutual Fund – Category.

User-Friendly: in computers, a term used to indicate that a certain program or system is easy to use. *See also* Computer.

U.S. Money Market Fund: 1. *see* Foreign Money Market Fund. **2.** *see* Mutual Fund – Category.

U.S. Small to Mid Cap Equity Fund: one of the 31 Canadian categories developed by the Investment Funds Standards Committee. Mutual funds in this category must have a minimum of 50 percent of the total assets, and 75 percent of the non-cash assets, of the portfolio, based on individual market value, in

U.S. equities that have a market capitalization of less than $6 billion U.S. The calculations to determine whether a mutual fund fits this definition are based on median values from fund data over three years, unless otherwise noted. The derivatives are weighted on an extended value basis. Each of the categories may be refined by the fund manager (e.g., a Canadian Large Cap Equity Fund might be described as "growth" or "value" to reflect the manager's style). Also known as American Equity Fund, Mid Cap Equity Fund, Small Cap Equity Fund, U.S. Common Stock Fund. *See also* Extended Value, Mutual Fund – Category.

Usufruct: in law, the temporary right to use, enjoy and derive income from someone else's property without damaging or destroying it.

Usurer: one who lends money and charges exorbitant or illegal interest rates. *See also* Usury.

Usury: the lending of money at exorbitant or illegal interest rates. *See also* Usurer.

Utility: *see* Public Utility.

V: in Roman numerals, the number five.

Vacancy: 1. the condition of a dwelling that is not occupied. *See also* Occupancy. **2.** a description of a job or position that is available to be filled.

Vacancy Rate: the extent to which a rental property is not rented. Calculated as 100 percent less the occupancy rate. *See also* Occupancy Rate.

Valid: having legal effect, as in a "valid will."

Valuables: *see* High Ticket Items.

Valuation: the act of assessing or determining the value or price of an asset.

Valuation Day (V-Day): before 1972, there was no tax on capital gains in Canada. Therefore, to avoid paying taxes on any capital gain that was already in place before 1972, the cost of such an asset can be adjusted to its value on December 31, 1971, or Valuation Day. *See also* Valuation Day Value.

Valuation Day Value: the value of an asset on December 31, 1971 (Valuation Day). *See also* Valuation Day.

Value: 1. the monetary worth of something. **2.** the worth of something compared to the price paid for it. *See also* Value Investor. **3.** to assess the worth of an asset, as in "I need it valued for insurance purposes."

Value-Added Tax (VAT): a tax added to a product at each stage of its production and on the end selling price. The Goods & Services Tax is a value-added tax. Also known as Consumption Tax. *See also* Goods & Services Tax.

Value Investment: an investment valued relative to asset value or cash value, as opposed to growth potential (e.g., a stock trading below net asset value per share). *See also* Magic Sixes.

Value Investor: an investor who focuses on value investment as opposed to growth investments. Also referred to as Value. *See also* Bottom-Up, Growth Investor, Portfolio Management Style, Sector Rotation, Top Down, Value Investment, Value Stock.

Value of Trading: the number of shares traded multiplied by the price of each trade totalled for a given period. The calculation can apply to an individual stock, a group of stocks or the overall market.

Also known as Market Value of Trading. *See also* Volume of Trading.

Value Stock: a share of a company that is primarily attractive because of some underlying tangible asset value (e.g., a high value of real estate per share) or a below-average price to earnings ratio or both. *See also* Growth Stock, Magic Sixes.

Vancouver Stock Exchange (VSE): a stock exchange located in Vancouver, British Columbia, it was founded in 1907. In 1990, the VSE became the first fully automated stock exchange in North America. Generally, the VSE is associated with trading the shares of smaller or more venturesome Canadian companies, especially those active in resources or high technology. Under an agreement in principle announced in March 1999, the VSE will merge with the Alberta Stock Exchange to form a national junior equities market known as the Canadian Venture Exchange. The Toronto Stock Exchange will become the senior securities market and the Montreal Exchange will focus exclusively on futures and derivatives trading. Web site: www.vse.com *See also* Alberta Stock Exchange, Canadian Venture Exchange, Montreal Exchange, Toronto Stock Exchange.

Vancouver Stock Exchange Composite Index: a market capitalization weighted stock price index for the Vancouver Stock Exchange. The composite index combines the resource, commercial/industrial and venture indexes.

Vancouver Stock Exchange Resource Index: a market capitalization weighted index of resource companies listed on the Vancouver Stock Exchange.

Vancouver Stock Exchange Commercial/Industrial Index: a market capitalization weighted index of commercial and industrial companies listed on the Vancouver Stock Exchange.

Vancouver Stock Exchange Venture Index: a market capitalization weighted index of venture companies listed on the Vancouver Stock Exchange.

Vanilla Offering: a routine offering that has no special or unusual features.

Variability: the fluctuations in rates of return on investment.

Variable Annuity: an annuity in which the income changes depending on the performance of a portfolio of securities. *See also* Annuity, Deferred Variable Annuity, Fixed Annuity, Segregated Fund.

Variable Contract: a contract under which at least some benefits are not fixed and vary with market conditions (usually, a portfolio of common stocks).

Variable Cost: an operating cost of a company that rise and fall as production rises and falls. Fuel costs are a variable cost in that they go up and down with production, unlike rental expenses, which are fixed each month and do not vary with output. Also known as Variable Expense. *See also* Fixed Cost.

Variable Deferred Annuity: a variable annuity in which annuity payments to the investor are deferred. *See also* Annuity, Variable Annuity.

Variable Expense: *see* Variable Cost.

Variable Interest Rate: *see* Floating Interest Rate.

Variable Life Insurance: a form of whole life insurance that allows the cash value to be invested in the money market, bonds and stocks. The policy holder assumes the investment risk but is guaranteed a minimum amount of death benefit. With variable life insurance, the premium and death benefits cannot be changed. *See also* Life Insurance, Universal Life Insurance.

Variable Premium Life Insurance: a life insurance policy in which the premium changes, usually related to the age of the insured. *See also* Fixed Premium Life Insurance.

Variable Pay Program: *see* Bonus Plan.

Variable Rate: *see* Floating Rate.

Variable Rate Debt: *see* Floating Rate Debt.

Variable Rate Mortgage: *see* Floating Rate Mortgage.

Variable Rate Preferred Share: *see* Floating Rate Preferred Share.

Variance: 1. in real estate, an exemption from zoning regulations. **2.** in finance, the difference between a budget amount and the actual amount. **3.** the changes from period to period in specific items in financial statements (e.g., revenue).

Variation: a change in a previous court order, it reflects new or changed circumstances.

VAT: *see* Value-Added Tax.

Vatu: the primary currency of Vanuatu.

Vault Cash: cash held in financial institution vaults for cash payments to customers. The total cash held by an institution is vault cash plus till money. *See also* Till Money.

V-Chip: an electronic device added to or built into a television, it can be programmed to block out or scramble any programs containing unacceptable language, violence or explicit sex. Also known as ViewControl Device.

V-Day: *see* Valuation Day.

VDT: *see* Video Display Terminal.

Vehicle-Currency Trade: a trade that takes place between two parties that use a third currency for settlement (e.g., it may be difficult to settle directly from Swiss francs to Japanese yen, so each converts into and settles in U.S. dollars).

Vein: a long, narrow deposit of metallic material in or under the ground.

Velocity of Money: a theoretical economic calculation that measures the rate at which money changes hands. The higher the velocity of money, the more support a given amount of money supply can give to the economy.

Vendee: the buyer. *See also* Vendor.

Vendor: the seller. *See also* Vendee.

Vendor Financing: this occurs when a buyer cannot get a loan to purchase an asset and the seller agrees to provide both a second mortgage or similar funding and to take regular payments rather than a lump sum. Also known as Balance of Sale, Seller Financing, Vendor Take-Back Mortgage. *See also* Mortgage, Second Mortgage.

Vendor Take-Back Mortgage: *see* Vendor Financing.

Venezuela Stock Market Capital General Index: a stock market index of shares traded in Venezuela. *See also* Caracas Stock Exchange.

Venture Capital: money available for investment in new businesses, often before a product or service is proven. As this is high risk money, the cost to a new company will be comparatively high, either because shares issued are priced at a low level or interest charged on a loan is high. Venture capital is raised after seed capital and carries a business to the mezzanine level. A listing of venture capital providers, *Sources of Venture Capital: A Canadian Guide and Sources of Funds Index,* is available from the federal government. *See also* Adventure Capital, Mezzanine Level, Seed Financing.

Venture Capital Corporation: 1. a special investment in which investors receive a tax credit on the amount invested (usually, 20 percent from the federal government and 20 percent from the provincial government). The investment cannot be sold for a fixed period and the assets invested in must meet guidelines and be preapproved. **2.** *see* Labour Sponsored Venture Capital Corporation.

Venture Capital Fund: a fund, similar to a mutual fund, that invests in new businesses. *See also* Mutual Fund – Other.

Venture Capitalist: a person who seeks out venture capital investments.

Verbal Contract: an agreement between two parties that has been spoken but is not in writing. In many cases, verbal contracts are legally enforceable. Also known as Oral Contract.

Verbal Will: *see* Nuncupative Will.

Verdict: in law, the decision of a jury.

Veronica: an acronym for **V**ery **E**asy **R**odent-**O**riented **N**etwide **I**ndex to **C**omputerized **A**rchives. An index that searches for Gopher archives by keywords. *See also* Gopher.

Vertical Analysis: a method of analysis that entails comparing an item on a financial statement with a different item on the same statement (e.g., current assets compared with current liabilities). *See also* Horizontal Analysis.

Vertical Integration: the act of expanding a company's operations into businesses that are at different points on the same production path (e.g., a car company expanding into tire manufacturing). *See also* Horizontal Integration.

Vertical Merger: a merger between two firms involved at different points in the same production path (e.g., a clothing retailer and a clothing manufacturer). *See also* Horizontal Merger.

Vertical Spread: the simultaneous purchase and sale of more than one option of the same type (e.g., calls, puts) on the same underlying security with the same expiration date but different strike prices. *See also* Option, Calendar Spread.

Very High Frequency: radio frequency of 30 to 300 megahertz. *See also* High Frequency, Low Frequency, Ultra-High Frequency, Very Low Frequency.

Very Low Frequency: radiowave frequency of 3 to 30 kilohertz. *See also* Low Frequency, Ultra-High Frequency. *See also* High Frequency, Low Frequency, Ultra-High Frequency, Very High Frequency.

Vested: fixed or absolute. Not subject to anything (e.g., a vested pension plan). *See also* Vested Interest.

Vested Interest: one's personal or financial right or interest in a property or transaction. *See also* Vested.

Vesting: the process of becoming vested. Also known as Accrued Benefits.

V-Formation: a sharp drop followed by an immediate recovery on a security price chart.

Viager: a French real estate arrangement in which, in return for a down payment and regular cash payments for the remainder of his/her life, a homeowner agrees to surrender title in his/her property at death.

Viatical Contract: an agreement in which a terminally ill person agrees to sell the death benefit of his/her life insurance for less than its full value. The seller wants the money to spend during his/her limited life expectancy; the buyer is making an investment with an uncertain term to maturity. *See also* Critical Illness Insurance, Living Benefit, Life Insurance.

Vicarious Liability: the liability incurred by an employer for the actions of an employee.

Vice-President (VP): in a company, the position, office or person holding the position that is normally immediately below president and acting for or representing the president in his/her absence. The vice-

president is often identified as the person who will replace the president at the appropriate time. *See also* Chief Executive Officer, Chief Operating Officer, President.

Vicious Cycle: a negative economic trend that feeds on itself (e.g., low consumer confidence produces a decline in corporate profits, which triggers a decline in stock prices, which further affects consumer confidence in a negative fashion).

Video Display Terminal (VDT): a terminal that includes a cathode-ray tube and a keyboard. *See also* Cathode-Ray Tube, Computer.

Video Game: an electronic or computer-based game that uses images on a display screen. The video game industry is dominated by Japanese firms such as Sony Corporation and Nintendo Company Ltd.

Vienna Stock Exchange: the major stock exchange of Austria, located in its capital, Vienna. Also known as Wiener Borsekammer. Web site: www.vienna-stock-exchange.at/boerse/ *See also* Austrian Trade Index.

ViewControl Device: *see* V-Chip.

Vignette: the unique illustration often found on a stock certificate.

Viral Marketing: an Internet marketing phenomenon in which visitors to an Internet site are induced to recruit friends, relatives and associates to visit the site as well. *See also* Internet.

Virtual Banking: a totally computerized banking service in which almost all banking facilities exist electronically but not physically. *See also* Internet.

Virtual Mall: an Internet site that features merchants offering goods and services. *See also* Internet.

Virtual Private Network: security measures on a public network, such as the Internet, that ensure that messages are as free from unauthorized interference as they would be on a private network. *See also* Internet.

Virtual Reality (VR): a computer-simulated three-dimensional environment that exists electronically but not physically. *See also* Computer.

Virus: a small self-replicating program that can cause serious damage to a computer system. A virus is capable of spreading its "infection" by hiding inside otherwise innocuous programs that may be copied to other systems. *See also* Computer, Good Times Virus, Infect, Michelangelo Virus.

Visa: an official document sometimes required to gain entry to a country or region.

Visibility: in investment, predictability, as in a "high degree of earnings visibility."

Visible Gold: in mining, the presence of gold that can be seen by the naked eye.

Vital Statistics: data concerning births, deaths, marriages and migration.

Viz.: from the Latin *videlicit* (literally, "it is permitted to see"), it means "that is to say," or "to wit."

Vocation: *see* Occupation.

Vocational School: a school that offers instruction in skilled trades (e.g., mechanics).

Voice Print: an electronically recorded graphic representation of a person's voice.

Void: having no legal force.

Voidable: capable of being annulled.

Voir Dire: a preliminary examination of the competence of a witness by the court, it requires him/her to speak the truth. From the Old French *voir*, meaning "true" or "truth," and *dire*, meaning "to say."

Volatility: a tendency to be subject to many, and perhaps large, fluctuations. Volatility is often used as a measure of risk. *See also* Beta.

Volcanic: pertaining to rocks formed by heat, fusion and crystallization of lava near the surface. Generally, the opposite of Plutonic. *See also* Craton, Plutonic.

Volume: *see* Volume of Trading.

Volume Alert: in technical analysis, this occurs when the volume of trading for a stock or financial market suddenly increases to above-normal levels. This is taken as a sign of an impending change in price trend. *See also* Technical Analysis.

Volume Discount: 1. a reduction in commission rate charged on a large order. **2.** generally, a price discount or other reduction offered on a large order.

Volume of Trading: the total number of shares traded within a given period. The calculation can apply to an individual stock, a group of stocks or the overall market. Also known as Market Volume of Trading, Volume. *See also* Value of Trading.

Voluntary Accumulation Plan: a plan offered by mutual funds in which an investor agrees to invest a predetermined amount at regular intervals. The investor is not contractually bound by the plan. *See also* Accumulation Plan, Contractual Plan, Mutual Fund, Periodic Payment Plan, Systematic Savings Plan.

Voluntary Bankruptcy: this occurs when a debtor declares bankruptcy before creditors force the issue. *See also* Bankruptcy.

Voluntary Settlement: an out-of-court settlement with creditors. A voluntary settlement avoids many of the costs of bankruptcy and may leave the business involved, in a position to continue operations or to realize better prices when liquidating remaining assets. *See also* Bankruptcy.

Voluntary Trading Halt: *see* Trading Halt.

Vote: the method by which a preference (e.g., for a candidate) is made known. *See also* Secret Ballot, Straw Vote, Transferable Vote.

Voting Rights of the European Council: members of the European Council have votes according to the population of the 15 member countries. For most legislation, 62 out of 87 votes are needed for approval. *See also* European Council.

Voting Stock: a security that carries the right to vote on corporate matters. *See also* Non-Voting Shares.

Voting Trust: the accumulation of many owners' shares of a company in a trust, to be used to control the company.

Voucher: a written record of an expenditure or transaction.

Vox Populi: popular or prevailing opinion. Latin for "the voice of the people."

VP: *see* Vice-President.

VR: *see* Virtual Reality.

VSE: *see* Vancouver Stock Exchange.

Vulture Capital: capital invested in a company with excellent prospects but no money, the intent of the investor being to wrest control from the owner. *See also* Vulture Capitalist.

Vulture Capitalist: a person who earns a living investing vulture capital. *See also* Vulture Capital.

Vulture Fund: a reference to a business that buys property or other assets from a distressed seller, usually at a deep discount, often in the hope of taking advantage of the latter's difficult circumstances. *See also* Mutual Fund – Other.

W3: *see* World Wide Web.

WACC: *see* Weighted Average Cost of Capital.

Wafer: a thin, flat piece of semiconductor on which an integrated circuit is printed. *See also* Integrated Circuit.

Wage: payment to a worker for labour. Wage often implies payment for physical labour. *See also* Compensation, Salary.

Wage and Price Controls: a government policy used to restrict wage and price increases during periods of high inflation. Wage and price controls were enforced in Canada during the 1970s. Also known as Wage Controls. *See also* Price Freeze.

Wage Controls: *see* Wage and Price Controls.

Waiting Period: *see* Elimination Period.

Waiver: the act of not insisting on a right, claim or privilege.

Waiver of Premium: an option often attached to a life insurance policy, it calls for a moratorium on premium payments if the insured becomes totally and permanently disabled. *See also* Life Insurance.

Walk Away Mortgage: a mortgage in which the lender's security is restricted to the property securing the mortgage. *See also* Mortgage.

Walking Papers: written notification of dismissal from a job. *See also* Pink Slip.

Walkout: 1. a labour strike. *See also* Labour Union, Sickout, Sit-Down, Strike, Work-to-Rule. **2.** to leave a meeting or negotiation as a sign of protest.

Walk the Walk: this occurs when a policy change that was earlier suggested, usually by a central banker or a politician, is put into action. *See also* Talk the Talk.

Wallflower: an out-of-favour security, company or industry. *See also* Fallen Angel, Orphan Stock.

Wall of Worry: this refers to the expression, "the stock market must climb a wall of worry," which indicates that stock prices can only rise if actual results are better than expected. The more things investors worry about, the more likely it is that actual results will be able to exceed expectations and stock prices will rise. *See also* Contrarian, Contrary Market Indicator.

Wallpaper: a worthless share certificate belonging to a company that has gone out of business. *See also* Scripophily.

Wall Street: 1. the main financial district of New York and the location of the New York Stock Exchange. *See also* Bay Street, Howe Street, Main Street, Threadneedle Street. **2.** a general reference to the investment community, as in "Wall Street doesn't like higher interest rates."

Wall Street Journal: the major daily financial publication in the U.S. and often the largest selling newspaper of any kind. *See also* Dow Jones & Company, Inc.

Wall Street Lawyer: *see* Philadelphia Lawyer.

War Babies: securities issued by companies in the defence industry.

War Chest: an accumulation of funds for the purpose of waging a battle (e.g., money available to a union that is preparing for a prolonged strike).

War Debt Income Tax Act: *see* Income Tax Act.

Ward-Heeler: a local worker in a political machine.

Warehouse Receipt: a document that gives evidence of ownership of commodities held in a warehouse, it enables investors to transfer title without moving the physical commodity.

Warehouse Receipt Financing: lending against a finished goods inventory where the lender maintains careful records of the items in stock.

Warrant: *see* Share Purchase Warrant.

Warranty: a legally binding guarantee for a product or service.

Warsaw Stock Exchange: the major stock exchange of Poland, located in its capital, Warsaw. Also known as Gielda Papierow Wartosclowych w Warszawle SA. Web site: www.fuw.edu.pl/gielda.eng.html/

Washed Out: a condition that exists in financial markets, or for a particular share, when a significant amount of selling is over.

Wash Trading: 1. the illegal practice of an investor simultaneously buying and selling a security through two different brokers in order to create the illusion of activity. Also known as Matched Orders. *See also* Acting in Concert, Daisy Chain, Surveillance Department. **2.** *See* Superficial Loss.

Waste to Ore Ratio: in mining, the ratio of the amount of waste removed for each ton of ore mined.

Wasting Asset: 1. a fixed asset that depreciates in value. **2.** a security (e.g., an option contract) in which the value diminishes as the expiry date nears. *See also* Option.

Wasting Trust: a trust in which the capital value is declining because assets are being gradually distributed to beneficiaries. *See also* Trust.

Watchdog: often, a reference to a regulatory authority.

Watered Stock: stock issued at a price that is well above the value of the assets that underlie it. This term is said to derive from the practice of cowboys allowing cattle to drink substantial amounts of water just before delivery to market because value was based on weight. *See also* Dilution.

Watt: the unit of power equal to the work done at the rate of one joule per second. *See also* Joule.

WCB: *see* Workers' Compensation Board.

Weak Hands: a person (or institution) who holds an investment that he/she may be forced to sell (e.g., by a margin call). *See also* Strong Hands.

Weak Market: a market that is consistently declining. *See also* Strong Market.

Weak Sister: a weak link (e.g., the weakest stock in a portfolio).

Wear and Tear: depreciation due to normal use.

Web Browser: a program that accesses files and information on the World Wide Web. Also known as Browser. *See also* Internet, World Wide Web.

Web Page: a document on the World Wide Web that is accessed by a unique uniform resource locator address. *See also* Hits, Internet, Uniform Resource Locator, World Wide Web.

Web Site: a group of related documents on the World Wide Web that is accessed by a unique uniform resource locator address. *See also* Internet, Uniform Resource Locator, World Wide Web.

Weekend Effect: the tendency of securities to perform better on Fridays than on Mondays. In the 1990s, Mondays have been better than Fridays.

Weighted Average: an average in which individual components have a different proportionate contribution.

Weighted Average Cost of Capital (WACC): a calculation of a company's cost of capital made by weighting the cost of each category of capital employed, such as bank loans, bonds, preferred shares and common shares, by the proportion of each. *See also* Cost of Capital.

Weighting: the proportionate contribution to the total allocated to each component (e.g., in mid-1999, Toronto-Dominion Bank's weighting in the Toronto Stock Exchange 300 Index was approximately 3.8 percent compared with 1.5 percent for the Canadian National Railway Co.). *See also* Toronto Stock Exchange 300 Index.

Welfare: financial or other aid provided to people in need, mainly by the government. *See also* Social Safety Net, Welfare State, Workfare.

Welfare State: a social system in which the government assumes primary responsibility for the welfare of its citizens. *See also* Welfare.

Well: a deep hole sunk into the ground, mainly to find water, oil or natural gas.

Well-Fixed: financially secure.

Wellhead: 1. specifically, the set of valves and gauges that control production from an oil or gas well. Also known as Christmas Tree. **2.** generally, the structure erected above an oil or gas well. Also known as Christmas Tree.

Went to the Wall: a person (or company) who suffered serious financial reversals. The term implies that the experience has been survived.

West Texas Intermediate Crude Oil: a light, sweet grade of crude oil produced in Oklahoma and Texas. The West Texas Intermediate Crude Oil price is often used as a benchmark for oil prices. *See also* Brent Crude Oil.

W Formation: *see* Double Bottom.

Wharfage: the fee charged for use of a wharf.

"What-If" Evaluation: using a computer to provide information under different assumptions. *See also* Computer.

What You See Is What You Get (WYSIWYG): in computers, a term that is used when something displayed on the screen is shown exactly as it will be printed. *See also* Computer.

Wheel: 1. a force that provides energy, as in "The wheels of commerce." **2.** a person of power and influence, as in "a big wheel." *See also* Wheeler Dealer.

Wheeler Dealer: an aggressive, often unscrupulous, business operator.

When, and if, Issued: a term used to describe trading in a security before it is cleared for trading, the stipulation being that settlement will occur when approval is given. The trade will be cancelled if approval is not received. Also known as When Issued. *See also* When Distributed.

When Distributed: a security issued before the final certificate is available. Settlement is completed when the certificate is printed and distributed. *See also* When, and if, Issued.

When Issued: *see* When, and if, Issued.

Whipped: *see* Whipsaw.

Whipsaw: a term used to describe a securities transaction, usually made in response to an initial transaction, that immediately goes wrong (e.g., after buying a stock and having it fall in price, selling the stock, only to have it immediately rise in price). Also known as Whipped.

Whisper: an unofficial forecast (e.g., an analyst's published estimate is earnings per share of $1.00 but his/her "whisper" is $1.05 per share).

Whisper Stock: shares of a company rumoured to be the target of a takeover offer.

Whistle Blower: an employee or other person inside a company, organization or government that reveals wrongdoing.

White-Collar: employment of a non-manual nature. *See also* Blue-Collar, Profession.

White-Collar Crime: a term used to describe commercial crime, usually of a financial, nonviolent nature.

White Elephant: an asset or investment that no one wants because it is a money loser.

White Gold: 1. an alloy of approximately five parts silver to one part gold. *See also* Gold, Precious Metal. **2.** an alloy of gold and nickel, palladium, platinum or zinc. *See also* Gold, Precious Metal.

White Knight: a party that makes a friendly takeover offer for control of a target company faced with a hostile takeover offer from another party. *See also* Black Knight, Grey Knight, Hostile Takeover Offer, Yellow Knight.

White List: a list, often kept by unions, of individuals suitable for hiring or businesses suitable for business transactions.

Whitemail: this occurs when a takeover target sells a large number of shares to a friendly party at a price well below the unwanted offer. This discourages the takeover because the acquiring company will have to purchase these shares as well. *See also* Bankmail, Blackmail, Greenmail.

White Pages Directory: an Internet database of names and e-mail addresses. *See also* E-Mail Address, Internet.

White Sheets: a daily over-the-counter price publication for market makers, it is put out by the National Quotation Bureau. *See also* Market Maker, National Quotation Bureau, Pink Sheets, Yellow Sheets.

White Squire: an investor who supports management and who holds or purchases a less than control block of stock in a company that is, or could be, subject to an unfriendly takeover. *See also* White Squire Defence.

White Squire Defence: an anti-takeover strategy in which a takeover target places a large block of its stock in the hands of an investor who is supportive of management. *See also* Poison Pill.

Whois: an Internet service, offered by certain organizations, that provides e-mail addresses and other information in the organization's database. *See also* Internet, Electronic Mail.

Whole Life Insurance: a cash value insurance policy that requires a fixed annual premium. Also known as Cash Value Life Insurance, Straight Life Insurance. *See also* Life Insurance.

Wholesale: the sale of goods in large quantities, the idea being that they will be resold by a retailer.

Wholesaler: 1. in mutual funds, an employee of a mutual fund company who markets his/her employer's products to agents and brokers. *See also* Mutual Fund, Retail. **2.** the sale of goods to an intermediary. *See also* Wholesale.

Wholesale Financing: *see* Inventory Financing.

Wholesale Price Index (WPI): *see* Producers' Price Index.

WHOOPS: the nickname for the Washington Public Power Supply System, it was the largest municipal bond failure in U.S. history.

Widget: a hypothetical product often used to illustrate economic theories of production.

Widely Held: 1. a term used to describe shares of a company that are owned by many shareholders. **2.** a public company. *See also* Public Company.

Widows and Orphans: a term used to refer to investors who take very little risk (or who should take very little risk).

Widows and Orphans Stock: a high-quality stock with very low volatility.

Wiener Borsekammer: *see* Vienna Stock Exchange.

Wildcat: a well drilled in an area in which there has been minimal exploration drilling.

Wildcat Drilling: speculative oil or gas drilling outside an area or structure that is currently producing.

Wildcat Scheme: a speculative investment doomed to failure.

Will: a legal document in which a person determines the distribution of his/her assets after his/her death. Also known as Testament. *See also* Ademption, Administrator, Beneficiary, Bequeath, Bequest, Codicil, Common Disaster Clause, Conditional Will, Coparceners, Defeasance, Devisee, Devisor, Die Without Issue, Domicile, English Form Will, Escheat, Estate, Estate Creation, Estate Freeze, Estate Liquidity, Estate Planning, Estate Preservation, Estate Tax, Executor, Executrix, Exoneration Clause, Failure of Issue, Fee Tail, First Devisee, Health-Care Directive, Heir, Heir Apparent, Heiress, Holographic Will, Inherit, Inheritance, International Will, Intestacy, Intestate, Intestate Succession, Letters Probate, Living Will, Next Devisee, Notarial Will, Nuncupative Will, Oral Will, Other Wills, Ratable Distribution, Revocation by Destruction, Revocation by Marriage, Revocation by Subsequent Testamentary Instrument, Specific Bequest, Specific Devise, Statutory Next-of-Kin, Testacy, Testamentary Capacity, Testamentary Trust, Testate, Testator, Testatrix, Ultimate Beneficiary, Will Variation.

Will Variation: generally, laws in place to allow legally married spouses and children to contest wills if they are not adequately provided for by the will. *See also* Will.

Windfall Profit: an unexpected, lucky profit or gambling win.

Windfall Profits Tax: a tax levied on windfall profits.

Window Dressing: adding and deleting securities in a portfolio before a reporting period to make the portfolio appear better to investors. Also known as Dress Up, Portfolio Dressing.

Windows: a computer operating system that has a stranglehold in the personal computer market. Windows is a brand name of Microsoft Corp. Other brand names include Windows 95 and Windows NT. *See also* Gates, William (Bill) H.

Window Settlement: the settlement of a securities transaction by the physical delivery of securities. *See also* Securities Cage.

Wind Up: to take steps to liquidate a business.

Winnipeg Commodity Exchange: an exchange located in Winnipeg, Manitoba, for trading commodity futures.

Winnipeg Stock Exchange: a now inactive stock exchange located in Winnipeg, Manitoba, it was incorporated in 1903. It was Canada's only agricultural commodities and futures exchange.

Win-Win: an agreement, transaction or settlement in which all parties benefit. *See also* Lose-Lose.

Wire Transfer: the transfer of funds from one person's account to another, usually in different geographic locations.

Witching Hour: the last chance to trade before financial options and financial futures expire. *See also* Double Witching Hour, Option, Triple Witching Hour.

Withdrawal: 1. money removed from a bank account. *See also* Deposit. **2.** in law, to remove a case from the judicial process.

Withholding Tax: 1. a tax levied by some countries on interest and dividend payments paid to non-residents. **2.** a portion of income that an employer is required to hold back from an employee and remit to Canada Customs and Revenue Agency. **3.** with certain gambling winnings in the U.S., an amount of tax taken from the winnings and remitted directly to the Internal Revenue Service.

Without: indicates that no quotation is available, as in "The stock was offered at $6 without."

Without Prejudice: in law, a term used to indicate that a matter is not closed. *See also* With Prejudice.

With Prejudice: in law, a term used to indicate that a matter is closed. *See also* Without Prejudice.

Wolf: 1. an experienced investor. **2.** an investor who preys on others.

Wolf Pack: this forms when one investor buys shares in a company and tells others to do the same, the expectation being that the company is a takeover target.

Won: the prime currency of North and South Korea.

Wooden Nickel: something that is counterfeit or false.

Wooden Ticket: a term used to describe the illegal practice of a broker confirming a trade to a client before the trade has been completed. If the trade is completed at a more favourable price, the broker pockets the difference.

Word: in computers, a set of bits that make up the smallest unit of addressable memory (usually 16 or 32 bits). *See also* Addressable, Bit, Computer.

Word Processing: the entering and editing of text on a personal computer. *See also* Computer.

Word Processor: 1. a personal computer dedicated to word processing. *See also* Computer. **2.** a term often used to refer to a particular word processing program.

Worker Capitalism: a system in which employees own part or all of the firm for which they work.

Wills

A will is a legal document in which a person determines the distribution of his or her personal assets after his or her death. Anything given to one person by another through a will is called a bequest.

A person leaving a valid will is known as testate; a person who dies without a will is referred to as intestate.

A person who gives a gift of real property through a will is a devisor. A person who receives property is the heir, beneficiary or devisee.

A will should appoint an executor to carry out its terms. A will should also appoint guardians for children in the event of the parents' simultaneous deaths.

When a person dies testate, the court is asked to grant letters probate, which confirms both the executor named in the will and the latter's validity. If an executor is not appointed, or the person dies intestate, the court will appoint an administrator to carry out executor functions.

A valid will is an essential part of every person's financial plan. The benefits of a lifetime of hard work can be lost in the absence of a will. A properly conceived will can save money and protect loved ones from potential hardship at a most difficult time.

Workers' Compensation Act: various provincial statutes that establish the liabilities of an employer for on-the-job injuries to employees.

Workers' Compensation Board (WCB): a board established by provincial statutes to oversee the payment of benefits to employees for on-the-job injuries. The WCB assesses employers an amount each year to cover operating costs and benefits. A particular WCB may or may not have sufficient capital to offset actuarial liabilities.

Workfare: a form of welfare in which recipients are required to perform some type of work or training in order to receive benefits. *See also* Welfare.

Workforce: in any given region, the total number of people working or looking for work.

Working Capital: *see* Net Current Assets.

Working Capital Loan: a loan to finance day-to-day operations of a business. The loan may not be used to purchase fixed assets or long-term investments. *See also* Business Expansion Loan.

Working Control: ownership of a block of a firm's voting stock, less than 50 percent but sufficient to influence corporate policy.

Working Interest: a financial interest in an oil or gas property, generally one in which the owner is responsible for his or her share of the costs in relation to ownership.

Working Order: an order to a broker to buy or sell a large block of securities gradually so as to not impact the market price. *See also* Order.

Work in Progress: an accounting category for partially finished goods that are held in inventory awaiting completion and eventual sale.

Work Off: *see* Work Out.

Work Out: 1. to execute a sell order by gradually selling shares into the market in a way that does not disturb pricing or cause prices to fall. Also known as Work Off. *See also* Working Order. **2.** A term used to describe a situation (e.g., a bad loan) in which cooperative steps are being taken to correct the situation.

Work Out Market: an estimated average price at which a security can be sold through a work out strategy.

Work Slowdown: *see* Work-to-Rule.

Workstation: 1. an area, usually in an office, set up for one worker. It often includes a computer terminal. **2.** *see* Network Computer.

Work-to-Rule: a bargaining strategy used by dissatisfied workers that involves reducing productivity and output until demands are met. Also known as Slowdown, Work Slowdown. *See also* Labour Union, Sickout, Sit-Down, Strike, Walkout.

World Bank: formerly known as the International Bank for Reconstruction and Development, it is an agency of the United Nations and was set up to finance the rebuilding of Europe after the Second World War. The World Bank now helps developing nations to build infrastructure and is the most important lending agency in the area of international development. *See also* United Nations.

World Court: the principal judicial organization of the United Nations, it adjudicates disputes between sovereign states in accordance with international law. Also known as International Court of Justice.

World Reserve: in an auction, the minimum amount the seller will accept for all the items offered. *See also* As is; As Is, Where is; Auction; Reserve Bid.

World Trade Organization (WTO): an international body comprised of 134 member governments that monitors global trading practices. Created in 1994 as a successor to the General Agreement on Tariff and Trade.

Worldwide Income: for Canadian tax purposes, total income (regardless of where it is earned). *See also* Taxes.

World Wide Web (W3, WWW): the total set of files that uses Hypertext Markup Language (HTML) and resides on Hypertext Transfer Protocol (HTTP) servers connected throughout the world. Different files on different servers are accessed by "clicking" on the hypertext links (called hyperlinks) embedded into each server's Web pages. *See also* Internet.

Worth: relating to material or market value, wealth, riches or the qualities that make something valuable.

WPI: *see* Wholesale Price Index.

Wrap Account: a service offered by Canadian brokerage firms to large clients, it uses professional money manager inputs to determine which securities are bought and sold for individual accounts.

Wrap-Around Mortgage: a second mortgage that is made up of an assumable mortgage from the vendor and a new loan. *See also* Assumable Mortgage, Mortgage, Second Mortgage.

Wrinkle: an unusual feature in a security.

Writ: in law, a written command.

Write: 1. to sell a put or call option in an opening transaction. *See also* Option. **2.** in computers, to record data on a storage device. *See also* Computer.

Writedown: to reduce the value of an asset carried on the books, with the reduction charged against earnings.

Write Off: to eliminate the value of an asset carried on the books, with the reduction charged against earnings.

Write-Off: a poor or unsuccessful investment.

Write Up: 1. to increase the book value of an asset, as substantiated by an appraisal. **2.** to prepare a brokerage company research report on a company. **3.** a written report (e.g., a research report).

Writing Naked: *see* Uncovered Writing.

Writ of Seizure and Sale: an instrument that allows a creditor to direct a sheriff to seize and sell certain assets of a debtor in order to satisfy the debt.

Wrongful Dismissal: the unjust firing of an employee from a job. An employee has remedies for such dismissal available through the courts. *See also* Age Discrimination, Constructive Dismissal, Dismissal for Cause, Severance, Severance Pay.

WTO: *see* World Trade Organization.

WWW: *see* World Wide Web.

WYSIWYG: *see* What You See Is What You Get.

X: in Roman numerals, the number 10.

X-Axis: the horizontal scale of a two-dimensional coordinate system. *See also* Y-Axis, Z-Axis.

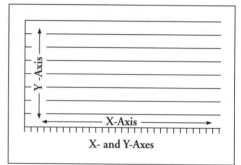

X- and Y-Axes

XD: a notation meaning ex dividend. *See also* Ex Dividend.

X-Div.: a notation meaning ex dividend. *See also* Ex Dividend.

X-Efficiency: a term used to describe how efficiently a business is managed.

Xenocurrency: a currency that is traded in money markets outside its own country.

Xerography: a dry copying process in which a negative image on an electrically charged plate is thermally fixed onto paper. This process is used in photocopiers and laser printers. Also known as Electrophotography.

X Factor: an unknown quantity or quality.

XTS: *see* Automated Exchange Trade System.

Y

Y2K: the year 2000. *See also* Year 2,000 Problem.

Yankee Bond: a foreign bond in U.S. dollars offered for sale in the U.S. *See also* Bond, Dragon Bond, Eurobond, Gilt, Samurai Bond, Shogun Bond.

Yankee: a U.S. security traded in London.

Yard: a measure of length equal to three feet, or .91 metre. *See also* Foot.

Yard Sale: *see* Garage Sale.

Yardstick: generally, any standard used in making a comparison or in assessing performance.

Y-Axis: the vertical scale of a two-dimensional coordinate system. *See also* X-Axis, Z-Axis.

Year 2000 Conversion: any solution to the Year 2000 Problem, namely one that will enable computers to distinguish between the 1900s and the 2000s. *See also* Bug, Computer, Leap Year Bug, Year 2000 Problem.

Year 2000 Problem

Also known as the Millennium Bug, the Year 2000 Problem refers to a computer glitch that may cause serious difficulties at the turn of the century.

The problem is almost trivial. Many computers have been programmed to recognize the year as a two-digit number. In other words, 88 is understood as 1988, 97 as 1997. Under such a program, the year 2000, entered as 00, will be read by computer systems as the year 1900.

Why is this an issue? A credit card, for example, that expires on June 30, 2000, will be read by computers as having expired on June 30, 1900. Between January 1 and June 30, 2000, one's credit may be declined because computer systems will assume that one's card expired a century earlier.

In the U.S., it is estimated that correcting the Year 2000 Problem will consume 700,000 person-years of work. The resources needed to correct the problem will reduce economic growth by .3 percent in 1999 and by .5 percent in 2000 and into early 2001. It is estimated that it will cost the U.S. $119 billion in lost economic output by the year 2001.

Year 2000 Problem: a significant computer hardware problem caused by equipment that allows only two digits to note the year. After the turn of the century, these computers may assume that the year "00" is 1900 rather than 2000. Also known as Millennium Bug. *See also* Bug, Computer, Leap Year Bug, Year 2000 Conversion.

Year-End Audit: *see* Annual Audit.

Year-End Rally: the tendency for common stock prices to be strong in the months shortly before and after the calendar year end. Because of the season, this is sometimes referred to as the Santa Claus Rally. *See also* Seasonal Trend.

Year over Year: a comparison of results from a reporting period in a current year with results from the same period in the previous year (e.g., first half of 1999 to the first half of 1998). *See also* Quarter over Quarter, Year to Year.

Year to Year: a comparison of results for the latest year compared with the previous year (e.g., 1999 to 1998). *See also* Quarter to Quarter, Year over Year.

Yellow Knight: a term used to describe a situation in which a company making a takeover attempt ends up discussing a merger with the target company. *See also* Black Knight, Grey Knight, White Knight.

Yellow Market Indicator: a tongue-in-cheek indicator that holds that the stock market will rise when the colour yellow is popular. *See also* Aspirin Count Theory, Boston Snow Indicator, Frivolity Theory, Hemline Indicator, SuperBowl Indicator, Tie Theory.

Yellow Sheets: a daily over-the-counter corporate bond price publication for market makers, it is published by the National Quotation Bureau. *See also* Market Maker, National Quotation Bureau, Pink Sheets, Yellow Sheets.

Yen: the prime currency of Japan.

Yield: the return, in most cases restricted to income, on an investment expressed as a percent per annum.

Yield Burning: an illegal practice engaged in by some U.S. underwriters refunding municipal bonds. Yield burning involves over-charging for the treasury bonds in which funds must be invested until the municipal bonds can be redeemed.

Yield Curve: a plotting of interest rates (e.g., bond yields) on the vertical axis and of term to maturity on the horizontal axis. Most often, interest rates at shorter terms to maturity are lower than interest rates at longer terms to maturity. Also known as Term Structure (of Interest Rates). *See also* Negative Yield Curve, Positive Yield Curve.

Yield Equivalent: the interest yield needed to provide the same after-tax income as a dividend yield. Since dividends are taxed less than is interest, to obtain the same after-tax income as a 3 percent dividend yield, a 4.1 percent interest yield is required. *See also* Interest Equivalent Ratio.

Yield Equivalent Ratio: to determine the equivalent interest yield needed to provide the same after-tax income as a dividend yield, the latter must be multiplied by the yield equivalent factor, which is 1.35 in 1999. If the tax rate on either interest or dividends is changed, the yield equivalent factor will change. *See also* Interest Equivalent Ratio.

Yield Pickup: a gain in yield realized by selling one bond and buying another. Also referred to as a Pickup.

Yield Spread: the difference in yield between two securities. *See also* Spread

Yield to Lessor: the rate of return earned by a property owner from a lease. *See also* Lease, Lessor.

Yield to Maturity: the yield of a bond calculated with the assumption it will be owned until maturity and interest payments are reinvested at the yield to maturity rate. *See also* Bond, Cash Yield, Duration, Nominal Yield, Realized Yield.

Yield to Redemption: the yield of a bond (or preferred share) calculated with the assumption it is owned until the nearest redemption date at which time it is redeemed at the applicable redemption price. *See also* Redeemable Bond, Redeemable Preferred Share.

YMMV: Internet acronym for "your mileage may vary." This is a warning that instructions just given may not work exactly as described.

Yo-Yo: a market that moves up and down with great volatility.

Yukon: *see* Canada's Provinces and Territories.

Zagreb Stock Exchange: the major stock exchange of Croatia, located in its capital, Zagreb. Web site www.zse.hr *See also* Croation CROBEX Index.

Zaire: the prime currency of Congo (formerly Zaire).

Z-Axis: the third axis in a three-dimensional coordinate system, used in computer graphics to represent depth. *See also* X-Axis, Y-Axis.

Zero: *see* Zero Coupon Bond.

Zero Based Budgeting: a method of budgeting in which (1) each item of income and each expense starts from a base of zero for each new period and (2) the entire budget must be justified. Usually, managers are required to justify increased or decreased spending only from the year before. Zero based budgeting is encouraged for government budgets because expenditures can run out of control if it is automatically assumed that what was spent last year will be spent this year.

Zero Coupon Bond: a bond that provides its return by being sold at a large discount from the value at which it matures. A zero coupon bond does not pay regular interest. Also known as Zero, Zeroes. *See also* Bond.

Zeroes: *see* Zero Coupon Bond.

Zero-Minus Tick: this occurs when a security trades at the same price as that of the immediately preceding trade but below the last different trade price. A short sale is not permitted on a zero-minus tick. *See also* Closing Tick, Downtick, Minus Tick, Plus Tick, Short Sale, Tick, Zero-Plus Tick, Zero Tick.

Zero Net Position: a term used to describe a portfolio or a security position that has zero net exposure to market price changes (e.g., a short position that offsets a long position). *See also* Flat.

Zero-Plus Tick: this occurs when a security trades at the same price as that of the immediately preceding trade but above the last different trade price. A short sale is permitted on a zero-plus tick. *See also* Closing Tick, Downtick, Minus Tick, Plus Tick, Short Sale, Tick, Zero-Minus Tick, Zero Tick.

Zero Population Growth (ZPG): a rate of birth sufficient to maintain, but not to increase, the population.

Zero-Sum Game: a situation in which whatever is gained by one side is lost by the other, so that the net change is always zero. Excluding costs, options are an example of a zero-sum game.

Zero Tick: this occurs when a security trades at the same price as that of the immediately preceding trade. *See also* Downtick, Minus Tick, Plus Tick, Zero-Minus Tick, Zero-Plus Tick.

Zimbabwe Stock Exchange: the major stock exchange of Zimbabwe, located in its capital, Harare.

Zimbabwe Stock Exchange Indexes: Zimbabwe has only two indexes: the Zimbabwe Industrials Index and the Mining Index. Both are market capitalization weighted indexes.

Zloty: the prime currency of Poland.

Zombies: companies that continue to operate even though they are insolvent. Also known as Living Dead.

Zoning: often refers to the building and other development restrictions a municipality sets on real property (e.g., minimum lot size, land use). *See also* Conforming Use, Non-Conforming Use.

ZPG: *see* Zero Population Growth.

Z-Score: an analytical tool used by lenders (e.g., banks, credit card issuers) to estimate the creditworthiness of potential customers. The Z-Score takes information such as age, type of accommodation and employment record and reduces it to a number. The higher the Z-Score, the more creditworthy the applicant. *See also* Credit Score.

Zurich Stock Exchange: the major stock exchange of Switzerland, located in Zurich. Web site: www.bourse.ch

ZZZZ Best: the name of a contracting company owned by Barry Minkow in the 1980s. Using all manner of deceit, including forgery and theft, Minkow (who was just a teenager at the time) appeared to be building a multimillion dollar enterprise. ZZZZ Best went public in December 1986, reached a market value of $100 million by April 1987 and reached a peak of $200 million. In December 1988, Minkow was eventually sentenced to 25 years in prison. *See also* Bre-X Minerals Ltd., Equity Funding Corporation, Ponzi Scheme, Prime Bank Note, Salad Oil Scandal.